MAGILL'S
SURVEY
OF
SCIENCE

MAGILL'S SURVEY OF SCIENCE

EARTH SCIENCE SERIES

Volume 3
1079-1680
Hot Spots and Volcanic Island Chains—Micropaleontology

Edited by
FRANK N. MAGILL

Consulting Editor
Dr. James A. Woodhead

SALEM PRESS
Pasadena, California   Englewood Cliffs, New Jersey

Library of Congress Cataloging-in-Publication Data
Magill's survey of science. Earth science series/edited
by Frank N. Magill.
    p. cm.
    Includes bibliographical references.
    1. Earth sciences. I. Magill, Frank Northen,
1907-   .
QE28.M33   1990   89-10923
550—dc20   CIP
ISBN 0-89356-606-3 (set)
ISBN 0-89356-609-8 (volume 3)

PRINTED IN THE UNITED STATES OF AMERICA

CONTENTS

CONTENTS

MAGILL'S
SURVEY
OF
SCIENCE

HOT SPOTS AND VOLCANIC ISLAND CHAINS

Type of earth science: Geology
Field of study: Tectonics

Crustal hot spots and volcanic island chains are geologic features that result from the mechanisms associated with plate tectonics. A few hot spots are found on the continents, but most are associated with oceanic plates. Both types of hot spots are related to rising magma plumes. Hot spots are generally isolated near plate centers and remain relatively stationary. Volcanic island chains are formed along plate margins and result from the sinking and melting of oceanic plates.

Principal terms

ASTHENOSPHERE: a layer of the earth's mantle (about 50-200 kilometers beneath the surface) where the shock waves of earthquakes travel at reduced speeds, probably because of its low rigidity

CONVERGENT PLATE BOUNDARY: the boundary between two plates that are moving toward each other, which may result in island arc development or volcanic arcs on land

DEEP-OCEAN TRENCH: an elongate depression in the sea floor produced by bending oceanic crust during subduction; examples include the Mariana, Puerto Rico, and Aleutian trenches

DIVERGENT PLATE BOUNDARY: the boundary where two plates move apart, resulting in the upwelling of magma from the mantle; the Mid-Atlantic Ridge is a good example

HOT SPOT: a concentration of heat in the mantle, capable of producing magma that, under certain circumstances, can extrude onto the earth's surface

ISLAND ARC: a curved chain of volcanic islands generally located a few hundred kilometers from a trench where active subduction of one oceanic plate under another is occurring

MAGMA: a body of molten rock material found at depth and capable of intrusion and extrusion; igneous rocks are derived from this material through the process of solidification

MANTLE: the 2,885-kilometer-thick portion of the earth's interior located beneath the crust; it is believed to consist of ultramafic material

PLATE TECTONICS: the theory which proposes that the earth's outer layer consists of a series of individual plates that interact and thereby produce earthquakes, volcanoes, and mountain building and recycle the crust

PLUME: a generally isolated convection cell believed to carry heat and mantle material from lower levels up to the crust, resulting in hot spots at the surface

SUBDUCTION ZONE: an area where oceanic crustal plates plunge into the mantle along a convergent zone; examples include Japan and the Aleutian Islands

Summary of the Phenomenon

In the late 1960's, a theory emerged which suggested that all continents were once joined as a supercontinent that later broke apart. This theory had been debated for decades but finally achieved acceptance on the basis of information by the Deep Sea Drilling Project (begun in 1969). The theory of plate tectonics envisioned that the earth's crust consists of continental and oceanic components that are mobile and "float" upon a semiliquid mantle. The element of mobility offers various explanations for mountain building, volcanism, and earthquake activity. More significant, the theory enabled scientists to see how most geological processes fit into a single unifying mechanism that shapes the earth.

The big question of what caused plate movement, however, had yet to be answered. One theory proposed that convection cells existed in the upper portion of the mantle. In this process, hot, less dense, semisolid material rises up toward the crust, where lower temperature and pressure conditions exist. Contact with the solid crust results in both an upward stress and lateral movement (deflection) of this material. Occasionally, the crust fractures and volcanism results. The lateral movement of the convection cell drags the crust away from the volcanic centers, thus giving the appearance of continental drift if continents are present. The Mid-Atlantic Ridge is an excellent example of a spreading ridge pushing plates apart, and it typifies the convection cell process.

One of the more interesting aspects of plate tectonics involves the occurrence of hot spots. A hot spot is a relatively small region (a few hundred kilometers in diameter at most) of higher than average temperatures that produces melting in the mantle and volcanic activity above. Hot spots occur under both oceanic and continental plates, but they are more common under oceanic plates. Most hot spots are found along spreading ridges, such as those found in Iceland and the Azores. A few do exist at the centers of plates, including the hot spot of the Hawaiian Islands. Although quite rare, hot spots do occur on land, including the hot spot at Yellowstone National Park.

The origin and nature of hot spots are still something of a mystery to scientists. Hot spots undoubtedly have their origin within the earth's mantle and extrude magma up through the crust. It is believed that a hot spot originates beneath the convective flow zone of the mantle and is localized at a much deeper position. This situation could cause the rise of less dense material upward along cylindrical channels called plumes. Plumes can be relatively isolated and produce a single volcanic structure when melting takes place at shallower depths and magma extrudes to the surface. This process is in contrast to the more elongate upwelling associated with spreading axes such as the Mid-Atlantic Ridge. Hot spots and plumes may be the mechanism that initiates plate spreading through development of new plate boundaries.

Over the last several years, more than one hundred hot spots have been identified as having been active during the past 10 million years. This suggests that hot mantle material rises and spreads out laterally in the asthenosphere from perhaps twenty major thermal plumes. These plumes in turn give rise to hot spots with associated volcanic activity. Such hot spots appear to be stable because they occupy the same positions relative to each other as the overlying mobile crust passes over. This stability became quite apparent when sea-floor mapping of the Pacific Ocean basin revealed a linear chain of volcanic structures stretching from the Hawaiian Islands to the Aleutian trench southwest of Alaska. Most of these are submerged sea-mounts, while others such as Midway Island break the surface. Collectively, these islands and seamounts form the Hawaiian-Emperor chain.

When rocks from the Hawaiian-Emperor chain were dated by the potassium-argon method, an unusual sequence of dates emerged. The Suike seamount, positioned near the Aleutian trench, proved to be 65 million years old, while the island of Hawaii at the opposite end of the chain was less than 1 million years old. The implication was clear: During its continual movement, the overlying Pacific plate was passing over a stationary hot spot that was extruding magma to the surface and thereby building up large volcanic structures. As the plate carried an older lava pile away, a new one would arise to take its place over the hot spot. In this way, the entire chain was built up over time.

As the Hawaiian Islands typify an oceanic hot spot setting, Yellowstone National Park is an example of a continental setting. The basic mechanism for each type of hot spot is similar. The generation of a basaltic magma through partial melting of mantle material is responsible for the volcanism both at Yellowstone and at Hawaii. The mantle at both places can be found at relatively shallow depths, which permits the partial melting of materials with low melting points. Unlike the crust at Hawaii, where there is no significant variation in crustal composition, the crust under Yellowstone is composed of material higher in silica content, easily subjected to partial melting. Magma thus formed is of a much lower density and is capable of rapid upward movement. The eventual volcanism was of a greater explosive nature than that of Hawaii, and in fact did create the giant explosion caldera that is Yellowstone today.

Although the "rising magma plume" explanation for hot spot development is an attractive theory, there are notable objections. One problem is that hot spots remain stationary for extremely long periods of time (more than 50 million years). Recent studies have shown some movement (a few millimeters per year) that resembles the motion of a swaying palm tree. This motion, however, seems rather insignificant in relation to the larger plate tectonics picture. Seismic studies have not strongly supported the existence of mantle plumes but merely offer mild evidence suggestive of their presence.

Presently, the best evidence for the existence of deep mantle plumes comes from chemical comparisons of the lavas extruded. The volcanism of most oceanic hot spots like Hawaii tends to be of an alkali basaltic nature (rich in sodium-potassium), while that of the oceanic spreading ridges is mostly tholeiitic (with little or no olivine present). This fact supports widely separated sources for the respective magmas and tends to isolate the hot spot phenomenon from the more common volcanism characteristic of plate boundaries. Scientists presently cannot offer a conclusive explanation for the existence of hot spots or how they fit into the overall mechanism of plate tectonics.

In contrast to the hot spot phenomenon, much is known about volcanic island chains and their associated plate boundaries. One plate descends beneath the other; as it penetrates into the asthenosphere, partial melting occurs, with low-melting-temperature materials forming an upwelling magma. Quite often, these magmas break through the crust and form a chain of small volcanic islands arranged in an arc pattern relative to the nearby trench. These islands are usually located a few hundred kilometers behind the trench and are collectively called an island arc system. The Aleutian, Mariana, and Tonga islands are excellent examples.

The geological situation that produces a volcanic island chain always occurs at plate boundaries where two oceanic plates are converging. This area is also referred to as a subduction zone, as one of the plates is pushed under the margin of the other. The immediate result is the formation of a trench, and the movement of the descending plate generates an inclined zone of seismic activity. This movement can be seen on seismic reflection profiles because the solid material must reach a considerable depth (more than 50 kilometers) before it melts and remains intact for a long period of time. The descending plate itself is composed of three basic layers: unconsolidated sediment, lithified sediment, and basalt. The top layer of unconsolidated sediment is scraped off by the overriding plate and piles up to form an accretionary prism. Both the lithified sediment and the basaltic layers are eventually remelted and give rise to the volcanism that will create the island arc.

The material that eventually is remelted in the asthenosphere consists of relatively cold, wet oceanic crust. Water, which was originally absorbed during the long journey from the spreading ridge to the trench, is driven off during various stages of increasing temperature initially derived from metamorphic reactions. As the water-rich melt rises into the surrounding mantle, it acts as a flux that lowers the melting temperature sufficiently to produce magma distinctive to subduction zones. Andesite is the principal rock formed, with various other forms of silica-rich rock also present. Even in the case of remelting of the basaltic layer of the plate, differentiation (separation by density) and remelting of digested crustal material would also produce these silica-enriched magmas.

Given sufficient time and continued volcanic activity, a rather large and geologically mature landmass may result from an island arc beginning. Volcanism, coupled with the buoyancy of the intrusive rock being emplaced within the crust below, will gradually increase the surface area and elevation of the island arc. As the island arc grows, greater erosion will increase the amount of sediment being accumulated offshore. Through various transportation means (such as currents and mudslides), some of these sediments will reach the trench and will be subjected to metamorphism and even be melted by the compressional forces of the converging plates. In this way, a geologically mature island arc will result that has all the familiar forms of volcanic and intrusive igneous, sedimentary, and folded metamorphic rocks present. Good examples of a mature island arc system are the Alaska Peninsula, the Philippines, and Japan.

A continental equivalent of an island arc system exists. Here, an oceanic plate is being subducted beneath continental crust, resulting in a trench lying in front of the margin and a series of andesitic volcanoes present a few hundred kilometers inland. This situation would also produce deformation of the continental margin into folded mountain belts. The resulting metamorphism and partial melting of the descending plate would produce high-grade metamorphic rocks, along with granitic intrusions on the overlying plate. A fine example is the Andean mountain chain and is referred to as an Andean-type arc. In some cases, such arcs may be covered by seas and may somewhat resemble island arcs. Examples can be seen in some of the eastern-end Aleutian islands and in Sumatra, Indonesia.

Methods of Study

The methods employed to study crustal hot spots and volcanic island chains involve both direct and indirect approaches. Both geologic features are part of the plate tectonics theory and must be explained in the light of that concept. Hot spots and volcanic island chains therefore must be examined from the perspective of a localized occurrence as well as a global situation. Only when the two are blended will a detailed picture emerge showing their close relationship in both origin and formation processes.

The search for a better understanding of hot spots and volcanic island chains began shortly after World War II, when sonar, a radio pulse used to detect submarines, was used to measure the topography of the sea floor. The time it takes for a sonar signal to strike an underwater object and reflect back to its source is measured, and the rate of return plots the highs and lows of the sea floor. By using this technique, scientists were able to measure accurately ocean depths and discover the geological features that constitute the sea floor. Long mountain chains, deep trenches, and flat abyssal plains were revealed, giving the sea floor a geological characteristic as complex and interesting as the continental surfaces. It was in this manner that the Hawaiian Islands were revealed to be a related series of volcanic seamounts that stretch several thousand kilometers across the Pacific Ocean basin. As a result of such discoveries, the theory of continental drift was given new consideration.

Once the nature of the sea floor was characterized, other techniques were employed to investigate the nature of the crust that underlies the deep ocean sediment. The earliest studies employed a combination of sediment penetrators to collect samples and limited drilling along the continental shelves. These first studies— partly a result of offshore oil exploration—began to reveal a somewhat different view of the sea floor. Later studies made by the research vessel *Glomar Challenger* provided long core sections of both the sediment accumulation on the sea floor and the underlying rock. Samples were taken from numerous worldwide locations, and comparisons were made that revealed a much clearer picture of the global implications of plate tectonics.

The deep-ocean core samples provided scientists with direct evidence of the underlying oceanic crust. From this evidence, age determinations were made by using radioisotope dating techniques. These studies revealed that rocks found near the oceanic volcanic ridges were much younger than those found in front of the deep oceanic trenches. A progression of younger to older rocks was clearly evident and provided direct evidence for plate movement. It became apparent that new crust originated at the spreading centers along the submerged ridges as active volcanoes, with the older crust being pushed aside toward the distant trenches. Collision with a thicker plate would cause the older, thinner crust to be diverted downward, thus producing the trench. As the older rock plunges deeper into the mantle, it melts and separates into denser (sinking) and less dense (rising) material. It is this less dense material that rises and later forms the volcanic island chains behind the trenches.

An additional research technique that provides evidence to support this scenario is seismic reflection profiling. In this method, shock waves are generated from a controlled explosion. Because different shock waves travel at different speeds and behave differently as they pass through rocks of varying densities, these aspects can be used to determine the nature of the underlying rock. Primary shock waves, or P waves, travel faster than secondary shock waves, or S waves: P waves can penetrate liquids that S waves cannot. Each has its specific velocity as it passes through rocks of varying densities, and this difference is used to recognize specific rock types. In some situations, the shock waves can bounce off a particular rock material and thus give an image of its shape and thickness. This image is seen clearly where a trench and island arc are present. The seismic-reflection images reveal a relatively thin oceanic plate being diverted underneath the thicker plate's edge, upon which the island arc chain forms from the volcanic activity generated by the melting plate.

Perhaps the final piece of evidence needed to understand hot spots and volcanic island chains comes from the study of the chemistry and petrology of the rocks. Their chemistry and mineral compositions can reveal much about the depth, temperature, and pressure conditions that existed when the original magma formed. Experimental studies dealing with the melting and the recrystallization of the rocks can provide much evidence for the rocks' origin and formative processes. When rocks from widely separated locations are studied, the resulting data reveal the rather complex yet uniform mechanisms governing plate tectonics.

Context

The understanding of the mechanisms of crustal hot spots and volcanic island chains not only is important for scientific purposes but also has a bearing on everyday life. Associated with both geological occurrences are earthquakes and volcanic activity. Hundreds of millions of people live in areas threatened by intense earthquake activity. Every year, several earthquakes of large magnitude rock the earth and cause the loss of life and inflict great property damage. Although scientists have collected much information on seismic activity, there is no reliable means for predicting earthquakes.

In contrast, hot spots and volcanic island chains occur in areas of sustained earthquake activity, and much can be learned from their constant monitoring. Where the frequency of earthquake activity is high, patterns can develop over relatively short periods of time, and theories can be tested. The large number of earthquakes that would normally occur over millions of years happen relatively quickly in these active regions. The greater the amount of available data, the better the chances for making more accurate predictions. If earthquake predictions can eventually be made with a high degree of accuracy for these localized areas, then perhaps the process could be extended to include all earthquake-prone regions. Loss of life could then be greatly reduced. Perhaps even a method of earthquake prevention could be developed from a better understanding of what occurs at hot spots and volcanic island chains.

Volcanoes do not present the same danger that an earthquake does, as their impending eruptions are usually quite predictable. Loss of life caused by volcanic activity therefore is generally much less. What is gained from volcanic studies is a greater awareness of the physical processes responsible for continuous crustal renewal and the development of new landmasses. The study of volcanoes has also provided evidence to show how volcanic activity can influence the weather and global climatic patterns. Most of the volcanic activity that occurs over hot spots such as Hawaii is rather gentle and quite predictable. It slowly continues to increase the surface area of the islands and replenish the soil with new mineral nutrients. Volcanism that occurs along plate boundaries and forms island arc chains can be very explosive and has produced some of the world's greatest and most destructive eruptions. The hot spot that currently lies beneath Yellowstone National Park once erupted with a tremendous explosive force and covered most of North America with ash. It represented a plate boundary at that time.

Perhaps the greatest benefit from the study of hot spots and volcanic island chains is the realization of how the earth works over relatively short periods of time. A volcanic eruption or an earthquake demonstrates the enormous energy contained within the earth and how that energy is released. Over the great span of time, this energy has shifted plates and led to the development and breakup of a supercontinent. From scientific observations, the earth can be seen as a living organism as it recycles its surface materials. In the eruption of a Hawaiian volcano, the past and the future come together in a demonstration of earth processes. Such events are dramatic reminders that the earth is a dynamic, evolving planet.

Bibliography

Burke, Kevin C., and J. Tuzo Wilson. "Hot Spots on the Earth's Surface." *Scientific*

American 235 (February, 1976): 46-57. An excellent discussion on the worldwide occurrences of crustal hot spots. Emphasizes the mechanisms of hot spot genera-tion, along with worldwide geographical distribution. The relationship between hot spots and plate tectonics is dealt with quite well. Excellent maps and dia-grams. Best suited for advanced high school and undergraduate college students.

Condie, K. C. *Plate Tectonics and Crustal Evolution*. Elmsford, N.Y.: Pergamon Press, 1976. This book presents a good basic summary of the development of continental and oceanic crust, based on the principles of plate tectonics and continental drift. Good background information that is necessary to understand hot spot development and its various occurrences. Well illustrated. Suitable in part for high school through graduate levels.

Cox, A., and R. Hart. *Plate Tectonics: How It Works*. Palo Alto, Calif.: Blackwell Scientific, 1986. Incorporates most of the latest developments in the theory of plate tectonics and provides a good overview as well as an in-depth look into the mechanisms behind plate tectonics. Included are discussions on hot spots and related volcanic island arcs. Best suited for advanced high school and under-graduate college students.

Heezen, Bruce C., and Ian D. MacGregor. "The Evolution of the Pacific." In *Readings from Scientific American Ocean Science.* San Francisco: W. H. Free-man, 1977. This article presents results from the Deep Sea Drilling Project, which deals with the evolutionary history of the Pacific sea floor as a result of plate tectonic processes. Good information is presented on the techniques of data collection and the acquired results. Discussions of trench and seamount develop-ment, along with the varying ages of deep-sea sediment, give a good picture of the true nature of the Pacific Ocean basin. Suitable for advanced high school and undergraduate college students.

Macdonald, G. A., A. T. Abbott, and F. L. Peterson. *Volcanoes in the Sea: The Geology of the Hawaiian Islands*. 2d ed. Honolulu: University of Hawaii Press, 1983. This book deals specifically with the geology of the Hawaiian Islands, which represents one of the earth's most active hot spots. Among the many topics covered are past and present volcanism on Hawaii and how it fits into the overall picture of global plate tectonics. A detailed reference to the many geolog-ical activities involved in the formation and continued evolution of the Hawaiian Islands as a stationary hot spot center. Best suited for undergraduate college students.

Van Andel, T. H. *New Views on an Old Planet: Continental Drift and the History of the Earth*. New York: Cambridge University Press, 1985. This book provides a general and popularized history of the earth and the evolution of scientific ideas. Provides a good discussion of continental drift and plate tectonics to aid the reader in better understanding those concepts. Presents a rather different ap-proach not found in standard references on these topics. Recommended for college students.

Wilson, J. Tuzo, ed. *Continents Adrift and Continents Aground*. San Francisco:

W. H. Freeman, 1976. This work is a collection of articles on plate tectonics which originally appeared in the journal *Scientific American*. The articles provide both an overview and specifics of plate tectonics in a way that is understandable for most readers with a basic interest in earth sciences. Well illustrated through its use of maps, charts, and diagrams. Best suited for high school and undergraduate college levels.

Wyllie, Peter J. *The Way the Earth Works*. New York: John Wiley & Sons, 1976. An often-cited work that is highly readable and well illustrated, dealing with various tectonic subjects. Coverage of continental drift and plate tectonics is extensive and should provide the reader with the background knowledge needed to understand crustal hot spots. Best suited for advanced high school and undergraduate college students.

Paul P. Sipiera

Cross-References

Geothermal Phenomena and Heat Transport, 906; Heat Sources and Heat Flow, 1065; Island Arcs, 1261; The Origin of Magmas, 1428; Ocean Basins, 1785; Ocean-Floor Exploration, 1813; The Ocean Ridge System, 1826; Plate Tectonics, 2079; Seamounts, 2274; Seismic Reflection Profiling, 2333; Volcanism at Spreading Centers, 2607; Volcanoes: The Hawaiian Islands, 2638; Yellowstone National Park, 2757.

HURRICANES AND MONSOONS

Field of study: Atmospheric sciences and meteorology

The hurricane, a deadly natural phenomenon, is more understood now than ever before, although some aspects of its behavior still remain a mystery. Monsoons are highly important to the agriculture of Asian societies, which rely on the storm-carrying winds to irrigate crops at precise times of the year.

Principal terms

CYCLONE: another name for a hurricane

EYE: the calm central region of a hurricane; it is composed of a tunnel with strong sides

HURRICANE: a severe tropical storm with winds exceeding 119 kilometers per hour which originates in tropical regions

JET STREAM: a narrow current of high-speed winds in the upper atmosphere

MONSOON: any large wind system that blows from cold to warm regions

PARABOLIC PATH: a nearly semicircular curve in a plane; it is the path of a hurricane turning back in the direction from which it came

PRECIPITATION: water droplets or ice particles that form in the atmosphere or in clouds and fall to earth

TROPICAL STORM: a severe tropical storm with winds ranging from 45 to 120 kilometers per hour

VORTEX: a flow of fluid about a central axis that draws material into its center

Summary of the Phenomenon

A hurricane is a cyclonic disturbance in the tropics that rotates about a low-pressure center, or "eye." Hurricanes begin as tropical storms; when the internal winds reach 119 kilometers per hour, the storm becomes a hurricane. As the velocity of the winds increases, the hurricane is upgraded according to a set scale ranging from force 1, which begins at 119 kilometers per hour, to force 5, which begins at 281 kilometers per hour. There are three types of motion in a hurricane: forward movement over the earth's surface, internal motion, and spin. A hurricane's speed of movement over the surface of the earth is its forward velocity; this speed varies between 8 and 80 kilometers per hour and can be erratic. The air speed inside the hurricane is called internal velocity; these winds sometimes reach a rate of more than 320 kilometers per hour, although they seldom reach as much as 240 kilometers per hour. The spin's speed is called rotational velocity and usually is relatively slow. All three movements occur simultaneously.

Hurricanes always begin over water and come to an end when they encounter cold water or land; they need to be "fed" by warm water to survive. In addition,

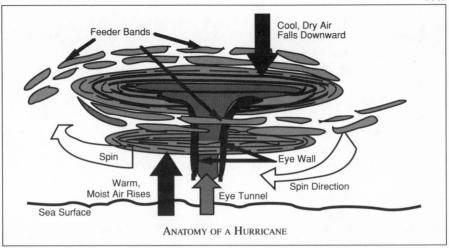

Feeder Bands

Cool, Dry Air
Falls Downward

Spin

Eye Wall

Warm,
Moist Air Rises

Spin Direction

Sea Surface

Eye Tunnel

ANATOMY OF A HURRICANE

hurricanes always form in a region of the earth that has come to be called the Hurricane Belt, an area adjacent to the equator and extending north and south to about 40° latitude. In the creation of a hurricane, the sun shining on the ocean heats the water, which in turn heats the air immediately above it. Three or four kilometers up, the temperature is much lower; the heated lower air is lifted upward, creating convection. The air then begins a constant upward drain and at the same time starts to spin; the hurricane is born. Hurricanes in the Northern Hemisphere spin counterclockwise; those in the Southern Hemisphere spin clockwise. When this mixing mass of air reaches an altitude of about 5 kilometers, gravity pulls it downward to the ocean. There, it is warmed and moistened, becoming light and buoyant once more, and the whole cycle repeats itself. The process continues until the hurricane encounters land and dies.

The force that gives the hurricane its forward motion is the general atmospheric movement in the region where the hurricane is created. Strong winds can push a hurricane in this or that direction. Meteorologists have determined that hurricanes are mostly generated close to the equator; that they follow parabolic paths (curving back in the direction from which they came); that when a hurricane pauses, it is about to change direction; that only one of every ten potential hurricanes actually matures and becomes a real hurricane; and that hurricanes usually last about five to seven days.

Hurricanes are invisible because they are winds; what is usually identified as a hurricane is its exhaust—the clouds that shape themselves to follow the action of the swirling winds spinning around the central eye. It is through this seemingly empty eye that the hot air drives upward, causing a partial vacuum at the surface of the sea and drawing inward cool air that spills over from the top of the eye. All the incoming air moves up this column, and it is the flow of air up the column that brings about the sudden drop in barometric pressure. The drop lessens the weight of the atmosphere on the sea, the sea level rises, and wind-battered waves keep piling up more water as the storm moves closer to the coast. These actions create what is called a "storm surge": a wall of rolling water that can reach heights of more than 8 meters. It is the combination of storm surge and fierce winds that accounts for a hurricane's fury.

Hurricanes tend to conform to seasonal schedules. Most hurricanes occur in the late summer and early fall, when ocean temperatures are highest. By the start of the winter, cool winds begin to affect the warm areas, and the frequency of hurricanes begins to decrease. The Western Caribbean, Bay of Bengal, and Arabian Sea are notable exceptions. Most notable are the September and October hurricanes that skirt across the equator directly through the Caribbean Sea, causing some of the most widespread destruction of the hurricane season.

Hurricanes starting in the Northern Hemisphere tend to curve northward; those in the Southern Hemisphere curve southward. The paths of nearly all hurricanes are parabolic, and it has been determined that hurricanes reach their greatest intensity just before or at the place where they curve backward. (One exception to this rule was Hurricane Gilbert, which, in September, 1988, took an almost straight path from Africa to inland Mexico.) Once a hurricane begins its reverse journey, it immediately loses intensity in the coolness of the higher latitudes, even when over water. The storms almost always move from east to west during their lifetimes, and they tend to be drawn toward the pole in their own hemisphere. Finally, on North American coastlines, a hurricane picks up speed once it makes its first curve northward, and it will not slow until it makes its reverse curve and starts back toward the direction from which it first came.

Although the usual lifetime of a hurricane is five to seven days, that time may be lengthened by as much as two or three days by its erratic behavior. It is not unusual for a hurricane to stop dead in its tracks and remain motionless for a time before suddenly moving onward again. A hurricane may double back on itself, making an imprecise loop, and then continue onward in the direction in which it was originally moving.

Studies of hurricane frequency have revealed some statistical tendencies. The western North Pacific (a very large area) has been the leader in the number of hurricane occurrences, with twenty-six per year, followed by the East Pacific, with fifteen, and the North Atlantic, with eight. East Pacific hurricanes, however, often derive directly from Atlantic hurricanes, which cross over the Central American chain and then enter the Pacific Ocean region. Some meteorologists believe that the hurricane will take a path across the part of the Central American land bridge that exhibits the leanest profile and offers the moist exposure to water. Experience with hurricane pathways strongly supports this belief.

Mature hurricanes are usually covered by a layer of clouds containing a significant amount of moisture. The most intense part of the storm is located off center to the right of the direction of forward motion, and it is here that both wind and rain are concentrated. Precipitation from a hurricane can measure anywhere from a trace to a whole meter coming in one downpour. Since the eye, wind, and rain are often close together, they occur at ground level almost simultaneously. Strong winds drive the rain as the hurricane moves along its path, followed by the calm and motionless eye. In other instances, rain bands occur toward the outer fringes of the mass and can extend over as much as 300 kilometers, dumping record-setting amounts of rainfall. Occasionally, when a hurricane comes to a full stop, the amount of rainfall at ground level can be catastrophic, causing heavy flooding. During the stop, however, the hurricane begins to lose much of its intensity.

Although the eye is a region of relative calm, it should always be regarded as an unstable feature. A period of sunshine may occur, the wind may die, and the temperature may even rise—perhaps as much as 10 degrees Celsius. This situation fools people into thinking that the storm has passed when, in fact, the second half of the hurricane, usually much worse than the first half, is still to come. Since the eye's diameter and the hurricane's forward velocity vary, the time it takes the eye to pass also varies—from a few minutes to several hours. Other events that occur in the eye include large downward flows of ice crystals, almost like waterfalls. Little accumulations of puffy clouds frequently build up at some level, sometimes very thin and at other times quite thick. The clouds come and go unpredictably.

"Monsoon" was first used in India to indicate winds that blew southwest in summer and northeast in winter. The term, which comes from the Arabian word *mausim* (season), has been broadened to include any large wind system that blows from cold to warm regions. In the Arabian Sea and the Bay of Bengal, the season of advance is in May and June, and the season of retreat is in September and October. Monsoons inevitably bring heavy rains, on which agrarian cultures depend for irrigation. In fact, for the Japanese, the coming of a monsoon is a time for celebration.

Monsoons are driven by the presence or absence of jet streams, which themselves are created by changes in temperature. In the summertime, the temperature at the North Pole is about zero degrees Celsius, and the usual jet streams all but vanish. It is at this time that an easterly jet stream, moving at or above the 16-kilometer level, takes advantage of this absence and forms across southern Asia and Africa, bringing the monsoon rains. This jet stream has no counterpart in the Southern Hemisphere and is aided by the seasonal flow of cool, moist ocean air over the hot land. Any delay in this seasonal shift can have catastrophic effects, including the starvation of millions of people who rely on the monsoon for crop watering.

As summer temperatures build day after day, rising hot air causes low-pressure areas that extend for millions of square kilometers across the planet. Cool sea air blows across the hot continents. During this period, the low-pressure areas produce hurricanes in the Hurricane Belt as well as monsoons. In winter, the process reverses itself: The land cools off and the sea breezes become warmer, bringing about the next cycle in the monsoon schedule.

Monsoon rains appear almost the same as the sheets of rain emanating from hurricanes, but there is no devastating, driving wind behind them. Rather, they simply pour down in large amounts. They do little damage, except for flooding, and in this case, flooding is welcomed as a water source for waiting fields of crops.

Methods of Study

Hurricanes and monsoons are studied on the ground as well as in the air. Rain gauges measure amounts of rainfall, weather vanes monitor wind direction, and barometers record changes in barometric pressure. Since wind is the principal physical force in these storms, however, it usually is necessary to go above the ground to study the features that these winds create. Scientists working with the National Oceanic and Atmospheric Administration have purposely flown into the eyes of numerous hurricanes to study their structure. These studies allow scientists to make measurements of wind velocities, water saturation and volume, wind direction, and barometric pressure. Since the eye is mostly without movement and since it can reach as much as 130 kilometers in diameter, the researchers are not in extreme danger unless their aircraft gets too close to the wall of the eye. Not all hurricanes have well-defined eye walls, however, and in many hurricanes, the eye wall changes constantly during the life of the storm. This erratic eye-wall behavior makes study flights very risky. Nevertheless, the study of hurricane eyes has contributed significantly to the understanding of hurricane behavior, and not a single scientist has been killed in the process. Advances in technology have yielded better airborne and spaceborne methods of study, however, including satellites and high-altitude radar and photographic reconnaissance planes.

Weather-satellite imaging, especially, has been a major tool in these studies, because it allows not only extremely broad coverage (literally, an entire side of the planet at once) but also close-up views. In addition, the photographic paper prints made from satellite digital imagery can be enlarged to study fine detail or kept at their original size to study weather relationships across sweeping expanses of the planet. One can see the entire Atlantic and Pacific oceans on either side of a major continental mass and compare weather systems in the two oceans.

Radar has been used extensively, not only to study the layered structure of hurricanes but also to aid in the creation of numerical and computer models of hurricanes. Radar has the capacity to measure dense portions precisely and to include the wide panorama of a large hurricane, furnishing numerical data that are used to construct three-dimensional illustrations of, especially, the tops of hurricanes. By collecting these numerical data over a long period, meteorologists can construct a sequence of pictures that follows the hurricane from birth to death.

Despite these advances in technology, high-flying aircraft and weather balloons are still essential to measuring the weather and its effects. Helium-filled weather balloons ascend to high altitudes, carrying temperature and chemical sensing gear. The balloons are transported by wind systems and can be tracked by radio to determine their speed and direction. An aircraft, on the other hand, is controlled by a pilot, and the onboard instruments can be carried directly into a storm, for example.

Manned spacecraft, such as the U.S. space shuttle orbiter and the Soviet space stations Salyut and Mir, act as orbiting platforms at lower altitudes than satellites. Astronauts and cosmonauts can take very detailed photographs of major weather systems and can even pinpoint photographically the ground effects of severe storms as the spacecraft make successive passes over the surface of the planet. The United States' Skylab space station, from 1972 to 1974, allowed onboard astronauts to photograph numerous tropical storms and hurricanes by means of successive passes over almost the same area of the earth.

The instrument that has contributed most to knowledge of weather patterns and systems has been the desktop computer, which allows scientists to record, analyze, compare, and compile enormous amounts of data. Historical accounts, measurements, and other information representing centuries of data can be put into computers by meteorological researchers. Major patterns, previously unnoticed, become clear as these analytical tools are used to study the earth's weather machine. In some cases, it is even possible to go back into history and create computer models of single storm systems. Using the models, scientists are better able to predict future weather trends and their effects on populations, agriculture, geography, and climate.

Context

People who live in coastal cities and towns are always affected by hurricanes and monsoons. Hurricanes, especially, can devastate large areas of land and take many lives. Hurricane Camille, which hit the U.S. Gulf coast states of Mississippi, Louisiana, and Alabama to vanish off the coast of Virginia, left as many as 400 dead or presumed dead in August, 1969. A hurricane along the coast is not an isolated event. The temperature, barometric pressures, and winds can cause catastrophic events to take place far inland, away from the hurricane itself. In 1986, for example, Hurricane Diana entered the eastern coastline curve of Florida on September 8 and began a slow drive directly up the coast all the way to Newfoundland. On that particular day, a warm front moving north from the Gulf of Mexico combined with a cold front moving south from Canada, meeting the westward-moving temperature and pressure from Hurricane Diana. All three systems came together over Missouri. The result was a raking thunderstorm the size of the entire state which lashed wind-driven rain in huge amounts from Kansas City to St. Louis and into Illinois, causing considerable damage from hail, flooding, and lightning.

The National Weather Service is able to advise citizens and the news media about severe weather and specific storms. It is not unusual now for mobile camera crews and reporters to go to the scene of a hurricane in progress for live television coverage of all aspects of the storm. The entire lifetime of Hurricane Gilbert in September, 1988, was covered by television camera crews, including on-board interviews and photographic coverage of scientific airplanes making their descent into the eye of the hurricane.

Bibliography

Bernard, Harold W., Jr. *Weather Watch: How to Make the Most of America's Changing Climate*. New York: Walker, 1979. This unusual view of the major components of weather and their effects includes much useful information for anyone interested in the subject of weather in general or severe storms in particular. Diagrams, charts, and sketches help explain concepts and provide needed visual support. Bernard writes clearly about the problems of the next millennium that can be charged to major changes in the weather machine. Good reading for high school and college-level readers.

Green, Fitzhugh. *A Change in the Weather*. New York: W. W. Norton, 1977. Green describes and illustrates the unusual tools that have been developed for weather modification. Stopping hurricanes, seeding clouds, dispersing fog, and dealing with problems of thunder and lightning are only some of the topics in this fascinating book. Good photographs and diagrams help the reader understand the scope of these new technologies. Includes bibliography. For general audiences.

The Illustrated Encyclopedia of the Planet Earth. New York: Exeter Books, 1979. Highly accurate in science and technology, this source covers the entire scope of earth science. Earth's physical aspects are carefully explained and illustrated. A full-color atlas section is illuminating. Hundreds of photographs are supported by diagrams and sketches. For students from junior high school through college.

Simpson, Robert H., and H. Riehl. *The Hurricane and Its Impact*. Baton Rouge: Louisiana State University Press, 1981. The authors have packed an astounding amount of detailed information about hurricanes, monsoons, and other weather systems into this volume. For those interested in the hurricane as a scientific subject, this source is the place to begin. An excellent index and many graphs, charts, and satellite images enhance the text. For general audiences.

Thurman, Harold V. *Introductory Oceanography*. 5th ed. Columbus, Ohio: Merrill, 1988. This textbook contains a brief section entitled "Hurricanes: Nature's Safety Valves." It includes a diagram of the path followed by Hurricane David in 1979, satellite photographs of hurricanes, and several descriptions of famous hurricanes and the damage they caused.

Young, Louise B. *Earth's Aura*. New York: Alfred A. Knopf, 1977. Science writer Young clearly explains the fragile envelope that surrounds the earth. The book is a survey of the weather machine that affects daily life. It is lacking in illustration, but the writing style is delightful. For readers of all ages.

Thomas W. Becker

Cross-References

HYDROELECTRIC POWER

Field of study: Economic geology

Hydroelectric power is the one renewable energy resource that is environmentally nondestructive. The water that contains the potential energy can be generated numerous times as it flows downstream. This form of energy can be stored and shaped to the needs of millions of people.

Principal terms

ELECTRICITY: a flow of subatomic charged particles called electrons

ENERGY: the capacity for doing work; power (usually measured in kilowatts) multiplied by the duration (usually expressed in hours, sometimes in days)

FLOW RATE: the amount of water that passes a reference point in a specific amount of time (liters per second)

GENERATOR: the machine that converts mechanical energy to electrical energy

HEAD: the vertical height that water falls or the distance between the reservoir above and the turbine below

HYDROELECTRIC POWER: energy produced by employing falling water to turn a turbine-generator

KILOWATT: a thousand watts; a unit of measuring electric power

MEGAWATT: a million watts; a unit of measuring electric power

PENSTOCKS: the tube that carries water from the reservoir to the turbine

POWER: the rate that energy is transferred or produced

PUMPED HYDRO: a storage technique that utilizes surplus electricity to pump water into an elevated storage pond to be released later when more electricity is needed

TURBINE: a device with movable blades, mounted on a shaft, that converts mechanical energy to electrical energy by the force of water directed against the blades

Summary of the Methodology

Even though running water has been used by people for centuries to turn the wheels of gristmills and sawmills, it was not until the end of the nineteenth century that waterpower began to be employed to generate electricity. Hydroelectric projects can be as small as a waterwheel supplying energy to a single household or as large as a system of dams and storage projects that supply electricity to many cities and millions of people. Electric energy, generated by water-powered turbines, is transported to houses, factories, mills, and other sites of consumption along high-energy transmission lines that may extend for more than 1,500 kilometers. These transmission lines are either alternating current (AC), the type of electricity used in houses, or direct current (DC), the type of electricity used in batteries, and contain up to 500 megawatts of electrical energy. In the United States, agreements between states, regions, and Canada have created a network of transmission lines that allows the flow of electricity from one part of North America to another. This ability to transport electricity from one place to another was one of the driving forces behind the relocation of factories and mills from along the rivers to adjacent to sources of raw materials. The mobility of electricity has also allowed for the growth of numerous cities located away from sources of energy.

The easiest way to harness a river for the purpose of generating hydroelectric power is to construct a dam across a river and funnel the water through a turbine that creates electricity. A dam with a large reservoir of water behind it is best for generating electricity, because both the amount of water in the river and the demand for electricity vary throughout the year. For example, in the Columbia River system in the Pacific Northwest, the river reaches peak flow during the spring snowmelt, but demand for electricity is greatest during the late winter (for heating of homes) and summer (for air conditioning). The ability to store large volumes of water behind each of the dams in the system allows the electric utilities to meet summer and winter demands for electricity by "storing" the water until electricity is needed. Water from spring runoff is stored and then released to generate electricity to power air conditioners in the summer and to heat homes in the winter.

Large storage dams also allow a utility to increase or decrease electric generation to match the demand. Electrical demand in the morning is met by releasing extra water, while at night, when the demand is less, water is either kept in the reservoir or passed through the turbines using a process called spinning. Spinning is the method in which water passes through a turbine but no electricity is produced. In a matter of seconds, the spinning turbine can be engaged and electricity produced.

Another form of stored hydroelectric power is pumped storage. During the period from midnight to six in the morning, when energy demand is at its lowest, hydroelectric projects must maintain a minimum outflow of water for navigation, agriculture, mining interests, recreational interests, fish breeding, and water quality. A utility may choose to use the electricity produced by minimum stream flow regulations to pump water into a storage pond. Then, during the day, when energy demand increases, the pumped water is released and electricity generated.

During the late 1980's, pumped hydro required 1.3-1.4 kilowatt hours for every 1 kilowatt hour produced. That may not seem economic, but because the water is pumped using surplus energy (energy that cannot be saved), the utility is able to postpone generation until demand is present. Another consideration is the difference in the cost of energy at peak and nonpeak hours. Electricity sold by the utility during peak demand may be several times the cost of electricity sold during nonpeak hours. Some utilities have even pumped water into excavated caverns. Hydroelectric power produced by the pumped-hydro plants amounts to thousands of megawatts.

Applications of the Method

Hydroelectric power is produced by converting the potential power of natural streamflow into energy. That is commonly done by employing falling water to turn turbines, which drive generators and produce electricity. The amount of electric power produced is dependent upon the flow rate of the water and the head.

The flow rate of water is the volume of water that moves past a point during a specific period of time. The quantity of water is commonly measured by first determining the cross-sectional area (width and depth) of the river; second, the speed of the water is measured by defining a reference length of river to monitor, dropping a float at the upper end of the reference length, and recording the length of time the float takes to travel down the reference length of the river. Then, if one calculates the volume of water (length × width × depth) divided by the time the float took to travel down the reference length of the river, the result is volume per time—the stream velocity, or flow rate.

The head of a stream is the vertical height through which the water falls. The head measurement of a hydroelectric project is the elevation difference between where the water enters the intake pipe, or penstock, and the turbine below. When waterwheels are employed to produce electricity, the head measurement is the total distance that water falls to the waterwheel. As with all energy conversions, friction results in some loss. The type of turbine or waterwheel utilized can also contribute to greater or lesser losses of energy. The amount of electric power that can be produced is equal to the head, measured in meters, multiplied by the flow rate divided by 102, a "fudge" factor that takes into account some inherent energy losses. Efficiencies (actual energy produced divided by the amount of energy available in the flowing water) for hydropower plants (turbines, waterwheels) vary from a high of 97 percent, claimed by manufacturers of large turbines, to less than 25 percent for some waterwheels.

Two devices used to convert the potential energy of water to mechanical energy are the waterwheel and the water turbine. The type of waterwheel or turbine used is dependent upon the flow and head. The ideal situation is high head (more than 18 meters) and high flow, but it is feasible to produce electric energy with any combination of high head and low flow or low head and high flow. With head at less than 1 meter, it is not economical to generate electricity, although outside the United States, some projects with very large volumes of water available do operate at the lower limits.

Waterwheels are the simplest machines employed to generate hydroelectric power. The central shaft of the waterwheel, which in the past was directly connected to a grindstone, is hooked to a generator to produce electricity. Efficiency has been claimed by waterwheel manufacturers to be around 90 percent but the usual efficiency ranges from 60 percent down to around 20 percent. The most efficient is the overshot wheel, in which water falls onto the top of the wheel and turns it. The wheel is suspended over the tailwater (the water on the downstream side of the wheel) and is not resting in the water but is suspended above the water surface. This type of waterwheel requires at least a 2-meter head of water.

Three other types of waterwheels are able to operate at lower heads than does the overshot wheel, but all three are costly to construct. The first type, the low and high breast wheels, are turned by water striking the wheel at a point one-third to over one-half of the height of the wheel. The "low" or "high" defines the level at which the water enters the wheel. The second type, the undershot wheel, is probably the oldest style presently in use. The wheel is turned by water running under the wheel. Although this type of waterwheel has an efficiency of less than 25 percent, it can operate with less than a third of a meter head. The third low-head waterwheel is the Poncelet wheel, which is an improved undershot that rests just at the water level and depends upon the velocity of the water to turn the wheel. Because it forces the water through narrow openings on the wheel, it is suitable for heads of less than 2 meters, but it is easily damaged by debris carried in the water.

Because the waterwheel rotates at a slow rate, the gear box, which transfers the rotation energy to the turbine, is a very costly, complex collection of gears. This expense is a major disadvantage. Another disadvantage is the large size of a waterwheel—given the large amount of time and material involved and the low efficiency, the rate of monetary return is low. Overshot wheels, however, have the advantage of being able to operate with fluctuating water flows better than do water turbines. A second advantage is that once set up, an overshot wheel requires little repair and is not damaged by grit or clogged by leaves as the low-head water turbines are.

Two types of hydraulic turbines are in existence: impulse turbines, which utilize water that is exposed to normal atmospheric pressure, and reaction turbines, which use water under pressure to drive them. The Pelton impulse wheel was designed in 1880 and is the crossover from waterwheels to turbines. The Pelton wheel is composed of a disk with buckets attached to the outside of the wheel. This wheel requires a head of at least 18 meters but can operate under low flow rates because the water is forced under its own pressure through a nozzle to strike the buckets. The water striking the buckets causes the wheel to spin. Because operating efficiencies are commonly over 80 percent, this wheel is still a favorite of many small utilities in North America. The turgo impulse wheel represents an improvement over the Pelton. The water jet is aimed at the buckets at a low angle, thus allowing the stream of water to strike several buckets at once. That results in higher efficiencies with smaller wheels and lower flow rates than those needed for the Pelton. The turgo has an efficiency reported over 80 percent and is suited for use with heads greater than 10 meters. The cross-flow turbine is a drum-shaped impulse turbine with blades fixed along its outer edge. The drum design allows water to pass over the blades twice: once from the outside to the inside, then (after entering the drum) back outside again. The net result is up to 88 percent efficiency in large units and the ability to operate with heads as low as 1 meter. The cross-flow turbine is in widespread use around the world. It is simple to operate and largely self-cleaning.

Reaction turbines are normally used in the large hydroelectric projects; a single unit at Grand Coulee Dam can produce 825 megawatts. Reaction turbines work by placing the whole runner (which is what is left of the "wheel" and resembles all blades set into a central shaft) into the flow of water. The water is carried to the turbines from the reservoir by a long tube called a penstock. The penstock can be more than 10 meters in diameter and tens of meters long. A propeller turbine is a reaction type of turbine that resembles a boat propeller in a tube. This type of turbine may be set either horizontally or vertically, depending on the design of the system. The Kaplan turbine is a turbine with adjustable blades on the propeller to allow operation at different flow rates. The water pressure in this system must be constant or the runner will become unbalanced. Very large hydroelectric plants usually install the Francis turbine. This type of turbine is designed to be set up and adjusted for the specific site. It can be used with a head of 2 meters and has an efficiency rating over 80 percent. The turbine spins as water is introduced just above the runner and directed onto the blades, causing the blades to rotate. The water then falls through and out a draft tube. A complicated mechanical governor is often used to guide the water around the runner.

Most existing dams (98 percent) have been built for irrigation and flood control purposes and are therefore not utilized as generating facilities. These dams could be fitted with turbines to generate electricity and replace the more expensive fossil-fuel generating plants. Many of the existing hydroelectric power facilities are not generating to capacity because of nonpower constraints such as fish, navigation, and recreation. Many of the small irrigation and flood control projects could be fitted with impulse turbines or even waterwheel generating systems.

Context

Hydroelectric power is the one clean, renewable energy source available today. Large storage dams allow utilities to supply energy when it is needed at costs lower than those incurred by burning fossil fuels or using nuclear fusion. By pumping water into a secondary reservoir during nonpeak hours, energy can be stored. Hydroelectric plants do not face the high cost of environmental clean-up like those associated with the use of uranium and fossil fuels. That allows even small hydroelectric power plants to be economical. Other alternate power sources such as solar, wind, and geothermal still need research and development to make them economically feasible.

During the late 1980's, government and private industry studies were still identifying many regions in the world that could be developed with hydroelectric power plants. The available technology allowed for construction of dams that would permit unhindered fish migration, coexistence of fish hatcheries and hydroelectric projects, and maintenance of natural fish and wildlife populations. Concerns about commercial and sport fishing populations have resulted in the close monitoring of hydroelectric power plant operation by biologists to ensure fish survival.

A major obstacle to the development of new hydroelectric power plants is the large amount of paperwork involved. The cost of environmental impact studies can exceed the cost of actual construction of the projects. Dams must be licensed by the federal government and must meet hundreds of county and state regulations. The amount of water allowed to flow downstream is regulated to ensure that agriculture, sport and commercial fisheries, recreation, environmental considerations, and Native American water rights are satisfied. These competing interests for water imply that no single user of the river will determine how much or when water is moved through the dams.

Bibliography

Alward, Ron, Sherry Elisenbart, and John Volkman. *Micro-Hydro Power: Reviewing an Old Concept*. Butte, Mont.: National Center for Appropriate Technology, 1979. Delineates all the components of a hydroelectric system with detailed but easy to understand pictures. Although the title refers to micro-systems, this publication also includes pictures of turbines used on larger hydroelectric projects. It contains an international list of manufacturers and suppliers of hydroelectric system components as well as a well-written bibliography.

Freeze, R. Allan, and John A. Cherry. *Groundwater*. Englewood Cliffs, N.J.: Prentice-Hall, 1979. The leading groundwater hydrology text. The subject is presented in an interdisciplinary manner with practical sampling methods, and tests are explained. (It is important to understand the relationships between surface and subsurface water systems before understanding hydroelectric systems.)

McGuigan, Dermott. *Harnessing Water Power for Home Energy*. Pownal, Vt.: Garden Way Publishing, 1978. Explains how to build any type of small to microscale hydroelectric facility. Lists manufacturers in the United States and United Kingdom as well as the 1989 cost of the equipment.

Palmer, Tim. *Endangered Rivers and the Conservation Movement*. Berkeley: University of California Press, 1986. Examines the "flip side" of hydroelectric power: the river. Palmer details the conservation battles that people fought to preserve rivers in their natural states. This book is based on hundreds of interviews and was reviewed by a number of environmentalists and politicians. Easy, enjoyable reading.

Sullivan, Charles W. *Small-Hydropower Development: The Process, Pitfalls, and Experience*. 4 vols. Palo Alto, Calif.: Electric Power Research Institute, 1985-1986. This four-volume Electric Power Research Institute (EPRI) work explains hydroelectric power plants, how to determine where to place them, cost, regulations, environmental impact, and a number of other related topics. This study was completed under contract with the U.S. Department of Energy and is complete to the point of suggesting which computer programs one might utilize when organizing data. This complete study is detailed enough for any group wanting to build a hydroelectric plant and simple enough to read and understand for the nontechnical individual.

United States. Bonneville Power Administration. *Columbia River Power for the People: History of Policies of the Bonneville Power Administration*. Portland, Oreg.: Author, 1980. This publication provides a good description of the development of one of the largest hydroelectric systems in the world. Documents the harnessing and development of the Columbia River and the politics involved. Helps the reader to understand the social, economic, and cultural forces that must be pacified in order to create a successful hydroelectric system.

United States Federal Power Commission. *Hydroelectric Power Resources of the United States, Developed and Undeveloped.* Washington, D.C.: Government Printing Office, 1976. This Federal Power Commission reported on the electric power resources both developed and undeveloped as of 1976. Lists the state, project owner, river, developed and undeveloped generation capacity, and gross static head of all projects that are licensed by the United States federal government.

Susan D. Owen

Cross-References

Dams and Flood Control, 309; Drainage Basins, 384; Floods, 719; The Hydrologic Cycle, 1102; River Valleys, 2210; Earth Resources, 2175; Future Resources, 2182; Surface Water, 2504.

THE HYDROLOGIC CYCLE

Type of earth science: Hydrology

Water circulates through a system called the hydrologic cycle. This cycle operates through vegetation, in the atmosphere and in the earth, and on land, lakes, rivers, and oceans. The sun and the force of gravity provide the energy to drive the cycle that provides clean, pure water at the earth's surface.

Principal terms

BASE FLOW: that part of a stream's discharge derived from groundwater seeping into the stream

CAPILLARY FORCE: a form of water surface tension, forcing water to move through tiny pores in rock or soil, caused by molecular attraction between the water and earth materials

EVAPORATION: the process by which water is changed from a liquid or solid into vapor

INFILTRATION: the movement of water into and through the soil

INTERCEPTION: the process by which precipitation is captured on the surfaces of vegetation before it reaches the land surface

OVERLAND FLOW: the flow of water over the land surface caused by direct precipitation

PRECIPITATION: atmospheric water in the form of hail, mist, rain, sleet, or snow that falls to the earth's surface

RUNOFF: the total amount of water flowing in a stream, including overland flow, return flow, interflow, and base flow

SOIL MOISTURE: the water contained in the unsaturated zone above the water table

TRANSPIRATION: the process by which plants give off water vapor through their leaves

Summary of the Phenomenon

The unending circulation of water on earth is called the hydrologic cycle (see figure). This system is driven by the heat energy produced by the sun. Gravity pulls water that falls on the earth back to the oceans to be recycled once again. The total amount of water on earth is an estimated 1.36 billion cubic kilometers. Most of this vast amount of water—97.2 percent—is found in the earth's oceans. The Greenland and Antarctic ice caps and glaciers contain 2.15 percent of the earth's water. The remainder—0.65 percent—is divided among rivers (0.0001 percent), freshwater and saline lakes (0.017 percent), groundwater (0.61 percent), soil moisture (0.005 percent), the atmosphere (0.001 percent), and the biosphere and groundwater below 4,000 meters (0.0169 percent). While the percentage of water appears small for each of these water reservoirs, the total volume of water contained in each is immense.

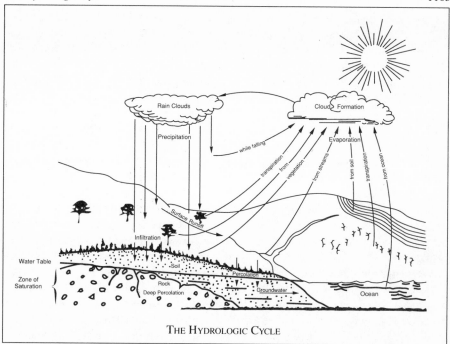

THE HYDROLOGIC CYCLE

SOURCE: U.S. Dept. of Agriculture, *Yearbook of Agriculture* (Washington, D.C.: Government Printing Office, 1955).

Description of the hydrologic cycle must begin with the oceans, as most of the earth's water is located there. Each year, about 320,000 cubic kilometers of water evaporate from the world's oceans. Evaporation is the process whereby a liquid or solid is changed to a gas. Adding heat to the water causes the water molecules to become increasingly energized and to move more rapidly, weakening the chemical force that binds them together. Eventually, as the temperature increases, water molecules tend to move from the ocean's surface into the overlying air. Factors that influence the rate of evaporation from free water surfaces are radiation, temperature, humidity, and wind velocity. It is estimated that an additional 60,000 cubic kilometers of water evaporate either from rivers, streams, and lakes or are transpired by plants every year. A total of about 380,000 cubic kilometers of water is evapotranspired from the earth's surface every year.

Wind may transport the moisture-laden air long distances. The amount of water vapor the air can hold depends upon the temperature. The higher the temperature, the more vapor the air can hold. As the vapor-laden air is lifted and cooled at higher altitudes, the vapor condenses to form droplets of water. Condensation is aided by the ever-present small dust and salt particles or nuclei in the atmosphere. As droplets collide and coalesce, raindrops begin to form and precipitation begins. Most precipitation events are the result of three causal factors: frontal precipitation, or the lifting of an air mass over a moving weather front; convectional precipitation related to the uneven heating of the earth's surface, causing warm air masses to rise and cool; and orographic precipitation, resulting from a moving air mass being forced to move upward over a mountain range, cooling the air as it rises. Each year, about 284,000 cubic kilometers of precipitation fall on the world's oceans. This water has completed its cycle and is ready to begin a new cycle. Approximately 96,000 cubic kilometers of precipitation fall upon the land surface each year. This precipitation follows a number of different pathways in the hydrologic cycle. It is estimated that 60,000 cubic kilometers evaporate from the surface of lakes or streams or transpire directly back into the atmosphere. The remainder—about 36,000 cubic kilometers—is intercepted by human structures or vegetation, is infiltrated into the soil or bedrock, or becomes surface runoff.

Although the amount of water intercepted by and evaporated from human structures—the surfaces of buildings and other artificial surfaces—may approach 100 percent, much urban water is co'' ʹted in storm sewers or drains that lead to a surface drainage system or is spread over the land surface to infiltrate the subsoil. Interception loss from vegetation is dependent upon interception capacity (the ability of the vegetation to collect and retain falling precipitation), wind speed (the higher the wind speed, the greater the rate of evaporation), and rainfall duration (the interception loss will decrease with the duration of rainfall, as the vegetative canopy will become saturated with water after a period of time). Broad leaf forests may intercept 15-25 percent of annual precipitation, and a bluegrass lawn may intercept 15-20 percent of precipitation during a growing season.

When the duration and intensity of the rainfall is greater than the earth's ability to absorb it, the excess water begins to run off, a process termed overland flow. Overland flow will begin only if the precipitation rate exceeds the infiltration capacity of the soil. Infiltration is the process whereby water sinks into the soil surface or into fractures of rocks. It is dependent upon the characteristics of the soil or rock type and upon the nature of the vegetative cover. Sandy soils have infiltration rates of 3.6-3.8 centimeters per hour, clay rock soils average 2.0-2.3 centimeters per hour. Nonporous rock would have an infiltration rate of zero, and all precipitation would become runoff. The presence of vegetation impedes surface runoff and increases the potential for infiltration to occur.

Water infiltrating into the soil or bedrock encounters two forces: capillary force and gravitational force. A capillary force is the tendency of the water in the subsurface to adhere to the surface of soil or sediment particles. This tendency may draw the water upward against the downward pull of gravity. Capillary forces are responsible for the soil moisture found a few inches below the land surface.

Growing plants are continuously extracting soil moisture and passing it into the atmosphere through a process called transpiration. Soil moisture is drawn into the plant rootlet because of osmotic pressure. The water moves through the plant to the leaves, where it is passed into the atmosphere through the leaf openings, or stomata. The plant uses less than 1 percent of the soil moisture in its metabolism; thus, transpiration is responsible for most water vapor loss from the land in the hydrologic cycle. For example, an oak tree may transpire 151,200 liters per year.

The water that continues to move downward under the force of gravity through the pores, cracks, and fissures of rocks or sediments will eventually enter a zone of water saturation. This source of underground water is called an aquifer—a rock or soil layer that is porous and permeable enough to hold and transport water. The top of this aquifer, or saturated zone, is the water table. This water is slowly moving toward a point where it is discharged to a lake, spring, or stream. Groundwater that augments the flow of a stream is called base flow. Base flow enables streams to continue to flow during droughts and winter months. Groundwater may flow directly into the oceans along coastlines.

When the infiltration capacity of the earth's surface is exceeded, overland flow begins as broad, thin sheets of water a few millimeters thick called sheet flow. After flowing a few meters, the sheets break up into threads of current that flow in tiny channels called rills. The rills coalesce into gullies and, finally, into streams and rivers. While evaporation losses occur from the stream surface, much of the water is returned to the world's oceans, thus completing the hydrologic cycle.

Scientists are interested in how long it takes water to move through the hydrologic cycle. The term "residence time" refers to how long a molecule of water would remain in the various components of the hydrologic cycle. The average length of time that a water molecule would stay in the atmosphere is about one week. Two weeks is the average residence time for a water molecule in a river and ten years in a lake. It would take four thousand years for all the water molecules in the oceans to be recycled. Groundwater may require anywhere from a few weeks to thousands of years to move through the cycle. This time period may appear extremely long to humans; yet it suggests that every water molecule has been recycled millions of times.

Methods of Study

Scientists have developed a vast array of mathematical equations and instruments to collect data to quantify the complexities of the hydrologic cycle. The geographic, secular, and seasonal variations in temperature, precipitation, evapotranspiration, solar radiation, vegetative cover, and soil and bedrock type, among other factors, must be evaluated to understand the local, regional, or global hydrologic cycle.

Precipitation, an extremely variable phenomenon, must be accurately measured to determine its input into the hydrologic cycle. The United States has some thirteen thousand precipitation stations equipped with rain gauges placed strategically to compensate for wind and splash losses. Techniques have been developed to determine the average depth of precipitation falling on a given area or drainage basin. The effective uniform depth method utilizes a rain-gauge network of uniform density to determine the arithmetic mean for rainfall in the area. The isohyetal and polygonal methods are used to determine the arithmetic mean for an area or basin with a nonuniform distribution of rain gauges. The amount of water in a snowpack is estimated by snow surveys. The depth and water content of the snowpack are measured and the extent of the snow cover mapped using satellite photography.

The amount of precipitation lost by interception can be measured and evaluated. Interception is equal to the type of vegetation, the amount of evaporation that occurs during the storm, and the length of the storm. Most often, interception is determined by measuring the amount above the vegetative canopy and at the earth's surface. The difference would be lost to interception.

The volume of water flowing by a given point at a given time in an open stream channel, measured in cubic meters per second (CMS), is called discharge. Discharge is determined by measuring the velocity of water in the stream channel with a current meter. The Price meter and the pygmy-Price meter meet the specifications of the U.S. Geological Survey. The cross-sectional area of the stream channel is determined at a specific point and multiplied by the stream velocity to determine discharge. Automated stream-gauging stations are located on most streams to supply data for various hydrologic investigations.

The U.S. Weather Bureau maintains about 500 stations using Class A land pans to measure free-water evaporation. These pans are 122 centimeters in diameter and 254 centimeters deep, and they are made of unpainted galvanized metal. Water depths of 17-20 centimeters are maintained. The wind velocity is also determined. Errors may result from splashing by raindrops or from birds. Because the metal pan will also heat and cool more rapidly than will a natural reservoir, a pan coefficient must be employed to compensate for this phenomenon. A lake evaporation nomograph is employed to determine daily lake evaporation. The mean daily temperature, wind velocity in kilometers per day, solar radiation, and mean daily dew point are the variables required to determine daily lake evaporation.

The amount of evapotranspiration can be measured using a lysimeter—a large container holding soil and living plants. The lysimeter is set outside, and the initial soil moisture is determined. All precipitation or irrigation is measured accurately. Changes in the soil moisture storage determine the amount of evapotranspiration.

Those techniques are utilized to determine the water budget for different geographic areas. Collectively, these data enable scientists to estimate the total water budget of the earth's hydrologic cycle.

Context

Water is necessary for life. It flushes waste, nourishes crops and animal life, and generates electricity. The amount of water on earth is immense—an estimated 1.36 billion cubic kilometers. The world's oceans contain 97.2 percent of all water on earth; 2.15 percent is located in ice caps, inaccessible to humans. The remaining 0.65 percent is located in streams, lakes, groundwater, and the atmosphere. This water is not uniformly distributed, resulting in water shortages in many sections of the earth. These water shortages may be the result of climate, overuse, or environmental degradation.

Water from the ocean and, to a lesser extent, the land is constantly evaporating or being transpired by plants into the atmosphere. Winds carry this moisture-laden air over the continents, where the air is cooled to form clouds; precipitation occurs as the moisture-laden air continues to cool. Precipitation in the form of snow may be stored in ice caps or glaciers and effectively removed from the hydrologic cycle for hundreds to tens of thousands of years. When rain falls upon the surface of the continents, some of the water will infiltrate into the earth to become soil moisture. The soil moisture may continue to move downward under the force of gravity to recharge the groundwater. Plant roots may extract large amounts of the soil moisture for use in metabolic processes. When the precipitation duration and intensity exceed the infiltration rate of the earth's surface, overland flow begins. The water is moved downslope under the force of gravity to augment streams and rivers; the river water will return to the ocean within a few days after the runoff event, thus completing this phase of what is known as the hydrologic cycle. All water on earth is involved in this constant, never-ending cycle.

Bibliography

Cunningham, Floyd F. *1001 Questions Answered About Water Resources*. New York: Dodd, Mead, 1967. Chapter 3, "The Water Cycle," provides forty-nine questions and answers characterizing the hydrologic cycle. There is a short introduction describing the cycle. The answers to each question are well conceived, short, and easily understood by the general public.

Fetter, C. W., Jr. *Applied Hydrogeology*. Westerville, Ohio: Charles E. Merrill, 1980. Chapter 1, "Water," provides a brief overview of the science of hydrogeology. An excellent, but brief, description of the hydrologic cycle is presented. This chapter provides an excellent introduction for the nonscientist.

Leopold, Luna B. *Water: A Primer*. San Francisco: W. H. Freeman, 1974. An excellent introduction to water science for the general public. The book discusses the general principles of hydrology for the reader who desires an overview of the discipline. Suitable for high school readers.

Lutgens, Frederick K., and Edward J. Tarbuck. *Essentials of Geology*. 3d ed. Westerville, Ohio: Charles E. Merrill, 1989. Chapter 6, "Mass Wasting and the Work of Running Water," provides an excellent discussion of the hydrologic cycle and the earth's water balance. Designed for the college student.

Smith, David G., ed. *The Cambridge Encyclopedia of Earth Sciences*. New York: Crown, 1981. Chapter 17, "Atmosphere, Water and Weather," presents a brief overview of the hydrologic cycle and water budget. The text is suited to the reader with a technical background. An excellent and complete reference volume.

Samuel F. Huffman

Cross-References

HYDROTHERMAL MINERALIZATION

Type of earth science: Economic geology

Hydrothermal mineralization refers to the formation of minerals from the interaction of hot aqueous (water) solutions with ordinary rocks. The minerals could form by precipitating directly out of the solutions, or they could result from the replacement of minerals by other minerals.

Principal terms

ANION: a negatively charged ion

BRINE: a solution that contains dissolved ions, including halogens such as chlorine, in excess of 3.5 percent

DIFFUSION: the movement of ions or molecules through a medium (solid, liquid, or gaseous) from a location of high concentration to that of a lower concentration

FLUID INCLUSION: a bubble, within a mineral, filled partly with liquid and partly with gas

ION PAIR: a loose combination of two or more ions, such that the combination acts as a single ion having a neutral, negative, or positive charge

IONS: atoms that have either gained or lost electrons

ISOTOPES: atoms of the same element with different numbers of neutrons in their nuclei

MINERAL: a natural substance with a definite chemical composition and with an ordered internal arrangement of atoms

REDUCED SULFUR: a negatively charged sulfur ion

SULFIDE: a mineral type containing reduced sulfur, as in zinc sulfide

Summary of the Phenomenon

Within certain zones of rocks, economic minerals exist in large enough amounts that they can be mined for profit. In other areas, these minerals and their constituent elements may be found in trace amounts. The question becomes one of understanding the characteristic differences between zones where there are abundant economic minerals and the bulk of rocks where there are virtually none. Is it possible for the trace elements that occur in ordinary rocks to be mobilized and then deposited in a concentrated form at those places where economic deposits are found? If so, how are these trace amounts removed from rocks, transported, and then deposited? The study of hydrothermal mineralization seeks to answer such questions.

A mineral is a natural substance with a definite chemical composition and an ordered internal arrangement of atoms. Commonly, economic hydrothermal minerals are dominated by the mineral group called sulfides. Sulfides are a combination of metallic ions such as those of copper, zinc, and lead with the sulfur ion. Ions are atoms that have lost electrons and are thus positively charged or that have gained electrons and are characterized by negative charges. The negatively charged sulfur ion is also called reduced sulfur. Examples of sulfides include chalcopyrite, a golden-colored copper-iron sulfide; sphalerite, a greenish-brown zinc sulfide; and galena, a shiny, silver-colored and heavy lead sulfide.

Many economic deposits exhibit textures indicating that the minerals formed by precipitation from solutions. In some places, hydrothermal solutions may have dissolved certain rock layers and caused the breakup of overlying rocks. The ensuing rock fragments (breccia) may be cemented together by minerals, including economic minerals, that precipitated from a later phase of hot aqueous solution processes.

Aqueous solutions can be classified into the following types: meteoric waters, which include river, lake, snow, and rain waters; seawater; juvenile waters, which originate from magmas; and connate waters, which are trapped in the pore spaces of rocks. Some connate waters have a concentration of dissolved ions exceeding 3.5 percent, a concentration greater than that found in normal seawater. Such waters are called brines.

Both the heat and the ions for juvenile waters originate from magmas. The other aqueous solutions become hot because the rocks within which they are trapped are buried deep within the earth or because such rocks are close to a hot magma. Metallic ions may be leached (removed by diffusion) from rocks by hot solutions that circulate through the rocks. These aqueous solutions can be distinguished by their isotope ratios. Isotopes of the same element have an identical number of protons, but they have different atomic weights because of the difference in the number of neutrons in their nuclei. From a study of isotope ratios in minerals, scientists can determine whether a single solution or a mixture of solutions was responsible for the formation of minerals and what the proportions of the component solutions in a mixture are.

Hydrothermal solutions circulate in various ways through permeable and fractured rocks because of differences in the effects of gravity, heat, or pressure between different places. Dense brines may seep essentially downward to replace light solutions below. Meteoric waters may move downward through fractures and interconnected pore spaces by the action of gravity and leach ions from rocks in their route. Such movement (hydrodynamics) readily explains why some economic deposits, including those found in some intrusive igneous rocks—rocks formed at depth from a cooling magma—contain isotopic ratios similar to those of meteoric waters.

Solutions expand and become buoyant (less dense) and rise upward to areas of lower gravity when they are heated at depth. Such hydrodynamics is better illustrated by what takes place in oceanic rocks. At the midpoints of oceans there are mid-ocean ridges (MORs). At an MOR, the oceanic crust is fractured, and hot magma ascends through these fractures and cools into rocks at the same time that cold seawater descends and is heated. Sodium and components of water molecules diffuse from the hot seawater into the rocks and change the nature of minerals as other ions diffuse from the rock into the solution. By such a mechanism, often called sub-sea-floor metamorphism, the original igneous rocks are changed into metamorphic rocks. What is more significant, ions leached from rock of the oceanic crust are transported in steam and ascend to the ocean floor. Scientists have observed from submarines that the ascending steams that gush out through fractures are comparatively dark, and they call such fractures "black smokers." The availability of reduced sulfur is key for the formation of sulfide deposits from black smokers.

Circulation of hydrothermal solution because of differences in heat between different places is exemplified by what happens when hot magmas intrude into cold rocks. A dramatic reaction results when a magma intrudes into a limestone, a light-colored rock composed predominantly of calcium carbonate minerals. Juvenile waters containing ions of iron, magnesium, silicon, and aluminum convert carbonate minerals into dark-colored silicate minerals as heat causes carbon to be removed in the form of carbon dioxide. Such a process of metamorphism of a rock is called contact metasomatism. By contact metasomatism, a light-colored limestone is changed to a dark-colored rock, called a skarn. A later hydrothermal solution may deposit economic minerals in the skarn.

Circulation of hydrothermal solutions caused by differences in pressure exerted at different places may explain what happens to connate waters trapped in the pore spaces of thick sequences of rocks. The weight of overlying thick sequences of rocks could cause enough pressure to squeeze out solutions from pore spaces of lower formations. The pressure for squeezing out these solutions could equally well come from lateral forces, such as those exerted during the collision of continents or similar rigid tectonic plates. Typically, such pressures cause hydrothermal solutions to move from lower levels of rock basins to higher levels of basin rims and beyond these rims. (Basins are depressions in which there is a thick sequence of rocks.)

In the circulating hydrothermal solutions, the atoms necessary for the formation of economic minerals are dissolved in the form of ions. Metallic ions and reduced sulfur combine readily, however, to form sulfide minerals, which should settle out from the solutions. Thus, it is not easy to transport metallic ions and reduced sulfur in the same solution. Some scientists believe that metallic ions combine with other ions to form pairs that act as single ions. In such ion pairs, the metals are kept in solution and then transported. There is no agreement among scientists, however, about the nature of these ion pairs or whether metallic ions and reduced sulfur are transported in the same or different solutions.

From the circulating hydrothermal solutions, minerals precipitate out and form economic deposits at certain places. Appropriate geologic settings for viable economic deposits include the following: a plumbing system that is continuous up to the source areas from which the mineralizing ions enter the hydrothermal solution; a rock sequence that slows down the circulation of hydrothermal solution so that minerals, some of which are extremely coarse-grained, can precipitate out; or a place where different conditions combine to cause the precipitation of minerals.

Scientists have suggested that the following conditions are possibilities that lead to the precipitation of minerals: the mixing of a metallic ion-carrying solution with a reduced sulfur-carrying solution; a hot solution encountering cold conditions; solutions encountering conditions where their hydrogen ion content (pH) must change; or solutions encountering conditions that lead to the breaking of ion-pairing mechanisms that had kept metallic ions dissolved. In some localities, the common rocks might serve as essentially passive places where the conditions that cause mineral precipitation are mingling. In other places, the rocks are reactive, and the formation of economic deposits results from solution-rock interaction. Scientists can infer the geologic conditions and processes that led to the precipitation of economic mineral deposits from stable isotope ratios in the minerals.

Methods of Study

Hydrothermal mineralization may be inferred from the analysis of minerals by using a variety of methods and instruments: petrographic microscopes for distinguishing mineral types, heating- and freezing-stage microscopes for estimating temperature and salinity of fluids, mass spectrometers for estimating geologic conditions and processes, and radiant-energy emission-measuring instruments such as electron microprobes, X-ray fluorescence spectrometers, and instrumental neutron activation analysis equipment for determining elemental composition.

Rocks can be sliced into extremely thin sections (0.03 millimeter thick) after they have been mounted on transparent glass. In these thin sections, some minerals allow the transmission of light through them; they are called transparent minerals. Others, such as sulfides, reflect light and are opaque. Such optical properties can be used for identifying minerals under appropriate microscopes. Reflected-light microscopes are used to identify opaque minerals, and transmitted-light microscopes are used for transparent minerals.

In some transparent minerals, spherical and ellipsoidal bubbles, filled partly by a liquid phase and partly by gas, are observed. These are fluid inclusions. A thin section containing fluid inclusions is placed on a heating and cooling stage, a specially designed stage, of a transmitted-light microscope. On the heating stage, the heat is increased until the bubbles in a thin section are filled with a homogeneous phase—that is, until there is no more separation between liquid and gas in the fluid inclusions. The temperature of homogenization of the fluids in the bubbles is then recorded and is deduced to be the minimum temperature of the fluid from which the enclosing mineral was formed. The fluid may be examined in place or extracted for further chemical analysis—for example, to determine the type and amount of dissolved ions. Other samples from the same rock, containing identical bubbles, may be frozen until the fluids in the bubbles become solids. The freezing temperature is recorded, and scientists use this temperature to infer the amount of salts that were dissolved in the solution.

Geologic conditions and processes that led to the formation of minerals may be determined from isotopes in minerals. For this analysis, selected samples are powdered and dissolved in acids, producing gases. The gas container is then attached to a mass spectrometer, and the gases are made to enter a chamber. In this chamber, the gases are bombarded with electrons so that atoms (including isotopes) in the gases lose electrons and are converted into positive ions. The ionized isotopes are accelerated and made to pass through a magnetic field before they arrive at a detector. Electrical signals from the detector can be digitized or displayed on a strip-chart recorder. A series of peaks, each representing an isotope (the peak height being proportional to the abundance of the isotope), can be recorded by adjusting the accelerating voltage or the magnetic field. This technique permits the identification of isotopes and determination of their relative abundance. If the isotopes are stable isotopes (isotopes that do not change into other ones), then isotope ratios in rocks yield information on geologic conditions. Geologic conditions such as oxidation-reduction reactions, temperature, or diffusion, as well as the type of solution that led to the formation of hydrothermal minerals, can be extrapolated from stable isotope ratios in rocks. If the isotopes are naturally radioactive, they can be used to determine the age of formation of hydrothermal minerals.

Change in the composition of a hydrothermal solution during the growth of a mineral may be estimated by using an electron microprobe (EMP). The EMP is a powerful tool for determining the variation of composition within a single mineral, because several analyses can be conducted on one surface of a mineral. For an EMP analysis, polished rock samples are placed on the stage of a special microscope, which is fitted with an X-ray spectrometer for the determination of elemental composition of a sample. The polished sample is carbon-coated and then bombarded with electrons, causing electrons from the sample to be excited to higher energy levels. Upon deexcitation, irradiated X rays are guided to a crystal that will cause separation of the rays so that they may be detected by X-ray counting devices or displayed on strip-chart records as peaks and valleys. The peak positions on the charts correspond to the elements in the rock sample, and the peak heights are proportional to the concentration of the elements.

An analytical technique that is similar to the EMP is the use of the X-ray fluorescence spectrometer (XRF). For an XRF analysis, selected samples are powdered and then bombarded with X rays. The elements in the sample then irradiate X rays, which can be analyzed as in the EMP method. Major and trace elements in minerals can be identified by this method, which will provide comprehensive information about the hydrothermal solution from which the minerals were formed.

Detailed information on hydrothermal mineralization may be determined from elements that occur in extremely small amounts and cannot be determined by the methods discussed above. Instrumental neutron activation analysis (INAA) can circumvent this problem. For the INAA, selected samples are powdered and placed in small containers. The samples are then placed in a chamber where they are bombarded by neutrons supplied by a nuclear reactor or a particle accelerator. The atoms in the sample incorporate these neutrons and become artificially induced heavy and unstable (radioactive) isotopes. The samples are removed and placed in a chamber where the activity of gamma rays emitted by the decay of the artificial radioactive isotopes can be detected by a recording device. The elements are identified from the decay constants and half-lives of the isotopes.

Context

Hydrothermal mineralization is the formation of minerals from naturally hot aqueous solutions. Minerals that form at the mouths of hot springs (geysers) are hydrothermal minerals. Such minerals are usually banded and colorful. Hot springs produce banded calcium carbonate rocks, called travertine, which are used as building stones. In the Old Faithful geyser of Yellowstone National Park, Wyoming, a famous tourist attraction, hydrothermal solutions spout out episodically. Cold water descends to hot levels during those minutes when the geyser is quiet. As the descending cold water is heated, it turns into steam, ascends through the same fractures, and becomes a fountain of hot water and steam.

Hydrothermal solutions can be a source of wealth through means other than tourism. The circulation of hydrothermal solutions can be interrupted in such a way as to cause the rotation of turbines and associated instrumentation for the generation of geothermal electric power. Such geothermal energy, a clean source of energy, is utilized in those regions where there is ample near-surface circulation of hydrothermal solutions, such as in Iceland and in western California.

Some economic mineral deposits are formed by hydrothermal mineralization processes. Economic mineral deposits are commonly exploited for their metallic components. The properties of metals are such that they have many applications. Furniture; materials for electrical wiring, cables, and plumbing systems; kitchen utensils; and the framework of buildings can be partly or completely made of metals. Automobiles, trucks, trains, ships, submarines, airplanes, rockets, guns, and munitions are almost entirely made of metals. Jewelry, too, is commonly metallic. Metallic coins serve as currencies. Clearly, metals have profound impact on civilization. Economic mineral deposits are not sought only for their metals. Certain economic minerals, because of their industrial applications, are called industrial minerals. Industrial minerals may be used as insulators of heat and electric current, as cement and concrete for buildings, or as fertilizers.

Because economic mineral deposits have a variety of applications for the advancement of humankind, deposit-rich regions are of special interest to all societies. The presence of economic mineral deposits may not necessarily be beneficial, however, to the societies that inhabit the deposit-rich regions. Depending on the sociocultural background of a society, its economic mineral deposits may help it to become economically advanced or may cause it to be colonized and exploited by others. Moreover, the mere abundance of economic mineral deposits in a region does not mean that the minerals will be mined. The extraction of minerals from the ground depends on a variety of factors, including the quality of the economic infrastructure such as roads, water, and electric power; the existence of a nearby mineral concentrator; the proximity to markets; and the political stability of the society.

Hydrothermal mineralization leading to the formation of economic mineral deposits is important to human beings, so much so that governments and private companies invest substantial sums of money and effort to find such deposits. Native elements such as gold, copper, silver, and sulfur are so easy to identify that even the ancients knew how to mine for them. Similarly, soils and rocks rich in iron oxide are relatively easy to identify by their rusty coloration. The ancients knew how to extract these deposits and how to smelt them for metallic iron. The minerals that are found on the surface of the earth have by now been mostly mined. The current effort is to extract economic minerals from beneath the surface of the earth. The modern search for mineral deposits requires the utilization of sophisticated tools.

Bibliography

Barnes, H. L., ed. *Geochemistry of Hydrothermal Ore Deposits*. 2d ed. New York: Wiley-Interscience, 1979. An excellent collection of basic articles on ore-forming processes.

Dear, W. A., R. A. Howie, and J. Zussman. *Rock Forming Minerals*. Vol. 5, *Non-Silicates*. 4th ed. London: Longmans, 1965. This work describes nonsilicate minerals such as sulfides, oxides, and carbonates. Useful for advanced students and research workers.

Guilbert, John M., and Charles F. Park, Jr. *The Geology of Ore Deposits*. New York: W. H. Freeman, 1985. One of the textbooks used in colleges for the study of ore deposits. Provides an excellent description of hydrothermal fluids, their migration, and other processes that lead to the formation of deposits. Chapters 2 through 5 describe various aspects of hydrothermal processes.

Sawkins, F. J., ed. *Metal Deposits in Relation to Plate Tectonics*. New York: Springer-Verlag, 1984. No specific chapter is devoted to hydrothermal solutions in this book. Yet discussions of mineral deposit types in the book address hydrothermal fluid movement and deposition. Provides an excellent survey of the geologic settings in which mineral deposits occur.

Skinner, B. J., ed. *Economic Geology: Seventy-fifth Anniversary Volume, 1905-1980*. Lancaster, Pa.: Economic Geology, 1981. An excellent collection of articles. Useful for advanced students and researchers in the geological sciences.

Stanton, R. L. *Ore Petrology*. New York: McGraw-Hill, 1972. A very helpful college-level book on ore deposits. Stanton emphasizes the association of mineral deposits with ordinary rocks. Hydrothermal solutions are discussed in chapter 6.

Habte Giorgis Churnet

Cross-References

Fluid Inclusions, 726; Gem Minerals, 802; Geothermal Phenomena and Heat Transport, 906; Geysers and Hot Springs, 929; Groundwater Movement, 1020; Heat Sources and Heat Flow, 1065; Crystallization of Magmas, 1420; Water in Magmas, 1433; Metamorphism: Metasomatism, 1599; Sub-Sea-Floor Metamorphism, 1614; Pegmatites, 2025; Stable Isotopes: Water-Rock Interactions, 2462.

ICE AGES

Type of earth science: Paleontology and earth history

Several periods of earth's history were marked by major glacial episodes. Possible causes of these episodes include the movement of the earth's continental areas into higher latitudes, changes in atmospheric composition and motion, and changes in the earth's orbit. Effects of the ice ages included substantial changes in sea level and coastal topography, alteration of lake and river drainage, and the shifting of plants and animals accompanying the changing climates.

Principal terms

ALBEDO: the amount of solar energy reflected by the earth's surface back into space; an increase in albedo is believed to lead to lower temperatures and stimulates the expansion of glaciers

GLACIATION: a major formation of land ice and the period in which it occurs

GLACIER: an accumulation of ice that flows viscously as a result of its own weight; it forms when snowfall accumulates and recrystallizes into a granular snow (firn, or névé), which becomes compacted and converted into solid, interlocking glacial ice

INTERGLACIAL PERIOD: the interval of milder climate between two major glacial episodes

PLEISTOCENE: the epoch of earth history characterized by the presence of large ice sheets in the higher latitudes of the Northern Hemisphere, approximately 2 million to 10,000 years before the present

SCABLAND: a region characterized by rocky, elevated tracts of land with little soil cover and by postglacial dry stream channels

Summary of the Phenomenon

There have been several periods in earth history in which large glaciers have covered substantial portions of the earth's surface. These "ice ages" were created during times in which more snow fell during the winter than was lost by ablation (melting, evaporation, and loss of ice chunks in water) during the summer. Approximately 2 billion years ago, during the Proterozoic eon, large ice sheets covered substantial portions of North America, Finland, India, and southern Africa as indicated by glacially deposited sediments termed tillites. Such glacial deposits have also been found in rocks of late Ordovician and early Silurian age in northern Africa, approximately 440-420 million years before the present. Glacial episodes intensified on the Gondwanaland continent during the Carboniferous (Mississippian and Pennsylvanian periods of North American classification) and Permian periods, as tillites and glacially scoured areas indicate the presence of vast ice sheets over large areas within the southern portions of South America, Africa, India, and Australia. Antarctica was probably almost completely covered with ice sheets at this time, and there are indications that the ice sheets expanded and retreated at intervals within these periods, spanning some 360 to 245 million years before the present. Although these earlier glacial episodes may represent substantial cooling periods for portions of the earth's surface, the term "ice ages" has almost become synonymous with the last great glacial episode at the end of the Cenozoic era. There is evidence that within South America, this glaciation began somewhere between 7 and 4.6 million years ago. In most areas, the major glacial episodes spanned the latter part of the Pliocene and the Pleistocene epochs, a period between 3 million and 10,000 years before the present. During this interval, ice sheets with thicknesses of 3 kilometers or more accumulated over much of the higher latitudes of the Northern Hemisphere.

Traditionally, these late Cenozoic ice ages have been separated into four subdivisions. In the European Alps, these included, from oldest to youngest, the Gunz, Mindel, Riss, and Würm glacials. These periods were believed to be separated by warmer interglacial periods termed the Gunz-Mindel, Mindel-Riss, and Riss-Würm. In North America, a fourfold subdivision was also utilized, which included (from oldest to youngest) the Nebraskan, Kansan, Illinoian, and Wisconsin glacials. These were divided by the Aftonian, Yarmouth, and Sangamon interglacials respectively. This fourfold subdivision seemed to be represented in other global regions as well. By the late 1970's, however, studies on deep-sea sediments indicated that the Alpine glacial sequence covered at least eight glacial cycles rather than four or five. Because severity of glaciation depends on both latitude and altitude as well as on local climatic factors, it has become apparent that such a simplistic classification for the last great ice age is untenable. Interdisciplinary studies are better establishing these glacial episodes and more precisely dating the glacial-interglacial cycles.

The causes of the ice ages may be quite varied. One possible explanation seems to be related to the distribution of continental areas as a result of plate tectonics. According to this theory, the earth is divided into a series of rigid plates that shift their position relative to one another because of the movement of underlying ductile material. Calculations on the position of Gondwanaland during the Carboniferous-Permian glaciation indicates that the southern portion of the supercontinent was situated over the South Pole. Such a position stimulated the growth of large ice sheets. The position of the continents during the last great ice age may also have caused the growth of ice sheets, as the most prominent glacial areas were at higher latitudes. Plate tectonics cannot, however, entirely account for late Cenozoic glaciation, as several glacial-interglacial periods have been recorded during a relatively brief period in which the earth's plates could not have been repeatedly repositioned in "colder" and "warmer" latitudes. Therefore, other explanations need to be sought to determine the specific causes of the last ice age.

Another explanation for the initiation of ice ages is that at certain intervals, the sun's luminosity decreases. Proposed mechanisms have been the movement of the sun through a dense interstellar cloud of gases and particles or fluctuations in the energy output of the sun. Other suggestions have concerned the earth's albedo, or the amount of solar energy reflected back into space. Twice during the nineteenth century, eruption of volcanoes in Indonesia resulted in colder winter temperatures worldwide as the result of a blockage of the sun's radiation by particles of floating volcanic ash. Short intervals of declining temperatures following these volcanic eruptions led to the hypothesis that severe climate changes could have been caused by more severe volcanism. It has also been suggested that the emergence of land areas during a relative drop in sea level also increases albedo because of the greater reflectivity of terrestrial surfaces. Such episodes may lead to a decrease in the relative temperature at the earth's surface. The greenhouse effect, in which an increase in carbon dioxide content in the atmosphere leads to greater temperatures, may also indirectly result in increased albedo. The higher temperatures may cause greater evaporation rates, and therefore more clouds would form. In turn, the tops of the clouds would reflect the sun's energy, possibly leading to a drop in temperature and initiating glaciation. A decrease in carbon dioxide content, however, could lead directly to the ice ages, because a decrease in this heat-trapping gas would cause a concomitant decrease in temperature. Another hypothesis suggests that mountain building along continental margins, where the earth's lithospheric plates collide, may have resulted in the formation of substantial mountain glaciers at the higher altitudes. The increased albedo resulting from the presence of these highly reflective ice surfaces may have resulted in cooler temperatures and more ice buildup, setting off a chain reaction leading to larger continental glaciers and major glacial episodes. There is no direct evidence, however, that volcanic eruptions, interstellar clouds and solar phenomena, emergence of landmasses, creation of mountain chains, or carbon dioxide fluctuations have led to glacial episodes.

Two hypotheses seem to fit the evidence better as pertains to the initiation of glaciation. Approximately 3.5 million years ago, the Isthmus of Panama emerged, apparently resulting in the strengthening of the Gulf Stream's northward flow. This strengthening may have fed more moisture to the northern high latitudes, therefore creating more snowfall and thus a buildup in glaciation. One of the most widely accepted theories concerning the origin of the ice ages was proposed by a Yugoslavian mathematician, Milutin Milankovitch. During the 1920's and 1930's, Milankovitch studied the possible effects of variations in the earth's orbit upon the timing of glacial episodes. These effects include the angle of the ecliptic (axial tilt), the precession of the equinoxes, and the eccentricity of the earth's orbit. At present, the earth's axial tilt is approximately 23.5 degrees from the perpendicular to the plane of the earth's orbit around the sun. According to Milankovitch's calculations, the earth's axial tilt would vary from approximately 22.1 to 24.5 degrees every 41,000 years. As the angle of the ecliptic is the primary factor producing the seasons, such cyclicity may lead to significant climate change. The second possible cause of climate change involves a variance in the eccentricity of the earth's orbit. A complete cycle between times of maximum orbital eccentricity occurs at approximately 93,000-year intervals, which closely corresponds to the twenty cold-warm cycles recorded in deep-sea cores from the last ice age. The final cycle theorized by

Milankovitch involved the precession of the equinoxes: The movement of the earth's axis would approximate the wobbling of a spinning top, with a periodicity of 21,000 years, which would cause a slow shift in the position of the solstices and equinoxes through time. As the earth's climate may be affected by each of these three cycles, the combination of their effects may at times create significant climate changes. As evidence from deep-sea cores seems to support the theory that Milankovitch's cycles correspond to glacial periodicity during the last ice age, this theory has become especially popular for explaining the origin of the major glacial periods.

Whatever caused the initiation of the ice ages, once large glaciers began forming, their presence may have stimulated further ice buildup. With more ice, the earth's albedo would increase, with resulting lower temperatures. Also, a drop in sea level accompanying glacial buildup would likely have led to variation in oceanic and atmospheric circulation patterns, along with a relative rise in altitude of the land-masses. Such a cycle may have been self-perpetuating, with more ice buildup creating more severe glaciation.

The effects of widespread glaciation were varied and profound. One result was a relative decrease in sea level, as more moisture became locked within the glacial ice. Estimations vary as to the amount of sea-level drop, although many scientists believe that it was 75 meters or more. This drop resulted in many changes in shoreline topography. Land bridges were formed between the British Isles and Europe, as well as between Asia and North America across the Bering Strait. The ice ages also greatly affected regional drainage patterns. Prior to Pleistocene glaciation, the northern portions of the Missouri and Ohio rivers drained toward the northeast. With incursion by the great ice sheet, called the Laurentide ice sheet, drainage patterns changed, eventually resulting in the modern southward drainage patterns. Because of this ice sheet's great weight, the continental crust beneath the glacial areas was depressed as much as 300 meters. As the glaciers melted and receded, the Great Lakes were formed within these basins. Even outside glacial areas, large lakes were formed because of the increased rainfall in certain areas. One of the largest of these pluvial lakes was Lake Bonneville, the remnant of which constitutes the Great Salt Lake of Utah. Glaciers also created large lakes by damming watercourses. In the Pacific Northwest, glacial Lake Missoula was a glacially dammed lake covering an area almost 8,000 square kilometers in extent. The disastrous collapse of the dam occurred during glacial retreat, with the ensuing catastrophic flooding creating the Channeled Scabland of eastern Washington. Another effect of glaciation is downcutting and subsequent erosion by rivers as a result of the lowering of sea level. Once the glaciers melt, sea level again rises, and rivers deposit large amounts of sediment in their floodplains.

Even in areas not covered by glacial ice, climates were affected. Studies indicate that glacial periods in the higher latitudes corresponded to drier (interpluvial) periods in temperate and tropical regions. Pluvial periods were essentially equivalent to the interglacials of higher latitudes.

Another possible effect of changing climates within and between glacial periods may be the selective extinction of animal species. At the end of the last great ice age, especially in North America, many types of large mammals became extinct. These extinctions have been theorized as resulting from the direct or indirect influence of climate change or, alternatively, as the result of the invasion of North America by Paleo-Indians across the Bering Strait land bridge. A seemingly less disastrous change that occurred during the Pleistocene—but one which is just as crucial for understanding the climate changes during the past glacial-interglacial periods—involves the displacement of plants and animals. The distributions through time of a wide variety of Pleistocene invertebrates, vertebrates, and plants have been documented. During periods of glaciation, forests diminished and desert areas, steppes, and grasslands increased in size. The peculiar presence of seemingly cold- and warm-climate species of mammals within the same deposits have led some scientists to speculate that some areas in front of the glaciers had a moderate climate. The winters were warmer (allowing the warm-climate species to live within the area) and the summers were cooler (enabling the cold-climate species also to become established in the same region). The fossil distributions of plants and animals during the past ice age indicate that they were often quite different from those observed at present.

Methods of Study

The concept of ice ages was first popularized by the naturalist Louis Agassiz during the mid-1800's. Building upon the work of other European scientists, Agassiz postulated that erratics (rocks removed far from their points of origin) and moraines (mounds or ridges of unsorted rock debris and sediment) were created and transported through the action of glaciers. Although initially rejected by most scientists, subsequent studies of glacially produced landforms verified the action of large ice sheets during the last glacial epoch.

One of the primary methods of documenting glacial events involves the study of changing climates. Paleontological studies, involving the distribution of fossil plants and animals, play an important role in this research. Fossil mammals have been especially important in the study of changes in climate, with analyses of the distribution of warm- versus cold-preferring types. Similarly, invertebrate animals have been utilized, including bivalves, snails, beetles, and especially the one-celled foraminiferans and coccoliths. Studies of the leaves, wood, seeds, pollen, and spores of fossil plants have also documented periods of climate change during the glacial-interglacial periods. Charts showing changes in pollen distributions within regions through time have been especially important in documenting climate variation. Another method of showing changes in temperature involves chemical techniques, especially the utilization of oxygen isotopes. There are three isotopes of oxygen, the most important being oxygen 16 (the normal form) and oxygen 18 (the "heavier" isotope). When water evaporates, the "lighter" isotope, oxygen 16, is preferentially sampled. The locking of this water in ice sheets during the great ice ages led to a slight increase in the amount of oxygen 18 within seawater. The isotopic compositions of the ice ages were preserved within the ice sheets or in calcium carbonate oceanic deposits. The study of deep-sea cores or cores from Antarctic glaciers reveals a history of changing climate during the Late Tertiary and Quaternary periods of earth history.

Chronological studies are very important in the study of the ice ages, as each glacial-interglacial cycle must be differentiated in order to be properly documented. Initially, relative dating techniques were used to document these changes. Paleontological studies, which established the changing plant and animal compositions throughout the glacial epochs, proved very important for formulating a relative chronology. Also of major importance were stratigraphic studies, in which the sequence of glacial- and interglacial-age rock and sediment layers was established. These relative dating techniques, however, have proven ineffective for precise dating of individual climate events. Therefore, absolute dating techniques (in which the age of sediments is determined in terms of years) have proven very important for determining the sequence of events. Varves—annual couplets of light- and dark-colored sediments formed in lakes located immediately outside the glacial areas—have been used for dating glacial events in regions such as Scandinavia. Of more importance is the utilization of radioactive isotopes for dating glacial-interglacial events. These radiometric techniques assume that the decay of a parent isotope to its daughter product is constant. The period in which half of the parent isotopes decay is termed the half-life. Three isotope pairs that have been especially useful for dating glacial events are potassium 40/argon 40 (with a half-life of approximately 1.31 billion years), uranium 235/lead 207 (with a half-life of approximately 700 million years), and carbon 14/nitrogen 14 (with a half-life of approximately 5,730 years). The most accurate of these techniques is carbon 14/nitrogen 14, although because of its relatively short half-life, it can only be utilized effectively for samples less than 70,000 years old.

Using data gathered from deep-sea cores, scientists have also established a paleomagnetic time scale for the last ice age. The earth's magnetic field changes polarity, apparently at random. The matching of these polarity changes with a known absolute date (usually established radiometrically) allows the stratigrapher to establish the date of an iron-bearing sediment in which the paleomagnetic record is preserved. Similarly, the study of the sequence of "heavy" and "light" oxygen isotope periods has allowed the construction of oxygen isotope stages for the Pleistocene.

Context

Within the higher latitudes, glacial landforms created during the Pleistocene ice ages greatly influence the decisions of urban planners and environmental scientists. Many of the buried glacial landforms constitute major aquifers (water-bearing strata of permeable rock, sand, or gravel), which supply water for farms and cities in many regions. The selection of landfills and toxic waste dumps must also take into account the distribution of glacially formed sand and gravel bodies, which may act as conduits for redistribution of toxic substances. Study of buried glacial landforms must be conducted in order to maintain a safe environment. Also, much glacially derived sand and gravel is utilized within the higher latitudes in construction of buildings and highways. Glacial landforms provide relatively inexpensive and substantial supplies of these materials.

The study of the earth's past climates is important in any study concerning the prediction of future climates. The belief that the earth's climate is cyclical, as established by the studies of Milutin Milankovitch during the 1920's and 1930's, is important for understanding future climate cycles. As human existence on earth is dependent on future climates, such studies may be critical for the survival of humankind. Studies of ancient climate changes will provide the basis for long-term climate prediction.

Another important aspect of studies of ice ages is to test the hypothesis of nuclear winter. It is believed that nuclear war would cause a tremendous increase in particulate matter in the atmosphere because of the throwing of dust into the atmosphere and the burning of cities and vegetated areas initiated by the intense heat of the nuclear blasts. As this would increase the earth's albedo (a result of the formation of huge dust clouds), it is hypothesized that the earth's temperatures would plummet. This temperature decrease would probably lead to the mass extinction of many plants and animals. It is clearly impractical to test the nuclear winter hypothesis directly. Therefore, the effects of severe climate change upon the plants and animals of the earth (including humans) must be tested based on past climate change. As the Pleistocene ice age is the best documented of these severe climate episodes, scientists are especially interested in it as a model for predicting the effects of nuclear war upon the earth's climate and inhabitants.

During the last set of glacial-interglacial cycles, many changes took place in human evolution. Social organization, major inventions (such as fire and hunting paraphernalia), and art were molded during the Pleistocene epoch. For understanding the origins of our culture, the study of the ice ages is of utmost importance.

Bibliography

Imbrie, J., and K. P. Imbrie. *Ice Ages: Solving the Mystery.* Cambridge, Mass.: Harvard University Press, 1979. This well-written book (it won the Phi Beta Kappa Science Writing Award) is a readily comprehended guide to the growth of knowledge that led to the modern understanding of the Pleistocene ice ages. A discussion of the history of study of the ice ages enables the reader to develop a general knowledge of their characteristics and possible causes.

Kurtén, B. *The Ice Age.* London: Rupert Hart-Davis, 1972. This book can be easily understood by high school students with little training in biology or geology. The primary topic covered is the changing mammalian faunas of the ice ages. The text is complemented by many black-and-white illustrations and color reconstructions of Pleistocene animals and their environments.

Lowe, J. J., and M. J. C. Walker. *Reconstructing Quaternary Environments*. London: Longman Group, 1984. This volume outlines the techniques for analyzing the environments and ecology of the Quaternary period. Included are discussions of landforms and characteristic sediments of the Quaternary, as well as dating techniques and analyses of plants and animals. Although the text would most easily be read by students with introductory training in geology and biology, all terms are thoroughly defined, and it could thus be comprehended by a general audience.

Nilsson, T. *The Pleistocene: Geology and Life in the Quaternary Ice Age*. Stuttgart: Ferdinand Enke Verlag, 1983. One of the most thorough accounts of the ice ages available. The bulk of the text concerns continental reviews as to the extent and characteristics of Pleistocene glaciation, as well as the mammal faunas and human fossils found. Emphasis is on the European record, although chapters are devoted to each of the other continents. Although all terms are thoroughly defined, the text is primarily designed for upper-level students of biology, paleontology, and geology.

Porter, S. C. *The Late Pleistocene*. Vol. 1 of *Late-Quaternary Environments of the United States*, edited by H. E. Wright, Jr. Minneapolis: University of Minnesota Press, 1983. This volume is a technical account of the Wisconsin glacial episode and its effects on the landmasses of the United States. Detailed chapters on Laurentide and Cordilleran glaciation, nonglacial terrestrial environments, coastal and marine environments, and Pleistocene climatology and plants and animals are included.

Sutcliffe, A. J. *On the Track of Ice Age Mammals*. Cambridge, Mass.: Harvard University Press, 1985. This volume is written for a general audience with no formal training in geology or paleontology. Well written, it avoids unnecessary scientific jargon and is profusely illustrated. Several chapters give a detailed summary of the chronology and general features of the ice ages. Other chapters cover the general characteristics of Pleistocene mammals, modes of preservation, and regional accounts of Pleistocene mammalian faunas.

Turekian, K. K., ed. *The Late Cenozoic Glacial Ages*. New Haven, Conn.: Yale University Press, 1971. This compilation of papers concerning Late Cenozoic glaciation is a technical account primarily designed for professional geologists and glaciologists. In general, it is a regional account of the history of Late Cenozoic glaciation and its effects on vegetation and mammalian faunas.

Wright, A. E., and F. Moseley, eds. *Ice Ages: Ancient and Modern*. Liverpool: Seel House Press, 1975. This volume represents the proceedings of the Twenty-first Inter-University Geological Congress held at the University of Birmingham (England) in 1974. It is designed for the specialist in geology and glacial studies. Approximately half of the text is devoted to non-Pleistocene glacial episodes and provides an important synthesis of these less well known ice ages.

Phillip A. Murry

Cross-References

IGNEOUS AND CONTACT METAMORPHIC MINERAL DEPOSITS

Type of earth science: Economic geology

Igneous rock is formed deep in the earth when magma cools and crystallizes; it yields massive mineral deposits and is an important commodity in the world market. Contact metamorphism is a process that alters preexisting rock through heat; resulting mineral deposits are usually small but contain valuable and rare minerals.

Principal terms

AUREOLE: a ring-shaped zone around an igneous intrusion; a zone of alteration

GANGUE: the worthless rock or vein matter in which valuable metals or minerals occur

IGNEOUS ROCKS: rocks formed by solidification of molten magma

METAMORPHIC ROCKS: rocks that are alteration products of preexisting rock forms that were exposed to unusual circumstances and changed as a result

METASOMATISM: metamorphism that involves changes in the chemical composition as well as in the texture of the rock

MINERAL: a solid homogenous crystalline chemical element or compound that results from the inorganic processes of nature

PYROCLASTIC: formed by or involving fragmentation as a result of volcanic or igneous action

VESICLE: a small cavity in a mineral or rock

Summary of the Phenomenon

A mineral deposit can be defined as valuable concentrations or accumulations of one or more useful minerals; if a miner thinks the deposit can be recovered at a profit or a metallurgist thinks it can be treated for a profit, then it is an ore. There are about fourteen hundred mineral species, of which roughly two hundred are considered economic minerals. To determine if a rock is an economic mineral, the miner or metallurgist examines its market value and physical and chemical properties. Although minerals exist to an extent in all rocks, the quantity and quality are not always valuable to the miner or metallurgist.

There are three broad classifications of rocks: igneous, metamorphic, and sedimentary. Metamorphic rocks are a link between the divergent igneous and sedimentary rock forms because they are alteration products of preexisting rock forms that were exposed to unusual circumstances and changed as a result. There are three types of metamorphism; only one of them, contact metamorphism, uses thermal energy exclusively as the catalyst of change. Igneous rock formation also uses thermal energy as the prime cause of formation, only on a much more intense scale than contact metamorphism.

Originating at depths of 200 kilometers within the earth and formed by cooling and recrystallizing magma, igneous rocks have a unique composition of silicate minerals and gaseous elements trapped by rock pressure. Igneous rocks are classified into groups based on mode of origin (formation conditions), mineral constituents (composition), and size and arrangement of mineral crystals (texture). The first group of igneous rocks is granite: large crystalline, quartz-bearing, light-colored rocks. The next group includes basalt and diabase, grouped together because of occurrences close in proximity and similar in composition; quartz-free, dark, and heavy, these rocks are at the opposite end of the igneous spectrum from granite. The third type of rock is pumice and pumicite (volcanic ash): vesicular, glassy, pyroclastic rocks. The fourth and last type of rock, perlite, is sometimes classified with pumice and pumicite because of its similar glassy and vesicular features; however, it has a unique composition that is partly primary (original) and partly an alteration product of rhyolite or obsidian.

Plutons are structures resulting from the emplacement of igneous materials at depth, and they can be studied only after uplifting and erosion, millions or hundreds of millions of years after formation. Plutons are associated with volcanic activity and can be either tabular or massive, discordant or concordant (cutting across existing structures or parallel to existing structures). Dikes are tabular discordant masses that occur where magma is injected into fractures that most likely were vertical pathways followed by molten rock to the surface. Sills—tabular plutons occurring where magma is injected, usually, but not always, horizontally along sedimentary bedding surfaces—can be a mixture of concordant and discordant. Sills force the overlying rock up to a height equal to the sill's thickness. Because of the amount of force needed to push an overlying structure upward, sills form at shallow depths and are easy to spot owing to the deformation of the surrounding surface area. When magma is intruded between layers of sedimentary rock in a near-surface environment, laccoliths form. Like sills, they are easily spotted by the trained eye because of the dome created on the surface by the lens-shaped mass of magma. Batholiths are the largest intrusive igneous bodies to be found; a linear formation, they are sometimes the core of an extinct mountain system.

The formation of a mineral deposit is dependent on the chemical composition of the magma, the time of formation, heat pressure, and the rate of cooling. Experimental data on the factors present during formation were sought in the nineteenth century by N. L. Bowen; his attempt was to determine melting temperatures of rocks and silicate phases. The product of his work was a reaction chart of mineral crystallization behavior. His results indicate the order of minerals formed under specific conditions. Olivine is the first mineral to form and it remains in the melt, reacting with free atoms to become pyroxene (augite), which becomes amphibole (hornblende), which becomes biotite mica, the last mineral to form in this sequence, named the "discontinuous series" because each mineral has a different crystal structure. The "continuous series" begins with the formation of calcium-rich feldspar crystals, which react with sodium ions in the melt until sodium-rich feldspar is produced; quick cooling is prohibitive of a complete transformation to sodium-rich feldspar and results instead in calcium-rich interiors surrounded by zones progressively richer in sodium. Both series occur simultaneously. In the last stages of crystallization, most of the magma is solid, and the remaining melt forms the minerals quartz, muscovite (mica), and potassium feldspar. Basaltic rocks contain the first minerals to crystallize: calcium feldspar, pyroxene, and olivine. Basalts are high in iron, magnesium, and calcium but are low in silicon. Granitic rocks are predominantly composed of the last minerals to crystallize: potassium feldspar and quartz. Andesitic rocks are composed of minerals near the middle of Bowen's table: amphibole and intermediate plagioclase feldspars. Gradations exist in each general mineral composition that distinguish one deposit from the other.

Another rock produced from high temperatures is contact metamorphic. Although contact metamorphism involves high temperatures, complete melting never occurs, for that is the realm of igneous rocks. Contact, or thermal, metamorphism is the intrusion of molten magmas into the earth's crust, accompanied by the exuding of heat and gases that profoundly alter the invaded rocks and give rise to an aureole. The further away the aureole is from the magma body, the lower the grade of its mineral. The size of the altered zone appears to be governed by the size of the rock formation. Contact metamorphism is distinguishable only when it occurs at the surface or in a near-surface environment where the temperature difference between the host rock and environment is great.

There are two kinds of contact metamorphism. Normal contact metamorphism involves recrystallization and reconstruction of the original constituents of the invaded rock: in this process, no additional material is added to the host rock. The second type of contact metamorphism, pneumatolytic, is the one of interest to miners and metallurgists because it involves the same processes of recrystallization and reconstruction as does normal contact metamorphism, in addition to a gaseous transfer of materials from the invading magma. Unlike normal contact metamorphism, the pneumatolytic type involves the formation of new minerals, combining the old constituents with new ones. Rock products yielded are fine-grained, dense, tough rocks of various chemical compositions. Pneumatolytic contact metamorphism occasionally results in economic mineral deposits, which are characterized by an assemblage of very distinctive high-temperature minerals.

The actual mineral deposits are distinguished by the unusual mixture of ores and gangue. Perhaps one of the most unusual features about this comparatively rare phenomenon is the distinctive, high-temperature gangue minerals found with the ores. The deposits usually consist of two or more disconnected bodies, on the average of 100-400 feet, yielding tens of thousands to hundreds of thousands of tons; in a very few cases, the yield has been in the millions of tons. The small size of the deposits also makes them hard to find, necessitating costly exploration and development. The exploitation of the deposits can be annoying because of the size, the random distribution of minerals in the aureole, and the sudden termination of the mineral vein. Occurrence of deposits is within the contact aureole, most often within 100 yards or so of the intrusive contact. The deposits are irregular in outline, taking any shape, and are fairly equidimensional. Their texture is coarse, commonly containing large crystals or clusters of crystals, although very few of the minerals show a crystal outline except garnet, which appears in sugarlike masses of irregular outline.

Methods of Study

The methods of studying rocks range across several fields of earth science. For example, a physicist might use spectroscopy, a method of radiation measurement, where a chemist might use laboratory techniques to determine mineral or elemental constituents of a sample rock. Other methods of study span from laboratory techniques to field examination; a partial list includes assaying, chemical analysis, microscopic examination, X-ray examination, infrared scanning, and physical tests. An economic geologist's area of interest, however, would lie in the geology of rocks and the value of mineral deposits within a rock as a commodity to be exploited at the least cost and the most profit. The geologist identifies rocks primarily by noting places of origin, formation, distinctive features, and rock associations; keeping in mind the fact that igneous and contact metamorphic rocks formed hidden from view in the earth's crust thousands and millions of years in the past, these observable details help the geologist to piece together the mysterious history of the rock's formation and to hypothesize which minerals the rocks contain.

The best way to study rocks is to examine the conditions under which they were formed: temperature, pressure, volatile content, and volatile composition. One can study these components in two ways. Relative conditions compare the formation of one rock to another by using petrology and microscopic examination to determine their characteristic positions in the field. Absolute conditions—exact temperature and pressure—of masses of minerals can be calculated to a degree using experimental synthesis, experimental determination of the conditions of reactions between groups of minerals, and the thermodynamic stability field of a mineral; the last method would be of particular interest in the study of contact metamorphism.

Texture is extremely useful as a key element in learning the order in which the minerals of metamorphic rocks crystallized and the sequence of events that occurred during formation. The texture of a rock refers to shape, size, orientation, and arrangement of mineral grains in a rock. Grain sizes vary from phaneritic (large) to aphanitic (small). The rate of cooling is a primary factor in the development of a rock's texture. A few textures that indicate planar or linear elements in the crystal grains in relation to one another are foliation, a parallel arrangement or distribution of minerals, rather like layering; schistosity, a parallel arrangement of mica or other platy minerals such as slate; and gneissosity, a pattern of alternating light and dark layers. Three textures that denote equidimensional grains are hornfelsic, nondirectional, and fine-grained (containing dark spots consisting of clusters of grains in common); granoblastic, a mosaic of coarser grains of equal size; and polygonal, equal-sized, interlocking grains of a single mineral that form triple junctions of 120-degree angles. Rocks that contain larger grains are denoted by five textures: euhedral porphyroblast (similar to phenocrysts in igneous rocks, a large crystal surrounded by smaller grains of other minerals); idioblast, a porphyroblast with well-developed crystal faces; xenoblast, an anhedral (irregularly formed) porphyroblast; porphyroclast, a broken fragment of a phenocryst or porphyroblast in a fine-grained matrix; and augen, feldspar porphyroclast with an eyelike shape in a fine-grained gneissic matrix. Other textures of importance include ones that indicate planar features (which deform schistosity), inclusions within or rims on a porphyroblast, concentric features, and the fragmental nature of the whole rock.

Igneous rocks also are studied by the conditions under which they formed. The heat and the composition of the magma involved are key factors to the diversity of mineral deposits. Laboratory experiments have shown that different minerals form under different temperatures; Bowen's reaction chart is one of the many possible igneous rock formation patterns. Magma is a hot liquid that consists, in most cases, of eight elements that are the primary constituents of silicate minerals. The ions in magma are free and unordered until cooling prompts crystallization. Atoms are reformed and arranged in an orderly pattern when cooling restricts rotational and vibrational movement, forcing ions to pack together and chemically rebond. As the magma cools, it does not solidify at once; instead, embryo crystals form and become centers of growth, capturing free ions. The result of the process is a mass of interlocking crystals. The crystal size is directly affected by the rate of cooling; slow cooling produces large crystals with a crystalline network, and rapid cooling results in very small, intergrown crystals with randomly distributed ions and no crystalline network.

Context

An economic mineral deposit is one that can be exploited profitably and one in which the ores are of industrial value. The value of the ore is determined by utilizing standards specific to the ore, such as hardness, cleavage, rift, and grain. Because mineral deposits of the contact metamorphic kind occur rarely, the resulting minerals are often valuable; two examples are garnet, a high-temperature mineral, and crystalline calcite in marble, an alteration mineral. Igneous rocks are more common and yield larger deposits of minerals that are most often used in construction and as abrasives; one common igneous rock is granite, a heavy, sturdy rock that is a very popular building material.

The commercial classification of granite refers to any light-colored, coarse-grained, heavy rock. True granite is a product of the solidification of liquid magma, but some granite, such as granite gneiss, indicates a formation process called metasomatism, which produces a nonigneous granitic rock through pervasively soaking preexisting solid rock via plutonic solutions. The resulting rock is formed without the liquid stage associated with true igneous rocks and, therefore, is a hybrid rock. In industry, granite is desired in one of two forms: crushed or dimension.

The important industrial properties of crushed stone granite are resistance to impact (toughness), to abrasion (hardness), and to disintegration from repeated freezing and thawing (soundness). Crushed granite is used most often for road metal and railroad ballast and as concrete aggregate. One of the minor uses of crushed granite is as poultry grit. Dimension granite has more rigorous properties than does crushed granite. Some important ones are hardness; soundness; compressive strength, the load per unit of area under which the rock fails by shearing or splitting; color, which must be uniform throughout a deposit; texture, of which grain size and distribution of minerals must be uniform; and scaling, or flaking, which occurs on all granite blocks. Dimensional granite is used most often in monuments, memorials, and buildings and as curbstones and paving blocks.

The uses of the other types of igneous rocks are varied according to the class. Basalt and diabase are used in the form of crushed stone for abrasives and aggregates; high-density aggregate is used in nuclear reactors. Some diabase is polished for use as dimension stone and is called black granite. Pumice and pumicite are used primarily as abrasives and lightweight aggregates, as is perlite. Perlite has a unique property that increases its commerical value: the ability to suddenly expand when rapidly heated. The use of contact metamorphic rocks is also varied; two examples are garnet and marble. Garnet, a gemstone, is used in industry as a cutting tool and for decorative purposes. Marble is used in place of other, more common, less attractive stones in the structure of buildings or as decoration. The numerous other products of igneous and contact metamorphic mineral deposits have varied industrial use and range in value, demand, and rarity. While metamorphic mineral deposits are less profitable and yield fewer tons of product, they contribute to the industrial field in a proportion nearly equal to that of igneous rock deposits.

Bibliography

Bateman, Alan M. *Economic Mineral Deposits*. New York: John Wiley & Sons, 1942. Although the text is outdated, the field of economic geology is one in which there is little change in fundamentals. Bateman's book is a good introduction, in very understandable terms, to different types of industrial, or economic, rocks. Not only does he discuss the value of the rock to the industries in which it is used, but he also describes the properties of the rock for which professionals look as well as the origins and occurrences of the rock.

Bates, Robert L. *Geology of the Industrial Rocks and Minerals*. Mineola, N.Y.: Dover, 1960. This text is meant for use by the professional geologist more than the layperson; however, it is written in terms that are easy to understand; any technical terms can be found in a standard dictionary. This book dovetails nicely with Bateman's work; both are formatted in a very similar fashion, though the tones and stresses of the works are very different.

Gillson, Joseph L. *Industrial Minerals and Rocks (Nonmetallics Other Than Fuels)*. 3d ed. New York: American Institute of Mining, Metallurgical, and Petroleum Engineers, 1960. An excellent reference written by professionals and giving a brief but thorough synopsis of a mineral's composition, origin, uses, quarrying, and even industrial properties. Although it is a professional publication, it can supply nonprofessionals with general but crucial facts.

Hyndman, Donald W. *Petrology of Igneous and Metamorphic Rocks*. New York: McGraw-Hill, 1985. Hyndman's work is the best source for general study of igneous and metamorphic rocks. Discusses the latest theories and examines the evolution of the two rocks. Includes some technical, scientific information, with the most technical data being appended. Much information is poured into each section of the book, and graphs and illustrations are included when needed.

Lutgens, Frederick K., and Edward J. Tarbuck. *The Earth: An Introduction to Physical Geology*. Columbus, Ohio: Charles E. Merrill, 1984. An introductory-level college text that contains cursory information on several items of interest: magma and its rock forms; igneous rock origins, occurrences, and classifications; and the three kinds of metamorphism.

United States. Bureau of Mines. *Minerals Yearbook*. Vol. 2, *Metals and Minerals*. Washington, D.C.: Government Printing Office, 1986. An economic evaluation of minerals as commodities, including domestic, foreign, and world production; price; value; supply; demand; technology; uses; and comparisons to earlier years in terms of increase and decrease in percentage. A public document published annually.

Earl G. Hoover

Cross-References

Gem Minerals, 802; Igneous Rock Bodies, 1131; Igneous Rock Classification, 1138; Ionic Substitution in Minerals, 1245; Crystallization of Magmas, 1420; Metamorphic Rock Classification, 1553; Metamorphic Textures, 1578; Contact Metamorphism, 1594; Metamorphism: Metasomatism, 1599; Silica Minerals, 2365.

IGNEOUS ROCK BODIES

Type of earth science: Geology
Field of study: Petrology, igneous

The geometry of the bodies in which igneous rocks are found can provide useful information about the physical characteristics of the magmas or lavas that produced them and about the stress field that was active in the region at the time of their formation.

Principal terms

ASH: solid particles from an erupting volcano, usually formed as ejected molten material cools during its flight through the atmosphere

CONCORDANT: having sides (contacts) that are nearly parallel to the layering in the country rock

COUNTRY ROCK: the rock into which magma is injected to form an intrusion

DIKE: a discordant sheet intrusion

DISCORDANT: having sides (contacts) that are at a substantial angle to the layering in the country rock

LACCOLITH: a concordant, nearly horizontal intrusion that has lifted the country rock above it into a dome-shaped geometry

LAVA: molten rock at or above the surface of the earth

MAGMA: molten rock, still beneath the surface of the earth

SHEET INTRUSION: an intrusion that is tabular, or sheetlike, in shape

SILL: a concordant sheet intrusion

Summary of the Phenomenon

Igneous rocks form as molten rock cools and solidifies. If this happens at or above the surface of the earth—during a volcanic eruption, for example—the extrusive rock bodies that result are lava flows and ash fall deposits. If it happens beneath the surface of the earth, the resulting rock bodies are called intrusions or plutons. The igneous rocks involved can have a wide range of compositions and textures, and hence a great variety of names. Common ones include basalt and granite; less common ones are monchiquite and lamprophyre. Igneous petrologists study the rock itself, seeking information about how, where, and from what it melted and how it might have been modified prior to its final solidification. Their emphasis is on chemical and mineralogical composition, and they employ phase diagrams and chemical reactions in their work. Information obtained from the body itself—its size, shape, and orientation—is also worth studying. Extrusive rock bodies can also be studied to learn about former volcanoes. A volcano's location, some of the characteristics of its lava, and even details of the topography at the time it was active can be reconstructed long after the volcano has stopped erupting, and even after it has eroded completely away.

Lava flows develop as fluid lava moves downhill, but lava is not a simple fluid. Its behavior is complex. How easily a fluid flows (how "thick" it is) is a function of its strength and its viscosity. A sensitive function of composition, lava viscosities range from those similar to motor oil to those more like asphalt. Within a single flow, strength and viscosity will vary with temperature, gas content, and flow rate—all of which change as the lava is moving. At the edges of flows, cooler lava may form natural levees, confining the flow. Within the flow itself, tubes may develop beneath the surface through which quickly flowing lava can move with little cooling. At the surface, the loss of heat and gases can result in a nearly solid rind that deforms by cracking and breaking.

An ash fall deposit is thickest near the site of the eruption. Its areal extent will be influenced by the winds prevailing at the time of the eruption and the height reached by the ash before its descent. Being blown by the wind, ash may accumulate beneath areas of stagnant air. If still sufficiently hot, particles of ash may weld together as they settle, producing a hard rock that resists the forces of erosion.

Molten rock that has not reached the surface is called magma. As complex as lava, magma moves from regions of higher pressure to areas where the pressure is lower, rather than flowing downhill. During this process, magma may wedge apart solid rock and intrude into the crack it produces. In this way, magma can forge its own subsurface path for many kilometers. Eventually, this forging may bring it to the surface, where an eruption will ensue. An eruption will permit much greater flow through the crack. Flow will be easiest and fastest where the crack is widest. The flowing magma erodes the walls of the crack; the walls near the fastest-flowing magma will erode most quickly. In the narrow parts of the crack, flow will be much less, the magma will be harder to deform, and it will cool and solidify. Thus, the magma conduit, which initially was a fluid-filled crack, transforms during the eruption into a nearly cylindrical form. At any point in this process, the flow of magma may be interrupted, permitting the magma within the conduit system to solidify. The form taken by this frozen magma will be inherited from the walls of the conduits, just as a casting takes its form from a mold.

There are many names for different intrusive forms, and their classification is not very systematic. If the sides of the intrusion are generally parallel to the layering in the rock into which it intrudes (the country rock), it is said to be concordant. If its sides are at a significant angle to that layering, the intrusion is said to be discordant. The names for irregularly shaped discordant intrusions are based on size. Batholiths are huge; stocks are much smaller. Perhaps more important than the sizes which define them, though, are the differences in depths of formation. Batholiths form at great depths, where the temperatures are so high that the country rock behaves in a fairly ductile fashion, whereas many stocks are thought to be remains of the subsurface cylindrical conduits which fed volcanoes.

Commonly, igneous intrusions will form tabular bodies, with one dimension much smaller than the other two. These sheet intrusions are called dikes if they are discordant and sills if they are concordant. These names originated in coal mines, where they were useful in mapping the underground workings. It is now understood that the orientation of a sheet intrusion is more likely to be controlled by the direction of least compression than by attitude of existing layers.

A simple experiment can help to show how the orientation of sheet intrusions is determined by the direction of least compression in the region. The experiment involves a cube made up of several rectangular wooden blocks. In between some of the blocks are uninflated balloons that are all attached to the same source of compressed air, turned off at the beginning of the experiment. Some balloons are horizontal, some are vertical in north-south planes, and some are vertical in east-west planes. If there is pressure on the blocks in an east-west direction, pressure in a north-south direction, and still more pressure surging downward, the balloons that inflate when the compressed air is gradually turned on will resist the pressure the most. Similarly, when molten rock is forced into the crust, it forms dikes or sills depending on which direction is under the least compression. At the surface of the earth, the direction of least compression must be either horizontal or vertical. Sheet intrusions that form near the surface, then, will be emplaced in either a vertical or a horizontal position. Because sedimentary strata are commonly nearly horizontal, a horizontal sheet intruded into such strata is concordant, while a vertical one is discordant. As magma pushes the sides of a sheet intrusion away from each other, stress is concentrated at the tip of the crack. When this stress exceeds the strength of the rock, the rock splits apart and the crack grows longer. The longer crack fills with fluid under pressure, forcing the sides farther apart. Now, with even greater leverage acting on it, the crack tip fails again. The process is repeated as long as there is enough fluid pressure.

The country rock ahead of a sheet intrusion fails in extension. The fracture produced is much like a joint and as such will have many of the surface decorations common to joints. One of these decorations, called plumose structure or twist hackle, occurs when the crack breaks into a number of smaller cracks, each slightly rotated from the parent crack to produce a series of parallel offset cracks. These are called *en echelon* cracks. If they become filled with magma, a set of *en echelon* dikes will result. Continued propagation of the crack and filling with magma will cause the individual segments to coalesce. The resulting intrusion will be a dike with a series of matching offsets along its edges, showing where individual *en echelon* segments existed earlier. Such offsets can be used to infer the direction in which the crack initially grew.

As the area over which the pressure acts increases, the force produced by that pressure increases also. This is the principle behind pneumatic jacks. In the case of a horizontal sill not too far beneath the surface of the earth, the force pushing up increases with area, while the resisting forces increase with the perimeter. Because area grows faster than does perimeter, there may come a time when the rock lying above the sill will be domed up, producing a laccolith: a concordant intrusion, with a flat floor and a domed roof. Many other names have been assigned to intrusions with different geometries. Lopoliths, sphenoliths, bysmaliths, phacoliths, ductoliths, harpoliths, akmoliths, and even cactoliths have been described. Yet, it is not clear whether such nomenclature has useful general applicability, and the use of these terms has fallen out of favor. Indeed, even the distinction between dikes and sills is often no longer made, the phrase "sheet intrusions" being preferred by many geologists.

Methods of Study

Lava flows and ash fall deposits are usually studied in the field. If the outcrops are favorable, detailed maps are constructed, often on top of aerial photographs. These might show variations in thickness, locations, and orientations of lava tubes, levees, and surface fracture patterns. From the patterns that emerge and by radiometric dating of the deposits, geologists seek to understand the history of the volcanoes involved. Which vents were active when? How large was the largest flow? The smallest? What is the average rate at which lava has been produced by this volcano?

Even if the deposits are buried under thousands of feet of sedimentary rock, they may still be susceptible to study where they are exposed in canyons or encountered in wells. Most of the detail will have been obliterated, but trends in the variation of their thickness can still be used to indicate where the eruptions that produced them occurred. This study has been conducted on rocks hundreds of millions of years old, enhancing the understanding of the earth's tectonic history.

Intrusions are also studied in the field. Measurements are made of the size and shape of the body being studied. Because much of the intrusion is usually buried and much of it has been removed by erosion, reconstructing the original shape may not be easy. Yet, even a thin slice of data through an intrusion can provide important information. When examined carefully, many dikes show an asymmetric cross section, something like a long, thin teardrop. This cross section has been interpreted to indicate gradients in magma pressure or regional stresses active during emplacement. The edges of sheet intrusions frequently display offsets and occasionally grooves, which are thought to indicate the direction in which the crack occupied by the intrusion initially grew. Such information can be utilized to help reconstruct the three-dimensional form of the intrusion and to define the sequence of events that produced it. The transition from sill to laccolith represents a particularly opportune situation. Estimates of the depth of overburden, strength, and resistance to bending of the overlying rock, and the pressure and mechanical behavior of the magma may all be derived if sufficient data are available for a substantial number of laccoliths and sills in an area.

Dikes often occur in groups, called dike swarms. By mapping such swarms, geologists may find that they reveal systematic patterns that can be interpreted as images of the stress field in the region. The next step is to use computers and the theory of elasticity to analyze such stress fields, and then try to find causes for the stresses discovered. Because the igneous rock making up the intrusions can often be dated, a stress history of the region may be developed.

To understand field exposures, geologists may construct models representing the intrusions they wish to study. Some of these models are physical, with motor oil or petroleum jelly acting as magma and being intruded under pressure into gelatin, plaster, or clay. Conditions can be controlled, and the experiments can be halted to make measurements, photographs, and even films of the process. Another way to model intrusions is on a computer. Using a system of equations derived from the theory of elasticity, geologists can predict the stresses and displacements in the vicinity of an intrusion with a given shape, containing a magma with known properties, and surrounded by rock with known elastic behavior subjected to a known stress field. By letting each of these variables change, their effects can be studied independently.

Laboratory simulations can suggest which field measurements are most likely to be significant in learning about the conditions at the time of intrusion. Armed with an intuition developed in the lab, the field geologist is better prepared to understand field exposures. Field data, in turn, often pose dilemmas that yield to analysis in the laboratory.

Context

A volcanic eruption is certainly one of nature's most spectacular displays. For reasons ranging from fascination and curiosity to hazard mitigation and self-preservation, people have studied volcanoes for centuries from many different perspectives. One rewarding approach has been to examine the exhumed remains of the deposits and underground plumbing systems of former volcanoes. The sizes, shapes, orientations, and distribution of such igneous rock bodies have been interpreted to reveal important physical characteristics of the molten rocks that produced them, as well as the conditions prevailing at the time of their formation.

By studying the composition and textures of igneous rocks, scientists are able to decipher much about the rocks from which they melted and some of the details about how the melt changed between its initial formation and its final emplacement. Such study, however, usually does not provide much information on the physical processes involved. Some of this information can be obtained by a study of the rock body as a whole, instead of the rock of which it is composed. From the shape of a dike or a sill (a sheet intrusion), it may be possible to determine the direction in which the intrusion initially grew and something about the pressure of the molten rock. From the dimensions of another type of intrusion called a laccolith, it may be possible to make estimates of the fluid pressure of the magma and the original depth of emplacement.

Because they are useful pressure gauges, igneous rock bodies can also provide information about the stresses active at the time of their emplacement. Patterns produced by swarms of dikes have been interpreted in terms of the horizontal stresses acting throughout the region. Such information has direct bearing on questions concerning the mechanism of mountain building, plate tectonics, and the history of the earth in general.

Finally, owing to the fact that igneous rock is frequently more resistant to weathering and erosion than is the sedimentary rock into which it may have been emplaced, igneous rock bodies often form impressive scenic features. Devils Postpile in California, the Henry Mountains of Utah, Ship Rock in New Mexico, and the Palisades Sill across the Hudson from New York City are some of the scenic attractions produced by igneous rock bodies. Appreciation of these and similar features is enhanced when one understands something about their formation.

Bibliography

Billings, Marland P. *Structural Geology.* 3d ed. Englewood Cliffs, N.J.: Prentice-Hall, 1972. Chapter 16, "Intrusive Igneous Rocks," presents classic descriptions of many different intrusive rock bodies. There is little emphasis on the mechanisms of formation or on the interpretation of the bodies described, but each is defined and most are illustrated. Descriptive, with little prior knowledge assumed, this book is suitable for the general reader.

Decker, Robert, and Barbara Decker. *Volcanoes.* San Francisco: W. H. Freeman, 1981. Suitable for the general reader, this book provides useful background for the understanding of igneous rock bodies. Of particular interest are chapter 10, "Roots of Volcanoes," and chapter 8, "Lava, Ash, and Bombs."

Hargraves, R. B., ed. *Physics of Magmatic Processes.* Princeton, N.J.: Princeton University Press, 1980. This book is a fairly technical review of much of the work in progress at the time of its publication. The first seventeen pages of chapter 6, "The Fracture Mechanisms of Magma Transport from the Mantle to the Surface," by Herbert R. Shaw, are very informative and easily understood by the general reader. Most readers will also learn much from chapter 7, "Aspects of Magma Transport," by Frank J. Spera, which describes some of the complexities of magma behavior.

Hunt, Charles B., Paul Averitt, and Ralph L. Miller. *Geology and Geography of the Henry Mountain Region, Utah.* U.S. Geological Survey Professional Paper 228. Washington, D.C.: Government Printing Office, 1953. A classic paper, this 234-page report describes the laccoliths of this region in detail. Profusely illustrated and accompanied by maps and cross sections, the information presented will provide the reader with an excellent sense of what these laccoliths look like and the map patterns they produce. There is little, however, in the way of a convincing discussion concerning how they formed or what inferences may be drawn from their locations or geometries. Suitable for the general reader.

Johnson, Arvid M. *Physical Processes in Geology.* San Francisco: Freeman, Cooper, 1970. This book has strongly influenced the way igneous rock bodies have been studied ever since its publication. Building on an approach developed to study the formation of laccoliths, Johnson leads the reader through discussions of elasticity and viscosity and proceeds to apply some of the results obtained to problems of dike intrusion and the flow of magma. Although differential and integral calculus are needed to follow the derivations, much of the general approach can be appreciated by those with less mathematical training. Suitable for the technically oriented college student.

Suppe, John. *Principles of Structural Geology.* Englewood Cliffs, N.J.: Prentice-Hall, 1985. Chapter 7, "Intrusive and Extrusive Structures," shows how the emphasis in the study of igneous rock bodies has shifted since publication of Billings' book. In this text, there is little in the way of categorizing bodies in terms of their shapes and much more on their interpretation in terms of the physical conditions existing during the time of their emplacement. Although mechanically sound, the math used is not intimidating. Suitable for the general reader.

Williams, Howel, and Alexander R. McBirney. *Volcanology.* San Francisco: Freeman, Cooper, 1979. This book is a general text on volcanoes. Chapter 5, "Lava Flows," and chapter 6, "Airfall and Intrusive Pyroclastic Deposits," are most relevant to igneous rock bodies. The writing seems to put an unnecessary stress on terminology. Suitable for college students with some background in geology.

Otto H. Muller

Cross-References

Geothermal Power, 915; Igneous and Contact Metamorphic Mineral Deposits, 1124; Igneous Rock Classification, 1138; Joints, 1276; The Origin of Magmas, 1428; Contact Metamorphism, 1594; Pyroclastic Rocks, 2131; Stress and Strain, 2490; Volcanic Hazards, 2601; Volcanoes: Eruption Forecasting, 2622; Volcanoes: Flood Basalts, 2630; Volcanoes: The Hawaiian Islands, 2638; Volcanoes: Recent Eruptions, 2673; Volcanoes: Types of Eruption, 2695.

IGNEOUS ROCK CLASSIFICATION

Type of earth science: Geology
Field of study: Petrology, igneous

The classification of igneous rocks depends on their texture and composition. "Texture" refers to the grain size of the constituent minerals of the rock and depends on how slowly or quickly a magma cooled to form the igneous rock. "Composition" refers to both chemical and mineralogical features.

Principal terms

COLOR INDEX: the percentage by volume of dark minerals in a rock; it is used for quick identification of rocks

EXTRUSIVE ROCK: a fine-grained, or glassy, rock which was formed from a magma that cooled on the surface of the earth

FELSIC: characterized by a light-colored mineral such as feldspar or quartz, or a light-colored rock dominantly composed of such minerals

INTRUSIVE ROCK: an igneous rock which was formed from a magma that cooled below the surface of the earth; it is commonly coarse-grained

MAFIC: characterized by a dark-colored mineral such as olivine, pyroxene, amphibole, or biotite, or a rock composed of such minerals

MAGMA: a molten rock material largely composed of silicate ions

MINERAL: a natural substance with a definite chemical composition and an ordered internal arrangement of atoms

MODE: the type and amount of minerals actually observed in a rock

NORM: the type and amount of minerals derived by a set of calculations from a chemical analysis of a rock

SILICA: silicon dioxide, or quartz

Summary of the Phenomenon

Igneous rocks are classified according to their texture and composition. With regard to texture, there are two groups: fine-grained, or glassy, and coarse-grained. With regard to composition, the rocks can be classed chemically or mineralogically. Chemically, they can be grouped according to their silicon dioxide content or their combination of oxides; mineralogically, they can be grouped according to mode, norm, or color index.

Rocks that are formed from magmas that cool beneath the surface of the earth are called "intrusives." Depending on grain size, intrusives are grouped into plutonics, hypabyssal rocks, and pegmatites. Plutonics are coarse-grained igneous rocks that are formed from magmas that cooled slowly deep beneath the surface of the earth. Hypabyssal rocks are fine-grained, because of a magma's comparatively rapid rate of cooling at a shallow depth. A variety of intrusive which commonly occurs as a tabular body that cuts across other rocks is a pegmatite. A pegmatite is a light-colored and extremely coarse-grained rock.

Igneous rocks which are formed from a magma that has extruded onto the surface of the earth are known as either "extrusives" or "volcanics." In such environments, the magmas cool rapidly, so the minerals are fine-grained. In some cases, a magma may cool so rapidly that minerals may not form at all. Instead, the magmas turn into rocks with no ordered arrangement of atoms, and as such with no crystalline structure. Such an amorphous and unorganized arrangement of atoms characterizes glass. A rock composed of glass is called "obsidian" and generally is black.

Extrusives are subdivided into "pyroclastics" and "lavas." Pyroclastics are formed by the forcible extrusion of highly gas-charged magmas. The top portion of such magma is full of gas and frothy, much like the top part of beer that is poured into a glass. The melt that surrounds the spherical gas bubbles cools into glass shards, yielding a "pumice" rock while, or soon after, the magma is extruded. Glass shards, pumice fragments, early formed crystals, fragmented magma, and rocks that surround the conduit may be ejected into the atmosphere or flow laterally. An accumulation of such fireborne fragmentary material is called a "pyroclastic rock." Commonly, the fragments are flattened and welded together because of heat and overlying weight, which produces a "welded tuff." When very fine-grained glass shards which were explosively ejected into the atmosphere rain down and settle on the ground, they produce volcanic ash, or ash fall tuff. Occasionally, a rising magma may encounter a mass of water which creates steam and causes a powerful phreatomagmatic eruption. In such a case, a ring-shaped cloud of steam with minor solid particles moves swiftly away from a vertical eruption column above the vent. Rocks that are formed from the ring of cloud are called "base surge deposits" and show many structures similar to sedimentary rocks.

Lavas are volcanic rocks formed from magmas that flow gently. "Lava" is also a name for the magma itself. Such magmas do not contain much gas. The gas that may be derived from dewatering vegetation and soil over which the magma moves ascends to the top surface of the cooling magma body, so the top part of a lava rock may contain air bubbles, or vesicles. When there are abundant vesicles in the rock, the lava is called a "scoria." In some lavas, the vesicles may be filled by secondary minerals which precipitated from groundwater. Such rocks are called "amygdaloi-dal lavas." Some magmas erupt and flow beneath a body of water. The ensuing lavas have a texture that resembles pillows and are therefore called "pillow lavas." Depending on their composition, they are pillow basalts (fine-grained, dark rocks) or spilites (greenish rocks). In the latter, the basalt is altered by interaction with the surrounding body of water.

Some igneous rocks are porphyritic, in that a few minerals in the rock are coarser-grained than the majority of the minerals. The coarse-grained minerals formed first and probably at greater depths than the fine-grained ones; commonly, the term "porphyritic" is used as a prefix or suffix of a rock name, as in porphyritic lava or lava porphyry.

Although a few igneous rocks are identified only by their textural characteristics, most are classified on the basis of their composition. The composition of an igneous rock depends on the magma from which the rock was derived. A magma is itself derived by the melting of some portion of the top part of the earth. This part of the earth is composed primarily of the following eight major elements: oxygen, silicon, aluminum, iron, calcium, sodium, potassium, and magnesium. Oxygen and silicon together comprise about 75 percent of the top part of the earth. Thus, the combination of silicon and oxygen dominates rocks which are formed from this part. When igneous rocks are chemically analyzed, the results are dominated by seven different oxides, including silicon dioxide. These oxides are used to classify igneous rocks.

The most common parameter used for classifying igneous rocks is the silicon dioxide, or silica, content of a rock. Based on its weight percent of silica, a rock could be placed in one of the following four major classes of igneous rocks: felsic (greater than 66 percent), intermediate (52 to 66 percent), mafic (45 to 52 percent), and ultramafic (less than 45 percent). These four major groups of igneous rocks can also be identified by the percentage of dark minerals, or the color index (CI): Felsics have a CI of less than 30 percent; intermediates, 30 to 60 percent; mafics, 60 to 90 percent; and ultramafics, more than 90 percent. An uncommon group of rocks called "carbonatites" are dominantly composed of carbonate minerals instead of silica minerals.

The combination of the seven oxides in igneous rocks is used as another chemical classification scheme. The exact definition of the types of igneous rock distinguished by such a classification scheme requires using graphs that show the variation of the selected oxides. Such a graph is augmented by trace element and isotope ratios of elements in the rocks. Essentially, however, the method classes igneous rocks into alkaline, peralkaline, and subalkaline rocks. The subalkaline rocks are divisible into tholeiitic and calc-alkali rocks. Generally, the tholeiitic rocks have mafic to ultramafic rock associations as a predominant component. In calc-alkali rocks, felsic to intermediate rock associations are most abundant. Alkaline and subalkaline rocks can form at any place where a deep-seated magma source, or a hot spot, penetrates the surface of the earth, such as in Hawaii. More commonly, though, igneous rock associations are formed at plate boundaries, zones that separate adjacent shifting plates.

Scientists believe that the top part of the earth is compartmentalized into tectonic plates that are in constant motion with respect to one another. The plate boundaries are the geologic settings in which igneous rock associations are formed. Adjacent tectonic plates may move toward each other and converge at their mutual boundary. This geologic setting is called a convergent plate boundary, and the igneous rocks that form in such a setting are in the calc-alkali class. The group of igneous rocks found in the Andes of South America or the mountains of the Caribbean islands are examples of such igneous rocks. In another geologic setting, adjacent plates move away from each other and a rising molten rock material pushes upward at their mutual boundary. This mutual boundary is called a divergent plate boundary, and there are two types of igneous rock association that can form in such a geologic setting. In continental areas, where the plate motion has not succeeded in tearing apart the continent and where there is a continental bulge with a depression at its center (called a rift valley), the igneous rocks at the boundary are of the alkaline class. The East African Rift Valley is an example of a place where alkaline rocks are found. In contrast, where plate motion has succeeded in tearing apart a continent and has created an intervening oceanic floor, the igneous rocks are of the tholeiitic class, particularly the mafic-ultramafic associations.

Another compositional parameter used for classifying igneous rocks is mineralogic composition. The mineral composition is dependent on the chemical composition of the parental magma. A magma is commonly called a silicate melt, because it is composed mainly of silicon and oxygen that are combined to form the silicate ion. This ion has a four-sided configuration, with oxygens at the corners and silicon at the center. The charge on the corner oxygens of a silica tetrahedron is such that the oxygen atoms can bond with equal strength to adjacent tetrahedra. Thus, silica tetrahedra have the capacity to link, or to polymerize. It is the polymerization of the silica tetrahedra that explains why a magma has more resistance to flow, or is more viscous, than liquid water. The degree to which a magma is polymerized determines its viscosity. Felsic magmas are more viscous, so they form volcanic domes; the less viscous, mafic magmas form lava flows. Silicates are a class of minerals that contain the silicate ion in their composition. The resulting silicates are divisible into groups based on how many of their oxygen atoms are shared among adjacent tetrahedra.

Felsic minerals are composed of oxygen, silicon, aluminum, sodium, potassium, and calcium. They are silicates in which all oxygen atoms are shared among adjacent tetrahedra. Felsic minerals include quartz (silicon dioxide), which is commonly colorless to transparent; feldspars, such as potassic feldspar, sodic feldspar, and calcic feldspar; and feldspathoids, such as nepheline and leucite. In general, the felsic minerals are light-colored, because they may not contain transition metals. Transition metals are elements whose atomic numbers range from 21 to 30 and whose outer electrons can be excited by light to the same energy levels that correspond to the colors of visible light. Thus, felsic igneous rocks that are dominantly composed of felsic minerals are light-colored, or leucocratic, with a color index of less than 30 percent. A felsic rock is formed from the cooling of a felsic magma, a highly polymerized and viscous magma. Typically, a magma is such that it either does or does not have sufficient silicon dioxide to form quartz; in the latter case, feldspathoids form. In other words, feldspathoids and quartz are incompatible minerals and are not to be found in the same igneous rock.

In contrast to felsic minerals, mafic minerals are dominantly composed of magnesium and iron. These minerals have a structure in which a maximum of three oxygens are shared among adjacent silica tetrahedra; the unshared oxygens are bonded with magnesium and iron. The mafic minerals include olivine, green and equidimensional; pyroxene, dark green or black, and stout; amphibole, black and elongate; and biotite, black and tabular. In most cases, the mafic minerals are dark-colored as a result of the presence of transition metals such as iron. A mafic igneous rock which is dominantly composed of these silicates is therefore also dark-colored.

The visible mineralogic composition, or the mode, is used to classify a rock if it consists of minerals of sizes that can be identified and amounts that can be counted; however, some rocks are very fine-grained, or they contain glass, so their mineral composition cannot be estimated even after magnification under a microscope. In such cases, the rocks are analyzed for their major element content, and the minerals that would have formed had the magma cooled slowly are obtained by calculation. The minerals and their amounts determined by calculation give the norm of a rock, and the individual minerals are normative minerals. The normative mineral composition can be used for classification purposes in the same way as the modal composition.

Methods of Study

Division into coarse-grained intrusives and fine-grained, or glassy, extrusives is done by visual examination of the texture of the igneous rock. Further classification of these is undertaken by determining the mode or the norm of the rock and applying a classification scheme.

The mode may be determined by trained persons who can identify the minerals in a rock with the naked eye or after magnifying the minerals ten to thirty times with a magnifying glass, such as a pocket-sized hand lens or a binocular microscope. Better mineral identification is done by scientists after a rock is cut to a small size, mounted on glass, and then ground until a very thin section (0.03 millimeter) of the rock, capable of transmitting light, is prepared. The thin section is placed on a stage of a transmitted light polarizing microscope. A lens below the stage polarizes light by allowing the transmission only of light which vibrates in one direction—for example, east to west. A lens above the stage allows the passage of light vibrating in a north-south direction. When glass is placed on the stage and the lower polarizer is inserted across the transmission of light, the color of the glass is seen. When the upper polarizer is also inserted, the glass appears dark, because no light is transmitted. The properties of most minerals with respect to the transmission of light (optical properties) are different from those of glass.

Other accessories are used in addition to the polarizing lenses in order to characterize accurately the optical properties of minerals. Magnification by the microscope permits better determination of the physical properties of minerals, such as their shape and cleavage. Cleavage refers to a set of planes along which minerals break, and it is related to the ordered internal arrangement of the atoms of a mineral. The felsic minerals are used to classify the non-ultramafic rocks. A rock sample or thin section of such a rock may be inserted into a dye that stains one of the felsics, usually the alkali feldspars. This method simplifies the counting of minerals for classification.

The norm of a rock is calculated from the major elements obtained by chemical analysis. Modern methods of chemical analysis use emission or absorption of radiant energy that is unique to each atom and therefore can lead to the identification of that atom. There are four such methods: X-ray fluorescence (XRF) spectrometry, electron microprobe (EMP) analysis, instrumental neutron activation analysis (INAA), and atomic absorption spectrometry (AAS).

In the XRF method, radiant energy is focused on a sample of a rock. This energy removes electrons from the lower electron-energy levels of the atoms. The place of the removed electrons may be taken by other electrons, which fall from higher energy levels by emitting radiant energy. Depending on the energy levels from which the electrons fall, X rays of different energy are released from one element, and the spectrum of these is unique to that element. The X rays from many elements are guided to a crystal, which diffracts and disperses them for easy detection by an X-ray counter. The counter triggers electronic signals, which may be either recorded digitally and interfaced to computers or displayed on strip-chart recorders as separate peaks. The peak positions on the chart correspond to the elements in the rock sample. The peak heights are related to the concentration of the elements, the exact amount being determined by a comparison to that of a standard element admixed to the rock sample.

In EMP analysis, electrons are used as the radiant energy source, and this energy is focused on a rock sample that is polished and coated with carbon. It is a nondestructive analytical method that is better suited for determining the compositional variation within a mineral. In INAA, the sample is bombarded by neutrons supplied by either a nuclear reactor or an accelerator. Atoms in a sample acquire neutrons and become heavy and unstable (radioactive) isotopes. The samples are removed and placed in a chamber, where the emitted radiant energy (gamma rays) resulting from the decay of the artificially induced radioactive isotopes is guided to a crystal which separates the sample rays for easy detection by a recording device. This method is suitable for detecting the type and concentration of even those elements which may be found only in trace amounts.

In AAS, one uses the radiant energy emitted from a known element in a cathode-ray tube to detect the presence of an element in a sample by noting whether the energy is reduced and by how much. A rock sample is dissolved in a solution and then heated until chemical bonds are broken and the solution contains individual atoms. When radiant energy is made to pass through the atomized sample, the energy will be absorbed by the sample if there are elements in the sample that are identical to those in the cathode. This absorption of energy by the sample causes a reduction in the detection of the source radiant energy, and the reduction corresponds to the amount of the element in the sample.

The XRF method is by far the most widely used technique for analyzing chemical composition. The other techniques have their application in the determination of trace elements that are used to facilitate the classification of igneous rocks by igneous rock association, such as alkaline or subalkaline.

Context

Igneous rocks are one of the three major types of rock, the others being sedimentary and metamorphic rocks. In some regions, igneous rocks are the only types of rock that are found. Inhabitants of such regions have reason to know the varieties of igneous rocks; moreover, many tourists visit sites of igneous rocks, such as the granites of Stone Mountain, Georgia, and of Yosemite National Park, California, and marvel at the beauty of the rocks and the landscape in which they are found.

Humans throughout the centuries have used igneous rocks for a variety of purposes. Prehistoric man used, and certain tribesmen of the Third World still use, obsidian to fashion axes for cutting softer material, and arrowheads or spearheads for hunting. Many kinds of igneous rock, especially plutonic rocks, are used as grinding stones to produce flour for preparing bread and other foods. Monuments are often made of igneous rock. Typically, granite and granodiorite, which are light-colored rocks, are used for tombstones. Other igneous rocks, such as diorite and gabbro, which are black, have been selected for dark-colored monuments, such as the Vietnam Memorial in Washington, D.C. In some cultures, obelisks and places of worship are hewn from solid igneous plutons, irrespective of their hardness. The three-thousand-year-old obelisks at Axum, Ethiopia, were carved out of granodiorite plutons. Many other types of building can be completely or partly constructed with igneous rock. Architects and masons choose the rock's color, type, and dimensions. In general, granite is the igneous rock most often used for expensive structures.

The classification of igneous rocks has its most useful application in the search for economic metal deposits. Ultramafic and mafic rocks are associated with chromium, platinum, palladium, iridium, osmium, rhodium, ruthium, nickel, iron, titanium, and gold deposits. Intermediate and felsic rocks are associated with copper, molybdenum, tin, tungsten, silver, lead, and zinc deposits. Alkaline rocks, particularly the kimberlites, are associated with diamonds. These different igneous associations are found in different geologic environments. Knowing the geologic environment, then, helps both in classifying the rocks and in anticipating the types of metallic deposit that could be sought in such regions.

Bibliography

Best, Myron G. *Igneous and Metamorphic Petrology.* New York: W. H. Freeman, 1982. An easy-to-read book that provides classification as well as description of igneous rocks.

Carmichael, Ian S., Francis J. Turner, and Joan Verhoogen. *Igneous Petrology.* New York: McGraw-Hill, 1974. An excellent book on the classification and description of igneous rocks for college-level students.

Hutchison, Charles S. *Laboratory Handbook of Petrographic Techniques.* New York: John Wiley & Sons, 1974. This book provides a discussion of technique used in the laboratory for identifying minerals and rocks.

Klein, Cornelis, and C. S. Hurlbut, Jr. *Manual of Mineralogy.* 20th ed. New York:

John Wiley & Sons, 1985. A useful book for study of minerals. Chapter 12 provides a succinct treatment of igneous rocks.

Prinz, Martin, et al., eds. *Simon & Schuster's Guide to Rocks and Minerals*. New York: Simon & Schuster, 1978. Rocks and minerals are described in this easy-to-read book. Illustrated in color.

Zussman, J., ed. *Physical Methods in Determinative Mineralogy*. 2d ed. London: Academic Press, 1978. An excellent collection of articles on microscopy and instrumental analytical methods. Suitable for advanced students and research geologists.

Habte Giorgis Churnet

Cross-References

Feldspars, 698; Igneous and Contact Metamorphic Mineral Deposits, 1124; Igneous Rock Bodies, 1131; Igneous Rocks: Andesitic, 1146; Igneous Rocks: Anorthosites, 1152; Igneous Rocks: Basaltic, 1158; Igneous Rocks: Carbonatites, 1173; Igneous Rocks: Granitic, 1180; Igneous Rocks: Ultramafic, 1207; Crystallization of Magmas, 1420; The Origin of Magmas, 1428; Physical Properties of Minerals, 1681; Pyroclastic Rocks, 2131; Physical Properties of Rocks, 2225; Silica Minerals, 2365.

IGNEOUS ROCKS: ANDESITIC

Type of earth science: Geology
Field of study: Petrology, igneous

Andesite is an intermediate extrusive igneous rock. It is porphyritic and contains phenocrysts of plagioclase, little or no quartz, and no sanidine or feldspathoid. Active volcanoes on the earth erupt andesite more than any other rock type. Andesites are primarily associated with subduction zones along convergent tectonic plate boundaries.

Principal terms

BOWEN'S REACTION PRINCIPLE: a principle by which a series of minerals forming early in a melt react with the remaining melt to yield a new mineral in an established sequence

EXTRUSIVE ROCK: igneous rock that has been erupted onto the surface of the earth

GROUNDMASS: the fine-grained material between phenocrysts of a porphyritic igneous rock

INTERMEDIATE ROCK: an igneous rock that is transitional between a basic and a silicic rock, having a silica content between 54 and 64 percent

PHENOCRYST: a large, conspicuous crystal in a porphyritic rock

PLUTONIC ROCK: igneous rock formed at great depth within the earth

PORPHYRY: an igneous rock in which phenocrysts are set in a finer-grained groundmass

STRATOVOLCANO: a volcano composed of alternating layers of lava flows and ash; also called a composite volcano

SUBDUCTION ZONE: a convergent plate boundary

VISCOSITY: a substance's ability to flow; the lower the viscosity, the greater the ability to flow

Summary of the Phenomenon

Andesite takes its name from lavas in the Andes mountains of South America. To most geologists, andesites are light gray porphyritic volcanic rocks containing phenocrysts of plagioclase but little or no quartz and no sanidine or feldspathoid. Despite their lackluster appearance, andesites are of great interest to geologists for several reasons. First, active volcanoes on the earth erupt andesite more than any other rock type; andesite is the main rock type at 61 percent of the world's active volcanoes. Second, andesites have a distinctive tectonic setting. They are primarily associated with convergent plate boundaries and occur elsewhere only in limited amounts. Of the active volcanoes that occur within 500 kilometers of a subduction zone, 78 percent include andesite; only three active volcanoes not near a destructive plate boundary include it. Third, andesites have bulk compositions similar to estimates of the composition of continental crust. This similarity, in association with the tectonic setting of andesites, suggests that they may play an important role in the development of terrestrial crust. Fourth, the development and movement of andesitic magma seem to be closely related to the formation of many ore deposits. It appears that andesite genesis is the source of these metals.

Rocks are classified chemically according to how much silica they contain; rocks rich in silica (more than 64 percent) are called silicic. They consist mostly of quartz and feldspars, with minor amounts of mica and amphibole. Rocks low in silica (less than 54 percent),˙ with no free quartz but high in feldspar, pyroxene, olivine, and oxides, are called basic. Basic rocks, free of quartz, tend to be dark, while silicic rocks are lighter and contain only isolated flecks of dark minerals. Basalts are examples of silicic volcanic rocks. Andesites, having a silica content of about 60 percent, are volcanic rocks termed intermediate. Andesite's plutonic equivalent is diorite. There is no cut-and-dried difference between basalt and andesite or between andesite and rhyolite. Instead, there is a broad transitional group of rocks that carry names such as "basaltic andesite" or "andesitic rhyolite."

Nevertheless, some generalizations can be applied to the lavas and magmas that form these rocks. One generalization has to do with viscosity. Andesite lavas are more viscous than are basalt lavas and less viscous than are rhyolite lavas. This difference is primarily an effect of the lava's composition, and to a certain extent it is a result of the high portion of phenocrysts present in the more viscous lavas.

Different minerals crystallize at different temperatures. As a basalt magma cools, a sequence of minerals appears. The first mineral to crystallize is usually olivine, which continues to crystallize as the magma cools until a temperature is reached at which a second mineral, pyroxene, begins to crystallize. As the temperature continues to drop, these two continue to crystallize. Cooling continues until a temperature is reached when a third mineral, feldspar, crystallizes. This chain of cooling and mineral crystallization is known as Bowen's reaction principle. Often, olivine and pyroxene crystallize out early in the process, so they may be present in the final rock as large crystals, up to a centimeter across. These crystals are called phenocrysts. The size of these phenocrysts is in direct contrast to the fine-grained crystals of the groundmass. Igneous rocks with phenocrysts in a fine-grained groundmass are known as porphyries. Most volcanic rocks contain some phenocrysts. The groundmass crystals form when the lava cools on reaching the surface. If the lava has a low viscosity, reaches the surface, spreads out, and cools quickly, individual crystals do not have enough time to grow. The overall rock remains fine-grained. The phenocrysts crystallized out much earlier, while the magma was still underground. There, they had plenty of time to grow and were then carried to the surface with the magma during eruption.

Basalts, as a result of their low viscosity, tend to produce thin lava flows that readily spread over large areas. They rarely exceed 30 meters in thickness. Andesite flows, by contrast, are massive and may be as much as 55 meters thick. The largest single andesite flow described, which is in northern Chile, has an approximate volume of 24 cubic kilometers. Because of their low viscosity, basalt flows can advance at considerable rates; speeds up to 8 kilometers per hour have been measured. Andesite flows often move only a matter of tens of meters over several hours. As a result of higher viscosity, andesite flows show none of the surface features of more "liquid" lavas. Flow features such as wave forms, swirls, or ropy textures often associated with basalt flows never occur in andesite flows. Andesite flows tend to be blocky, with large, angular, smooth-sided chunks of solid lava. The flow tends to behave as a plastic rather than a liquid. An outer, chilled surface develops on the slow-moving flow, with the interior still molten. Plasticity within the flow increases toward the still-molten inner portion. As the flow slowly shifts, moves, and cools, the hard, brittle outer layer breaks into the large angular blocks characteristic of andesite lava flows. As the flow slowly moves, the blocks collide and override one another to form piles of angular andesite blocks.

The differences between basalts and andesites reflect their differences in composition, which is a function of the environment in which their source lavas occur. Basalts are typically formed at mid-ocean ridges and form oceanic crust. The generation of andesite magma is characteristic of destructive plate margins. Here, oceanic plates are being subducted below continental plates. Destructive plate boundaries tend to produce a greater variety of lavas than do spreading zones (ocean ridges). The close association of andesite with convergent plate boundaries is the significance of the "Andesite Line" often drawn around the Pacific Ocean

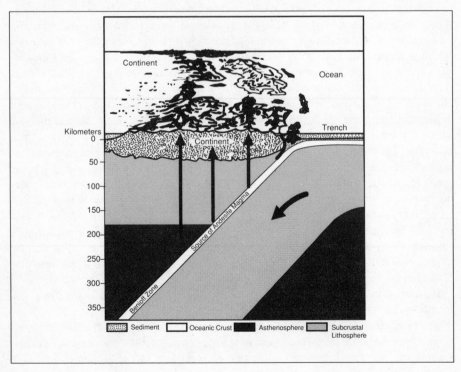

basin (see figure). This fairly well-defined line separates two major petrographic regions. Inside this line and inside the main ocean basin, no andesites occur. All active volcanoes inside the line erupt basaltic magma, and all volcanic rocks associated with dormant volcanoes within this region are basaltic. Outside the line, andesite is common. The Andesite Line is the western and northern boundary of the Pacific plate and the eastern boundary of the Juan de Fuca, Cocos, and Nazca plates. The Andesite Line parallels the major island arc systems, the subducting edges of the tectonic plates listed above, and a chain of prominent and infamous stratovolcanoes known as the Ring of Fire. These stratovolcanoes are exemplified by Mount Rainier and other volcanoes of the western United States, El Chichón of Mexico, San Pedro of Chile, Mounts Egmont and Taupo of New Zealand, Krakatoa and Tambora of the Indonesian Arc, Fujiyama of Japan, Bezymianny of Kamchatka, and the Valley of Ten Thousand Smokes in Alaska.

The viscous nature of andesite lavas is responsible for many classic volcanic features. Most notable is the symmetrical cone shape of the stratovolcanoes of the Circum-Pacific region. Short, viscous andesitic flows pouring down the flanks of these volcanoes are alternately covered by pyroclastic material and work to build the steep central cone characteristic of composite stratovolcanoes. When an andesite's silica content rises to a point that it approaches rhyolite composition, it is termed a dacite. Dacite is often so viscous that it cannot flow and blocks the vent of the volcano. This dacite plug is called a lava dome. Such a dome can be seen in pictures of Mount St. Helens. If the plugged volcano becomes active again, the lava dome does not allow for a release of accumulating pressure and explosive gases. Pressure builds until the volcano finally erupts with great force and violence.

The Benioff zone is a plane dipping at an angle of 45 degrees below a continent, marking the path of a subducting oceanic plate at the destructive plate margin. It is a region of intense earthquake activity. At the Benioff zone, the subducting plate melts, producing a chemically complex, destructive margin magma (andesitic). As andesitic magma is formed at the Benioff zone and begins its slow rise toward the surface, it passes through and comes in contact with regions of the asthenosphere, lithosphere, and continental crust. During its rise, the magma also comes in contact with circulating meteoric water, and new magmatically derived fluids are formed. Because andesitic magma rises through a variety of host rocks, the variety of minerals that enrich the new fluids is increased. The rising magma also stresses the surrounding host rocks, causing them to fracture. These fractures and similar open spaces are filled with mineral-rich water and magmatically derived fluids. As the fluids cool, mineral ores precipitate from the solutions and fill the open spaces. These filled spaces often become mineral-rich dikes and sills.

Methods of Study

The study and interpretation of andesitic rocks is accomplished in three basic ways: fieldwork, in which researchers travel to locations to assess and interpret a specific region of the earth that is known or suspected of being andesitic terrain;

petrological studies, which use all available methods of study to ascertain the history, origin, conditions, alterations, and decay of the rocks collected during fieldwork; and mineralogical studies, which through intensive laboratory investigations identify the specific mineral characteristic of a sample.

If a scientist is interested in andesitic rocks and knows, or suspects, that a region of the earth is andesitic terrain, travel to this location to do fieldwork is likely. There, the researcher will most likely collect a large number of samples. The location from which each sample is taken is carefully recorded on a map. Additional data describing the stratigraphic interval from which the sample is taken are recorded. These data include thickness, areal extent, weathering, and strike and dip of the location. Photographs are also commonly used to record the surrounding environment of the sample location. Samples are usually given preliminary study at the researcher's field camp.

When the fieldwork is over, the researcher returns with the samples to a laboratory setting. In the laboratory, petrological and mineralogical investigations begin. A petrological study of an andesitic sample will include both a petrographic and petrogenetic analysis. The petrographic analysis will describe the sample and attempt to place it within the standard systematic classification of igneous rocks. Identification of the sample is accomplished by means of examining a thinly sliced and polished portion of the sample under a petrographic microscope—a process known as thin-section analysis. The information obtained by microscopic examination gives a breakdown of the type and amount of mineral composition within the sample. Knowing the conditions under which these minerals form allows the researcher to make a petrogenetic assessment. Petrogenesis deals with the origin and formation of rocks. If a mineral is known to form only at certain depths, temperatures, or pressures, its presence within a sample allows the researcher to draw some specific conclusions concerning the rock's formation and history.

Mineralogical studies of field-gathered samples aid in the petrogenetic portion of the analysis. Mineralogy involves the study of how a mineral forms, its physical properties, chemical composition, and occurrence. Minerals can exist in a stable form over only a narrow range of pressure and temperature. Experimental confirmation of this range enables the researcher to make a correlation between the occurrence of a mineral in a rock and the conditions under which the rock was formed. In this sense, mineralogical and petrological analyses complement each other and work to formulate a concise history of a given sample.

When data gathered from the field and laboratory are combined, the geological history of a given field area can begin to be interpreted. When areas of similar igneous rock types, ages, and mineral compositions are plotted on a map, they form a petrographic province. A petrographic province indicates an area of similar rocks that formed during the same period of igneous activity. On a global scale, the Andesite Line marks the boundary between two great provinces: the basaltic oceanic crust and the andesitic continental crust. Both crustal forms have distinctly different geological histories and mineral compositions.

Context

Andesitic magmas are responsible for the formation of new continental crust. The crust grows by progressive accumulation from the eruptions of andesitic volcanoes on the surface and from dioritic intrusions below ground. In addition, the understanding of andesitic volcanism and its relationship to convergent plate boundaries has aided in the exploration of economic minerals. Certain economically important ores are associated with andesitic rocks and zones of andesitic volcanism. Plotting on a map the locations of the world's major molybdenum and porphyry copper deposits shows that they are situated along the Andesite Line. The deposits are in direct correlation with convergent plate boundaries and with andesitic volcanism. These ores are the result of hydrothermal activity associated with igneous bodies emplaced at high levels in the earth's crust.

Bibliography

Bowen, N. L. *The Evolution of Igneous Rocks*. Mineola, N.Y.: Dover, 1956. An unmatched source and reference book on igneous rocks, written by the father of modern petrology. This book is the basis of Bowen's Reaction Principle. Written for graduate students and professional scientists.

Carmichael, I. S. E., F. J. Turner, and J. Verhoogen. *Igneous Petrology*. New York: McGraw-Hill, 1974. A college-level textbook on the formation and development of igneous rocks. Very detailed and complete.

Gill, J. B. *Orogenic Andesite and Plate Tectonics*. New York: Springer-Verlag, 1981. A well-documented summary of the entire field of andesite genesis. Written for graduate students and professional earth scientists.

Klein, Cornelis, and Cornelius S. Hurlbut, Jr. *Manual of Mineralogy*. 18th ed. New York: John Wiley & Sons, 1971. A comprehensive physical and chemical description of andesite. For high school and general readers.

Williams, H., and A. R. McBirney. *Volcanology*. San Francisco: Freeman, Cooper, 1979. A classic textbook on volcanoes and volcanology. Well illustrated and very descriptive. Written for the undergraduate or graduate student.

Windley, B. F. *The Evolving Continents*. New York: John Wiley & Sons, 1977. An excellent reference book on plate tectonics and tectonic processes. Written for the college-level reader.

Randall L. Milstein

Cross-References

IGNEOUS ROCKS: ANORTHOSITES

Type of earth science: Geology
Field of study: Petrology, igneous

Anorthosites are coarse-grained, intrusive rocks composed principally of plagioclase feldspar. They are useful for what they reveal about the early crustal evolution of the earth, and they are the source of several economic commodities.

Principal terms

CRUST: the upper layer of the earth and other "rocky" planets; it is composed mostly of relatively low-density silicate rocks

GABBRO: coarse-grained, iron-magnesium-rich, plutonic igneous rock; anorthosite is an unusual variety of gabbro

HYPERSTHENE: a low-calcium pyroxene mineral

MAGMA: molten silicate liquid plus any crystals, rock inclusions, or gases trapped in that liquid

MANTLE: a layer in the earth extending from about 5 to 50 kilometers below the crust

MASSIF: a French term used in geology to describe very large, usually igneous intrusive bodies

NORITE: gabbro in which hypersthene is the principal pyroxene; it is commonly associated with anorthosites

PERIDOTITE: the most common rock type in the upper mantle, where basalt magma is produced

PLAGIOCLASE: a silicate mineral found in many rocks; it is a member of the feldspar group

PLUTONIC: formed by solidification of magma deep within the earth and crystalline throughout

PRECAMBRIAN EON: a large span of geologic time extending from early planetary origins to about 600 million years ago

Summary of the Phenomenon

Anorthosites are igneous rocks that are composed primarily of plagioclase feldspar (calcium-sodium-aluminum silicate). Minor minerals in these rocks may include pyroxene minerals (calcium-iron-magnesium silicates), iron-titanium oxides, and, in metamorphosed varieties, garnet. All anorthosites are coarse-grained, plutonic rocks (they crystallize at depth), and they may have plagioclase crystals 10 centimeters or more in length. Because the color of plagioclase changes with minor changes in chemical composition, anorthosites come in a variety of colors. Light gray is the most common, but dark gray, black, light blue, green, and brown varieties are known.

In the earth, there are two types of anorthosite, massif-type anorthosites and layered intrusive anorthosites. The former occur as large, lens-shaped or dome-shaped intrusions that may be exposed by erosion over an area of several square kilometers. The latter variety is associated with intrusions of gabbroic (iron-rich, low-silica) magma that has segregated into mineralogically distinct layers, anorthosite occurring in the uppermost layers. The lighter areas on the moon, known as the "lunar highlands," are composed of anorthosite that originated in a similar manner to terrestrial, layered intrusive anorthosites.

Massif-type anorthosites are unusual among igneous rocks in their restricted distribution in time and space and their composition. They contain at least 85 percent plagioclase, the other silicate minerals being either augite (high-calcium pyroxene), hypersthene (low-calcium pyroxene), or both. Ilmenite and apatite commonly occur as minor accessory minerals. Massif anorthosites are found almost exclusively in a wide belt from the southwestern United States through Labrador and on the other side of the Atlantic through Sweden and Norway. Another belt extends from Brazil, through Africa (Angola, Tanzania, Malagasy), through Queen Maud Land in Antarctica, and across Bengal, India, to Australia (a pre-continental drift reconstruction). The best examples of massif anorthosites in the United States are in the Adirondack Mountains in northeastern New York State. In Canada, the Nain and Kiglapait intrusions are notable for their excellent surface exposures of anorthosite and associated rocks.

Ages determined with radiometric dating techniques demonstrate that nearly all anorthosites, including the layered-intrusion varieties, are Precambrian; most are between about 1,700 million and 1,100 million years old. No lava flows of anorthositic composition are known; they are exclusively plutonic. In addition, experimental evidence shows that liquids of anorthositic composition cannot be produced by any known process of melting at depth in the earth. Although specific mechanisms are not fully understood, it is generally accepted that anorthosites form from concentrated plagioclase crystals that had previously crystallized from gabbroic or other magmas. Massif anorthosites are commonly associated with gabbroic rocks called "norites" (gabbro in which the pyroxene mineral is hypersthene), and it can be demonstrated in most cases that anorthosite is produced by adding progressively more plagioclase to norite magma.

Anorthosites in layered intrusives clearly result from the same processes that produce the other layered rocks associated with the anorthosite layers. Layered intrusives, commonly termed "layered complexes," are generally tabular bodies that vary in thickness from a few hundred to thousands of meters thick. They consist of extremely iron- and magnesium-rich rocks called peridotites in their lower reaches but grade upward into gabbros and, in some cases, anorthosites in their upper extents. This layering of different rock types is attributed to the gravitationally controlled settling of dense minerals to the bottom of a large body of originally gabbroic magma. Rock layers of different compositions are built up over time as different minerals crystallize and are deposited on the chamber floor. Plagioclase generally crystallizes relatively late in this process and, depending on its composition and that of the enclosing silicate liquid, may actually float to the top of the magma chamber instead of settling to the bottom. Anorthosite deposits are known to have been formed by both settled and floated plagioclase. In both cases, anorthosite results from the concentration of plagioclase by mechanical processes after crystallization.

Layered intrusive anorthosites occur in the early Precambrian Stillwater Complex of western Montana and late Precambrian Duluth Complex that parallels the north shore of Lake Superior in northern Minnesota. The Stillwater contains three anorthosite units, each about 400 to 500 meters thick. In contrast, the Duluth Complex, about 40 kilometers thick, is mostly anorthosites and "gabbroic anorthosites" (somewhat richer in iron-magnesium silicates than anorthosites), with a mostly unexposed, relatively thin peridotite unit at its base. Norites and troctolites (olivine plus plagioclase) occur as minor associated rocks. Other layered anorthosites occur in the Bushveld Complex in South Africa, the Fiskenaesset Complex in Greenland, and the Dore Lake and Bell River complexes in Ontario, Canada, among others. All the layered intrusions in the United States are Precambrian.

Without question, the most obvious (but least accessible) exposures of anorthosite occur on the moon. Relatively rare on earth, anorthosite is the dominant rock type on the moon, where it forms the bulk of the rocks in the lunar highlands. The lunar highlands are the moon's ancient, highly cratered, light-colored areas. The dark areas are basalt (iron-rich silicate rock) lava flows that fill huge craters blasted in the highlands by large meteorite collisions. Ever since the first moon rocks were returned to earth by the Apollo 11 astronauts in 1969, scientists have studied lunar anorthosites and associated rocks for clues to how the moon's crust and interior originated and evolved. The generally accepted model postulates that early in its history, more than 4 billion years ago, the entire surface of the moon became molten to a depth of several kilometers. This "magma ocean" then cooled, and as it cooled, it crystallized various silicate and oxide minerals. The heavier, iron-rich minerals, being denser than the silicate magma, sank to form deep-seated layers, similar to the peridotite layers in the Stillwater and Bushveld complexes noted above. Plagioclase, on the other hand, was less dense than the iron-rich liquid, so it floated to the top, solidifying to form the early lunar highland anorthosites. Over time, the highlands became increasingly cratered by the meteorite impacts, until they acquired their present appearance about 3 billion years ago. Since that time, meteorite impacts have been sporadic. Interestingly, lunar highland anorthosite occurs with minor quantities of norite and troctolite, two rock types that also are commonly associated with terrestrial anorthosites. To lunar scientists, this peculiar group of associated rocks is the "ANT suite"; ANT is an acronym for anorthosite, norite, troctolite.

Methods of Study

Paradoxically, the origin of terrestrial anorthosites is not as clear-cut as the origin of lunar anorthosites, and many models and hypotheses have been offered to explain their unique composition and space-time relationships. No explanation is readily accepted as applying to all or most anorthosite occurrences, but enough is known about anorthosite bodies to allow some good, educated guesses. Scientific work on anorthosites has included numerous field-mapping projects to determine their spatial extent and structure. Laboratory work has included radiochemical dating studies to determine the absolute ages of anorthosites and associated rocks and experimental studies that have explored possible parent materials and melting environments of anorthosite magmas.

Several factors must be considered in assessing the origin and significance of anorthosite bodies, specifically the massif varieties. First, anorthosites are restricted, for the most part, to the very narrow time band between about 1.7 and 1.1 billion years, as determined mostly by potassium-argon, uranium-lead, and rubidium-strontium dating. Second, they occur in belts where orogeny (mountain building) may have occurred before or after their emplacement but where they intruded during anorogenic times or during rifting. They are unequivocally igneous as opposed to metamorphic; that is, they did not result from some other type of rock that changed in the solid state but rather from molten magmas. This fact is determined in the field by examining anorthosite contacts with older rocks to see whether these rocks show evidence of thermal heating caused by intrusion or hot magma. Anorthosites lack minerals that contain water in their structures, so water was not an important constituent of anorthosite parent magmas. Finally, many anorthosite complexes, such as those in New York's Adirondack Mountains, show an association not only with norites and troctolites but also with pyroxene-bearing granitic rocks called "charnockites."

Although experimental evidence shows that a liquid of plagioclase composition cannot be generated under high pressures from any known earth materials, magmas can form from rocks in the mantle or lower crust that—under anhydrous conditions—are capable of generating the plagioclase "mush" (crystals plus a small amount of liquid) by plagioclase flotation. Laboratory melting experiments show that one type of magma, called "quartz diorite" (relatively siliceous magma of the type erupted in 1980 by Mount St. Helens), could produce a plagioclase mush at great pressures. Intrusion of this mush at higher levels in the crust could squeeze out some of the interstitial liquid, which would crystallize as charnockites. Norites and gabbroic anorthosites represent cases where the plagioclase mush has trapped greater or smaller amounts of more iron-rich silicate liquid.

Other scenarios are possible, and others have been proposed to explain anorthosite bodies. Whatever the precise mechanism might have been, it produced large volumes of a very unusual suite of rocks over a geologically brief time interval. No doubt this extensive melting event required higher heat flow in the crust and mantle than is now present in areas of anorthosite occurrences or in most other areas of the earth. The explanation for anorthosites therefore requires an evaluation of what unique thermal or cataclysmic event they record in earth history. About that, geologists can only conjecture.

Context

Anorthosites are not very common in the earth's crust, and most people are not as familiar with this stone as they are with the more common building stones, granite and marble. Ironically, anyone who has ever seen the moon has seen huge spans of anorthosite; it is the principal rock type composing the lunar highlands, the dominant light-colored areas of the moon.

Anorthosite is used as a building stone or for decorative building facings. A beautiful variety composed mostly of the high-calcium plagioclase known as labradorite is in particular demand. Labradorite exhibits blue, violet, or green iridescence that varies in color with the angle of incidence of light. Anorthosite composed of labradorite plagioclase is sometimes polished and used in table tops and floor or wall panels. It has other decorative and practical applications as well. Like other feldspar-rich rocks, anorthosite can be used to make ceramic products. Porcelain bath fixtures, insulators, and dining ware are made from finely pulverized feldspar that is heated to very high temperatures. The resistance to heat and electricity and the general durability of porcelain come from the same properties inherent in feldspar.

Anorthosites and associated rocks are also the sites of economically exploitable iron-titanium deposits in some localities. The ore occurs mostly as ilmenite (iron-titanium oxide) and magnetite (iron oxide), mostly concentrated in associated rocks such as norite. Some notable deposits occur at Lofoten, in northern Norway; Allard Lake, in Quebec; Iron Mountain, in the Laramie Range of Wyoming; Duluth, Minnesota; and Sanford Lake (near Tahawus), in the Adirondacks of New York State.

Bibliography

Carmichael, Ian S. E., F. J. Turner, and John Verhoogan. *Igneous Petrology.* New York: McGraw-Hill, 1974. This textbook is designed for upper-level undergraduates and graduate students; the section on anorthosites does an excellent job of summarizing their occurrences and the problems associated with their interpretation and geologic significance. Much of this section can be comprehended by anyone with a minimal background in geology. Critical references from the scientific literature are listed in full near the end of the book.

Isachsen, Yngvar W., ed. *Origin of Anorthosite and Related Rocks.* Memoir 18. Albany, N.Y.: State Department of Education of New York, 1968. A massive compendium of articles presented at the Second Annual George H. Hudson Symposium, held at Plattsburg, New York, in 1966. The conference was devoted to massif anorthosite bodies and problems of their origins and was attended by experts on anorthosites as well as those with general interest in their study. It is without question one of the most extensive and comprehensive works on anorthosites ever prepared. It includes a very detailed appendix, and each article has an extensive reference list at the end. For students who are interested in the details of anorthosites, this book is the best place to start.

Taylor, G. Jeffrey. *A Close Look at the Moon*. New York: Dodd, Mead, 1980. This book is designed for junior and senior high school readers. It has a very good section on lunar rocks by an author who is one of the world's authorities on lunar rocks and lunar crustal evolution. Excellent cross-sectional diagrams trace the history of the lunar highlands (anorthosite-rich areas) and the lunar crust in general. The book contains photographs of moon rocks, including some taken through a microscope. A brief volume, but one packed with useful information about one of the most familiar anorthosite bodies, the moon.

Windley, Brian F. *The Evolving Continents*. New York: John Wiley & Sons, 1977. An advanced text that focuses on the evolution of the earth's continental crust as revealed by its complex geology. The section on anorthosite bodies is very descriptive and should be comprehensible to most nonspecialists. The book also contains a brief description of economic commodities associated with anorthosites, and other references to various anorthosite occurrences and problems may be found in the index. Includes a complete listing of technical references for those who wish to dig deeper.

John L. Berkley

Cross-References

Building Stone, 178; Feldspars, 698; Igneous and Contact Metamorphic Mineral Deposits, 1124; Igneous Rock Bodies, 1131; Igneous Rock Classification, 1138; Industrial Metals, 1216; Iron Deposits, 1254; Lunar History, 1400; Lunar Rocks, 1414; Mountain Belts, 1725.

IGNEOUS ROCKS: BASALTIC

Type of earth science: Geology
Field of study: Petrology, igneous

"Basalt" is the term applied to dark, iron-rich volcanic rocks that occur everywhere on the ocean floors, as oceanic islands, and in certain areas on continents. It is the parent material from which nearly any other igneous rock can be generated by various natural processes.

Principal terms

AUGITE: an essential mineral in most basalts, a member of the pyroxene group of silicates

CRUST: the upper layer of the earth and the other "rocky" planets; it is composed mostly of relatively low-density silicate rocks

LITHOSPHERIC PLATES: giant slabs composed of crust and upper mantle; they move about laterally to produce volcanism, mountain building, and earthquakes

MAGMA: molten silicate liquid, including any crystals, rock inclusions, or gases trapped in that liquid

MANTLE: a layer beginning at about 5 to 50 kilometers below the crust and extending to the earth's metallic core

OCEANIC RIDGES: a system of mostly underwater rift mountains that bisect all the ocean basins; basalt is extruded along their central axes

OLIVINE: a silicate mineral found in mantle and some basalts, particularly the alkaline varieties

PERIDOTITE: the most common rock type in the upper mantle, where basalt magma is produced

PLAGIOCLASE: one of the principal silicate minerals in basalt, a member of the feldspar group

SUBDUCTION ZONES: areas marginal to continents where lithospheric plates collide

Summary of the Phenomenon

Basalt is a dark, commonly black, volcanic rock. It is sometimes called "trap" or "traprock," from the Swedish term *trapp*, which means "steplike." On cooling, basalt tends to form hexagonal columns, which in turn form steplike structures after erosion. Excellent examples can be seen at Devils Postpile, in the Sierra Nevada in central California, and the Giant's Causeway, in County Antrim, Ireland. The term "trap," however, is used mostly by miners and nonspecialists; scientists prefer the word "basalt" for the fine-grained, volcanic rock that forms by the solidification of lava flows. Basaltic magma that crystallizes more slowly below the earth's surface, thus making larger mineral grains, is called "gabbro."

The importance of basalt to the evolution of planets like the earth cannot be overemphasized. Basalt is considered to be a "primary silicate liquid," in that the first liquids to form by the melting of the original minerals that made up all the so-called rocky planets (those composed mostly of silicates) were basaltic in composition. In turn, basalt contains all the necessary ingredients to make all the other rocks that may eventually form in a planet's crust. Furthermore, many meteorites (which are believed to represent fragments of planetoids or asteroids) are basaltic or contain basalt fragments, and the surfaces of the moon and the planets Mercury, Venus, and Mars are known to be covered to various degrees by basalt lava flows.

Like most rocks in the earth's crust, basalt is composed of silicate minerals, substances whose principal component is the silica molecule. Compared with other silicate rocks, basalts contain large amounts of iron and magnesium and small amounts of silicon. This characteristic is reflected in the minerals in basalts, which are mostly pyroxene minerals (dark-colored, calcium-iron-magnesium silicates, such as augite) and certain feldspar minerals called plagioclase (light-colored, calcium-sodium-aluminum silicates). Pyroxenes and plagioclase are essential minerals in basalts, but some types of basalt also contain the mineral olivine (a green, iron-magnesium silicate). The high abundance of dark green or black pyroxene and, in some cases, olivine gives basalts their characteristic dark color. This color is mainly attributable to the high iron content in pyroxene and olivine.

Basalt is the most common type of igneous rock (rock formed by the crystallization of magma) on or near the surface of the earth. Relatively rare on continents, it is the principal rock in the ocean floors. Drilling into the sea floor by specially designed oceanographic research ships reveals that basalt invariably lies just below a thin cover of fine, sedimentary mud. Ocean floor basalt flows out of mid-ocean ridges, a system of underwater mountain ranges that spans the globe. These ridges commonly trend roughly down the middle of ocean basins, and they represent places where the earth's lithospheric plates are being literally split apart. In this process, basalt magma is generated below the "rift mountains"; it flows onto the cold ocean floor and solidifies. Although oceanic ridges are normally hidden from view under the oceans, a segment of the Mid-Atlantic Ridge emerges above the waves as the island of Iceland.

Oceanic islands are also composed of basalt. The islands of Hawaii, Fiji, Mariana, Tonga, and Samoa, among others, are large volcanoes or groups of volcanoes that rise above water from the ocean floor. Unlike the basalts that cover the ocean floors, however, these volcanoes do not occur at oceanic ridges but instead rise directly from the sea floor. Basalt is also a fairly common rock type on island arcs, volcanic islands that occur near continental margins. These curvilinear island chains arise from melting along subduction zones, areas where the earth's lithospheric plates are colliding. This process generally involves material from the ocean basins diving under the more massive continents; andesite (a light-colored rock) volcanoes are the main result, but some basalt erupts there as well. The Japanese, Philippine, and Aleutian island chains are examples of island arcs, as are the island countries of New Zealand and Indonesia.

Basalt lava flows are not nearly as common on continents as in oceanic areas. Andesites, rhyolites, and related igneous rocks are far more abundant than basalt in continental settings. In North America, basalt lava flows and volcanoes are best exposed to view in the western United States and Canadian provinces, western Mexico, Central America, and western South America. The greatest accumulations of basalt lava flows in the United States are in the Columbia Plateau of Washington, Oregon, and Idaho. In this large area, a series of basalt lava flows have built up hundreds of feet of nearly flat-lying basalt flows over a few million years. These "fissure flows" result from lava's pouring out of long cracks, or fissures, in the crust. They are similar in many respects to the basalt flows produced at oceanic ridges, because no actual volcanic cones are produced—only layer after layer of black basalt. The Snake River Plain in southern Idaho has a similar origin, and other extensive basalt plateaus occur in the Deccan area of southern India, the Karroo area of South Africa, and Paraná State in Brazil.

Not all basalt is erupted as lava flows. If the lava is particularly rich in volatiles such as water and carbon dioxide, it will be explosively ejected from the volcano as glowing fountains of incandescent particles that rain down on the surrounding area. Conical volcanoes composed almost exclusively of basalt ejecta particles are called cinder cones. Good examples of cinder cones are Sunset Crater in northern Arizona, the numerous cinder cones in Hawaii and Iceland, and the very active volcano in Italy known as Stromboli. In fact, the rather violent eruptions that produce cinder cones are called "strombolian eruptions."

Although basaltic rocks may all look alike to the nonspecialist, there are actually many different kinds of basalt. They are arranged by scientists into a generally accepted classification scheme based on chemistry and, to some extent, mineralogy. To begin with, basalt can be distinguished from the other major silicate igneous rocks by its relatively low (about 50 percent) silica content. Within the basalt clan itself, however, other means of classification are used. Basalts are divided into two major groups, the alkaline basalts and the subalkaline basalts. Alkaline basalts contain high amounts of the alkali metal ions potassium and sodium but relatively low amounts of silica. In contrast, subalkaline basalts contain less potassium and sodium and more silica. As might be expected, this chemical difference translates into differences in the mineral content of the basalt types as well. For example, all alkaline basalts contain one or more minerals called "feldspathoids" in addition to plagioclase feldspar. They also commonly contain significant olivine. Subalkaline basalts, on the other hand, do not contain feldspathoids, although some contain olivine, and they may be capable of crystallizing very tiny amounts of the mineral quartz. The presence of this very silica-rich mineral reflects the relatively high silica content of subalkaline basalt magmas versus alkaline basalt magmas. Within these two major groups are many subtypes, too numerous to discuss here.

Methods of Study

Like other igneous rocks, basalts are analyzed and studied by many techniques.

Individual studies may include extensive field mapping, in which the distribution of various types of basalt is plotted on maps. Especially if geologic maps of basalt types are correlated with absolute ages determined through radiometric dating techniques, the history of magma generation and its relation to tectonic history (earth movements) can be reconstructed for a particular area. Good examples of such studies are those conducted in recent years on the Hawaiian Islands. These studies indicate that the alkaline basalts on any given island are generally older than the subalkaline basalts, showing that magma production has moved upward, to lower pressure areas, in the mantle with time. This finding supports the idea that oceanic island basalts such as those in Hawaii are generated within so-called mantle plumes, roughly balloon-shaped, slowly rising masses of mantle material made buoyant by localized "hot spots."

Samples of basalt are also analyzed in the laboratory. The age of crystallization of basalt is obtained by means of radiometric dating techniques that involve the use of mass spectrometers to determine the abundances of critical isotopes, such as potassium 40 and argon 40 or rubidium 87 and strontium 86 and 87. To obtain information on how basalt magma is generated and how it subsequently changes in composition before extrusion as a lava flow, scientists place finely powdered samples in metallic, graphite, or ceramic capsules and subject them to heating and cooling under various conditions of pressure. Such procedures are known as experimental petrology. It has been proved that nearly any other igneous magma composition can be derived from basalt magma by the process of crystal fractionation. Widely believed to be the major factor influencing chemical variation among igneous rocks, this process results in ever-changing liquid compositions as the various silicate minerals crystallize, and are thus removed from the liquid, over time. Basalt's parental role gives it enormous importance in the discipline of igneous petrology.

Another fruitful avenue of research is trace element analysis of basalts. Trace elements occur in such low abundances in rocks that their concentrations must usually be expressed in terms of parts per million or even parts per billion. Among the most useful substances for tracing the history of basalt are the rare earth elements. Chromium, vanadium, nickel, phosphorus, strontium, zirconium, scandium, and hafnium are also used. There are many methods for measuring these elements, but the most common, and most accurate, is neutron activation. This method involves irradiating samples in a small nuclear reactor and then electronically counting the gamma-ray pulses generated by the samples. Since different elements tend to emit gamma rays at characteristic energies, these specific energies can be measured and the intensity of gamma pulses translated into elemental concentrations.

Once determined for a particular basalt sample, trace element abundances are sensitive indicators of events that have transpired during the evolution of the basalt. There are two reasons for this sensitivity. First, trace elements are present in such low concentrations as compared with major elements (iron, aluminum, calcium, silicon, and the like) that any small change in abundance caused by changes in the environment of basalt production will be readily noticed. Second, different minerals, including those crystallizing in the magma and those in the source peridotite, incorporate a given trace element into their structures or reject it to the surrounding liquid to widely varying degrees. Therefore, trace element concentrations can be used to show which minerals were involved in producing certain observed chemical signatures in basalts and which were likely not involved.

For example, it is well known that the mineral garnet readily accepts the rare earth element lutecium into its structure but tends to reject most lanthanum to any adjacent liquid. Basalts with very little lutecium but much lanthanum were therefore probably derived by the melting of garnet-bearing mantle rocks. Since garnet-bearing mantle rocks can exist only at great depth, basalts with such trace element patterns must have originated by melting at these depths in the mantle. In fact, that is one of the most important lines of evidence that alkaline basalts originate at high-pressure regions in the mantle.

Context

Basaltic islands, particularly in the Pacific basin, are some of the most popular tourist stops in the world. More important, however, basalt magma contains low concentrations of valuable metals that, when concentrated by various natural processes, provide the source for many important ores. Copper, nickel, lead, zinc, gold, silver, and other metals have been recovered from ore bodies centered in basaltic terrains. Some of the richest mines of metallic ores in the world are located in Canada, where ores are found associated with extemely old basaltic rocks, called "greenstones," from long-vanished oceans. The richest of these mines is Kidd Creek, in northern Ontario. These ore-bearing basalts were first extruded more than 2 billion years ago, during what geologists call Precambrian times (the period from 4.6 billion to about 600 million years ago). Other notable ore deposits include the native, or metallic, copper in late Precambrian basalts that was mined for many years in the Keweenaw Peninsula of northern Michigan. In addition, the island of Crete in the Mediterranean Sea has copper mines that were mined thousands of years ago during the "copper" and "bronze" ages of human history. The basalt enclosing these ores is believed to have erupted from an ancient mid-ocean ridge trending between Africa and Europe.

Basalt can also be used as a building stone or raw material for sculptures, but its high iron content makes it susceptible to rust stains. It is also ground up to make road gravel, especially in the western United States, and it is used as decorative stone in yards and gardens.

Bibliography

Ballard, Robert D. *Exploring Our Living Planet.* Washington, D.C.: National Geographic Society, 1983. This book covers every aspect of the earth's volcanic and tectonic features and is lavishly illustrated with color photographs, illustrations, and diagrams. The sections on "spreading" and "hotspots" largely deal with basalt volcanism and its relationship to plate tectonic theory. Well written and indexed, the text will be easily understood and appreciated by specialists and laypersons alike.

Decker, Robert, and Barbara Decker. *Volcanoes.* New York: W. H. Freeman, 1981. This brief book gives a comprehensive treatment of volcanic phenomena. It is illustrated with numerous black-and-white photographs and diagrams. Chapters 1, 2, 3, and 6 deal almost exclusively with basalt volcanism. The last four chapters deal with human aspects of volcanic phenomena, such as the obtaining of energy and raw materials, and the effect of volcanic eruptions on weather. Includes an excellent chapter-by-chapter bibliography. Suitable for high school and college students.

Lewis, Thomas A., ed. *Volcano.* Alexandria, Va.: Time-Life Books, 1982. One of the volumes of the Planet Earth series, this book is written with the nonspecialist in mind. Wonderful color photographs, well-conceived color diagrams, and a readable narrative guide the reader through the world of volcanism. The book is especially good for its descriptions of past eruptions and their effects on humankind. Basalt is covered mainly in the chapter on Hawaii and the chapter on Heimaey, Iceland. Has a surprisingly extensive bibliography and index for a book of this kind.

Macdonald, Gordon A. *Volcanoes.* Englewood Cliffs, N.J.: Prentice-Hall, 1972. Written by one of the premier volcanologists in the world, this book is ideal for those desiring a serious but not overly technical treatment. Every conceivable aspect of volcanic phenomena is covered, but the sections on basalt (particularly as it occurs in Hawaii) are particularly good. Includes suggested readings, a comprehensive list of references, a very good index, and an appendix that lists the active volcanoes of the world. Somewhat lengthy.

Putnam, William C. *Geology.* 2d ed. New York: Oxford University Press, 1971. A comprehensive and accessible text. Chapter 4, "Igneous Rocks and Igneous Processes," uses a vivid description of the 1883 eruption of Krakatoa as a way of introducing the formation processes of igneous rocks. Other famous volcanic eruptions are also discussed. The rocks' classification and composition are described in detail. The chapter concludes with a list of references. Illustrated.

Tarbuck, Edward J., and Frederick K. Lutgens. *The Earth: An Introduction to Physical Geology.* 2d ed. Columbus, Ohio: Merrill, 1987. Aimed at the reader with little or no college-level science experience, this textbook includes a chapter devoted to igneous rocks and their textures, mineral compositions, classification, and formation. Illustrated with photographs and diagrams. Includes review questions and list of key terms.

John L. Berkley

Cross-References

IGNEOUS ROCKS: BATHOLITHS

Type of earth science: Geology
Field of study: Petrology, igneous

Batholiths are gigantic bodies of granitic rock that are located in mobile belts sur-rounding the ancient cores of the continents. The growth of continental crust dur-ing the past 2.5 billion years is intimately related to the origin and emplacement of major volumes of granitic magma that solidify as batholiths.

Principal terms

CRYSTALLIZATION: the solidification of molten rock as a result of heat loss; slow heat loss results in the growth of crystals, but rapid heat loss can cause glass to form

GRANITIC/GRANITOID: descriptive terms for plutonic rock types having quartz and feldspar as major mineral phases, including rocks ranging from quartz diorite (tonolite) to true granite

I-TYPE GRANITOID: granitic rock formed from magma generated by partial melting of igneous rocks in the upper mantle or lowermost crust

MAGMA: molten rock material that crystallizes to form igneous rocks

MIGMATITE: a rock exhibiting both metamorphic and plutonic textural traits

MOBILE BELT: a linear belt of igneous and deformed metamorphic rocks produced by plate collision at a continental margin; relatively young mobile belts form major mountain ranges

PARTIAL MELTING: a process undergone by rocks as their temperature rises and metamorphism occurs; magmas are derived by the partial melting of preexisting rock; also known as ultrametamorphism or anatexis

PLUTON: a generic term for an igneous body that solidifies well below the earth's surface; plutonic rocks are coarse-grained because they cool slowly

S-TYPE GRANITOID: granitic rock formed from magma generated by partial melting of sedimentary rocks within the crust

Summary of the Phenomenon

Batholiths are large composite masses of granitoid rock formed by numerous individual bodies of magma that have risen from deep source areas in molten form and solidified near enough to the surface to be exposed by erosion. The resulting rocks are relatively coarse-grained in texture and markedly heterogeneous in chemi-cal and mineralogical composition. A well-studied example is that of the coastal batholith of Peru, which forms an almost continuous outcrop 1,100 kilometers long and 50 kilometers wide along the western flank of the Andes between 8° and 16° south latitude. This enormous body has steep walls and a flat roof. It is composed of more than one thousand individual plutons emplaced along a narrow belt parallel to the present coastline during a volcanic-plutonic event that extended over a period of 70 million years. Many such batholiths are known in the mountainous areas of the world, but few are as large or as magnificently exposed to view as that in Peru. Geological glossaries often define a batholith as a "coarse-textured igneous mass with an exposed surface area in excess of 100 square kilometers"; this description has the virtue of simplicity but is misleading because it encompasses granitic plutons, and even nongranitic plutons, which form under conditions quite removed from those associated with the world's major batholiths.

In most instances, there is evidence to indicate that the individual plutons of a batholith were emplaced as hot, viscous melts containing suspended crystals. This molten material is called magma. Cooling and crystallization occur during the surfaceward ascent of magma and gradually transform it to solid rock, which prevents further upward movement. The depth at which total solidification occurs varies and is strongly dependent upon the initial temperature and water content of the magma. Extreme levels of ascent, within 3 to 5 kilometers of the surface, are possible only for very hot magmas with very low initial water contents. Most granitic plutons complete their crystallization at depths in the range of 8 to 20 kilometers. The characteristic coarse textures observed in most granitic plutons are the result of slow cooling, which, in turn, implies that the rate of magma ascent is also slow. These traits distinguish plutonic rocks from their volcanic counterparts. As would be expected, the formation of a batholith is a complex and lengthy event that is the sum of the processes responsible for the emplacement of each member pluton. Each member pluton has an individual history involving the generation of magma in the source region, ascent and partial crystallization, physical displacement of overlying solid rock, chemical interaction with the solid rocks encountered during ascent, and the terminal crystallization phase. Consequently, each member pluton of a batholith can be expected to exhibit a combination of textural, mineralogical, and chemical variations that are peculiar to itself.

It has long been recognized that major batholiths are confined to narrow zones elongated parallel to the margins of older continental crust. In such zones, granitic melts intrude either thick sequences of chemically related volcanic rocks or highly deformed and metamorphosed sedimentary rocks. These granite-dominated zones are called mobile belts. The ancient cores of continents are all older than 2.5 billion years. They are surrounded by mobile belts that become successively younger away from the core. The most recent mobile belts form major mountain chains along continental margins. The resulting age pattern clearly shows that continents grow larger with time by the marginal accretion of mobile belts. In the late 1960's, the emergence of plate tectonic theory provided a basis for understanding how mobile belts form and are accreted to preexisting continent margins. The impetus provided by this theory sparked intensive study of the world's mobile belts. These studies amply show that logical time-space relationships exist between plate collisions, deformation styles, and rock types that occur in mobile belts. Two distinct types of mobile belts are now recognized, and each is dominated by granitic batholiths. These batholiths, however, are very different in terms of granitic rock types, modes of pluton emplacement, rock associations, metamorphic effects, and the metallic ores they host. The batholiths of the two mobile belt types are called I-type and S-type batholiths.

Mobile belts along the eastern margin of the Pacific Ocean contain I-type batholiths exclusively. Their size and collective volume is staggering. The Peruvian batholith is an example already mentioned. Others of this type include the Sierra Nevada batholith, the Idaho batholith, and the tremendous Coast Range batholith, which extends from northern Washington to the Alaska-Yukon border. In contrast, the western margin of the Pacific Ocean is dominated by mobile belts with S-type batholiths, although some I-types are also present. The batholiths of Western Europe are also mainly of the S-type. In southeastern Australia, where the two types of batholiths were first recognized, S-type and I-type granitoids form a paired belt parallel to the coastline. Although their geographical distribution is uneven, both I-type and S-type batholiths occur worldwide.

The most distinctive trait of I-type batholiths is the broad range of granitic rock types they contain. In these batholiths, the rock types gabbro-diorite, quartz diorite-granodiorite, and granite occur in the approximate proportions of 15:50:35. This means that quartz diorite (also called tonalite) and granodiorite jointly comprise 50 percent of I-type batholiths, and true granite is a subordinate component in them. This wide compositional spectrum not only characterizes an entire I-type batholith but also is typical of the individual member plutons. Usually the major plutons are concentrically zoned with small central cores of true granite enveloped by extensive zones of granodiorite that grade outward into margins of quartz diorite. Small plutons in the compositional range of gabbro-diorite are common but subordinate to the zoned granitic bodies. Most member plutons of I-type batholiths have domal or cylindrical shapes and very steep contacts with the surrounding rock. Others may have a steeply tilted sheetlike form, but, regardless of shape, most I-type plutons cut through the preexisting rock layers at a steep angle. The emplacement of these plutons appears to be controlled by near-vertical fractures that may extend downward to the base of the crust. In younger I-type batholiths such as that in Peru, the granitoids have intruded into a roof of chemically related volcanic rocks that show the same compositional spectrum as the granitic plutons. This volcanic pile, dominated by andesite, may be 3 to 5 kilometers thick at the time of pluton emplacement. Gradually, this volcanic roof is stripped away by erosion so that in older, deeply eroded batholiths, volcanic rocks are generally absent. The grade of regional metamorphism in the rocks enclosing I-type batholiths is relatively low, and there is little evidence of large-scale horizontal compression or crustal shortening. Structural displacements and the movements of rising plutons are dominantly vertical and typically occur over a time span of 50 to 100 million years.

S-type batholiths contrast with I-types in almost every respect. To begin with, the ratio of gabbro-diorite to quartz diorite-granodiorite to granite is 2:18:80 in S-type batholiths. These plutonic complexes are very much dominated by true granite, and gabbro-diorite plutons are rare or absent. In many cases, S-type granites are the distinctive "two mica granites," which contain both biotite and muscovite and are frequently associated with major tin and tungsten ore deposits. The batholiths of northern Portugal are typical examples of this association. S-type batholiths, as well as their member plutons, lack the concentric zoning that characterizes I-type plutons. Compositional homogeneity is their trademark. S-type plutons are intruded into thick sequences of regionally metamorphosed sedimentary rocks. The metamorphic grade ranges from moderate to very high, and, frequently, the granites are located within the zone of highest metamorphic grade. In such cases, migmatites are often present. The enclosing metamorphosed rocks are intensely folded in response to marked crustal compression, and volcanic rocks are conspicuously absent. S-type batholiths are smaller in volume and form over a shorter period of time (usually less than 20 million years) than their I-type counterparts.

The many contrasting traits of I-type and S-type batholiths are an indication that the conditions of magma generation and emplacement are very different in the mobile belts in which they are found. In the case of I-type batholiths, it appears that magmas are generated at relatively great depths and above the subduction zones formed at destructive plate boundaries. The magmas are derived by partial melting of upper-mantle basic igneous rocks and, perhaps, lower crustal igneous rocks. The melts rise along the steep fractures produced by crustal tension over the subduction zone. The igneous ancestry of these melts is the reason for calling the resulting plutons "I-type." The hottest and driest of these I-type magmas will reach the surface to produce extensive fields of volcanic rocks and large calderas. In some cases, like the Peruvian batholith, the rise of magma was "passive" in the sense that room was provided for the rising plutons by gravitational subsidence of the overlying roof rock. This is the process of cauldron subsidence. In the case of the Sierra Nevada batholith, however, it appears that I-type magmas were emplaced by "forceful injection." In this process, rising magma makes room for itself by shouldering aside the surrounding solid rock. On the other hand, the evidence suggests that S-type magmas originate by partial melting of metamorphosed sedimentary rocks. This sedimentary parentage of the magmas is the reason for designating them as "S-type." Melting is made possible by dehydration of water-bearing minerals under conditions of intense metamorphism. The frequent presence of migmatites is evidence for this transition from metamorphic conditions to magmatic conditions. The essential requirements for relatively high-level crustal melting are high temperatures, intense horizontal compression to produce deep sedimentary basins, and a thick pile of sediments to fill these basins. Such conditions are best met in back-arc basins, which also form at destructive plate margins but considerably inland from the volcanic-plutonic environment of I-type batholiths. This may explain why some I-type and S-type batholiths occur in paired belts parallel to a continental margin, as in southeastern Australia. The collision environment that arises when continent meets continent in the terminal stage of subduction may also provide suitable conditions for S-type magma production. The magmas that result will be relatively cool and wet and will not be able to rise far above their zone of melting. During this limited ascent, the S-type magmas tend to assume the shape of a light bulb, with a neck tapering down to the zone of melting. Because of their limited capacity for vertical movement, S-type plutons require no special mechanisms to provide additional space for them.

Methods of Study

The study of a batholith begins with the study of its individual member plutons. This always involves fieldwork, laboratory analysis of rock samples returned from the field, and comparison of the resulting data with those obtained from other batholiths. Because of their great size, batholiths present special problems for field study. The most informative studies are those in mountainous areas, such as the Peruvian Andes, where erosion has exposed the batholith roof contact and cut steep canyons between and through individual plutons. High topographic relief is essential if the geologist is to learn anything about the variation in shape and composition with depth in the plutons. Most studies are in remote mountain ranges where climatic factors and the absence of roads are obstacles to fieldwork. Often, the summer, snow-free period is as short as four weeks, and, even during this period, winter snow and glaciers may cover much of the study area. A well-financed project may employ helicopters to supply remote base camps and transport geologists to sites that are virtually inaccessible by other means. This saves precious field time, which must otherwise be devoted to supply logistics and slower modes of transportation, such as backpacking, animal transport, and (where roads exist) four-wheel drive vehicles.

Study of even a small portion of a major batholith requires several well-trained geologists working intensively during the short field seasons over a period of several years. The geologists make traverses on foot across and around the individual plutons as topography permits, and they record the textural, mineralogical, and structural features observed on maps or aerial photographs of the area. These maps eventually reveal the overall shape of plutons and the patterns of concentric zoning within them. Special maps are prepared to show the distribution of fractures and flow structures within individual plutons. These features indicate how fluid the magma was at the time of emplacement. Contacts between the plutons and older enclosing rocks are closely examined for deformation effects and evidence of thermal and chemical interaction with the magma. Fragments of older rock engulfed by magma are often preserved in a recrystallized state, and these are scrutinized carefully, since they provide clues as to whether the emplacement process was passive or forceful. As the end of the field season draws near, the mapped plutons are sampled. Large, fresh samples must be collected from each recognized zone of each pluton for subsequent laboratory study. The number of samples collected from a single pluton depends upon its size and homogeneity but is frequently in the range of one hundred to five hundred samples. A smaller number of samples is collected from the host rocks at varying distances from the plutonic contact in order to study the thermal effects produced by the pluton. The field description, identifying number, and exact location of each sample site must be meticulously recorded. If, at the end of the field season, several plutons have been studied and sampled, there may be several thousand rock samples to label, pack securely, and ship to the laboratory, where they will receive further study.

At the laboratory, the samples are usually cut in half and labeled in a permanent fashion. One half of each sample is stored for future reference, and the other is prepared for the laboratory procedures. Paper-thin slices of each sample are glued to glass slides for examination under a petrographic microscope. The microscopist identifies the mineral phases present in each slide and determines the abundance of each. The texture of each rock, as revealed under the microscope, is carefully described and interpreted in terms of crystallization sequence and deformation history. When the microscopic study is complete, certain samples, perhaps fifty to one hundred, are chosen for chemical analysis. Most will be analyzed because they are judged to be representative of major zones of a pluton; a few may be analyzed because they exhibit unusual minerals or some peculiar trait not explained by the microscopic study. If the age of a pluton is not known, a few samples (one to ten) will be shipped to a laboratory that specializes in age determinations by radio-isotope methods.

Finally, on the basis of the field observations, microscopic examinations, and chemical data, the investigators will assemble rival hypotheses, or scenarios, for the origin and emplacement of the plutons that have been studied. Any scenario that conflicts seriously with known facts is discarded. Those remaining are compared with well-known laboratory melting-crystallization experiments on synthetic and natural rock systems. The size and shape of the plutons, as determined by the field mapping, can be compared with those of "model plutons" derived through sophisticated, but idealized, centrifuge experiments in laboratory settings. The investigators will compare their data, in detail, with data reported in the geological literature by workers in other parts of the world. They will also compare their results with earlier studies of the same plutons, or studies in the same region, if they exist. Ideally, this approach leads to elimination of all hypotheses for the origin and emplacement of the plutons but one. In the majority of cases, particularly those where the study of a major batholith is still in its infancy, it is found that two or even several rival hypotheses explain the known facts equally well. This is an indication that the scope of the study must be enlarged to include even more member plutons of the batholith. As additional plutons are studied in detail, more constraints on the mode of origin and emplacement of the batholith are obtained.

Context

Mobile belts, dominated by immense granitic batholiths, have been systematically accreted to the ancient continental cores for the last 2.5 billion years of earth history. Modern plate tectonic theory has provided the basis for understanding the periodic nature of mobile belt accretion and the ways in which crustal and mantle materials are recycled. It is evident that the emplacement of batholiths is at present, and has been for at least 2.5 billion years, the major cause for progressive crustal growth. It is also clear that the rate at which batholiths formed during this lengthy period has far exceeded the rate of continental reduction by erosion. The generation of large volumes of granitic magma and its subsequent rise to form batholiths a few kilometers below the crustal surface must be viewed as fundamental to crustal growth. Batholiths play a major role in the formation of mountain systems and are the most important element in the complex rock and metallic ore associations of mobile belts. The very existence of continents is, in fact, a result of the long-standing process of batholith emplacement.

Bibliography

Atherton, Michael P., and J. Tarney, eds. *Origin of Granite Batholiths: Geochemical Evidence.* Orpington, England: Shiva Publishing, 1979. A summary of the views of major authorities on the origin of batholiths. Suitable for advanced students of geology.

Best, Myron G. *Igneous and Metamorphic Petrology.* New York: W. H. Freeman, 1982. A popular university text for undergraduate majors in geology. A well-illustrated and fairly detailed treatment of the origin, distribution, and characteristics of igneous and metamorphic rocks. Chapter 4 covers granite plutons and batholiths.

Hamilton, Warren B., and W. Bradley Meyers. *The Nature of Batholiths.* Professional Paper 554-C. Denver, Colo.: U.S. Geological Survey, 1967. In this classic paper, the authors propose their controversial "shallow batholith model." The account is short and very descriptive and can be followed by college-level readers. This and the following article influenced many geologists to abandon the traditional view of batholiths.

_____. "Nature of the Boulder Batholith of Montana." *Geological Society of America Bulletin* 85 (1974): 365-378. The authors apply their 1967 model to the Boulder batholith and reply to the heated criticism of colleagues who did the fieldwork on this batholith. This work is aimed at professionals but can be understood by those with moderate knowledge of plutonic processes.

Judson, S., M. E. Kauffman, and L. D. Leet. *Physical Geology.* 7th ed. Englewood Cliffs, N.J.: Prentice-Hall, 1987. A traditional text for beginning geology courses. Simplified but suitable for high school readers. Contains a good index, illustrations, and an extensive glossary. Chapter 3 treats igneous processes and rocks. Chapters 4, 7, 9, and 11 examine fundamental processes related to mountain building, metamorphism, volcanism, and plate tectonics.

Meyers, J. S. "Cauldron Subsidence and Fluidization: Mechanisms of Intrusion of the Coastal Batholith of Peru into Its Own Volcanic Ejecta." *Geological Society of America Bulletin* 86 (1975): 1209–1220. Possibly the best available account of a major batholith. The excellent cross-section diagrams clearly indicate that the author was influenced by the model of Hamilton and Myers. Aimed at professionals but can be understood by college-level readers with some background in geology.

Press, F., and R. Siever. *Earth.* 4th ed. New York: W. H. Freeman, 1986. Chapter 5, "Plutonism," is a more thorough treatment of the subject than that in Judson et al. but requires a slightly higher level of reading. This is one of the best university-level texts for a first course in geology.

Smith, David G., ed. *The Cambridge Encyclopedia of Earth Sciences*. New York: Crown, 1981. More of a super-text than an encyclopedia. The authors skillfully place their fields of expertise in the plate tectonic context and provide a modern overview of the entire field of earth science. Includes comprehensive index and glossary as well as high-quality maps, tables, and photographs. For both general and college-level readers.

Gary R. Lowell

Cross-References

Continental Crust, 261; Continental Growth, 268; Igneous Rock Bodies, 1131; Igneous Rock Classification, 1138; Igneous Rocks: Granitic, 1180; Crystallization of Magmas, 1420; The Origin of Magmas, 1428; Water in Magmas, 1433; Mountain Belts, 1725; Plate Tectonics, 2079; Subduction and Orogeny, 2497.

IGNEOUS ROCKS: CARBONATITES

Type of earth science: Geology
Field of study: Petrology, igneous

Carbonatites are composed of carbonate minerals that appear to have formed from carbonate liquids. They typically contain many minerals of unusual composition that are seldom found elsewhere. Carbonatites have been mined for a variety of elements, including the rare earth elements, niobium, and thorium. The rare earths are used as phosphors in television picture tubes and in high-quality magnets in stereo systems; niobium is used in steel to make it resist high temperature.

Principal terms

CALCITE: a mineral composed of calcium carbonate

DIKE: a tabular igneous rock formed by the injection of molten rock material through another solid rock

DOLOMITE: a mineral composed of calcium magnesium carbonate

IGNEOUS ROCKS: rocks formed from liquid or molten rock material

IJOLITE: a dark-colored silicate rock containing the minerals nepheline (sodium aluminum silicate) and pyroxene (calcium, magnesium, and iron silicate)

ISOTOPES: different atoms of the same element that have different numbers of neutrons (neutral particles) in their nuclei

LIMESTONE: a sedimentary rock composed mostly of calcium carbonate formed by organisms or by calcite precipitation in warm, shallow seas

MINERAL: a naturally occurring element or compound with a more or less definite chemical composition

ROCK: a naturally occurring, consolidated material that usually consists of two or more minerals; sometimes, as in carbonatites, the rock may consist mainly of one mineral

SILICATE MINERAL: a mineral composed of silicon, oxygen, and other metals, such as iron, magnesium, potassium, and sodium

Summary of the Phenomenon

Carbonatites are unusual igneous rocks because they are not primarily composed of silicate minerals, as are most other rocks formed from molten rock material. Instead, carbonatites are composed mostly of carbonate minerals and of minor amounts of other minerals that are rare in other rocks. The carbonate minerals composing carbonatites are usually calcite (calcium carbonate) or dolomite (calcium magnesium carbonate). The other minerals found in carbonatites often contain large concentrations of elements that rarely become concentrated enough to form these minerals in other rocks.

Carbonatites often occur as small bodies of various size and shape that cut across the surrounding rocks. Often, they occur as dikes that may be only a few feet to tens of feet wide, but they may be greater in length. An example of carbonatites occurring as dikes is found at Gem Park near Westcliffe, Colorado. Carbonatites sometimes occur as somewhat equidimensional bodies that are larger than those forming dikes. The Sulfide Queen carbonatite at Mountain Pass, California, for example, is about 800 meters long and 230 meters wide. Often, carbonatites contain foreign rock fragments. The cross-cutting relations and foreign rocks found within the carbonatites suggest to many geologists that these carbonatites form by the injection or intrusion of molten carbonate into the surrounding solid rock. The foreign rock fragments within the carbonatite could be solid rocks ripped off the walls by the moving molten carbonate material as it was injected through solid rock.

The occurrence of molten carbonate at the active volcano at Ol Doinyo Lengai in northern Tanzania, Africa, confirms that such material exists. The abundance of recently formed volcanic material composed of carbonatite at Ol Doinyo Lengai and at other locations indicates that considerable carbonatite can form at the surface. The carbonatite liquids at the surface may flow as a lava out of the volcano or be ejected explosively into the air, similar to that of other volcanoes formed mostly from silicate liquids. Carbonatites of volcanic origin are especially abundant in Africa along a portion of the continent called the East African rift zone. There, Africa is slowly being ripped apart by forces within the earth. Some carbonatites that intruded below the surface as dikes may also have fed volcanoes at the surface at one time. Erosion of the extinct volcano and associated silicate rocks may have exposed the dikes composed of solidified carbonatite.

Carbonatites are often associated with rare silicate rocks injected at about the same time as the carbonatites. These silicate rocks are unusual, as they normally lack feldspars (calcium, sodium, and potassium aluminum silicate minerals), which are abundant in most igneous rocks formed within the earth. Instead of feldspar, many of these silicate rocks contain varied amounts of the minerals nepheline (sodium aluminum silicate) and clinopyroxene (calcium, magnesium, iron silicate) and minor amounts of minerals not commonly found in other igneous rocks. The silicate rock consisting of more or less equal amounts of nepheline and clinopyroxene is called ijolite.

The carbonatites, ijolites, and other associated igneous rocks that formed at the same place and were injected at about the same time are called complexes. These complexes have small areas of exposure at the surface; most are exposed over a surface area of only about 1-35 square kilometers. The Magnet Cove complex in Arkansas, for example, has about a 16-square-kilometer exposure. The Gem Park complex in Colorado is only about 6 square kilometers in area. The associated silicate rocks usually compose most of the area of the exposed complex; only a small portion is carbonatite. The overall shape of these complexes is often circular, elliptical, or oval, but departures from these shapes are common. Often, the different rock types within a complex are built of concentric zones much like the layers of an onion.

Examples of these complexes include Seabrook Lake, Canada, where the complex is roughly circular and is about 0.8 kilometer across. Its "tail," however, extends from the main circular body to about 1.2 kilometers to the south. The central core of carbonatite, composed mostly of calcite, is about 0.3 kilometer across. Smaller carbonatite dikes can be found within other rocks. The largest carbonatite body is surrounded by a dark rock containing angular blocks composed mostly of carbonate, clinopyroxene, or biotite (a dark, shiny potassium, iron, magnesium, and aluminum silicate). This latter body is surrounded by a mixture of ijolite and pyroxenite (a rock containing only pyroxene). The ijolite and pyroxenite also compose much of the tail to the south. Close to the complex, the solid rock into which the partially molten material was intruded has been highly altered to other minerals. This alteration is believed to have been caused by water vapor or carbon dioxide vapor bubbling out of the molten material into the surrounding rocks, changing the original minerals to new ones.

Another complex is located at Gem Park in Colorado. Gem Park is oval in shape, roughly 2 by 3.3 kilometers. There is no central carbonatite there. Instead, scores of small, dolomite-rich carbonatites have intruded as dikes across the silicate rocks of the complex. The main silicate rocks of the complex are pyroxenite and a feldspar-clinopyroxene rock called gabbro. The pyroxenite and gabbro form concentric rings with one another. The large amount of gabbro makes this complex unusual, as gabbros are seldom present with carbonatite in the same complex.

The complexes at Gem Park and Seabrook Lake are rather simple, as they contain very few rock types. A wide variety of minerals can be found in some complexes, resulting in a large number of rock types. The Magnet Cove complex in Arkansas, for example, has twenty-eight major rock types listed on the geologic map. (The reading accompanying the map extends the total rock types to an even greater number.) A large proportion of the rock names in geology are generated by the wide variation of minerals found in these complexes that compose merely a tiny portion of the earth's surface.

Methods of Study

Up until the 1950's, geologists believed that carbonatites were limestones that melted and were intruded as molten rock material or that circulating waters formed carbonatites by replacing carbonate minerals with silicate minerals. Some geologists thought that carbonatites could have formed from limestones that were remobilized by a solid, plastic flow—much like the flow of toothpaste squeezed out of a tube.

A major problem with the suggestion that carbonate material could melt, however, was the apparently high melting point of pure calcite or dolomite. Few geologists could believe that the temperature within the earth was high enough to melt calcite or dolomite. Another problem concerning the belief that limestones were the source of carbonatite was that in some areas, no limestones could be found anywhere near the occurrences of carbonatites. Also, the concept of the intrusion of limestones by plastic flow of a solid was difficult to reconcile with many observations of carbonatites, including the occurrence of foreign igneous rock fragments composed of silicate minerals within them. The absence of fossils in the "limestone" also was noted as unusual, as most limestones have abundant fossils. The lack of fossils could be explained, however, by the melting hypothesis: The fossil evidence would have been destroyed during the melting.

Experiments in furnaces at temperatures and pressures similar to those expected deep within the earth have done much to support the melting hypothesis for the igneous formation of carbonatites. Several experiments in the late 1950's showed that carbonate minerals could melt at reasonably low temperatures (about 600 degrees Celsius) if abundant carbon dioxide and water vapor coexisted with the carbonate minerals. This dispelled the notion that molten carbonate could not exist within the earth. Also, the discovery of a volcano in Africa in 1960 that was extruding carbonate lavas confirmed that carbonate liquids could exist within the earth. Similar experiments at high temperature and pressure on the composition of carbon dioxide or water vapor suggested that their composition could not produce carbonatites by replacement of silicate minerals with carbonate minerals.

These experiments, combined with field observations (including the way carbonatites cross-cut surrounding rocks and the presence of foreign rock fragments), confirmed that most carbonatites formed by the intrusion of carbonate liquids. Even so, the experiments fell short of dispelling the notion that carbonate liquids could have been derived from melted limestones. The melted limestone hypothesis met objections, because isotopic and element concentrations in carbonatites were much different from those observed in limestones. For example, the ratio of strontium 87 to strontium 86 in most limestones ranges from 0.707 to 0.711. If carbonatites were derived by melting limestones, then the strontium 87-strontium 86 ratios of carbonatites should be within the same range as those of limestones. Instead, they are significantly lower (0.702-0.705 is the common range in carbonatites). The concentration range of many elements is also much larger in carbonatites than those observed in limestones. For example, the elements lanthanum and niobium are hundreds of times more concentrated in carbonatites than they are in limestones. No way known can produce this magnitude of enrichment of the elements by melting or by leaching of the carbonate liquid from the solid rock through which it moved. Such observations have caused the limestone origin of carbonatites to be rejected by most geologists.

Scientists continue to try to understand how carbonatites form. Experiments in furnaces suggest that some carbonate liquids may separate from some silicate liquids similar to those occurring with carbonatites. This process would be like the separation of oil and water as immiscible liquids. Other experiments in furnaces suggest that rocks more than 80 kilometers deep within the earth may melt in small amounts and produce the carbonate liquids and associated silicate liquids similar in composition to those observed in the natural rocks. Although these experiments fail to prove that carbonate liquids form in these ways, several other lines of evidence have convinced geologists that either of these possibilities could produce carbonatites in nature. For example, some possible source rocks that could melt and produce carbonatites or associated silicate rocks are sometimes carried up with lava from deep within the earth. The strontium 87-strontium 86 ratios and element contents of these possible source rocks have been measured and are similar to those expected for rocks that would melt and produce carbonate and silicate liquids.

Context

Their unusually high concentrations of some elements in certain minerals make carbonatites potential ores for these elements. Carbonatites have high concentrations of niobium, thorium, and the rare earth elements of lower atomic number (such as lanthanum and cerium). Iron, titanium, copper, and manganese also have been mined from carbonatites.

Niobium has been economically extracted from the mineral pyrochlore at Fen, Norway, at Kaiserstuhl, West Germany, and at the Kola Peninsula in the Soviet Union. Niobium is used as an alloy in steel to resist high temperature, used in gas turbines, rockets, and atomic power plants. Rare earth elements have been mined from the large carbonatite at Mountain Pass, California. The reserves of rare earths are enormous at Mountain Pass—averaging about 7 percent—compared to other carbonatites. Other carbonatites enriched with rare earths occur in Malawi in Africa. The rare earths are concentrated in many minerals, including perovskite, monazite, xenotime, and a variety of rare earth carbonate minerals. The rare earths are used as color phosphors in television picture tubes and as components in high-quality magnets used in stereo speakers and headphones. Thorium, often enriched along with the rare earths in many carbonatites, tends to concentrate in the same minerals and deposits as do the rare earths. Thorium is radioactive and has been used as a source of atomic energy. It has also been used for the manufacture of mantles for incandescent gas lights.

Geologists want to understand how carbonatites form partly because of their economic importance. Thus, they can design better strategies to find carbonatites or the associated silicate rocks that are as yet undiscovered. For example, carbonatites are very small targets to find on the surface of the earth; therefore, if geologists know that the silicate rocks associated with carbonatites contain abundant magnetic minerals, they can fly an airplane systematically across the surface of the area and detect high magnetic fields by using a device designed to detect the magnetism. Once geologists find areas with magnetic anomalies, they can collect soil or stream samples in the area to see if any unusual minerals associated with carbonatites or the associated silicate rocks are present. They could also drill the area to see if any carbonatites were below the surface.

Bibliography

Deer, W. A., R. A. Howie, and J. Zussman. *Rock-Forming Minerals.* 5 vols. New York: Longman, 1962, 1982, 1986. There is also a shortened one-volume condensation of this five-volume set. Using this source, the layperson can look up the composition of a mineral and how to identify it in a carbonatite. There are sections, however, that may be too technical for the layperson.

Heinrich, E. William. *The Geology of Carbonatites.* Skokie, Ill.: Rand McNally, 1966. A layperson can gain useful information from this volume designed for specialists. Of special interest are sections on the history of carbonatite studies (chapter 1), the economic aspects of carbonatites (chapter 9), and descriptions and locations of carbonatites of the world (chapters 11-16).

Kapustin, Yuri L. *Mineralogy of Carbonatites.* Washington, D.C.: Amerind, 1980. This book summarizes the vast variety of minerals that have been found in carbonatites. Much geologic jargon, but a reader with some geologic background or a mineral collector will find it useful.

Larsen, Esper Signius. *Alkalic Rocks of Iron Hill, Gunnison County, Colorado.* Geological Survey Professional Paper 197-A. Washington, D.C.: Government Printing Office, 1942. This publication describes the wide variety of minerals and rocks at this complex containing carbonatite. The rocks are located on a geologic map. The area is easy to visit to collect the minerals, so a mineral collector would find this publication useful.

Menzies, L. A. D., and J. M. Martins. "The Jacupiranga Mine, São Paulo, Brazil." *The Mineralogical Record* 15 (1984): 261-270. *The Mineralogical Record* is a journal for the lay reader or mineral collector that summarizes the geologic occurrence of minerals with a minimum of technical language. It often contains beautiful photographs of minerals. This article is an example of one on carbonatite minerals at a specific location.

Olsen, J. C., D. R. Shawe, L. C. Pray, and W. N. Sharp. *Rare Earth Mineral Deposits of the Mountain Pass District, San Bernardino County, California.* U.S. Geological Survey Professional Paper 261. Washington, D.C.: Government Printing Office, 1954. An excellent description of the rare earth carbonatite at Mountain Pass. Many detailed rock and mineral names, but a geologic map of the rock locations is included, so a mineral collector might find this source useful.

Parker, Raymond L., and William N. Sharp. *Mafic-Ultramafic Igneous Rocks and Associated Carbonatites of the Gem Park Complex, Custer and Fremont Counties, Colorado.* U.S. Geological Survey Professional Paper 649. Washington, D.C.: Government Printing Office, 1970. This publication gives a detailed description of the large number of minerals and the rocks found at Gem Park. Useful for a mineral collector. A layperson could read it with a dictionary of mineral and rock names. Photographs of some of the minerals are included.

Roberts, W. L., G. R. Rapp, and J. Weber. *Encyclopedia of Minerals.* New York: Van Nostrand Reinhold, 1974. One of a variety of mineral references available to the layperson that gives common properties, composition, and color photographs of many minerals, including some found in carbonatites. Also provided is a best reference for a mineral.

Tuttle, O. F., and J. Gittins. *Carbonatites.* New York: Wiley-Interscience, 1966.

Another fairly technical book, but it could be useful to a layperson who is not intimidated by mineral and rock names. One interesting section describes the only active volcano extruding carbonate lava by the person who first descended into the volcanic vent. A section on the location and description of carbonatites around the world is also included.

Robert L. Cullers

Cross-References

Carbonates, 190; Igneous and Contact Metamorphic Mineral Deposits, 1124; Igneous Rock Bodies, 1131; Igneous Rock Classification, 1138; Igneous Rocks: Ultramafic, 1207; Crystallization of Magmas, 1420; The Origin of Magmas, 1428; The Structure of Minerals, 1693.

IGNEOUS ROCKS: GRANITIC

Type of earth science: Geology
Field of study: Petrology, igneous

Granitic rocks are coarse-grained igneous rocks consisting mainly of quartz, sodic plagioclase, and alkali feldspar, with various accessory minerals. These rock types occur primarily as large intrusive bodies that have solidified from magma at great depths. Granitic rocks can also occur to a lesser degree as a result of metamorphism, a process referred to as granitization.

Principal terms

APHANITIC: a textural term that applies to an igneous rock composed of crystals that are microscopic in size

CRYSTAL: a solid made up of a regular periodic arrangement of atoms

CRYSTALLIZATION: the formation and growth of a crystalline solid from a liquid or gas

GRANITIZATION: the process of converting rock into granite; it is thought to occur when hot, ion-rich fluids migrate through a rock and chemically alter its composition

ISOTOPES: atoms of the same element with identical numbers of protons but different numbers of neutrons, thus giving them a different mass

MAGMA: a body of molten rock typically found at depth, including any dissolved gases and crystals

MIGMATITE: a rock exhibiting both igneous and metamorphic characteristics, which forms when light-colored silicate minerals melt and then crystallize, while the dark silicate minerals remain solid

PHANERITIC: a textural term that applies to an igneous rock composed of crystals that are macroscopic in size, ranging from about 1 millimeter to more than 5 millimeters in diameter

PLUTON: a structure that results from the emplacement and crystallization of magma beneath the surface of the earth

PORPHYRITIC: a texture characteristic of an igneous rock in which macroscopic crystals are embedded in a fine phaneritic or even aphanitic matrix

Summary of the Phenomenon

The term "granitic rocks" generally refers to the whole range of plutonic rocks that contain at least 10 percent quartz. They are the main component of continental shields and also occur as great compound batholiths in folded geosynclinal belts. Granitic rocks are so widespread, and their occurrence and relation to the tectonic environment are so varied, that generalizations often obscure their complexity. Basically, major granitic complexes are a continental phenomenon occurring in the form of batholiths and migmatite complexes.

When large masses of magma solidify deep below the ground surface, they form igneous rocks that exhibit a coarse-grained texture described as phaneritic. These rocks have the appearance of being composed of a mass of intergrown crystals large enough to be identified with the unaided eye. A large mass of magma situated at depth may require tens of thousands, or even millions, of years to solidify. Because phaneritic rocks form deep within the crust, their exposure at ground surface reflects regional uplift and erosion, which has removed the overlying rocks that once surrounded the now-solidified magma chamber.

As with other rock types, granitic rocks are classified on the basis of both mineral composition and fabric or texture. The mineral makeup of an igneous rock is ultimately determined by the chemical composition of the magma from which it crystallized. Feldspar-bearing phaneritic rocks containing conspicuous quartz (greater than 10 percent in total volume) in addition to large amounts of feldspar can be designated as granitic rocks. This nonspecific term is useful where the type of feldspar is not recognizable because of alteration or weathering, for purposes of quick reconnaissance field studies, or for general discussion.

Granitic rocks consist of two general groups of minerals: essential minerals and accessory minerals. Essential minerals are those required to be present for the rock to be assigned a specific name based on a classification scheme. Essential minerals in most granitic rocks are quartz, sodic plagioclase, and potassium-rich alkali plagioclase (either orthoclase or microcline). Accessory minerals include biotite, muscovite, hornblende, and pyroxene.

When an initial phase of slow cooling and crystallization at great depths is followed by more rapid cooling at shallower depths or at the surface, porphyritic texture develops, as is evident in the presence of large crystals enveloped in a finer-grained matrix or groundmass. The presence of porphyritic texture is evidence that crystallization occurs over a range of temperatures, and magmas are commonly emplaced or erupted as mixtures of liquid and early-formed crystals.

Classification of granitic rocks can be based either on the bulk chemical composition or on the mineral composition. Chemical analysis units are in the weight percent of oxides, whereas mineral composition units are in approximate percent in total volume. The mineral composition of granitic rocks, unlike that of volcanic rocks, provides a reliable basis for classification. Because the two primary feldspars may be difficult to distinguish as a result of extensive solid solution and unmixing, the chemical composition of the rock in terms of the normalized proportions of quartz, plagioclase, and alkali feldspar is recast. Thus, specific rock types are defined on the basis of their ratios. Accessory minerals may or may not be present in a rock of a given type, but the presence of certain accessory minerals may be indicated in the form of a modifier (such as biotite granite).

Granitic rocks include granodiorite, quartz monzonite granite, soda granite, and vein rocks of pegmatite and aplite. The mineralogy of these vary, and the distinction between different granitic rocks can be gradational. Granodiorite is composed predominantly of andesine-oligoclase feldspar, with subordinate potassium feldspar and biotite, hornblende, or both as accessory minerals. Quartz monzonite is composed of subequal amounts of potassium and oligoclase-andesine feldspars, with biotite, hornblende, or both as accessory minerals. Granite is composed predominantly of potassium feldspar with subordinate oligoclase feldspar and biotite alone or with hornblende or muscovite as accessory minerals. Soda granite is composed predominantly of albite or albite-oligoclase feldspar, with small amounts of algerine pyroxene or sodic amphibole.

Pegmatite is a very coarse-grained and mineralogically complex rock. Structurally, pegmatites occur as dikes associated with large plutonic rock masses. Dikes are tabular-shaped intrusive features that cut through the surrounding rock. The large crystals are inferred to reflect crystallization in a water-rich environment. Aplite is a very fine-grained, light-colored granitic rock that also occurs as a dike and consists of quartz, albite, potassium feldspar, and muscovite, with almandine garnet as an occasional accessory mineral. Most pegmatites can be mineralogically simple, consisting primarily of quartz and alkali feldspar, with lesser amounts of muscovite, tourmaline, and garnet; they are referred to as simple pegmatites. Other pegmatites can be very complex and contain other elements that slowly crystallize from residual, deeply seated magma bodies. High concentrations of these residual elements can result in the formation of minerals such as topaz, beryl, and rare earth elements, in addition to quartz and feldspar.

Other rocks that are occasionally grouped with granitic rocks are migmatites. Migmatites, meaning mixed rocks, are heterogeneous granitic rocks which, on a large scale, occur within regions of high-grade metamorphism or as broad migmatitic zones bordering major plutons. Migmatites appear as alternating light and dark bands. The light-colored bands are broadly granitic in mineralogy and chemistry, while the darker bands are clearly metamorphic.

Geochemically, granitic rocks vary in several ways, including isotopic composition; proportion of low-melting constituents, such as quartz and alkali feldspars, to high-melting constituents, such as biotite, hornblende, and calcic plagioclase; relative proportion of the low-melting constituents; alumina saturation; and accessory mineral content. Granitic rocks can further be divided into two groups, S-types, and I-types, according to whether they were derived from predominantly sedimentary or igneous sources, respectively. This distinction is based on strontium isotope ratios. For example, a sedimentary source is characterized by a high initial ratio, whereas an igneous source is characterized by a low initial ratio. Most isotope applications are conditional on the magma not having been subsequently contaminated by crystal material. Thus, isotopic composition in granitic rocks must be used with caution when attempting to identify source rocks or locate source regions at specific levels within the mantle or deep crust. S-type granites occur in some regionally metamorphic and migmatitic complexes. Enormous volumes of I-type granites, which constitute most plutons, occur along continental margins overriding subducting oceanic material.

A common feature of granitic rocks, notably in granodiorite to dioritic plutons, is the presence of inclusions or rock fragments that differ in fabric and/or composition from the main pluton itself. The term "inclusions" indicates that they originated in different ways. Foreign rock inclusions, called xenoliths, include blocks of wall rocks that have been mechanically incorporated into the magma body. This process is referred to as stopping. Some mafic inclusions are early-formed crystals precipitated from the magma itself after segregation along the margin of the pluton, which cools first. These inclusions are called antoliths. Other inclusions may reflect clots of solidified mantle-derived magma that ascended into the granitic source region or residual material that accompanied the magma during its ascent.

Along continental margins, belts of granitic rocks developed as batholiths composed of hundreds of individual plutons. Formation of batholithic volumes of granitic magmas generally appears to require continental settings. Some of the more prominent batholiths in North America are the Coast Range, Boulder-Idaho, Sierra Nevada, and Baja California. The largest are more than 1,500 kilometers long and 200 kilometers wide, and have a composite structure. The Sierra Nevada, for example, is composed of about 200 plutons separated by many smaller plutons, some only a few kilometers wide.

Methods of Study

Granitic rocks are widespread, but the greatest volume is in areas underlain by continental crust in orogenic regions (that is, where mountain building has occurred). Granitic magmas can be derived from a number of sources, notably the melting of continental crust, the melting of subducted oceanic crust or mantle, and differentiation. The problem facing the geologist is to decide on the importance of these sources in relation to their tectonic environment. To accomplish this objective, both petrographic and geochemical information is used.

The standard method of mineral identification and study of textural features and crystal relationships is by the use of rock thin-sections. A thin-section is an oriented wafer-thin portion of rock 0.03 millimeter in thickness that is mounted on a glass slide. The rock thin-section shows mineral content, abundance and association, grain size, structure, and texture. The thin-section also provides a permanent record of a given rock that may be filed for future reference.

Thin-sections are studied with the use of a petrographic microscope, which is a modification of the conventional compound microscope commonly used in laboratories. The modifications that render the petrographic microscope suitable to study the optical behavior of transparent crystalline substances are a rotating stage, an upper polarizer or lower polarizer, and a Bertrand lens, used to observe light patterns formed on the upper surface of the objective lens. With a magnification that ranges from about 30 to 500 times, the petrographic microscope allows one to examine the optical behavior of transparent crystalline substances or, in this case, crystals that make up granitic rocks.

The study of granitic rocks may be greatly facilitated by various staining techniques of both hand specimens and thin-sections. Staining is employed occasionally to distinguish potassium feldspar from plagioclase and quartz, the three main mineral constituents of granitic rocks. A flat surface on the rock is produced by sawing and then polishing. The rock surface is etched using hydrofluoric acid. This step is followed by a water rinse and immersion in a solution of sodium cobaltinitrate. The potassium feldspars will then turn bright yellow. After rinsing with water and covering the surface with rhodizonate reagent, the plagioclase becomes brick red in color. Staining techniques are available for other minerals, including certain accessory minerals such as cordierite, anorthoclase, and feldspathoids.

Measurement of the relative amounts of various mineral components of a rock is called modal analysis. The relative area occupied by the individual minerals is estimated or measured on a flat surface (on a flat-sawed surface, on a flat outcrop surface, or in thin-section) and then related to the relative volume. Caution must be used, because the relative area occupied by any mineral species on a particular planal surface is not always equal to the modal (volume) percentage of that mineral on the rock mass.

When a rock specimen is crushed to a homogeneous powder and chemically analyzed, the bulk chemical composition of the rock is derived. Chemical analyses are normally expressed as oxides of the respective elements, which reflects the overwhelming abundance of oxygen. Analysis of granitic rocks shows them to be typically rich in silica potassium and sodium, with lesser amounts of basic oxides such as magnesium, iron, and calcium oxides. Magnesium, iron, and calcium oxides are present in higher abundance in basalts, which contain plagioclase feldspar, pyroxene, and olivine.

Isotopes such as strontium, oxygen, and lead can also be used as tools in evaluating granitic magma sources such as a mantle origin and crustal melting of certain rock types. Some accessory minerals reflect the trace element content of the magma and thus the possible nature of their source. Some, such as garnet or topaz, are products of contamination, while others, such as andalusite, magnetite, or limenite, are products of late hydrothermal alteration. Much research is focused on chemical tracers. Tracers help distinguish the source region of a granitic magma, such as lower-crustal igneous or sedimentary rock or mantle material.

Context

Granitic rocks have been used as dimension stones for many years. Dimension stones are blocks of rock with roughly even surfaces of specified shape and size used for the foundation and facing of expensive buildings. When crushed, granitic rocks can be used as aggregate in the cement and lime industry. In addition to these uses, granitic rocks are valued because of their geographic association with gold. Gold ores are found in close proximity to the contacts of the granitic bodies within both the granitic rocks and surrounding rocks.

Pegmatites can also be very valuable. Simple pegmatites are exploited for large volumes of quartz and feldspar, used in the glass and ceramic industries. Complex pegmatites can also be a source of gem minerals, including tourmaline, beryl, topaz, and chrysoberyl. In spite of varied mineral composition, relatively small size, and unpredictable occurrence, pegmatites constitute the world's main source of high-grade feldspar, electrical-grade mica, certain metals (including beryllium, lithium, niobium, and tantalum), and some piezoelectric quartz.

Bibliography

Carmichael, Ian S., Francis J. Turner, and John Verhoogen. *Igneous Petrology*. New York: McGraw-Hill, 1974. A well-known reference presenting both the mineralogical and geochemical diversity of granitic rocks and their respective geologic settings. Chapter 2, "Classification and Variety of Igneous Rocks," and chapter 12, "Rocks of Continental Plutonic Provinces," are particularly recommended.

Hutchison, Charles S. *Laboratory Handbook of Petrographic Techniques*. New York: John Wiley & Sons, 1974. Stresses the practical aspects of laboratory and petrographic methods and techniques.

Phillips, William Revell. *Mineral Optics: Principles and Techniques*. San Francisco: W. H. Freeman, 1971. A standard textbook discussing mineral optic theory and the petrographic microscope and its use in the study of minerals and rocks.

Smith, David G., ed. *The Cambridge Encyclopedia of Earth Sciences*. New York: Crown, 1981. Chapter 5, "Earth Materials: Minerals and Rocks," gives a good discussion of the processes involved in the formation of granitic rocks and description of the mineral and chemical composition of granitic rocks. A well-illustrated and carefully indexed reference volume.

Stephen M. Testa

Cross-References

Building Stone, 178; Continental Crust, 261; Feldspars, 698; Fold Belts, 734; Igneous and Contact Metamorphic Mineral Deposits, 1124; Igneous Rock Bodies, 1131; Igneous Rock Classification, 1138; Crystallization of Magmas, 1420; The Origin of Magmas, 1428; Physical Properties of Minerals, 1681; Mountain Belts, 1725; Pegmatites, 2025; Petrographic Microscopes, 2034.

IGNEOUS ROCKS: KIMBERLITES

Type of earth science: Geology
Field of study: Petrology, igneous

Kimberlite is a variety of ultramafic rock that is fine- to medium-grained, with a dull gray-green to bluish color. Often referred to as a mica peridotite, kimberlite originates in the upper mantle under high temperature and pressure conditions. It often occurs at the earth's surface as old volcanic diatremes and dikes. Kimberlite can be the source rock for diamonds.

Principal terms

BLUE GROUND: the slaty blue or blue-green kimberlite breccia of the South African diamond pipes

DIAMOND: a high-pressure, high-temperature mineral consisting of the element carbon; it is the hardest naturally occurring substance and is valued for its brilliant luster

DIATREME: a volcanic vent or pipe formed as the explosive energy of gas-charged magmas break through crustal rocks

DIKE: a tabular body of igneous rock that intrudes vertically through the structure of the existing rock layers above

MAGMA: a semiliquid, semisolid rock material that exists at high temperatures and pressures and that is mobile and capable of intrusion and extrusion; igneous rocks are formed from magma as it cools

MANTLE: the layer of the earth's interior that lies between the crust and the core; it is believed to consist of ultramafic material and is the source of magma

PERIDOTITE: any of a group of plutonic rocks that essentially consist of olivine and other mafic minerals, such as pyroxenes and amphiboles

ULTRAMAFIC: a term used to describe certain igneous rocks and most meteorites that contain less than 45 percent silica; they contain virtually no quartz or feldspar and are mainly of ferromagnesian silicates, metallic oxides and sulfides, and native metals

XENOCRYSTS: minerals found as either crystals or fragments in some volcanic rocks; they are foreign to the body of the rock in which they occur

XENOLITHS: various rock fragments that are foreign to the igneous body in which they are present

Summary of the Phenomenon

The rock known as kimberlite is a variety of mica-bearing peridotite and is characterized by the minerals olivine, phlogopite (mica), and the accessory minerals pyroxene, apatite, perovskite, and various opaque oxides such as chromite and ilmenite. Chemically, kimberlite is recognized by its extraordinarily low silicon dioxide content (25-30 percent), high magnesia content (30-35 percent), high titanium dioxide content (3-4 percent), and the presence of up to 10 percent carbon dioxide. It is a dark, heavy rock that often exhibits numerous crystals of olivine within a serpentinized groundmass. Upon weathering, kimberlite is commonly altered to a mixture of chlorite, talc, and various carbonates and is known as blue ground by diamond miners. Occasionally, kimberlites contain large quantities of diamonds, which makes them important economically.

"Kimberlite" was first used in 1887 by Carvill Lewis to describe the diamond-bearing rock found at Kimberly, South Africa. There, it primarily occurs as a breccia found in several deeply eroded volcanic pipes and also in an occasional dike. Unfortunately, the kimberlite is so thoroughly brecciated and chemically altered that it does not lend itself to detailed petrographic study. Instead, the kimberlite of Kimberly, like kimberlite elsewhere, is more often noted for the varied assortment of exotic xenoliths and megacrysts it contains. The explosive nature of a kimberlite pipe leads to the removal of country rock (rock surrounding an igneous intrusion) as the magma passes thorough the crust and thus can provide scientists with samples of material that originated at great depths. Among the many xenoliths found in the kimberlite breccia pipes are ultramafic rocks such as garnet-peridotites and eclogites, along with a variety of high-grade metamorphic rocks. These specimens provide scientists with an excellent vertical profile of the rock strata at various locations, serve to construct a model of the earth's crust at various depths, and provide information on the chemical variations in magma.

The geological occurrence of kimberlite, clearly volcanic in origin, takes the form of diatremes, dikes, and sills of relatively small size. In shape, kimberlite diatremes usually have a rounded or oval appearance but can occur in a variety of forms. Quite often, diatremes occur in clusters or as individuals scattered along an elongated zone. They rarely attain a surface area greater than a kilometer but in profile will resemble an inverted cone that descends to a great depth. When it occurs as a dike, kimberlite is quite small—often not more than a few meters wide. It may occur as a simple ring dike or in swarms of parallel dikes. Kimberlite's occurrence as a sill is quite rare and will have a wide variability in thickness.

The emplacement of kimberlite—seen as a calcite-rich kimberlite magma that has intruded rapidly up through a network of deep-seated fractures—clearly attests its volcanic nature. The magma's rate of upward mobility must have been rapid, as evidenced by the positioning of high-density xenoliths such as eclogite and peridotite within the kimberlite pipes. The final breakthrough of the kimberlite magma may have taken place from a depth of 2-3 kilometers, where contact with groundwater contributed to its propulsion and explosive nature. Brecciation rapidly followed, along with vent enlargement by hydrologic fracturing of the country rock. Fragments of deep-seated rock, along with other country rocks, were then incorporated within the kimberlite magma.

As a rock, kimberlite is very complex. Not only does it contain its own principal mineral phases, but also it has multicrystalline fragments or single crystals derived from the various fragmented xenoliths that it collected along the way. These fragments represent upper mantle and deep crustal origins and are further complicated by the intermixing with the mineralogy of a highly volatile fluid. As a result, no two kimberlite pipes have the same mineralogy. The continued alteration of the high-temperature phases after crystallization can produce a third mineralogy that can affect the interpretation of a particular kimberlite's occurrence.

The characteristic texture of kimberlite is inequigranular because of the presence of xenoliths and megacrysts within an otherwise fine-grained matrix. In relation to kimberlite, the term "megacryst" refers to both large xenocrysts and phenocrysts, with no genetic distinctions. Among the more common megacrysts present are olivine (often altered to serpentine), picro-ilmenite, mica (commonly phlogopite), pyroxene, and garnet. These megacrysts are usually contained in a finer-grained matrix of carbonate and serpentine-group minerals that crystallized at considerably lower temperatures. Among the more common matrix minerals are phlogopite, perovskite, apatite, calcite, and a very characteristic spinel. Found within the textures of these matrix minerals are examples of both rapid and protracted cooling, with the latter evidenced by zoning. Zoning indicates that the matrix liquid cooled after emplacement and that there was sufficient time for crystals present to react with the remaining liquid, which is common to the megacrysts as well. In addition, the megacrysts exhibit an unusual, generally rounded shape that is believed to be a result of their rapid transport to the surface during the eruptive phase.

As compared to other types of igneous rocks, the occurrence of kimberlite is considered to be quite rare. Based on factors such as specific matrix color, density, mineral content, and xenolith size, shape, and number, distinction between a certain kimberlite and a specific occurrence can be made. Aside from their scientific value, most kimberlites are economically worthless, except when they contain diamonds.

Of the many minerals that constitute kimberlite, diamond is the most noteworthy because of its great economic value. Not all kimberlite contains diamonds, and when diamonds are present, they are not always of gem quality. Even in the most diamondiferous kimberlites, the crystals and cleavage fragments are rare and highly dispersed. Diamond mining from kimberlite requires the removal and processing of enormous amounts of rock to produce relatively few diamonds. This method is expensive and can be dangerous. A much better rate of return can be gained from the placer mining of riverbeds and shorelines where nature has weathered out the diamonds and concentrated them in more readily accessible areas. The discovery of a large diamond in a riverbed in 1866 led to the eventual search for the source rock that produced diamonds. Up to that time, diamonds were recovered only from alluvial deposits and not from the host rock. In 1872, as miners were removing a diamond-bearing gravel, they uncovered a hard bluish-green rock that also contained diamonds. Further mining revealed the now familiar circular structure of the diatreme that continued downward to an undetermined depth. In 1887, the first petrographic description was made of the rock now known as kimberlite, and it was then recognized to be similar to other volcanic breccias from around the world.

Diamond-bearing kimberlite locations can be found around the world, the most famous being in South Africa. The diamond pipes of South Africa have been the leading producer of diamonds for well over a hundred years and are still unrivaled in terms of world production. Other locations of kimberlites that produce diamonds include the pipes of Siberia, western Australia, and Arkansas. Alluvial deposits rich in diamonds are known to exist in Zaire, West Africa, Venezuela, Brazil, Borneo, and the Soviet Union (in the Urals); their kimberlite source locations, however, are unknown at present.

The chemistry and mineralogy characteristic of kimberlite indicate a very complex set of conditions that existed during their emplacement and subsequent crystallization. This fact, combined with kimberlite's limited occurrence and the altered nature of its matrix, makes kimberlite a puzzle to scientists. Three hypotheses have been proposed to explain its origin. A zone-refining hypothesis describes a liquid generated at great depth (600 kilometers) that is dynamically unstable and, as a result, rises toward the surface. As it reaches specific lower pressures, its composition is altered through partial crystallization and fractionation. A second hypothesis envisions a residual process: Partial melting of a garnet-peridotite parent, at depths of 80-100 kilometers, produces fractional crystallization of a picritic basalt (olivine-rich, or more than 50 percent olivine) at high pressure, which could lead to the formation of ecologite cumulates and a residual liquid of kimberlite composition. The third hypothesis describes kimberlite as either the residual end product of a long fractionation process or the product of a limited amount of partial melting. Each of the three hypotheses has merit but falls short of providing a definitive answer, partly because the near-surface environment where kimberlites are found is one of complex chemical reactions, which makes interpretation difficult.

Although kimberlites tantalize scientists with their complexity, the xenoliths and megacrysts that arise with the kimberlites provide substantial data on the relationship between the lower crust and the upper mantle. Kimberlites show the earth's upper mantle to be petrographically very complex and define both large- and small-scale areas of chemical and textural heterogeneities. Pressure and temperature conditions have been accurately established for depths down to 200 kilometers through studies based on the specimens brought up during kimberlite eruptions.

Methods of Study

To make a definitive evaluation of a rock specimen, the scientist must employ the tools of the geologist, chemist, and physicist. Analysis of a rock such as kimberlite begins with the collection of a fresh specimen (as unaltered by weathering as possible) and continues with the preparation of a series of thin sections and microprobe sections. In this process, a slice of rock is cut with a diamond saw and glued to a glass plate. A second cut is then made to reduce the specimen's thickness to nearly 0.03 millimeter. A final polishing will achieve this thickness, which will permit light to pass through the specimen and provide the opportunity for microscopic examination. A similar procedure will produce a microprobe-thin section, but it requires extra polishing to assure a uniform surface.

Once the thin sections have been prepared, a geologist uses a petrographic microscope, which employs polarized light, to make proper identification of the mineral phases present, along with their specific optical parameters. Opaque minerals require reflective light study. Microscopic examination is usually the first step in classifying a rock, and it may include an actual point count of the minerals present to determine their individual ratios. Afterward, an electron microprobe or electron microscope is used to give specific chemical compositions for individual mineral phases. With this device, the scientist can analyze mineral grains as small as a few microns with a high degree of accuracy. Mineral grains or crystals that are smaller require an analyzing electron microscope to reveal their composition and fine detail. If the individual minerals are large enough and can be extracted, then X-ray diffraction can be used for a definitive identification of a particular mineral phase.

It is also important to understand the bulk chemistry of a rock specimen. Here, the scientist can select several different methods, including neutron activation analysis (NAA) and atomic absorption spectrometry (AAS). Both techniques provide excellent sensitivity and precision for a wide range of elements. A third method, X-ray fluorescence (XRF), is also commonly used and provides an accurate and quick means for analysis.

In NAA, a specimen is activated by thermal neutrons generated in a nuclear reactor. In this process, radioisotopes formed by neutron bombardment decay with characteristic half-lives and are measured by gamma-ray spectrometry. In AAS, a specimen is first dissolved in solution and then identified element by element. XRF, which provides sensitivity and precision for quantitative determination of a wide range of elements (best for those above atomic number 12), is the principal method used by most geologists to gather element amounts in both rocks and minerals.

After all the bulk chemical analyses have been gathered and run through various computer programs to determine mineral compositions, the data are compared to the microscopy results for evaluation and classification of the rock. This evaluation is compared to similar data from other locations. A final check and comparison to other rock types and strata in the field collection area complete the analysis. The analysis of a single rock specimen represents the marriage between chemical and geological laboratory studies with actual fieldwork. As a result, it provides a detailed evaluation of the specimen and its relationship to the larger geological picture of the area.

Context

Although some kimberlites have economic value in their diamond content, most do not. No dramatic breakthroughs from the study of kimberlites will make diamonds more abundant or cheaper in price. The result of these studies is a better understanding of the processes and conditions under which diamonds and semiprecious minerals such as garnet are formed. This knowledge has led to the development of synthetic gems that can be used for industrial applications.

The study of kimberlites also has a direct bearing on scientists' understanding of volcanic activity. The prediction of eruptions is an aim of geology, as it affects the hundreds of thousands of people who live near potentially dangerous volcanoes. Kimberlite magma, by the nature of its chemical composition, is a very explosive material and can produce violent eruptions. Even so, it is true that most kimberlite magmas do not reach the surface, and when they do, they affect only a small area. Kimberlite magmas are more effective at depth, where rock is being fractured by the rising magma and by the hydraulic pressures exerted by the various gases moving through the magma. By examining the results of the movement of a kimberlite magma, scientists can gain a better understanding of volcanic behavior.

As is the case in many specialized areas of science, as more questions are answered, new questions arise. To help answer some of these new questions, technology must continue to provide advanced methods of obtaining physical and chemical data from the earth materials being studied. The study of kimberlites has revealed that a complex set of conditions is responsible for its formation. Studies have also shown what happens to kimberlite as it rises through the crust, interacting with country rock and groundwater. Scientists are learning much from the trace elements and various isotopes present in the kimberlite minerals and matrix, although they occur in only minor amounts. To obtain these data, sophisticated instrumentation is required in both analytical and computer technologies. These developments can then be used for other industrial applications. By studying kimberlites, scientists have been able to examine the conditions that exist deep in the earth's interior. Scientists have also learned how and where diamonds form as well as how phenomena once thought unrelated in fact interact significantly. The basic geological and chemical principles behind volcanism are understood, and reasonably accurate predictions can be made.

Bibliography

Basaltic Volcanism Study Project. *Basaltic Volcanism on the Terrestrial Planets*. Elmsford, N.Y.: Pergamon Press, 1981. This work represents the efforts of a team of scientists to provide the most up-to-date review of the subject of basalt and its relationship to planetary structure. Included are good references to kimberlites. Best suited for undergraduate and graduate students.

Blackburn, William H., and William H. Dennen. *Principles of Mineralogy*. Dubuque, Iowa: Wm. C. Brown, 1988. A basic textbook on the subject of mineralogy. Provides an excellent review of the principles of mineralogy and crystallography, along with the various techniques used in their study. Offers the reader both a broad overview and specific references to mineral families and their relationship to rock groups. Suitable for undergraduate and graduate students.

Boyd, F. R., and H. O. A. Meyer, eds. *Kimberlites, Diatremes, and Diamonds: Their*

Geology, Petrology, and Geochemistry. Washington, D.C.: American Geophysical Union, 1979.

_____. *The Mantle Sample: Inclusions in Kimberlites and Other Volcanics.* Washington, D.C.: American Geophysical Union, 1979. Each is part of a two-volume set that examines the many aspects of kimberlites and their formation conditions. Specialized articles cover a wide range of related geochemical, petrological, and mineralogical topics. Volume 2 also provides an in-depth study of the minerals and foreign rocks brought up by the kimberlite pipes. An excellent reference set suitable for undergraduate and graduate students.

Dawson, J. Barry. *Kimberlites and Their Xenoliths.* New York: Springer-Verlag, 1980. A very technical work that examines the geochemistry and mineralogy of kimberlites, along with their relationship to the other rock types. Complete and detailed in its approach. Bibliography provides a wealth of journal article references. An excellent review source on kimberlites for the undergraduate and graduate student.

Nixon, Peter H., ed. *Mantle Xenoliths.* New York: John Wiley & Sons, 1987. This collection of highly technical articles covers a wide range of topics that are related to kimberlites. Considerable attention is paid to regional kimberlite occurrences and to the foreign rocks that are brought up by the kimberlite diatremes. Several of the articles are general enough to suit a beginning reader, but the work is best suited for the undergraduate and graduate student.

Wyllie, P. J., ed. *Ultramafic and Related Rocks.* New York: John Wiley & Sons, 1967. A collection of specialized articles that deal with the various types of rock that are derived from mantle material. Several of the articles focus specifically on kimberlites, especially as an overall review of the subject. Best suited as a reference work for undergraduate and graduate students.

Paul P. Sipiera

Cross-References

Diamonds, 362; Gem Minerals, 802; Igneous Rock Bodies, 1131; Igneous Rock Classification, 1138; Igneous Rocks: Carbonatites, 1173; Igneous Rocks: Ultramafic, 1207; Crystallization of Magmas, 1420; The Origin of Magmas, 1428; Pyroclastic Rocks, 2131; Volcanoes: Types of Eruption, 2695.

IGNEOUS ROCKS: KOMATIITES

Type of earth science: Geology
Field of study: Petrology, igneous

Komatiites are volcanic rocks with abundant olivine and pyroxene and little or no feldspar. They also contain large magnesium-oxide concentrations (greater than 18 percent). They are most abundant in the lower portion of exceedingly old piles of volcanic rocks. Economic deposits of nickel, copper, platinum group minerals, antimony, and gold have been found in some komatiites.

Principal terms

BASALT: a dark rock containing olivine, pyroxene, and feldspar, in which the minerals often are very small

CRUST: the veneer of rocks on the surface of the earth above the Moho; it is about 12 kilometers thick in the oceans and 30-50 kilometers thick on the continents

FELDSPAR: calcium, potassium, and sodium aluminum silicate minerals

IGNEOUS ROCK: a rock solidified from molten rock material

METAMORPHISM: the process in which a rock is buried in high temperature and pressure so that the original minerals are transformed into new minerals in the solid state

MOHOROVIČIĆ DISCONTINUITY (MOHO): the region in which seismic waves given off by earthquakes sharply increase, marking the boundary between the earth's mantle and crust

OLIVINE: a magnesium and iron silicate mineral

PYROXENE: a calcium, magnesium, and iron silicate mineral

SILICATE MINERAL: a naturally occurring element or compound composed of silicon and oxygen with other positive ions to maintain charge balance

SKELETAL CRYSTALS: elongate mineral grains that may resemble chains, plates, or feathers

UPPER MANTLE: the region of earth immediately below the Moho, believed to be composed largely of periodotite (olivine and pyroxene rock), which is thought to melt to form basaltic liquids

Summary of the Phenomenon

Komatiites are unusual volcanic rocks. They contain mostly large grains of olivine (magnesium and iron silicate mineral) and pyroxene (calcium, iron, and magnesium silicate mineral) scattered among fine mineral grains that at one time were mostly glass. The glass was unstable and in time slowly converted into individual minerals. The larger minerals often form elongate grains composed of olivine, pyroxene, or chromite (a magnesium, chromium oxide mineral) called skeletal grains at the top of some lava flows. No other rocks form these skeletal grains. The skeletal grains are believed to have formed by quick cooling at the top of the lava flow. The glass must have also formed by quick cooling of the lava, often in contact with water. Because most igneous rocks contain feldspar (calcium, sodium, and potassium aluminum silicate minerals), the lack of feldspar in komatiites also makes them unusual. They also contain magnesium concentrations (magnesium-oxide greater than 18 percent) larger than most other igneous rocks. Komatiites have been studied in detail only since 1969. They were discovered in the late 1960's in exceedingly old Archean rocks (more than 2.5 billion years old) in Zimbabwe and South Africa. Other occurrences of komatiites have been found in Western Australia, Canada, India, Finland, and Russia.

Most occurrences of komatiites are in Archean rocks. Only a few komatiites occur in younger rocks. One unusual occurrence of a young komatiite is located on Gorgona Island off the coast of Colombia. Komatiites typically occur in the lower or older portions of vast piles of volcanic rocks containing many layers of different lava flows. Komatiites gradually become less abundant further up the volcanic pile and in younger volcanic rocks. Other dark, feldspar-rich, volcanic rocks called basalt (calcium-rich feldspar and pyroxene rock) are interlayered with komatiites. Basalts gradually become more abundant in the younger volcanic flows, along with more light-colored and more silica-rich rocks such as andesite. Small amounts of sedimentary rocks may be interlayered with the volcanic rocks. Sedimentary rocks are derived by water reworking the volcanic rocks. Komatiites eventually disappear in the upper portions of these volcanic piles.

Each individual lava flow of a komatiite may be a meter to tens of meters thick. A given lava flow can often be traced for a long distance without much variation in thickness. Some of the lava flows contain rounded or bulbous portions called pillows. Pillows can be formed only by extrusion of the lava into water. As lava breaks out of the solid front of a flow, it is quickly cooled into a rounded pillow. Since this process continually takes place, numerous pillows form as the lava advances. The more magnesium-rich komatiites occur as lava flows in the lower portions of these volcanic piles. They gradually become less magnesium-rich in the younger or upper portions of these volcanic piles.

The mineralogy and observed mineral shapes can vary vertically through a given lava flow. The most spectacular and beautiful komatiite lava flows are the ones in which the upper portions contain the skeletal olivine and pyroxene grains. Skeletal grains may resemble chains, plates, or feathers. Some grains grow as large as 3 centimeters. The thickness of these lava flows varies from about 1 meter to 20 meters. In one type of vertical variation, there are abundant fine minerals formed from the original glass at the top of these flows, along with irregular fractures caused by quick cooling at the top of the lava. Underlying this quickly cooled zone is a layer of the larger skeletal grains of olivine and pyroxene that increase in grain size downward. These skeletal crystals probably form very rapidly in the lava by growth from the top downward.

The lower portion of these komatiite flows often contains abundant olivine grains that are much more rounded and less elongated than those of the upper zone. The more rounded grains are believed to have formed by slow crystallization of the olivine from the liquid lava. As the olivine formed from the liquid, the grains slowly sank and piled up on the bottom of the flow until the lava solidified. The base of the lava also may contain very fine-grained, skeletal grains of olivine with irregular cracks, much like the top of the flow. Presumably, the base of the flow formed by quick cooling, as did the top portion.

Observing several cross sections shows how komatiite flows can vary. There is, for example, a considerable difference in the amount of the flow that contains the skeletal minerals from that containing the more rounded minerals. Most komatiite flows do not contain any skeletal minerals. Instead, they consist mostly of the more rounded mineral grains and have irregular fractures extending throughout the lava flow. These differences could be caused by different cooling rates or by the lava's viscosity (how easily it flows). Other flows are composed mostly of rounded pillows.

Komatiite lava flows are often interbedded with rocks composed of angular fragments that came from all parts of the lavas. Some of these rocks show features that might be found along the edge of a body of water, such as ripples formed by wave action. These rocks have formed by the action of waves breaking up some of the solidified lavas and reworking them after they were deposited. (Rocks that have been reworked by water are sedimentary rocks.)

Many komatiites are located in rather inaccessible regions. One area that is accessible is the Vermilion district of northeastern Minnesota in the vicinity of Little Long, Bass, Low, Cedar, Shajawa, and Fall lakes. The age of the district is 2.7 billion years old. Here, there are no true komatiites with magnesium-oxide concentrations greater than 18 percent. There are, however, very magnesium-rich basalts that contain the skeletal crystals found in true komatiites. All the rocks have been buried deep enough that the original minerals were changed or metamorphosed to new minerals in response to the high temperature and pressure. The temperature of metamorphism was still low enough that the original igneous relations may still be observed.

The lower or oldest portions of these old rocks are mostly basaltic lavas with pillows or tabular basaltic bodies called sills that intruded horizontally within the lava flows after they solidified. The lava flows are only 2-4 meters thick, but the sills are 100-400 meters thick and up to 6 kilometers long. The sills are among the zoned rock types that vary considerably in mineralogy vertically through the sill. The top and bottom of the sills consist of abundant skeletal crystals embedded in altered glass. This material represents the portions of the sill that were quickly chilled when first intruded. As the magma slowly cooled, the minerals of olivine and clinopyroxene slowly cooled as well and settled to the bottom, forming both the olivine-clinopyroxene and pyroxene-rich layers. The last magma to crystallize formed a feldspar-olivine-clinopyroxene rock. The lower basaltic lavas and sills gradually grade upward into lighter-colored and more silica-rich lavas and pyroclastic rocks that exploded out of volcanoes. Some of these lavas and pyroclastic rocks were reworked by moving water and formed sedimentary layers.

A second example of a komatiite sequence is located at Brett's Cove in Newfoundland. The komatiites here are much younger than most komatiites (formed during the Ordovician, about 450 million years ago). These komatiites formed within layers of rocks called ophiolites, which are believed to be sections of ruptured and tilted oceanic crust and part of the upper mantle. The lower part of the ophiolites contains an olivine and/or pyroxene mineralogy thought to compose much of the upper mantle of the earth. Overlying the upper-mantle rocks are rocks of basaltic composition containing coarse crystals of olivine, pyroxene, and feldspar. These rocks probably formed by slow cooling of basaltic magma below the land surface. Above these rocks are numerous basaltic lavas that were extruded at the surface and that built up large piles of lavas on the ocean floor. Some komatiite lavas are interbedded in the lower portion of these mainly basaltic lavas. These komatiite flows have a lower zone rich in pyroxene and an upper pillow lava that contains skeletal crystals of pyroxene.

Methods of Study

Komatiites were only clearly defined in 1969, although various observations alluded to their possible occurrence as early as 1913. In that year, one observer actually described a komatiite with skeletal crystals of pyroxene. Several prominent geologists recognized then that the upper-mantle rocks that were needed to produce komatiite magma would have to be raised to very high temperatures. For years, this recognition prevented acceptance of the idea that komatiites could form by the melting of upper mantle rocks. In the late 1920's, several geologists in South Africa and Canada independently described and analyzed volcanic rocks with skeletal olivine and pyroxene embedded in altered glass. These rocks were classified in a group of rocks where they did not really belong; thus, their significance was obscured. In the 1930's, several geologists suggested that high water vapor or iron in rocks of the upper mantle might lower their melting point. If that were true, then upper mantle rocks could melt and form komatiite magmas. Again, several prominent geologists rejected this concept. Nothing more was said about these rocks until the late 1960's, when komatiites were "rediscovered." As often happens in geology, once a new rock type is discovered, it begins to be found in many places. Subsequent to the "rediscovery" of komatiites, there has been much study and discussion about them.

The characteristics of komatiites that are exposed at the surface are described carefully during a field study. These characteristics can suggest how komatiites form at the surface. For example, features such as abundant pillows indicate that the komatiite lava was extruded into water. A small amount of reworking of the lavas by moving water suggests that there was little time between eruptions. A sign of a rapid eruption is the spread of lava over a great distance and at a gentle flow rate.

In addition to the field characteristics of komatiites, geologists study their chemical characteristics in order to understand how they form and evolve. Komatiites are igneous rocks, so they form by the melting of another rock. Experiments using furnaces suggest that much of the rock called peridotite (olivine-pyroxene rock) must melt to form high-magnesium magmas. The magma then may evolve or change in composition by processes such as the crystallization of minerals from the magma, by dissolving some of the solid rock through which it moves, or by mixing with magma of a different composition. The komatiite may even change composition after the magma solidifies because of water vapor or carbon dioxide-rich solutions moving through the solid. It is difficult to assess the relative importance of these processes to modify the composition of a given komatiite.

One way to test for mineral crystallization of the magma is to plot the elemental concentrations of several analyzed rocks from the same general area against another element, such as magnesium. If the concentration of all elements systematically increases or decreases with increasing magnesium concentrations, then the lavas were probably related by fractional crystallization. The formation and settling of olivine from lava appear to control the concentration of most elements. For example, magnesium, chromium, nickel, and cobalt all concentrate in lava-related olivine; thus, a plot of chromium, nickel, and cobalt shows smooth and systematic decreases when compared to magnesium. Elements such as calcium, titanium, aluminum, silicon, iron, and scandium are rejected from lava-related olivine; they gradually increase with decreasing magnesium. Some elements, such as sodium, potassium, barium, rubidium, and strontium, should also systematically increase with decreasing magnesium, as they are also rejected from lava-related olivine. Instead, these elements are greatly scattered when they are plotted relative to magnesium. These elements are notorious for being moved by carbon dioxide or by water-vapor-rich fluids. Thus, it is assumed that the scatter of these elements is a result of movement by these fluids. The fractionation of these elements because of olivine crystallization, therefore, is obscured.

A few changes in elemental concentrations in komatiite lavas cannot be explained by crystallization or alteration processes. For example, a rare earth element with a lower atomic number, such as lanthanum, should not systematically increase more than a rare earth element with a higher atomic number, such as lutetium, with olivine crystallization, as olivine should not fractionate these elements. (The atomic number of an element is the number of protons in its nucleus.) Either the theory is incorrect or some other process produces this variation. Some geologists believe that melting processes control the lanthanum concentration relative to that of lutetium. This melting control may be attributable to a combination of differences in composition of the rock that melts to form komatiites and by the degree and nature of the rock's melting process.

Context

Komatiites contain several types of economic deposits. They may contain important deposits of nickel sulfides, along with large concentrations of platinum group elements (such as platinum and palladium) and copper. The nickel sulfide was probably formed from a sulfide liquid that separated as an immiscible liquid from the komatiite liquid. This is similar to the way oil and water separate when they are mixed together. Nickel sulfide ores have been found in Western Australia, Canada, and Zimbabwe. The most important deposits are found in the komatiite lava flows in the lower portion of a lava pile. The nickel sulfide ore is concentrated in a portion of the base of a lava flow where it is thicker than other portions of the flow. The immiscible and dense nickel-sulfide liquid may have settled in a thick portion of the flow that was not stirred as much as other portions of the flow. The platinum group metals have a stronger affinity for the sulfide liquid than for the komatiite liquid; consequently, they concentrate in the sulfide liquid.

Gold, antimony, and a few other elements are concentrated in some komatiite flows. Running water may alter and rework some komatiite lavas and form sedimentary rocks. Examples of these deposits occur northeast of Johannesburg in South Africa. There, the lower portion of the rock pile is mostly layers of successive komatiite or basaltic lava flows. This portion is overlain by sedimentary rocks composed of mudrocks changed, at high temperature and pressure, into metamorphic rocks. Some quartz-carbonate rocks within the sedimentary rocks probably formed by the alteration of komatiites. The quartz-carbonate rocks contain high concentrations of antimony in the mineral stibnite and small particles of gold. Solutions moving through the komatiites probably altered the komatiites, leaving the high concentrations of these elements.

Komatiite liquids are of interest because they depict the nature of the earth during the Archean eon, about 2.5-3.8 billion years ago. Most komatiites are found only in rocks from this period. Exceedingly high temperatures must be reached before enough peridotite melts to form these komatiite liquids. It may be that the temperature within the earth was higher during the Archean than it is now, making it possible to reach the exceedingly high temperature necessary to form komatiite magma.

Bibliography

Arndt, N. T., D. Frances, and A. J. Hynes. "The Field Characteristics and Petrology of Archean and Proterozoic Komatiites." *Canadian Mineralogist* 17 (1985): 147-163. An advanced article summarizing the way komatiite lavas occur. A number of diagrammatic representations of these lavas make it easier to visualize what they look like. A college student with a petrology course could read the discussion; someone with a course in introductory geology could read it if he or she were willing to look up terminology in a geologic dictionary.

Arndt, N. T., and E. G. Nisbet. *Komatiites*. Winchester, Mass.: Allen & Unwin, 1982. An advanced book reviewing many aspects of komatiites. Much of the book could be read by someone who has had a petrology course. Someone taking an introductory geology course could read chapters 1 and 2 on the history and definition of komatiites. A mineral collector can find references to the location of komatiites. The skeletal crystals developed by some komatiites may be especially beautiful; there are black-and-white photographs of some of the skeletal crystals in the book.

Best, M. G. *Igneous and Metamorphic Petrology*. San Francisco: W. H. Freeman, 1982. This petrology book has a short section on komatiites. Several photographs of the skeletal olivine and pyroxene crystals and a diagrammatic cross section of a komatiite lava flow are included. A person taking an introductory geology course could read the text with the help of a geologic dictionary.

Hyndman, D. W. *Petrology of Igneous and Metamorphic Rocks*. New York: McGraw-Hill, 1985. This petrology book contains a short section on komatiites, including a section on the economic importance of komatiites. A black-and-white photo of the skeletal crystals is provided. A person taking an introductory geology course could read this section with the help of a geologic dictionary.

Robert L. Cullers

Cross-References

Gold and Silver, 975; Igneous Rock Bodies, 1131; Igneous Rock Classification, 1138; Igneous Rocks: Basaltic, 1158; Crystallization of Magmas, 1420; The Origin of Magmas, 1428; Water in Magmas, 1433; Regional Metamorphism, 1606; Phase Changes, 2042; Platinum Group Metals, 2086.

IGNEOUS ROCKS: LAMPROITES

Type of earth science: Geology
Field of study: Petrology, igneous

Lamproites are potassium-rich and magnesium-rich rocks. They contain the highest ratios of potassium to sodium oxides and potassium to aluminum oxides of any igneous rocks. Some lamproites in Australia have the world's largest concentrations of diamonds, exceeding those from South Africa by factors of seven to thirty.

Principal terms

AMPHIBOLE: a calcium, magnesium, iron, and aluminum silicate and hydroxide mineral, which may have a variety of other elements
CLINOPYROXENE: a calcium, magnesium, and iron silicate mineral
DIKE: a tabular igneous rock body that cuts across the fabric of the solid rocks
IGNEOUS ROCK: a rock formed from molten rock material or magma
MAGMA: molten rock material usually of silicate composition
MICA: a potassium, magnesium, iron, and aluminum silicate mineral
MINERAL: a naturally occurring element or compound that has a more or less constant composition and arrangement of atoms
OLIVINE: a magnesium and iron silicate mineral
ROCK: a material usually composed of two or more minerals
SILL: a tabular igneous rock body that is parallel to the fabric of the solid rocks; the fabric is commonly the sedimentary layering in these kinds of rocks

Summary of the Phenomenon

Lamproites are unusual igneous rocks (formed from molten rock material) because they contain little or no feldspar (potassium, calcium, and sodium silicate). In this respect, lamproites are like kimberlites, carbonatites, or komatiites. Instead of feldspar, they contain potassium- and magnesium-rich minerals such as magnesium-rich olivine and clinopyroxene, magnesium- and titanium-rich mica, and potassium- and magnesium-rich amphiboles. A variety of other, normally scarce, minerals may also occur in lamproites. Often, their original minerals are transformed by water-vapor- and carbon-dioxide-rich fluids into a wide variety of hydrous or carbonate minerals. Lamproites, besides being enriched in potassium and magnesium, are depleted in aluminum and sodium compared to other igneous rocks. They have the highest ratios of potassium to sodium oxide (greater than 3:1) and potassium to aluminum oxide of any igneous rocks.

Lamproites are frequently confused with lamprophyres, kimberlites, and other sodium- and potassium-rich igneous rocks. Lamprophyres are dark-colored, igneous rocks found in dikes that have large, dark minerals with many fine, dark minerals of similar composition. The dark minerals in lamprophyres also are found as well-developed geometric solids with smooth, planar surfaces. Unlike lamproites, the finer minerals often contain feldspars. Kimberlites contain large minerals such as magnesium-rich ilmenite (magnesium, iron, and titanium oxide), titanium-rich pyrope (magnesium and aluminum silicate), olivine, clinopyroxene, and magnesium-rich mica surrounded by abundant smaller minerals of olivine, magnesium-rich mica, clinopyroxene, or minerals formed when the original minerals were transformed by later fluids. The lamproites contain much higher potassium-to-aluminum and potassium-to-sodium ratios than those of lamprophyres or kimberlites. Lamproites also contain much higher silicon contents than do kimberlites. Compared with lamprophyres and kimberlites, lamproites contain a higher average concentration of the trace elements rubidium, strontium, uranium, zirconium, and the rare earths. (Trace elements are those elements that substitute in small amounts for other elements composing the bulk of the minerals in a rock.) The range of concentrations of some trace elements, however, often overlap among these rock types.

Geologists have known about lamproites for some time. Prior to the late 1970's, however, lamproites were believed to be rare rocks without any economic importance. The discovery of large concentrations of diamonds in lamproites from northwestern Australia has elevated them to an important economic position. Thus, the study of lamproites, and the technical literature written about them, has increased. Lamproites occur in more than twenty regions in the world, including the United States, Greenland, Canada, Australia, Europe, Africa, Antarctica, Asia, and Brazil. Although not restricted to any given time period, they appear to have formed most abundantly during the Cretaceous (about 70 million years ago).

Lamproites often occur as lavas. The lava flows are often associated with rocks with other typical volcanic features, such as pyroclastic material thrown out of the volcano into the air. Some pyroclastic material may build up high enough around the vent to create a volcano called a cinder cone. These types of lamproites occur at Leucite Hills, Wyoming, and in the Antarctic. Pyroclastic material formed by the settling of fine volcanic ash is present in some deposits, including those at Prairie Creek, Arkansas, and with lavas and cinder cones at Leucite Hills.

Lamproites commonly occur as tabular igneous rock bodies called dikes. Dikes cut across the layering of other solid rocks (sedimentary rock layers) into which the magma was injected below the land surface. Some lamproites occur as tabular bodies, called sills, that are parallel to the layering into which the magma was injected. The lamproites in Woodson County, Kansas, are horizontal sills parallel to the sedimentary rock layers.

Lamproites also occur as vertical pipelike bodies below the land surface. Lamproite pipes occur at Prairie Creek and at Argyle and the Fitzroy Basin in Western Australia. Lamproite pipes differ from kimberlite pipes as they are shaped like inverted cones, with approximately 0.5 kilometer of flaring outward near the surface. In contrast, kimberlite pipes are more funnel-shaped, with several kilometers of flaring near the surface. The flaring is probably produced by the magma as it begins to boil and explode near the surface when carbon-dioxide- and water-vapor-rich gases are rapidly lost. The explosive activity probably occurs much like shaking a capped soft drink container and suddenly taking off the cap. The kimberlites probably contain more carbon dioxide or water vapor than do the lamproites, and they thus lose these fluids at a greater depth than do the lamproites.

Lamproites vary in size, but they are generally small in surface outcrop area compared to many bodies of igneous rock. The smaller bodies are sills and dikes and may be only a few meters wide. The pipes sometimes flare outward as much as 100 meters. Some volcanic cinder cones rise several hundreds of meters around the surroundings and are hundreds to several thousand meters wide.

All known lamproites are found on continents. Most of them occur nearer the edge of continents than do most kimberlites, but it is impossible to relate them to plate tectonic processes such as subduction (the movement of one crustal plate below another) or rifting (the ripping apart of the crust by tension). The lamproite occurrences in the United States and Australia illustrate the range of field relations in these rocks.

Lamproite is exposed over a 400-square-kilometer area in Leucite Hills, Wyoming, where it occurs as volcanic rocks and as shallow magma bodies that crystallized only a million years ago—making them among the youngest of any lamproites. The volcanic rocks originated as lava flows and pyroclastic rocks. In some places, erosion has exposed magma bodies that had solidified below the surface. These intrusive rocks occur as dikes or pipes. The common minerals in these rocks consist of a combination of magnesium-rich mica, magnesium-rich clinopyroxene, magnesium-rich olivine, and leucite (potassium and aluminum silicate).

Lamproite sills that were intruded horizontally about 70 million years ago into limestones and shales are found in Woodson County, Kansas. The sills—a few meters to approximately 30 meters thick—mostly have been located by drilling 330 meters below the surface. One near-surface exposure is being mined for alleged "growth nutrients," which could be added to animal feed. Large granite (quartz and feldspar rock) boulders are exposed at the surface at another location where lamproite is very close to the surface. Apparently, the granite was carried up as a solid by the molten lamproite magma. The granite was probably ripped off the sides of the magma conduit in the lower crust and carried upward by the lamproite magma to become accidental foreign rock fragments in the lamproite. The largest minerals found in the lamproite are magnesium-rich mica, magnesium-rich clinopyroxene, potassium-rich amphibole, and altered magnesium-rich olivine located in an altered mass of much smaller minerals. The overlying and underlying shales and limestones show evidence of having been "baked" or metamorphosed by the heat emitted by the hot magma. For example, minerals in the shale have been changed to sanidine, a potassium-rich feldspar formed only at very high temperatures. Movement of water vapor-rich fluids has apparently carried barium, potassium, and rubidium from the magma into the overlying shales.

Lamproite also is found in the Prairie Creek area and in the Crater of Diamonds

Park close to Murfreesboro, Arkansas. The lamproite at Prairie Creek occurs as pipes, dikes, pyroclastic deposits, and ash deposits. The intrusion at the Crater of Diamonds is a pipelike body. Diamonds have been found in both areas. The pipes and dikes are composed of large, altered olivine grains with other small minerals of magnesium-rich mica, potassium-rich amphibole, chromium-rich spinel (magnesium and chromium oxide), magnesium-rich clinopyroxene, magnetite (iron oxide), and other altered minerals. The ash deposit contains magnesium-rich mica, sanidine, and quartz (silicon oxide), with small minerals of carbonate and clays (aluminum silicate minerals with a wide variety of metallic elements).

Lamproites also exist in the northern portion of Western Australia at more than 100 locations. Diamonds are found at approximately 30 sites. Most of these lamproites are quite young (formed 17-25 million years ago), but some may be Precambrian (older than 600 million years). The intrusive lamproites occur as dikes, sills, pipes, and larger bodies of various shapes. The extrusive lamproites occur as fine-to-coarse volcanic material which was thrown into the air rather than extruded as lava. The diamond-bearing lamproites contain large olivine grains with smaller minerals of olivine, magnesium-rich mica, magnesium-rich clinopyroxene, potassium-rich amphibole, and various minor minerals. The lamproites that do not contain diamonds have the mineral leucite along with many of the minerals found in diamond-bearing lamproites.

One of the olivine-rich lamproites at Argyle contains incredible concentrations and amounts of diamonds. Erosion has also concentrated diamonds in stream deposits adjacent to this lamproite. The rocks here are a mixed ash and sand deposit formed by ejection of material into the air and by dikes formed by injection of lamproite into the other rocks. The ash-sand deposit consists mostly of sand-sized pieces of lamproite and volcanic ash. The lamproite contains large olivine and magnesium-rich mica grains with fine grains of magnesium-rich mica, anatase (titanium oxide), sphene (calcium and titanium silicate), perovskite (calcium and titanium oxide), and other minor minerals.

Methods of Study

The field relationships, mineral relationships, and chemical composition of lamproites may be used to infer something about their origin. Experiments using furnaces also may help to explain how lamproites form and evolve.

Lamproites in the form of pipes, sills, and dikes are thought to have intruded as magma into solidified rocks, especially if the age of the lamproite is younger than the rocks above or below it. Lamproites were probably injected while they were very hot and contained fluids. These fluids bubbled out and altered the overlying and underlying rocks as observed in the sills at Woodson County, Kansas. The shales into which the lamproite was intruded were "baked" so that the original minerals were tranformed into minerals such as sanidine.

The large minerals coexisting with very fine minerals in the lamproite indicate the cooling history of the rocks. The larger minerals often form by slow crystallization of the mineral from the magma at great depth. If the magma-mineral mixture rapidly moves upward into cooler rocks at lower pressure, the mixture may suddenly cool and quickly form much smaller minerals or even glass. The rapid rise of the lamproite magma to lower pressure may cause rapid water vapor loss. This loss suddenly raises the crystallization temperature of the magma, thus favoring the rapid crystallization of the magma.

The presence of lamproite material located at or near a volcano may be used to infer its volcanic origin. In older rocks, the volcanic cone may have eroded long ago; in this case, the volcanic origin of the rocks may be obscure. Other features must be used to infer their volcanic origin. For example, the presence of fine ash or angular fragments (bombs) that may have been blown out of a volcano suggest a volcanic origin. The presence of glass or altered glass suggests quick cooling of the magma, which is also consistent with a volcanic origin. Other rocks deposited over the volcanic lamproites would not be baked, as they would have been in sills.

The distinctive chemical composition of lamproites helps a geologist to understand what kind of rock melts to form a lamproite magma. The high potassium and magnesium combined with low aluminum and sodium are simply not found in other igneous rocks, so there must be something distinctive about the rocks that melt to form lamproites. Only peridotite, a rock deep within the earth that contains olivine, pyroxene, garnet (magnesium and aluminum silicate), and magnesium-rich mica, may melt to form the major constituents in the lamproite magma. For example, about 60 percent of the magnesium-rich mica and 40 percent of the pyroxene must have melted to form the major element content of the lamproite at Woodson County, Kansas. This is also consistent with experiments in furnaces in which rocks of similar composition have been melted to produce such magma. In addition, the lamproite magmas contain exceedingly large concentrations of certain trace constituents, such as lanthanum, rubidium, barium, and strontium. It is impossible to melt most peridotites (peridotite is carried up as foreign rock fragments in some magmas) and produce such large concentrations of these trace constituents. Mica peridotites have been found, however, that contain enriched amounts of these trace constituents. If these mica peridotites were to melt, they would produce the large concentrations of those trace constituents found in the lamproite magmas. The presence of diamonds in some lamproites proves that the magma must have formed very deep within the earth. Diamond is stable only at depths greater than 150 kilometers below the earth's surface. The magma must have ascended rapidly; otherwise, the diamonds would have had time to decompose as they rose to the surface.

The concentration of some elements may also be changed as lamproite magmas rise from deep within the earth to where they finally solidify. Indeed, the local variation in many element concentrations across one small sill in Woodson County, Kansas, is as great as the variation in element concentrations among all lamproites in the world. Here, much of this chemical variation is produced by two processes. One process involves the concentration of the larger mineral grains toward the center of the sills by rapid flow of the mineral-magma mixture. This process produced a concentration of some elements in the middle of the sills that concentrate in large minerals. Another process involves the movement of elements in water-vapor-rich fluids that seem to concentrate toward the ends and tops of the sills. In portions of some sills, for example, the barium content is as high as 3 percent. This percentage is exceedingly high, as most lamproites contain only about 0.5 percent barium, and most other igneous rocks contain only about 0.05 percent barium.

Context

The world's largest concentrations of diamonds have been found in lamproites from the northern portion of Western Australia. Diamonds have also been found in lamproites at Prairie Creek, Arkansas; the Luangwa graben, Zambia; and at Bobi and Séguéla, Ivory Coast. There is little information on lamproites in Zambia and the Ivory Coast, but the others have been well studied. The grade of diamonds at the more than twenty locations known to contain diamonds in Australia varies from about 5 to 680 carats per ton. The largest known reserves are at Argyle, where there are at least 61 million tons of known reserves at 680 carats per ton: These reserves are seven to thirty times more enriched in diamonds than the kimberlites in South Africa. Other reserves at Argyle contain lower concentrations of diamonds.

Diamonds have been valued for their beauty for at least twenty-four centuries. More recently, diamonds have become important for industrial purposes, as they are exceedingly hard. Indeed, this elemental form of carbon is the hardest substance in nature. Diamonds are also one of the most expensive natural materials. Even industrial diamonds typically cost $10,000 per pound. Until the 1970's, most of the world's diamond supply and the price of diamonds were controlled by the De Beers Corporation. In the 1980's, the selling of investor diamonds on the world market and the opening of large new diamond mines in Australia led to a new supply of diamonds. De Beers, while trying to maintain its high prices by buying many of these diamonds, considerably strained its resources.

About 20 percent of diamonds are used for gemstones. Prices vary depending on the demand for diamonds of differing size, clarity (lack of impurities), and color. The other 80 percent of diamonds are used for industrial purposes. Diamond is used as an abrasive to cut, polish, or grind a variety of materials. They also are used in tools such as diamond saws, glass cutters, grinding wheels, and drilling bits. Diamond powder or dust is used for polishing and lapping. Many industrial diamonds are produced from graphite (another form of carbon) at exceedingly high pressure and temperature. In the 1980's, the production of artificial industrial diamonds far outpaced the production of natural industrial diamonds.

Bibliography

Bates, R. L. *Geology of the Industrial Rocks and Minerals*. Mineola, N.Y.: Dover, 1969. The author discusses many types of economic deposits, including diamonds. The reader should have had an introductory course in geology, as the author assumes the reader is familiar with common geologic terms. No glossary; few illustrations.

Bergman, S. C. "Lamproites and Other Potassium-Rich Igneous Rocks: A Review of Their Occurrence, Mineralogy, and Geochemistry." In *Alkaline Igneous Rocks*, edited by J. G. Fitton. Boston: Blackwell Scientific for the Geological Society, 1987. This technical discussion of lamproites is suited for the advanced student or the mineral collector who wishes to locate known lamproites: There is often a geologic map of the lamproite and many references.

Craig, J. R., D. J. Vaughan, and B. J. Skinner. *Resources of the Earth*. Englewood Cliffs, N.J.: Prentice-Hall, 1988. A well-written book on economic deposits, for persons with little technical background. Numerous figures and pictures. Includes a glossary and several sections on diamonds.

Cross, C. W. "The Igneous Rocks of the Leucite Hills and Pilot Butte, Wyoming." *American Journal of Science* 4 (1987): 115-141. This article gives the main rock types of this area and locates them on a map. Suitable for a mineral collector who is not intimidated by complex rock names.

Cullers, R. L., et. al. "Geochemistry and Petrogenesis of Lamproites, Late Cretaceous Age, Woodson County, Kansas, U.S.A." *Geochimica et Cosmochimica Acta* 49 (1985): 1383-1402. A technical paper suitable for an advanced student. A mineral collector can find the location and the minerals found in this lamproite.

Steele, K., and G. H. Wagner. "Relationship of the Murfreesboro Kimberlite and Other Igneous Rocks of Arkansas, U.S.A." In *Kimberlites, Diatremes, and Diamonds: Their Geology, Petrology, and Geochemistry*, edited by H. R. Boyd and H. O. A. Myers. Washington, D.C.: American Geophysical Union, 1979. The reading is appropriate for a college student with a course in petrology. A mineral collector can find the locations of the lamproites.

Robert L. Cullers

Cross-References

Diamonds, 362; Igneous Rock Bodies, 1131; Igneous Rock Classification, 1138; Igneous Rocks: Kimberlites, 1186; Crystallization of Magmas, 1420; The Origin of Magmas, 1428; Water in Magmas, 1433; Contact Metamorphism, 1594; Phase Changes, 2042; Phase Equilibria, 2049; Pyroclastic Rocks, 2131; Silica Minerals, 2365; Volcanoes: Types of Eruption, 2695.

IGNEOUS ROCKS: ULTRAMAFIC

Type of earth science: Geology
Field of study: Petrology, igneous

Ultramafic rocks are dense, dark-colored, iron- and magnesium-rich silicate rocks composed primarily of the minerals olivine and pyroxene. They are the dominant rocks in the earth's mantle but also occur in some areas of the crust. From a scientific standpoint, ultramafic rocks are important for what they contribute to the understanding of crust and mantle evolution. They also serve as an important source of economic commodities such as chromium, platinum, nickel, and diamonds, as well as talc, asbestos, and various decorative building stones.

Principal terms

CRUST: the upper layer of the earth, composed primarily of silicate rocks of relatively low density compared to those of the mantle

MANTLE: the middle layer of the earth, composed of dense, ultramafic rocks, located from about 5-50 kilometers below the crust and extending to the metallic core

OLIVINE: a silicate mineral abundant in many ultramafic rocks; gem-quality, clear green olivine is called peridot

PERIDOTITE: a principal type of ultramafic rock, composed mostly of the minerals olivine and pyroxene

PYROXENE: a group of calcium-iron-magnesium silicate minerals that are important constituents of ultramafic and mafic rocks

Summary of the Phenomenon

Ultramafic rocks are dense, dark-colored, iron- and magnesium-rich rocks that constitute a volumetrically and scientifically important class of earth material. To qualify as ultramafic, a rock must contain 90 percent or more of the so-called mafic minerals, olivine and pyroxene. The term "mafic" is derived from "magnesium" and "ferric" (the latter meaning "derived from iron"); "ultramafic" is an appropriate term for these minerals as they are very rich in both magnesium and iron. Another class of common rocks in the earth's crust, the mafic rocks (including the black lava called basalt), are also rich in magnesium and iron but not to the extent shown by ultramafic rocks. A typical basalt may contain an average of about 20 percent iron plus magnesium (as the oxides ferrous oxide and magnesium oxide), but typical ultramafic rocks may contain more than twice that amount. Thus, the prefix "ultra" is well deserved. In addition, ultramafic rocks are generally—but not always—lower in silica than are mafic rocks, which is particularly true for olivine-rich ultramafic rocks, which average less than 45 percent silica; basaltic rocks average about 50 percent silica.

Although petrologists (geologists who study rocks) recognize several types of ultramafic rocks, the type called peridotite is the most common and, thus, considered the most important of all ultramafic rocks. Peridotites consist of more than 40 percent of the light green mineral olivine, an iron-magnesium silicate. The gem-quality variety of olivine is called peridot, from which the term "peridotite" is derived. The remaining minerals consist of various pyroxene minerals or hornblende. Pyroxene is a group of silicate minerals that contain calcium, iron, and magnesium as principal constituents; hornblende is similar to high-calcium varieties of pyroxene, but it contains water as part of its chemical structure. Variable amounts of spinel-group minerals (oxides of chromium, magnesium, iron, and aluminum), garnet, and other minerals commonly occur in minor amounts in peridotites. Peridotite is the principal constituent of the earth's upper mantle, which makes it one of the most abundant types of rock in the earth. In the crust, however, peridotite is relatively rare, occurring only in specific geological environments. It is this property of peridotites, among others, that makes these rocks so important and interesting as subjects of scientific investigation.

Peridotite is not the only type of ultramafic rock. Another important category of ultramafic rocks is the pyroxenites, which, as the name implies, are rocks composed mostly of pyroxene (greater than 90 percent). Pyroxene is not one mineral but is rather a family of related minerals, all having single chains of silicon-oxygen tetrahedra as their central structural aspect. This mineral group consists of two principal structural-chemical types: the low-calcium orthopyroxenes (with orthorhombic crystal symmetry) and the high-calcium clinopyroxenes (with monoclinic crystal symmetry). Pyroxenites can have variable amounts of either of these two pyroxene types or may have one more or less exclusive of the other. Orthopyroxenites contain mostly orthopyroxene and clinopyroxenites contain mostly clinopyroxene; the term "websterite" is used to describe pyroxenites that contain an appreciable mixture of both minerals.

Peridotites can also be subdivided into different types based on their pyroxene components. Those that contain mostly orthopyroxene as their pyroxene type are called hartzburgites. If the major pyroxene is clinopyroxene, the rock is called wehrlite; if both pyroxenes occur along with olivine, the rock is called lherzolite. One special and fairly rare type of peridotite is dunite: a nearly pyroxene-free, olivine-rich peridotite (90 percent or greater olivine). Most peridotites from the mantle contain minor amounts of an aluminum-rich mineral, generally either plagioclase (calcium-sodium aluminum silicate), spinel (magnesium-aluminum oxide), or pyrope garnet (magnesium-iron aluminum silicate). Many of the peridotites formed in the crust by igneous processes commonly contain the chromium-iron spinel-group mineral called chromite, the principal ore of chromium metal.

Geologists' knowledge of mantle rocks comes predominantly from either of two sources: chunks of rock torn from the walls of deep mantle conduits by molten magma that eventually carries these mantle "xenoliths" (Greek for "stranger rock") out of the earth enclosed in lava flows, or thick slices of ultramafic mantle material that were thrust up to the surface during mountain-building processes. Scientific examination of these mantle samples shows that most of them are metamorphic rocks that crystallized under high pressures and temperatures in the solid state. Some mantle samples, however, show evidence of an earlier history of crystallization from molten magma.

Ultramafic rocks that formed in the crust mostly originated by purely igneous processes and thus show evidence of crystallization from magma. Most crustal ultramafic rocks are found in layered complexes: crystallized bodies of magma trapped deep within the crust that display a "layer-cake" structure, with different kinds of igneous rocks composing the various layers. The production of many kinds of rocks from a single parent magma is called differentiation; the differentiation involved in the formation of layered complexes largely results from the process of gravity differentiation. In this process, early-formed minerals sink to the lower reaches of the magma reservoir, with later minerals forming progressively higher layers until the magma is wholly crystallized. The parent magma from which all layered complexes form is basaltic in composition—the same material that forms the islands of Hawaii, for example, or the steep cliffs of the Columbia River gorge in Washington State. Because the iron-magnesium-rich (mafic) minerals, olivine and pyroxene, form relatively early in basalt magmas, these minerals collect in the first-formed, lower layers of layered complexes. Resulting rocks in these layers are typically peridotites and pyroxenites. The igneous rocks that form later, above the dark ultramafic rocks, consist of gabbros (plagioclase-pyroxene rocks) and other mafic rocks. Knowledge of the ultramafic and other rocks in layered complexes comes from the fact that some of these deep-seated, crystallized magma bodies have been uplifted in mountainous areas and uncovered by erosion.

Where one would travel to see examples of ultramafic rocks would depend upon which of the two major categories—mantle or crustal—is of interest. In North America, the best places to see mantle-type ultramafic rocks are the Coast Ranges and the Sierra Nevada of California and the Klamath Mountains of western Oregon. Belts of ultramafic rocks are also found in some areas of the Canadian Rocky Mountains and on Canada's east coast, particularly in Quebec and Newfoundland. Exposures of ultramafic rocks also occur at various locations within the Appalachian Mountains in the United States, particularly in Vermont and Virginia. Worldwide, the Mediterranean area lays claim to some of the most impressive areas of exposed mantle-derived ultramafic rocks, notably the Troodos complex in Cyprus and the Vourinos complex in Greece. Similar ultramafic belts extend in scattered exposures from France and Italy eastward to Turkey and Iran. Other prominent occurrences are known from India, Tibet, and China. Most if not all of these exposures are known as ophiolite complexes. Ophiolites are slices of ocean crust (basalt and sediments) and underlying mantle (mostly hartzburgite and lherzolite peridotite and some ultramafic gravity-stratified rocks) that become involved in mountain-building activities where two lithospheric plates (consisting of upper mantle and crust) collide. This collision area, called a subduction zone, is commonly located near continental margins, which is why ophiolites generally occur in mountain belts (like the Coast Ranges or Appalachians) that parallel a coast. The Mediterranean ophiolites are thrust up in an area that is being deformed by the collision of Africa (on a lithospheric plate moving slowly northward) with Eurasia. Unfortunately for the scientists wishing to study them, most ultramafic rocks in ophiolites, especially the peridotites, are altered to varying degrees to serpentine (a hydrated magnesium silicate similar structurally to clay), producing a metamorphic rock called serpentinite. It is produced before or during mountain building by the interaction of olivine with water, much of which probably consists of seawater trapped in peridotites and associated rocks as they lay below the ocean floor.

Another source of mantle-derived ultramafic rocks are the xenoliths brought to the surface by lava flows. These mantle samples are particularly valuable as objects for scientific study and as potential sources of gem-quality peridot because they commonly show few if any effects of alteration to hydrous minerals such as serpentine. Well known to scientists who study ultramafic rocks are the excellent xenolith localities at San Carlos, Arizona; Salt Lake crater, Hawaii; Sunset crater near Flagstaff, Arizona; and the garnet-bearing xenoliths incorporated in diamond-bearing kimberlite deposits in South Africa. Kimberlite deposits are chaotic masses of broken fragments of ultramafic rocks and their constituent minerals mixed with serpentine, other hydrated silicate minerals, and carbonate minerals (mostly calcite and calcium carbonate). They originate in the upper mantle, between about 150 and 200 kilometers depth. Propelled rapidly upward as carbon-dioxide- and water-charged mixtures of mantle and crustal rocks encountered during their ascent, they explode violently at the surface and form large craters. The eroded remnants of these kimberlite pipes (also called diatremes) are mined for diamonds, which form at very high pressures and temperatures in the mantle. Diamond-bearing kimberlites occur in the United States in Arkansas; diamond-free kimberlites occur in Missouri, Oklahoma, and Kansas.

Large layered complexes containing ultramafic rocks are exposed in only a few places on the world's continents. Probably the best example in the United States is the Stillwater complex, located in the Beartooth Mountains of western Montana. Estimated to have originally measured 8 kilometers thick, it is now exposed as a 5-kilometer-thick strip approximately 30 kilometers long. The Stillwater has been the object of intense scientific research over several years and is a source of economic chromium deposits. Platinum deposits also occur within the ultramafic rocks of the Stillwater. An even more intensely studied layered intrusive body is the Skaergaard intrusion of eastern Greenland. Discovered in 1930, it is exposed over an area of glaciated outcrops 3.2 kilometers thick. It is believed to represent basaltic magma trapped beneath a rift zone created as the North Atlantic ocean basin opened up about 50 million years ago. This magma differentiated into a complicated layered zone consisting of various kinds of peridotites, pyroxenites, and gabbros.

No discussion of layered ultramafic complexes would be complete without mentioning the famous Bushveld complex of South Africa. Measuring 270 by 450 kilometers in area, it is estimated to have been originally about 8 kilometers thick, like the Stillwater. Much of the world's supply of chromium comes from the chromite deposits associated with peridotites in this monstrous intrusive body. The Bushveld is also the world's largest source of platinum, contained in a 1- to 5-meter-thick assemblage of olivine, chromite, orthopyroxene, and sulfides known as the Merensky Reef. This single, thin unit extends for a total of 300 kilometers. Other notable layered complexes with well-studied ultramafic rocks are the funnel-shaped Muskox intrusion in northern Canada and the Great Dyke of central Zimbabwe. With an average width of 5.8 kilometers, the Great Dyke extends for 480 kilometers. Like the Bushveld, it is a source of chromium ore.

Another type of crustal ultramafic rock is the rare but very important komatiite ultramafic lava flow. Mostly restricted to very old Precambrian terrains (most komatiite ages lie between about 2.0 and 2.5 billion years), these rocks represent nearly completely melted mantle material, a feat that requires extremely high temperatures. Present temperatures in the upper mantle are not sufficient to produce komatiites; basalt magma is produced instead by much lower degrees of melting of mantle peridotite. The restriction of komatiites to Precambrian terrains suggests that the mantle was much hotter billions of years ago compared to more recent times. Excellent exposures of these ultramafic lava flows occur at Yilgarn Block, Australia, and the Barberton Mountains, South Africa.

Methods of Study

Ultramafic rocks are studied using analytical techniques commonly applied to any kind of igneous or metamorphic rock type. These techniques include detailed microscopic analysis; analyses for major (1 percent or more by weight), minor (less than 1 percent), and trace (measured in terms of parts per million or parts per billion) elements; and analysis for various critical isotopes, such as those of rubidium and strontium, and the rare earth elements neodymium and samarium. The latter isotope systems are the most commonly used to date ultramafic rocks by radiometric methods. What kinds of analyses are performed on any given ultramafic rock depends upon the type of ultramafic rock in question and the objectives of the specific research project. For example, ultramafic rocks from the mantle would probably not be approached from the same scientific aspect as would ultramafic rocks formed in the crust. Analysis of mantle samples might reveal clues as to how the early earth formed originally and then differentiated into a core, mantle, and crust. Because many igneous magmas now residing as igneous rocks in the crust (especially those of basaltic composition) were originally produced by partial melting of ultramafic mantle rocks, the study of mantle samples provides a glimpse into how the earth's crust evolved. The detailed analysis of layered complexes, komatiites, kimberlites, and associated crustal rocks gives information about the complexities of igneous differentiation (making many kinds of rocks from a common parent) and also bears on the processes involved in crustal formation. These studies can also be applied to some ultramafic meteorites to show how other planets evolved in comparison to the earth.

Because many crustal rocks ultimately originated in the mantle, mantle ultra-mafic rocks have been subjected to laboratory experiments that seek to simulate the production of various magmas in the mantle. In these experiments, mantle samples (or artificially concocted facsimiles) are heated to the point of melting at pressures calculated to occur at different depths in the mantle. These experiments have shown that different kinds of basaltic magma can be produced by simply changing the pressure (thus, the depth) at which mantle materials melt. Varying the proportions of constituents such as water and carbon dioxide can also produce different magma compositions for a given pressure. These experiments have been correlated with rocks collected in the field and their particular environments of emplacement. For example, experimental evidence shows that rocks like kimberlites and alkaline lavas (high in potassium and sodium, very low in silica) originate at great depth in areas of the mantle enriched in carbon dioxide, which helps to explain the explosive, gas-rich nature of kimberlite deposits and the high carbon dioxide contents in gases released upon extrusion by alkaline lavas. More silica-rich lavas, like the basalt that floors the earth's oceans, originate at much shallower depth, and thus at lower pressures, than do alkaline-type lavas.

Mantle samples also give scientists clues as to the very early history of the planet, because their geochemistry records the earliest differentiation events, including the formation of the nickel-iron core. Trace element analyses of mantle samples show that certain elements generally expected to sink into the core along with the nickel and iron are depleted in the mantle. Some of these elements are gold, osmium, iridium, and platinum. Obviously, not all these elements sank to the core during the time about 4.5 billion years ago when the earth was much hotter than it is now; otherwise, the abundances of these elements (including iron) in the crust would not be seen. The process of core formation was not perfect; some elements that could have gone to the core stayed in the mantle, later to be erupted to the crust by volcanoes and other igneous processes. At the same time, geochemists note that laboratory analyses of some other elements show abundances similar to certain very old, "primitive" meteorites called chondrites. These meteorites are believed to have crystallized from gas that made up the solar nebula, the gaseous cloud from which the solar system eventually evolved. Chondrites are considered primitive because they contain abundances and ratios of most elements that are similar to those measured for the sun. Thus, chondrites are the rocky building blocks of most planets and asteroids. Analysis of mantle ultramafic rocks shows that their calcium-aluminum ratio, for example, is similar to that of chondrites, suggesting that mantle materials were originally composed of chondrites or chondritelike material that later differentiated to make the core and crust. Interestingly, the mineralogical makeup of chondrites is similar to that of the mantle: mostly olivine and pyroxene. Much of the mantle, therefore, probably represents highly metamorphosed chondritic meteorites or similar precursor rocks.

Layered complexes, such as the Skaergaard, Bushveld, and Stillwater, have been extensively studied as models for how magmas can differentiate into other kinds of magmas. These processes, in turn, demonstrate why the earth contains so many different types of igneous rocks compared to other planets and satellites, such as the moon. Experimental studies have been conducted on basaltic magmas in which the liquids are allowed to cool slowly as they would at great depth in the crust. By observing the kinds of minerals that crystallize at various temperatures and analyzing the chemical compositions of coexisting liquids, petrologists can attempt to explain the order and mineral compositions of the various layers in layered complexes. Experiments like these can also be used to show why minerals such as chromite and platinum-rich sulfides may concentrate in particularly thick layers that can be mined for these economically important minerals.

Context

Although ultramafic rocks are not commonplace constituents of the earth's crust, most people have seen examples of them, as they are used as building stone in large department stores, churches, banks, and various public buildings. The best known of these decorative stones is verde antique, which literally means "old green." Verde antique is considered to be a type of marble, but it mostly consists of dark green serpentine (a hydrous alteration of olivine) swirled together with white, gray, or pink calcite (calcium carbonate) that may also crosscut the serpentine as thin veins.

Ultramafic rocks may also serve as a source of gemstones. The semiprecious gemstone peridot originates as large, perfectly clear, green olivine crystals in peridotites, which can be incorporated into rings, bracelets, and necklaces, some of the finest examples being the silver with peridot jewelry made by members of the San Carlos (Arizona) Apache Tribe. These Native Americans own one of the world's richest sites for peridotite nodules incorporated in lava flows on the reservation. Some of the peridot crystals that they recover are as big as an adult thumb.

Perhaps the most important commercial use for ultramafic rocks lies in their tendency to harbor rich deposits of certain metallic ores, namely chromium, vanadium, platinum, and nickel. Chromium and vanadium (in the mineral chromite) are mined from peridotite units, usually from chromite-rich seams. The Stillwater complex in western Montana and the Bushveld complex in South Africa are some of the richest sources of this ore. Platinum is mined as native platinum (metallic) and as various platinum sulfides from the Bushveld, the Yilgarn Block area of Western Australia, and in the Ural Mountains and other sites in the Soviet Union. Nickel is commonly associated with platinum deposits in ultramafic rocks, but large quantities of nickel are also contained in so-called lateritic nickel deposits. These deposits form by intensive weathering of ultramafic rocks in tropical areas, causing the nickel to be released from olivine as it reacts with water to form serpentine and clay. Important nickel laterite deposits occur in Cuba, the Dominican Republic, Indonesia, and the southern Soviet Union.

Finally, certain nonmetallic minerals, particularly talc and asbestos, are also mined or quarried from ultramafic deposits. These include the talc deposits in Vermont and Virginia. In Virginia, the talc occurs in soapstone, a corrosion-resistant, durable stone commonly used for laboratory tables or for artistic carvings. Large talc deposits also occur in Italy and France. The principal form of asbestos fibers, chrysotile serpentine, also comes from ultramafic rocks. Large deposits occur in Quebec, as well as in the Soviet Union, Zimbabwe, and South Africa. In the United States, asbestos occurs in ultramafic deposits in California, Vermont, and Alaska.

Bibliography

Ballard, Robert D. *Exploring Our Living Planet*. Washington, D.C.: National Geographic Society, 1983. This book is an excellent guide to the dynamic processes that shape the earth. It does not have specific sections on ultramafic rocks, except for a brief item on the Bushveld complex. On the other hand, it is one of the best resources for the layperson on plate tectonics and volcanism, both of which involve ultramafic rocks. Extensively illustrated with color photographs and well-drafted, easily understood diagrams to show how the mantle is involved in processes of mountain building and volcanism. Includes an adequate glossary and extensive index.

Smith, David G., ed. *The Cambridge Encyclopedia of Earth Sciences*. New York: Cambridge University Press, 1981. This compendium of knowledge about the earth is a useful reference for laypersons and specialists alike. The color and black-and-white photographs are excellent, as are the color diagrams and charts. The section on peridotites and other mantle rocks is sufficiently comprehensive to include stable isotopes and trace elements. Contains an extensive glossary and index.

Symes, R. F. *Rocks and Minerals*. Toronto: Stoddart, 1988. This book, written by Dr. Symes and the staff of the Natural History Museum of London primarily with the young reader in mind, is lavishly illustrated with colored photographs and diagrams on every page. The photographs of museum rock and mineral specimens are combined with descriptive text giving characteristics, occurrences, and uses of the illustrated specimens. Most of the rocks and minerals important to the subject of ultramafic rocks are described and illustrated, including olivine and pyroxene, peridotite and serpentine, and basalt/gabbro. A visual delight, this book is highly recommended.

Wyllie, Peter J., ed. *Ultramafic and Related Rocks*. Huntington, N.Y.: Robert E. Krieger, 1979. This compendium of several articles by a number of authors is one of the most comprehensive works on ultramafic rocks for more advanced readers. Every chapter is preceded by a foreword by Dr. Wyllie, summarizing the content and significance of the article. Has an extensive list of references (all pre-1967, the original publication year) and an author and subject index. This volume is an ideal source of seminal information on ultramafic rocks for the serious student, but there are a few topics not covered concerning ultramafic and associated rocks.

Most college-educated persons should gain an appreciation for the significance and complexity of ultramafic rock associations by at least a cursory scanning of this book.

John L. Berkley

Cross-References

Diamonds, 362; The Evolution of Earth's Composition, 496; Experimental Petrology, 662; Igneous and Contact Metamorphic Mineral Deposits, 1124; Igneous Rock Bodies, 1131; Igneous Rock Classification, 1138; Igneous Rocks: Basaltic, 1158; Igneous Rocks: Kimberlites, 1186; Igneous Rocks: Komatiites, 1193; Crystallization of Magmas, 1420; The Origin of Magmas, 1428; Ophiolites, 1954; Platinum Group Metals, 2086.

INDUSTRIAL METALS

Type of earth science: Economic geology

Metals have played a major role not only in human survival but also in the high standard of living that most cultures enjoy today. Man has developed an understanding of the geologic conditions under which minerals form in nature and has learned to prospect for and produce those minerals from which metals are derived. A use for virtually every metallic element has been found.

Principal terms

BASIC: a term to describe dark-colored, iron- and magnesium-rich igneous rocks that crystallize at high temperatures, such as basalt

BY-PRODUCT: a mineral or metal that is mined or produced in addition to the major metal of interest

GRANITE: a light-colored, coarse-grained igneous rock that crystallizes at relatively low temperatures; it is rich in quartz, feldspar, and mica

HYDROTHERMAL SOLUTION: a watery fluid, rich in dissolved ions, that is the last stage in the crystallization of a magma

LATERITE: a deep red soil, rich in iron and aluminum oxides and formed by intense chemical weathering in a humid tropical climate

NODULE: a spherical to irregularly shaped, chemically precipitated mass of rock; nodules of economic interest are the "manganese nodules" which cover large parts of the ocean basin floor, especially in the North Pacific

ORE MINERAL: any mineral that can be mined and refined for its metal content at a profit

PEGMATITE: a very coarse-grained igneous rock that forms late in the crystallization of a magma; its overall composition is usually granitic, but it is also enriched in many rare elements and gem minerals

PLACER: a surface mineral deposit formed by the settling from a water current of heavy mineral particles, usually along a stream channel or a beach; gold, tin, and diamonds often occur in this manner

PRIMARY: a term to describe minerals that crystallize at the time that the enclosing rock is formed; hydrothermal vein minerals are examples

REFRACTORY: a term to describe minerals or manufactured materials that resist breakdown; most silicate minerals and furnace brick are examples

RESERVE: that part of the mineral resource base that can be extracted profitably with existing technology and under current economic conditions

RESOURCE: a naturally occurring substance in such form that it can be currently or potentially extracted economically

SECONDARY: a mineral formed later than the enclosing rock, either by metamorphism or by weathering and transport; placers are examples

VEIN: a mineral-filled fault or fracture in rock; veins represent late crystallization, most commonly in association with granite

Summary of the Phenomenon

The industrial metals occur in a wide variety of geologic environments and find use in a great many applications. They may, for convenience, be divided into three groups: the major nonferrous metals, the ferroalloys, and the minor metals. The major metals are copper, tin, lead, and zinc. All are essential to modern civilization, and some have been used since antiquity. Copper has been used longer than any metal except gold. It occurs in at least 160 different minerals, of which chalcopyrite is the most abundant ore. The world's most important source of copper is in large masses of granite rock known as porphyry copper bodies, which are found throughout the western United States but are especially numerous in southern Arizona. Hydrothermal solutions deposited copper-bearing minerals in openings and cracks throughout these masses. These minerals are low-grade ores and are mined by large-tonnage, open-pit operations. Copper also occurs in sedimentary rocks. Such deposits account for more than one-fourth of the world's copper reserves, with the best examples in the Zambian-Zairean copper belt of Africa. A future resource is the copper in manganese nodules that cover large portions of the ocean floor, especially in the North Pacific. These chemically precipitated masses contain as much as 1.5 percent copper. Chile, the United States, Canada, and the Soviet Union, in that order, are the world's leading producers of copper.

Like copper, tin was one of the first metals to be used by humans. Phoenician traders carried tin from the mines at Cornwall, England, to the Mediterranean world before 1500 B.C. The principal ore mineral of tin is the oxide cassiterite, "tinstone." Primary tin-bearing deposits include granite pegmatites and hydrothermal veins. Much more important from a commercial standpoint, however, are secondary stream placer deposits. The United States consumes approximately 30 percent of the annual free world production of tin. Domestic mine production is negligible, but the United States is the world's leading producer of recycled tin. World leaders in the mining of tin are Malaysia, Brazil, the Soviet Union, Indonesia, Thailand, China, and Bolivia.

While geologic conditions favor the joint occurrence of lead and zinc, the history of usage of each has been very different. Lead, one of the first metals smelted and used by humans, predates the use of iron. It was widely used in the Roman Empire for water systems and storage containers for wine. The decline and fall of the Roman Empire has been attributed by some scholars to a progressive, debilitating lead poisoning of the upper classes through these uses. Zinc, on the other hand, was discovered much later. Zinc and lead now rank just behind copper and aluminum as essential nonferrous (not containing iron) metals in modern industry. The most important geologic occurrences of lead and zinc are within stratified layers of metamorphic or carbonate rocks. The deposits at Ducktown, Tennessee, and Franklin, New Jersey, are in metamorphic rocks, while those in the upper Mississippi Valley, southeastern Missouri (the Virburnum Trend), and the Tri-State mineral district (Missouri-Oklahoma-Kansas) are found in carbonate rocks. This latter type of occurrence is now referred to as Mississippi Valley-type deposits. The principal ore minerals for lead and zinc are the sulfides galena and sphalerite (zinc blende), respectively. These minerals were probably emplaced in the host rocks by later hydrothermal solutions. The United States is a major producer of lead, with most coming from the Virburnum Trend. Recycled lead is also very important in the United States, accounting for more production than mining. Other major lead-producing countries are the Soviet Union, Australia, Canada, Peru, and Mexico. Canada ranks as the world's leading producer of zinc, followed by the Soviet Union, Australia, Peru, Mexico, and the United States.

The ferroalloys are a group of metals whose chief economic use is for alloying with iron in the production of carbon and various specialty steels. Manganese is the most important of the ferroalloys, and it occurs principally in sandstone deposits such as those at Nikopol and Chiaturi in the Soviet Union. Chemically precipitated nodules on the ocean floor contain up to 20 percent manganese and represent an important potential resource.

The elements chromium, nickel, titanium, vanadium, and cobalt most commonly occur in basic igneous rocks such as gabbro. These deposits are often layered, of great lateral extent, and are formed during an early stage of crystallization by the settling out of the minerals that contain these metals. Examples of such deposits are the Stillwater complex of Montana and the Bushveldt complex of South Africa. The Bushveldt is the largest such body in the world, and it holds most of the world's chromium reserves. Nickel ranks second in importance to manganese among the ferroalloys. The large igneous deposits at Sudbury, Ontario, Canada, have been the world's major supplier. Prior to the Sudbury ore discovery, the nickel-rich laterites of New Caledonia, formed by the tropical weathering of igneous rock, supplied most of the world's needs. The most important economic occurrences of titanium are in secondary placer deposits, notably the rutile beach sands of Australia and the ilmenite sands of northern Florida. In addition to its occurrence in dark igneous rocks, vanadium is found as a weathering product in uranium-bearing sandstones such as those of the Colorado Plateau region of the United States. Vanadium is also produced from the residues of petroleum refining and from the processing of phosphate rock. While the primary occurrence of cobalt is in dark igneous rocks, it also is produced from laterites and as a by-product of the sedimentary copper deposits of the African copper belt.

Molybdenum, tungsten, niobium, and tantalum occur commonly in quartz veins and granite pegmatites. Most molybdenum production comes from the very large, but low-grade, porphyry deposits at Climax, Colorado, and as a by-product of the porphyry copper deposits at Bingham Canyon, Utah. Production of the minerals scheelite and wolframite from quartz veins accounts for more than one-half of the world's production of tungsten. Because of their rarity, there is no mining operation solely for the production of either niobium (also known as columbium) or tantalum. Both are always produced as by-products of the mining of other metals.

The United States is self-sufficient and a net exporter only with respect to molybdenum. It is almost totally dependent on foreign sources for manganese, chromium, nickel, cobalt, niobium, and tantalum, and to a lesser degree for vanadium, tungsten, and titanium.

There are a number of metallic elements that are rare in nature or have relatively limited uses in industry. Most of these have a primary origin in hydrothermal veins or granite pegmatites and are produced either from such deposits (antimony, cadmium, beryllium, bismuth, arsenic, lithium, cesium, rubidium, and mercury) or from placer deposits that resulted from the weathering and erosion of the pegmatites (zirconium, hafnium, thorium, and the rare earth elements). The sole exception is magnesium, which is produced mostly from natural brines in wells and lakes, as at Great Salt Lake in Utah, or from seawater.

Most elements in this group are produced exclusively as by-products of the mining and processing of other metals. Antimony, in the mineral stibnite, is closely associated with lead ores in Mississippi Valley-type deposits, and most antimony is produced as a by-product of the mining and processing of lead, copper, and silver ores. China is the world's leading producer of antimony, and the United States must import most of what it consumes. Cadmium is a trace element that is similar to zinc and therefore substitutes for zinc in some minerals. All cadmium is produced from the mineral sphalerite as a by-product of zinc production. Large but untapped potential resources of cadmium exist in the zinc-bearing coal deposits of the central United States. There are no specific ore minerals of bismuth, and virtually all production is from the processing of residues from lead smelting. Mercury, or quicksilver, is the only metal that is a liquid at ordinary temperatures. It is produced from the sulfide mineral cinnabar and is marketed in steel "flasks," each flask containing 76 pounds of liquid mercury. The mines at Almaden, Spain, have been the leading producers. Magnesium is the lightest metal and is especially strong for its weight. It is an abundant metal, both in the earth's crust and in seawater. Lithium, cesium, and rubidium are often classified as the rare alkali metals, the abundant alkali metals being sodium and potassium. Like magnesium, lithium is abundant enough in brines and evaporite deposits to be processed economically from these sources. The rare earths, or lanthanide elements, are a group of chemically similar elements, of which cerium is the most abundant and widely used. Thorium is a heavy metal, the parent element of a series of radioactive decay products that end in a stable isotope of lead. It is not an abundant element, but it is widespread, occurring in veins, placers, and sedimentary rocks.

The United States is well endowed with some of these minor metals, including beryllium, lithium, magnesium, and the rare earths. On the other hand, it must import virtually all of its supplies of cadmium, bismuth, mercury, arsenic, and rubidium, and one-half of its annual consumption of zirconium and thorium ores and products.

Methods of Study

It is a fair assumption that all the large and easily accessible metallic ore bodies have been discovered. Emphasis in the years ahead will be on the detection of deposits that are in more remote localities, are concealed, or are of lower grade. While research provides more sophisticated tools, the basic exploration approach remains the same. Four main prospecting techniques are employed: geological, geochemical, geophysical, and direct. Geological exploration generally involves plotting the locations of rock types, faults, folds, fractures, and areas of mineralization on base maps. Examples of deposits that have been discovered by simple surface exploration and mapping are chromite, which is resistant to weathering and "crops out"; manganese-bearing minerals, which oxidize to a black color; and molybdenite with its characteristic silver color. Because ore minerals are known to be associated with rocks formed in certain geologic environments, the focus of study today is on understanding such associations as clues to locating mineral deposits.

Geochemical exploration consists of chemically analyzing soil, rock, stream, and vegetation samples. Concentrations of metallic elements in the surface environment are assumed to be representative of similar concentrations in the rocks below. Areas of low mineral potential can be eliminated, while targets for further study and testing can be outlined. In some instances, it is necessary to trace metals back through the surface environment to their points of origin. Research is being done not only on the movement and concentration of the economically important metallic elements, but also on other elements that are often associated with them but that, for various reasons, can be more easily moved and concentrated by nature. Cobalt, for example, is mobile, moving through rocks and sediments easily. It may be possible to trace this element back to its source and in the process locate other associated metals.

Geophysical techniques range from large-scale reconnaissance surveys to detailed local analysis. These techniques detect contrasts in physical properties between the ore bodies and the surrounding host rocks. Airborne magnetic and electromagnetic surveys are useful for rapid coverage of remote and inaccessible terrain and of areas where ore bodies are covered by glacial sediments. Ultrabasic rock bodies with concentrations of magnetic minerals have been located. Some massive sulfide bodies and zinc-bearing laterites will give high gravity readings because they are denser than the host rocks. Radiometric surveys can be used to detect concentrations of radioisotopes and have been effective in locating deposits of thorium, zirconium, and vanadium-bearing minerals. Other applications of geophysical techniques include seismic and gravity studies to determine the thickness of overburden, airborne infrared imagery to detect residual heat in igneous deposits, light reflectance of vegetation, side-looking radar, and aerial and satellite photography. In general, all airborne reconnaissance techniques are followed by detailed geological, geochemical, or geophysical ground surveys.

The final stage in the exploration process is the direct stage. Here, a prospect is directly sampled by drill, pit, trench, or mine to determine its potential. This step is the most expensive. It is the purpose of geological, geochemical, and geophysical prospecting to narrow the possibilities, lower the odds, and thereby reduce the final cost by selecting the most likely prospects for direct sampling.

In addition to the difficulties of exploration, the industrial metals pose other inherent problems. All ore minerals must be processed, and this technology is undergoing constant change. Research continues into the techniques of removing bismuth from smelter products and coal ash and into the recovery of mercury, tungsten, titanium, manganese, chromium, and nickel from low-grade ores and industrial wastes. Innovative techniques are being applied to find new ways to extract magnesium from a variety of natural sources, to increase the efficiency of recovery, and to develop stronger refractories and alloys. Work is being done to develop more uses and better markets for metals such as titanium and thorium that are produced as by-products.

Another research concern involves the manganese nodules which are present on the sea floor as enormous but subeconomic deposits. These provide a potential source of not only manganese, but also of titanium, zirconium, cobalt, nickel, and copper. Once legal questions concerned with ownership and sea-floor mining rights are resolved, the technology must still be developed to dredge the nodules from the sea floor on a large scale and to separate the metallic components into marketable commodities.

Context

Iron, in the form of various specialty steel products, accounts for the great bulk of all metal consumed by industry. There are, however, a number of other metallic commodities that are extensively used, upon which depends the high standard of living enjoyed by modern society—the industrial metals. The principal metals within this group are copper, tin, lead, and zinc, and their uses are many and varied.

The great value of copper derives from its high thermal and electrical conductivities, its corrosion resistance, its ductility, and its strength. It alloys easily, especially with zinc to form brass and with tin and zinc to form bronze. Principal uses of tin are plating on cans and containers, in solder, in bronze, and with nickel in superconducting alloys. Restrictions on the use of lead in pipes and solder should lead to an increase in tin consumption as a lead replacement. Bottle and can deposit laws, enacted in a number of states, will increase the use of scrap (recycled) tin. The principal use of lead is in automobile batteries, but cable sheathing, type metal, and ammunition are other important applications. Zinc uses include galvanizing for iron and steel, die castings, and brass and bronze.

As a group, the economic life of the ferroalloys is closely tied to that of steel.

These elements impart to steel such properties as strength at high temperatures (especially titanium and molybdenum), making them vital for aerospace applications; hardness (tungsten and manganese), for use in armor plate, structural steel, and high-speed cutting tools; and resistance to corrosion (chromium and nickel), for plating. The most important of these elements is manganese, for which there is no substitute. It acts as a scavenger during smelting to remove oxygen and sulfur and it is alloyed with the steel for hardness.

The ferroalloys also find important applications in industry beyond their use in steel. Manganese is widely used in dry batteries, pigments, and fertilizers. Chromium is used in refractory brick for high-temperature furnaces. Molybdenum, nickel, and vanadium compounds are catalysts in a number of chemical processes, and molybdenum is used in industrial lubricants. Tungsten carbide is the hardest cutting and polishing agent after diamond, and metallic tungsten is commonly the filament in electric light bulbs. Titanium oxide is an important pigment. It is opaque and forms the whitest of all paints. Nickel is used in coinage, batteries, and insecticides as well as for plating and catalysts. Cobalt is used in magnetic alloys and as a blue pigment in glass and ceramics. The radioisotope cobalt 60 has a number of medical applications. The rare ferroalloy tantalum is used for capacitors and rectifiers in the electronics industry.

The minor metals have a variety of applications in industry, both as metals and in chemical compounds. Antimony is used primarily as a fire retardant, but it is also alloyed with lead for corrosion resistance and as a hardening agent. This last characteristic is important for military ordnance and cable sheathing. Cadmium is used in the electroplating of steel for corrosion resistance, in solar cells, and as an orange pigment. Beryllium is alloyed with aluminum and copper to provide strength and fatigue resistance and is widely used in the aerospace industry. It is a "nonsparking" metal that can be used in electrical equipment. Oxides of beryllium are found in lasers, as refractories, in ceramics, and as insulators. The principal use of bismuth is in the pharmaceutical industry. It soothes digestive disorders and heals wounds. Salts of bismuth are widely used in cosmetics because of their smoothness. Bismuth metal lowers the melting points of alloys so that they will melt in a hot room. This allows them to be used in automatic water sprinkler systems and in safety plugs and fuses.

Mercury, because it is a liquid at room temperature, has applications in thermometers, electrical switches, and, with rubidium, in vapor lamps. It is also used in insecticides and fungicides and has medical and dental applications. Magnesium is alloyed in aircraft with aluminum to reduce weight and at the same time provide high rigidity and greater strength. The metal also burns at low temperature, which makes it suitable for flash bulbs, fireworks, flares, and incendiary bombs. The largest use of magnesium is in the oxide magnesia for refractory bricks. Arsenic is mostly used in chemical compounds as a wood preservative and in insecticides and herbicides. Lithium-based greases have wide application in aircraft, the military, and the marine environment, as they retain their lubricating properties over a wide temperature range and are resistant to water and hardening. Metallic lithium, as well as magnesium, is alloyed with aluminum for aerospace applications. Cesium is used in magnetohydrodynamic (MHD) electric power generators, in photoelectric cells (automatic door openers), and in solar voltaic cells. Zirconium is used as a refractory in crucibles and brick, as an abrasive and polisher, and for jewelry (cubic zirconium). The rare earth cerium has applications in photography and as a "colorizer" in television tubes. Most of the thorium consumption in the United States is by the nuclear fuel industry.

Bibliography

Evans, Anthony M. *An Introduction to Ore Geology.* 2d ed. Oxford: Blackwell Scientific Publications, 1987. A "slimmed down" text compared to others in the field, intended for undergraduate students and written at a somewhat lower level than most. Emphasis is on types of deposits and their environments of formation, with specific examples. Well illustrated and includes an extensive bibliography.

Hutchison, Charles S. *Economic Deposits and Their Tectonic Setting.* New York: John Wiley & Sons, 1983. This text covers the origin and occurrence of all major types of ore deposits, but from the standpoint of their formation within specific plate tectonic environments (such as oceanic spreading centers and subduction zones). Well illustrated, with numerous examples and an extensive bibliography. In addition, there is a brief summary of each of the important mineral resources. Can be read with understanding by a geologic novice.

Jensen, Mead L., and Alan M. Bateman. *Economic Mineral Deposits.* 3d rev. ed. New York: John Wiley & Sons, 1981. Although older, this text is probably the most complete and at the same time the most understandable. Contains good introductory chapters on the origins of ore minerals, followed by well-written descriptions of each of the individual metallic and nonmetallic resources. An excellent reference and one that can easily be used by a beginner.

Lamey, C. A. *Metallic and Industrial Mineral Deposits.* New York: McGraw-Hill, 1966. An older, but standard, reference in the field, which may still be used profitably. Includes an initial summary of geologic origins of mineral deposits, followed by a discussion of each individual mineral resource. This style of organization makes the book easier to use if the reader is interested in information about a particular commodity. Suitable for the reader with a limited geological background.

U.S. Bureau of Mines. *Mineral Commodity Summaries, 1987.* Washington, D.C.: Government Printing Office, 1987. This volume contains up-to-date summaries for eighty-eight nonfuel mineral commodities. For each, information is presented on use; domestic production; price; import quantities, sources, and tariffs; depletion allowances (if any); recycling; stockpiles; world production and reserve base; world resources; significant trends and events; and possible industrial substitutes. Most information is given in tabular summaries. An excellent source of information for research at any level.

_____. *Minerals Yearbook, 1986*. Vol. 1, *Metals and Minerals*. Washington, D.C.: Government Printing Office, 1988. The latest in a series of yearly summary of the various metallic and nonmetallic resources. Information on each commodity includes uses, consumers, domestic and world production figures, import and export data, prices, and technological advances. The book includes voluminous tables and charts and is probably the finest source of data for economic mineral study at any level.

U.S. Geological Survey. *United States Mineral Resources*. Professional Paper 820. Washington, D.C.: Government Printing Office, 1973. This volume includes an excellent summary for each mineral resource. Some of the data are obsolete, but the summaries are much more complete than those of the Bureau of Mines publications. For each resource, an extensive discussion includes uses, environmental problems, history of exploitation, ore minerals and geologic occurrence, reserves and resources, prospecting techniques, and research methods. An extensive bibliography is included for each resource. Some tables and graphs are included, but no illustrations or diagrams. An excellent source of information, especially for those with some background in geology.

Donald J. Thompson

Cross-References

Aluminum Deposits, 46; Elemental Distribution in the Earth, 391; Gold and Silver, 975; Hydrothermal Mineralization, 1108; Igneous and Contact Metamorphic Mineral Deposits, 1124; Iron Deposits, 1254; Manganese Nodules, 1459; Pegmatites, 2025; Platinum Group Metals, 2086; Earth Resources, 2175; Future Resources, 2182; Strategic Resources, 2188; Sedimentary Mineral Deposits, 2296; Weathering and Erosion, 2723.

INDUSTRIAL NONMETALS

Type of earth science: Economic geology

The nonmetallic earth resources consist of fertilizer minerals, raw materials for the chemical industry, abrasives, gemstones, and building materials for the construction industry. Although these substances mostly lack the glamour of gold and platinum or oil and uranium, they provide the necessary base for a technological society.

Principal terms

ASBESTOSIS: deterioration of the lungs caused by the inhalation of very fine particles of asbestos dust

CATALYST: a chemical substance that speeds up a chemical reaction without being permanently affected by that reaction

GUANO: fossilized bird excrement, found in great abundance on some coasts or islands

METAL: a shiny element or alloy that conducts heat and/or electricity; metals are both malleable and ductile

PROVEN RESERVE: a reserve supply of a valuable mineral substance that can be exploited at a future time

SEDIMENTARY ROCK: rock formed from the accumulation of fragments weathered from preexisting rocks or by the precipitation of dissolved materials in water

STAR SAPPHIRE/RUBY: a gem that has a starlike effect when viewed in reflected light because of fibrous structure within the mineral

STRATEGIC RESOURCE: an earth resource, such as manganese or oil, that would be essential to a nation's defense in wartime

Summary of the Phenomenon

The modern, technological society is heavily dependent for its existence on a wide variety of earth resources. Dependence on these resources came about very gradually at first, then with great rapidity during the Industrial Revolution, beginning in the mid-eighteenth century. These essential earth resources are divided by the economic geologist into three categories: metals, nonmetals, and energy resources.

The definition of a nonmetal is problematic. To the chemist, a nonmetal is any element not having the character of a metal, including solid elements, such as carbon and sulfur, and gaseous elements, such as nitrogen and oxygen. That is the definition found in most dictionaries. To the economic geologist, however, a nonmetal is any solid material extracted from the earth that is neither a metal nor a source of energy. It is valued because of the nonmetallic chemical elements that it contains or because it has some highly desirable physical or chemical characteristic.

Economic geologists consider the following to be major nonmetallic earth resources: fertilizers, raw materials for the chemical industry, abrasives, gemstones, and building materials. As can readily be seen, with the exception of the gemstones, the nonmetallic earth resources lack the glamour associated with metals such as gold and platinum or energy sources such as oil and uranium. Nevertheless, nonmetallic earth resources play an essential role in the world economy.

Except for gemstones, the nonmetallic earth resources have certain common characteristics. First, they tend to be more abundant in the earth's crust than the metals and are therefore lower in price. Nevertheless, most of them are needed in much larger quantities, so the total value of the substances produced is considerable. That is particularly true of the building materials needed for the construction industry. Second, nonmetallic earth materials tend to be taken from local sources. Most of them are needed in such large quantities that transportation costs would be excessive if they were brought long distances. As a result, regional variations occur in the types of rock used for building stone and crushed rock. Third, problems of supply are not generally associated with nonmetallic earth materials. Most of them are fairly abundant at the earth's surface, and few major industrial nations are without deposits of each of them. None of these resources is classified as a strategic material by the United States, for example. Finally, nonmetallic earth materials tend to require very little processing before being sent to market. In fact, most of them are used in the raw state.

The first category of major nonmetallic earth resources is the fertilizers. These substances are absolutely essential to a nation's agriculture and therefore to its food supply. The three most important elements for plant growth are nitrogen, potassium, and phosphorus. For years, nitrogen was obtained from nitrogen-rich earth materials—either from the famous guano deposits in Peru, which were built up by accumulated bird droppings on coastal islands, or from the nitrate deposits in Chile, which cover the floor of a desert. In 1900, however, a German chemist discovered a way of manufacturing nitrates synthetically, using nitrogen extracted directly from the atmosphere. Today, the synthetic nitrate industry provides 99.8 percent of the world's nitrogen needs.

The potassium required for fertilizers was originally obtained from wood ashes, and in many underdeveloped nations, it still is. In 1857, however, potassium-bearing salt beds were discovered in Germany. These had formed as a result of the evaporation of lakes in an arid climate, and they were the world's major source of potassium until 1915, when Germany placed a wartime embargo on their shipment. This embargo forced other countries to explore for replacement deposits, and similar salt beds were eventually found in the Soviet Union, Canada, and the western United States.

The third element required for fertilizers, phosphorus, was originally obtained from guano or from bones. These sources have been replaced by natural phosphate rock deposits, which are widely distributed around the world. Most of these deposits occur in marine sedimentary rocks, and it is believed that deposition of the phosphate resulted when cool, phosphorus-bearing waters upwelled from the sea floor and were carried into shallow environments, where the phosphorus was precipitated. The largest U.S. phosphate deposits are found in Florida and North Carolina.

The second major category of nonmetallic earth resources is that made up of the raw materials for the chemical industry. In terms of total production, the most important of these is salt, for which the mineral name is halite. In addition to its use as a dietary ingredient, salt is the raw material from which a number of important chemicals are made, including chlorine gas, hydrochloric acid, and lye. In colder climates, salt is also used for snow and ice control on roads. Salt is produced by the evaporation of seawater and by the mining of underground salt deposits. Although underground salt commonly occurs as deeply buried layers, nature has an interesting way of bringing the salt to the surface. Since salt is lighter in weight than the overlying rocks and is capable of plastic flow, it rises through the surrounding rocks as a salt plug with a circular cross section, known as a salt dome. Salt domes are particularly common along the Louisiana and Texas Gulf Coast.

Another important raw material for the chemical industry is sulfur, a soft yellow substance that burns with a blue flame. The major industrial use for sulfur is in the production of sulfuric acid. Large quantities of sulfuric acid are used in converting phosphate rock to fertilizer. Sulfur also has important uses in the manufacture of insecticides. Most of the sulfur used in the United States comes from the salt domes of the Louisana and Texas coast, where it is found in the upper part of the dome. Superheated steam is pumped down through drill holes to melt the sulfur, and the liquid sulfur is then brought to the surface by the pressure of compressed air. Additional raw materials for the chemical industry include several that are obtained from the beds of dry desert lakes: sodium carbonate and sodium sulfate, which are used in the manufacture of glass, soaps, dyes, and paper; and borax, which is used in making detergents. Another product is sodium bicarbonate, the familiar baking soda.

The third major category of nonmetallic earth resources is the abrasives, which are materials used for grinding, cleaning, polishing, and removing solid material from other substances. Most abrasives are very hard, but those used for cleaning porcelain sinks and silverware need to be fairly soft, so as not to scratch. Abrasives can be either natural or man-made. The natural abrasives are rock and mineral substances that have been extracted from the earth and that are then either used in the raw state, such as a block of pumice, or pulverized and bonded into sandpapers, wheels, saws, drill bits, and the like. Artificially made abrasives, however, are gradually coming to dominate the market.

The most common abrasive is diamond, which has a hardness of 10 on a scale of 1 to 10 and is the hardest known natural substance. Most natural diamonds are unsuitable for use as gems, however, so about 80 percent of them are used as abrasives. In 1955, General Electric developed a process to make industrial diamonds synthetically, and by 1986 two-thirds of the world's industrial diamonds were produced synthetically. Other important natural abrasives include corundum, the second hardest natural substance, with a hardness of 9; emery, a gray-to-black mixture of corundum and the iron mineral known as magnetite; and garnet, a reddish-brown mineral, with a hardness of approximately 7, that is commonly used in sandpaper. Ninety-five percent of the world's garnet comes from the Adirondack Mountains in New York State.

The fourth major category of nonmetallic earth resources is the gemstones. These are used primarily for adornment and decoration. Unlike the other nonmetals, they are generally not abundant, have a moderate-to-high value, come in small quantities only, are rarely of local origin, and are often in short supply. Desirable properties in a gem are color, brilliance, transparency, hardness, and rarity. Gems are categorized into two principal groups. The precious gems are diamond, ruby, sapphire, emerald, and pearl. All of these can be produced synthetically, except for high-quality gem diamonds. Ruby and sapphire are varieties of corundum and may exhibit "stars." Emerald is a variety of beryl wth a hardness of 7½ to 8. Pearls have a hardness of 3 and are technically not true minerals, because they are produced by a living organism. The semiprecious gems include some one hundred different substances. Most are minerals, except for amber (hardened resin from a pine tree), jet (a dense variety of coal), and black coral (a substance produced by a living organism).

The fifth major category of nonmetallic earth resources is building materials for the construction industry. They include the familiar building stones obtained from quarries, such as granite, sandstone, limestone, marble, and slate. There is also a high demand for crushed rock, which is used in highway roadbeds, and for concrete aggregate. Sand and gravel are also used in making concrete. In addition, many useful products are prepared from earth materials, such as cement, which is made from a mixture of limestone and clay; plaster, which comes from the mineral gypsum; brick and ceramics, which use clay as their raw material; glass, which is made from very pure sand or sandstone rock; and asbestos, which is obtained from flame-resistant mineral fibers that can be woven into fireproof cloth or mixed with other substances to make fireproof roofing shingles and floor tiles. Concerns about health hazards related to the use of asbestos arose in the 1970's. The very fine particles of asbestos dust can lodge in the lungs, causing asbestosis and lung cancer. As a result, the U.S. consumption of asbestos has declined markedly since the 1970's.

Methods of Study

An important way in which nonmetallic earth resources are studied is through the analysis of current production trends and usage figures. In this way, nations can determine the extent to which they rely on imports to meet their needs for specific nonmetallic resources. In 1980, for example, the United States imported 85 percent of the asbestos it used. Given the health hazards involved in mining and processing asbestos, however, and the rapidly declining consumption of asbestos, this statistic is probably not an alarming one.

One can also analyze the proven reserves of the various nonmetallic earth resources. Proven reserves are supplies of a mineral substance that still remain in the ground and are available to be taken out at some future time. When experts compare the present rates of production of various nonmetallic earth resources with the proven reserves of these substances, they can predict which resources may someday be in short supply. In the case of the phosphate rock used in making fertilizers, for example, analysts have found that the United States' phosphate reserves will be exhausted around the year 2010. In 1985, the United States was the world's largest exporter of phosphate; by 2010, it will be the world's largest importer. Clearly, a major exploration program is necessary.

Economic geologists also study ways to assure that adequate supplies of nonmetallic earth resources will be available for future needs. In the case of phosphate, for example, the need for such studies is critical. Such a program of exploration for new phosphate supplies, or for any other nonmetallic resource, must begin with a full understanding of the ways in which the mineral resource originates. Only when geologists understand the conditions under which valuable concentrations of mineral substances form can they successfully search for them.

In the case of phosphate, careful scientific study has shown that the cold waters found in the deep ocean contain thirty times as much dissolved phosphorus as do the warm shallow waters. This observation suggests that when the cold, deep waters are brought to the surface and warmed, by upwelling from the ocean floor and flowing across shallow submarine banks into coastal zones, the warming effect makes the phosphorus less soluble, and it precipitates. As a result, scientists are exploring for phosphates along present or former continental margins, where such upwelling might have taken place.

Another way in which adequate future supplies of nonmetallic earth resources can be assured is by creating nonmetals synthetically in the laboratory. A good example of this process was the successful synthesis of industrial diamonds by General Electric in 1955. Before then, the United States had no industrial diamond production or reserves and was totally dependent on supplies purchased in the world market, which was controlled by the De Beers group of companies in South Africa. General Electric was able to create diamonds synthetically by subjecting the mineral graphite—which is composed of pure carbon, as is diamond—to incredibly high temperatures and pressures in a special sealed vessel, using molten nickel as a catalyst. By 1986, two-thirds of the world's industrial diamonds were being produced by this process, and the De Beers monopoly on industrial diamond production was broken.

Context

The United States is fortunate in having a plentiful food supply, and most Americans rarely think about the importance of fertilizers. They are essential, however, for successful agricultural operations. Plant growth requires ample mineral matter, partly decomposed organic matter (humus), water, air, and sunlight. Of these, mineral matter is crucial, because it provides the nitrates and phosphates essential for healthy plant growth. These substances are quickly used or washed away, and they must be replenished regularly so that the soil does not become worn out and infertile. Worn-out soils are frequently encountered in developing nations, where farmers are often too poor to buy fertilizers.

Industrial chemicals such as salt, sulfur, and borax appear on grocery shelves in their pure state, but they are also present as ingredients in products where one would never suspect their existence. In addition, they are frequently needed to manufacture everyday products, such as drinking glasses or writing paper. Salt is a good example. In addition to its use as table salt, it is also an ingredient in almost every prepared food item on the grocery shelf: soup, nuts, bread, crackers, canned meats, bottled olives, frozen dinners. . . . The list goes on almost indefinitely. Abrasives, too, are common on grocery shelves, although the word abrasive may not be written on the package. They are in toothpaste, silver polish, bathroom cleanser, pumice stones, sandpaper, and emery boards.

Nonmetals are used in many common construction materials. The beautiful white buildings in Washington, D.C., are made of pure white Vermont marble. Granite, on the other hand, is preferred for tombstones, because it resists weathering better. It is also used for curbstones in northern cities, because it holds up best under the repeated impacts from snowplow blades. The day of buildings faced with cut stone, however, is on the wane; production and transportation costs are simply too high. Today's private dwelling is more likely to be built of cinder blocks, manufactured at a plant outside the city, and downtown office towers are sheathed with walls of glass and prefabricated concrete.

Bibliography

Bartholomew, John C., ed. *The Times Atlas of the World*. New York: Times Books, 1980. An overview entitled "Resources of the World" is followed by a large world minerals map printed in eight colors. It shows the world distribution of diamonds, chemical and fertilizer minerals, asbestos, clay, magnesite, and talc. The relative importance of each mineral deposit is indicated. Suitable for high school students.

Bramwell, M., ed. *The Rand McNally Atlas of the Oceans*. Skokie, Ill.: Rand McNally, 1977. A well-written and beautifully illustrated atlas. The section entitled "The Great Resource" has an excellent discussion of nonmetallic resources that can be obtained from the sea, such as phosphorite, salt, sulfur, diamond, shell sands, sand, and gravel. There are color photographs, maps, and line drawings. Suitable for high school students.

Craig, J. R., D. J. Vaughan, and B. J. Skinner. *Resources of the Earth*. Englewood Cliffs, N.J.: Prentice-Hall, 1988. A well-illustrated text with numerous black-and-white photographs, color plates, tables, charts, maps, and line drawings. It covers the major categories of nonmetallic earth resources: fertilizer minerals, chemical minerals, abrasives, gemstones, and building materials. Suitable for college-level readers or the interested layperson.

Fisher, P. J. *The Science of Gems*. New York: Charles Scribner's Sons, 1966. This book has excellent color photographs of the well-known gems. Topics covered include the history of gems, their origins, their characteristics, gem cutting, and gem identification. There is also a glossary of terms and a useful appendix giving detailed information relating to each type of gem. Written for general audiences.

Jensen, M. L., and A. M. Bateman. *Economic Mineral Deposits*. 3d ed. New York: John Wiley & Sons, 1979. This economic geology text provides detailed information on the different metallic and nonmetallic mineral deposits and their modes of formation. There are excellent sections on the history of mineral use and the exploration and development of mineral properties. Cross sections of individual deposits are provided. Suitable for college-level readers.

Skinner, B. J. *Earth Resources*. 3d ed. Englewood Cliffs, N.J.: Prentice-Hall, 1986. An excellent overview of the earth's nonmetallic resources. It is well written and contains helpful line drawings, maps, tables, and charts, although photographs are few. There are suggestions for further reading and a list of the principal nonmetallic minerals and their production figures for 1982. For college-level readers.

Tennissen, A. C. *The Nature of Earth Materials*. 2d ed. Englewood Cliffs, N.J.: Prentice-Hall, 1983. This useful reference book contains detailed descriptions of 110 common minerals, with a black-and-white photograph of each. Chapter 7, entitled "Utility of Earth Materials," contains helpful sections on the distribution of mineral deposits and the utilization of various earth materals. Suitable for the layperson.

Donald W. Lovejoy

Cross-References

Building Stone, 178; Cement, 196; Diamonds, 362; Evaporites, 631; Fertilizers, 706; Gem Minerals, 802; Igneous and Contact Metamorphic Mineral Deposits, 1124; Earth Resources, 2175; Future Resources, 2182; Strategic Resources, 2188; Sand, 2253; Sedimentary Mineral Deposits, 2296.

INFRARED SPECTRA

Type of earth science: Geochemistry
Field of study: Analytical techniques

The infrared spectrum is part of the electromagnetic spectrum that lies beyond the red color that human eyes perceive as visible light. Every body emits some energy in the infrared or near infrared. Detection of infrared radiation by special instruments can be applied to various fields, including medicine, mapping, defense, communication, and astronomy.

Principal terms

ANGSTROM: a unit of wavelength of light equal to one ten-billionth of a meter

MACROSCOPIC: large enough to be observed by the naked eye

PHOTON: a quantum of radiant energy

SPECTROGRAPH: an instrument for dispersing radiation (as electromagnetic radiation) into a spectrum and photographing or mapping the spectrum

SPECTROMETER: an instrument used in determining the index of refraction; a spectroscope fitted for measurements of the observed spectra

SPECTROPHOTOMETER: a photometer for measuring the relative intensities of the light in different parts of a spectrum

SPECTROSCOPY: the subdiscipline of physics that deals with the theory and interpretation of the interactions of matter and radiation (as electromagnetic radiation)

SPECTRUM: an array of the components of an emission or wave separated and arranged in the order of some varying characteristic (such as wavelength, mass, or energy)

SPECTRUM ANALYSIS: the determination of the constitution of bodies and substances by means of the spectra they produce

Summary of the Methodology

The small bands of infrared radiation seeping through the atmosphere were accidentally discovered in 1800 by William Herschel; when measuring the temperatures of the visible light spectra, he found a source of greater heat and wavelength radiation beyond the color red. It was not until 1881, however, when Samuel Pierpont Langley developed the bolometer, that the first in-depth studies of the infrared were possible. Max Planck's development of the quantum theory and his discovery of photons in 1900 led to the development of quantum detectors, which further advanced the study of the infrared; these early detectors have resulted in the modern spectroscopes, spectrometers, and spectrophotometers. The electromagnetic spectrum comprises visible light and five forms of invisible radiation: radio, infrared, ultraviolet, X, and gamma rays. All spectra travel at the speed of light in waves of energy bundles called photons and can be reflected, refracted, transmitted, absorbed, and emitted.

Infrared spectrometry encompasses the study of wavelengths in the electromagnetic spectrum that range between 0.7 microns in the near-infrared photographic region and 500 microns in the far-infrared rotation region. Wavelengths of the infrared spectra are most useful for detecting certain atoms and ions visible only in the infrared, such as hydrogen, the most abundant element in the universe. Infrared rays differ from the other components of the electromagnetic spectrum: Radio waves are propagated through the atmosphere and have a wavelength of between 30,000 meters and 1 millimeter; X rays are extremely short wavelengths, approximately 1 angstrom unit, and are generated by a sudden change in the velocity of an electrical charge; gamma rays are similar to X rays but are of a higher frequency and penetrating power; ultraviolet rays are beyond violet in the spectrum and have wavelengths shorter than 400 angstrom units.

Infrared radiation is emitted in some amount by every macroscopic body in the universe that has a temperature above absolute zero (or -273 degrees Celsius). In each macroscopic body, molecules not only are moving in all directions but also are rotating, and at the same time the individual atoms within the molecule are vibrating with respect to one another. It is the interaction of molecules with radiation that is the essence of the study of infrared.

For a molecule to absorb radiation, it must have a vibrational or rotational frequency the same as that of the electromagnetic radiation. In addition, a change in the magnitude and/or direction of the dipole moment must take place. The dipole moment is a vector that is oriented from the center of gravity of the positive charges to that of the negative charges, and it is defined as the product of the size and the distance between these charges. Corresponding frequencies between radiation and molecules are possible because radiation, in addition to having a magnetic component, has an electrical component. On the other hand, a molecule has an electrical field. When the electrical field of the molecule is rotating or vibrating at the same frequency as is the incoming radiation, then it is possible for a transfer of energy to take place.

The second requirement for the study of infrared, the dipole moment change, must have something to couple the energy from the radiation to the molecule. If atoms differ in their electronegativity and they combine to form a molecule, the centers of the positive and negative electrical charges may not coincide, producing a permanent dipole moment; the energy to produce this work can come from the absorption of the incoming radiation by the molecule. A permanent dipole is also necessary for inducing rotation. Rotation is accomplished by the fact that the electric fields are not the same on each side, thereby allowing for a transfer of energy; when energy is transferred in this manner, a rotator will rotate faster under certain rotational frequencies, while a vibrator will not change its frequency but will increase its amplitude of vibration. Because vibrational frequencies are of the order of 10^{14} cycles per second and rotational frequencies are 10^{11} cycles, they fall within the infrared region. Absorption bands for rotational spectra are quite sharp, but the bands for vibrational spectra tend to become broader because of the rotational levels associated with each vibrational level.

Detectors, either thermal or quantum, are commonly used to study the infrared. Each type uses a different property of electromagnetic radiation to convert the infrared to an electrical signal with intensity equivalent to the amount of infrared striking the detector. A thermal detector measures heat-induced changes in a property of a material, usually electrical resistance. A quantum detector also measures change, although it uses a photon, not heat, to create successive events when it strikes a material. There are three types of quantum detectors, and each one uses a separation, or diffusion, of different types of electrons as a catalyst for an event. In brief, the photoconductive effect uses incidental radiation to increase electrical conductivity, the photovoltaic effect uses a special junction for diffusion which creates voltage from charge separation, and the photoelectromagnetic effect uses radiation falling on a semiconductor with a magnetic field. In addition to detectors, there are various other instruments used in the study and application of the infrared, such as the radiometer, the comparator, the collimeter, and modulators, all of which perform unique and valuable tasks.

Applications of the Method

Basic for understanding how the infrared spectra works is the spectrometer. All spectrometers use certain elementary components: namely, a source of radiation, a condensing source for focusing energy onto the monochromatic (pertaining to one color or one wavelength) slit, a monochromator to isolate a narrow spectral range, a radiation detector, and some form of amplifying system and output recorder. Single-beam spectrometers record energy versus wavelength, whereas a double-beam spectrometer measures the ratio between energy transmitted by the sample and energy incident on the sample, and plot transmittance or a related quantity as a function of wavelength or wavenumber. One micron is equal to one-millionth of a meter, and wavenumber is obtained by dividing 10,000 by the wavelengths in microns.

An application of the method can be illustrated by emission spectrography, which allows the determination of major, minor, and trace elements in many materials. Approximately seventy elements can be determined in rocks and other geologic materials. When a sample of material is correctly excited by an electric arc or a spark, each element in the sample emits light of a characteristic wavelength. The light enters the spectrograph via a narrow opening and falls on a diffraction grating, which is a band of equidistant parallel lines (from ten thousand to thirty thousand or more to the inch) ruled on a surface of glass or polished metal used for obtaining optical spectra. The grating separates the reflected light of each wavelength by a different angle. The dispersed light is focused and registered on a photographic plate in the form of lines of the spectrum.

The comparator-densitometer is used to measure the intensity, or darkness, of the spectrum lines registered on the spectrograph photographic plate. Using standard films or plates for each element, scientists change the spectrograph markings to indicate the percent concentration of each element. For a visual estimate, a special screen permits a comparison of the spectrum of the sample with the spectra of standards containing known element concentrations. A direct-reading emission spectrometer is one that is tied in with a computer in which are stored electronic signals from specific parts of the spectrum during the burn of a sample. The stored signals are emitted in sequence to an electronic system that measures the intensities of the spectral lines.

The widest applications for the infrared spectra are in remote sensing, which is the process of detecting chemical and physical properties of an area by measuring its reflected and emitted radiation. Infrared is related to geophysics, geomorphology, structural geology, and exploration as well as to geochemistry. Specific areas in which the infrared spectra have been used in geochemical research include the study of the bonds between atoms in minerals and the gaining of unique information on features of the structure, including the family of minerals to which the specimen belongs, the mixture of isomorphic substituents, the distinction of molecular water from the constitutional hydroxyl, the degree of regularity in the structure, and the presence of both crystalline and noncrystalline impurities. For example, chalcedony, including flint, chert, and agate, has been shown by infrared spectroscopy and X-ray studies to contain hydroxyl in structural sites as well as in several types of nonstructural water that can be held by internal surfaces and pores. The content of the structural hydroxyl varies zonally in chalcedony fibers and in both natural and synthetic crystals of the same spectral type as chalcedony. The varieties of chalcedony, as well as rock crystal and amethyst formed at low temperatures and in association with chalcedony, together with crystals of synthetic quartz, show a distinctive infrared absorption spectrum in the region of 2.78-3.12 microns; natural quartz crystals formed at higher temperatures give a spectrum in this region. Structural hydroxyl is housed by different mechanisms in the two types of quartz. The fibrose nature of the low-temperature quartz may derive from the hydroxyl content and its effect on dislocations.

Remote sensing has been a great aid to geologists in their study of the earth. Thermal infrared scanning has been used to monitor and update mine waste embankment data and to locate faults and fracture zones. Landsat thematic mapper and airborne thermal infrared multispectral scanner data have been used to do surface rock mapping in Nevada. Advanced visible and infrared imaging spectrometers and other remotely sensed data have been used to locate water-producing zones beneath the surface in parts of the Great Plains region. Infrared reflectance surveys have been used to locate an extinct hot spring system in the Idaho batholith. Infrared surveys have also included quantitative measurement of thermal radiation from localized heat-flow in Long Valley, California, as well as surveys of the lava dome on Mount St. Helens, Washington. Reflectance variations related to petrographic texture and impurities of carbonate rocks have been analyzed by visible and near-infrared spectra.

Context

On a large-scale, national defense system, infrared is used in secret communications, night reconnaissance, missile guidance, and gun sitings and tracking. Weather and pollution control are accomplished by using infrared to detect levels of radiation and chemicals. The use of infrared in medicine is associated with finding hot areas on the surface of the human body as indicative of possible areas of disease. Studies have revealed positive applications in the detection of, for example, breast cancer, skin burns, frostbite, tumors, abscesses, and appendicitis. As an analyzer, infrared can pinpoint damage in semiconductors that results from overheating. It can also study electrical circuit performance while in operation, detect underrated components in regular circuits, and predict component failure or shortened lifetime: These uses are only a few that demonstrate infrared's analytical ability. In space technology, infrared can be used in telescopes for locating new cosmic bodies, observing star formation, studying planet temperatures, and determining the chemical and/or physical nature of distant sources of infrared radiation. Other major uses of infrared include detecting forest infiltrations and spotting welding defects; other fields that utilize infrared include photography and organic chemistry.

The widest application of the infrared is in the field of remote sensing. Infrared surveys and photography of volcanic zones around Mauna Loa and Kilauea were used to obtain information impossible to gather from the ground. The effects of the 1977 earthquake in Nicaragua were surveyed by infrared photography in order to find access and evacuation routes as well as safe areas for temporary camps; in addition, the photographs provided geomorphological information for future study. Infrared surveying has been used to study California's San Andreas fault. In one section near the Indio Hills, the fault trace is not topographically distinguishable but can be located by a margin of vegetation on the northeast side of the fault. Infrared sensing verified its location by imaging a band of alluvium kept cool by the water dammed up by the displaced rock.

Miscellaneous uses of infrared are as widely varied as the major uses already discussed. Infrared photography can reveal original charcoal sketches under oil paintings. Ecologists can study the thermodynamic world on the planet and observe the animals and plants as they adapt to the volatile thermal balance. They can also track schools of fish by mapping "warm" areas on the water's surface. Criminologists and police can use night vision to survey high crime areas in the dark without the use of a spotlight. Warm air masses associated with turbulence can be detected and avoided, resulting in smoother, safer airplane flights. Infrared studies are contributing to improved telecommunications as a result of the introduction of fiber optics, which uses glass as opposed to copper and other scarce metals. Other uses of the infrared are highly technical and are found in many fields, including geology, biology, agriculture, engineering, and defense.

Bibliography

Bernard, Burton. *ABC's of Infrared*. New York: Howard W. Sams, 1970. Bernard's book deals mostly with the theory and application of infrared but also includes segments on physics and optics. Written in the format of a college-level textbook, with questions at the ends of the chapters. While technical data are included, any reader can follow the carefully explained examples.

Brownlow, Arthur H. *Geochemistry*. Englewood Cliffs, N.J.: Prentice-Hall, 1979. This book is intended as an introductory text on geochemistry. Each chapter is devoted to a specific area of geochemistry. Pertinent chemical principles and concepts are reviewed. The basic data are summarized, and examples of applications to geological problems are given.

Conn, George Keith. *Infrared Methods, Principles, and Applications*. New York: Academic Press, 1960. An introduction to infrared studies, this book is divided into two parts: principles of the chief components used in studying the infrared region and practical applications. Although the text is heavily weighted in mathematics and physics, it can be understood by the layperson.

Gibson, Henry Louis. *Photography by Infrared: Its Principles and Applications*. 3d ed. New York: Wiley, 1978. This book's main topic is infrared photography. There are some aspects of indirect longwave infrared recording in which the image is formed by electronic or other means and copied on ordinary film. Discusses how infrared photography can be used by geologists and geomorphologists.

Sabins, Floyd F. *Remote Sensing: Principles and Interpretation*. San Francisco: W. H. Freeman, 1978. This book is an overview of remote sensing for people with no previous training in that process. The presentation attempts to strike a balance between the physical principles that control remote sensing and the practical interpretation and use of the imagery for a variety of applications. The first chapter summarizes the important characteristics of electromagnetic radiation and the reactions with matter that are basic to all forms of remote sensing.

Siegal, Frederick R. *Applied Geochemistry*. New York: Wiley, 1975. A very good general text on applied geochemistry, with a brief discussion of emission spectrography. Written in an understandable format for the layperson, requiring a minimum background in mathematics and chemistry. Very good references.

Strahler, Alan H., and Arthur N. Strahler. *Environmental Geoscience: Interaction Between Natural Systems and Man*. Santa Barbara: Hamilton, 1973. A college text on a basic introductory level, this book contains good illustrations and general information on the earth sciences.

Earl G. Hoover

Cross-References

IO

Type of earth science: Planetology
Field of study: Large solar system bodies

Io, one of Jupiter's four Galilean moons, has one of the most unusual planetary surfaces in the known solar system. Most of the knowledge concerning Io was obtained by the Pioneer and Voyager spacecraft that flew through the Jovian system.

Principal terms

CALDERA: a volcanic crater caused primarily by collapse; it may or may not have a raised rim generated by eruptive processes

GALILEAN MOONS: the four largest moons of Jupiter, discovered by Galileo in the seventeenth century

INTERVENT PLAINS: regions between active volcanic areas where fallout from plumes is deposited

LAYERED PLAINS: smooth, flat regions believed to be composed of materials other than sulfur compounds

MOUNTAIN MATERIAL: high-standing blocks of rugged relief

VENTS: calderas and fissures from which gaseous material from the interior may escape through the surface

VOLCANIC PLUMES: material thrown up from the surface by eruptions; they indicate high volcanic activity

VOYAGER: the name of several unmanned spacecraft that flew through the Jovian system, relaying high-resolution photographs and other experimental data to Earth

Summary of the Phenomenon

Io is the fifth most distant of Jupiter's known moons. Io's orbit is essentially circular, with a radius of 442,000 kilometers and an inclination of only 0.03 degree with respect to the Jovian equator. It has a mass of 8.89×10^{22} kilograms (1.5 percent of the earth's mass) and a 1,820-kilometer radius. Io revolves around Jupiter every 1.769 days. It takes the satellite the same amount of time to rotate around its axis; thus, it continually presents the same face toward Jupiter, in the same way that the Moon does to Earth, as it completes its orbital motion. Io's mean density is 3,530 kilograms per cubic meter; it has an albedo, or reflectivity, of 0.63. Escape velocity at Io's surface is 2.56 kilometers per second. Io has a tenuous atmosphere composed mainly of sulfur dioxide.

Even at 1-kilometer resolution, photographs of Io are not able to indicate evidence of impact cratering. Io should have received the greatest flux of impact-crater-producing debris of the four Galilean moons, because of the focusing effect of Jovian gravity. Yet, instead of a highly pockmarked look (like that of Callisto, the outermost of the Galilean moons), Io presents one of the youngest surfaces in the solar system, a surface constantly reworked by volcanic activity.

Eruptions spew from fresh volcanoes, spreading plumes of sulfur high above the Ionian surface. These plumes, umbrella-like in shape because of a lack of atmospheric interference, distribute fresh material that covers the effects of older volcanic eruptions. As active volcanoes become extinct, new ones arise to continue the resurfacing process. Extensive surface flows are evident on Io, spreading out from dark volcanic areas in fans roughly 100 kilometers wide or winding out in long, sinuous lines. Volcanic flows can be lighter or darker in color than the surrounding material. Volcanic eruptions deposit an average of one meter of material every one thousand years, thereby obliterating any record of the era of intense impact cratering.

The volcanic centers, dark regions more than 10 kilometers wide, are generally surrounded by irregular halos nearly as dark as the centers themselves. Circular, oval, or heart-shaped markings surround many of the large volcanoes. These areas are likely condensed sulfur or sulfur dioxide deposited on the surface around active volcanic centers, like the ejecta blankets produced by impact craters.

Sulfur is a nonmetallic element (atomic number 16 and atomic weight 32.06) common on the earth. Sulfur has two crystalline forms: a yellow rhombic phase that is stable below 96 degrees Celsius and a pale-yellow monoclinic phase that is stable between 96 and 119 degrees. It also has an amorphous phase that forms when molten sulfur cools rapidly. The latter phase exhibits colors ranging from red to black and when cooled becomes syrupy and gumlike. On Io's surface are yellowish, red, orange, black, and white regions resulting from various forms of sulfur and sulfur compounds. (Sulfur dioxide on Io's surface is white.)

Sulfur is also found surrounding Io. A cloud of sodium gas was detected in the vicinity of Io before the Voyager program began. This "flux tube" is composed primarily of sulfur, sodium, and oxygen and is spread out along Io's orbit. This formation is easy to understand in terms of the relationship of average molecular speeds for given temperatures to the escape velocity from Io. The average surface temperature on Io is 125 to 135 Kelvins. The temperature of warm spots is 270 to 310 Kelvins, and the temperatures of active erupting regions vary between 385 and 600 Kelvins. One can calculate the average speeds of sulfur in these regions: 317 meters per second on average, 474 meters per second in the warm spots, and 546 to 681 meters per second in active regions. Given the ratio of these speeds to Io's surface escape speed, 2,560 meters per second, significant amounts of sulfur gas will be lost to space. The escape velocity from Jupiter at the distance of Io's orbit, however, is 24,500 meters per second. Therefore, sulfur liberated from Io (and having an orbital speed of 17,320 meters per second) cannot escape totally and becomes trapped along the orbit of Io in a torus with a width equal to several times the diameter of Io. A similar argument can be made for the loss of lighter elements that Io may once have had. Over the eons, lighter elements have escaped, leaving Io with a greater density than the other Galilean moons.

Io's surface physiography can be separated into three categories: plains, vent-related features, and mountains. Although plains and vents are certainly related to volcanic activity, mountain features may be composed of crystal materials not directly arising from volcanism.

The most widespread feature on Io is the plain. Colors of plain regions range from reds to yellows and black to white. Various types of plain feature are found. The most prevalent are intervent plains; they represent 40 percent of the area of Io mapped by the Voyager probes. Intervent plains have smooth surfaces and intermediate albedo values and are interpreted as a combination of ejecta and flows from volcanic centers. Layered plains reveal a more complex structure and evolution, consisting of smooth surfaces with grabens and scarps as high as 1.7 kilometers. This stratigraphy indicates that layered plains may contain materials other than pure sulfur. Layered plains are intersected by faults and overlap other plains. They exhibit depositional and erosional features; it has been suggested that liquid sulfur dioxide is responsible for the erosion.

Vent-related features include calderas and fissures. Such features represent only 5 percent of Io's mapped area. More than three hundred vents were identified in the images. Although apparently randomly distributed rather than localized, the number and diameter of calderas on Io varies with latitude. Equatorial calderas are largest, with a maximum diameter of 250 kilometers, and most frequent. The average caldera is about 40 kilometers wide. The maximum diameter of calderas in the south polar region is nearly 100 kilometers. Lack of correlation of calderas across the surface indicates that the vents are not determined by highly patterned convection cells beneath the surface.

Mountain materials appear to be the oldest surface features. Such material is distributed evenly across Io. This material forms blocks of rugged terrain that can be as wide as 100 kilometers and as high as 9 kilometers. Because of the properties of sulfur and its compounds, mountainous material higher than 1,000 meters cannot be composed of sulfur and still be self-supporting. Io's mountain material probably consists, therefore, of silicate materials.

The Voyager data suggest a rather unusual model for Io's interior. Io contains virtually no ice; rather, it has a solid sulfur lithosphere about one kilometer thick floating on an asthenosphere composed of molten sulfur and sulfur dioxide. This molten layer is only about one hundred kilometers thick, according to the model. The asthenosphere is underlain by a thick mantle of molten or solid silicates and a dense core rich in iron sulfide. The core might account for as much as 20 percent of Io's total mass. Convection in the asthenosphere transports internal heat from the core and mantle to power the sulfur eruptions on the lithosphere, which leave the crust sulfur-rich and ice-free.

The heat that powers Io's extraordinary volcanic activity results from the satellite's proximity to the huge gravitational presence of Jupiter. Io is slowly flexed, much like a basketball being dribbled on a court, as its orbit undergoes perturbations caused by the other large, Galilean satellites. This flexing warms Io's interior; frictional forces dissipate energy as subsurface layers rub over each other. Tidal flexing becomes less significant the farther a satellite's orbit is from its planetary body. On Europa, tidal flexing could have provided sufficient heating to crack the surface, sending geysers of water across its icy face. On Io, tidal flexing is sufficient to power the volcanism that continuously alters the surface physiography.

Methods of Study

The earth's moon and Io have roughly the same size and density. It was therefore once believed that Io might have a silicate-like composition. Considering Jupiter's strong gravitational field and Io's proximity to the asteroids, astronomers thought Io would be a heavily cratered world, its surface highly preserved. Yet, earthbound observations of Io suggested that it was quite different from this simple picture. It was a very red world, and spectral analysis indicated the presence of sulfur. Observers reported detection of strong infrared emissions emanating from Io which lasted for several hours and then diminished. Suggestive of a 50-kilometer, 600-degree hot spot, these emissions were the first indication of volcanic activity on Io.

Most of what is known about Io was obtained by the Voyager 1 and 2 spacecraft, which made scientific measurements and returned high-resolution images as they passed through the Jovian system in 1979. The Voyager program objectives included measurements of the infrared and ultraviolet radiation, radio emissions, magnetic fields, plasma particles and waves, cosmic-ray particles, and low-energy charged particles in the vicinity of Jupiter (and later Saturn, Uranus, and Neptune). The most important objective with regard to Io, however, was the collection of high-resolution images.

Voyager included both narrow- and wide-angle multicolor television camera systems. The wide-angle camera used a 200-millimeter focal length optical system to generate images with a 3-degree field of view. The narrow-angle camera used a 1,500-millimeter focal length optical system to produce images with only a 0.4-degree field of view. The imaging system was designed to provide the highest possible resolution with minimum distortion and maximum stability.

Images of Io were taken with both the wide-angle and narrow-angle optical systems. Both television cameras used rotating filter wheels to select the desired viewing wavelength regions. The wide-angle camera filter wheel had violet, blue, green, orange, and clear filters and means for observing sodium and methane emissions. The narrow-angle camera filter wheel had ultraviolet, violet, blue, green, orange, and clear filters. Color images were created when the cameras photographed targets using the blue, green, and orange filters in rapid succession. Selenium-sulfur vidicon television tubes were used as detectors in the imaging system rather than ordinary photographic film. These detectors were designed for slow-scan readout, with forty-eight seconds needed for each photograph. Exposures as short as fractions of a second or as long as several minutes were possible.

Voyager 1 transmitted a high-resolution photograph of Jupiter on February 26, 1979, that included the entire disk of Io as viewed from 8 million kilometers. Even at this distance, Io displayed unusual features. As the probe approached Io, its low-energy charged particle experiment detected high-speed sulfur at a distance ten times as large as Io's sulfur torus. The cosmic-ray experiment began detecting both sulfur and oxygen. The plasma experiment also detected sulfur. All these data pointed to Io as the sulfur's source.

On March 5, 1979, Voyager 1 made its closest approach to Io, coming within 22,000 kilometers of the bizarre surface. The near-encounter images verified the tantalizing features partially revealed in earlier, more distant images. The largest, most conspicuous surface feature (about 1,000 kilometers wide) was a heart-shaped oval called Pele, reddish in color with a black center and some areas of mottled white. Smaller, similar features covered the surface. Impact craters were absent, and an explanation of the observed surface features initially eluded Voyager scientists.

A clue to understanding the origin of Pele and similar features was obtained in an image taken on March 8 at 5:00 A.M. from a distance of 4.5 million kilometers. This image was a long exposure taken for navigational purposes. At the limb of Io was a crescent-shaped cloud, indicative of a volcanic eruption on an atmosphereless world. Within a week of near-encounter, a total of eight active volcanic eruptions were identified in Voyager 1 images. Volcanic ash was photographed rising 300 kilometers above Pele.

Voyager 2 entered the vicinity of Io in early July, 1979. Although it did not pass as close to Io as Voyager 1, Voyager 2 provided more photographic evidence of spectacular volcanic activity. Pele was no longer active. There had been dramatic filling of the indentation of Pele's ejecta ring between the visits of Voyager 1 and 2. Pele had assumed a more symmetric oval shape, and about 10,000 square kilometers of the feature had changed. Ultraviolet studies of the feature called Loki indicated that its activity had increased. Loki's volcanic plume rose to 175 kilometers and exhibited a twin-column nature. The other six known volcanic eruptions were still active, roughly unchanged since Voyager 1 had revealed them. Although Voyager 2 searched Io for plumes as low as 40 kilometers in height, no new eruptions were discovered.

Context

Io, innermost of the Galilean moons and the third largest of Jupiter's sixteen known moons, is by far the most geologically active world in the solar system. Galileo first observed this unusual world in the early 1600's, using a primitive telescope. Not only did Galileo observe color variations on Jupiter, but he saw four points of light which changed position with respect to each other as well as Jupiter. Galileo named these moving points of light the Medician stars to honor his patron, Cosimo de' Medici. Except in Italy, Io and the others—Europa, Ganymede, and Callisto—are now known as the Galilean moons of Jupiter. Observations of Io with increasingly sophisticated telescopes provided few further details until the twentieth century. Io did give astronomers a hint of its bizarre nature, appearing quite reddish in color—almost as strongly red as Mars.

By the 1950's, techniques of modern polarimetry and spectrophotometry could be applied to the study of Io's color and albedo, and near-infrared photometry was available to reveal information about Io's surface compositions. Several unusual observations of Io have been recorded since then. Astronomers reported that Io was unusually brilliant for about a quarter of an hour after some Jovian eclipses in 1964 and subsequent years. Correlated to the position of Io's orbit relative to the earth, Jovian radio emission bursts were discovered for the first time in 1964. Analysis of spectral data revealed Io to be radically different from the other Galilean moons, lacking water frost and surface ice. In 1973, high-resolution telescopic images showed surface regions colored red and white. That same year, a thin, glowing yellow cloud of sodium was observed extending along Io's orbit. The width of this torus-shaped gas tube is several Io diameters. Later, investigators found evidence of sulfur and oxygen also spreading out along Io's Jovian orbit. This collection of gas is too faint for earth-based telescopic observation; however, an observer on Io would observe aurora-like effects generated by this gaseous collection. In the late 1970's, flare-ups of infrared emissions on Io were noted, but their significance was not deciphered.

A pair of Voyager spacecraft generated more interest in and data about Io during close-up flybys in 1979 than had all the previous observations combined. Io presented a mottled surface of red, orange, yellow, black, and white regions to the Voyager high-resolution cameras. Voyager 1's most important discovery about Io was made almost accidentally. A number of navigational images, analyzed by Linda Morabito at the Jet Propulsion Laboratory, Pasadena, California, revealed a peculiar bright pattern emanating from Io's surface. Fountainlike clouds of material were seen extending in umbrella shapes as high as 260 kilometers above Io's surface. Voyager 2 images confirmed Io's active volcanism. Several of the geysers detected by Voyager 1 were still active several months later, when Voyager 2 passed by Io. The observation of active volcanism explained why Io exhibited a young-looking surface virtually free of impact craters.

Bibliography

Beatty, J. Kelly, Brian O'Leary, and Andrew Chaikin. *The New Solar System.* Cambridge, England: Cambridge University Press, 1981. A series of chapters, written by various investigators on spacecraft planetary programs, on solar system bodies, both large and small. Contains numerous spacecraft photographs of the planets and their moons and ring systems. Includes atmospheric and geologic analyses. Easily understood maps and numerous further references.

Greeley, Ronald. *Planetary Landscapes.* Boston: Allen & Unwin, 1985. An excellent reference for the serious layman. It is highly technical but clearly written. Photographs are abundant and well described. Includes graphs, charts, diagrams, and an extensive list of further references. Essential reading for those interested in planetary geology.

Hartmann, William K. *Moons and Planets.* 2d ed. Belmont, Calif.: Wadsworth, 1983. A text on solar system astronomy and the planets, complete with problem sets. Photographs, charts, and diagrams are abundant. Includes planetary data tables and an extensive reference list. For the college-level reader.

Hunt, Garry, and Patrick Moore. *Jupiter.* Skokie, Ill.: Rand McNally, 1981. This source includes maps, graphs, and Voyager photographs and covers all aspects of the Jovian system. Extraordinarily good treatments of Jupiter's Galilean moons. Astronomical tables, useful glossary.

Morrison, David, and Jane Samz. *Voyage to Jupiter.* NASA SP-439. Washington, D.C.: Government Printing Office, 1980. A beautifully illustrated account of the Voyager encounters with the Jovian system, this book reviews the knowledge gained as a result of the Pioneer 10 and 11 flybys. Contains maps of the Jovian moons. Well written and easily understood.

Wilson, Andrew. *Solar System Log.* New York: Jane's, 1987. An excellent reference on the unmanned spacecraft planetary missions of all spacefaring nations. It offers pictures of spacecraft photographic targets, diagrams of spacecraft design and encounter trajectories, and tables of program details. Chronologically arranged by launch date. Solar system data appendix.

David G. Fisher

Cross References

Geysers and Hot Springs, 929; The Jovian Planets' Satellites, 1303; Elemental Distribution in the Solar System, 2434; Volcanoes: Calderas, 2614; Volcanoes: Eruption Forecasting, 2622; Volcanoes: Recent Eruptions, 2673; Volcanoes: Shield Volcanoes, 2681; Volcanoes: Types of Eruption, 2695.

IONIC SUBSTITUTION IN MINERALS

Type of earth science: Geology
Field of study: Mineralogy and crystallography

Ionic substitution varies the chemical composition of minerals by replacing atoms with other atoms of similar size, electrical charge, and chemical properties. Because of ionic substitution, many minerals are not distinct substances but are members of series whose composition varies over a wide range.

Principal terms

ANGSTROM UNIT: a unit of size often used for describing the dimensions of atoms, equal to one one-hundred-millionth (10^{-8}) centimeter

ANION: an atom that has gained electrons and thus acquired a negative electrical charge

CATION: an atom that has lost electrons; it has a positive charge because it has more protons than electrons

END MEMBER: any of the pure materials that make up a solid solution; a mineral intermediate in composition between two end members is called intermediate

ION: an atom that is electrically charged because it has gained or lost electrons

IONIC RADIUS: the effective radius of an ion in a mineral; ionic radius for a given ion can vary depending on the number and type of ions around it

OXIDATION STATE: the number of electrons gained or lost by an ion, usually specified as the electric charge on the ion; also called valence

SOLID SOLUTION: a mixture of two or more solid materials on the atomic scale, which can occur if the materials have very similar atomic structures

Summary of the Phenomenon

Ionic substitution is the substitution of one atom for another in minerals. Although minerals are naturally occurring, inorganic chemical compounds, which ideally should have definite, fixed compositions, the compositions of minerals are often far from definite. Much of the variability of mineral compositions results from ionic substitution. Ionic substitution is governed chiefly by the size, electric charge, and bonding behavior of the ions in minerals. In order to understand the patterns of ionic substitution, it is necessary first to understand the behavior of atoms within minerals.

Minerals, and solids in general, are held together, or bonded, by the sharing of electrons among atoms. Bonding results from the interaction of two forces within atoms. The familiar electromagnetic force causes particles of opposite electrical charge to attract and those of like charge to repel one another. A strong, short-range force called the weak nuclear force causes the electrons that orbit atoms to group into distinct levels called shells. The electromagnetic force requires that the number of electrons (negative) and protons (positive) in a material be equal. The weak nuclear force causes electron shells to gain or lose electrons in order to acquire a more stable structure. Atoms manage to satisfy both tendencies by sharing electrons, and this sharing bonds the atoms together.

Most of the bonding in minerals is ionic bonding: If some atoms in a mineral can lose electrons easily to become cations, and others can acquire electrons to become anions, their opposing electrical charges hold them together. Table salt, or halite, is a common material with ionic bonding: Each sodium atom loses an electron, while each chlorine atom acquires an electron. The sodium cations and chlorine anions are then bonded together by their opposite electric charges. In covalent bonding, electrons orbit adjacent atoms and fill out the electron shells of both atoms simultaneously. The most important example in geology is the bond between silicon and oxygen. This bond is partially ionic and partially covalent. That is, electrons spend most of the time attached to the oxygen anion, but there is also some sharing of electrons between oxygen and silicon. In metallic bonding, electrons wander freely through the metal. In effect, the metal consists of cations held together by a negatively charged electron "gas." The free electrons cause metals to be such good conductors of heat and electricity. Gold is a mineral with metallic bonding.

Each chemical element has a specific electron structure and tends to gain or lose a characteristic number of electrons in chemical reactions; that is, they have a characteristic valence or oxidation state. Most elements in minerals tend to have a single oxidation state. For example, sodium almost always occurs in the $+1$ oxidation state and silicon in the $+4$ state. A few elements, notably iron, occur in more than one state in minerals. Iron occurs as ferrous iron ($+2$) or ferric iron ($+3$).

Elements with similar electron arrangements in their outermost shells have similar chemical properties, a relationship that is illustrated in the periodic table of the elements. In the periodic table, elements with similar electron structures fall into vertical columns, called groups. The periodic table helps greatly in understanding ionic substitution in minerals. For example, all the common anions in minerals (oxygen, sulfur, fluorine, chlorine) are in Groups VIA and VIIA. A few elements can be either anions or cations. These elements—arsenic, selenium, antimony, and tellurium—are close together in the periodic table. Some cations often group with oxygen to form radicals that behave like anions. These elements are also clustered. One cluster consists of boron, carbon, nitrogen, silicon, phosphorus, and sulfur. Another, less important, cluster consists of titanium, vanadium, chromium, molybdenum, and tungsten.

In minerals an ion generally behaves as a rigid sphere of definite size, or ionic radius. Anions are generally larger than cations for two reasons. First, cations often form when atoms lose their outermost shell of electrons, whereas anions form by adding atoms to their outermost shell. Second, cations have more protons than electrons, so the positively charged nucleus of the atom pulls the remaining electrons in closer. Anions, on the other hand, have more electrons than protons. The extra electrons repel one another, and the electrons are pushed farther apart. In effect, the electron shells around an anion become slightly inflated. Ionic radius is also closely related to the position of an element in the periodic table. Cations become larger as their atomic number increases, simply because each row in the periodic table has one more electron shell than does the row above. Also, cations are largest in Groups IA and IB and become smaller in higher-numbered groups.

The size difference between the cations and anions has some interesting consequences. The most abundant element in the earth's crust, oxygen, is an anion in minerals. Its ionic radius is two to three times that of the commonest cations and its volume about twenty-five times as great. Oxygen accounts for fully 95 percent of the volume of all atoms in the earth's crust. The structure of minerals can often be pictured in terms of stacking spheres of various sizes in the right proportions. Because anions are so large, minerals often consist of anions packed in various ways, with the smaller cations filling the voids between. Frequently, the atomic arrangement of a mineral remains unchanged if one cation is substituted for another. Thus, it is usually more useful to classify minerals, and chemical compounds in general, according to their anions rather than their cations. For example, magnesium sulfate (epsomite) is very soft and soluble in water; magnesium carbonate (magnesite) is harder and insoluble in water but soluble in acid; and magnesium silicate (forsterite) is hard, glassy, and insoluble in water or acid. Magnesium minerals, as a group, have no properties in common. On the other hand, the carbonates of magnesium, calcium (calcite), iron (siderite), and manganese (rhodochrosite) are all quite similar in their density, hardness, crystal form, and many other physical properties.

In addition to size, the other important property of ions that governs the structure of minerals is electric charge. Size and electric charge dictate the degree of substitution of elements in minerals. Sometimes, elements with very different chemistries are similar enough in size and charge to substitute for each other. For example, nickel and magnesium are very different chemically, but they have nearly identical ionic radii and valences and substitute easily for each other in minerals.

The more different two ions are in radius, the less likely they are to substitute for each other. The difficulty is compounded if the ions have different charges. For an ion of one charge to substitute for another, some additional ionic substitution must be made to restore electrical charge balance. For example, in the plagioclase feldspars, sodium ($+1$) and calcium ($+2$) substitute, but the extra charge on the calcium ion is balanced by substituting aluminum ($+3$) for silicon ($+4$). Finally, the bonding behavior of some elements affects substitution. For example, silicon is bonded to oxygen partly by electrical attraction (ionic bonding) but also partly by sharing electrons (covalent bonding). Silicon usually bonds to four neighboring oxygen atoms in a tetrahedral (triangular pyramid) arrangement. Other elements can and do substitute for silicon but only in a limited way, because they lack silicon's distinctive bonding behavior. In some cases, ions are different enough in size, charge, and bonding behavior that they can substitute only to a limited degree. In other cases, ions substitute freely. A mineral series that varies over a wide range of composition because of free ionic substitution is called a solid solution. The ideal pure minerals at the extremes of the composition range are called end members of the series.

Elements that substitute for one another generally occupy distinct portions of the periodic table. These groups are usually atoms of similar size and valence. One important group includes the alkali metals: potassium, rubidium, and cesium. These ions all have charges of +1 and large ionic radii (greater than 1.0 angstrom unit). Another important group is the alkaline earth elements: calcium, strontium, and barium. These ions also have large ionic radii, but they have charges of +2. Sodium is often too small to substitute for the other alkali metals but commonly substitutes for calcium. Another group of large cations that substitute readily for one another are the lanthanide and actinide rare earth elements, mostly with valences of +3 or +4.

There are many medium-sized cations (ionic radii 0.6-0.8 angstrom unit) that substitute for one another. One large group consists of cations with +2 valence, mostly from the middle of the periodic table: iron, nickel, cobalt, manganese, magnesium, and sometimes copper and zinc. Iron and magnesium are perhaps the most important ionic substitution in minerals. If there is enough room in the mineral structure, calcium will sometimes substitute for some of these elements. Among the smaller cations, substitution is common among valence +3 cations of small to medium size: aluminum, chromium, and ferric iron. Another important group of elements are silicon and other small cations (with ionic radii of less than 0.6 angstrom unit) that substitute for it in mineral structures: aluminum, beryllium boron, and titanium. These ions have charges of +3 to +5.

Among the anions, ionic substitution occurs most commonly among the halogens: fluorine, chlorine, bromine, and iodine. These have charges of −1 and large ionic radii. The hydroxyl radical (OH) also has a charge of −1 (−2 for oxygen, plus +1 for hydrogen) and a large ionic radius. Fluorine often substitutes for the hydroxyl radical.

The variability of mineral compositions requires new ways of writing chemical formulas. Elements that substitute for one another are written in parentheses. For example, the mineral olivine is a solid solution of iron (Fe) and magnesium (Mg) silicate: Its formula is $(Mg,Fe)_2SiO_4$. In more complex cases, one can write the formula using arbitrary symbols to represent groups of elements. For example, the spinel group of minerals has the formula XY_2O_4, where X can be ferrous iron, magnesium, or, more rarely, nickel or zinc, and Y can be aluminum, chromium, or ferric iron. O, of course, is still oxygen. (Note that the element yttrium also has the symbol Y; it is usually clear from context whether a single letter is a specific or generic symbol.) Spinel minerals include the gem mineral spinel (X is magnesium, Y is aluminum), magnetite (X is ferrous iron, Y is ferric iron), and the important ore mineral chromite (X is ferrous iron, Y is chromium).

Among the non-silicates, perhaps the most important series are the spinel minerals, noted above, and the simple carbonates, all with the formula XCO_3, where X can be calcium (calcite), magnesium (magnesite), ferrous iron (siderite), manganese (rhodochrosite), zinc (smithsonite), or cobalt (sphaerocobaltite). The most important intermediate carbonate is dolomite $(CaMg(CO_3)_2)$. Carbonates with complex mixtures of elements are sometimes given the generic name "ankerite."

Among the silicates, the most important series include olivine, described above, and garnet, pyroxene, amphibole, micas and clay minerals, and plagioclase feldspars. The general formula for garnet is $X_3Y_2(SiO_4)_3$. There are two series: In one, X is calcium and Y is ferric iron, chromium, or aluminum; in the other, X is ferrous iron, magnesium, or manganese and Y is aluminum. The general formula for pyroxene is XYZ_2O_6. There are three main series: X and Y are calcium, magnesium, or ferrous iron and Z is silicon; X is calcium or sodium, Y is magnesium or ferrous iron, and Z is silicon or aluminum; X is sodium or lithium, Y is aluminum or ferric iron, and Z is silicon. Amphibole is a very complex group with the general formula $W_{0-1}X_2Y_5Z_8O_{22}(OH,F)$. W, which may not be present, is sodium or potassium, X is a medium or large ion with charge $+1$ or $+2$ (calcium, sodium, manganese, ferrous iron, magnesium, or lithium), Y is a medium-sized cation of charge $+2$, $+3$, or $+4$ (manganese, iron, magnesium, aluminum, or titanium), and Z is silicon or aluminum. Micas and clay minerals have a sheetlike atomic structure with sheets of aluminum or magnesium hydroxide interspersed with layers of silica. Ferrous iron and manganese sometimes substitute for magnesium, ferric iron or chromium for aluminum. In some minerals, large cations such as sodium, potassium, or calcium occur between the sheets; these ions substitute rather freely. Plagioclase feldspars are composed of a solid solution of albite $(NaAlSi_3O_8)$ and anorthite $(CaAl_2Si_2O_8)$. Potassium may substitute for sodium to a limited extent (freely at high temperatures), and barium sometimes substitutes for calcium.

In some minerals, cations are attached so weakly that they can be easily removed and replaced by other cations. This process, called ion exchange, occurs commonly among a group of silicates called the zeolites as well as among clay minerals. The ion-exchange capacity of zeolites was once widely exploited in water-softeners. One method of prospecting for mineral deposits involves collecting clay from stream deposits and analyzing it for any unusual elements that may have weathered out of a nearby ore deposit and attached to the clay by ion exchange.

If ionic substitution occurs on a small scale, the substitute ion is considered an impurity rather than a major chemical component. Nevertheless, impurities can be geologically and economically significant. One of the most conspicuous effects of impurities in minerals is to create or modify their color. In their pure state, the gem minerals quartz, corundum, beryl, and diamond are all colorless. Colored gem varieties of these minerals are the result of small ionic substitutions. For example, the green of emerald (beryl) and the red of ruby (corundum) both result from tiny amounts of chromium substituting for aluminum. Amethyst (purple quartz) owes its color to ferric iron, rose quartz (pink) to manganese or titanium. Only certain atoms are capable of producing color in minerals. Most electrons in atoms are paired, attracted to each other by the weak nuclear force so strongly that visible light lacks enough energy to affect them. Only those atoms with unpaired electrons can absorb visible light, and of the most abundant elements in the earth's crust (oxygen, silicon, aluminum, iron, magnesium, sodium, potassium, and calcium), only iron has unpaired electrons. Iron is the dominant coloring agent in most rocks and many minerals. Ferric iron imparts various shades of red, yellow, or brown; ferrous iron tends to color minerals green or black.

For some elements, ionic substitution is so effective that the element occurs only as impurities in other minerals. Rubidium is much more abundant in the earth's crust than are vital metals such as copper or zinc, yet there are no rubidium minerals. Instead, rubidium substitutes for potassium. Similarly, gallium substitutes for aluminum, hafnium for zirconium. Such elements are said to be dispersed.

Without ionic substitution, radiometric dating of rocks and minerals would be far more difficult. Radiometric dating relies on the decay of radioactive atoms at a known rate and the accumulation of the resulting decay products. Two of the major dating systems are based on elements that occur as impurities. The rubidium-strontium method is based on the decay of rubidium 87, which occurs as an impurity in potassium minerals. The uranium-lead dating method can make use of uranium minerals but is most frequently applied to zircon, in which the uranium occurs as an impurity substituting for zirconium.

Methods of Study

The study of ionic substitution in minerals requires an understanding of both the chemical composition of minerals and the geometric arrangement of atoms within them. The atomic structure of a mineral dictates how large or small an ion can be to fit in a particular site.

The basic understanding of mineral chemistry was acquired by methods that are now considered primitive: Minerals were dissolved in solvents, and the individual components were separated by chemical reactions and weighed. From this information, the chemical formula of the mineral could be calculated. Ionic substitution in most common minerals was first detected by such means. These techniques require great care, are time consuming, and are limited to an accuracy of about 0.1 percent.

Modern methods of chemical analysis include the electron microprobe and X-ray fluorescence. Both methods rely on bombarding a specimen with radiation (electrons or X rays, respectively), and analyzing the wavelengths of X rays emitted by the specimen. Each chemical element emits characteristic X-ray wavelengths, so that the X rays emitted by a specimen are a direct indicator of its composition. These methods can be easily automated, do not damage the specimen, and can be used on very tiny samples. It is thus possible to study mineral chemistry in much greater detail than early methods allowed and to detect far smaller concentrations of elements.

For some simple minerals, it has been possible to infer their atomic structure using geometrical reasoning and such clues as the crystal form of the mineral. For example, table salt (halite) always cleaves into cubic fragments, and it has a simple formula: equal numbers of sodium and chlorine atoms. It is reasonable (and correct) to surmise that sodium and chlorine atoms alternate in a simple cubic pattern.

Complex minerals, including many of the silicates, are far too complex for such methods. Atomic structures of complex minerals are usually determined by X-ray diffraction. When a specimen is bombarded by X rays, X rays scatter or diffract off atoms in the specimen. When the wavelength of the X rays, the angle at which the X rays strike, and the arrangements of atoms are just right, the diffracted X rays emerge in a particularly strong beam. The intensity of the X rays depends both on the geometry of the diffraction and on the chemical elements involved. There are many ways to make use of X-ray diffraction to determine the atomic structure of minerals. These methods can show not only the locations of atoms but also subtle details such as distortions that result from the substitution of unusually large or small ions. A computer is required to handle the complex computations needed for such studies.

Context

Ionic substitution in minerals enriches the variety of the mineral world and has played a significant role in the chemical evolution of the earth. Although the crust of the earth makes up only one three-hundredth of the total mass of the earth, it contains more than 1 percent of the earth's total potassium and half or more of the entire earth's rubidium, uranium, thorium, and some rare earth elements. These elements are enriched in the crust because they do not substitute easily for the iron and magnesium that are principal components of minerals in the earth's mantle, the layer beneath the crust. Whenever rocks in the interior of the earth melted, these "misfit" elements concentrated in the molten rock and eventually accumulated in the crust.

Ionic substitution is responsible for the color of many of the most valuable gemstones. In addition, some mineral deposits are the result of ionic substitution. For example, nickel commonly substitutes for magnesium. Weathering of magnesium-rich rocks dissolves away the magnesium and concentrates the nickel; many nickel deposits in tropical countries formed in this way. Other materials are more economical to recover as by-products than to mine directly. For example, there are several cadmium minerals, but cadmium is usually recovered as a by-product of zinc mining, because cadmium substitutes for zinc in the zinc ores.

Bibliography

Blackburn, William H., and William H. Dennen. *Principles of Mineralogy.* Dubuque, Iowa: Wm. C. Brown, 1988. A college-level mineralogy text, with chapters on mineralogical theory and methods, as well as descriptions of common minerals. Chapters 4, 5, and 6 describe the chemistry and atomic structure of minerals, with considerable detail on atomic bonding. Chapter 12 is useful for its good coverage of modern analytical techniques used in the study of minerals.

Bloss, F. D. *Crystallography and Crystal Chemistry*. New York: Holt, Rinehart and Winston, 1971. A text for advanced college students that covers crystal form, atomic structure, physical properties of minerals, and X-ray methods. Although the mathematics can be complex, there are also many passages where important concepts are explained in clear and simple terms. Illustrations are abundant and highly informative.

Chen, Philip S. *A New Handbook of Chemistry*. Camarillo, Calif.: Chemical Elements Publishing, 1975. A concise and simplified chemical reference book for introductory college chemistry courses. Although a general chemical reference, it contains much useful information including ionic radii, abundances of isotopes, and oxidation states of the elements for earth scientists.

Day, Frank H. *The Chemical Elements in Nature*. New York: Van Nostrand Reinhold, 1964. A survey of the occurrence of the elements in the earth and atmosphere as well as their biological and economic significance. The treatment is simple and nonmathematical. Some remarks on the chemistry of other planets are dated and a few are now known to be incorrect. On the whole, however, the book is a good survey for the layperson.

Deer, William A., R. A. Howie, and J. Zussman. *Rock-Forming Minerals*. 5 vols. New York: John Wiley & Sons, 1988.

_____. *An Introduction to Rock-Forming Minerals*. New York: Halsted Press, 1973. Standard references on mineralogy for advanced college students and above. Each chapter contains detailed descriptions of chemistry and crystal structure, usually with chemical analyses. Discussions of chemical variations in minerals are extensive. *An Introduction to Rock-Forming Minerals* is a condensation of the five-volume set.

Klein, Cornelis, and Cornelius S. Hurlbut, Jr. *Manual of Mineralogy*. 20th ed. New York: John Wiley & Sons, 1985. One of the most widely used college mineralogy texts. Contains chapters on most mineralogical methods, as well as descriptions of common minerals. Particularly good for its attractive illustrations of atomic structure of minerals and its survey of research on the causes of color in minerals. Chapter 4 contains many useful chemical tables and a good description of the way chemical analyses are converted into chemical formulas.

Muecke, Gunter K., and Peter Möller. "The Not-So-Rare Earths." *Scientific American* 258 (January, 1988): 72-77. A survey of one important group of elements that commonly substitute in minerals. The article explores the variations in their natural occurrence and shows how variations in ionic radius and valence allow the rare earths to be used as tracers for many geologic processes. *Scientific American* is written for nonspecialists at a college reading level.

O'Nions, R. K., P. J. Hamilton, and N. M. Evensen. "Chemical Evolution of the Earth's Mantle." *Scientific American* 242 (May, 1980): 120-135. This article, written for nonspecialists at a college reading level, shows how trace elements and isotopes in minerals can be used to deduce the chemical history of the earth's interior. In particular, elements with large ionic radii have become concentrated in the earth's crust.

Turekian, Karl K. *Chemistry of the Earth*. New York: Holt, Rinehart and Winston, 1972. A short but information-packed summary of geochemistry, written for college students at an introductory level. The description of mineral structure, bonding, and ionic substitution is well illustrated.

Steven I. Dutch

Cross-References

Carbonates, 190; Electron Microprobes, 596; Feldspars, 698; Gem Minerals, 802; Geochronology: Rb-Sr Dating, 848; Geochronology: U-Th-Pb Dating, 862; Physical Properties of Minerals, 1681; The Structure of Minerals, 1693; Neutron Activation Analysis, 1734; Oxides, 1976; Stable Isotopes: Fractionation Processes, 2449; X-Ray Fluorescence, 2744; X-Ray Powder Diffraction, 2751.

IRON DEPOSITS

Type of earth science: Economic geology

Local exploitation of iron deposits made possible both the Industrial Revolution of Europe in the eighteenth century and the rapid industrial growth of the northern United States at the start of the twentieth century. The mining of iron deposits has moved from these areas during the past half-century to become concentrated within thirty latitudinal degrees of the equator.

Principal terms

GOETHITE: the most common iron-hydroxide mineral

HEMATITE: a mineral composed of oxygen and fully oxidized iron but no hydrogen

IRON FORMATION: a layered rock deposit that consists mostly of ironstone

IRON HYDROXIDE: a mineral that contains oxygen, hydrogen, and fully oxidized iron

IRON SILICATE: a mineral that contains silicon, oxygen, hydrogen, and abundant iron

IRONSTONE: a chemically precipitated sedimentary rock which contains more than 15 percent iron

MAGNETITE: a mineral composed of oxygen and iron but no hydrogen; the iron occurs in two oxidation states: oxidized and reduced

OOID: a small round grain that is layered internally, like an onion; it typically has a diameter comparable to that of a mineral grain on a sandy beach

REGOLITH: the weathered surface of the earth; soil is the upper portion of regolith and includes plant roots

SIDERITE: a mineral composed of iron, carbon, and oxygen

SILICA: silicon with two oxygen atoms; essentially, naturally precipitated glass

Summary of the Phenomenon

Most young iron deposits contain marine fossils. Iron formations, therefore, usually are attributed to precipitation from ancient seawater, but the nature of the iron-concentrating process remains unclear. Iron is extremely insoluble within both oxidized and chemically reduced seawater. In a billion parts of seawater, there are only about three parts of iron. The only modern body of seawater with any appreciable dissolved iron is a deep, salty body under the northern Gulf of Mexico, called the Orca basin, which contains 1.6 parts of iron in a million parts of seawater. Given the lack of iron in all other seawater, it is not surprising that modern oceans lack significant iron deposits on the sea floor. In fact, it is extremely difficult to conceive of any reasonable mechanism to produce the enormous ancient iron deposits from seawater. Nevertheless, the very size of the ancient iron formations seems to record precipitation on an oceanic sea floor. Moreover, many ancient iron formations are closely associated with voluminous limestone, which also apparently precipitated from seawater.

The largest iron deposits (iron formations) occur in rocks which are older than 600 million years. Many of the largest iron deposits formed during the Early Proterozoic eon (between 2,500 and 2,000 million years ago) and are therefore about half as old as the earth itself. Rocks which are older than 2,000 million years constitute less than 5 percent of the surface area of the earth, because subsequent geologic processes either have destroyed the rocks by erosion or melting or have buried them under a thick cover of younger rocks. Deeply buried rocks cannot be mined profitably. Modern industrial society, therefore, depends on exposed remnants of the early earth that have survived an extremely long time.

No iron is being concentrated on the modern earth into a significant deposit (a large iron formation), and almost nothing is being produced currently that resembles the ironstone (iron-rich rock) in large iron formations. Ancient iron deposits accumulated within large water bodies, almost certainly oceans, but little is known about the nature of these ancient oceans, as they contained no fish or other animal life which would provide fossil records indicating environmental conditions. There is therefore little agreement among geologists as to the origin of ancient iron deposits.

Iron deposits can be traced laterally for as much as 1,000 kilometers through ancient rock sequences. An individual iron formation may exceed 100 meters in thickness. Large iron formations accumulated on extensive platforms that were not receiving any sediment from rivers. Otherwise, they would not be such pure chemical precipitates. The largest iron formations contain little other than iron, silicon, oxygen, and carbon. Sediment supplied by rivers always contains a wide variety of other chemical elements.

Some of the platforms on which iron formations have accumulated probably lie offshore from a continent, just as the modern Bahama platforms lie off the southeastern United States. The Bahama platform that lies closest to North America is separated from Florida by a deep-water channel, which prevents any continental sediment from reaching the shallow marine platform. The only sediments that are accumulating on the platform are precipitating from calcium and carbon-oxygen molecules dissolved in seawater. Ancient iron formations presumably also precipitated from chemical elements dissolved in seawater.

The most voluminous iron formations always contain as much chemically precipitated silica (similar to glass) as they do iron minerals. This silica is concentrated into thin layers that alternate with layers of iron-bearing minerals. The thinnest of these layers commonly ranges from 1 millimeter to 1 centimeter in thickness. In unweathered iron deposits, a common iron mineral is siderite, the iron-carbon-oxygen mineral. However, this mineral is particularly susceptible to weathering and readily becomes oxidized to an iron-oxygen-hydrogen mineral—for example, goethite. Within a well-drained, elevated plateau, weathering of chemically reduced minerals to goethite may occur to great depths, and a large volume of rock may become weathered without being removed by erosion. The weathered deposit subsequently may become deeply buried if the plateau subsides under the ocean, and a thick mantle of marine sediment may then accumulate over the area. If goethite becomes deeply buried, it may become transformed to hematite or magnetite under the great heat and pressure which characterize the deep earth. Some of the richest iron deposits appear to have experienced such ancient deep weathering and burial prior to becoming exposed to modern weathering.

Geologists who are interested in the origin of iron formations study only the unweathered iron formations. Unweathered iron formations are particularly well exposed around the western end of Lake Superior, in both Canada and the United States. There geologists have found fossils of some of the oldest known living cells, enclosed within layers of silica. The iron formations that contain these cells also exhibit large growth forms of ancient photosynthesizing bacteria, or cyanobacteria. These cyanobacteria produced mats that were folded upward from the shallow sea floor, like a crumpled carpet, stretching toward the ancient sunlight. Similarly folded mats are extremely rare on the modern sea floor.

The great bulk of the thin layering (also called banding) in voluminous iron formations is not crumpled but flat. The origin of the alternation between iron-rich and iron-poor (silica-rich) layers has been controversial, because only one other type of chemical sedimentary rock persistently displays such a systematic alternation of layers. This other rock type is calcium-bearing salt that has accumulated under deep water. Salt typically precipitates because of evaporation of seawater, but it is difficult to imagine how a chemical element that is as inherently insoluble as iron could behave like the highly soluble elements that precipitate in salt beds—for example, sodium and calcium.

Small iron deposits that are younger than 600 million years old typically do not exhibit layering. One explanation is that burrowing animals, which have proliferated on the sea floor during the past 600 million years, have disrupted any layering. Indeed, many young iron deposits contain remnants of animal burrows. The animals that constructed these burrows presumably required oxygen to breathe, but the young iron deposits contain chemically reduced, iron-bearing minerals that could precipitate only in the complete absence of molecular oxygen. The origin of young iron deposits is therefore no better understood than that of the larger old deposits.

Virtually all young iron deposits that are of ore grade exhibit a characteristic texture, which consists of tiny, onion-shaped spheres that are called ooids. Ooids are so beautifully formed that they were thought to be fossil fish eggs by ancient Greek investigators. Although geologists now know that they are not eggs, the origin of iron-rich ooids remains a mystery. Iron-rich ooids are extremely scarce in modern sediment, and the few modern localities where they occur have not yet been thoroughly studied.

Besides the scarcity of silica in young iron deposits, they also differ from old iron deposits in that they typically contain more aluminum. This aluminum occurs within an iron-rich clay mineral. Clay minerals are less abundant in old iron deposits, and the clay minerals that do exist in ancient deposits generally contain no aluminum. Phosphorus is abundant in young iron deposits, which contain an average of 0.5 percent phosphorus, whereas only about one-tenth of this concentration occurs in the old deposits. Old iron formations in Finland are exceptional in that they contain as much phosphorus as do typical young iron deposits. Iron deposits of all ages contain amounts of manganese, but all other metals—for example, copper—characteristically are scarce.

In addition to aluminum-rich silicate minerals, young iron deposits generally contain either goethite, a hydrogen-bearing oxide of iron, or hematite, an iron oxide that lacks hydrogen. It is easy to tell which mineral predominates because goethite imparts a yellow-brown color, whereas hematite is bright red. All iron-bearing silicates are green, regardless of whether they are aluminum-rich.

Young iron deposits in the United States are best known near Clinton, New York, and Birmingham, Alabama. The Clinton deposits are about 430 million years old. In northern Europe, young deposits range from about 150 to 200 million years old. Production of young deposits appears to have been somewhat episodic, as was production of old iron deposits. Although the most voluminous iron deposits formed on the ancient earth, there have been long stretches of ancient earth history when production of iron deposits was relatively depressed—for example, between 2,000 and 1,000 million years ago. An eventual understanding of the cyclicity of iron sedimentation probably will provide fundamental information about the global evolution of the earth.

Methods of Study

Iron deposits are studied both from an economic viewpoint and from an academic viewpoint. The academic potential of an iron formation is related to its state of preservation and the diversity of features it may exhibit. The prime economic criteria for mining of an iron deposit are ore composition, mining costs, and distance from market. Good ore contains not only a high percentage of iron but also a low percentage of certain chemical elements that would interfere with steel production. Most academic studies of iron formations focus on the information that they may provide about ancient earth environments, such as the temperature and composition of the earth's ancient atmosphere and oceans. Iron formations that are suitable for these studies have not been changed much by heat or pressure deep in the earth and have not experienced much weathering.

The initial step in studying an iron formation is to make thin slices of the various rock types. Each slice is abraded to be so thin that light will pass through the minerals when the slice is placed under a high-power microscope. Microscopic study allows for the identification of all minerals and any fossils of ancient life forms. Identification of life forms is facilitated by using an electron-beam microscope, which can achieve higher magnification than does a visible-light microscope.

A complete chemical analysis of an iron formation reveals the degree of concentration of the chemically precipitated elements relative to the composition of average rocks in the earth's crust. Some chemical elements—for example, carbon and oxygen—occur in more than one variety, called isotopes, and the ratio of these isotopes may indicate something about the chemical process that precipitated these elements. It is already well known that the ratios of oxygen and carbon isotopes in iron formations generally are distinct from those in common chemical sedimentary rocks—for example, limestone—of the same age as the iron formations, although a clear explanation of this distinction remains elusive to geologists.

Context

Voluminous silica-rich iron formations are the only major type of rock body that has not formed since complex life appeared on earth between 600 and 800 million years ago. An understanding of the origin of these ancient iron formations, therefore, may explain why the ancient earth did not support complex life. Although modern society depends on voluminous iron formations as a source of iron ore, modern accumulation of a voluminous iron formation may require the chemical composition of the atmosphere and oceans to become toxic to human life.

The present Iron Age, the portion of human history during which tools have been made of iron, started about 1000 B.C. Exploitation of iron deposits has increased roughly exponentially since that time. The fact that civilization continues to expand exponentially partly results from the continuing availability of both voluminous iron deposits and the fuels which are needed to convert iron ore into steel. Reserves of iron ore are becoming depleted less rapidly than the known reserves of fuel.

Bibliography

Holland, Heinrich D. *The Chemical Evolution of the Atmosphere and Oceans*. Princeton, N.J.: Princeton University Press, 1984. Only a small portion of this book (pages 374-407) is devoted to a discussion of the origin of iron deposits. Nevertheless, Holland provides a particularly lucid discussion about the importance of understanding iron-concentrating processes if geologists are to achieve a general understanding of the evolution of environmental conditions on earth.

James, H. L. "Chemistry of the Iron-Rich Sedimentary Rocks." In *Data of Geochemistry*, edited by M. Fleischer. Professional Paper 440-W. Denver, Colo.: U.S. Geological Survey, 1966. This classic publication remains valuable because it includes unchanging data on iron-rich minerals and chemical compositions of iron deposits.

James, H. L., and P. K. Sims, eds. *Economic Geology* 68, no. 7 (1973): 913-1179. This issue of the foremost journal of economic geology is entirely devoted to hypotheses about the origin of the largest iron deposits. A dozen renowned geologists present remarkably diverse explanations of the same rocks. The diversity itself is an indication of how difficult it is to explain the origin of iron deposits.

Kimberley, M. M. "Paleoenvironmental Classification of Iron Formations." *Economic Geology* 73 (1978): 215-229. Prior to this paper, nomenclature for iron deposits had become complicated by the local usage of poorly defined terms. This paper proposes simple definitions of the two most basic terms, "ironstone" and "iron formation," and a global classification scheme for iron deposits. The evolution of iron formations through earth history is apparent in a chronological listing of the classified types of iron deposits.

Maynard, J. B. *Geochemistry of Sedimentary Ore Deposits.* New York: Springer-Verlag, 1983. Although the largest iron deposits are older than 600 million years, there are several small iron deposits, which have formed more recently, as reviewed in this textbook.

Mel'nik, Yu. P. *Precambrian Banded Iron Formations: Physicochemical Conditions of Formation.* New York: Elsevier, 1982. The rise of the Soviet Union as an industrial power has depended partly on exploitation of its iron deposits. This translation from the Russian describes some of the major iron deposits of the Soviet Union as well as some of the Soviet theories about the processes that formed them.

Morris, R. C. "Genesis of Iron Ore in Banded Iron-Formation by Supergene and Supergene-Metamorphic Processes: A Conceptual Model." In *Handbook of Strata-Bound and Stratiform Ore Deposits.* Vol. 13, edited by K. H. Wolf. New York: Elsevier, 1985. A thorough discussion of the chemical alteration of iron formations. All voluminous iron formations contain as much silicon as iron when unaltered, but alteration (weathering under humid tropical conditions), preferentially removes the silicon, leaving iron within a porous regolith that may be mined readily.

Trendall, A. F. and R. C. Morris, eds. *Iron-Formation: Facts and Problems.* New York: Elsevier, 1983. The papers collected in this volume provide a good review of iron formations in western Australia and North America. Provides a description of how, over the past three decades, exploitation of iron deposits in western Australia has expanded greatly, while exploitation in North America has decreased correspondingly.

United Nations Educational, Scientific, and Cultural Organization. *Genesis of Precambrian Iron and Manganese Deposits.* Paris: Author, 1973. The thirty-eight papers in this book record the most international of all major symposia on the origin of large iron deposits, a symposium which occurred in Kiev, Soviet Union, in 1970. Offers the most comprehensive descriptions of iron deposits from around the globe.

Michael M. Kimberley

Cross-References

1976; Petrographic Microscopes, 2034; Prokaryotes, 2115; Earth Resources, 2175; Strategic Resources, 2188; Sedimentary Mineral Deposits, 2296; Sedimentary Rocks: Biogenic, 2312; Sedimentary Rocks: Chemical Precipitates, 2318; Silica Minerals, 2365; Stratigraphic Correlation, 2485; Weathering and Erosion, 2723.

ISLAND ARCS

Type of earth science: Geology
Field of study: Tectonics

Island arcs are arc-shaped chains of volcanic islands formed by the collision of two oceanic plates. They are the sites of most of the world's explosive volcanic eruptions and large earthquakes. Tsunami and ash clouds generated by these events can affect people around the globe.

Principal terms

ANDESITE: a light-colored volcanic rock rich in sodium and calcium feldspar, with some darker minerals

BASALT: a dark-colored igneous rock containing minerals such as feldspar and pyroxene, high in iron and magnesium

BENIOFF ZONE: the dipping zone of earthquake foci found below island arcs, named after Hugo Benioff, the seismologist who first defined it

EARTHQUAKE FOCUS: the region in the earth that marks the starting site of an earthquake

GRANITE: a light-colored igneous rock containing feldspar, quartz, and small amounts of darker minerals

GRAVITY ANOMALIES: differences between observed gravity readings and expected values after accounting for known irregularities

LITHOSPHERE: the rigid outer shell of the earth, composed of a number of plates

SUBDUCTION: the process by which a lithospheric plate containing oceanic crust is pushed under another plate

TSUNAMI: a seismic sea wave generated by vertical movement of the ocean floor, caused by an earthquake or volcanic eruption

Summary of the Phenomenon

An island arc is a long, arcuate chain of volcanic islands with an ocean on the convex (or outer) side of the arc. Paralleling the arc lies a long, narrow trench with steeply sloping sides that descend far below the normal ocean floor. A map of the world shows that many island arcs occur in and around the Pacific Ocean, such as the Aleutians, Japan, Tonga, Indonesia, New Zealand, and the Marianas. The West Indies are an island arc bordering the Atlantic Ocean. The associated trenches contain the deepest places on earth. The Marianas trench near the island of Guam reaches a maximum depth of 10,924 meters. This is farther below sea level than Mount Everest (at 8,848 meters) is above sea level. These island arc features, though merely topographic ones, demonstrate that island arcs and deep-sea trenches are parts of the same earth structure. There are six basic features common to island arc-trench systems: chains of volcanoes, deep ocean trenches, earthquake belts, a shallow sea behind the island arc, large negative gravity anomalies, and rock deformation in later geologic time. Some features are better displayed in one arc than another, but all are present.

All island arcs consist of an arc-shaped chain of volcanoes and volcanic islands. Many volcanoes are currently active or have been active in the recent geologic past. Some scientists group island arcs into two types: island arcs composed of volcanic islands located on oceanic crust (such as the Aleutians, Kurils, Marianas, and West Indies) and chains of volcanoes on small pieces of continental crust (such as Japan, Indonesia, New Zealand, and the Philippines). The main difference is that the continental-type arc is older, has had a more complex geologic history, and thus represents a later stage in the evolution of island arcs. The volcanoes of both types produce andesitic magma. Andesite is a light-colored, fine-grained igneous rock composed primarily of sodium- and calcium-rich feldspar. In composition, andesite lies midway between quartz-rich granites and iron- and magnesium-rich basalts. The andesitic magma also contains large amounts of gases that cause extremely explosive and destructive eruptions. Examples of island arc volcanic eruptions are Krakatoa, Indonesia, in 1883; Mount Pelée, Martinique, in 1902; and La Soufrière, St. Vincent, in 1902.

On the ocean side of all island arcs lie deep-sea trenches, long, narrow features that parallel the island chains. They have steep, sloping sides extending to great depths. Minor differences occur. Some trenches, such as the Marianas and the Kuril, have V-shaped cross sections and are rock-floored to their bottom. Others, such as the Puerto Rico and southwest Japan trenches, have a flat bottom. Detailed studies have shown that these flat-bottomed trenches are sediment-filled and that the underlying rock floor is also V-shaped.

Island arcs are active seismic regions and the sites of many of the world's largest and deepest earthquakes. The region in which an earthquake begins is called its focus. The foci of earthquakes in arc regions lie along a narrow, well-defined zone that dips from near the trench below the island arc. The number of earthquakes generally decreases with depth, with some foci reaching 600-700 kilometers below sea level. This dipping seismic zone is called the Benioff zone, after the seismologist Hugo Benioff, who first defined it.

Behind the island arc lies a shallow marginal sea; examples are the Sea of Japan, the Philippine Sea, and the Caribbean Sea. Below some marginal seas, the crust is partly continental but becomes oceanic toward the arc. Below other seas, the crust is entirely oceanic. The composition of the oceanic crust beneath the marginal seas is more like andesite than the basalt of the normal ocean floor.

Also common to arc-trench regions are large negative gravity anomalies. Geophysicists have found that the value of gravity over the earth's surface varies by slight amounts. Most of the variations can be accounted for and result from irregularities in altitude and topography. After observed gravity readings are corrected, however, variations called gravity anomalies still remain. These are caused by differences in rock density from place to place below the earth's surface. A negative anomaly shows that a greater volume of lighter (less dense) rocks is present in one area than in surrounding ones. Large negative anomalies are associated with the deep-sea trench and imply the presence of a great volume of low-density rocks at depth.

Deformation of rocks in the recent geologic history of an island arc is common. Some rocks have been folded, others metamorphosed. Areas of local uplift and subsidence are found that may also be related to shallow earthquakes and to faulting. These features are more easily seen and studied on the island arcs located on continental crust, such as Japan or New Zealand. Deformation, however, is present in all island arcs.

Earth scientists have long sought to explain the origin of island arcs. The remains of ancient marine volcanic islands and volcano-derived sediments are found in the core of the present-day Appalachian Mountains. These rocks and large amounts of continental sediments were compressed, faulted, and folded to form the ancient Appalachians. Yet, the relation of the volcanic islands to the mountain-building process was unclear. The development of the concept of plate tectonics has provided an explanation.

The outer portion of the earth is composed of a number of rigid lithospheric plates. Driven by forces in the mantle, the plates are pushed and shoved about the face of the earth. A lithospheric plate may contain continental crust, oceanic crust, or (more commonly) both. Island arcs form when the ocean portion of two colliding plates forces one plate under the other. The continuing collision of the plates may eventually result in the creation of a new mountain range, such as the ancient Appalachians. The process in which oceanic lithosphere is pushed under another plate is called subduction. Subduction of the plate causes the geological and geophysical features observed in the island arc system. (It should be noted that oceanic plates can also be subducted beneath continental plate margins. The resulting features are similar to those found in island arcs except that the andesite volcanoes form along the edge of the overriding continental margin. The Andes and Cascade mountains are the island arc equivalent for subduction beneath a continent. Mount St. Helens is an andesite volcano.)

As the two plates converge, one bends and is pushed under the other. The line of initial subduction is marked by a deep ocean trench. Subduction is not a smooth process. Friction between the subducting plate and the overriding plate and between the downgoing plate and the mantle tries to prevent movement. When frictional forces are overcome, an earthquake occurs. The location of earthquake foci outlines the subducting lithospheric plate. As subduction continues, earthquakes occur at greater depths. The lack of earthquakes below 700 kilometers suggests that this is the maximum depth that the plate can reach before it becomes part of the mantle. The downgoing oceanic plate drags along any deep-sea sediments that have been deposited on it or in the trench area. Both the plate and the sediments are heated, primarily by friction and by the surrounding hotter mantle. At about a depth of 100 kilometers, partial melting occurs, giving a magma rich in sodium, calcium, and silica. This magma mixes with the iron- and magnesium-rich mantle, creating a magma less dense than is the surrounding mantle. Forcing its way upward through zones of weakness in the overlying plate, the magma generates andesite volcanoes. The gravity anomaly associated with the trench is caused by the light crustal rocks of the subducting plate being held (or pushed) down by the overriding plate. The increased volume of less dense rocks produces a large negative anomaly.

Also common to island arc systems are recently deformed rocks. The overriding plate does not slip smoothly over the subducting plate. Rocks in the leading edge of the plate are compressed (pushed together), causing faulting, folding, and uplift. Pieces of the subducting plate can be broken off and folded into the island arc. Heat from the mantle causes metamorphism in the overlying rocks. Behind the island arc, shallow faulting caused by tension (pulling apart) creates earthquakes.

The marginal sea between the island arc and the continent is called the back-arc basin. The presence of these basins is not totally understood. Some, such as the Aleutian and the Philippine basins, were formed from pieces of preexisting ocean. Others have features suggesting that they were once continental crust that has been turned into oceanic crust. Still other basins appear to have been created by interarc spreading, like that seen along mid-ocean ridges. The origin of back-arc basins is a topic of active geologic research.

Methods of Study

In studying island arcs, scientists use a wide range of geological and geophysical techniques. The geological methods generally study the accessible portions of island arcs and include mapping and sample collection and analysis. The geophysical methods study the deep features of island arcs using earthquake and explosion seismology, gravity surveys, and heat-flow measurements. Computers aid in the analysis of data and in the generation of island arc models. Earth scientists studying certain aspects or features of island arcs select a combination of tools most appropriate to their region of interest.

Geologic mapping requires direct access to the rocks forming island arcs. The geologist surveys a region, recording the type of rock found and its extent and the orientation of observed faults and folds. Rock samples are collected for later study. These may be supplemented by drilling to sample rocks below the surface. The field data are transferred to a topographic map and, with the aid of aerial photographs, a geologic map is drawn. Aerial and satellite photographs have become increasingly helpful in the mapping of regions covered by vegetation. The traces of faults and the effects of changing bedrock can be reflected in surface features visible from high altitudes.

The rock samples collected are subjected to chemical and mineralogical analyses. The presence of trace elements or certain minerals can provide clues to the source region of a rock's components or to the thermal history of the rock since it was formed. Minerals containing radioactive elements, such as potassium 40 and rubidium 87, can be used to obtain the age of the rock units. Microscopic analysis of the rocks yields information on their thermal and deformational history. Direct collection of rock samples is limited to the exposed portions of island arcs. Dredging is used for sample collection in shallow ocean regions such as the back-arc basins. The use of submersibles, such as the *Alvin*, operated by Woods Hole Oceanographic Institution, has allowed scientists to photograph and collect rocks and other data from the ocean floor far below sea level, enabling them to extend the study of island arcs. These methods, however, do not reach the regions far below the earth's surface.

Indirect methods are used by geophysicists to study the deeper island arc regions. The two most widely used methods are earthquake and explosion seismology. Earthquake seismology studies the seismic waves generated by earthquakes and provides an average velocity structure of the crust and mantle. The distribution of earthquakes in arc regions, particularly Japan, led to the discovery of the dipping seismic zone beneath the arc. Scientists also study plate movements to learn the mechanism causing earthquakes.

Explosion seismology uses seismic waves generated by controlled explosions to study the detailed crustal and lithospheric structure of island arcs. Within the ocean regions, this technique has revealed the steep topography of the deep-sea trenches and the deformed rock layers near the base of the overriding plate.

Measurements of the earth's gravity field can be obtained on land and at sea. The data are corrected for irregularities in altitude and terrain. Remaining differences relate to density variations deep in the crust. The negative anomalies in the trench areas reflect the great thickness of crustal rocks at the plate boundary. In other areas, such as Japan, gravity data suggest a thicker crust or a less dense mantle below the back-arc basin (Sea of Japan) than below the Pacific Ocean.

Heat-flow measurements also reflect regional features. On the average, heat flow is the same over both continental and oceanic regions as a result of a deep, common source. In Japan, one of the most thoroughly studied island arc areas, a region of high heat flow coincides with the distribution of volcanoes and hot springs. A second high below the Sea of Japan suggests that the mantle is hotter than average, perhaps as a result of an interarc spreading center. A zone of low heat flow occurs on the Pacific side of the arc.

Earth scientists seek to unravel the history of island arcs to understand their formation. Computers are used to form models of island arcs so that theories of arc formation can be tested. By modifying the model to fit the observed geological and geophysical data, scientists can increase their overall understanding of the island arc system.

Context

Formed by the subduction of one oceanic plate beneath another, island arcs are active volcanic and seismic regions. Understanding island arcs aids earth scientists in unraveling the processes by which geologic features are formed. Knowledge of island arcs is also important to the nonscientist for two reasons: volcanoes and earthquakes. Though of greatest importance to people living in island arc regions, these active geologic zones can have far-reaching effects.

Subduction zone volcanism, in island arcs and in continental margins, accounts for 88 percent of known fatal eruptions. The high gas content of andesitic magma often results in abrupt and highly explosive eruptions, such as the eruption of Mount Pelée, Martinique, in 1902, which destroyed the town of St. Pierre and killed most of its inhabitants. The effects of eruptions can be far-reaching. In 1883, Krakatoa, Indonesia, erupted, sending volcanic ash over a 700,000-square-kilometer area. Fine dust from the explosion rose high in the atmosphere, where it stayed for several years, lowering the earth's average annual temperature a few degrees by partially blocking solar radiation. The explosion also generated a tsunami (a seismic sea wave), which washed away 165 villages in the Sunda Strait and was recorded as far away as the English Channel. In addition to having climatic effects, the presence of large amounts of ash and dust today can pose a hazard to aircraft navigation.

Many of the world's greatest earthquakes, such as those in Tokyo in 1923 and Alaska in 1964, originate in island arc regions. The danger posed is especially great in highly populated arcs, such as Japan or southern California. Ground movements caused by earthquakes and related landslides damage rigid structures—buildings, bridges, and pipelines—which disrupts basic health and safety services as well as economic production. More than 40 percent of the deaths in Tokyo in 1923 resulted from uncontrollable fires indirectly caused by the earthquake. Vertical movement of the sea floor associated with an earthquake can also generate tsunamis. Tsunamis caused by the 1964 Alaskan earthquake heavily damaged towns in the Gulf of Alaska. Tsunamis from the same earthquake also killed twelve people in Crescent City, California.

Understanding island arc processes can lead to better evaluation of the earthquake and volcanic hazard potential for nearby citizens. Identification and evaluation of events that are harbingers of earthquakes and volcanic eruptions may eventually lead to the prediction of both. The far-reaching effects of earthquakes and volcanic eruptions cannot be predicted. Tsunamis and ash clouds, however, may take several hours to reach distant cities. The Seismic Sea Wave Warning System, established in 1946 to reduce the danger from Pacific tsunamis, issues international warnings when tsunami risk from an earthquake is high. A volcanic watch service has been set up by the Federal Aviation Administration and the National Oceanic and Atmospheric Administration. Using satellite imagery and ground stations, the program will provide warnings to aircraft when dangerous ash clouds from volcanic eruptions are present.

Bibliography

Bolt, Bruce A. *Earthquakes*. New York: W. H. Freeman, 1988. A popular book on the many aspects of earthquakes. Chapters cover distribution of earthquakes, tsunamis, earthquake prediction, and hazard protection planning. Illustrated, with bibliography and index. Suitable for the general reader.

Decker, Robert, and Barbara Decker. *Volcanoes and the Earth's Interior*. San Francisco: W. H. Freeman, 1982. A series of articles on studies in volcanism. The first article, "The Subduction of the Lithosphere," discusses the relationship between subduction zones and island arcs. Illustrated, with bibliography. Suitable for the general reader.

King, Philip B. *The Evolution of North America*. Rev. ed. Princeton, N.J.: Princeton University Press, 1977. A revised edition of the classic book on the geology of North America. An excellent discussion of features of an island arc-trench system (the West Indies) appears on pages 84-90. Requires some knowledge of geology.

Lambert, David. *The Field Guide to Geology*. New York: Facts on File, 1988. A concise introduction to basic geologic terms and concepts. Chapter 2 explores the structure of the lithosphere. Chapter 3 discusses volcanoes and igneous rocks. A well-illustrated book suitable for high school students or beginning students at any level. Index and bibliography.

Miller, Russell. *Continents in Collision*. Alexandria, Va.: Time-Life Books, 1983. An extensively illustrated introduction to plate tectonics. Traces the historical development of the theory, with color illustrations and photographs. Index and bibliography. Suitable for the general reader.

National Research Council. *Explosive Volcanism: Inception, Evolution, and Hazards*. Washington, D.C.: National Academy Press, 1984. A study on all types explosive volcanism, prepared for the National Academy of Sciences. Includes a series of background reports on various aspects of explosive volcanism, including Mount St. Helens and Kilauea. Recommends plans for future research and emergency planning in the United States. Reports are technical but suitable for the knowledgeable reader.

Press, Frank, and Raymond Siever. *Earth*. 2d ed. San Francisco: W. H. Freeman, 1978. A book for the beginning reader in geology. Of interest are chapters 15, 17, and 19 for an overall view of earthquakes, volcanism, and plate tectonics. Illustrated and supplemented with numerous marginal notes. Chapter bibliographies and glossary.

Talwani, Manik, and Walter C. Pitman III, eds. *Island Arcs, Deep Sea Trenches, and Back-Arc Basins*. Washington, D.C.: American Geophysical Union, 1977. Series of technical papers from a symposium on island arcs, held in 1976. Papers cover a wide range of active research areas of the island arc-trench-back-arc system. Suitable for the college student or knowledgeable reader. Extensive references.

Walker, Bryce S. *Earthquake*. Alexandria, Va.: Time-Life Books, 1982. Extensively illustrated book on earthquakes, their causes, and their effects on humans. Chapter 1 covers the cause and effects of the 1964 Alaskan earthquake. Traces the historical development of scientific attempts to understand earthquakes and to predict them. Index and bibliography. Suitable for the general reader.

Pamela R. Justice

Cross-References

ISOSTASY

Type of earth science: Geophysics
Field of study: Geodesy and gravity

Isostasy is a principle that describes the vertical positioning of segments of the earth's lithosphere relative to one another in terms of the elevation of the land and depth to the top of the asthenosphere. It is, in effect, a restatement of Archimedes' principle or an application of that principle to the outer layers of the earth.

Principal terms

ARCHIMEDES' PRINCIPLE: the notion that a solid, floating body displaces a mass of water equal to its own mass

ASTHENOSPHERE: the layer immediately underneath the lithosphere, which acts geologically like a fluid

COLUMN: a cylindrical segment of the earth oriented on a line from the center of the earth to any point on its surface, beginning somewhere in the asthenosphere and ending somewhere within the atmosphere

DENSITY: the amount of mass per unit volume of a substance

LITHOSPHERE: the outermost solid layer of the earth

SEA LEVEL: the position of the surface of the ocean relative to the surface of land

SUBSIDENCE: the sinking of the earth's surface or a decrease in the distance between the earth's surface and its center

UPLIFT: the rising of the earth's surface or the increase in distance between the earth's surface and its center

VISCOSITY: the ability of a fluid to flow

Summary of the Phenomenon

Isostasy, sometimes called the doctrine or principle of isostasy, is a fundamental principle of the earth sciences that describes the spacial positioning of lithospheric mass within the earth. Isostasy requires that the total mass of air, water, and rock within any vertical column extending from within the asthenosphere, through the lithosphere, to within the atmosphere is equal to the total mass of any other column in the same area of the earth, extending from the same depth in the asthenosphere to the same elevation in the atmosphere. The concept of isostasy is analogous to the concept of buoyancy in physics. Buoyancy was first explained by Archimedes, who, as legend tells it, lowered himself into bathwater, observed the level of the water rise against the wall of the bath pool, and thus realized that ships float because they displace a mass of water equal to the mass of the ship. This discovery came to be known as Archimedes' principle.

Many centuries later, scholars realized that Archimedes' principle could be used to explain why the earth has both high mountain ranges and deep ocean basins. The main obstacle to the acceptance of the principle was the belief of early scholars that the earth was a solid, rigid body. The idea that the ground on which they stood could be compared to a boat floating on the sea was totally beyond their comprehension. The knowledge needed to draw that analogy did not become available until the mid-nineteenth century, when British surveyors under the direction of Sir George Everest were engaged in the trigonometrical survey of India near the Himalaya. The surveyors noted that the distance between the towns of Kalianpur and Kaliana, when measured by triangulation methods, differed by 5.236 seconds of arc, or about 160 meters from the distance when measured by astronomical methods. Two British scholars, George Biddell Airy and John Henry Pratt, realized the cause of this apparent error, though each provided different interpretations of the geologic conditions that gave rise to the difference in distances. Their interpretations later came to be known as the Airy hypothesis and the Pratt hypothesis of isostasy.

The discrepancy resulting from the two survey methods lies in the method of the triangulation survey. In a triangulation survey, the instrument, a transit, is positioned on a tripod directly over a reference station marked on the ground surface. To position the transit directly over the station mark, a string with a conical-shaped lead weight known as a plumb bob is attached to the center of the transit and allowed to hang down. In this way, the plumb bob and string trace a vertical line to the ground. The plumb bob pulls on the string under the force of gravity. If that force were truly vertical, as the surveyors had assumed, the string would have made a vertical line between the instrument and the survey mark. What both Airy and Pratt had realized after reviewing the results of the survey was that the force of gravity in the area of the Himalaya was not truly vertical and the plumb bob was pulled off at a very slight angle from vertical. Therefore, each time the surveyors had repositioned their instrument, they had introduced a small but systematic error into their measurements. Those several thousand tiny errors added up to the difference in distance determined by the two survey methods. Both Airy and Pratt attributed the deviation in the pull of gravity to reduced rock densities below the Himalaya. That reduction in the distribution of mass in and below the mountains caused the plumb bob to be pulled away from the area of the mountains and toward the denser rock of the low-lying areas adjacent to the mountains.

While both Airy and Pratt applied the Archimedes' principle to explain the elevation of the Himalaya and the discrepancy in distance between the two survey methods, their hypotheses differed in the way they explained how the mass is distributed below the mountains. Airy viewed that apparent mass deficiency below the mountains as a result of the mountains having a root of low-density rock that extends well into a lower-lying, denser, fluid layer upon which the mountains and all other surficial rock layers float. This lower-density mountain and mountain root combination were envisioned as being like a boat floating upon a denser fluid, which Airy thought was lava. The "boat" was thus made buoyant by the root's displacing a mass of the fluid equal in mass to the combined mountain and mountain root. To Airy, the higher the mountain, the deeper the root must extend to compensate for the elevated mass. By analogy, of two vessels of the same areal extent, one tall and the other of low profile, the tall vessel projects deeper into and rises higher out of the water. Pratt saw the situation somewhat differently. He maintained that the position of the base of the solid crust must be the same everywhere. The differences in surficial elevations, Pratt thought, arise from some areas having experienced less "contraction" than other areas during the cooling of the earth. These areas of less contraction are also of less density and float higher in accordance with Archimedes' principle. Regional variations in surface elevation, according to the Airy hypothesis, result from variations in the thickness of the solid outer layer of the earth. Airy thought the density of the outer layer was the same everywhere, but the position of the base varies according to the magnitude of surface elevation. According to the Pratt hypothesis, the regional variations in surface elevation result from variations in density of the solid outer layer, with the base of that layer being of equal position everywhere. The Pratt model has a flat-bottomed crust.

Elevated terrains in both the Airy and the Pratt models have less mass near the surface than low-lying terrains. Therefore, according to these hypotheses, the plumb bob was pulled by gravity away from the area of the mountains and toward the lower-lying plains of India. Clarence Edward Dutton in 1889 recognized the significance of this variation in the amount of mass near the surface and concluded, "Where the lighter matter was accumulated there would be a tendency to bulge, and where the denser matter existed there would be a tendency to flatten or depress the surface." Dutton coined the term "isostasy" for this definition between land surface elevation and rock mass as mandated by Archimedes' principle.

Earth scientists acknowledge the validity of both the Airy and the Pratt hypotheses. They consider large-scale or regional land surface elevation variation to result from variations in density and thickness of the lithosphere and also from variations in density of the asthenosphere. Furthermore, earth scientists recognize that the density and/or thickness of the lithosphere at any particular place can change through time and thus result in vertical movements of lithospheric plates to compensate for these changes. If one were to heat a solid object, such as a steel pipe, it would expand and thus decrease its density and increase its length. If a segment of the lithosphere of the earth were to be heated, the rock within that segment would also become less dense, the thickness of the lithospheric segment would increase, and the elevation of the land surface of that segment would rise in accordance with both the Airy and the Pratt hypotheses. This rising of the land surface is known as uplift. Similarly, if a segment of the lithosphere were to cool, the rock would increase in density, the thickness would be reduced, and the elevation of the surface would be reduced. This reduction of land surface elevation through time is referred to as subsidence. If cargo were added to the deck of a boat, it would be seen to ride lower in the water. The top of the cargo, however, would be at a greater distance above the water. Removing deck cargo has the opposite effect. If a segment of the lithosphere were to have sediment deposited on its surface, its base would project a greater distance into the asthenosphere, and its top would be described as being at a greater elevation. If material is removed from the lithosphere by erosion, the base of the lithosphere rises and the land surface elevation decreases.

The vertical adjustments in the position of the lithosphere to maintain equilibrium are referred to as isostatic compensations. To be in equilibrium, the total amount of mass within a column of the earth that extends from within the atmosphere, through the hydrosphere and lithosphere, and into the asthenosphere must be equal to the total mass of any other column of the same areal range that extends from the same elevation in the atmosphere to the same depth in the asthenosphere. A change in the lithosphere within a column in terms of mass or density will be compensated by changes in the mass of the atmosphere, hydrosphere, and asthenosphere.

When sediment or rock is deposited or eroded from the top of the lithosphere, mass is added or subtracted from the lithosphere, and isostatic adjustments are made to compensate for this change. If sediment is deposited upon the surface of the lithosphere, the added load displaces some of the asthenosphere; thus, there is less asthenospheric mass in the column. If the top of the lithosphere were below sea level, then hydrospheric mass would also be displaced; if sediment accumulated until it were stacked above sea level, then mass within the atmosphere would be displaced also. If sediment or rock is eroded from the top of the lithosphere, the base of the lithosphere rises, and mass is added to the asthenospheric portion of the column. If the top of the column were initially above sea level, then the mass of the atmospheric portion of the column would increase; if erosion cut below sea level, then hydrospheric mass would be added to the column. Depositional isostatic subsidence is seen along continental margins such as the Gulf Coast of Texas, where there are great accumulations of sediment. Isostatic rebound is associated with erosion (melting) of the Pleistocene ice sheets. Such glacio-isostatic rebounds have been measured in eastern North America and Northern Europe.

When the lithosphere is warmed or cooled, the situation becomes more complex. The warming or cooling of the lithosphere is geologically accomplished by changes in the temperature of the asthenosphere. Therefore, the density of both the lithosphere and asthenosphere would be expected to vary with temperature changes. If temperature change is the only process operating, then the mass of the lithosphere is constant regardless of its temperature; its thickness and density, however, would have changed. If the lithosphere is warmed, the mass in the hydrosphere and/or atmospheric portions of the column would have decreased in an amount equal to the increase in mass of the asthenospheric portion. The net effect is an increase in the elevation of the land surface, or thermo-isostatic uplift. If the lithospheric portion of the column were to cool, there would be an increase in the mass of the hydrospheric and/or atmospheric portions of the column and a decrease in the asthenospheric portion. The net effect would be a decrease in land elevation, or thermo-isostatic subsidence. Isostatic uplift is seen in the area of the Mid-Atlantic

Ridge, the greatest mountain range on the surface of the earth. It also may explain why the continent of Africa has such a greater average elevation relative to sea level than do the other continents. Isostatic subsidence has been suggested to be the underlying mechanism for the formation of the thick sediment accumulations within continental areas. The Michigan Basin and the Williston Basin in North America are examples of these accumulations.

The processes that give rise to isostatic adjustments take millions of years. The resulting isostatic adjustments are also very slow to occur. When a person steps onto a boat, it instantly rides lower in the water, because the compensation of the boat for the additional load is immediate. The medium upon which the boat floats, water, has a very low viscosity. If the boat were afloat in a more viscous fluid, such as cold molasses, the adjustment to the added mass would be noticeably slower, perhaps taking a minute or more. The asthenosphere is very viscous. Consequently, isostatic adjustments to lithospheric changes may take tens of thousands of years. A notable example is the glacio-isostatic rebound that is occurring today, resulting from the melt of the North American glaciers, which was largely completed 6,500 years ago.

Methods of Study

Isostasy is a principle or law of the earth sciences, and, as such, it cannot be collected, observed, or quantified. What can be observed or quantified are the results of lithospheric segments satisfying or attempting to establish isostatic equilibrium. If a geologic process changes the mass or density of a segment of the lithosphere, vertical adjustments in the position of the lithosphere are necessary to reestablish the equilibrium. These vertical adjustments are slow; 1 centimeter per year would be considered fast. To measure the changes in lithosphere position caused by isostatic compensation, one needs a hypothetical measuring stick and a clock. The "stick" in nearly all cases measures the distance between the top of the lithospheric segment and sea level. Because the time over which the adjustment process occurs is quite long, the clock that is used is the decay of radioisotopes, such as carbon 14, potassium 40, and uranium 238.

The application of these tools to the study of isostatic compensation can be illustrated with the evaluation of the phenomenon of glacio-isostatic rebound. During the last glaciation, the Wisconsin, vast sheets of ice covered portions of Antarctica, North America, Europe, and the southern tip of South America. That ice constituted a load on the decks of several lithospheric boats. From 18,000 to 6,500 years ago, most of the ice sheets in North America, Europe, and South America melted. The meltwater increased the volume of water in the oceans. Consequently, the level of the oceans rose 100 meters relative to a fixed point on a landmass that was not glaciated, such as the island of Cuba. From 6,500 years ago to the present, little additional ice has melted. Thus, the amount of water in the oceans has been constant. Sea level, therefore, should have been constant worldwide. During this period of time, however, sea level has not been constant in those areas where glacial ice had once loaded the lithosphere. In those areas, fixed points on the land surface are rising relative to sea level. Some areas are currently rising at the rate of 2 centimeters per year; other areas have already risen nearly 140 meters. Scientists can determine how far and how fast the lithosphere has rebounded or is rebounding by examining the locations of exposed shoreline sediments or marine terraces. The sediments would have been deposited and the terraces formed by waves on a beach when sea level was at that land point. Part of that sediment would have been the remains of plants and animals that were alive at the time of deposition of the sediment. By surveying the current difference in elevation between the ancient shoreline sediments and the present sea level, scientists can determine the amount vertical uplift since the sediment was deposited. By determining the radiometric age of the remains of organic life using carbon 14 dating methods, scientists can calculate the length of the time over which that amount of rebound occurred. Several different shoreline deposits or terraces in the same region can reveal different land positions relative to sea level and how the rate of rebound has changed with time. Geologists can therefore determine the viscosity of the asthenosphere, project how much rebound will occur in the future, and estimate how much rebound will have occurred when isostatic equilibrium is established. This estimate can be translated into how thick the ice was when the glaciers were present. Ice thickness equals the product of the total rebound times the ratio of the density of the asthenosphere to the density of the ice.

Context

The relationship between isostasy and the surface of the land is analogous to the relationship between buoyancy and the deck of a ship. Humans can overload the deck of a ship and sink it into the sea, but they cannot overload the lithosphere and sink it into the asthenosphere. This area of nature is one of the few that is not heavily influenced by human activity. If all the engineers of the world used all the earth-moving equipment in the world to pile soil, sediment, and rock in one huge mound, they could not in their lifetimes cause a segment of the lithosphere to ride 1 millimeter lower in the asthenosphere. Nature, however, in a few hundred millennia can pile enough snow and ice on Antarctica to sink land surface so substantially that most of the subice rock surface (the preglaciation top of the lithosphere) now lies below sea level, several hundred meters below where it originally was. Besides geologists and geophysicists, isostasy touches the lives of very few people directly. The notable exceptions are those few historians who ponder why certain Viking harbors in Scandinavia are now situated above sea level: The answer pertains to glacio-isostatic rebound.

Bibliography

Dockal, J. A., R. A. Laws, and T. R. Worsley. "A General Mathematical Model for Balanced Global Isostasy." *Mathematical Geology* 21 (March, 1989): 147. A comprehensive mathematical treatment of isostasy. Discusses the connection between isostatic adjustments and global sea-level changes. Suitable for college-level students with a working knowledge of algebra.

Hart, P. J., ed. *The Earth's Crust and Upper Mantle*. Washington, D.C.: American Geophysical Union, 1969. A somewhat technical book that gathers together many aspects of the crust and mantle or lithosphere and asthenosphere. A chapter by E. V. Artyushkov and Y. U. A. Mescherikov deals quite well with recent isostatic movements and provides a good bibliography of the foreign literature on isostasy. Suitable for college-level students.

Jordan, Thomas H. "The Deep Structure of the Continents." *Scientific American* 240 (January, 1979): 92-107. Discusses new ideas on the makeup and nature of the lithosphere and asthenosphere. Provides considerable insight into how knowlege of the deep earth is obtained. Suitable for college-level students.

Mather, K. F., ed. *A Source Book in Geology, 1900-1950*. Cambridge, Mass.: Harvard University Press, 1967. A collection of major landmark geologic works dating from 1900 to 1950. Included in this collection is Joseph Barrell's "The Status of the Theory of Isostasy," which summarizes much of the early thinking on isostasy. Other relevant works include the two studies of the properties of the asthenosphere, one by Felix Vening Meinesz and the other by Beno Gutenberg. Suitable for high school and college-level students.

Mather, K. F., and S. L. Mason, eds. *A Source Book in Geology, 1400-1900*. Cambridge, Mass.: Harvard University Press, 1970. A collection of major landmark geologic works dating from 1400 to 1900. Each paper is condensed from its original length. The collection includes the works of G. B. Airy, J. H. Pratt, and C. E. Dutton. Brief biographic sketches are given for the authors. Suitable for high school and college-level students.

Walcott, R. I. "Late Quaternary Vertical Movements in Eastern North America: Quantitative Evidence of Glacio-Isostatic Rebound." *Review of Geophysics and Space Physics* 10 (November, 1972): 849-884. A review paper that collects and evaluates from published sources the evidence of vertical movements of the lithosphere that are attributed to glacio-isostatic rebound. Charts present accumulated data for sea-level changes in North America. Maps portray the magnitude of rebound. Contains an excellent bibliography on glacio-isostatic rebound. Suitable in part for advanced high school and college-level readers.

James A. Dockal

Cross-References

JOINTS

Type of earth science: Geology
Field of study: Structural geology

Joints form when rocks undergo brittle failure, usually during expansion. Their orientations, physical features, and patterns of occurrence can be used to help infer the physical conditions present at the time of failure. Because joints are important conduits for fluids, particularly oil and water, that move beneath the surface, understanding their formation and occurrence has economic benefits.

Principal terms

CHEMICAL WEATHERING: changes in rocks produced by reactions with fluids near the surface of the earth

COLUMNAR JOINTING: the formation of columns, often with hexagonal cross sections, as joints grow inward from the outer surfaces of cooling igneous rock bodies

CONJUGATE SHEAR SETS: two sets of joints that make angles with each other of something close to 60 degrees and 120 degrees

EXFOLIATION: the splitting off of curving sheets from the outside of a body of rock; also called sheeting

EXTENSION: expansion, or stretching apart, of rocks

FRACTOGRAPHY: the study of fracture surfaces to determine the propagation history of the crack

JOINT: a fracture in a rock across which there has been no substantial slip parallel to the fracture

Summary of the Phenomenon

Joints are the ubiquitous cracks found in nearly every outcrop. They are unquestionably the most common structure at the surface of the earth. They vary in size from microscopic fractures visible only within an individual grain in a rock to fractures kilometers in length, some of which are responsible for the magnificent scenery of Arches National Park. If one smashes a rock with a hammer, one produces joints. Joints also form as molten rocks solidify and cool, as weathering alters the volume of the outer layers of a rock, and even as erosion removes overlying layers, reducing the weight on the layers below and permitting them to expand and crack.

There is no appreciable slip across a joint. (Failure surfaces accommodating large amounts of slip are faults.) Often, the same mineral grain can be observed on both sides of a joint, neatly cut in two but otherwise not disturbed. This indicates failure in extension; such joints are sometimes called extension joints. The sides of the fracture moved away from each other but did not slide past each other at all. The forces producing such joints were literally pulling the rock apart. An engineer might call these tensile forces. Geologists work with rocks that are nearly always in a state of compression, however, and true tension is uncommon. Therefore, geologists usually call such forces the forces of least compression. The direction of least compression is the direction in which extension occurs. That is, as the crack opens and the sides move away from each other, they will move in the direction of the least compressive force. Consequently, the plane of an extension joint will be perpendicular to the direction of the least compressive force.

Such extension may be produced in a variety of ways. Most obvious are mechanisms involving large-scale deformation of the rock. The folding of a unit of rock causes extension on the outside of the fold. Often, extension joints are found fanning around the "nose" of a fold. The injection of molten rock into cooler rock, and its subsequent cooling, can fracture the cooler rock, producing joints. Extension is also produced during weathering when, because of chemical reactions at the surface of a rock, the surface layer expands more than the interior does. This expanded surface pulls away from the rest of the rock much as an onionskin pulls off the outside of an onion. This process is called exfoliation or sheeting. One classic example of this is Half Dome, in Yosemite National Park.

Contraction, too, can cause joints. The familiar cracks that form in dried-up mud puddles are an example: Moist mud contracts as it dries, and cracks in the surface result when the forces involved in this contraction overcome the cohesive strength of the mud. As rock cools, such as when a molten, igneous rock body solidifies and then cools further, it contracts. The cooling and contraction are greatest at the surface of such a body. The polygonal patterns of cracks that form on such surfaces are very similar to those seen in dried mud. As the hot rock continues to cool, these cracks extend into the interior of the body. This may result in spectacular columns, such as those seen at Devils Postpile. The process is called columnar jointing.

The most common way joints form, however, is probably when rocks that equilibrated at depth are brought to the surface, either by mountain-building forces or when erosion removes the overlying rocks. This means of forming joints was proposed by Neville Price in his 1966 book *Fault and Joint Development in Brittle and Semi-Brittle Rock*. Although the model cannot be applied directly at any particular location because the deformation history, local topography, and other factors vary too much from place to place, it is instructive to consider the process in general terms.

How can vertical uplift produce horizontal extension? Consider large suspension bridges such as the Verrazano Narrows in New York City or the Golden Gate Bridge in San Francisco. The vertical towers supporting these bridges diverge from one another by about a hundredth of a degree, because of the curvature of the earth. The tops of these towers are farther apart than their bases, so a rope that exactly reached between the bases would have to stretch a bit if it were raised to their tops. If it were unable to stretch, it would break.

Would uplift of 5 kilometers be sufficient to produce joints in a typical rock? If the earth's circumference is 40,074 kilometers, the circumference of a circle lying 5 kilometers beneath the surface would be 40,043 kilometers. If that circle were brought to the surface, it would have to be stretched by 31 kilometers, or by 0.078 percent. This amount of stretch might not seem like much, as a block of rock 100 meters long would need to extend only 7.8 centimeters. But if one tried to stretch that block of rock by attaching a gigantic pulling apparatus on it, experimental data show that the block would break before stretching that much. In addition to this geometric extension, the rock would generally cool as it came up to the surface, contracting and making more joints in the process. Because the state of compression at depth would likely be different from that at the surface, the changes that occur during uplift might encourage or inhibit joint formation, depending on local conditions. Still, if all the joints currently at the surface of the earth are considered, it appears as if the majority of extension joints may form by uplift. The fact that joints form during uplift and erosion does not mean, however, that they are necessarily unrelated to the structural history of the rocks in which they occur. Deformed rocks often contain stored-up energy, much like the energy stored in a spring, which was caused by the deformation. This energy, usually called residual stress, can influence the development of joints. Thus, joints that form hundreds of millions of years after a rock was initially deformed will often occur in patterns and orientations clearly related to that deformation.

Some joints are not formed strictly by extension. These joints develop as a series of cracks, called shear joints, which break the rock into diamond-shaped pieces. These pieces slide slightly past one another, accommodating the deformation. Careful examination of these joints may show some slight offset of grains across the joint, but the displacement across any one joint is small. The cumulative effect across hundreds of joints, however, can be considerable. Often, these joints occur in two parallel sets, with angles of about 60 degrees and 120 degrees between them. Such sets are called conjugate shear sets. Shear joints are not perpendicular to the direction of least compression, but it is possible to determine the direction of compression from the orientation of the conjugate shear sets. The direction of intermediate compression is indicated by the line of intersection of the joints. The direction of least compression bisects the obtuse angle between the sets, and the direction of maximum compression bisects the acute angle. In terms of a diamond-shaped piece, the direction of least compression is the short way across the diamond, and the direction of greatest compression is the long way across the diamond. It is not uncommon for conjugate shear sets to occur in conjunction with extension joints. In this case, the extension joints will be parallel to the long axes of the diamonds.

Consider the joints that might be associated with a fold that forms in a horizontal layer of rock not too far beneath the surface. The fold will form as the layer buckles in response to forces acting along it—in the north-south direction, for example— which is similar to the way a playing card flexes when one squeezes the edges between one's fingers. Early in the deformation process, least compression in the east-west direction results in extension joints running north-south and shear joints running northeast and northwest at a 30-degree angle. Eventually a buckle develops, folding the layer and producing extension fractures in the east-west direction. Much later, erosion and uplift may bring parts of this layer to the surface. The direction of the least compression at that time, which may have no relation at all to the forces that originally produced the fold, will control the vertical extension joints that develop because of this uplift. Finally, weathering and the vagaries of the topography at the time the rock is exposed to weathering control the exfoliation joints that will follow the shape of the exposed surface.

Fracture "decorations" — patterns — on the joint surfaces can yield useful information about the speed of fracture growth and the direction in which it grew. This field of study is called fractography and has been developed by ceramic engineers concerned with reconstructing the brittle failure of glass and ceramic objects in order to improve their design. It can be directly applied to the study of joint surfaces.

When a fracture begins to grow, it starts with a low velocity but accelerates quickly. While it is moving slowly, the front of the fracture is usually a smooth curve, and the decoration it leaves on the fracture surface may be perfectly smooth, called the mirror region, or slightly frosted in appearance, in which case it is called mist hackle. If the crack grows intermittently, arrest lines may result. These curves show where the crack front was at different times when it temporarily stopped growing. As it increases in speed, the fracture front divides into a number of fingerlike projections. These commonly move a bit beyond the initial plane of the fracture as the fracture continues to grow. The result is a pattern on the surface of the fracture that has long been called plumose structure by geologists but is known as twist hackle by fractographers. It looks very much like a feather. The directions in which the fracture grew are shown by the directions of each slightly offset, curving element. Many of these features can be seen on building stones, flagstones, and slate floor tiles.

Joints provide conduits for the movement of fluids beneath the surface. Just as cracks in a pot permit water to leak through the pot, joints in the bedrock greatly enhance the rate at which water, oil, natural gas, and other fluids move through it. Near the surface, water is the fluid most likely to move through joints. As it does so, it is likely to attack the rock on both sides of the joint, chemically weathering it. This process enlarges the joint, increasing the flow of water through it, which in turn causes it to be weathered further, and the process continues. When the jointed rocks are limestone, the result may be elaborate systems of caverns, such as Carlsbad Caverns and other famous caves. Maps of such caves clearly demonstrate that joints controlled their development. In areas underlain by less soluble rock, joints may provide access to groundwater resources. By studying joint patterns displayed on geologic maps, aerial photographs, or satellite images, hydrologists are sometimes able to see where the natural underground flow of water may be greatest, and they can exploit this knowledge in their search for water. Similarly, petroleum geologists seek conditions where joints may facilitate the movement of oil and gas toward potential well sites. Because the rocks of interest to them are often much deeper than those with useful water resources, petroleum geologists may be forced to guess the location of joints at depth. Although the surface traces of joints seen on maps can help, it is often necessary to apply an understanding of how and why joints form in order to predict where they may be at depth. In some cases, artificial joints are produced by pumping fluids under very high pressure into the rocks.

Methods of Study

Joints can be studied at a variety of different scales. Sometimes a regional picture is sought, in which case aerial photographs or topographic maps can be used to see where joint surfaces intersect the surface of the earth. These lines are called the traces of the joints. The advantage of this technique is that large areas can be studied easily, with no need to be in the field. The disadvantages include the fact that vertical and other very steep joints may be well represented, but horizontal or gently dipping joints may not be visible. Knowledge that such biases exist enable useful results to be derived from such studies; however, care must be exercised. The significance—or even existence—of physical causes for the lines and lineaments perceived in such studies is often open to question.

When more three-dimensional information is sought, the orientations of joint planes can be measured in the field and plotted on maps. Approaches vary from visually estimating which joints on an outcrop are significant and then measuring only a representative sample of them (the selection method) to establishing a grid of stations so that every joint within a circle of a certain radius is measured (the inventory method). If the study involves a large number of joints, statistical techniques are employed, such as plotting the data on a graphic device called a stereonet and contouring the results.

If the details of the propagation history of the joints are important, exposed joint surfaces are studied and mapped. Careful measurement of joint openings and offsets (if they exist) can give an estimate of strain. Traces on the outcrop surface can be studied to determine the extent and significance of joint interactions. Finally, the forces that had the greatest influence in the joint development can be isolated, and their magnitudes can be estimated.

Context

Joints are fractures in solid rock. Unlike faults, which are also fractures, there is little or no slip across joints. In many ways, joints are like cracks in a pane of glass. If a baseball hits a window hard enough to crack it, but not hard enough to go through it, it may produce a set of fractures, radiating from the point of impact, which look a bit like a spider's web. That pattern strongly suggests an impact and is not what would be expected from a more gradual process, such as the settling of a house. Similarly, the orientations of some joints can be used to infer the directions of the stresses and forces in the outer part of the earth during the time they formed. This information may help in predicting where the walls and ceilings of mines might collapse and where earthquakes will occur in the future.

Many joints are controlled by stresses locked into the rock long before it fractures. The tempered glass in the rear window of a car always shatters the same way, regardless of how it is broken; the characteristic net of cracks results from the high stresses locked into that type of glass when it was manufactured. The patterns produced by such joints in rocks can provide useful insights into deformations that occurred millions of years ago.

Because they are planes of weakness, joints often control how rocks weather and erode. Cliffs, caves, and mountaintops often owe their shapes to joints. When rocks fail and landslides or rockslides result, joints usually influence where the failure occurs. Fluids utilize joints in order to move through otherwise impermeable rock. In cold climates, near the surface of the earth, water can freeze inside joints, wedging them apart. Water moving through joints frequently reacts chemically with the rock it contacts, weathering the rock and weakening it. This process can be a factor in the formation of additional joints.

At greater depths, joints provide conduits through which water—and also oil and gas—can migrate. Scientists seeking water resources use aerial photographs, satellite images, and topographic maps to locate areas where joints are prevalent. Petroleum geologists study complicated models of deformation deep within the earth in order to guess where naturally produced jointing may increase the flow of oil and gas. If necessary, engineers can increase fluid flow rates, producing joints by pumping fluids into the earth under high pressure.

The surface of the earth would look much different, weather and erode at much lower rates, and have much slower movement of fluids within it, if it were not for the millions and millions of joints that fracture it so pervasively.

Bibliography

Billings, Marland P. *Structural Geology*. 3d ed. Englewood Cliffs, N.J.: Prentice-Hall, 1972. Chapter 7, "Joints" (33 pages), gives a general description of joints and how they are studied. Includes four photographs and a discussion of brittle failure. Suitable for college students.

Davis, George H. *Structural Geology of Rocks and Regions*. New York: John Wiley & Sons, 1984. Chapter 10, "Joints" (28 pages), covers the subject from a generally field-oriented perspective. The discussion of field methods is clear and comprehensive. Includes a section on joint-related structures, including veins and stylolitic joints. Largely descriptive, easily read, and suitable for anyone interested in joints and the study of joints.

Johnson, Arvid M. *Physical Processes in Geology*. San Francisco: Freeman, Cooper, 1970. Chapter 10, "Formation of Sheet Structure in Granite," shows how a particular variety of joints has been studied using a quantitative approach. A technical approach that reveals how interesting some of the questions raised by jointing become when studied in detail. Appropriate for technically oriented college students.

Marshak, Stephen, and Gautam Mitra, eds. *Basic Methods of Structural Geology*.

Englewood Cliffs, N.J.: Prentice-Hall, 1988. Chapter 12, "Analysis of Fracture Array Geometry," by Arthur Goldstein and Stephen Marshak (18 pages), gives a good description of joint surface morphology, an overview of the field methods that have been used in studying them, and a summary of graphing and statistical techniques. The treatments are brief, but references are complete. Seems to have been designed for the reader who already knows something about joints but wishes to learn more about how to study them. College level.

Price, Neville J. *Fault and Joint Development in Brittle and Semi-Brittle Rock.* London: Pergamon Press, 1966. This 176-page book is a classic in its field. Most of the work done on joints since its publication has been done by people who have read this book, so its influence is great. Suffers, however, from having been written before modern experimental methods for studying rock deformation had been fully developed and from its use of the British system of measurement. Contains only four photographs, of somewhat limited usefulness, and other figures are schematic, though clear. Not overly technical, with a minimum of mathematical derivations, this book gives a fair summary of what was know about joints at the time it was written. Suitable for college-level students.

Suppe, John, ed. *Principles of Structural Geology.* Englewood Cliffs, N.J.: Prentice-Hall, 1985. Chapter 6, "Joints," presents an excellent overview of the classification, appearance, and formation of joints. The sixteen photographs show all manner of joints at a variety of scales, and some of the fourteen line drawings provide good examples of how joint studies have been used in interpreting structures and the state of stress in the crust. At times, the discussion becomes a bit technical, and several references are made to chapter 4, "Fracture and Brittle Behavior," which is more technical yet. A useful digression concerns the state of stress in the upper and lower crust and in the mantle. College-level reading.

Otto H. Muller

Cross-References

Aerial Photography, 17; Aquifers, 71; Building Stone, 178; Continental Rift Zones, 275; Folds, 739; Groundwater Movement, 1020; Igneous Rock Bodies, 1131; Karst Topography, 1310; Landsat, 1358; Landslides and Slope Stability, 1365; Underground Mining Techniques, 1710; Oil and Gas Exploration, 1878; Stress and Strain, 2490; Weathering and Erosion, 2723.

THE JOVIAN PLANETS

Type of earth science: Planetology
Field of study: Large solar system bodies

The Jovian planets—Jupiter (Jove), Saturn, Uranus, and Neptune—are gigantic solar bodies of mass 15-320 times that of Earth, although they are of very low relative density. They are mainly gaseous and liquid, composed of relatively light elements such as hydrogen and helium. All of them are surrounded by ring systems and a host of diverse moons.

Principal terms
ASTRONOMICAL UNIT: 1.5×10^{11} meters, the distance between Earth and the sun
BELTS: low-pressure, sinking red-brown gases that circle Jovian planets above the equator
GREAT RED SPOT: a cyclonic disturbance in Jupiter's atmosphere that has existed for at least 300 years
LIQUID METALLIC HYDROGEN: hydrogen that behaves as a metal under pressure of about 5 million Earth atmospheres
MAGNETOSPHERE: the volume of space near a planet that is dominated by that planet's magnetic field
OBLATENESS: the fraction by which the equatorial diameter exceeds the polar diameter
SILICATE: a salt composed mainly of silicon and oxygen
SPECIFIC GRAVITY or DENSITY: the density of an object relative to that of water
WHITE SPOTS: atmospheric disturbances on Jovian planets, appearing at boundaries between zones and belts
ZONES: yellow-white high-pressure gases that circle Jovian planets

Summary of the Phenomenon

The four Jovian planets are totally different geologically and physically from the terrestrial planets, Mercury, Venus, Earth, and Mars. Massive gaseous and liquid giants composed primarily of hydrogen and helium, the Jovian planets are relatively rapid rotators (all rotate about their own axis in less than twenty-four hours), have low specific gravities, and have variegated ring systems and a series of diverse moons or satellites orbiting them.

The atmospheres of the Jovian planets—the feature that dominates observational work done on these planets—are very similar to one another in composition. Hydrogen represents about 90 percent of the atoms present, with helium making up the bulk of the remaining atmospheric gases. Methane and ammonia are also present, although the ammonia surrounding Jupiter and Saturn has most likely fallen out of the colder outer two planets, Uranus and Neptune. The weather systems that dominate these atmospheres, particularly in the case of Jupiter and Saturn, consist of rapidly rotating belts and zones that are visible from Earth. In the case of Jupiter, wind speeds on the order of 300 kilometers per hour are common, while on Saturn wind speeds of two to three times that speed have been measured. (On Earth, hurricane-force winds rarely exceed 150 kilometers per hour.)

Both Jupiter and Saturn are much hotter than might be expected in view of their distances from the sun. They have their own sources of heat deep in the planetary interiors and thus are able to produce extensive thermal cells to drive such high-speed winds. The source of the heat within these planets is not evident, and there is some evidence that even in the case of Uranus there may also be a heat-driven weather system resulting from a much more modest heat source on the planet. Indeed, images from Voyager 2 have shown that Neptune has an actively driven weather system.

Although there are no measurements to indicate what lies below these turbulent atmospheres, there is indirect evidence that toward the center of a typical Jovian planet, the pressures become higher; a portion of the interior is liquid. Toward the center of both Saturn and Jupiter, a very unusual state exists, that of liquid metallic hydrogen. This liquid metallic state would enhance both the thermal and electrical conductivity of the planetary interiors and no doubt is largely responsible for the strong magnetic fields associated with Jupiter and Saturn. The pressures necessary to create liquid metallic hydrogen are on the order of millions of times the atmospheric pressure at the surface of Earth. No such pressures have been sustainable under laboratory conditions on Earth, and so the liquid metallic hydrogen layer in the interiors of Jupiter and Saturn have effects that are not completely describable. Uranus and Neptune probably have no such layers, for their mass is not great enough to produce such interior pressures.

If one were proceeding inward toward a Jovian planetary center, one would next approach the core of the planet. Theorists disagree as to what might exist there, but the dominant opinion is that the cores would be largely solid and would contain relatively heavy metals such as iron, or they may be silicon in some high-pressure phase. In the case of Jupiter, such a solid core might have a mass twenty times greater than that of Earth, but this is a small fraction of the total mass of this planet—320 times that of Earth. Uranus and Neptune might have solid cores on the order of several Earth masses, while that of Saturn would be about five to ten Earth masses.

Little or nothing is known about planetary interiors experimentally; this is true even for Earth and its fellow terrestrials. Modeling planetary interiors, particularly on the scale necessary in the cases of Jupiter and Saturn, requires knowledge of pressure effects on bulk matter at pressures of millions of atmospheres and at alleged temperatures of 50,000 Kelvins or hotter. It is known, however, that all the Jovian planets have a very low density, or specific gravity. Specific gravity is a measure of relative density, using water as a unit of 1 gram per cubic centimeter or

1,000 kilograms per cubic meter. Saturn has a specific gravity or relative density of 0.7; this means that it would float if one could find an ocean big enough to place it on. It is by far the least dense of all the planets. Jupiter has an average density of 1.3 grams per cubic centimeter, while Uranus and Neptune have relative densities of 1.2 and 1.7 grams per cubic centimeter, respectively. A typical terrestrial planet has a density of about 5; Earth's is 5.5 grams per cubic centimeter. Overall, such relatively low density measurements indicate the predominance in the planetary structure of light elements such as hydrogen and helium.

Jupiter, above all the planets, has a very sizable magnetosphere as a result of its strong magnetic field, which is about ten times as strong as that of Earth. Jupiter's magnetosphere, which consists of trapped charged particles in amounts that would be lethal for humans, is so large that Saturn, which is 9.5 astronomical units (AU) from the sun, passes through it. Saturn is almost twice as far from the sun as is Jupiter (about 5.2 AU), yet its magnetosphere is very strongly influenced by that of Jupiter. Saturn itself has a magnetic field slightly larger than that of Earth.

All the Jovian planets rotate about their own axes rapidly in relation to the terrestrials, which take at least twenty-four hours to make one rotation. Earth is the fastest rotating terrestrial planet. All the Jovian planets thus exhibit oblateness. Saturn has an oblateness of about 0.1, which means that its equatorial diameter is about 10 percent bigger than its polar diameter, and thus it appears noticeably flattened at the poles. Saturn takes 10 hours and 13 minutes to make one complete rotation; Jupiter spins even faster, taking only 9 hours and 55 minutes to complete a rotation. Uranus takes 17 hours for one complete rotation, while Neptune takes about 18 hours (a figure that is subject to conjecture).

These rapid rotations are surprising for such gaseous and liquid planets, because the angular momentum principle of elementary physics would have bigger bodies rotate more slowly than smaller ones. Such rapid rotation rates, then, are a mystery of the first magnitude in solar physics and geophysics. The correlation between magnetic fields and rotation rates is not very strong, and why some planets have powerful magnetic fields and others have negligible ones is unknown. In general, however, if magnetic fields result from dynamo currents deep within planets, then rapid rotators should have strong magnetic fields, which is largely true in the case of both Jupiter and Saturn. Uranus has a magnetic field weaker than that of Saturn. Neptune has a magnetic field roughly comparable to that of Uranus.

Neptune and Uranus seem to be smaller and colder versions of Saturn and Jupiter. Uranus has a pale blue appearance, undoubtedly because of the presence of methane. Intense imaging from Voyager photographs has shown that Uranus has belts and zones, although they are not as spectacular as those of Jupiter and Saturn. The ammonia in the Uranian atmosphere and that of Neptune is thought to have precipitated to the surface. In August, 1989, Voyager 2 flew by Neptune and returned images of the planet and its atmosphere; no good photographs of Neptunian surface features can be made from Earth because of its distance (30 AU from the sun). Voyager 2 showed that Neptune is also a pale blue-green planet with marked bands in its atmosphere. It has a gigantic Black Spot, somewhat analogous to Jupiter's Great Red Spot, which seems to cause a tremendous sinking and upswelling of its atmospheric winds. This spot has a diameter about the same dimension as the diameter of Earth. In addition, extremely high clouds, about 50 kilometers above the (normal) Neptunian atmosphere, make its atmosphere different from those of the other Jovian planets. Winds on the order of 200 meters per second have been measured in the Neptunian atmosphere, with unique streams and band systems.

All the Jovian planets have several moons. By 1990, Neptune was discovered to have eight moons. Uranus has at least fifteen detected moons, while Saturn and Jupiter each have more than twenty. All the Jovian planets have rings as well, although they vary considerably in texture and content. What is a bit surprising is how these planets rotate so rapidly while at the same time having so many satellites. The presence of such satellites should have slowed down the rotation rates, if indeed the satellites and the primary planets had common origins. Nearly all the moons keep the same face toward their primary planet and thus are tidally locked.

Methods of Study

Galileo's 1610 discovery of the four large moons of Jupiter (Io, Europa, Ganymede, and Callisto, known as the Galilean moons) launched the age of modern science. By the 1650's, Christiaan Huygens in Holland and other astronomers in Italy had established conclusively that Saturn had rings and at least one large moon, Titan. The Great Red Spot on Jupiter had been noted by 1660, and the zones and belts on both Jupiter and Saturn had been clearly detected by enterprising visual astronomers. For three centuries, astronomers around the globe have tracked the Great Red Spot and noted the changes in the belts and zones of these two gigantic planets. Uranus, too, was viewed by many from the 1700's onward, but it was not clearly designated as a planet until the late eighteenth century.

With the advent of spectroscopy in the nineteenth century, helium was discovered first on the sun and shortly after on Jupiter and Saturn. In the early twentieth century, it was learned that methane and ammonia were present in the Jovian atmospheres as well. In the 1930's, radio astronomy detected radio signals coming from Jupiter's magnetosphere as well as from solar flares.

It was not until the 1970's, however, that the great discoveries on the Jovian planets were made. Data from Voyager 1 revealed the unexpected existence of rings around Jupiter. Earth-based observations showed rings around Uranus and Neptune, and images returned from Voyager 2 in the 1980's revealed ten moons circling Uranus and eight moons orbiting Neptune. Scientists continue to investigate the Jovian planets and to find surprising features either on the planets themselves or in their moons or ring systems.

Radio astronomy probes the 10-meter radio signals from Jupiter, which signal the extent of its magnetosphere and the relationship of its halo and its large interior moon, Io. Infrared astronomy has been very helpful in determining some of the features of the cold Jovian planets, Uranus and Neptune.

Many experimental techniques have been used to determine the size and extent of the ring systems surrounding these planets, and still there are many unanswered questions about these systems. The atmospheres of Jupiter and Saturn have been probed with all sorts of sensitive spectrometers, yet experimental information is valid only for a penetration depth of a few tens of kilometers. What lies below the turbulent, fast-moving atmosphere has not been experimentally detected; all that scientists can do is rely on the best theories and modeling techniques presently available.

The Pioneer probes found that Jupiter is a tremendous source of electrons and that it generates several times as much heat as it receives from the sun. The origin of these electrons and heat is far from clear to the most discriminating theorists in both physics and geophysics. There are no comparable conditions on Earth or the nearby terrestrial planets to produce such effects. The Hubble Space Telescope (HST) was expected to give much better images of Uranus and Neptune than had been previously available. Voyager 2 passed Neptune in August, 1989, and its use as a planetary probe effectively ceased. The Galileo probe was to visit Jupiter in the 1990's and examine details of the atmosphere and some of the interesting moons, and the Cassini probe will explore Saturn a few years later.

Context

It was expected that exploration of the Jovian planets and their extensive satellite systems would give good scientific clues as to how the solar system formed. Instead, a whole series of new mysteries has appeared.

For meteorologists, the weather systems evident in the atmospheres of both Jupiter and Saturn have provided much material for study. The Great Red Spot and several of the lesser white spots on both Saturn and Jupiter have proved to be cyclonic or anticyclonic storms that somehow are able to maintain themselves for decades—in the case of the Great Red Spot, for at least 350 years. Could such a massive storm system be maintained on Earth? What conditions on Jupiter contribute to the longevity of the Great Red Spot? In attempting to answer questions such as these, meteorologists have modeled all sorts of weather systems, which have proved to be useful in deciphering weather patterns on Earth. Thus Jupiter and Saturn have served as gigantic, high-pressure, turbulent laboratories for atmospheric modelers.

Even in the esoteric discipline of fluid mechanics, particularly in the study of turbulent flow, data from Jupiter and Saturn have been unexpectedly helpful. These studies are critical in air-frame design and, when coupled with modern computer modeling techniques, have proved to be very valuable in the design of supersonic air frames and high-speed hydrofoils. Neptune's Black Spot should provide fodder for both fluid mechanics and meteorology studies well into the twenty-first century. Many scientists believe that the solar system location most likely to host life, in some form or other, is either Jupiter's ice-covered moon, Europa, or the Jovian atmosphere itself. (Space probes have eliminated both Mars and Venus as possibilities.) Some sort of life systems could be operating in either of these locations, for the energy and chemical conditions seem suitable. Should some sort of complex organic molecules or anaerobic bacteria be found on either Jupiter or Europa, the perennial mystery as to how life formed on Earth and why it exists at all could be addressed intelligently for the first time. Neptune's moon Triton has appeared to contain some sort of liquid geyser, perhaps water geysers; the presence of such warm liquids could drive biological networks.

Signals from Jupiter's magnetosphere have been a reference measurement for radio astronomers since the 1930's, when both Karl Jansky at Bell Laboratories in New Jersey and Grote Reber in Wheaton, Illinois—the two founders of the science of radio astronomy—detected radio signals from Jupiter. Half a century later, Voyager 2 recorded the largest electrical current ever measured as it passed near Jupiter. In the first half of the twentieth century, most scientists did not realize that Earth, with its reasonably strong magnetic field, produced a magnetosphere just as Jupiter did. It was not until the early U.S. space probes discovered the Van Allen radiation belts that radio engineers, astronomers, and plasma physicists realized that Earth's magnetosphere was a smaller version of Jupiter's. The magnetospheres of Jupiter, Saturn, and even Earth are still not completely understood; what influence they might have had on planetary origins and developments is unknown. Eventually, studies of Jupiter and Saturn might provide clues regarding the forces and mechanisms behind the electrical storms, violent atmospheric electricity, and radio blackouts that can have pronounced effects on life on Earth.

Bibliography

American Association for the Advancement of Science. *Science* 233 (July 4, 1986). This special issue of the journal *Science* is nearly entirely devoted to the data obtained by Voyager 2 on its visit to Uranus. Articles in this issue deal with the composition of the Uranian atmosphere, constituents of the planet and its moons and rings, and peculiarities in the system. The issue represents a virtually comprehensive description of the Uranian system. Written so as to be understandable to most people interested in the science of the planets.

Hartmann, William K., ed. *Astronomy*. 4th ed. Belmont, Calif.: Wadsworth, 1989. Hartmann's section of this astronomy textbook, which should be accessible to high school and college students, examines the Jovian planets and other parts of the solar system. Besides discussing many late twentieth century findings, Hartmann lists various theories of planetary origins and natures, and he examines the strengths and weaknesses of each. Chapter 11 focuses on Jupiter, and chapter 12 compares Jupiter to the other Jovian planets. Well illustrated.

Ingersoll, Andrew P. "Uranus." *Scientific American* 256 (January, 1987): 38-45. An excellent general article on the findings of Voyager at Uranus. Written for the layperson.

King, Elbert A. *Space Geology: An Introduction*. New York: John Wiley & Sons,

1976. Although this book is somewhat dated, it is a classic for anyone investigating the geology of the planets. Does not incorporate the later Voyager data on the Jovian planets, but contains very informative sections on planetology in general and a good descriptive format for evolutionary geology. See especially chapters 10 and 11.

Kuhn, Karl F. *Astronomy: A Journey into Science*. St. Paul, Minn.: West, 1989. Kuhn's astronomy textbook makes use of much relevant material on the Jovian planets and their rings and atmospheres. Chapter 9 includes sections addressing the reason planets have rings, explaining the nature of satellites, and providing interesting historical notes on the discoveries of Uranus and Neptune. Includes many helpful illustrations. Can be read by any interested general reader.

Protheroe, W. M., E. R. Captiotti, and G. H. Newsom. *Exploring the Universe*. 4th ed. Westerville, Ohio: Charles E. Merrill, 1989. This astronomy textbook devotes several good chapters to the Jovian planets and their satellites and ring systems. Chapter 10 focuses on the nature of the Jovian planets, with findings from the Voyager probes clearly listed, and chapter 11 is mainly concerned with the satellite and ring systems. The book is very well written and contains extremely informative diagrams.

Seeds, Michael A. *Horizons: Exploring the Universe*. 3d ed. Belmont, Calif.: Wadsworth, 1989. Seeds uses some of the best available images of Jovian planet features, satellites, atmospheres, and ring systems. Chapter 19 is devoted to the Jovian planets. Well written and accessible to the general reader.

Snow, Theodore P. *Essentials of the Dynamic Universe*. 2d ed. St. Paul, Minn.: West, 1987. This book is a bit dated, but chapters 10 and 12 are valuable in giving a good historical development of discoveries relative to the Jovian planets and their satellites and ring systems. Snow uses an evolutionary-developmental approach, and chapter 12 is excellent in offering a likely scenario for the origin of the solar system, including the Jovian planets.

John P. Kenny

Cross-References

Asteroids, 98; The Atmosphere's Evolution, 114; Io, 1238; The Jovian Planets' Atmospheres, 1290; The Jovian Planets' Ring Systems, 1296; The Jovian Planets' Satellites, 1303; Elemental Distribution in the Solar System, 2434; The Origin of the Solar System, 2442.

THE JOVIAN PLANETS' ATMOSPHERES

Type of earth science: Planetology
Field of study: Large solar system bodies

As astronomers seek to discover the detailed history of the solar system, examination of the atmospheres of the planets provides clues about the type of chemistry that occurred. A study of the Jovian planets could provide information about the conditions that existed in the early days of the solar system.

Principal terms

CONVECTION: the transfer of energy by the movement of higher energy matter into a region of lower energy (usually warmer gases rising through the atmosphere)

INFRARED RADIATION: a form of energy associated with heat; it has less energy than visible light; used to determine the temperature of the atmosphere or surface of a planet

SPECTRUM: light from an object arranged in order of increasing energy

STRATOSPHERE: the layer of the atmosphere lying immediately above the troposphere

THERMAL INVERSION: a region in the atmosphere of a planet in which a change from decreasing temperature with increasing altitude to increasing temperature occurs

TROPOSPHERE: the layer of an atmosphere nearest the surface of the planet in which energy is transferred by convection

ULTRAVIOLET RADIATION: a form of energy that can cause chemical reactions; it has more energy than visible light

Summary of the Phenomenon

The study of the atmospheres of the Jovian planets began more than fifty years ago, when astronomers found methane on Jupiter and Saturn and ammonia on Jupiter. Since that time, extensive work has revealed much more detail of those atmospheres as well as those of Uranus and Neptune. Unlike Earth's atmosphere, where water is the only substance that condenses to form clouds, the lower temperatures and higher pressures of the atmospheres of the Jovian planets allow the formation of clouds of ammonia or methane. The challenge to modern astronomers has been to identify the substances present on these distant planets and then to describe the structure of an atmosphere that contains these materials and produces the physical effects seen.

The atmosphere of Jupiter displays a series of highly colored bands and a series of red, brown, or white spots. The five most abundant components are hydrogen, helium, methane, ammonia, and water vapor. Hydrogen and helium represent 86.1 and 13.8 percent of the atmosphere, respectively, but the visible portion, the clouds, forms from the remaining 0.1 percent of the gases present. Hydrogen and helium do not condense at the temperatures and pressures that exist in the atmosphere.

If Jupiter and the sun formed from the same gas and dust cloud, their compositions should be similar. Many elements exist in similar abundances, but oxygen and sulfur seem to be present in much smaller quantities on Jupiter than in the sun. The amount of water vapor (formed from oxygen and hydrogen) present is less than 1 percent of the amount expected, while less than 0.1 percent of the expected sulfur is found. The missing water vapor, if it exists, could be in tropospheric clouds or in the planet's core, and the sulfur could be bound up in one of the cloud layers. Yet, no evidence exists for the presence of either substance. Several unexpected compounds such as carbon monoxide and hydrogen cyanide are also present in trace amounts. These may form when ultraviolet light from the sun interacts with methane molecules. Similar reactions occur on Earth when sunlight reacts with atmospheric gases to produce smog.

The temperature in the lower troposphere may be as high as 500 Kelvins when the atmospheric pressure is greater than 450 pounds per square inch. Much of this heat energy is radiated by the planet into the atmosphere. The temperature and pressure decrease steadily moving up through the atmosphere, until the pressure is about 1.5 pounds per square inch and the temperature is about 110 Kelvins. At this point, a thermal inversion occurs, and the temperature begins to increase as one continues toward the top of the atmosphere. Absorption of ultraviolet sunlight by gases and small particles causes this increase.

The highest visible cloud layer is composed of ammonia ice crystals. The next cloud layer is colored and probably has a mixed composition. One possible component is ammonium hydrosulfide, although it is white and the clouds have a tawny color. This color could come from sulfur compounds, but the formation of these compounds is difficult to explain. The lowest layer is expected to be water clouds that have ammonia dissolved in them. These clouds have not been observed, and, since the existence of water in the atmosphere has not been confirmed, these clouds may not exist.

The source of the many colors in the atmosphere has not been discovered. Sulfur compounds, red phosphorus, and yellow phosphorus are some possible contributors, but none of these has been identified as being present. Final judgment must wait until the space probe on the Galileo mission performs a direct analysis of the atmospheric components. The cloud patterns shift regularly, but the underlying currents seem to be stable for extended periods of time. The atmosphere shows an eastward-flowing equatorial jet stream with a velocity of about 300 kilometers per hour. An alternating east/west pattern of wind flows with velocities of about 75-100 kilometers per hour exists in the higher latitudes. These currents may represent the outermost edges of concentric cylinders of gas that run through the entire planet.

One of the most interesting features of the atmosphere is the Great Red Spot. This feature is almost three hundred years old, and, while it undergoes small color changes and periodically shifts its position, it may last another one thousand years. It appears to be an enormous storm whose center must be a region of locally high pressure. It is about 13,000 kilometers wide and extends several kilometers below and above the adjacent cloud layer. White ovals about the size of Mars have existed for more than forty years. Dark brown clouds and blue-gray areas also exist. These are smaller storms that will not last as long as the Great Red Spot. Lightning discharges provide additional evidence of storm activity. Scientists have concluded that the larger the storm, the longer it will last. Drawing a parallel to storms on Earth, one notices that a hurricane gains strength over the seas and dissipates over the continents. Since Jupiter has no continents, its storms would have little to keep them from intensifying or continuing. These storms may be formed from the inter-action of two adjacent currents moving rapidly in opposite directions. Laboratory experiments and computer calculations support this explanation. No seasonal varia-tion is seen in Jupiter's atmosphere.

Saturn's atmosphere contains more hydrogen (92.4 percent), less helium (7.4 percent), and more methane (0.2 percent) than does Jupiter's. The structure of the atmosphere is similar to that of Jupiter. The temperature drops from 143 Kelvins in the upper stratosphere to a minimum of 93 Kelvins when the pressure is 1 pound per square inch. A thermal inversion occurs and the temperature steadily increases into the atmosphere, reaching 133 Kelvins at 14.6 pounds per square inch and going to 300 Kelvins in the lower troposphere.

A thin layer of photochemical smog lies above the first visible clouds made of ammonia ice. Additional cloud layers presumably lie below the first layer, but they have not been observed. Some may contain ammonium hydrosulfide, while others may be largely water and ammonia. The substances from which clouds form on Saturn are not colored; therefore, the colors observed must come from very small amounts of chemical compounds of unknown composition.

The wind patterns on Saturn differ greatly from those found on Jupiter. Most of the winds flow eastward, with speeds up to 1,500 kilometers per hour. The section of the atmosphere found between latitudes of ± 35 degrees forms a single equatorial jet stream traveling four times faster than the strongest winds on Jupiter. At higher latitudes, an alternating east- and west-flow pattern exists, with the majority of the air movement toward the east. Storms form in the regions where the winds are not severe. These storms look much like the white ovals found on Jupiter but are much smaller. They tend to be high-pressure systems in contrast to the low-pressure cyclones that dominate the temperate zones of Earth. Thermal energy from the interior is transformed into atmospheric energy through the storms that power the horizontal jet streams.

The atmosphere of Uranus contains 84 percent hydrogen, 14 percent helium, and 2 percent methane, and has a blue-green color. The upper part of the visible atmosphere is frozen methane and has a temperature of 52 Kelvins. Very few clouds are visible above this layer. The atmosphere above the methane layer contains very few particles, but these reach a temperature of 750 Kelvins. Absorption of sunlight alone cannot cause a temperature this high, but the other source of energy has not been identified.

Uranus is the only Jovian planet whose atmosphere does not have a thermal inversion. The temperature increases from 52 to 210 Kelvins, although the increase is not as steady as it is in Jupiter's and Saturn's atmospheres. The temperatures of the atmosphere when the pressure was 8.8 pounds per square inch was 64 Kelvins at both poles and at the equator and is only one or two degrees lower in the midlatitudes of both hemispheres. The wind currents in the thin methane clouds show a banded pattern lying along the latitude lines, similar to Jupiter and Saturn. These winds move slightly faster than the planet rotates.

The atmosphere of Neptune contains about 84 percent hydrogen and 2-3 percent methane. The amounts of other gases present have not been determined, although scientists expect that most of the remaining gas will be helium. There are few clouds present, and the blue-green color of the planet suggests that frozen methane forms the outermost visible portion of the atmosphere. The temperature of this outer layer is about 50 Kelvins. The cloud cover changes globally in a matter of days, but the process that causes this rapid condensation or haze formation is not known. Huge storm systems, one about the size of the earth, have been detected, evidencing winds of up to 1,126 kilometers per hour.

Methods of Study

Astronomers, unlike many other scientists, are not able to make direct measurements on the objects of their studies. Since the substances that exist on Earth could exist on the planets and in the stars, however, an astronomer can study the characteristics of hydrogen on Earth, for example, and then look for those characteristics in the atmosphere of a planet or a star. The information from these distant objects comes to Earth in the form of infrared, ultraviolet, or light energy.

Each element or compound has an identifying characteristic associated with the energy it will absorb and emit. Some molecules will absorb infrared (heat) energy when they vibrate. Other substances have electrons that can absorb or emit energy. An astronomer can study the energy spectrum coming from a planet and can identify the substances that have interacted with the light as it left the planet. The presence of methane and ammonia in the atmosphere of Jupiter more than fifty years ago was established when the spectrum obtained from Jupiter was compared to spectra of methane and ammonia recorded in an earth-based laboratory.

The technique called occultation uses the decrease in intensity of radio signals passing through an atmosphere or ring system to determine the density of the material blocking the signal. As the Pioneer and Voyager spacecraft passed behind Jupiter and Saturn, the radio signal being sent back to Earth had to pass through thicker and thicker layers of atmosphere. The decrease in signal strength provided a measure of the increase in atmospheric density, which in turn is determined by the gases present and their temperature and pressure. Occultation has also been used to study the rings of Saturn.

Wind patterns can be determined by photography. Earth-based photographs often lack the resolution to establish patterns, but close-up camera work from a space probe such as Voyager 1 or 2 can provide much detail and can show changes that occur over a short time span. The use of film sensitive to infrared or ultraviolet energy can also provide valuable information about the structure of an atmosphere. Movement of some small storms around the Great Red Spot was detected by a series of photographs taken by Voyager 2 as it approached Jupiter; photographs from Voyager 2 also revealed the storm systems of Neptune's atmosphere.

Astronomers trying to find thin clouds on Uranus made photographs of the planet and then, using computers, subtracted the light that would be expected to come from a planet with no clouds. The new photographs showed several bands of clouds, which allowed astronomers to evaluate and develop theories explaining the motion of the Uranus' upper atmosphere.

Context

The Jovian planets, Jupiter, Saturn, Uranus, and Neptune, are of special interest to astronomers as they seek information about the history of the solar system. Scientists believe that these planets have changed more slowly during their histories than the four planets nearest the sun.

Examination of the atmospheres of the Jovian planets shows that Jupiter, Uranus, and Neptune have about 85 percent hydrogen, while Saturn has more than 92 percent. The sun contains about 76 percent hydrogen. The presence or absence of several other materials has been of special interest to astronomers. The exceptionally low concentrations of water and sulfur compounds detected on Jupiter and Saturn are a mystery. Scientists hypothesize that these compounds are trapped in clouds deep in the atmosphere but have no evidence that this is the case.

The presence of compounds such as carbon monoxide, acetylene, hydrogen cyanide, and other compounds containing carbon and hydrogen (hydrocarbons) in the Jovian atmospheres was unexpected. These could not have formed with the energy supplied by the planets themselves. Photochemical reactions occur when ultraviolet radiation from the sun breaks methane molecules apart and the parts combine in various ways to produce the hydrocarbons. Similar reactions occur in Earth's atmosphere when sunlight interacts with oxygen molecules to form ozone. Lightning discharges contribute to the formation of hydrogen cyanide. Carbon monoxide is presumably formed from methane and water vapor deep in the atmosphere, where the temperature is about 1,200 Kelvins and pressure is high. Much of the missing sulfur is thought to exist in ammonium hydrosulfide clouds in the tropospheres, although there is no way to explain the formation of the compound at that level of the atmosphere.

These data as well as information about the temperatures and pressures that exist in these atmospheres provide clues as to what changes have occurred and what types of chemical reactions can occur in the colder regions of the solar system. Ultimately, scientists are searching for a process that could generate molecules that could come together under the right conditions to form life. This search has so far been futile but will continue.

Bibliography

Fimmel, Richard O., James Van Allen, and Eric Burgess. *Pioneer: First to Jupiter, Saturn, and Beyond.* Washington, D.C.: National Aeronautics and Space Administration, 1980. A summary of the flight, spacecraft, and results of the Pioneer missions. Contains an excellent set of photographs of the instruments used in collecting data and of the planets and their moons. For a general audience.

Hunt, Garry, and Patrick Moore. *Jupiter.* Skokie, Ill.: Rand McNally, 1981. This is an astronomical atlas that gives detailed information about the structure, composition, history, rings, and satellites of Jupiter. Maps of the satellites combined with photomosaics of the rings and satellites make this an excellent source for details of this system. Good for a general audience.

_____. *Saturn.* Skokie, Ill.: Rand McNally, 1982. This astronomical atlas provides information about Saturn's structure, composition, history, rings, and satellites. Like the authors' book on Jupiter, this book is an excellent source containing useful maps and photomosaics.

Morrison, David. *Voyages to Saturn.* Washington, D.C.: National Aeronautics and Space Administration, 1982. The discussion includes all the important discoveries of the Pioneer and Voyager missions and presents the voyages from the perspective of the individuals controlling the spacecraft and collecting the data. Excellent collection of information with many photographs of the Saturnian system.

Morrison, David, and Tobias Owen. *The Planetary System.* Reading, Mass.: Addison-Wesley, 1987. Excellent descriptions of each of the planets and their satellites accompany many photographs and drawings. Although the format is that of a textbook, it provides good reading for anyone with an interest in solar system astronomy.

Morrison, David, and Jane Samz. *Voyage to Jupiter.* Washington, D.C.: National Aeronautics and Space Administration, 1980. This book includes a review of the Pioneer and Voyager missions in the context of the scientists involved in collecting the data. An excellent collection of data and photographs of the Jovian system.

Trejo, P. E. *Introductory Astronomy: The Solar System.* Dubuque, Iowa: Kendall/Hunt, 1986. General astronomical principles are discussed before the details of the solar system are given. Some photographs and line drawings are included. The planetary data are summarized well.

Dennis R. Flentge

Cross-References

THE JOVIAN PLANETS' RING SYSTEMS

Type of earth science: Planetology
Field of study: Large solar system bodies

Rings apparently are persistent features of Jovian-type planets, for Jupiter, Saturn, Uranus, and Neptune all have ring systems. These ring systems exhibit remarkable diversity in spatial extent, constituents, and optical properties. Why rings should exist at all is a mystery. It is thought that an understanding of such systems provides insight into how the early solar system formed.

Principal terms

ACCRETION: a process by which smaller particles cohere and become larger bodies

ALBEDO: the fraction of incident light on a surface which is reflected back in all directions

EPHEMERAL RINGS: rings of changing size, albedo, and constituents that are continually forming and disintegrating

OPACITY: the light flux or energy incident on a surface divided by the light transmitted through the surface

ROCHE LIMIT: the closest orbit at which a planet's satellite can maintain its structure without being torn asunder by gravitational tidal forces

SHEPHERD SATELLITES: the satellites that influence a planet's ring structure by removing debris from certain orbits

SILICATE: any compound containing the chemical element silicon; often an oxide of silicon

SPECTROPHOTOMETRY: the measurement of reflected light and also near light frequencies (ultraviolet and infrared) coming from celestial bodies

SPOKES: dark radial features, similar to the spokes on a bicycle wheel, noted on the Saturnian ring system

STELLAR EXTINCTION: a technique of astronomical study whereby a star's output is carefully measured as a planet, moon, or ring system passes between the star and the earth

TIDAL DISRUPTION: a gravitational mechanism which keeps ring particles from accreting into larger bodies by tearing them apart

Summary of the Phenomenon

The four Jovian planets are each surrounded by a system of rings whose size, optical properties, composition, and general structure are quite diverse. Why these planets have rings and how they can be maintained over long periods of time is a mystery of the first magnitude in solar system studies. If, as many scientists think, such a primordial ring system around the sun resulted in planetary formation, there is still the question of how, after so many billions of years, a ring system can be maintained around these large planets. Moreover, why do the terrestrial planets (Mercury, Venus, Earth, Mars) have no rings? Did the terrestrial planets have ring systems at some time in the distant past?

Saturn's ring system is by far the largest and the most spectacular of all the ring systems. Many historians believe that it was discovered by Galileo in the winter of 1611, but it is Christiaan Huygens who usually is credited with outlining the features of these rings, with his sighting of both the rings and Saturn's large moon Titan in 1656. It was soon recognized that the Saturnian rings had to be a series of satellites encircling the primary planet. By 1700, Gottfried W. Leibniz and Sir Isaac Newton had invented the calculus, and Newton's law of universal gravitation described such satellite motions. In addition, in the early 1700's, bigger and better telescopes were being built, and it was not long until two and later three divisions were noted in the Saturnian ring system. Around 1857, James Clerk Maxwell, perhaps the greatest mathematical physicist ever to work on planetary and satellite problems, wrote a theoretical paper establishing the fact that the rings were swarms of small satellites encircling Saturn. He also suggested reasons for the existence of "Cassini's division," a dark separation in the rings discovered by Jean-Dominique Cassini in 1675. Maxwell explained the phenomenon in terms of orbital resonances with some of Saturn's larger moons.

Until the 1970's there were arguments regarding whether Saturn had three, four, or five distinct rings. By convention, the rings, beginning with the outermost, have been labeled the A, B, C, and D rings. A and B, the two brightest rings, are separated by the Cassini division. The four rings range in extent from an inner radius for the D ring of 1.2 Saturnian radii to the outer edge of the A ring at about 2.5 Saturnian radii. Those who view Saturn with a small telescope generally see only the A and B rings because of their relatively high albedo. As is the case with all the planets and their satellites, the rings can be observed visually only via the amount of solar light they reflect, for they have no source of light within them.

In the 1970's, Pioneer probes and later Voyager 1 and Voyager 2 gave indications that the Saturnian ring system consisted of thousands of ringlets. The data from Voyager 1 and particularly Voyager 2 conclusively established that there are many ringlets in the dark regions and even discovered several more ring systems, which generally became known as the F ring (just outside the outer edge of the A ring, at about 2.5 planetary radii), the G ring at about 3 radii, and the E ring at slightly more than 4 planetary radii. This latter ring is almost exactly in the orbit of a sizable moon, Enceladus, and the G ring is between the orbits of the moon Mimas and two very small moons called 1980S1 and 1980S3, respectively.

Voyager 2 was able to pass by Saturn and its rings and to measure the amount of light and radiation that passed through the rings from the sun. The data thus gathered showed that these thousands of ringlets vary considerably in opacity. This variation suggests that the material of the various rings differs in nature or in the sizes of its particles.

Prior to Voyager 2, ring detection had depended primarily on albedo. That is, the sunlight reflected from the ring particles was what showed the existence of a ring. The one exception was the discovery of the Uranian ring system in the late 1970's via stellar occultation: As Uranus passed in front of a well-known star, there were variations in the stellar light reaching the earth as each ring passed before it. Nine distinct rings were discovered on Uranus through such measurements, and by the time Voyager 2 reached this planet in 1986, their existence was firmly established.

Voyager data showed that some of the wide and brighter Uranian rings, like those of Saturn, consist of many smaller ringlets, although Uranus' diversity is not as great as Saturn's. Most of the rings in the Uranian system are between 1.6 and 2 times the planetary radius. The Uranian rings are very narrow, probably as a result of the presence of shepherding satellites (small moons between the rings); only the outer ring, called the epsilon ring, has a width much greater than 20 kilometers. It was within this outer ring that images from Voyager 2 revealed the existence of a significant ringlet structure.

Jupiter's rings are the smallest and perhaps least interesting of all the ring systems because of their low albedo. They are centered at about 1.8 planetary radii from the center of Jupiter and extend for a distance of only 6,000 kilometers, which makes them the narrowest ring system of the four. The relative darkness (or low albedo) of Jupiter's rings is attributed by many to the considerable charges they pick up from the magnetosphere, which would cause any carbon compounds in the rings to take on a black, sooty appearance. Measurements indicate that Jupiter's rings contain particles as large as 1 meter in diameter, but apparently most of the ring constituents are granular, very much like grains of sand. The rings were discovered rather accidentally, after Voyager passed by Jupiter and took some final photographs of the gigantic planet; for this reason, the detailed imaging of the Voyager photos on these rings is far from complete.

From Earth observations, Neptune's rings appeared to be arc-type—that is, they do not make complete rings around the planet. Voyager 2 visited Neptune in August, 1989, and new pictures of Neptune's rings were obtained. At least five diverse and distinct rings were observed by Voyager 2 on its Neptunian visit. That was another historical instance of a ring system proving to be different from what Earth-based measurements had suggested.

The matter of all the planets' ring systems is thought to be silicates and ices. There are indications that some of Saturn's rings are made of materials of density less than half that of water; this might indicate a structure similar to that of snowflakes. As it is Saturn's rings that have been studied most extensively, most of the Voyager findings have been extended as being relevant to the other systems. Some of Saturn's rings seem to be composed mainly of rather large chunks of matter, with radii of up to 10 meters (boxcar-sized). Others seem to be dominated by structures with radii of 1-3 meters (compact car-sized), and most of the others contain primarily small, granular pieces ranging from under 1 centimeter to 1 meter in radius. Voyager was able to make opacity measurements at both visible light and some radio frequencies; most of what is known about the sizes of ring particles is extrapolated from these measurements, but there is considerable controversy about some of the findings. Opacity is a measure of how well light or radiation is transmitted through the rings. Prior to these measurements, most ring information came from albedo readings—that is, reflected light and radiation.

What Voyager found that was truly surprising was that the depth of the rings was very small, perhaps as small as 10 to 100 meters. This shallowness explains the fact that for centuries, astronomers have been able to view stars through the Saturnian rings. Voyager obtained some remarkable photographs of the limb of the planet viewed through the rings.

Why there are rings at all has not been answered by Voyager results. It seems that particles in orbit would collide and accrete into sizable bodies, which then would be ripped apart by tidal forces. One might surmise that energy would be lost in such collisions and that very shortly (at least in terms of thousands of years) the rings would fall into the major planet. It is true that most of the rings are within the Roche limit of their primary planets (the Roche limit is the orbital radius at which a small moon or body would disintegrate as a result of tidal disruption). Most scientists think that Jupiter's ring system is debris from a small moon that was tidally disrupted rather recently (at least less than a million years ago). They believe that Jupiter's rings are spiraling into the planet and will gradually disappear. The nature of Saturn's vast ring system, however, challenges this interpretation. Some theorists think that electromagnetic effects play a dominant role in ring structure, while others view shock waves or acoustic modes as being responsible for the rich ringlet structure. It could be, on the other hand, that what is at work is a very large-scale gravitational effect that is at present incomprehensible to physicists and planetary scientists.

Methods of Study

Saturn's rings have a relatively high albedo and thus appear very bright for such small, fragile bodies. Yet it was not until Voyager 2 passed by Saturn in August, 1981, that conclusive opacity measurements at both visible and radio frequencies could be made.

Jupiter's rings were discovered rather accidentally. It was noted in the imaging headquarters that one of Voyager's last panoramic views of the planet showed some ringlike structures at the planetary limb. Voyager was already on its way to Saturn and could not be sent back to make a more resolved set of photographs. Immediately thereafter, Jupiter's rings were confirmed by stellar extinction measurements on Earth. For the stellar extinction method, Earth-based astronomers must wait until the planet being examined passes between Earth and a star whose spectrum is well known. The planet must pass at exactly the correct position relative to the ring plane. As the rings pass in front of the star, the amount of starlight passing through the rings rises and falls, depending on the amount of ring material present. Thus, photometric measurements of the star as the rings pass give a reasonably good image of the rings.

The rings of Uranus and Neptune were discovered by stellar extinction measurements of this type. As one might expect, stellar extinction measurements can be made only rarely, because they require that the planetary ring system pass exactly in front of a particular star when conditions on earth are just right for viewing. Furthermore, if there is not much material present in the rings, stellar extinction measurements are generally inconclusive.

Information on ring contents is obtained by means of spectrophotometry, a technique for analyzing light reflected off the rings to see what frequencies might be absent. If, for example, there is an absence of red light in the reflected spectrum, then astrochemists can assert that something in the rings is absorbing red light and suggest which molecules might be creating this effect. Saturn's rings exhibit spectrophotometric characteristics generally consistent with ices and silicates, or some mixture of the two. Opacity measurements can be made only rarely. Once Voyager or some known source of light or radiation gets past the rings, the amount of light or radiation transmitted through the rings can be measured. The opacity of Saturn's rings was measured in this way. There are difficulties in interpreting spectrophotometry and opacity data. The shape of the scattering ring material, whether smooth spheres or rough-edged grains of sand and ice, influences the interpretation of the results. Jagged-edged materials scatter radiation erratically, so that in such cases no conclusive notions can emerge regarding the content, size, and shape of the material doing the scattering. Such has proved to be the case with several of Saturn's rings.

No really conclusive measurements have been made on the rings. That probably will not happen until individual ring particles are captured, imaged with sufficient resolution, or chemically analyzed by some remote means. Even the Voyager 2 cameras could not come close to picturing individual ring particles. Yet techniques of imaging are being invented and improved continually. The Hubble Space Telescope (HST) was to be launched in 1989 and was expected to give a developmental view of how Saturn's and Jupiter's rings behave over a span of several years. Multiple-mirror telescopes based on Earth should aid in deciphering the infrared behavior of rings and give further clues as to their composition. In the middle 1990's, the Galileo probe was projected to provide a good picture of Jupiter's ring system as well as of the planet itself and some of its satellites.

Context

The rings of all the Jovian planets are a mystery in their shape, size, and very existence. Many scientists believe that once the sun was surrounded by a ring system like those of the giant planets and that from these rings, the planets and their satellites formed. The sun indeed is circled by rings—the asteroid belts located between Mars and Jupiter, at about 2.8 astronomical units (one astronomical unit is the earth-sun distance). These belts are similar to the rings of Saturn, with the gaps between them known as Kirkwood gaps. The asteroids, however, include very sizable bits of matter, some on the order of hundreds of kilometers in diameter. Since Voyager and Pioneer spacecraft passed through the asteroid belt, some insights have been gained on the nature of these bodies. The picture that is emerging is that the asteroids are mostly silicates that coagulated into rather rough-edged globules from several centimeters to hundreds of kilometers in diameter.

It appears that several nearby stars have rings or something equivalent to asteroid belts around them. Infrared measurements indicate that the stars Vega and Beta Pictoris, for example, have ringlike debris floating in orbit around them. It is speculated that they may be in the process of forming planets.

The only ring systems that can be examined in any detail are those of the Jovian planets. How can they maintain themselves after so many billions of years (assuming that they are primordial materials and as old as the planets themselves)? Most scientists claim that the ring systems cannot last much longer than hundreds or thousands of years, based on what is known about energy dissipation in collisions and tidal disruptions in classical orbits bound by gravity.

If electromagnetic effects dominate the ring structure, however, and if other conditions are right, some sort of plasmalike rings might be able to exist for long periods. (A plasma is a charged set of particles interacting with one another.) All the Jovian planets have magnetic fields and considerably large magnetospheres, so there might be some modes that are favored in some electromagnetic boundary situations. Then, too, these ring systems may involve some new physics—that is, if one assumes that they have circled these planets for millions or perhaps billions of years. A gravitational quantum effect might be selecting certain orbits, just as the Bohr quantum models had the hydrogen atom surrounded by electrons only in certain orbits. Most scientists are hesitant to advance such gravitational quantum explanations, because the gravitational effects are so weak compared to the electromagnetic effects that might be present. Still, this line of inquiry may eventually prove fruitful.

Scientists need to determine whether the ring systems of the planets are changing. Images from Voyager 1 showed spokes, dark radial bands, and a braided F ring in Saturn's ring system. When Voyager 2 passed by only ten months later, in August, 1981, the braid was gone, and the spokes had largely disappeared. What had happened in those 10 months? In addition, it has been shown that Neptune's rings have bright and dull sections, and it could be that a single ring might contain different types and sizes of constituents in sighted sections. Why that should be has mystified scientists. Answering such questions might ultimately shed light on how the earth was formed billions of years ago—if indeed the Jovian planets' rings are analogous to rings that circled the sun before the solar system was formed.

Bibliography

Greenberg, Richard, and Andre Brahic, eds. *Planetary Rings.* Tucson: University of Arizona Press, 1984. This 784-page work is the authoritative source on the rings of Saturn, the rings of Uranus, and theories of the origin and structure of the rings in general. It consists of eighteen articles written by the leading researchers in planetology and the astrophysics and geology of the outer planets and their ring systems. Some of the articles are for general readers, but this volume is the most thorough and complete exposition of the understanding of rings as of the year of its publication.

Hartmann, William K., ed. *Astronomy: The Cosmic Journey.* 4th ed. Belmont, Calif.: Wadsworth, 1989. The section of this astronomy textbook on the solar system, and the Jovian planets in particular, is well illustrated. Up-to-date at the time of its publication. A number of theories regarding the planets and rings are explored. Chapter 11 focuses on Jupiter, and the other Jovian planets are considered in chapter 12. Appropriate for high school and college-level readers.

Kuhn, Karl F. *Astronomy: A Journey into Science.* St. Paul, Minn.: West, 1989. Another textbook, this work is helpful for those seeking material on the Jovian planets and their rings. Chapter 9 takes up the question of why planets have rings, gives some history of Uranus and Neptune, and defines and describes shepherding satellites. Exellent illustrations. For the general reader.

Protheroe, W. M., E. R. Captiotti, and G. H. Newsom. *Exploring the Universe.* 4th ed. Westerville, Ohio: Charles E. Merrill, 1989. Several informative chapters in this textbook describe the Jovian planets and their satellites and ring systems. Chapter 11 is devoted mainly to the satellites and ring systems. Very well written, and features remarkably clear diagrams.

Science 233 (July 4, 1986). This special issue highlights Voyager 2 data from Uranus. The composition of the Uranian atmosphere, of the planet itself, and of its moons and rings is examined. For general readers.

Seeds, Michael A. *Horizons: Exploring the Universe.* 3d ed. Belmont, Calif.: Wadsworth, 1989. Seeds's work is notable for its very helpful illustrations and clear descriptions of planetary features, including ring systems. The Jovian planets are discussed in chapter 19. This book's style makes it accessible to a wide variety of readers.

Snow, Theodore P. *Essentials of the Dynamic Universe.* 2d ed. St. Paul, Minn.: West, 1987. Though the book is dated in some respects, chapters 10 and 12 provide valuable historical background on discoveries regarding the Jovian planets and their ring systems. In chapter 12, Snow envisions the formation of the solar system in one possible scenario.

John P. Kenny

Cross-References

Asteroids, 98; The Atmosphere's Evolution, 114; Io, 1238; The Jovian Planets, 1283; The Jovian Planets' Satellites, 1303; Remote Sensing and the Electromagnetic Spectrum, 2166; Elemental Distribution in the Solar System, 2434; The Origin of the Solar System, 2442.

THE JOVIAN PLANETS' SATELLITES

Type of earth science: Planetology
Field of study: Large solar system bodies

The study of the surfaces and atmospheres of the moons of the Jovian planets reveals information about the solar system's past and about the interaction of large bodies (the planets) with much smaller objects (the moons).

Principal terms

DIFFERENTIATED OBJECT: an object whose contents separated when the object was melted, with the densest material in the interior and the less dense material near the surface

INFRARED RADIATION: electromagnetic radiation with energy below that of visible light; usually associated with heat and used to find the temperature of the surface or atmosphere of a planet or moon

PLASTIC DEFORMATION: the change in the surface of an icy moon or planet as the ice flows like a very thick liquid and smooths out surface features such as craters and mountains

SATELLITE: an object that is in orbit around a larger body; may be either man-made, such as a communications satellite, or naturally occurring, such as a moon

SPECTRUM: light arranged in order of increasing energy

TIDAL HEATING: the heating of a moon as tides are raised in its crust

Summary of the Phenomenon

The Jovian planets, Jupiter, Saturn, Uranus, and Neptune, have a collection of moons, naturally occurring satellites that display a wide range of physical characteristics and histories. Many of these moons are very small, irregularly shaped objects that show no evidence of geologic activity other than collisions with meteorites. Jupiter has twelve moons with diameters of less than 200 kilometers and surfaces that reflect less than 4 percent of the light that strikes them. By contrast, Saturn's small inner moons are icy objects that reflect light very well. Many of these moons are closely associated with some of Saturn's rings, while others share orbits with its larger satellites. Phoebe, Saturn's outermost moon, reflects little light. Uranus has ten small moons that orbit inside its rings and reflect only 5-7 percent of the light that strikes them. The remaining satellites can be grouped into large (diameters of 3,100 to 5,300 kilometers) and medium (diameters of 400-1,600 kilometers) sizes. The six largest are Jupiter's Ganymede, Callisto, Europa, Io; Saturn's Titan; and Neptune's Triton.

The four large moons of Jupiter are called the Galilean moons because they were discovered by Galileo soon after he constructed his telescope. Callisto and Ganymede are about the same size and density and are about 50 percent water ice and 50 percent rocky material. Scientists believe that all of the Galilean moons are differentiated objects, with the denser, rocky material in the cores of the moons and the less dense water ice forming the crusts and mantles. Callisto's surface temperature ranges from 100 to 150 Kelvins. The icy surface reflects only 18 percent of the light striking it. The surface has about the same number of craters per square kilometer as do the mountains of Earth's moon and shows no evidence of internal processes destroying any of these craters. The craters' features have been softened by plastic deformation of the icy surface. A series of concentric circles could be the remnants of a large crater that has been almost consumed by plastic deformation.

About half of the surface of Ganymede, the largest moon in the solar system, is dark and heavily cratered like Callisto, but the other half contains lighter, less cratered areas. These lighter areas have mountains and valleys running parallel to one another. The mountains formed when tension in the icy crust caused long cracks to form. On Earth, mountains form by compression of the crust. The low areas look as if they have been flooded with liquid from Ganymede's interior. Light-colored material around some craters is probably clean ice that was splashed on the surface when the crater was formed. Internal processes that could cause the surface tension which led to mountain formation or which kept water liquid near the surface are not understood.

The two inner Galilean moons are of similar size and density, but they are very different in appearance and behavior. Europa is about 90 percent rocky material and 10 percent water and has a surface of relatively pure ice. The high purity of this surface and the absence of craters implies that some internal process resurfaces the moon periodically, making Europa the smoothest body in the solar system. Long lines a few kilometers wide and a few hundred meters tall formed when fluid from the interior squeezed up through cracks in the icy surface. Some scientists believe that there are large underground oceans of water present on Europa and that some exotic life form might exist in that water. This is pure speculation and cannot be verified without direct examination of Europa.

Io, the Galilean moon nearest Jupiter, has no water, and its multicolored surface has a high reflectivity. Some substances that could account for these colors are sulfur dioxide, sulfur, and sulfur-sodium compounds. Io captured the interest of scientists when active volcanoes were discovered by the interplanetary probe Voyager 1. While there are no impact craters on Io, many volcanic features are present, including lava plains, volcanic mountains, calderas, and vents. Plume eruptions and lava flows are the two forms of volcanism displayed. Violent, short-lived plume eruptions leave a dark red deposit that is probably elemental sulfur. A longer-lived, less violent eruption leaves a white deposit that is believed to be sulfur dioxide. Several volcanic hot spots, which can be detected on Earth, are also present on Io. Astronomers have found that these spots remain active for years and that the total heat energy released by Io comes from 1 or 2 percent of its surface. The relatively high temperature of Io arises from tidal heating. The strong gravitational pull of Jupiter raises a bulge several kilometers high on Io. The gravitational pulls of

Europa and Ganymede cause Io to twist back and forth as it orbits Jupiter. This twisting causes the crust to flex and to heat up. This process generates ten times as much energy as the total energy consumption of the people on Earth. The interior of Io is entirely liquid and the crust may be only 25 kilometers thick. Io is the only body in the solar system other than Earth that is still geologically active.

Titan's atmosphere, which has severely limited the gathering of information about the moon itself, is at least 82 percent nitrogen with at least 1 percent methane, and it exerts a pressure that is 50 percent greater than Earth's. The other major components have not been identified. Many astronomers, in their unwavering search for life in the solar system, believe that the composition of Titan's atmosphere and the chemistry taking place there may be similar to the composition and chemistry of Earth's early atmosphere. Several scientists suggest that heavy bombardment of an atmosphere of ammonia and methane by high-velocity meteors could have generated the current amount of nitrogen in Titan's atmosphere. These astronomers believe that Earth's first atmosphere contained large quantities of ammonia and methane and that over time these substances have been converted to nitrogen and other compounds. Because Titan's surface temperature is only 94 Kelvins, all water in the atmosphere would condense and form ice. Ethane and methane could be present as liquids. Limited data are available about Titan, however, and thus scientists can only speculate about its structure and geologic activity.

Estimates of the diameter of Neptune's Triton range from 2,200 to 5,000 kilometers, with most astronomers suggesting 3,600 kilometers as a likely value. Its atmosphere is mostly nitrogen, with some methane, and measures about 1,200 kilometers thick. Its surface temperature is about 30-35 Kelvins. Results from the August, 1989, flyby of Triton revealed a largely pinkish surface and indicated the presence of solid methane. From a geologic standpoint, the surface of the satellite is relatively young, as it evidences few meteor craters. The flyby did show craters of then-active volcanoes; these volcanoes, when they were first detected, were hypothesized to result from liquid nitrogen working its way to the surface of Triton and then solidifying as it would break through a fissure.

Saturn's six medium-sized moons—Rhea, Mimas, Tethys, Dione, Enceladus, and Iapetus—are approximately 50 percent water ice and 50 percent rocky material. Rhea, the largest of this group, is heavily cratered, very much as Earth's moon is. The low temperature (about 100 Kelvins) causes ice to behave much as rock does and not to undergo plastic deformation. Crater features can easily be preserved on this icy surface, while they were smoothed out on the warmer surface of Callisto. Most of the moons in the solar system rotate once about their axes during one orbit around the planet. Therefore, one side always "leads" the moon, while the other side "trails" the moon. The trailing side of Rhea shows bright streaks, known as wispy terrain, which may be remnants of a time when water was released from the interior and condensed on the surface.

Dione's surface is heavily cratered, and its trailing side displays prominent regions of wispy terrain. Much of the moon has been resurfaced, and valleys of unknown origin are found near the bright streaks. The bright material may have come to the surface through cracks in the crust and solidified on the cracks' edges to form the wispy terrain. Tethys, very much like Dione, contains only one giant valley system that stretches almost 75 percent of the way around the moon. This valley, called Ithaca Chasma, is about 100 kilometers wide and could have formed when internal changes caused an expansion of Tethys. Mimas is heavily cratered and shows no evidence of internal activity. It has one large crater, Herschel, whose diameter is about one-third the diameter of Mimas itself. Enceladus is about the same size as Mimas but is strikingly different. Its surface reflects almost 100 percent of the light reaching it. Enceladus is associated with Saturn's E ring and may have played a role in its formation. Most of the impact craters have been erased, and many of the surface features point to relatively recent volcanic activity. Scientists have yet to explain how Enceladus can maintain its internal activity. The last of Saturn's medium-sized moons is Iapetus, a satellite whose leading side has a reflectivity of 3 percent and its trailing side a reflectivity of 50 percent. Scientists believe, and have some evidence to support their belief, that the dark material is similar to dark carbon-containing material found on some meteorites. Scientists do not know why only this moon has the dark deposit over its icy crust.

Like Saturn's medium-sized moons, the composition of Uranus' moons is about half water ice and half rocky material. The five satellites—Miranda, Ariel, Umbriel, Titania, and Oberon—have water ice surfaces with a reflectivity of 20-30 percent. Titania, Oberon, and Umbriel are heavily cratered and display little evidence of any internal activity. Ariel shows cratering but also contains long valleys and smoother areas that appear to have been resurfaced. The surface features indicate that much geologic activity has occurred and that the moon may have expanded and cracked its crust. Scientists studied the photographs of the valley floors on Ariel and Miranda and concluded that ice volcanism filled the low areas. As the crust cracked, a plastic ice flowed to the surface, where it hardened before it could smooth itself out. The causes of the crustal cracking and the ice flow remain unexplained. Miranda has great valley systems, unusually shaped mountain ranges, craters with sharp features, craters with subdued features, and a large cliff. All these structures indicate much activity, but scientists are struggling to explain how that activity could occur on such a small object. One explanation is that Miranda was shattered after it differentiated and the pieces fell back together randomly.

Little is known about Nereid, Neptune's second moon. Recent earthbound studies have noted a change in its brightness as it orbits Neptune. These changes could be caused by the rotation of a spherical moon with one side four times brighter than the other. Alternatively, Nereid could be shaped like a potato, and as it rotates on its axis the surface area reflecting light to Earth changes and, therefore, its apparent brightness changes.

Methods of Study

Planetary scientists face the difficult task of studying their objects of interest at very great distances. Two techniques have been used over the years. The first involves analysis of energy coming to Earth from reflected light or from processes on the object that radiate energy. The second uses space probes to fly by the planets to collect data.

Chemical compounds interact with energy in such a way that each substance has an identifying "fingerprint" in its energy spectrum. As molecules vibrate, they interact with infrared (heat) energy. Electrons in compounds can absorb and emit ultraviolet energy. Substances that exist on Earth could be present on the planets. Therefore, scientists can find the fingerprints of substances on Earth and then compare them to fingerprints detected in energy sent to Earth or found by space probes. This process works for substances in an atmosphere or on a visible surface. The presence of water ice on the surface of many of the Jovian satellites and of methane on Titan and Triton was established using this technique.

Spacecraft such as Pioneers 1 and 2 and Voyagers 1 and 2 carry cameras in addition to the other sophisticated analytical equipment. Careful examination of the surface details in the photographs permits astronomers to develop models that describe the geologic history and relative age of the moon's surface. A moon that is heavily cratered over its entire surface probably has been geologically inactive for much of its life. Callisto is a moon whose surface contains many impact craters, no volcanic craters, and no evidence of internal activity. Approximately half of Ganymede, however, is lightly cratered and contains a series of mountain ranges and valleys. This indicates a period of significant geologic activity. Photographs of Io revealed its current volcanic activity. Voyager 2 measured the drop in brightness of the star Beta Canis Majoris as it passed through Triton's atmosphere to determine how much haze and what gases are present in the atmosphere. This technique, called occultation, was also used to measure the diameter of Triton as Voyager 2 passed behind the moon and temporarily lost contact with Earth and the sun.

Context

As astronomers try to piece together a history of the solar system, they turn to the outer planets and their moons to provide information because some of these groupings represent small solar systems. If the models are correct, the Jovian planets and their satellites should have retained much of their original components, while the four inner planets will have changed or lost material because of the energy they received from the sun. The moons without atmospheres can reveal much about the number and size of meteors and asteroids present during the younger days of the solar system, while the one moon with an atmosphere has scientists speculating about what kind of life could develop there.

Several challenges have arisen as the Jovian satellites have been studied. Callisto and Ganymede are about the same size and density and are located near each other in orbit around Jupiter, yet Callisto shows no evidence of internal activity, while Ganymede has been very active. Enceladus has properties very different from Mimas, even though they should be much alike. Iapetus has one hemisphere covered with a very dark material that is not found on other moons but resembles material found on meteorites. Ice volcanism has been found on Ariel and Miranda. Miranda has been very active geologically even though it is rather small.

These challenges illustrate both the strengths and weaknesses of the scientific method. In its most effective application, continued experimentation leads scientists to eliminate possibilities and then to make predictions about future events or conditions. Although the data gathered have been limited because of the difficulty of sending spacecraft to the outer reaches of the solar system, scientists have learned enough to describe the behavior of Io and the geologic activity of some of the other moons. Nevertheless, many of the observed phenomena have neither been explained nor accurately predicted. Scientists working with incomplete data sets may, and do, form incomplete or incorrect models. With information that will be gathered by Voyager 2, Galileo, and other space probes, a wealth of new insights are expected to be gathered by the early twenty-first century.

Bibliography

Fimmel, Richard O., James Van Allen, and Eric Burgess. *Pioneer: First to Jupiter, Saturn, and Beyond*. NASA SP-446. Washington, D.C.: Government Printing Office, 1980. A summary of the flight, the spacecraft, and the results of the Pioneer missions. Contains an excellent set of photos of the instruments used in collecting data and of the planets and their moons. For a general audience.

Hunt, Gary, and Patrick Moore. *Jupiter*. Skokie, Ill.: Rand McNally, 1981.

_____. *Saturn*. Skokie, Ill.: Rand McNally, 1982. Astronomical atlases that give detailed information about the structure, composition, history, rings, and satellites of Jupiter and Saturn, respectively. Maps of the satellites combined with photomosaics of the rings and satellites make this an excellent source for details of this system. For a general audience.

Mirabito, Michael M. *The Exploration of Outer Space with Cameras: A History of the NASA Unmanned Spacecraft Missions*. Jefferson, N.C.: McFarland, 1983. A survey of the types of cameras and their design criteria and an analysis of the photographs from all parts of the solar system that have been explored. Thirty-two black-and-white photos are included. Some science background for the reader is helpful, and a knowledge of cameras and lenses is important.

Morrison, David. *Voyages to Saturn*. NASA SP-451. Washington, D.C.: Government Printing Office, 1982. The discussion includes all the important discoveries of the Pioneer and Voyager missions and presents the voyages from the perspective of the individuals controlling the spacecraft and collecting the data. Excellent collection of information that includes many photographs of the Saturnian system. For a general audience.

Morrison, David, and Tobias Owen. *The Planetary System*. Reading, Mass.: Addison-Wesley, 1987. Excellent descriptions of each of the planets and their satellites accompany many photos and drawings. Although the format is that of a textbook, anyone with an interest in solar system astronomy will find good reading. A science background is helpful in understanding some sections.

Morrison, David, and Jane Samz. *Voyage to Jupiter.* NASA SP-439. Washington, D.C.: Government Printing Office, 1980. The discussion includes a review of the Pioneer and Voyager missions in the context of the scientists involved in collecting the data and running the program. Excellent collection of data and photographs of the Jovian system. For a general audience.

Trejo, P. E. *Introductory Astronomy: The Solar System.* Dubuque, Iowa: Kendall/ Hunt, 1986. General astronomical principles are discussed before details about the solar system are given. A limited number of photographs and line drawings. The planetary data are summarized well. For a general audience.

Dennis R. Flentge

Cross-References

The Atmosphere's Evolution, 114; Earth's Differentiation, 525; Infrared Spectra, 1232; Io, 1238; The Jovian Planets, 1283; The Jovian Planets' Atmospheres, 1290; The Jovian Planets' Ring Systems, 1296; Remote Sensing and the Electromagnetic Spectrum, 2166; Elemental Distribution in the Solar System, 2434; The Origin of the Solar System, 2442.

KARST TOPOGRAPHY

Type of earth science: Geology
Field of study: Geomorphology

Karst topography is a landform produced by the dissolving action of surface and groundwaters on the underlying bedrock of a region. The landforms produced are unique because they represent internal or underground drainage, forming such features as sinking streams, sinkholes, caves, natural bridges, and springs.

Principal terms

CARBONIC ACID: a weak acid formed by mixing water and carbon dioxide; it is important in the dissolving of the most common karst rock, limestone

CAVE: an opening or hole in the ground enterable by people; in karst topography, caves have been dissolved out and act (or once acted) as underground conduit flow routes for water

KARST: the international term for landforms dissolved from rock

LIMESTONE: a common sedimentary rock containing the mineral calcite; the calcite originated from fossil shells of marine plants and animals

NATURAL BRIDGE: a bridge over an abandoned or active watercourse; in karst topography, it may be a short cave or a remnant of an old, long cave

SINKHOLE: a hole or depression in the landscape produced by dissolving bedrock; sinkholes can range in size from a few meters across and deep to kilometers wide and hundreds of meters deep

SINKING STREAM: a stream or river that loses part or all of its water to pathways dissolved underground in the bedrock

SPRING: a place where groundwater reappears on the earth's surface; in karst topography, a spring represents the discharge point of a cave

Summary of the Phenomenon

Karst topography is a unique landscape produced by the dissolving of the bedrock of a region, with the consequent development of underground drainage. Most common bedrock materials, such as granite, sandstone, and shale, are resistant to the process of dissolving (also known as dissolution), and landscapes are carved into these bedrock materials by the mechanical action of water, wind, and ice. Some bedrock materials, such as limestone, dolomite, gypsum, and rock salt, dissolve relatively easily. Gypsum and rock salt are soluble in plain water and in most landscapes are chemically destroyed very quickly. Karst landscapes on these two rock types persist only in dryer climates, such as in the American Southwest. Gypsum and rock salt are also mechanically weak rocks and are destroyed rapidly by mechanical erosive activities. Limestone, and its close cousin dolomite, are mechanically strong rocks; therefore, they resist normal erosive activity. Yet, calcite, the mineral of which limestone is composed, is especially vulnerable to dissolving by water that is slightly acidic. Under normal conditions, the source of such acidity is from carbonic acid, a natural combination of carbon dixoide and water. Rain-water absorbs carbon dioxide from the atmosphere and is naturally slightly acidic (modern pollution has accentuated this natural tendency to produce acid rain). In the soil, organic activity can increase the amount of carbon dioxide to levels well above those found in the atmosphere, and water moving through such soils can become very acidic. When rainwater or soil water charged with carbonic acid meets limestone bedrock, it will slowly dissolve the limestone. Limestone, mechanically resistant, supports the development of karst topography well. Dolomite reacts more slowly to acid waters, and generally the karst features found on dolomites are subdued and take longer to form than those on limestones. Discussion of karst topography is therefore, in most situations, a discussion of the dissolving of lime-stone.

The rate at which limestone dissolves depends on the amount of water in the environment and the amount of carbon dioxide available. Atmospheric levels of carbon dioxide are similar worldwide, but the amount of carbon dioxide in the soil varies greatly. Organic activity controls the amount of carbon dioxide available, and for that reason, the most acid groundwater tends to be found in the warm, wet zones of the tropics, where organic activity is high. Dry, cold climates have erosion rates as little as a few millimeters per one thousand years, whereas warm, wet climates can have rates up to 150 millimeters per one thousand years. These erosion rates are averages of the rate of surface lowering for a region. Over the course of hundreds of thousands of years, significant landforms can be developed.

The dissolving action of carbon dioxide-charged water produces a number of etching patterns on exposed limestone bedrock, from microscopic features to large trough structures more than a meter deep and many meters long. Karst topography develops when the water penetrates down pores, cracks, and openings into the limestone. Once inside the rock, the water is capable, over long periods of time, of dissolving voids and passageways in the rock. These openings in the rock become integrated into underground flow networks similar to stream patterns on the earth's surface. The result is a series of underground passageways called caves, which collect water from sinkholes and sinking streams on the earth's surface and transmit the water back to the earth's surface at springs. While the flow pattern of caves is often similar to the pattern of surface streams, caves are tubes in bedrock and may migrate up and down, as well as from side to side, in a manner that surface streams cannot. As the cave system grows and matures, it can capture larger volumes of surface water and enlarge. Eventually it will not only carry material in solution but also mechanically transport sediment underground. On the land surface, this under-ground or internal drainage produces sinking streams and sinkholes. In mature systems, the sinkholes may be kilometers across and hundreds of meters deep, containing many sinking streams. Depending on the exact nature of the limestone, the climate, and the presence of mountains, a wide variety of karst landscapes may appear. The landscape may be as simple as rolling hills or a flat plain with mostly normal surface drainage and only a few scattered sinkholes, sinking streams, and caves. Other landscapes, however, may have no significant surface drainage and have sinkholes covering the land surface, producing a sinkhole plain. One of the best examples of a sinkhole plain is in the Mammoth Cave area of Kentucky. Under extreme conditions, usually associated with the tropics, the landscape is so altered by dissolution that the sinkholes deepen faster than they widen, producing a landscape of tall limestone towers and pinnacles standing above a flat plain. This landform is called tower karst and is best known from southern China, where thousands of towers several hundred meters high dot the landscape.

The ever-downward erosion by groundwater can produce cave systems at lower elevations, causing earlier, higher cave systems to become abandoned. These abandoned caves may persist for hundreds of thousands of years, developing complex mineral displays of stalactites, stalagmites, and other deposits. Animals and people may use the cave for shelter, leaving behind important fossil and cultural material. Continuing erosion of the land surface will eventually breach into underlying cave systems to produce new entrances and truncated cave fragments called natural bridges. Sinkholes become natural traps, collecting unwary animals as well as plant remains, soil, and pollen. The transport of material into the subsurface allows the material to be preserved from destruction in the earth's surface environment.

Like all landscapes, karst topography can go through a series of developmental stages. Karst development begins when the soluble rock is first exposed at the earth's surface. In some cases, groundwater reaches the soluble rock before it is ever exposed, and cave development can begin before the rock is present on the surface. In either case, the progressive development of a karst landscape by chemical and mechanical erosion will remove the layer of soluble rock responsible for the karst processes. In time, karst processes become less important in the landscape as the soluble bedrock disappears, and the landscape will begin to revert to a more typical, mechanically produced form.

In the United States, limestones form important areas of karst topography in the Virginias, Pennsylvania, Indiana, Kentucky, Tennessee, Alabama, Florida, Missouri, Arkansas, and Texas. Many other states have minor amounts of limestone karst, such as New York, Minnesota, Iowa, Colorado, and New Mexico. Some states have major cave systems located in minor areas of karst, such as Carlsbad Caverns in New Mexico and the Jewel and Wind Caves in South Dakota. Gypsum karst is locally important in Kansas, Oklahoma, and New Mexico, while dolomite karst is found in Missouri. Marble, limestone altered by heat and pressure, forms small karst areas in California, New England, and Oregon. Rock salt karst is very rare in the United States but can be found in Spain and the Middle East. Almost every state and every country has some form of karst development.

The unique features of karst topography can be mimicked by other landscapes in special cases. Such cases are called pseudokarst, because they imitate karst topography but are produced by other phenomena. For example, volcanic areas produce eruptive craters and lava tubes that look like sinkholes and caves from karst areas. In deserts, streams can dry up and appear to be sinking, and winds can produce excavated hollows in the sand. Glaciers can produce depressions in the ground that look like sinkholes. In fine-grained clay deposits—which can be seen in the Badlands of South Dakota—caves, bridges, and sinkholes are produced by mechanical flushing of the clay particles, a process called suffusion. Wave activity on rocky coastlines can carve sea caves in a variety of rock materials.

Karst topography is unique because of the chemical manner in which the bedrock is destroyed and because of the internal or underground drainage that results. Most karst is developed in limestone because of this rock's abundance, slow chemical dissolution rates, and great mechanical strength. In certain areas of the world, karst topography is the dominant landscape for thousands of square kilometers. Cave systems in excess of 500 kilometers of surveyed passage exist, and caves have been followed as deep as 1,700 meters beneath the surface.

Methods of Study

Karst topography is most easily recognized from topographic maps, which show the earth's elevations as a series of contour lines. Areas of karst topography will show internal drainage, with sinking streams, large sinkholes, and springs. Well-known caves will be listed on the map. Field examination of the area is necessary to prove that the bedrock involved has undergone chemical attack and has dissolved. Geologists determine the rate at which the landscape has formed by analyzing rock samples in the laboratory under controlled conditions to see how it dissolves under a variety of temperatures and acid concentrations. Measurements of soil carbon dioxide, regional rainfall and temperature, and amount of soluble rock present allow the rate of landscape formation to be established. Sinking streams and springs are measured to establish a water balance; how much water is entering the system and how much is leaving it. To understand the underground flow paths, a geologist will explore and map a cave system; in many cases, however, the cave system is blocked by collapse, sediment, or excess water, and the explorer is stopped. To define the water's underground flow paths completely requires stream tracing, in which a known quantity of dye is placed in a sinking stream; springs in the area are monitored to see where (and how much) of the dye returns to the surface. Special dyes are used that are safe, detectable in tiny quantities, and resistant to loss or destruction in the groundwater system. The dye is detected by automatic water samplers and a fluorometer, a device that can detect dyes even in parts per billion concentrations. The speed at which the dye transits the cave system and the degree to which it has become diluted can reveal the nature and configuration of the unexplored portion of the cave system.

The successful delineation of the cave systems of a karst area, along with data about the nature of the rock and climate, can show geologists what is happening in the present. In many cases, however, the geologist is also interested in the past development of the karst area in order to detect trends that allow prediction of the karst area in the future: Will the caves get bigger? Will sinkholes collapse? Will there be flooding? These are questions important to land use. Geologists often go to the abandoned caves to learn about the history of a karst landscape. Inside the caves, they find sediments that were washed in from the surface when the abandoned caves were active. The size and composition of those sediments reveal how much water was entering the cave and from what source areas. Animal fossils and human cultural remains can explain how the climate may have changed.

A special technique involving stalagmites, calcite mineral deposits that grow up from the floors of caves, can provide hard numerical data on past conditions. The calcite that makes up the stalagmites is deposited in layers, much like the growth rings in a tree trunk. Uranium, a radioactive element, is often present in trace amounts in the drip water that falls from the cave roof to make the stalagmite. As the calcite crystallizes to make the layering in the stalagmite, it traps small amounts of uranium with it. Through time, the radioactive uranium begins to decay into the element thorium. The older the stalagmite, the more calcite layers it has. The bottom layers of calcite will have both uranium and thorium in them: the uranium from the initial deposition and the thorium from decay of some of the uranium. Higher up in the stalagmite, each calcite layer is younger, and therefore the amount of thorium should be less. Since the rate of decay of uranium is well known, the ratio of uranium to thorium is a measure of how old the calcite layer is. The more thorium relative to uranium in the layer, the older it is. When these sorts of measurements were first done, a startling discovery was made. The age of many stalagmites, especially those from northern North America, did not get uniformly younger from the base of the stalagmite to the top. Instead, there were sudden jumps in age. The bottommost portion of the stalagmite might show a progression in age from older to younger layers, but then there would be an abrupt jump to a much younger age. Geologists reasoned that the sudden jumps in age meant that at certain times in the history of the stalagmite, it was not growing; the drip water feeding the stalagmite had become shut off. This was clearly a signal of climatic conditions on the surface of the earth. The earth was either too dry or too cold to allow liquid water into the cave ceiling, where it could drip and make the stalagmite. When the times of stalagmite growth and nongrowth were examined, it was found that for northern North American caves, the nongrowth occurred when the region had been covered by ice sheets during ice ages. The technique has since been refined to allow geologists to use the rate of stalagmite growth in caves to determine many aspects of the duration and intensity of climatic changes on the earth's surface above the caves. The stalagmite data, when joined to the sediment and fossil data, have allowed the history of many karst areas to be determined with a higher degree of accuracy than is possible in most nonkarst areas.

Context

About 25 percent of the world's population either lives on or obtains its water from areas of karst topography. Because of the internal, underground nature of landscape development and water flow, many environmental problems occur in karst areas that do not happen on other landscapes. The ability of limestone to react with acids means that soils in limestone karst areas are rarely acidic and are therefore often highly productive agriculturally.

Abandoned caves in karst areas preserve a wealth of information about past landscape history, extinct animals, and past human culture. Some of the most famous paleontological and archaeological sites in the world have been situated in or near caves. Cultural uses of caves have ranged from homes and churches to prisons and air-raid shelters. The earliest known human artworks have been found in caves of the Pyrenees Mountains of France and Spain, cave paintings produced more than thirty thousand years ago.

Karst areas are confronted with an unusual array of environmental problems. Sinkholes are convenient sites for waste disposal, yet they feed directly into the underground water supply. Unlike traditional underground water reservoirs or aquifers, water transmission underground in karst areas is through tubes in the bedrock, caves. There is no filtration in a cave system, as there is in an aquifer of porous sandstone. In addition, caves can transmit water long distances in very short periods of time. Cave streams often cross underneath surface divides to release groundwater at springs in a completely different valley from the one in which the water first sank underground. These unique aspects of groundwater flow in karst areas make groundwater pollution and contamination a serious problem. The pollution can travel rapidly with minimal alteration over long distances to unexpected locations.

In some regions, agricultural, industrial, and domestic use of water has resulted in the lowering of the water table in karst areas. Lowering of the water table can lead to sinkhole collapse with large-scale disruption on the land surface. In South Africa, Pennsylvania, Missouri, and most dramatically in Florida, excessive groundwater pumping has resulted in the loss of property and life. The collapse can be sudden or gradual, and special engineering techniques are required to restore the landscape to its original function.

Land use in areas of karst topography requires a complete understanding of karst processes and of the nature of the landscapes those processes produce. The list of engineering failures in karst areas is long: landfills that polluted a city's water supply, sewage lagoons that drained underground overnight, dams that collapsed, and reservoirs that never filled. Karst topography, because of caves, is tied directly to the early development of humans. The cryptic nature of the underground environment continues to lure amateur explorer and scientist alike.

Bibliography

Beck, B. F., and W. L. Wilson, eds. *Karst Hydrogeology: Engineering and Environmental Applications*. Boston: A. A. Balkema, 1987. This book is the proceedings volume of the Second Multidisciplinary Conference on Sinkholes and the Environmental Impacts of Karst and contains sixty-three papers on a variety of topics concerning human activity and karst, with an emphasis on the high rate of mistakes made as a result of ignorance of karst processes. Accessible to the nonspecialist.

Jennings, J. N. *Karst Geomorphology*. New York: Basil Blackwell, 1985. A college-level text that emphasizes karst processes overall, as opposed to only their role in cave formation. The text requires some knowledge of the basic sciences. It is interesting to read, as it uses many Australian examples and contains the lifetime knowledge of one of the world's leaders in karst research.

Middleton, John, and Anthony C. Waltham. *The Underground Atlas: A Gazetteer of the World's Cave Regions*. New York: St. Martin's Press, 1987. An easy-to-read guide to the famous long and deep caves of the world, this atlas covers the continents in a general review and then describes the cave resources of the world's countries, from Afghanistan to Zimbabwe. Simple maps are presented to portray the largest and deepest caves. The appendices supply a listing of record-holding caves in terms of length, depth, and volume, as well as data about caving organizations and sources of additional reading.

Moore, George W., and G. Nicholas Sullivan. *Speleology: The Study of Caves*. Teaneck, N.J.: Zephyrus Press, 1978. This text is designed to give a scientific introduction to caves and karst for nonscientists. It explores the chemistry, atmospherics, mineralogy, biology, and cultural uses of caves. Oriented to the American reader, examples are primarily from North America. Contains an appendix that lists caves open to the public throughout the United States.

Palmer, Arthur N. *A Geological Guide to Mammoth Cave National Park*. Teaneck, N.J.: Zephyrus Press, 1981. Mammoth Cave is the longest explored cave in the world, with more than 500 kilometers of surveyed passage. This very readable book explains subtle aspects of karst geology in a way understandable to the layperson but at the same time impressive to the specialist. Demonstrates how surface karst topography relates to the internal drainage of caves.

Sasowsky, I. D. *Cumulative Index for the National Speleological Society Bulletin, Volumes 1 Through 45, and Occasional Papers of the N.S.S., Numbers 1 Through 4*. Huntsville, Ala.: National Speleological Society, 1986. The Bulletin of the National Speleological Society is carried by many libraries and contains papers on the science of speleology and karst processes. This index to that journal allows quick access to published papers on specific topics, by topic, author, or geographical area.

Waltham, Anthony C. *Caves*. New York: Crown, 1974. An easy-to-read popular account of caves, how they form, what they contain, and how they are explored. The author is both an internationally recognized cave explorer and a top scientist in the area of karst topography. The text contains a good index and a bibliography and uses worldwide examples to explain the variety of features found above and below ground in karst areas.

White, William B. *Geomorphology and Hydrology of Karst Terrains*. New York: Oxford University Press, 1988. An advanced college textbook written by one of the leaders in karst research in North America, this volume contains a well-written and comprehensive discussion of karst topography.

John E. Mylroie

Cross-References

Aquifers, 71; Carbonates, 190; Drainage Basins, 384; Evaporites, 631; Fossilization and Taphonomy, 768; Freshwater Chemistry, 795; Geochronology: U-Th-Pb Dating, 862; Groundwater Movement, 1020; Groundwater Pollution, 1028; The Hydrologic Cycle, 1102; Reefs, 2158; Sedimentary Rocks: Biogenic, 2312; Sedimentary Rocks: Chemical Precipitates, 2318; Surface Water, 2504.

LAKES

Type of earth science: Geology
Field of study: Sedimentology

Lakes are geologically short-lived features, and sediments deposited in lakes (called lacustrine sediments) constitute only a tiny part of the sedimentary rocks of the earth's crust. Nevertheless, lake sediments are the most important sources of information about past climates. Several important economic resources, including oil shales, diatomaceous earth, salt, some limestones, and some coals, originate in lakes.

Principal terms

ALLOGENIC SEDIMENT: sediment that originates outside the place where it is finally deposited; sand silt and clay carried by a stream into a lake are examples

BIOGENIC SEDIMENT: sediment that originates from living organisms

CLASTIC SEDIMENTS: sediments composed of durable minerals that resist weathering

CLAY: a size term referring to any mineral particle less than 2 micrometers in diameter

CLAY MINERALS: a mineral group that consists of structures arranged in sandwichlike layers, usually sheets of aluminum hydroxides and silica, along with some potassium, sodium, or calcium ions

ENDOGENIC SEDIMENT: sediment produced within the water column of the body in which it is deposited; for example, calcite precipitated in a lake in summer

MINERAL: a solid with a constant chemical composition and a well-defined crystal structure

MINERALOID: a solid substance with a constant chemical composition but without a well-ordered crystal structure

PLANKTON: plant and animal organisms, most of which are microscopic, that live within the water column

SESTON: a general term that encompasses all types of suspended lake sediment, including minerals, mineraloids, plankton, and organic detritus

Summary of the Phenomenon

Several geologic mechanisms can provide the closed basins that are needed to impound water and produce lakes. The most important of these mechanisms include glaciers, landslides, volcanoes, rivers, subsidence, and tectonic processes.

Continental glaciers formed thousands of lakes by the damming of stream valleys with moraine materials. Glaciers also scoured depressions in softer bedrock, and these later filled with water to form lakes. Depressions called kettles formed when buried ice blocks melted. Mountain glaciers also produce numerous small, high alpine lakes by plucking away bedrock. The bowl-shaped depressions that occur as a result of this plucking are called cirques; lakes that occupy these cirques are called tarns. Sometimes, a mountain glacier moves down a valley and carves a series of depressions along the valley that, from above, look like a row of beads along a string. When these depressions later fill with water, the lakes are called paternoster lakes, the name coming from their similarity to beads on a rosary.

Landslides sometimes form natural dams across stream valleys. Large lakes then pond up behind the dam. Volcanoes may produce lava flows that dam stream valleys and produce lakes. A volcanic explosion crater may fill with water and make a lake. After an eruption, the area around the eruption vent may collapse to form a depression called a caldera. Some calderas, such as Crater Lake in Oregon, fill with water. Rivers produce lakes along their valleys when a tight loop of a meandering channel finally is eroded through and leaves behind an oxbow lake, isolated from the main channel. Sediment may accumulate at the mouth of a stream, and the resulting delta may build and bridge across irregularities in the shoreline to create a brackish coastal lake.

Natural subsidence creates closed basins in areas underlain by soluble limestones or evaporite deposits. As the underlying limestone is dissolved away, the earth above collapses to form a cavity (sinkhole), which later fills with water. Finally, large-scale (tectonic) downwarping of the earth's crust produces some very large lakes. Large basins result when the crust warps or sinks downward in response to deep forces. The subsidence produces very large closed basins that can hold water. A few immense lakes owe their origins to tectonic downwarping.

With few exceptions, most lakes exist in relatively small depressions and serve as the catch basins for sediment from the entire watershed around them. The natural process of sedimentation ensures that most lakes fill with sediment before very long periods of geologic time have passed. Lakes with areas of only a few square kilometers or less will fill within a few tens of thousands of years. Very large lakes, the inland seas, may endure for more than ten million years. Man-made lakes and reservoirs have unusually high sediment-fill rates in comparison with most natural lakes. Man-made lakes fill with sediment within a few decades to a few centuries.

Lake sediments come from four sources: allogenic clastic materials that are washed in from the surrounding watershed; endogenic chemical precipitates that are produced from dissolved substances in the lake waters; endogenic biogenic organic materials, produced by plants and animals living in the lake; and airborne substances, such as dust and pollen, transported to the lake in the atmosphere.

Allogenic clastic materials are mostly minerals; they are produced when rocks and soils in the drainage basin are weathered by mechanical and chemical processes to yield small particles. These particles are moved downslope by gravity and running water to enter streams, which then transport them to the lake. Clastic materials also enter the lake via waves, which erode the materials from the shoreline, and via landslides that directly enter the lake. In winter, ice formed on the lake can expand and push its way a few centimeters to a meter or so onto the shore. There, the ice may pick up large particles, such as gravel and cobbles. When spring thaw comes, waves can remove that ice, together with its enclosed particles, and float it out onto the lake. The process by which the large particles are transported out on the lake is called ice-rafting. As the ice melts, the large clastic particles drop to the bottom; they are termed dropstones when found in lake sediments. A landslide into a lake or a flood on a stream that feeds into the lake can produce water heavily laden with sediment. The sediment-laden water is more dense than is clean water and therefore can rush down and across the lake bottom at speeds sufficient to carry even coarse sand far out into the lake. These types of deposits are called turbidite deposits.

Endogenic chemical precipitates in freshwater lakes commonly consist of carbonate minerals (calcite, aragonite, or dolomite) and mineraloids that consist of oxides and hydroxides of iron, manganese, and aluminum. In some saline and brine lakes, the main sediments may be carbonates, together with sulfates such as gypsum (hydrated calcium sulfate), thenardite (sodium sulfate), epsomite (hydrated magnesium sulfate) or with chlorides such as halite (sodium chloride) or more complex salts. Of the endogenic precipitates, calcite is the most abundant. Its precipitation represents a balance between the composition of the atmosphere and that of the lake water. The mechanism that triggers the precipitation of calcite is usually an algal bloom, often of diatoms. Diatoms are distinctive microscopic algae that produce a frustule (a kind of shell) made of silica glass that is highly resistant to weathering. When seen under a high-powered microscope, diatom frustules appear to be artwork—beautiful and highly ornate saucer- and pen-shaped works of glass. A tiny spot of lake sediment may contain millions.

A lake's sediment may contain from less than 1 percent to more than 90 percent organic materials, depending upon the type of lake. Most organic matter in lake sediments is produced within the lake by plankton and consists of compounds such as carbohydrates, proteins, oils, and waxes that are made up of organic carbon, hydrogen, nitrogen, and oxygen, with a little phosphorus. Plankton, with an approximate bulk composition of 36 percent carbon, 7 percent hydrogen, 50 percent oxygen, 6 percent nitrogen, and 1 percent phosphorus (by weight), includes microscopic plants (phytoplankton) and microscopic animals (zooplankton) that live in the water column. Lakes that are very high in nutrients (eutrophic lakes) commonly have heavy blooms of algae, which contribute much organic matter to the bottom sediment. Terrestrial (land-derived) organic material such as leaves, bark, and twigs form a minor part of the organic matter found in most lakes. Terrestrial organic material is higher in carbon and lower in hydrogen, nitrogen, and phosphorus than is planktonic organic matter.

Airborne substances constitute only a tiny fraction of lake sediment. The most important material is pollen and spores. Pollen usually constitutes less than 1 percent of the total sediments, but that tiny amount is a very useful component for learning about the recent climates of the earth. Pollen is some of the most durable of all natural materials. It survives attack by air, water, and even strong acids and bases. Therefore, it remains in the sediment through geologic time. As pollen accumulates in the bottom sediment, the lake serves as a kind of tape recorder for the vegetation that exists around it at a given time. By taking a long core of the bottom sediment from certain types of lakes, a geologist may look at the pollen changes that have occurred through time and reconstruct the history of the climate and vegetation in an area.

Volcanic ash thrown into the atmosphere during eruptions enters lakes and forms a discrete layer of ash on the lake bottom. When Mount St. Helens erupted in 1980, it deposited several centimeters of ash in lakes more than 160 kilometers east of the volcano. Geologists have used layers of ash in lakes to reconstruct the history of volcanic eruptions in some areas. Although dust storms contribute sediment to lakes, such storms are usually too infrequent in most areas to contribute significant amounts.

Lake waters are driven into circulation by the agents of temperature and wind. Most freshwater lakes in temperate climates circulate completely twice each year; they are termed dimictic lakes. Circulation exerts a profound influence on water chemistry of the lake and the amount and type of sediment present within the water column. During summer stratification, the lake is thermally stratified into three zones. The upper layer of warm water (epilimnion) floats above the denser cold water and prevents wind-driven circulation from penetrating much below the epilimnion. The epilimnion is usually in circulation, is rich in oxygen (from algal photosynthesis and diffusion from the atmosphere), and is well lighted. This layer is where summer blooms of green and blue-green algae occur and calcite precipitation begins. The middle layer (thermocline) is a transition zone in which the water cools downward at a rate of greater than 1 degree Celsius per meter. The bottom layer (hypolimnion) is cold, dark, stagnant, and usually poor in oxygen. There, bacteria decompose the bottom sediment and release phosphorus, manganese, iron, silica, and other constituents into the hypolimnion.

Sediment deposited in summer includes a large amount of organic matter, clastic materials washed in during summer rainstorms, and endogenic carbonate minerals produced within the lake. The most common carbonate mineral is calcite (calcium carbonate). The regular deposition of calcite in the summer is an example of cyclic sedimentation, a sedimentary event that occurs at regular time intervals. This event occurs yearly in the summer season and takes place in the upper 2 or 3 meters of water. On satellite photos, it is even possible to see the summer events as whitings on large lakes, such as Lake Michigan.

As the sediment falls through the water column in summer, it passes through the thermocline, into the hypolimnion, and onto the lake bottom. As it sits on the bottom during the summer months, bacteria, particularly anaerobic bacteria (those that thrive in oxygen-poor environments), begin to decompose the organic matter. As this occurs, the dissolved carbon dioxide (CO_2) increases in the hypolimnion. If enough CO_2 is produced, the hypolimnion becomes slightly acidic, and calcite and other carbonates that fell to the bottom begin to dissolve. The acidic conditions also release dissolved phosphorus, calcium, iron, and manganese into the hypolimnion, as well as some trace metals. Clastic minerals such as quartz, feldspar, and clay minerals are not affected in such brief seasonal processes, but some silica from biogenic material such as diatom frustules can dissolve and enrich the hypolimnion in silica. As summer progresses, the hypolimnion becomes more and more enriched in dissolved metals and nutrients.

Autumn circulation begins when the water temperature cools and the density of the epilimnion increases until it reaches the same temperature and density as the deep water. Thereafter, there is no stratification to prevent the wind from circulating the entire lake. When this happens, the cold, stagnant hypolimnion, now rich in dissolved substances, is swept into circulation with the rest of the lake water. The dissolved materials from the hypolimnion are mixed into a well-oxygenated water column. Iron and manganese that formerly were present in dissolved form now oxidize to form tiny solid particles of manganese oxides, iron oxides, and hydroxides. The sediment therefore becomes enriched in iron, manganese, or both during the autumn overturn, the amount of enrichment depending upon the amount of dissolved iron and manganese that accumulated during summer in the hypolimnion. Dissolved silica is also swept from the hypolimnion into the entire water column. In the upper water column, where sunlight and dissolved silica become present in great abundance, diatom blooms occur. The diatoms convert the dissolved silica into solid opaline frustules.

As circulation proceeds, the currents may sweep over the lake bottom and actually resuspend a centimeter or more of sediment from the bottom and margins of the lake. The amount of resuspension that occurs each year in freshwater lakes is primarily the result of the shape of the lake basin. A lake that has a large surface area and is very shallow permits wind to keep the lake in constant circulation over long periods of the year.

As winter stratification comes, an ice cover forms over the lake and prevents any wind-induced circulation. Because the circulation is what keeps the lake sediment in suspension, most sediment quickly falls to the bottom; sedimentation then is minimal through the rest of winter. If light can penetrate the ice and snow, some algae and diatoms can utilize this weak light, present in the layer of water just below the ice, to reproduce. Their settling remains contribute small amounts of organic matter and diatom frustules. At the lake bottom, the most dense water (that at 4 degrees Celsius) accumulates. As in summer, some dissolved nutrients and metals can build up in this deep layer, but because the bacteria that are active in releasing these substances from the sediment are refrigerated, they work slowly, and not as much dissolved material builds up in the bottom waters.

When spring circulation begins, the ice at the surface melts, and the lake again goes into wind-driven circulation. Oxidation of iron and manganese occurs (as in autumn), although the amounts of dissolved materials available are likely to be less in spring. Once again, nutrients such as phosphorus and silica are circulated out of the dark bottom waters and become available to produce blooms of phytoplankton. Spring rains often hasten the melting, and runoff from rain and snowmelt in the drainage basin washes clastic materials into the lake. The period of spring thaw is likely to be the time of year when the maximum amount of new allogenic (externally derived) sediment enters the lake.

Spring diatom blooms continue until summer stratification prevents further replenishment of silica to the epilimnion. Thereafter, the diatoms are succeeded by summer blooms of green algae, closely followed by blooms of blue-green algae. Silica is usually the limiting nutrient for diatoms; phosphorus is the limiting nutrient for green and blue-green algae.

After sediments are buried, changes occur; this process of change after burial is termed diagenesis. Physical changes include compaction and dewatering. Bacteria decompose much organic matter and produce gases such as methane, hydrogen sulfide, and carbon dioxide. The "rotten-egg" odor of black lake sediments, often noticed on boat anchors, is the odor of hydrogen sulfide. After long periods of time, minerals such as quartz or calcite slowly fill the pores remaining after compaction.

One of the first diagenetic minerals to form is pyrite (iron sulfide, or FeS_2). Much pyrite occurs in microscopic spherical bodies that look like raspberries; these particles, called framboids, are probably formed by bacteria in areas with low oxygen within a few weeks. In fact, the black color of some lake muds and oozes results as much from iron sulfides as from organic matter. Other diagenetic changes include the conversion of mineraloid particles containing phosphorus into phosphate minerals such as vivianite and apatite. Manganese oxides may be converted into manganese carbonates (rhodochrosite) and, in a few rare cases, freshwater manganese oxide nodules may form.

Methods of Study

Scientists who study lakes (limnologists) must study all the natural sciences— physics, chemistry, biology, and geology—because lakes are complex systems that include biological communities, changing water chemistry, geological processes, and interaction between water, sunlight, and the atmosphere.

Modern lake sediments are collected from the water column in sediment traps (cylinders and funnels into which the suspended sediment settles over periods of days or weeks) or by filtering large quantities of lake water. Living material is often sampled with a plankton net. Older sediments that have accumulated on the bottom are collected with dredges and by coring, which involves pushing a sharpened hollow tube (usually about 2.5 centimeters in diameter) downward into the sediment. A special tip at the bottom of the tube prevents the soft sediment from falling out as the core is withdrawn from the lake bottom. Cores are valuable because they preserve the sediment in the order in which it was deposited, from oldest at the bottom to youngest at the top. Once the sample is collected, it is often frozen and taken to the laboratory. There, pollen and organisms may be examined by microscopy, minerals may be determined by X-ray diffraction, and chemical analyses may be made.

Varves are thin laminae that are deposited by cyclic processes. In freshwater lakes, each varve represents a year's deposit; it consists of a couplet with a dark layer of organic matter deposited in winter and a light-colored layer of calcite deposited in summer. Varves are deposited in lakes where annual circulations cannot resuspend bottom sediment and therefore cannot mix it to destroy the annual lamination. Some lakes that are small and very deep may produce varved sediments; Elk Lake in Minnesota is an example. In other lakes, the accumulation of dissolved salts on the bottom eventually produces a dense layer (monimolimnion), which prevents disturbance of the bottom by circulation in the overlying fresher waters. Soap Lake in Washington State is an example. Because each varve couplet represents a year, a geologist may core the sediments from a varved lake and count the couplets to determine the age of the sediment in any part of the core. The pollen, the chemistry, the diatoms, and other constituents may then be carefully examined to deduce what the lake was like during a given time period. The study is much like solving a mystery from a variety of clues. Eventually, the history of climate changes of the area can be known from the study of lake varves.

Context

Lake sediments (particularly varved sediments) are among the most important sources of information about how climates have changed over the past ten thousand to fifteen thousand years. The study of lake varves can show what the temperatures were and how much rainfall occurred. Scientists can thus use varves to look for periodicity, or repeating patterns of climate fluctuation. For example, the eleven-year period of the sunspot cycle produces a cyclic "fingerprint" in lake sediments, which show temperature and rainfall variations in accord with that cycle. Other longer-period variations have been noted, but the mechanisms that cause them have yet to be well understood. Clearly, such knowledge of the past is important for understanding present climate trends such as global warming and droughts.

Varved lakes also give scientists an opportunity to monitor environmental changes that have occurred in the earth as a result of human activities. For example, an increase in lead content in the upper layers of sediments in many lakes marks the time when leaded gasoline and automobiles became abundant. Careful measurements of radioactivity in lake sediments can detect the layers deposited during the years of nuclear weapons testing in the 1950's. Studies of varves can show whether lakes are becoming acidified in the present and if and when they had ever become acidic in prehistoric times through natural causes. Increased sedimentation often shows the effects of construction and mining. The alteration of vegetation is reflected within the pollen record. Therefore, lake sediments serve as a storehouse for vast amounts of information about the recent past of the planet.

Lake sediments sometimes yield valuable commercial deposits. Saline lakes such as the Great Salt Lake, Utah, yield a variety of evaporite salts, including the common table salt, halite. Commercial borate deposits that include borax (hydrated sodium borate) and other boron-containing minerals are found in lake sediments in California and also in Kashmir, Tibet, India, the Soviet Union, and Iran. Soda ash, used in the manufacture of glass, baking soda, and many chemicals, is the mineral trona (a complex salt of sodium carbonates and bicarbonates and water), which is mined in Wyoming from the lake deposits of the Green River formation.

After long burial under suitable geological conditions, the abundant hydrogen in lake plankton yields an organic matter, kerogen, that is conducive to the formation of petroleum. The world's oil shales mostly originate in lakes; the Green River formation of Utah and Wyoming is the largest and best known. Oil is produced when the volatile organic matter from these shales is heated and distilled. The Green River shales may contain over a trillion barrels of oil that can be recovered in this way. Clearly, these lake sediments constitute a major source of future fuel and petrochemicals.

Many coal beds are nonmarine and were deposited in lakes associated with swamps, marshes, and delta plains. Lakes also yield deposits of diatomaceous earth, which is simply a deposit of diatom frustules. The tiny pieces of broken diatom frustules pierce the outside of insects and kill them as they try to crawl through it; therefore, diatomaceous earth is used as a pesticide in shipment of seeds. It is also used as a filter medium and absorption medium in the manufacture of explosives.

Bibliography

Bailey, Ronald. *Rivers and Lakes*. New York: Time-Life Books, 1985. A book on lacustrine (lake) and fluvial (river) environments, suitable for general readers. Part of the Time-Life Planet Earth series.

Håkanson, Lars, and M. Jansson. *Principles of Lake Sedimentology*. New York: Springer-Verlag, 1983. Though this book is a reference for professionals in the field of lake sedimentology, parts of it may be understood by high school students. Most books on limnology focus on lake water; this reference is one of the few to focus on lake sediments in detail. Provides methods of sampling and discusses the influence of lake type and shape on the sediments formed in the lake, the circulation of lake waters, the chemistry of sediments, and the pollution of lakes.

Hutchinson, G. Evelyn. *A Treatise on Limnology*. 3 vols. New York: John Wiley & Sons, 1957-1975. A highly comprehensive reference about lakes. The set derives its information from worldwide sources and is well indexed by subject as well as by specific lakes and their geographic locations. Volume 1 (in two parts: *Geography and Physics of Lakes* and *Chemistry of Lakes*) discusses the geologic formation of lakes, lake types, the interaction of sunlight with lake waters, water color, heat distribution, and water circulation. The chemistry of lake waters is discussed in detail. Volume 2, *Introduction to Lake Biology and Limnoplankton*, covers plankton and the factors that influence their growth. Volume 3, *Limnological*

Botany, covers larger aquatic plants (macrophytes) and attached algae. Most of the treatise is readable by college undergraduates and high school seniors, but a few parts will be well understood only by specialists.

Lerman, Abraham, ed. *Lakes: Chemistry, Geology, Physics*. New York: Springer-Verlag, 1978. This book fills a gap in the Hutchinson treatise by focusing on the geologic processes of sedimentation in freshwater and brine lakes. The book is actually a compilation of chapters, each written by specialists. Particular attention is given to carbonate sediments, clastic and endogenic minerals, human influence on natural lakes, and organic compounds. The chapters on lake sediments and carbonate sedimentation are well illustrated. Most parts of these chapters are accessible to college undergraduates and high school students. Other chapters will be well understood only by specialists.

Stumm, Werner, ed. *Chemical Processes at the Particle-Water Interface*. New York: John Wiley & Sons, 1987. A highly technical reference book, designed for specialists and graduate students. Chapters are authored by a variety of experts, who focus on the chemical interactions that occur between sediment particles and the surrounding lake waters, the process of clotting of particles, and the role of particle surfaces in removing trace metals from water. Chapter 12, by Laura Sigg, focuses specifically on lake sediments and may be understood by undergraduates who have had rigorous courses in introductory chemistry and geology.

Wetzel, R. G., ed. *Limnology*. 2d ed. Philadelphia: Saunders, 1983. A very well written textbook typical of those used by undergraduates and graduates in their first limnology courses. Covers physical, biological, and chemical aspects of lakes. High school algebra, chemistry, physics, and biology courses will be necessary prerequisites to understand most of the text.

Edward B. Nuhfer

Cross-References

Coastal Processes and Beaches, 240; Dams and Flood Control, 309; Diagenesis, 354; Drainage Basins, 384; Evaporites, 631; Freshwater Chemistry, 795; The Geochemical Cycle, 818; The Hydrologic Cycle, 1102; Micropaleontology: Microfossils, 1674; Oil Shale and Tar Sands, 1939; Sedimentary Mineral Deposits, 2296; Sedimentary Rocks: Biogenic, 2312; Sedimentary Rocks: Chemical Precipitates, 2318; Surface Water, 2504; Volcanoes: Calderas, 2614.

LAND MANAGEMENT

Field of study: Soil science

Land management is essential to the proper maintenance and preservation of a natural resource of limited availability. There are both reversible and irreversible land uses, and their implementation will dictate the future availability of land as a natural resource at any given point in time.

Principal terms

LAND: any part of the earth's surface that may be owned as goods and everything annexed to it, such as water, forests, and buildings

LAND MANAGEMENT: an ongoing activity related to the planning and implementation of ideas aimed at establishing the best use of any tract of land

LAND USE: the application to which a tract of land is subjected

MULTIPLE USE: the use of land for more than one purpose or activity at the same time

SUBSURFACE: land features or characteristics that are not visible or apparent and that are beneath the land surface, such as minerals, oil and gas, and structural features

TAXATION: a land-management tool that usually reflects the perceived best use of land

TOPOGRAPHY: the collective physical features of a region or area, such as hills, valleys, streams, cliffs, and plains

ZONING: a land-management tool used to limit uses, conditions of use, and the extent of use

Summary of the Methodology

Land is not reproducible; it is present in only a fixed amount. In addition, its location—important to its use and value—cannot be changed. Aspects of land include its topography, which controls many uses; its soil, which is vital to agricultural and other applications; its subsurface structure and composition, which can prove to be either beneficial or problematic; and the availability of minerals, oil and gas, and other natural resources.

Conflicts are basic between humans and nature. Natural changes in land resulting from changes in climate and geologic evolution are compounded by human influence. Land management is the science that has developed in response to the need for control of land use and preservation. Land-management programs attempt to organize, plan, and manage land-use activities. Well-developed programs are concerned with land and water and address the issues of water-use rights, subsurface rights, surface rights, and above-surface rights. Land-management activities can take place at local, state, and federal levels. They can be geared to single or multipurpose land uses and can be oriented toward rural or urban settings.

Land uses can be either reversible or irreversible. Reversible uses—such as agricultural activities, grazing of livestock, forestry, recreation, and mining—can allow for reversion to former or alternate uses. These uses are frequently applied in multiple-use programs of land management and are generally compatible with one another. The purpose of programs such as these is to maximize use while allowing for the greatest good for the most people. Irreversible land uses result in permanent changes in the character of the land such that it cannot revert to a former condition or use. The filling-in of swamps or other water bodies, the building of cities, and the development of nonreclaimable surface mines result in irreversible, permanent changes. Activities such as these generally result in single-use situations and preclude the development of alternative-use plans.

All land-use issues can present or generate one or more uncertainties with respect to future applications of the land; represent a problem or an opportunity; be subject to the effects of supply and demand; and be dealt with systematically or conceptually. The degree of uncertainty in any land-use issue is a direct result of the availability of data regarding the use and prior experience with the issue. One of the focal points of well-developed land-management policies is to reduce or remove the uncertainties related to land use. Opportunities in land use are those activities that benefit a large segment of the population, either directly or indirectly. Examples range from the establishment of a national park to the development of a new airport. Problems in land use might include the subsurface disposal of radioactive waste or threatening a wildlife habitat by constructing a reservoir system. Supply will dictate how much land should be subjected to a specific use in response to the perceived demand.

Major land-use issues requiring the application of land-management policies can be identified as relating to new growth, declining growth, reclamation, resource exploitation and/or utilization, preservation of natural or cultural resources, plans for maintenance of stable populations, or environmental, economic, or social concerns. Each land-use issue and attendant land-management policy may require specialized knowledge and specific approaches. Science and technology are vital in developing land-use plans; science provides the knowledge, while technology provides the means to implement that knowledge.

Ecological diversity is an important aspect of land-use planning and also of land-management policies. The ultimate goal of all land-management programs should be to put land to its multiple best uses. In doing so, the ecological "carrying capacity" of a regional environment should not be exceeded. Natural resources should be maintained in a state of availability, and development should only be encouraged in areas best suited for it; development should be discouraged in areas of significant resource value. Development should also be discouraged in areas of natural or man-made hazards.

Land-management programs and policies are largely a result of the location of the land to be managed and the anticipated impact the programs might have on a given population. Economics will frequently dictate the preferred use of land, sometimes at the expense of wildlife, aesthetic beauty, and other ecological factors. Land-use issues can be addressed at different levels; factors that help to determine the level at which any particular issue might be addressed include the number of people and locality or localities that might be affected by the issue; the magnitude of the potential cumulative effects that may result from the issue; and the threshold at which an issue becomes significant. The availability (or lack) of water and the effect of water pollution are examples of factors that can have a cumulative effect, while air pollution or radioactive contamination (such as that which happened at the Chernobyl nuclear power plant in the Soviet Union in 1986) are examples of issues that reached a threshold, elevating them from local to international concerns.

Land management is an ongoing activity, and policies may require change and/or modification with time. Land has an intrinsic (cash or exchange) value and an extrinsic (inherent or judgmental) value, both of which must be considered when dealing with or formulating a management plan. Effective planning and subsequent management, public or private, require that land-use controls be regulated and supported by sufficient authority.

Lands are generally managed and their use controlled by taxation, police and regulatory powers, and strategic considerations. Taxation serves as a management tool because taxes levied are generally a reflection of the perceived best use. Changes in tax status frequently result in changes in land use, as in the case of agricultural land that is converted to urban use as a direct result of an increase in taxes and subsequent cessation of agricultural activities. Police and regulatory powers dictate what can and cannot be done on a specific piece of land. Subdivision regulations, environmental laws, and zoning ordinances are the most common form of regulatory land management. Master plans also control land use and are required by most local governments. They assist cities and counties in coordinating the regional implementation of statutes and/or regulations and include a statement of goals, an outline of societal needs, and a list of specific objectives. They are generally collective plans backed by extensive information and by many independent studies. Master plans also outline mechanisms by which the objectives are to be reached. Strategically located lands can affect the use of adjoining parcels. The presence of industrial areas could, for example, preclude adjoining residential development, while the existence of parks and golf courses could discourage adjacent industrial development. Airports, ski areas, forests, and rangelands can also have strategic value if situated properly.

Applications of the Method

Land management can be applied to virtually every use of land. The most familiar applications are those associated with the control of geologic hazards or the reclamation of disturbed lands. In these instances, land-management activities maintain a high profile and are widely publicized. Less visible or publicized activities are associated with agricultural endeavors; forest maintenance and preservation; the construction of recreational areas; the growth of cities, towns, and villages; and the preservation of wildlife habitats. The major land-use categories are forests, range-lands, croplands, and special uses, such as wilderness areas, parks, and wildlife habitat. Many activities take place within these areas, including mining, harvesting of forests and crops, development of urban areas, maintenance of reservoirs and watersheds, and recreation. Activities connected with coastal and inland waters must also be considered within the context of land use.

Federal and state land-management programs are widely recognized forms of land-use planning. These programs have a direct impact on the use of public land such as parks, forests, seashores, and inland waterways. The U.S. federal government has owned lands that were not required for its own activities since October 29, 1782. Approximately one-fifth of the public domain (lands owned by the federal government) was eventually granted to individual states. These lands were set aside for schools, hospitals, mental institutions, and transportation or were swamps and flooded lands—all part of an overall land-management plan.

The management of federal lands is largely custodial. It is carried out under the provisions of numerous statutes and regulations, including the Multiple Use-Sustained Yield Act of 1960, which legalized the multiple use of federal lands; the Wilderness Act of 1964, which set aside wilderness areas; the Classification and Multiple Use Act of 1964, which allowed for the classification of land for determining the best use and determining which lands should be retained or discarded; and the National Environmental Policy Act of 1969, which required the filing of an Environmental Impact Statement (EIS) for major actions that would significantly affect the quality of the human environment.

Grazing is the oldest use of federal lands, but oil and gas activities generate the largest revenues. Mining of nonfuel minerals is governed by the Mining Laws of 1866 and 1872, while the Mineral Leasing Act of 1920 provides for competitive and noncompetitive leasing of land containing oil and gas, oil shale, coal, phosphate, sodium, potash, and sulfur. The United States Forest Service administers all federal forest lands, while the Bureau of Land Management (BLM) administers all else.

Issues that must be addressed in all federal land-management programs include fraud and trespass (relating to illegal harvesting of timber or other valuable materials), resource depletion, reserved rights on lands that have been discarded, multiple use of lands, equity for future generations, the ability to maintain lands and retain their value, and the ideal of private land ownership. Policy issues that are closely related include how such land should be acquired by the federal government, how much land should be discarded, to whom the lands should be granted and what rights (such as access to minerals) should be retained and for how long, what should be the terms of land disposal, how much should be spent to maintain lands that are retained, to what use should retained lands be put, who should share in the benefits which accrue from lands retained, and who should develop the land-management plan and execute it. An important fact to remember is that policy issues change with time, as do approaches to land management.

Forests are an important target of land-management activities because they occupy approximately one-third of the total land area of the United States. Of that area, nearly two-thirds is occupied by commercial forests, while the remainder is reserved from harvest. Forests are used as watershed areas, renewable consumable resources, recreational areas, and wilderness preserves. Policy issues that affect the management of forests include questions regarding how much forest to maintain, how much to restore, how much to withdraw from use, and how they should be harvested. Several criteria must be met to establish practical forest policy. They are physical and biological feasibility of an action, economic efficiency, economic equity, social acceptability, and operational practicality. Not all uses of forests are compatible in a potential multiuse scenario; some uses will necessarily exclude others, which must be considered in a forest-management program. For example, interactive effects must be considered in the harvesting of timber, as it affects the watershed, soil, regenerative growth, and wildlife. Policy areas directly related to the maintenance and management of forest resources include taxation, often a large cost of forest ownership; housing programs, which affect the demand for forest products; foreign trade with attendant import duties, quotas, or tariffs affecting the merchantability of forest products; transportation, which affects the marketability of forest products; direct aids to forest development programs, such as research, education, and production subsidies; and the administration of public forests.

Coastal land management is as complex as the management of inland areas, if not more so. In Florida, for example, the value of shore properties frequently dictates the reclaiming of lost lands or the creation of new lands for urban use. Swamps and intertidal areas along coastlines may be filled in at the expense of what is frequently a fragile environment. At issue is whether development can take place in such a manner that people can live in an area without destroying the natural features and the beauty that attracted them in the first place. One approach has been to set aside areas of land to be used as parks or conservation areas. This approach is increasingly popular in the formulation of land-management policy.

Mining activities generally require extensive land-use planning and must be carried out under well-defined land-management policies. These policies control mining activities from the earliest stages of exploration through the actual mining and production of mineral materials and finally through reclamation. Most of the management policies are in place to help preserve the character of the land to the greatest possible degree. The route and design of access roads must generally be approved by either the Forest Service or the Bureau of Land Management when on federal lands. Some restrictions also apply on private lands, requiring special permits.

Mineral-exploration activities frequently must be limited in size on federal land so that they do not interfere with natural wildlife habitats or other approved uses of the land. Once a valuable deposit has been identified, mining permits must be applied for, EIS's may have to be prepared, and reclamation procedures must be outlined prior to the extraction of the deposit. Once mining has been completed, the land must be reclaimed in accordance with an approved plan. All these activities take place under the land-management plan affecting the mine area.

Context

A drive through cities and suburban developments shows that some areas have been relegated to industrial, commercial, or residential uses. These use areas are the result of zoning, taxation, and other management tools that attempt to encourage certain types of development in relation to the carrying capacity or suitability of the land and its annexed improvements. The availability of deep-water ports and rail transportation is, for example, more important to commercial and industrial development than to residential land use. By the same token, certain soils and other natural factors might favor residential development. Land reclamation, soil-erosion prevention measures, and imposed land-use limitations are all part of land management. The State of Georgia, for example, requires that all mine sites provide reclamation of as many acres as were actually mined during a given year, although the reclaimed acreage need not be that which was mined. Soil-erosion prevention programs are incorporated as part of nearly every development or activity plan that will result in disturbance or modification of a soil profile, including plans for wilderness or forest roads, residential subdivisions, construction along waterways or coastlines, and agricultural activities.

On a stroll along the beach, one may observe a fisherman standing on a jetty or surfcasting from the base of a seawall. Sailboats cruise the inner harbor, protected from the sea by the distant breakwater. All these physical structures—the jetty, seawall, and breakwater—are part of the coastal land-management program. The jetty attempts to prevent beach erosion by the longshore current that runs nearly parallel to the shoreline, while the seawall aids in the maintenance of a stable coastline that might otherwise erode under the constant battering of winter storms. The breakwater helps to maintain quiet waters in the shallow inner harbor area, otherwise subjected to high, frequently damaging waves.

Crop rotation and strip farming are land-management mechanisms employed in agriculture. Different crops require different kinds and levels of nutrients for proper development. Crop rotation, or changing the type of crop grown on a particular tract of land with each growing season, allows for the greatest yield of nutrients from the soil. Strip farming regenerates nutrients and also serves as a soil-erosion prevention measure. Early farming techniques put all lands under cultivation and, therefore, all were subject to wind erosion. Strip farming leaves alternating strips vegetated or cultivated, helping to prevent erosion.

Land is, indeed, a finite resource that must be maintained and preserved. The science of land management is elemental to this process, and it must be maintained as an ongoing activity, constantly responding and adjusting to changes in nature and in society.

Bibliography

Clawson, Marion. *The Federal Lands Revisited*. Washington, D.C.: Resources for the Future, 1983. A discussion of federal land policies and management. The author explores all aspects of land management and introduces many new concepts as solutions to the current problems in the field. Major policy issues and present usages are discussed, including wildlife, grazing, minerals extraction, oil and gas production, watershed protection, and recreation. Numerous data tables and figures are included in an easily understood format, and an index is provided. Written for the nonspecialist.

_____. *Forests for Whom and for What?* Baltimore: Johns Hopkins University Press, 1975. A well-developed discussion regarding forest management from both a public and a private viewpoint. Issues addressed include timber production, recreational usage, wildlife protection, and watershed management, as well as other economic, social, and environmental concerns. Public forest policy is discussed in detail, and impacts of land conversion, restoration, and clearcutting are considered. Includes several data tables, an index, and a bibliography. Geared toward an intellectual but nonspecialist audience.

_____. *Man, Land, and the Forest Environment.* Seattle: University of Washington Press, 1977. A compilation of three essays that were originally delivered as public lectures in 1976. The topics discussed include land-use planning and control, as well as the private and federal ownership of forested land. Suggestions for future land management are presented, as are discussions of past "mismanagement." A short bibliography is included along with several graphs and data tables. The essays are targeted toward an intellectual but nonspecialist audience.

The Conservation Foundation. *State of the Environment: An Assessment at Mid-Decade.* Washington, D.C.: Author, 1984. An insightful report on the status of the environment in 1984, this book deals with underlying trends in conditions and policy and addresses environmental contaminants, natural resources, future problems, and the assessment of environmental risks. An extensive bibliography and an index are included. Geared toward a diverse audience with interests in politics, statistics, and the environment.

Dasmann, Raymond F. *No Further Retreat.* New York: Macmillan, 1971. A discussion of the development of Florida from the late 1960's to 1971. Concentrates on coastal and inland waterway land-management efforts. Conservation efforts that are discussed include Everglade protection, wildlife preservation, and the development of the Florida Keys. Offers reasonable approaches for controlling land use and instituting proper planning. Includes several photographs and maps and is well-indexed. Suitable for any interested layperson, it uses no technical language.

Davis, Kenneth P. *Land Use.* New York: McGraw-Hill, 1976. This book discusses concepts of land, land ownership, land use and classification, and land-use controls. Examines the planning process with respect to land management and valuation, as well as the attendant decision-making processes. Several case histories are presented as examples. Appropriate for many levels of reader interest, from the layperson to the technical specialist.

Fabos, Julius Gy. *Land-Use Planning.* New York: Chapman and Hall, 1985. This book examines land-use planning from many perspectives. Planning issues are discussed in detail, as are the roles of science and technology in land-use planning. The evolution of land-use planning is addressed from the standpoint of interaction between disciplines, public versus private planning, and types of planning. Regional and local considerations are discussed, as are future prospects in land-use planning. Contains a good bibliography. Appropriate for all levels of interested readership.

Healy, Robert G. *Competition for Land in the American South*. Washington, D.C.: The Conservation Foundation, 1985. A carefully organized discussion of land use and development in the southern United States. Divided into chapters that address the issues of competition for land, the economic uses of agriculture, wood protection, animal agriculture, and human settlement. Each land use is analyzed with respect to future demands. The effects on soil, water, wildlife, and aesthetics are discussed. Contains a summary which is well thought-out. Includes a reference list as well as an index. Very readable, this book is targeted toward a nonspecialist audience.

Paddock, Joe, Nancy Paddock, and Carol Bly. *Soil and Survival*. San Francisco: Sierra Club Books, 1986. This book analyzes what the authors view as a lack of human commitment to the land. Examines the threats to American agriculture, the drive for greater land efficiencies at the expense of natural beauty, and the technical loss of land through erosion, chemical usage, and development. Attitudes about ethics are stressed, as is land stewardship and environmental concerns. Well indexed and contains footnotes. Geared toward an environmentalist audience.

Kyle L. Kayler

Cross-References

Alluvial Systems, 31; Coastal Processes and Beaches, 240; Dams and Flood Control, 309; Earthquake Hazards, 437; Environmental Health, 615; Groundwater Pollution, 1028; Hazardous Wastes, 1059; Land-Use Planning, 1335; Landfills, 1351; Mining Wastes and Reclamation, 1718; Nuclear Waste Disposal, 1758; Strategic Resources, 2188; Soil Erosion, 2387; Volcanic Hazards, 2601.

LAND-USE PLANNING

Field of study: Urban geology and geologic hazards

Land-use planning is that part of the broader process of comprehensive planning that deals with the types and locations of existing and future land uses and their impacts on the environment.

Principal terms

DATA FILE: a series of data collected and stored in an organized manner in a computer system

DERIVATIVE MAPS: maps that are prepared or derived by combining information from several other maps

GRID: a pattern of horizontal and vertical lines forming squares of uniform size

LANDSCAPE: the combination of natural and human features that characterize an area of the earth's surface

PROGRAM: a series of instructions that direct the computer to perform specific operations in order

REMOTE SENSING: any of a number of techniques, such as aerial photography, that can collect information by gathering energy reflected or emitted from a distant source

SCALE: the relationship between a distance on a map or diagram and the same distance on the earth

ZONING ORDINANCE: a legal method by which governments regulate private land

Summary of the Methodology

Land-use planning is a process that attempts to ensure the organized and wise use of land areas. Two things are certain: First, land has great value in modern society; second, there is only a limited amount of it. Land is indeed a valuable resource, deserving of careful management. It is also true that the physical environment influences the location and types of human settlements, transportation routes, and economic endeavors. The hills, ridges, valleys, and depressions of a landscape create potential opportunities and/or limitations for human use. It is important to realize that preexisting land uses likely will affect an area's future possibilities. Land-use planning is part of the master-planning process. Land-use planning deals with the types and the distribution of existing and future land uses, their relationship to other planning elements, such as transportation networks, and the interactions between land use and the environment.

This last point deserves elaboration. While it is certain that existing physical and cultural aspects of a landscape affect land use, humans have an enormous capacity to alter their surroundings. The behavior and wants of people greatly influence emerging land uses. Additionally, each land use affects not only the users but the nonusers as well. An industrial park, for example, may result in increased traffic, slower travel times for commuters passing through the area, and the eventual construction of a multilane highway requiring expenditure of public funds. Furthermore, the effects of land use tend to be cumulative: Even small changes can, over time, combine to produce large and long-lasting impacts.

Spangle and others in *Earth-Science Information in Land-Use Planning* recognize five separate phases of the land-use planning process. Although conceptually distinct, the phases are complexly interrelated and often overlap in practice. The accompanying figure concisely illustrates the sequence and relationships of these five phases: the identification of problems and definition of goals and objectives; data collection and interpretation; plan formulation; review and adoption of plans; and plan implementation. At each phase, feedback occurs so that modifications can be made as the process progresses. Even implemented plans are subject to review and redefinition as more information accumulates.

Once the goals and objectives have been defined, the problems of the acquisition and interpretation of the data on which the plan is based must be addressed. For example, earth science information, in the form of an Environmental Impact Statement (EIS), is needed throughout the planning process. At least a basic understanding of the climate, hydrology, geology, and soils of the area is essential. A considerable amount of data may already be available and need to be consolidated from existing sources, such as published reports. Most often, however, many of the

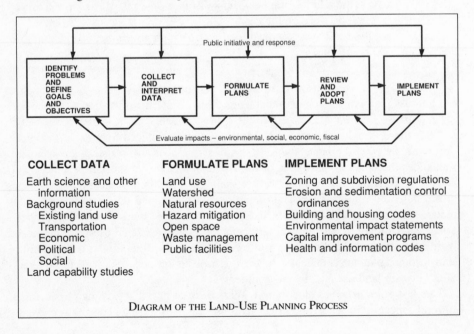

COLLECT DATA	FORMULATE PLANS	IMPLEMENT PLANS
Earth science and other information	Land use	Zoning and subdivision regulations
Background studies	Watershed	Erosion and sedimentation control ordinances
Existing land use	Natural resources	Building and housing codes
Transportation	Hazard mitigation	Environmental impact statements
Economic	Open space	Capital improvement programs
Political	Waste management	Health and information codes
Social	Public facilities	
Land capability studies		

DIAGRAM OF THE LAND-USE PLANNING PROCESS

needed data must be collected specifically for the proposed plan. All data—whether already available or newly developed—must be evaluated and analyzed. Not all information is of equal quality or compatible with the needs of the plan. Some data may be of poor quality and must be eliminated. Some is not useful although it may be of high quality. For example, in an assessment of an area's capability to support structures of various kinds, a list and discussion of the fossils found in the bedrock are not useful, whereas the engineering properties of the same rocks are important. Still other types of data may be incompatible with the needs of the plan because it was collected for different purposes, by different groups, or with different systems. EIS's also must be in sufficient detail and at the appropriate map scale (the relationship between the same distances on the map and on the land surface). Once the high quality and appropriate data are accumulated, they can be used to produce maps that show the capability of the area to support each potential use. These land-capability maps are analyzed together with projections and with economic, social, and political factors to evaluate alternative land-use patterns. The most desirable or feasible alternatives are adopted to prepare a suitable plan on which future decisions can be based. The proposed land uses and the plan in total are reviewed for environmental and other impacts and revised as necessary.

The formulated plan must then be reviewed and adopted by the commissioning agency or governmental body. At this phase, the technical personnel responsible for the development of the plan must be available to answer questions, respond to criticism, and make any further changes considered reasonable.

The final, and perhaps most critical, phase is that of plan implementation. Plans that are adopted, but not implemented, serve little purpose. There must be ways through which the plan influences the formal and informal processes of decision making. Zoning ordinances, construction regulations, and building codes based on the plan should be in place and enforced. Responsibilities and guidelines for preparation and evaluation of required reports, impact assessments, and proposals must be established. This requires a staff that not only reviews proposals but also requests additional information or modification of project proposals.

Applications of the Method

Agriculture and forestry comprise the most extensive land uses in the United States. Only a small percentage of land is used for urban development, transportation facilities, mining, or other uses. Although a relatively small area is affected by these activities, their importance is magnified because the areas are intensively used, large populations are often involved, and impacts on the environment are substantial. Moreover, the conversion of rural areas to urban and other uses is proceeding at the significant rate of about 1,600 square miles per year. An additional area, almost as large, is converted to less intensive uses, such as parks and wildlife areas. As farmlands and forests are converted to housing developments, shopping centers, highways, airports, and reservoirs, pressures intensify, problems increase, and the benefits of organization and reasonable control become apparent.

Maps are prime aids for land-use planning because they present the location, size, shape, and distribution patterns of landscape features. Specialized or derivative maps can be prepared by combining several environmental factors, such as geology, soil types, and slope, to illustrate the best possible use or specific problems of an area. Furthermore, maps can be used to guide further development by outlining areas reserved for particular land uses.

Data are collected for land-use planning purposes in many ways. Some information can be obtained through door-to-door or mailed surveys. Very often, technical personnel, such as geologists or hydrologists, will conduct field investigations in the area. Observations and measurements are made and recorded, and samples are collected for laboratory analysis. Water samples might be analyzed to determine the quality of the water resources, or rock and soil samples may be tested to yield information about engineering properties, such as strength.

Remote-sensing methods are among the most useful sources of collecting data for land-use studies. Remote sensing is a method of imaging the earth's surface with instruments operated from distant points, such as airplanes or satellites. Many different types of remote-sensing instruments, such as aerial photography equipment and radar, are applicable to land-use purposes. Basically, remote-sensing systems collect and record reflected or emitted energy from the land surface. Aerial photography, for example, collects visible light reflected from the earth's surface to produce images on film. Line-scanning systems can record a wide range of energy types. For example, infrared devices can be used to detect small differences in temperature, which reflect differences of soil, water, or vegetation on the earth's surface. Another technique, side-looking airborne radar (SLAR), uses pulses of microwave energy to locate surface objects by recording the time necessary for the energy transmitted to the object to be returned to the radar antenna.

Remote-sensing techniques are applicable to many data-collection efforts. Inventories of existing land uses, crop patterns, or vegetational types can be accomplished relatively quickly. Locations and extents of environmental hazards, such as floods or forest fires, can be delineated and landscape changes—crop rotations, shoreline shifts, and forest clearings—can be documented over a period of time.

Computers are assuming major roles in land-use planning. Because they can store and manipulate large data sets, computers are ideally suited to compare and combine many types of data into a final integrated or interpretive map. The application of a computer system to land-use planning is accomplished by changing EIS's and other data into a form that can be entered into the machine. The data can be entered manually or by more sophisticated optical scanning methods. One straightforward method uses a grid system to enter data. Basically, maps of the area of interest portraying different types of information can be subdivided into a grid formed by equally spaced east-west and north-south lines. The size of the grid squares depends on the purpose of the study and the nature of the data. The intersection points of the grid lines or the centers of the grid squares can be used as data entry locations. An illustration of this operation is the overlying of a grid on a map of soil types and the entry of the soil type at each line intersection or the dominant soil type in each square.

When all the available types of data are in the computer, they can be analyzed, combined, and applied to indicate areas best or least suited for a particular use. The information can also be used to make predictions. A planner may need to suggest the location of future solid-waste disposal sites. Although such a task involves knowledge of waste sources and waste volumes as well as of transportation distances, the performance capability of the various sites is a primary concern. The planner can select those data sets considered to be important to a site's capability to contain waste effectively and have the computer evaluate the area in terms of those factors. Bedrock geology, soil type and depth, distance to groundwater, distance from surface water bodies, and other factors may be selected. Each factor is assigned a weighted value which is a measure of its relative importance to the specific purpose. Depth to the water table, for example, might be considered more important than the distance to surface water bodies. The computer incorporates the relative ranking of the variables into the data analysis to produce a composite map of favorable and unfavorable areas for solid-waste disposal. Such comprehensive systems, known as geographic information systems (GIS), are being developed widely for many purposes. To summarize, a GIS consists of computer storage files of data, a program to analyze the data, and another program to map the stored data and produce several forms of output from the analysis program.

Land-use planning or management is still a controversial subject. Landowners, developers, environmentalists, and government agencies have very different views as to what is the best use of a parcel of land and who should make the decision. These are issues of individual-versus-group rights and benefits and they are not easily resolved. It is clear that as land resources dwindle and use pressures increase, some form of planning or management is necessary. It seems equally clear that while decisions among multiple use will often be difficult, the best decisions can only be based on sufficient high-quality data.

Context

Land-use planning attempts to ensure organized and reasonable development of areas as the pressures of potential multiple uses mount and the value of land increases. Planning must be based on a thorough understanding of the environment and of economic, political, and cultural factors to produce a prediction of future land-use needs and ways to satisfy those needs.

An effective land-use plan consists of four basic parts. First, it includes a discussion of land-use issues and a statement of goals and objectives. This section provides the background and establishes what the plan seeks to accomplish. Second, there is a discussion of the methods of data collection, evaluation, and analysis. This will include a description not only of the collection techniques, methodology, and the sources of the information, but also a consideration of the limitations of the data used in the study. Third, a land classification map is produced. The classification used to complete the map will depend on the goals of the plan and on the needs of each area. This map will serve as the basis for many kinds of decisions—from the location of new facilities to regulatory policies and tax structure. Finally, a report is included that provides a framework to the plan and discusses sensitive issues or areas. Any environmentally significant sites that may be adversely affected by change are considered, and appropriate policies are recommended.

Land-use decisions are made by individuals, groups, industry, and governmental bodies. Individuals want the freedom to choose where they live and what to do with their property, but most also do not want an incompatible land-use located next door. Land-use plans based on high-quality data and sound interpretations of that data, with abundant public input during formulation, adoption, and implementation of the land-use plan, can help to avoid costly and time-consuming confrontations. There will seldom be unanimous agreement, but planning can provide a framework in which to make decisions that will have far-ranging effects.

Almost without exception, everyone is affected by growth, development, and changing land-use patterns. Plans may determine how far residents must drive to shop, the location of a new park or school, or where houses may be built. Land-use plans may be as simple as efforts to protect citizens from hazardous locations. Such plans might call for setback zones along eroding sea cliffs that prohibit construction, thus preventing structures from being destroyed as the cliff retreats. Conversely, plans may be very complex attempts to guide and direct the types, rates, and locations of change in an area. Such plans have the potential to influence the area's economic and cultural characteristics, its environmental quality, and the way its residents live in the near and distant future.

Bibliography

Davidson, Donald A. *Soils and Land Use Planning*. New York: Longman, 1980. A short text for middle-level students that shows how soils information can be used in land-use planning.

Dluhy, Milan J., and Kan Chen, eds. *Interdisciplinary Planning: A Perspective for the Future*. New Brunswick, N.J.: Center for Urban Policy Research, 1986. Land-use planning is covered along with other types of planning. The complex nature of the planning process is illustrated.

McHarg, I. L. *Design with Nature*. Garden City, N.Y.: Doubleday, 1969. An older but still useful text. Provides the basis for environmentally based planning technologies.

Marsh, William M. *Landscape Planning: Environmental Applications*. New York: John Wiley & Sons, 1986. A useful introduction to landscape planning. A wide range of topics are discussed and numerous case histories are provided.

Rhind, D., and R. Hudson. *Land Use*. London: Methuen, 1980. This is a well-illustrated treatment of land-use issues and the planning process. Good discussions of data needs and planning models are included.

So, Frank S., ed. *The Practice of Local Government Planning*. 5th ed. Chicago:

American Planning Association, 1979. A thorough treatment of all aspects of planning at the level of cities and counties. Discussion is clear but advanced.

So, Frank S., Irving Hand, and Bruce McDowell. *The Practice of State and Regional Planning*. Chicago: Planners Press, 1986. Designed to be a companion volume to the work above. Thorough treatment of the practices of planning at higher government levels that are not as well defined.

Spangle, William, and Associates, F. Beach Leighton and Associates, and Baxter, McDonald and Company. *Earth-Science Information in Land-Use Planning: Guidelines for Earth Scientists and Planners*. Geological Survey Circular 721. Arlington, Va.: U.S. Department of the Interior, Geological Survey, 1976. An excellent discussion of the sources, accuracy, and applications of earth science information in the land-use planning process.

Ronald D. Stieglitz

Cross-References

Aerial Photography, 17; Dams and Flood Control, 309; Environmental Health, 615; Land Management, 1327; Landfills, 1351; Landslides and Slope Stability, 1365; Remote Sensing and the Electromagnetic Spectrum, 2166; Volcanic Hazards, 2601.

LAND-USE PLANNING IN THE COASTAL ZONE

Field of study: Urban geology and geologic hazards

In order to designate appropriate coastal land uses, policymakers must take into consideration geological processes, recognizing that the coastal zone is one of rapidly evolving landforms, sedimentary deposits, and environments. Much of the American coastal zone has undergone rapid development without the benefit of landscape evaluation. Future development, as well as corrective measures, must be grounded in the knowledge of the underlying geology and its climatic and oceanographic interactions.

Principal terms

COASTAL WETLANDS: shallow, wet, or flooded shelves that extend back from the freshwater-saltwater interface and may consist of marshes, bays, lagoons, tidal flats, or mangrove swamps

COASTAL ZONE: coastal waters and lands that exert a measurable influence on the uses of the sea and its ecology

ESTUARINE ZONE: an area near the coastline that consists of estuaries and coastal saltwater wetlands

ESTUARY: a thin zone along a coastline where freshwater system(s) and river(s) meet and mix with an ocean

GROUNDWATER: water that sinks into the soil, where it may be stored in slowly flowing underground reservoirs

LAND-USE PLANNING: a process for determining the best use of each parcel of land in an area

MASS WASTING: the downslope movement of earth materials under the direct influence of gravity

SALTWATER INTRUSION: aquifer contamination by salty waters that have migrated from deeper aquifers or from the sea

WATER TABLE: the level below the earth's surface at which the ground becomes saturated with water

Summary of the Methodology

The dependency of the United States on its coastal zone cannot be exaggerated, a lesson taught to national leaders in 1969 when the Stratton Report, "Our Nation and the Sea," revealed that coastal areas contained more than 50 percent of the nation's population (projected to reach 80 percent by the year 2000), seven of the nation's largest cities, 60 percent of the petroleum refineries, 40 percent of industry, and two out of three nuclear or coal-fired electrical generating plants. The report further concluded that more than one-third of the productive estuaries had been destroyed and another 24 percent severely impacted. Not surprisingly, the Stratton Report became the primary impetus for the passage of the National Coastal Zone Management Act (NCZMA) of 1972 and 1980. NCZMA provides federal aid to thirty coastal states and five territories for development and implementation of voluntary, comprehensive programs for the management and protection of coastlines. In 1982, Congress passed the Coastal Barrier Resource Act, which declared 195 acres of beachfront on various barrier islands ineligible for federal infrastructure funding.

The first step of all land-use planning, the provision of geologic information and analysis, is complicated in the coastal zone by the fact that the major value of the area is water. Indeed, water is the overwhelming determinant of intrinsic suitabilities of the various microenvironments under consideration. Landscape evaluation must also recognize that the zone is not static but is the locus of rapid geologic change. Such change involves a complex sediment dispersal system that responds rapidly to human modifications. The coastal zone also includes fundamental legal boundaries between private and public ownership that are also high-energy geological boundaries. The presence of barrier islands demands a highly specialized set of land-use practices for these dynamic systems. Natural hazards in the coastal zone include periodic hurricane attacks on the Atlantic and Gulf coasts and landslides on the cliffed coasts of the Pacific. Superimposed upon the dynamic processes of the coastal zone is a global sea-level rise, initiated some eighteen thousand years ago with the termination of the Late Wisconsin glaciation. Sea-level rise is currently accelerating, possibly in response to the "greenhouse effect," human-induced atmospheric change.

A major resource of the area is the estuarine zone, encompassing less than 10 percent of the total ocean area but containing 90 percent of all sea life. Estuaries trap the nutrients that rivers wash down from the land and use them to produce an extraordinary quantity of biomass that sustains a variety of marine life. It is estimated that 60-80 percent of all edible seafood is dependent on the estuary for survival. Estuarine zones and coastal wetlands also serve as natural flood control devices by absorbing the energy of damaging storm waves and storing floodwaters. If not overloaded, these wetlands have the ability to remove large quantities of pollutants from coastal waters. This contribution alone was conservatively valued at $75,000 an acre in 1989; with the addition of monies generated by sport and commercial fishing, an acre was worth $83,000.

The first consideration of coastal zone land-use planning is historical geology and its interactions with climate and hydrologic energy. Together, these forces have created the basic form of the coastal zone, which varies dramatically from sea to sea. The geologically stable Atlantic and Gulf coasts are depositional coasts, marked by broad coastal and deltaic plains, over which many large, long rivers meander toward the sea. Here, sedimentary strata, or layers of sands, clays, and marls, were laid on a bedrock base beginning in Cretaceous times, approximately 136 million years ago. These coastal plain sediments, derived from erosion of the Appalachian Mountains and interlayered with sediments of marine origin, dip gently seaward. The combination of this thick wedge of largely unconsolidated sediments and high precipitation rates has resulted in abundant groundwater resources and a high groundwater table. Nevertheless, excessive withdrawal of groundwater for irrigation, industry, and urban use has resulted in saltwater intrusion in many major aquifers along these coasts. Depositional coasts are tectonically subsiding, thereby compounding problems associated with sea-level rise. Shorelines of such coasts are invariably marked by barrier island chains oriented parallel to shore.

In contrast, the geologically active Pacific coast is a young mountain range coast, characterized by mountains of up to 1,500 meters related to the Cenozoic orogeny, mountain-building activity occurring between about 65 and 2.5 million years ago. The bedrock is principally composed of sediments of Tertiary age (about 65-7 million years ago) and volcanic rock. Much of the shoreline is characterized by steep cliffs and coastal mountains occasionally broken by valleys where short, high gradient rivers empty into the sea. Large seasonal changes in beach width are particularly common on the West Coast. The combination of largely unweathered bedrock at the surface and low precipitation rates has resulted in a sparse groundwater supply and a low water table. Excessive withdrawal of groundwater has caused much subsidence, or lowering of the earth's surface. The coastal zone of the West Coast is one of active tectonic uplift, subject to mass wasting in the form of slumping, rockfalls, and landslides.

The great financial potential of beachfront properties makes the consequences of beach erosion, as well as efforts to halt shoreline retreat, of vital concern in coastal zone land-use issues. Although some beach erosion is rightly attributed to sea-level rise, much is the direct result of human activities. The damming of major rivers has essentially cut off the sediment supply to the nation's beaches. Loss of dredged sediment through maintenance of shipping channels results in rapid erosion on the downdrift beaches to which wave action would normally deliver sands. Both jetties and groin fields act as dams to sediment transport and create erosion on adjacent beaches. Dune destruction removes the natural barriers to storm surges and reservoirs for sand storage. In addition to degradation of the aesthetic and recreational character of the shoreline, seawalls accelerate erosion by increasing wave energy. Emplacement of sand on the beach from offshore or inland sources (beach renourishment) and pumping sediment across navigation channels (inlet bypassing) represent more acceptable "soft engineering" alternatives to the armoring of the shoreline.

On the Atlantic and Gulf coasts, hurricanes account for much of the sediment distribution patterns. These tropical cyclones modify barrier islands by removal of beach sand offshore as well as over the dunes. Overwash, in which large quantities of sediment are moved inland, is the major means by which barrier islands retreat before the rising sea. The inevitability of hurricane attack mandates land use compatible with predicted flooding patterns, building codes based on hurricane-force winds and tidal storm surges, and up-to-date evacuation plans.

Retreat of the shoreline along the West Coast is more frequently related to seacliff erosion. Erosion along cliffed coasts is caused by a combination of wave scour at the base and landsliding higher on the bluffs. In winter, the large tides and waves force the rain-weakened cliffs to retreat. The degree of failure depends on wave energy, hardness of the cliff rock, and internal fractures and faults. Weathering processes further weaken rocks and aid erosion. Human activities that accelerate cliff retreat include storm runoff, septic tank leaching, landscape irrigation, alteration of drainage patterns, and introduction of nonnative vegetation.

Applications of the Method

Because every region within the coastal zone is the sum of dynamic physical, biological, and historical processes, each parcel of land demonstrates an inherent suitability for certain land uses. Some areas may be optimized for multiple land uses, such as water-based recreation and fishing, without compromise of the region's natural values. Other regions may be equally suitable for conflicting uses, such as passive recreation or low-density housing, forcing a choice by decision makers. Other vulnerable coastal zone resources, such as the salt marshes, are too valuable for any use but conservation.

The low, sandy Gulf and Atlantic coasts, characterized by estuaries, marshes, and inlets, are separated from the open ocean by barrier islands. Major values of the lower coastal plain include abundant forests, a diversity of land and water wildlife habitats, and a unique potential for water-based recreation. The area is largely unsuited for urbanization, because of the high water table, but remnant ancient barrier island chains, or "terraces," represent elevated sites suitable for building. The largely sandy soils are poorly suited for widespread agriculture, though some fertile alluvial, or river valley, soils are present. The high water table makes aquifer pollution an ever-present threat; the abundant forests, which support a major pulp and paper production region, are fire-prone.

Because the broad coastal plains of the depositional coasts were formed by barrier island migration during the sea-level fluctuations of the Pleistocene "ice ages," the resulting sediments are largely barrier island sands or marsh muds and peats. Rapid, unplanned growth in the coastal zone has resulted in widespread use of septic tanks in these unsuitable sandy soils, allowing waste water to percolate too rapidly and releasing improperly treated effluent. The degradation of coastal waters by septic tanks can be avoided by tertiary treatment of waste water, which may in turn be used for wetlands recharge or for irrigation. A sanitary landfill properly sited in mud or peat has low permeability, which limits the flow of leachate, contaminated landfill runoff. The most heavily developed resort areas, with the greatest need for landfill space, also have the highest land prices, making suitable land acquisition difficult.

The vast marshes of the coastal zone grade from fresh to brackish to salt water. The river-swamp system, interrelated with the marsh-estuary system through flows of water, sediments, and nutrients, plays a major role in determining the impact of inland development on the estuary. In their natural state, swamps buffer the coast from the many impacts of land-use activities. If drained, filled, or altered, this contribution is lost. An increase in stormwater runoff related to urbanization reduces their ability to hold and absorb floodwaters. This problem could be avoided by placing limits to development and requiring that nonhighway "paving" be of permeable material, such as crushed limestone, instead of asphalt. The river swamp's ability to filter and absorb pollutants also improves the quality and productivity of downstream coastal waters; if overloaded with pollutants from industrial effluents, agricultural practices, or improperly sited septic tanks and landfills, the closing of shellfish beds is inevitable.

The "low marsh," inundated daily by the tides, is well recognized as an area so valuable and productive that conservation is mandatory. Although protected by state laws, estuarine marshland continues to experience some destruction as a result of marina construction and the disposal of dredged sediments from navigation channels. Marshland is also lost to the boat-wake erosion that undercuts the banks, causing slumping of the rooted clays.

At a slightly higher elevation is the "high marsh," sandy marshland occasionally wetted by storms or extreme tides. This marsh, unprotected by law, is known to be an important wildlife habitat but has not been widely studied. Indeed, the role of the high marsh and its relationship to the low marsh is unknown. The widespread exploitation of this area for residential and commercial development will make it impossible for the low marsh to reestablish itself landward in response to sea-level rise. The resultant loss in areal extent of the salt marsh will cause a great decline in estuarine-dependent marine life and a corresponding rise in pollution.

The barrier islands that front low-lying coastal plains are such dynamic geologic features that they are clearly unsuited for widespread development. These islands are composed of unconsolidated sediments that continuously seek to establish equilibrium with the waves, winds, currents, and tides that shape them. Early settlements were wisely constructed on the landward-facing, or back-barrier, portion of the islands. The beachfront was considered too dangerous because of hurricanes.

Ideally, high-density barrier island development should be confined to the back-barrier part of the island, there protected from storms and hurricanes. Low-density development should thin out in both directions, and open island should be preserved along the high-energy beachfront. That would ensure the scenic and recreational value of the island, as well as the sand supply and the natural maintenance of the system. If stabilization of inlets for shipping is necessary, the sand built up on the updrift side should be bypassed downdrift to reenter the system. Many islands should be preserved totally free of development for sand storage, as well as for educational, recreational, and aesthetic benefits.

Prior to the development of Miami Beach in the 1920's, most beachfront construction was undertaken away from areas affected by hurricanes. The change in willingness to risk large investments along the beaches and trust to human ingenuity has generally resulted in critical erosion. The concept of "beach erosion," however, is dependent upon the presence of threatened human structures. Any beachfront construction should first be considered within the context of readily available historical shoreline change data. If the area under consideration has a suitable history of stability or accretion, development should be limited to a set-back line landward of the heavily vegetated, stable dunes. Construction should be compatible with historical hurricane storm surge data, and, at elevations below recorded storm surges, dwellings should be elevated on a foundation of pilings.

Access to the beach should be via dune walkovers to avoid damage to the plants that stabilize the fragile dune environment. The dunes that are closest to the ocean and tied to the beach for their windblown sand supply are constantly changing landforms. Storm waves scour away the front of the dunes, and fair-weather waves return the lost sand to the beach to rebuild the dunes. These ephemeral features, vital as buffers to storm attack, should be protected not only from construction but also from human activity of any sort.

The updrift and downdrift inlet beachfronts are best utilized as nature preserves or public beaches, free of construction, because of the natural instability of both zones. The updrift inlet is constantly reestablishing its channel in response to tide-deposited mounds of sand, causing alternating and far-flung advances and retreats of the north-end shoreline. The downdrift, or south end, represents the geologically young part of the island. Because the area is barely above sea level, hurricane storm surges can readily cut through an elongated south-end spit, creating a new inlet and freeing the sand to migrate downdrift.

The barrier island uplands, or high ground, consist of maritime forest on ancient oceanfront dune ridges; these dunes were left behind as the island built seaward, caused by a fortuitous combination of sediment supply and fluctuating sea level. This forested region is appropriate for environmentally sensitive development, if care is taken to conserve ample wildlife preserves. Freshwater sloughs and ponds are located in the low swale areas between dune ridges, where rainfall floats on salt water within the porous material of the island subsurface. These wetlands represent important wildlife habitat and, on developed islands, serve as natural treatment plants for storm runoff and as natural storage areas for floodwaters. They may also be recharged with tertiary treated waste water, if not overloaded. Unfortunately, there has been a great loss of freshwater wetlands, on the mainland as well as the islands, to developers who have drained and filled them to produce construction sites.

The geologic instability of the rocky Pacific coast demands land-use planning strategies that will protect its rugged beauty and minimize the threats of natural hazards. Development in the available coastal zone regions of cliff tops, dune fields, and beachfront are all potentially hazardous.

On the beachfront, a wide beach between cliff and shoreline should not be mistaken for a permanent feature. Developed beachfront areas at the bases of cliffs are subject to periodic floodings by large waves combined with high tides; after much of the beach sand is removed by the storm, the wave energy is expended against the buildings. Houses in this zone have collapsed when their foundations were undermined or have smashed through their pilings after being uplifted by waves. If beachfront development is allowed, it should be based on a comparison of the site elevation and expected tidal ranges, storm surges, and storm-wave heights. A secure piling foundation below any potential wave scour should elevate the structure above any maximum inundation.

Although the presence of dunefields is restricted on young mountain range coasts, existing dunes have not escaped urbanization, and the resultant problems are identical to those of the East Coast. Where homes and condominiums have been built on conventional foundations, periodic dune erosion has undermined and threatened the structures, forcing emplacement of sea walls constructed of boulders. The dynamic nature of sand dunes negates any notion of wise land-use planning other than prohibition.

The zone consisting of bluff or cliff tops represents the West Coast environment with the greatest potential for development. Construction should not proceed here without a large enough setback behind the cliff edge so that the structure should endure for at least one hundred years, based on long-term erosion rates. The increased runoff associated with urbanization, if not collected and diverted away from the seacliff, results in serious slope failure. Homes, patios, swimming pools, and other construction also decrease the stability of the seacliff by increasing the driving forces, forces that tend to make earth materials slide. Although seacliff erosion is a natural process that cannot be completely controlled, regardless of financial investment, it can be minimized by sound land-use practices.

Context

Accelerating development along North America's most dynamic environment, largely without the benefits of land-use planning, has posed a national dilemma. The inherent geological instability of the coastal zone is a product of constant reshaping of the interface between land and sea by waves, winds, tides, and storms. Much of the shoreline of each coastal state is eroding, caused by human activities and sea-level rise. The low, sandy Atlantic and Gulf coasts are subject to periodic hurricane attack, while the cliffed Pacific coasts face the threat of landslides.

In the twentieth century, the attraction of the coast combined with population pressures, widespread affluence, and demands for water-based recreation have accelerated the exploitation of North America's coastal zone. Growth and expansion without regard for environmental consequences have been motivated largely by the desire to develop harbors and coastal resources. As construction has intensified and sea-level rise has accelerated, shoreline protection costs have reached into the millions of dollars per mile. The staggering costs of shoreline protection have now forced communities to rely on state and federal subsidies. The heavy investment of public monies has led to a growing national concern over coastal zone management policy.

Adoption of coastal zone land-use planning strategies can ameliorate existing problems and avoid future ones. Landscape evaluation, in which evidence is gathered from the exact sciences of geology, hydrology, soils, and plant ecology, can prescribe potential land uses that accommodate necessary human structures while maintaining the existing natural order of the coastal zone. An important first step is the elimination of unseen government spending so that economic decisions are not based on direct or indirect subsidies. Corrective measures should be adopted for unwise development, such as removal of hard engineering structures that magnify both erosion and the costs of major storms. High-risk development should be replaced with safe development away from the beaches. Where natural beaches still exist, public access should be improved to meet recreational demands. Americans already possess the necessary technical, scientific, and legal tools to preserve and protect the nation's valuable coastal zone.

Bibliography

Dolan, Robert. "Barrier Islands: Natural and Controlled." In *Coastal Geomorphology*, edited by Donald R. Coates. Binghamton: State University of New York, 1972. A comparison of the stabilized islands (Cape Hatteras National Seashore) and the natural islands (Core Banks) of the Outer Banks of North Carolina. The responses of these two systems to coastal processes, particularly major storms, are of great interest for both preservation and management reasons. Suitable for college-level readers.

Griggs, Gary, and Lauret Savoy, eds. *Living with the California Coast*. Durham, N.C.: Duke University Press, 1985. This book, part of the Living with the Shore series (sponsored by the National Audobon Society), addresses the problems resulting from coastal development during a relatively storm-free period without analysis of historical storms or long-term erosion rates. It includes conclusions and recommendations of coastal geologists and other specialists. Suitable for those with an interest and concern for the California coast.

Kaufman, Wallace, and Orrin H. Pilkey, Jr. *The Beaches Are Moving: The Drowning of America's Shorelines*. Durham, N.C.: Duke University Press, 1983. An introduction to environmental coastal geology, nearshore processes, and the effects of human modifications on the shorelines of the United States, this book serves as background to the Living with the Shore series, covering the basic issues that are applied to specific shorelines. Suitable for those interested in the shorelines of the United States.

Keller, Edward A. *Environmental Geology*. 5th ed. Columbus, Ohio: Merrill, 1988. This work introduces physical principles basic to applied geology and reviews major natural processes and geologic hazards, including how society deals with them. Previous exposure to the geological sciences is not necessary for comprehension. Suitable for college-level readers.

McHarg, Ian L. *Design with Nature*. Garden City, N.Y.: Doubleday, 1971. An explanation of the ecological land-use planning method, proving that necessary human structures can be accommodated within the existing natural order. (National Book Award Nominee, 1971.) Suitable for high-school-level readers.

Neuman, A. Conrad. "Scenery for Sale." In his *Coastal Development and Areas of Environmental Concern*. Raleigh: North Carolina State University Press, 1975. A statement on the science, scenery, and selling of a barrier island system like the Outer Banks of North Carolina, cleverly illustrated by the author. Free of technical terminology and readable for all.

Martha M. Griffin

Cross-References

Aquifers, 71; Coastal Processes and Beaches, 240; The Geologic Time Scale, 874; Groundwater Movement, 1020; Groundwater Pollution, 1028; Groundwater Pollution Remediation, 1035; Groundwater: Saltwater Intrusion, 1042; Hurricanes and Monsoons, 1088; Land-Use Planning, 1335; Landslides and Slope Stability, 1365; Ocean Tides, 1832; Ocean Waves, 1839; Plate Tectonics, 2079; Sand Dunes, 2259; Sea Level, 2267; Sediment Transport and Deposition, 2290.

LANDFILLS

Field of study: Urban geology and geologic hazards

Humankind has found it convenient throughout history to dump unwanted wastes into nearby ravines, swamps, and pits. With increased emphasis on sanitation, the open dumps have been replaced with landfills in which wastes are placed into excavations and covered with soil. Landfilling is the most common method of disposing of garbage and other unwanted material generated by cities and industry.

Principal terms

AQUIFER: a porous, water-bearing zone beneath the surface of the earth that can be pumped for drinking water supply

CLAY: a term with three meanings: a particle size (less than 2 microns), a mineral type (including kaolin and illite), and a fine-grained soil that is puttylike when damp

GEOMEMBRANE: a synthetic sheet (plastic) with very low permeability used as a liner in landfills to prevent leakage from the excavation

GROUNDWATER: water found below the land surface

LEACHATE: water that has seeped down through the landfill refuse and has become polluted

PERMEABILITY: the ability of a soil or rock to allow water to flow through it; sands and other materials with large pores have high permeabilities, whereas clays have very low permeabilities

POLLUTION: a condition of air, soil, or water in which it contains substances that make it hazardous for human use

SATURATED ZONE: that zone beneath the land surface where all the pores in the soil or rock are filled with water rather than with air

VECTOR: a term used in waste disposal when referring to rats, flies, mosquitoes, and other disease-carrying insects and animals that infest dumps

WATER TABLE: the upper surface of the saturated zone; above the water table, the pores in the soil and rock contain both air and water

Summary of the Phenomenon

All human activities produce unwanted by-products called wastes. For normal household living, these unwanted wastes are garbage and trash. Stores, factories, gas stations, and all other businesses also create large amounts of waste materials. Waste materials are classified as hazardous and nonhazardous: Hazardous wastes contain chemicals and other constituents that, if inhaled, eaten, or absorbed by humans and other life forms, are detrimental to the health; nonhazardous wastes may contain small amounts of toxic or hazardous ingredients. They present no threat, however, to the welfare of society if disposed of correctly.

One of the primary methods of getting rid of wastes is by land disposal. Land disposal may be in the form of placing the unwanted material directly on the land surface, especially in low, swampy areas, ravines, and old gravel or other mined-out pits. These types of land disposal are known as dumps, or open dumps, because the unwanted wastes literally are haphazardly dumped at the site, and the waste piles often are not covered until some other use is made of the surface. The term "landfill," although sometimes used to describe dumps, refers to land disposal of wastes in which the disposal site is designed and operated to a specific plan. Modern landfills are designed to receive a certain amount of refuse over a specified period of time, such as twenty years. At the end of that period, the site is reclaimed and converted for a different land use.

In ancient times, when the earth's population was small, waste products were discarded on the ground surface or thrown into a stream at the campsite. The amount was small enough at that time so that there was no significant pollution or adverse effects on the environment. As the population grew and more people began to live in towns, trash and garbage often were thrown in ravines and in low, swampy areas as a way of filling in the land. This practice of open dumping has existed in the United States and other Western nations up to the present.

The earth's population has soared to more than 5 billion people, approximately 250 million of them living in the United States. The population concentration has shifted from rural to urban areas. To supply the demands of the public, industry has developed and produced a wide variety of materials and chemicals, such as plastics, that end up as waste products after use. More than 10 billion metric tons of solid waste are generated each year in the United States: Some 250 million metric tons are municipal generated rubbish and garbage, which amounts to 1 ton of nonindustrial waste per person per year.

As the amount of municipal wastes increased, more and more space was needed for open dumps. Many serious problems arose as the use of dumps conflicted with land use, sanitation, and aesthetics to the surrounding communities. Pollution of rivers and the groundwater was directly traced to uncontrolled dumping of toxic wastes in dumps and pits. The federal government, therefore, enacted a series of laws over the years to protect the environment and especially the surface and groundwaters from pollution. The result of the legislation was to define and separate wastes that were hazardous to humans from the municipal wastes in land disposal. Special restrictions were placed on the disposal of hazardous wastes in the earth. Although originally no special restrictions were placed on land disposal of municipal wastes, the protection of rivers and the groundwater from pollution required states to establish a permit process that set limits on where dumps and landfills could be located. Thus, disposal of municipal and industrial wastes has become expensive.

Modern disposal of wastes has evolved from the indiscriminant discarding of unwanted material in any convenient way at any available site at almost no cost to a community or business into methods that are environmentally constricted to protect the health and safety of the public. The escalating costs associated with waste disposal have focused attention on reducing the amount of waste generated. In spite of this emphasis, the amount of municipal wastes continues to increase. The principal disposal options are recycling, incineration, and land disposal.

The cheapest method of disposing of municipal and industrial nonhazardous wastes is by burial in the ground. There are more than 16,000 active nonhazardous waste landfills of various types in the United States. More than 6,000 of them are classified as municipal, which means that most of the waste placed in the landfill is from households or is general community refuse.

Modern landfills cover many acres. Some are more than 100 acres in size. Although the actual size and shape of each landfill depend upon the site geology and the amount of waste that is to go in it, landfill facilities generally are excavated into the ground to form a pit. The refuse is placed in the pit and gradually builds up throughout the life of the landfill to a predetermined vertical height above the original ground level. Once the design height is reached, a soil cover is added, and the ground surface is reclaimed to form a moundlike hill. The depth of excavation to form the pit will depend upon the thickness of low-permeability clay soils over a buried water-bearing deposit, called an aquifer, that supplies drinking water to households and towns. Enough clay soil must be left to prevent seepage of any leachate that may escape from the landfill into the aquifer and pollute it. (Leachate is rainwater that has seeped down through the landfill refuse and has become polluted.) Monitoring wells are placed around the landfill into the aquifer to ensure that no pollution occurs.

The figure shows a vertical slice through a landfill, illustrating some of the more important features. After the excavation has been dug to its intended depth, a protective liner is placed over the bottom and sides of the pit. The liner may be of compacted clay by a construction roller, or it may be a plastic sheet called a geomembrane. Waste material that is brought to the landfill daily is placed in

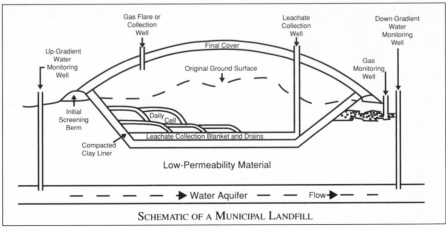

SCHEMATIC OF A MUNICIPAL LANDFILL

NOTE: Not to scale.

specified layers called cells. At the close of each day, the exposed waste is covered with soil to prevent odors, blowing debris, and infestation by vectors. "Vector" is a term used to collectively refer to any disease-carrying insects or animals, such as rats, flies, and birds, that would infest the waste material. The daily cells are stacked one on top of another until the final height is reached. Leachate and gas collection pipes are installed throughout the landfill to collect and dispose of dangerous gases and liquids. These perforated pipes are covered with a layer of gravel through which the leachate can easily flow from the landfill waste to the collection network.

Because of the severe environmental restrictions and legal liabilities associated with burying hazardous materials in the ground, recycling and incineration have become the principal disposal options for hazardous wastes. Sites at which toxic wastes are buried are tightly controlled and carefully monitored to ensure that no leakage occurs that could pollute the groundwaters.

Methods of Study

Before a landfill can be constructed and operated at a proposed location, the site must be evaluated to ensure that it satisfies all local, state, and federal regulations relating to protecting the environment and the health and welfare of the citizens. The landfill operator must collect and assess much information before applying to a state pollution control board or similar governing commission for a permit. The information must verify that the landfill will present no danger to the public or to the environment. A large number of factors must be evaluated and presented to the permit board.

By far the most important factor for determining whether a site is satisfactory for a landfill is the geology. The local geology must contain thick and continuous clay soils or their rock equivalents, shale. These deposits do not allow water or contaminated water from landfills (leachate) to flow rapidly through them; their low permeability will prevent any leachate that may escape from the pit from flowing into surface streams or to underlying aquifers that supply water to the surrounding communities. It is very important to protect these aquifers; once they become polluted, it is extremely difficult (and costly) to clean them up for public use in a short period of time. Compared to water in surface streams, groundwater in porous aquifers moves exceedingly slow. Also, because the aquifer is hidden beneath the surface, it is difficult to trace and clean up the polluted water flow. To evaluate the subsurface geology of the site and the surrounding region, the company proposing the landfill will drill holes around the area and take soil samples so that a geologist can identify the different soils and rocks and construct a cross section illustrating the thicknesses, types, and relationships of the different materials.

Besides the geology, other major factors that must be assessed are climate and weather, flooding, ecology, historical landmarks, nearness to airports, traffic, and land-use and zoning restrictions. The climate and weather describe the rainfall and winds to be expected. All landfills must be above the 100-year-flood height or have suitable flood protection. Special emphasis is placed on the ecology: A landfill cannot be built in protected wetlands or destroy the habitat of endangered species of plants and animals. Also, landfills are not allowed to destroy historical landmarks and archaeological sites. Municipal landfills attract birds; therefore, landfills must be more than a mile away from airports. Information on the road system and traffic volumes must be gathered to assess the impact of waste trucks adding both more traffic and greater loads to the roads. Landfills are not the most desirable land use and, therefore, such developments must prove they are compatible with the surrounding land use. Many communities have zoning restrictions that must be met. Thus, evaluating a proposed site for a landfill is a complex and time-consuming job.

A company must supply to the state permit board, in addition to information and assessment on the suitability of a proposed site, data and plans outlining the overall design, construction, operation, and reclamation when the landfill is closed. The design information must include drawings showing the depth and size of the pit area. The plans must give details on how the leachate is prevented from escaping from the pit and where monitoring wells will be drilled around the site to detect any leakage that may occur. Landfills that contain garbage and other organics will generate methane gas that must be collected and either flared into the atmosphere or piped away for fuel. Some landfills use the gas at the site for commercial and light industrial energy.

The final aspect in a landfill design is the closing of the operation and the reclaiming of the site for a different land use. As illustrated in the figure, a final soil cover is placed over all the waste to isolate it from the public. Five to ten feet in thickness, this layer of soil controls vectors, prevents odors, and beautifies the landfill's surface. Periodic checks are made by the owner after the landfill has been reclaimed to sample the monitoring wells and to repair any erosion features.

Context

Human activities have throughout time created undesirable materials called wastes. When the earth's population was small and no industrial technology existed, people could throw their garbage and other unwanted materials anywhere that was convenient with very little harm to the environment. As the population increased, however, and more resources were used to support living conditions, especially in towns and cities, the volume and toxic composition of the used, unwanted material increased to the point where it degraded the environment and posed a health hazard to the communities if disposed of haphazardly.

The federal government, the states, and communities have had to reevaluate their policies of uncontrolled dumping of municipal and industrial wastes because of serious pollution to the water supplies. With enactment of laws to protect the environment and to prevent pollution, land disposal of wastes is now controlled and monitored. Hazardous wastes are a severe threat to the health and welfare of communities. As a result, with few exceptions, land disposal of these wastes is no longer the primary disposal option.

Land disposal remains the primary method of disposing of nonhazardous wastes. Liquid nonhazardous wastes usually are disposed of in lagoons. Solid wastes, such as garbage and trash, are placed in landfills. For cities and other urban areas, large acreage of open land is scarce, and citizens generally object to having a landfill constructed nearby. Thus, cities and adjacent communities have been forced to cooperate on large regional landfills. It is therefore necessary for companies wanting to site new landfills to hunt for undeveloped land of a hundred acres or more where the geology is satisfactory to prevent pollution of the public water supplies. Even though municipal landfills, which often are called sanitary landfills, are considered nonhazardous, they will contain from 5 to 10 percent toxic material. If the landfill is small, such as in rural communities, the amount of hazardous leachate that may escape from the pit site is small and will thus have no appreciable detrimental effects on the environment and public health. The large landfills serving cities, however, do pose a threat to the public welfare and health if major amounts of leachate escape from the site. It is extremely difficult and costly to purify groundwater used for public water supplies if an aquifer becomes polluted. When households and communities lose their groundwater supply to pollution, the hardships to the citizens are both severe and costly. Some communities have had to transport water from other areas and to impose tight controls on how the water is used.

Waste disposal is a very important part of the life-style of modern society; with the quest for more and more conveniences and services, the unwanted by-products of civilization continue to increase and must be disposed of in some way. In addition, the natural environment has deteriorated to a point of serious concern. Therefore, landfilling must be done with the utmost care and planning in order to guard against pollution.

Bibliography

Cook, James. "Not in Anybody's Back Yard." *Forbes* 142 (November 28, 1988): 172-177. One of several articles that *Forbes* magazine has printed on waste disposal and pollution of the environment.

Foreman, T. L., and N. L. Ziemba. "Cleanup on a Large Scale." *Civil Engineering*, August, 1987. An example of a large number of articles published in technical journals on waste disposal and pollution. Although they can contain technical data and scientific details, the bulk of the texts are written in a very understandable way and provide an important source of information on landfills.

U.S. Environmental Protection Agency. *Subtitle D Study*. Washington, D.C.: Government Printing Office, 1986, 1988. This study on nonhazardous wastes is one of many reports by the U.S. Environmental Protection Agency on all aspects of waste disposal and pollution control. The agency is an excellent source of both general information and specific data. Interested readers can write to the U.S. Environmental Protection Agency, Office of Solid Waste (WH-562), 401 M Street S.W., Washington, D.C. 20460.

U.S. Geological Survey. *Toxic Waste—Groundwater Contamination*. Water Fact Sheet. Washington, D.C.: Government Printing Office, 1983. An informational brochure, or fact sheet, for the general public on groundwater supplies and pollution. Interested readers should write to the Hydrologic Information Unit, U.S. Geological Survey, 419 National Center, Reston, Virginia 22092.

N. B. Aughenbaugh

Cross-References

Aquifers, 71; Clays, 210; Engineering Geophysics, 607; Environmental Health, 615; Freshwater Chemistry, 795; Groundwater Movement, 1020; Groundwater Pollution, 1028; Groundwater Pollution Remediation, 1035; Hazardous Wastes, 1059; Land-Use Planning, 1335; Sand, 2253; Surface Water, 2504; Water Wells, 2708.

LANDSAT

Field of study: Remote sensing

The Landsats are space satellites that have collected data about the earth: its agriculture, forests, flat lands, minerals, waters, and environment. These were the first satellites to aid in earth sciences, helping to produce the best maps available and assisting farmers around the world to grow more and better crops.

Principal terms

MULTISPECTRAL SCANNER: a data-recording device in which a scanner mirror rocks from side to side, deflecting light from the ground into the detectors; it can be mounted on the bottom of a space satellite

SPACE SATELLITE: a man-made object sent into regular orbit around the earth

SUN-SYNCHRONOUS SATELLITE ORBIT: an orbit in which the space satellite moves around the earth at the same rate as the earth moves around the sun

THEMATIC MAPPER (TM): a remote sensing device on a spacecraft

VIDEO CAMERA: a device that can be used from a space satellite to gather information about changing features of the earth below

Summary of the Methodology

In 1970, the National Aeronautics and Space Administration (NASA) proceeded to develop a series of satellites specifically designed to obtain practical information about the surface of the earth that could be used on a routine and repetitive basis. In the early 1960's, the early weather satellites had taken pictures of the earth and had demonstrated to scientists the usefulness of orbital satellites for mapping and providing data about the earth itself. This type of satellite, originally named the Earth Resources Technology Satellite (ERTS), later became the Landsat series.

On July 23, 1972, Landsat 1, the first in the series, was launched, followed by Landsat 2 in 1975 and Landsat 3 in 1978. They were sent up on Delta rockets. The Landsat 1 spacecraft was manufactured at General Electric's Space Sciences Facility at Valley Forge, Pennsylvania. This spacecraft, an outgrowth of the Nimbus weather series of meteorological satellites, was designed to carry two remote-sensing systems and a system to collect data from sensors located in remote places on the earth.

Landsat 1, 2, and 3 satellites were placed in near-polar, sun-synchronous, near-circular orbits around the poles at an altitude of approximately 920 kilometers. Landsat's orbit is inclined 99 degrees, which means it is slightly (1 degree) off from a purely North-Pole-to-South-Pole rotation. A sun-synchronous orbit means that the satellite orbits the earth at the same rate as the earth moves around the sun. This feature enables the spacecraft to cross the equator daily at the same local time (between 9:30 to 10:00 A.M.) on the sunlit side of the earth; Landsat thus crosses the equator at exactly the same local time on every pass. At 9:30 A.M., there are shadows on the underlying ground, which help show up the topographical features more clearly. By passing over at exactly the same time every day, the sensors capture the information under conditions of light and shade that are as constant as possible. There are differences caused by varying amounts of cloud cover and the changing seasons of the year, but the sun-synchronous orbit minimizes the variations. In this orbit at this altitude, each satellite circles the globe fourteen times a day, taking 103.3 minutes for each orbit. That is, the satellite circles the globe slightly off center from a precisely north-south orbit. It is easiest to think of the earth as an enormous orange with fourteen sections; the Landsat satellites pass over each section twice a day, once in the daylight and once at night.

Programmed ground commands were sent from NASA's Goddard Space Flight Center, located in Greenbelt, Maryland. The orbit and field of view were such that any given place on the earth's surface was observed every eighteen days by the same satellite at the same local time. With the launching of Landsat 2, two satellites were phased in orbit so that the coverage of any spot on the globe could be obtained every nine days. At sites closer to the North and South poles, the coverage was even more frequent.

For their tasks, the Landsat satellites required electrical power, which they obtained from the sun. Banks of silicon cells converted the sunlight to electricity. With their sun-synchronous orbits, the Landsat satellites spent half their orbits in the dark, thus requiring some means of storing power. A series of batteries stored the power collected while the satellite traveled in the sunlight, releasing it when Landsat traveled in the dark. The first three Landsat spacecraft weighed about 950 kilograms, were approximately 3.3 meters tall, and were stabilized by gas jets so that if the orbit varied, the satellite could be repositioned. This crucial feature guaranteed that the images recorded would be consistent over time.

The Landsat 1, 2, and 3 spacecrafts did not carry cameras. Instead, each satellite was equipped with a multispectral scanner (MSS) as the principal sensing instrument, three special television cameras, and other data collection systems that obtain information from remote, surface-based, automatic platforms around the world. These platforms were able to monitor local conditions and to relay the data to central ground stations whenever the Landsat could simultaneously view the platform and a ground station.

On Landsat 1, the triplet of television cameras failed shortly after launch, so the key recording instrument became the multispectral scanner. This instrument had been tested on high-altitude aircraft, but Landsat 1 first tested it in space. A scanner mirror rocked from side to side some thirteen times per second. By deflecting light from the ground into the detectors, the mirror scanned the scene below in a series of parallel swatches, rather like someone walking along while sweeping with a broom. The sensors were mounted on the bottom of the spacecraft. The area in each image measured approximately 185 square kilometers.

The MSS was the Landsat's primary information gatherer. The advantage of this type of sensor over a traditional camera is that the information is sent back rapidly by radio waves to ground stations on earth instead of being recorded on the camera film, which would then have to be physically transported back to earth, a costly and complicated process. Moreover, scanners capture images at wavelengths—including the important infrared region of the electromagnetic spectrum—that are invisible to the human eye and to conventional cameras. Other variables that use of the MSS avoided included the different film-developing practices of various laboratories and the subjective eyes of scientists who interpret the information. On Landsat 3, the video equipment was greatly improved and, as a consequence, so was the quality of the image resolution.

These MSS data, and later video data, were principally in digital form; thus, the data could be rapidly processed with computers, which could analyze the information so it could be used quickly and precisely. NASA operates three ground stations to receive data from the Landsat satellites and control their operation. These stations are located in Greenbelt, Maryland; Goldstone, California; and Fairbanks, Alaska. Any one of these three stations can detect Landsat at any time it is over the continental United States. Additional coverage can be obtained from ground stations in Italy and Sweden, operated by the European Space Agency, and from stations in Canada, Brazil, Argentina, South Africa, India, Australia, Japan, Thailand, Indonesia, and mainland China, operated by their respective governments. In addition to the real-time coverage permitted by these stations (that is, transmission of information as it is collected), tape recorders on the satellites allow the recording of data from areas around the world that are outside the range of the ground stations. Since 1979, both Goddard and the Earth Resources Observation Satellite (EROS) Data Center in Sioux Falls, South Dakota, have shared the role of processing information, which is placed, as quickly as possible, into national data bases operated by the Department of the Interior and the Department of Agriculture.

Landsat 4 was launched in 1982 and used (as would Landsat 5) a multimission spacecraft, an improvement over the original Nimbus series used for Landsats 1, 2, and 3. With an improved launch vehicle (the 3920 Delta), Landsat 4 and Landsat 5 were fitted in size to 2,200 kilograms. Physically, the Landsat 4 flight vehicle consists of two major sections. An on-board computer controls the power and altitude. It is used also in monitoring flight and communication. In addition, the vehicle has a device which provides the capability to adjust the orbit periodically. The forward end of the spacecraft contains the thematic mapper (TM) and the MSS. The antenna mast is 13 feet high.

The Landsat 4 orbits are different from those of Landsats 1, 2, and 3. Most significant is the nominal altitude, which is 705 kilometers as opposed to the 900 kilometers of the first three Landsats. Additionally, Landsat 4 can circle the globe in sixteen instead of eighteen days.

Starting with the launch of Landsat 4 in July, 1982, a new page was turned in the history of remote sensing of the land surface of the globe. A thematic mapper on board the spacecraft imaged the earth with a resolution sufficient to detect geological features of interest in mineral exploration. The TM was designed to be most relevant to agriculture experiments that observe vegetation cover and measure crop acreages. Together with the MSS, the TM has thus provided information which is useful for both geology and agriculture. The resolution capability of the TM, an improvement over that of the MSS, was adopted to estimate crop acreages in regions with small fields, such as China, India, Europe, and the eastern United States. In addition, the TM sends data directly to the earth, in this case to White Sands, New Mexico.

The speed of data collection was improved for Landsats 4 and 5. The early programs of Landsats 1, 2, and 3 were primarily for researchers, and rapid transmission of data was not considered necessary. Landsats 1, 2, and 3 thus did not adopt digital data until 1978; Landsats 4 and 5 used it from the beginning.

Landsat 5, launched in early 1984, was the same size as Landsat 4 and fulfilled the same functions. Landsat 5 synchronizes with Landsat 4 to provide an eight-day full-coverage orbit of the earth. The orbit of Landsat 5 was targeted low intentionally, to ensure that no orbit-lowering maneuvers would be required. Between March 7, 1984, and April 4, 1984, a series of eight orbit-raising maneuvers were performed to correct the axis so that Landsat 4 and Landsat 5 would be coordinated to cover the entire globe in eight days. Landsat 5, like Landsat 4, has a sun-synchronous orbit and a sixteen-day tracking cycle around the world. The nominal orbits of the two are identical except for their phasing. An eight-day complete coverage of the earth is achieved when Landsat 4 and Landsat 5 are on opposite sides of the globe. This phasing also minimizes any interference between the two satellites.

Starting in January, 1983, the National Oceanic and Atmospheric Administration (NOAA) assumed the responsibility for operating the Landsat series of satellites. NOAA also produces and distributes the data and the data products.

Applications of the Method

The Landsat system was designed to gather information for better use of the earth's resources. The principal uses of Landsat data can be grouped into the following broad areas: agriculture, forestry, and rangeland; water resources; geology and mineral resources; land use and mapping; oceanography and marine resources; and environment.

Landsat makes it possible to discriminate the patterns of crops, lumber, and vegetation around the world. The satellites are able to measure crop acreage by species. Very precise estimates of the amount and type of lumber resources in the world can be obtained. In addition, soil conditions can be monitored as well as the extent of fire damage.

Landsat enabled scientists, for the first time, to make an exact determination of the water boundaries and surface water area and volume around the globe. Plans could be formulated to minimize the damage from flooding. Scientists were able also to survey snow areas of mountains and glacial features. The depths of the oceans, seas, lakes, and other bodies of water could be calculated and used to plan better use of water resources. On June 26, 1978, a new experimental satellite, Seasat, was launched; it was a modified Landsat system to research oceans, specifically. After merely four months of operation, however, the satellite failed, and the Landsat system continued this important function.

Mineral and petroleum exploration is made easier with precise geological data, as has been possible with Landsat. Maps of rocks and rock types can be made for all corners of the globe. Overall, the knowledge of geology was greatly expanded by data obtained from Landsat about rocks and soils, volcanoes, changing landforms, and precise land formations.

Landsat has helped to revolutionize the science of mapping of the earth. Surface mining can be monitored and land more productively reclaimed. Urban and rural demarcations have been corrected, significantly assisting regional planners. Transportation networks have been mapped as well as basic land uses and land and water boundaries. For the first time, the shape and scope of the planet are known with accuracy.

Floods can be monitored and measured and their damage delineated and repaired. In desert regions, possible water sources can be more easily identified. Water quality and change can be monitored. The patterns and movements of living ocean forms can be detected. Shoreline changes, shoals, and shallow areas, wave patterns, and ice patterns can be mapped.

With Landsat, researchers have been able to gather more precise data on air and water pollution and their sources and effects. Scientists can determine the scope and effects of natural disasters and can monitor the environmental effects of human population, such as defoliation.

Context

The Landsat series of satellites offered the first in a set of tools from space exploration which could be used to investigate and understand the earth itself. A single image obtained from space could encompass large-scale geological features that would otherwise take days or weeks to cover, even with aerial mapping. Additionally, such images could show patterns so extensive that they could never have been noticed from the ground and would be lost in the patchwork of aerial mosaics.

This family of satellites has proved to be a valuable component of a new approach to locating, monitoring, managing, and understanding many of the earth's resources. Before Landsat began systematic sensing of changing features of the earth, broad-scale land monitoring was nearly impossible to achieve at cost-effective means. Producing maps of comparable accuracy by conventional methods was costly, and by the time they were complete, such maps were already out of date.

In the areas of agriculture, oceanography, geology, and environmental studies, scientists were able to gather significant data from Landsat that could help both in fundamental research and in governmental decision making. Even in the most technologically advanced countries, up-to-date and complete assessments of total acreage of different crops were incomplete before the use of the Landsat system. Vast areas of Africa, Asia, and South America had been poorly, even incorrectly, mapped. After the launch of Landsat, mountain ranges, deserts, vegetable cover, and land use could be known for all parts of the earth. Forests could be managed for fire and for insect infestation. Wildlife habitats could be monitored and better conserved.

Since the mid-1970's, Landsat has marketed several million dollars worth of products each year to state governments and to the Departments of the Interior, Agriculture, and Commerce. With the use of sophisticated computers, the science of knowing the earth and its resources has far advanced. Private businesses that explore for minerals and petroleum have been quick to seize on Landsat images as cost effective. Private industry, for more than a decade after launch, has accounted for a third of Landsat sales of images.

Landsats 4 and 5 helped in gathering information about the nuclear accident at Chernobyl in the Soviet Union on April 26, 1986. This mission involved obtaining data about the surrounding air, soil, and water. Information gleaned from Landsat 5's thematic mapper of images of Chernobyl before and after the accident helped to determine the character and extent of the damage.

Bibliography

Barker, John. *Landsat 4 Science Investigations Summary.* NASA CP-2326. Springfield, Va.: National Technical Information Service, 1984. This volume provides a summary of the success of Landsat 4 in terms of its ability to map and survey the earth's resources. Some of the material is specifically written for geologists, but the volume does provide basic information and description helpful to the layperson.

Computer Sciences Corporation. *Landsat 5 Orbit Adjust Maneuver Report.* Greenbelt, Md.: Goddard Space Flight Center, 1984. An evaluation of the success of Landsat 5 in terms of its orbit and the technology aboard to map the earth. Many valuable diagrams help the reader to understand the functioning of Landsat 5.

Harper, Dorothy. *Eye in the Sky: Introduction to Remote Sensing.* 2d ed. Montreal: Multiscience Publications, 1983. This clear explanation of the use of satellites contains on pages 97-107 a survey explanation of the Landsat system. Aimed at those with little or no knowledge of space science.

Salomonson, Vincent V., and R. Kottler. *An Overview of Landsat 4: Status and Results.* Greenbelt, Md.: Goddard Space Flight Center, 1983. This source analyzes the success of the thematic mapper on Landsat 4. A number of helpful diagrams are included.

Salomonson, Vincent V., and Harry Mannheimer. *An Overview of the Evolution of Landsat 4.* Proceedings of the Eighth Pecora Symposium, Ann Arbor, Mich., October, 1983. A fine summary of the history of the development of the Landsat 4 program. A number of useful diagrams are included. The improvements over

Landsats 1, 2, and 3 are described in some detail.

Short, Nicholas M. *The Landsat Tutorial Workbook: Basics of Satellite Remote Sensing*. NASA RP-1078. Washington, D.C.: Government Printing Office, 1982. A basic guide to the uses of Landsats 1, 2, and 3. Aimed at the user of the data of the Landsat system, whether in agriculture, geology, or environmental control. Contains numerous charts and diagrams and provides references to numerous publications. Suitable for the college-level reader.

_____, et al. *Mission to Earth: Landsat Views the World*. NASA SP-360. Washington, D.C.: Government Printing Office, 1976. This picture book describes the Landsat program and presents a multitude of maps of the earth made from Landsat 1. A photo-laden book aimed at publicizing the Landsat program.

U.S. Congress. Senate. Committee on Aeronautical and Space Sciences. *An Analysis of the Future Landsat Effort*. 94th Congr., 2d sess., 1976. This comprehensive report provides much information on the Landsat program, its uses and shortcomings. Written for the Committee on Aeronautical and Space Science of the United States Senate.

U.S. Geological Survey. *Landsat Data Users Handbook*. 3d rev. ed. Washington, D.C.: Department of the Interior, 1979. A loose-leaf guide to the functions of Landsats 1, 2, and 3. Covers principally the various sensing and data-gathering devices, clearly describing the functions of the hardware.

Williams, Richard S. *ERTS-1: A New Window on Our Planet*. U.S. Geological Survey Professional Paper 929. Washington, D.C.: Government Printing Office, 1976. A short, comprehensive guide to the Earth Resources Technology Satellite, which later became known as Landsat 1. The pioneering work that delineated the uses of the satellite to map the earth and help plan its management. The professional predecessor to *Mission to Earth: Landsat Views the World*.

Douglas Gomery

Cross-References

Aerial Photography, 17; Dams and Flood Control, 309; Floods, 719; Land Management, 1327; Land-Use Planning, 1335; Remote Sensing and the Electromagnetic Spectrum, 2166; Earth Resources, 2175; Soil Erosion, 2387; Soil Formation, 2394.

LANDSLIDES AND SLOPE STABILITY

Field of study: Urban geology and geologic hazards

Each year, landslides cause extensive damage to highways and structures in the United States and the loss of roughly twenty-five lives. Elsewhere, in densely populated areas of the world, single landslide events cause death tolls in the thousands. Landslides occur under specific geological conditions that are usually detectable. Site assessments done by qualified geologists are important to land-use planning and engineering design; much of the tragedy and expense of landslides is preventable.

Principal terms

ANGLE OF REPOSE: the maximum angle of steepness that a pile of loose materials such as sand or rock can assume and remain stable; the angle varies with the size, shape, moisture, and angularity of the material

AVALANCHE: any large mass of snow, ice, rock, soil, or mixture of these materials that falls, slides, or flows rapidly downslope; velocities may reach in excess of 500 kilometers per hour

COHESION: the strength of a rock or soil imparted by the degree to which the particles or crystals of the material are bound to one another

CREEP: the slow, more or less continuous downslope movement of earth material

EARTHFLOW: a term applied to both the process and the landform characterized by fluid downslope movement of soil and rock over a discrete plane of failure; the landform has a hummocky surface and usually terminates in discrete lobes

HUMMOCKY: a topography characterized by a slope composed of many irregular mounds (hummocks) that are produced during sliding or flowage movements of earth and rock

LANDSLIDE: a general term that applies to any downslope movement of materials; landslides include avalanches, earthflows, mudflows, rockfalls, and slumps

MUDFLOW: both the process and the landform characterized by very fluid movement of fine-grained material with a high (sometimes more than 50 percent) water content

SLUMP: a term that applies to the rotational slippage of material and the mass of material actually moved; the mass has component parts called scarp, failure plane, head, foot, toe, and blocks; the toe may grade downslope into a flow

Summary of the Phenomenon

Slope failure, or landsliding, is the gravity-induced downward and outward movement of earth materials. Landslides involve the failure of earth materials under shear stress and/or flowage. When slope failures are rapid, they become serious hazards. Areas of the United States that are particularly susceptible to landslides include the West Coast, the Rocky Mountains of Colorado and Wyoming, the Mississippi Valley bluffs, the Appalachian Mountains, and the shorelines and bluffs around the Great Lakes. Downslope movement of soil and rock is a natural result of conditions on the planet's surface. The constant stress of gravity and the gradual weakening of earth materials through long-term chemical and physical weathering processes ensure that, through geologic time, downslope movement is inevitable.

Slope failures involve either the soil, the underlying bedrock, or both. Several types of movements (falling, sliding, or flowing) can take place during the failures. Simple rockfalls, or topples, may occur when rock overhangs a vertical road cut or cliff face. Other failures are massive and include flows (see figure 1) and slides (see figure 2). Slides involve failure along a discrete plane. The failure planes in soils are usually curved, as in the illustration of a rotational slide or slump. The failure planes in bedrock can be curved or straight. Failures often follow planes of weakness, such as thin clay seams, joints, or alignment of fabric in the rock. Slides may be slow or rapid but usually involve coherent blocks of dry material. Flows, on the other hand, behave more like a fluid and move downslope much like running water. Earthflows, mudflows, sand flows, debris flows, and avalanches occur when soils or other unconsolidated materials move rapidly downslope in a fluidlike manner. The movement destroys the vegetative cover and leaves a scar of hummocky deposits where the flow occurred. Although flows usually involve wet materials, rare

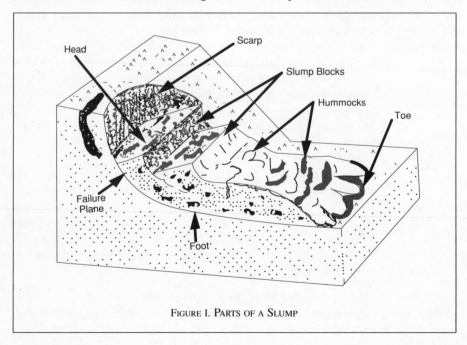

FIGURE 1. PARTS OF A SLUMP

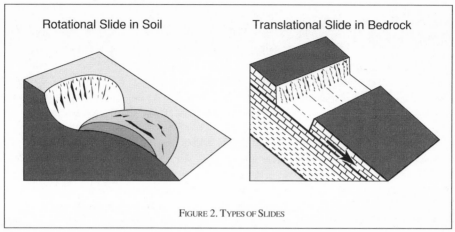

Rotational Slide in Soil   Translational Slide in Bedrock

FIGURE 2. TYPES OF SLIDES

exceptions, such as the destructive flows in Kansu, China, occur in certain types of dry materials.

Slides and flows are terms applied to failures that produce rapid movement. Rock slides are those slides that involve mostly fresh bedrock; debris slides include those movements which are mostly rock particles larger than sand grains but with significant amounts of finer materials; mudslides involve even finer material and water, but the failure plane is straight. Earthflows involve mostly the soil overburden and move over a slope or into a valley rather than failing along a rock bedding plane; mudflows involve more water than earthflows and have a downslope movement much like flowing water.

"Creep" is a term given to very slow movement of rock debris and soils. Creep in itself does not usually pose a life-threatening danger. When creep occurs beneath man-made structures, however, it leads to economic damage that requires repair or reconstruction in a new location. Examples include the gradual cracking and destruction of buildings, disalignment and breaking of power lines and fences, the filling of drains along highways, and the movement of topsoils into streams and reservoirs. Sometimes creep precedes a very rapid failure, and therefore new evidence of creep requires careful monitoring and an evaluation of the conditions that produce it.

Solifluction is a special type of creep that occurs in cold climates where the soil is frozen most of the year, permafrost regions. In summer, the ice in the upper layer of soil melts, and the soil becomes waterlogged and susceptible to downslope movement. Solifluction is an important consideration for the design of structures in cold climates: For example, the Alaska pipeline, used for conveyance of petroleum, could not be buried but had to be set above ground on supports that were anchored at a depth below the seasonal depth of thaw to escape solifluction movement. Houses and other buildings in such areas must be set on supports and insulated in order to keep heat from the structures from melting the underlying soils.

Water is an important agent in promoting instability in slopes. Where soils are saturated, water in large pores will flow naturally in a downward direction. The resulting pressure of the water pushing against the soil grains is called pore pressure. As pore pressures increase, the grains are forced apart and cohesion decreases. The saturated soils become easier to move downslope. Water flowing along a bedding plane or joint can also exert pressure on either side of the joint and decrease the cohesion there, thus causing the block above the discontinuity to move downslope.

Designers may unwittingly assemble, in a man-made structure, conditions that produce slope failures. Dry materials such as mine wastes have sometimes been stacked into piles that are steeper than their angle of repose after saturation. Much later, a rainstorm or earth tremor can send the piles into motion, destroying all structures around them. When man removes the supporting toe from the base of a slope, during excavations such as occur for a highway or building foundation, this action produces many landslides, evidence of which can be found on most highways constructed through hilly terrain. An unstable slope can be set into motion by loading the slope from above, which occurs when man builds a structure such as a building, a storage tank, or a highway on materials that cannot remain stable under the load. Human development alters the natural drainage of the area and increases runoff. Occasionally, water from storm drains, roof gutters, septic tanks, or leaking water mains reaches a sensitive slope and generates movement. This instability is particularly likely to occur where intensive housing development takes place in several levels on a long slope.

Methods of Study

The stability of slopes is evaluated over large regions from aerial photographs, satellite photographs, and images made by remote sensing techniques. Investigators look for telltale signs, such as hummocky topography and old scars left by slides, that may not be evident when viewed from the ground.

The regional study involves an evaluation of the history of past landslides within the region. That history often reveals particular geological formations that have an association with landslides. For example, the shales of the Pierre formation are well known by engineering geologists in the area of Denver, Colorado, as materials in which many slope failures occur. A geologic map that shows where this formation is exposed at the ground surface reveals potentially dangerous areas. Ignoring evidence of past landslides invites disaster.

The regional study also defines loose surficial materials that are likely to fail. Soils rich in clay minerals that swell and expand when wet are notorious for slumping and flowing. Usually, movement occurs in these soils in the spring, when the soil is very saturated from soil thaw and snowmelt. Other soils fail simply because they have low cohesion and large amounts of open space (pore space) between the tiny soil grains. Collapse of these soils requires no wetting; strong vibrations can trigger the movement. The most tragic example of this type took place in 1920, when thick deposits of fine loess (a type of soil deposited by the wind) settled rapidly during an earthquake in Kansu, China, and the resulting flows toppled and buried the many homes built upon them. More than 100,000 deaths resulted from the flows that occurred in the loess.

Loose volcanic materials often can absorb so much water that they flow quickly down even gentle slopes. A mudflow destroyed the Roman city of Herculaneum at the base of Mount Vesuvius in A.D. 79; mudflows generated during the Mount St. Helens eruption of May 18, 1980, destroyed many properties.

Regional studies also look at the earthquake history of an area, because a tremor, even a fairly mild one, can provide the *coup de grace* to a slope that has been resting for decades in a state of marginal instability. Almost thirty campers were killed when an earthquake triggered the 1959 landslide in the Madison Canyon of Montana. In excess of 130 million tons of debris covered Canada's Highway 3 when two small earthquakes triggered the Hope Mountain slide in British Columbia in 1965. Huge blocks of the shoreline slid beneath the ocean at Valdez, Alaska, during the 1964 earthquake when the rotational slumping of materials occurred below sea level. Landslides triggered by that same earthquake destroyed much of Anchorage, Alaska.

Finally, the regional study includes a history of weather events. When the right geological conditions exist, periods of intense rainfall can trigger the movement of unstable slopes. In one night in January of 1967, seventeen hundred people lost their lives in Brazil when a three-hour cloudburst converted green hills into mudflows and attractive stream valleys into flood torrents. In the southern and central Appalachian Mountains, periods of increased frequency of slides often coincide with severe local summer cloudbursts and thunderstorms. Intense rainfall events associated with hurricanes which have moved inland also trigger landslides over larger areas. Studies in the Canadian Rockies reveal a definite link between rainstorms and rockfalls, and landslides are particularly abundant during the rainy season along the West Coast of North America.

Once knowledge is collected on the region, more specific questions about the local site itself are considered. The investigator first looks at the steepness of the slopes and the earth materials present. In the case of loose materials and soils, the angle of repose is very important. Dry sand poured carefully onto a table to form an unsupported conical pile cannot achieve a cone with sides steeper than approximately 40 degrees, because the cohesion between loose dry sand grains is not strong enough to allow the material to support a steeper face. The 40-degree angle is the maximum angle of repose for dry sand. The angle of repose changes with water content, mineral content, compaction, grain shape, and sorting. Soils that contain clay may be tough and cohesive when dry and have natural repose angles greater than 40 degrees. When wet, their angle of repose may be only 10 degrees. This is particularly true if the soils contain clay minerals such as montmorillonite that absorb large amounts of water. Those soils, sometimes called "quick clays," can fail instantaneously and flow downslope almost as rapidly as pure water.

The orientation of discontinuities in rocks is as important in determining the stability of a slope as is the type of rock involved. Bedding planes that dip downslope serve as directions of weakness along which failure may occur (see translational slide shown in figure 2). Other planar weaknesses may develop along joints and faults and along parallel fabrics produced by the alignment of platy and rod-shaped minerals that are oriented downslope.

The investigator will check to see if natural processes are removing the supporting material at the bases of slopes. Landslides are particularly common along stream banks, reservoir shorelines, and large lake and seacoasts. The removal of supporting material by currents and waves at the base of a slope produces countless small slides each year. Particularly good examples are found in the soft glacial sediments along the shores of the Great Lakes of the United States and Canada.

Finally, the investigator will look for evidence of actual creep at the site. Damage to structures already on the site, curved tree trunks (where tilting occurring as a result of soil movement is compensated for by the tree's tendency to resume vertical growth), the offset of fences and power lines, or the presence of hummocky topography on slopes can demonstrate the presence of recent motion at the site.

Context

An annual economic loss of between $1 and $1.5 billion is a reasonable estimate for costs of landslides within the United States. Expenses include the loss of real estate around large lakes, rivers, and oceans; loss of productivity in agricultural and forest lands; depreciated real estate in areas of slide development; public aid for victims of large landslides; and the contribution of sediment to streams that decreases water quality, injures aquatic life, and results in the loss of reservoir storage space. In the United States, approximately twenty-five lives are lost each year from landslides. Occasional landslides in densely populated regions of the world cause death tolls in the thousands. The most tragic landslide in history claimed more than 100,000 lives in Kansu, China, in 1920.

Loss of life and many economic losses are caused by inadequate characterization or appreciation of the geological conditions of a construction site. Although evidence of past landslides abounded in the valley used for the impoundment of the Vaiont Reservoir in northern Italy, engineers ignored the implications and constructed the reservoir. In 1963 a huge landslide shot into the reservoir and sent a wave of water exceeding 100 meters in height across the reservoir and over the dam. The dam withstood the immense wave that overtopped it, its strength a credit to its designer; however, three thousand people caught in the path of the onrushing flood wave perished. Excellence in engineering design proved to be no substitute for a geological site investigation.

Catastrophic failures have occurred where mudflows were produced when dams built from mine tailings burst as a result of slope failure. The mine wastes used for these dams were susceptible to swelling, absorption of water, and weakening over time. These materials were often stacked in slopes steeper than their natural angle of repose. Although 144 people died in the Aberfan tailings flow in 1966, six years later, the same ignorance about the behavior of geological materials resulted in more than one hundred deaths when a dam constructed from mine wastes burst at Buffalo Hollow, West Virginia.

Unlike natural lakes, man-made reservoirs in steep valleys are usually subject to seasonal water level variations that may exceed 100 feet. When the reservoirs are lowered quickly after a high water period (usually in the spring), the water level in the reservoir drops faster than water can exit from the pores and capillaries of the formerly flooded rocks and soils. As a result, the soils are waterlogged and lie tenuously on steep banks from which they easily slump into the reservoir to be washed away by waves. Soon, all loose material is removed and the soils that lie on the slopes above have no downslope support. Sliding then develops upslope and contributes to abnormal sediment fill of the reservoir.

The remediation of slope stability problems involves contributions from both geologists in the investigation of the site and civil engineers in the design of the project. The geologist is the master of the site investigation. Because slope stability involves geological processes and geological materials, no professional is better qualified to recognize slope stability hazards than the geologist. At the general level, geologists serve as data gatherers, compilers, and organizers of basic information that will become available for reference in areas subject to development. In this capacity, geologists employed by state geological surveys and the U.S. Geological Survey provide a tremendous service by constructing geological and slope stability maps based on knowledge of the soils and rock formations, use of remote-sensing methods such as satellite and high-altitude photography, and by field study of suspect areas. These maps are made readily available to engineers, contractors, developers, and home owners. These maps show color-coded areas of active and potentially active landslides. Such maps have been produced for many areas with a high population density. Residents in the United States may contact their local state's geological survey, which serves as distributors for such maps.

Geologic examination of a site for slope stability should include: topographic evaluation of relief, steepness, and shape of the slope; type and condition of the bedrock that underlies the slope; the type and thickness of soils present; the angle and direction of bedding or rock fabric; the frequency and direction of joints; the amount and type of vegetation on the slope; moisture present and moisture-retaining properties of the materials; the nature of surface drainage; determination of the earthquake history of the area; evidence of past slides, flows, or rockfalls; and an evaluation of the possible volume of earth materials susceptible to failure, the possible styles in which they may fail, and the area that may be affected by failure.

After the geologist has evaluated a site, the engineer must make several decisions. In the case of discovery of a potential for a large disastrous landslide, the engineer may opt to relocate the project to a more favorable area. If the potential slides are likely to be small and more of an economic nuisance than a life-threatening situation, then the engineer may opt for some remediation measures, which include construction of retainer walls, building up the toe of an incipient slide with rock or stable soils, and diverting drainage away from the slide area.

Some landslide areas have been developed for educational use and converted into parks, monuments, or scientific preserves. One of the most expensive slides in history occurred near Thistle, Utah, in 1983 and required relocation of a major highway and railroad. The site of the $200-million slide is now used as an educational resource for the public and a classic area for scientific study. So also are the sites of the Madison Canyon landslide in Montana and the Gros Ventre landslide in Wyoming.

Bibliography

Close, Upton, and Elsie McCormick. "Where the Mountains Walked." *National Geographic* 41 (May, 1922): 445-464. Kansu, China, 1920 earthquakes and land-slides—a graphic account of the most devastating landslide in history.

Costa, J. E., and V. R. Baker. *Surficial Geology: Building with the Earth*. New York: John Wiley & Sons, 1981. A very well-written text for undergraduates in environmental geology and engineering geology courses. Its particular strength is the use of simple numerical problems to illustrate concepts quantitatively. It may be understood by students with a background in algebra, trigonometry, and introductory geology or earth science. It is well illustrated and contains a good bibliography.

Costa, J. E., and G. F. Wieczorek, eds. *Debris Flows—Avalanches: Process, Recognition, and Mitigation*. Reviews in Engineering Geology, vol. 7. Boulder, Colo.: Geological Society of America, 1987. A number of case studies from various parts of the United States, Canada, and Japan. The content of the text is intended for professionals, but there are many photographs and illustrations that will interest students and laymen.

Cummans, J. *Mudflows Resulting from the May 18, 1980, Eruption of Mount St. Helens*. U.S. Geological Survey Circular 850-B. Washington, D.C.: Government Printing Office, 1981. This is a good illustration of the devastation caused by mudslides associated with volcanism.

Hays, W. W. *Facing Geologic and Hydrologic Hazards*. U.S. Geological Survey Professional Paper 1240-B. Washington, D.C.: Government Printing Office, 1981. A well-written and beautifully illustrated booklet intended for students and laymen. It can be appreciated by readers from grade school through professionals.

Hoek, E., and J. W. Bray. *Rock Slope Engineering*. 3d ed. Brookfield, Vt.: IMM/North American Publications Center, 1981. This is an engineering reference often used by professionals. Although much of it involves a solid quantitative approach, the descriptive sections are graphic and well written. Some parts may be understood by secondary students, and most of the book may be understood by junior and senior undergraduates in geology and civil engineering.

Keefer, D. K. "Landslides Caused by Earthquakes." *Geological Society of America*

Bulletin 95 (April, 1984): 406-421. A good review of the relationship between earthquakes and major landslides.

Keller, E. A. *Environmental Geology.* 5th ed. Columbus, Ohio: Merrill, 1988. Chapter 7, on landslides and related phenomena, is highly recommended for beginners. It is well illustrated and written in a simple and descriptive manner. A good set of references follows each chapter.

Kennedy, Nathaniel T. "California's Trial by Mud and Water." *National Geographic* 136 (October, 1969): 552-573. A graphic account of the interaction between landslides, earthquakes, and heavy seasonal rainfall.

Kiersch, G. A. "Vaiont Reservoir Disaster." *Civil Engineering* 34 (1964): 32-39. An enthralling account of one of the world's most tragic landslides. Excerpts of Kiersch's original article have been reprinted in many engineering geology texts.

McDowell, Bart. "Avalanche!" *National Geographic* 121 (June, 1962): 855-880. A graphic account of avalanches in Peru.

Radbruch-Hall, Dorothy H. *Landslide Overview Map of the Conterminous United States.* U.S. Geological Survey Professional Paper 1183. Washington, D.C.: Government Printing Office, 1981. A map, with accompanying text, that illustrates the major landslide areas within the United States.

Rahn, P. H. *Engineering Geology, an Environmental Approach.* New York: Elsevier, 1986. This text is for the serious undergraduate or graduate student interested in a solid quantitative approach. The text is well illustrated and well referenced.

Schuster, Robert L., ed. *Landslide Dams: Processes, Risk, and Mitigation.* New York: American Society of Civil Engineers, 1986. A particularly interesting compilation of papers that includes case studies of slides at Thistle Creek, Utah, and the control of the new Spirit Lake, which was produced by a landslide at Mount St. Helens.

Edward B. Nuhfer

Cross-References

Aerial Photography, 17; Dams and Flood Control, 309; Earthquake Engineering, 430; Earthquake Hazards, 437; Foliation and Lineation, 747; Hurricanes and Monsoons, 1088; Land Management, 1327; Land-Use Planning, 1335; Marine Terraces, 1466; Mining Wastes and Reclamation, 1718; River Valleys, 2210; Soil Erosion, 2387; Soil Liquefaction, 2402; Expansive Soils, 2421; Stress and Strain, 2490; Volcanic Hazards, 2601; Weathering and Erosion, 2723.

LIGHTNING AND THUNDER

Field of study: Atmospheric sciences and meteorology

Lightning is the sudden discharge of electricity between a cloud and the ground, from cloud to cloud, or within a single cloud. The hot stroke of lightning heats the air, which expands to cause a thunderclap. Although quite predictable, lightning kills more than one hundred persons and injures several hundred in the United States each year.

Principal terms

CONDUCTOR: a substance, such as metal or salty solution, that allows the easy flow of electricity

CUMULONIMBUS: the tall, billowy variety of cloud with precipitation falling; lightning, hail, violent winds, and strong vertical wind drafts are common with this type of cloud

ELECTRON: a negatively charged particle that is part of all kinds of matter; freely moving electrons are measured as electrical current

INSULATOR: a substance, such as glass, rubber, or even air, that blocks the easy flow of electricity

LIGHTNING: the giant, visible spark that occurs when electricity is discharged in a thunderstorm

STATIC ELECTRICITY: an area, or field, of positive or negative electrical charge that is not in motion

THUNDER: the noise generated by the rapid heating and explosive expansion of air as a stroke of lightning passes through

Summary of the Phenomenon

There is a tremendous amount of energy in a developing thunderstorm. Evidence includes the strong winds, violent up/down drafts, and the rapid growth of the tall pile of clouds that signals the birth of a cumulonimbus cloud. One of the products of this energy is a powerful charge of static electricity. The base of a cumulonimbus cloud usually develops a strong negative charge, and other parts of the cloud will include areas of positive charge and additional areas of negative charge. When the charge is strong enough to jump the gap between the two charges, a spark (lightning stroke) occurs as electrons from the negative field race to the positive field to neutralize the two charges. The flash instantly heats the air to approximately 30,000 degrees Celsius. The lightning stroke is incredibly fast, appearing to be instantaneous. Most strokes happen so quickly that it is impossible to see if the stroke moves from the ground to the cloud or from cloud to ground. In the case of a cloud-to-ground stroke, the negative charge in the base of the cloud is able to jump the gap to the ground where a positive charge has built up and followed the movement of the cloud.

An individual lightning stroke is more complicated than the simple, blinding flash seen with the naked eye. Before the visible arc, there is an unseen bundle of electrons that begin the journey below the cloud. With this initial pathway started, more electrons probe the dry air below the cloud, moving in short pulses ("steps") of perhaps 50 meters at a time. The first movement is called a leader, and each subsequent addition to the probe is called a step leader. When a suitable pathway is prepared, a massive flow of current surges up the pathway in a "return stroke," which is the visible flash. Usually, several return strokes are needed to neutralize the heavily charged portions of the cloud. The whole process from leader through several return strokes takes less than half a second.

Lightning complies with the rules of basic physics. It occurs when a strong negative charge develops, and an opposing positive charge is generated to counter the negative charge. When the strength of these two opposing forces is great enough—that is, when the "potential" is great enough—the discharge can jump across the air space between the two areas and neutralize the two fields of potential energy. The buildup of a negative field can be measured with instruments, and scientists monitoring a thunderstorm often can predict within a few seconds when the next stroke of lightning will occur. The stroke will take the path of least resistance between the two charged fields and, because of variations in the temperature, composition, and humidity of the air, the stroke usually will not follow a straight line. The stroke usually flashes between the base of the cloud and the nearest conductor that is solidly connected to the ground. When lightning hits the ground, any tree, dry grass, or building that takes part of the stroke can be ignited immediately. A single thunderstorm in a dry season may start dozens of fires. The power of a lightning stroke can be awesome. Century-old trees can be splintered, and heavy steel wire burned like a giant sparkler. There are reports of deep trenches dug in soil and electrical appliances physically damaged, in addition to the melting of much of the electrical wiring inside. Fire alarms, electrical bank vaults, and computer cash registers in stores have been ruined by the electrical surges caused by lightning. Commercial buildings on hilltops and mountain passes often bristle with lightning rods every few meters along the roof. Most computer systems are made with antisurge circuits to protect against lightning and other power malfunctions.

Occasionally, a stroke of lightning will leave the top region of a massive thunderstorm and avoid the cloud to travel through clear air, striking the ground a considerable distance from the cloud. These "bolts from the blue" are called positive strokes, because they seem to be a discharge between the positive portion of the cloud and a rather distant region of negative charge in the ground. The flow of electricity may be from ground to cloud or the reverse. In fact, with most lightning strokes, the flash is not a simple, single spark. High-speed lightning cameras have shown that lightning that may appear to the naked eye as a long stroke that flickers bright and dim is in fact a series of up to ten individual strokes, each following approximately the same path through the air. The entire sequence of flashes lasts about 1 second, and the direction of current flow is often reversed with subsequent strokes.

Untrained observers have coined the names "sheet lightning" and "heat lightning" for flashes that differ from normal lightning. In sheet lightning, the individual strokes of light cannot be seen; instead, the light appears to be a rapidly expanding glow that rises to great heights. In sheet lightning, the individual lines of light are obscured by clouds between the flash and the observer, who is usually several kilometers away. Heat lightning is merely lightning that is too far away for the thunder to be heard. It may appear as individual flashes or as obscured sheets.

Ball lightning is a fascinating phenomenon. Trained observers have seldom seen ball lightning, because it is totally unpredictable and very rare. Nevertheless, bright spheres of light associated with violent lightning storms have been documented often enough by reliable sources to verify their existence. Ball lightning is usually about 20 centimeters in diameter, and it tends to hover or glide a few meters above the ground and last from less than 1 second to more than 10 seconds. Often, a loud popping sound occurs when the ball disappears, and a rather strong smell remains in the air afterward.

Before a lightning stroke can occur, a powerful charge of electricity must develop. This charge may cause the hair on exposed parts of the body to tingle and stand up, and it can be felt on the arms as well as the scalp. A brief warning signal may be heard. Hikers on mountain peaks have reported a ringing sound from their steel-handled ice axes a few seconds before the peak receives a hit from lightning, so there may be time to dash a few meters to a safer location or at least to crouch low and make one's body a less favorable target.

Thunder is the sound of the rapidly expanding air that is heated by the lightning flash. The temperature of the arc may reach 30,000 degrees Celsius, and the booming sound of the expanded air spreads in all directions at the speed of sound, which is about 330 meters per second. The sound travels about 1 kilometer in 3 seconds, so it is easy to estimate the distance to the violent part of the storm. If one counts 15 seconds between the flash and the thunder, the stroke occurred about 5 kilometers away; if the next strokes are progressively closer, the violent part of the storm is moving toward one, and safety should be sought. Thunder may continue to rumble for several seconds after the initial boom, because the lightning probably extended over several kilometers from beginning to end, and it takes the sound longer to reach the observer from the distant parts of the stroke.

Methods of Study

Weather scientists (meteorologists) must first find cumulonimbus clouds before they can study lightning. Except for bolts that are generated in a laboratory, lightning is rarely found without the towering cumulonimbus thundercloud. Thousands of weather stations worldwide supply data to map global weather patterns. The information is manipulated with a vast computer network in order to allow forecasters to predict rather accurately when and where thunderstorms will occur. Satellites provide continuous views of the global weather, and many of the stations launch balloons twice daily to measure temperature, humidity, air pressure, and wind conditions to 15 kilometers above the surface. When the thunderstorms are predicted, meteorologists have several ways to measure the electrical field or potential in a cloud. Instruments can be carried into position with balloons or kites or even flown in with specially equipped aircraft or small, remote-controlled planes. Research centers have been built on mountain peaks in lightning-prone areas, such as the eastern slope of the Rocky Mountains, and in other areas, such as Florida, where lightning is very common, with thunderstorms occurring more than one hundred days each year. In the hot humid areas near the equator, many stations report thunderstorm activity more than three hundred days per year. Global lightning activity is estimated to be a hundred strokes a second with possibly eighteen hundred thunderstorms in progress at any moment. The time-honored notion that lightning never strikes in the same place twice is untrue; if a tall building is the target once, it will likely be hit again. Repeated strikes to the same building, the same mountain peak, and even the same vehicle are reported constantly by weather specialists.

Despite intense study for hundreds of years, scientists are not certain how the electricity is generated in clouds. Friction from the rapid up/down drafts in a cumulonimbus cloud may cause the electricity. Other research suggests that the collisions of ice and water particles in the top of the cloud start an electric charge with negatively charged ice particles sweeping the water droplets out of the cloud. The ice particles become heavy enough for gravity to draw them downward in the cloud, thus increasing the negative charge toward the base. In turn, the top of the cloud is robbed of its negative charge and in effect becomes an area of positive charge. It is known that lightning does not begin in clouds until the top of the cloud has reached freezing temperatures.

With modern computer equipment, meteorologists are able to plot the position of each lightning stroke in many areas of the country. A massive storm at peak development may have one hundred strokes an hour. By knowing the areas of the most intense lightning, rangeland and forest managers can concentrate fire-watch programs in the areas most likely to have fires caused by lightning.

Context

Although many believe that lightning randomly, but very rarely, hurts someone, lightning kills more people than do hurricanes or tornadoes in most years, even in the United States, which has most of the world's tornadoes. Lightning is not random in its destruction; instead, it follows some predictable rules, and with a little understanding, an individual can eliminate most of the risk of being a victim of lightning.

A person, with dissolved salts in the blood and flesh, is an excellent conductor. Lightning can reach the ground with less resistance by passing first through a wet, tall tree than by traveling through the air directly to the wet soil. Air is a poor conductor, which requires a strong charge to develop before a lightning stroke can occur. Buildings, telephone poles, and other structures are protected by the installation of metal lightning rods, which are designed to attract lightning to a copper line or other good conductor that is buried deeply in the ground. If the lightning stroke can be lured into hitting the lightning rod, the force passes harmlessly into the ground. If there is no lightning rod, the stroke tends to hit sharp corners on metal objects or other conductors on the way to the ground. A metal umbrella frame or a steel-handled golf club acts the same as a lightning rod—drawing lightning to the person carrying such an object. A golfer wearing steel spikes in his shoes, standing in moist grass on a hill, and swinging a metal club to a vertical position high above the head tends to coax disaster if a thundercloud is overhead. Other dangerous activities during thunderstorms include participating in outdoor sports, driving exposed farm equipment, using an outdoor clothesline, riding a horse, or working on an elevated site such as a hill or rooftop.

When lightning strikes the ground, a strong current spreads along the surface to dissipate the energy of the stroke. Rather than lying on the ground with much of one's body in contact with the ground, it is safer to crouch low, using the fingertips to maintain balance. A closed automobile is among the safest places for shelter during a lightning storm; one should keep hands inside and avoid contact with the metal framework of the auto. Taking shelter inside a sturdy building is also good practice, although if lightning strikes a building, even one with a functioning lightning rod, some of the charge may enter the wiring or metal plumbing. Taking a bath or shower is particularly dangerous, because the plumbing usually goes to a deep metal drain that is a perfect connection to the electrical ground of the earth. The plumbing thus becomes a lightning rod, and a person in contact with the plumbing becomes part of the lightning rod. Telephones and hand-held electrical appliances such as an electric toothbrush, shaver, or hair dryer are equally dangerous.

If a person receives a shock from lightning, it is common to have the electrical impulses to the brain interrupted. Arm or leg movements are performed by muscles using tiny electrical signals from the brain. Therefore, if a strong electrical current enters the body, the muscles get a false signal and may cease to work properly. The heart and lungs may stop the coordinated rhythm that circulates the blood and recharges it with oxygen to sustain life. A shock may stop the heart and lung action, but cause no other injury. In many cases, such a victim of electrical shock can be revived with no permanent damage if proper treatment is given within about two minutes; after four minutes, few victims survive, or brain damage is likely at best.

Bibliography

Bailey, Bruce H. "Ball Lightning." *Weatherwise Magazine* 30 (June, 1977): 99-105. The monthly magazine *Weatherwise* is profusely illustrated and is written by specialists for the layperson who is interested in the daily phenomena of weather. Monthly and annual summaries are included to document both the normal and the unusual happenings of global weather. The Helen Dwight Reid Educational Foundation sponsors the magazine in association with the American Meteorological Society. In this article, the author has digested much technical material for easy reading by the layperson.

Battan, Louis J. *The Nature of Violent Storms*. Garden City, N.Y.: Doubleday, 1961. This very old, pocket-sized paperback is still included in reference lists for current books on meteorology. The discussions about lightning are only on ten pages of the book, but the index is very detailed and lists subentries, so the reader can find specific information quickly.

_____. *Weather in Your Life*. San Francisco: W. H. Freeman, 1983. In this 230-page paperback, lightning is discussed in relation to a number of weather subjects. Although the material on lightning is scattered, the book has a complete index, and the author has had considerable experience with writing successfully for laypersons. As an experienced research professor, the author knows the subject well and writes clearly without the threatening jargon and calculations that might intimidate a general reader.

Keen, Richard A. *Skywatch: The Western Weather Guide*. Golden, Colo.: Fulcrum, 1987. This beautifully illustrated paperback deals almost exclusively with weather phenomena of the Mountain States. The author presents the material that is critical to outdoor activities, especially mountaineering. Reproduction of color photography is superb.

Mogil, H. Michael. "Lightning." *Weatherwise Magazine* 32 (February, 1979): 17-20. The author is an emergency warnings meteorologist with the National Weather Service, and his article is intended to refute the misconceptions of lightning for the layperson.

National Oceanic and Atmospheric Administration. *Lightning*. Washington, D.C.: Government Printing Office, 1969.

_____. *Thunderstorms*. Washington, D.C.: Government Printing Office, 1976. These brochures are available at any federal weather station in the United States. Personal copies can be purchased from the Government Printing Office, Washington, D.C., 20402.

Dell R. Foutz

Cross-References

Clouds, 224; Precipitation, 2108; Storms, 2477; Weather Forecasting, 2717; Wind, 2730.

THE LITHOSPHERE

Type of earth science: Geophysics
Field of study: Seismology

Within the lithosphere, earthquakes occur, volcanoes erupt, mountains are built, and new oceans are formed. An understanding of the lithosphere's structure is needed in the search for oil and gas, for the prediction of earthquakes, and for the verification of a nuclear test ban treaty.

Principal terms

ASTHENOSPHERE: the partially molten weak zone in the mantle directly below the lithosphere

BASALT: a dark-colored igneous rock containing minerals, such as feldspar and pyroxene, high in iron and magnesium

CRUST: the rocky, outer "skin" of the earth, made up of the continents and ocean floor

GRANITE: a light-colored igneous rock containing feldspar, quartz, and small amounts of darker minerals

MANTLE: the thick, middle layer of the earth between the crust and the core

MOHOROVIČIĆ DISCONTINUITY (MOHO): the boundary between the crust and the mantle, named after the Yugoslavian seismologist Andrija Mohorovičić, who discovered it in 1909

PERIDOTITE: an igneous rock made up of iron- and magnesium-rich olivine, with some pyroxene but lacking feldspar

REFLECTED WAVE: a wave that is bounced off the interface between two materials of differing wave speeds

REFRACTED WAVE: a wave that is transmitted through the interface between two materials of differing wave speeds, causing a change in the direction of travel

Summary of the Phenomenon

The lithosphere is the rigid outer shell of the earth. It extends to a depth of 100 kilometers and is broken into about ten major lithospheric plates. These plates "float" upon an underlying zone of weakness called the asthenosphere. The phenomenon is somewhat like blocks of ice floating in a lake: As lake currents push the ice blocks around the lake, so do currents in the asthenosphere push the lithospheric plates. The plates carry continents and oceans with them as they form a continually changing jigsaw puzzle on the face of the earth.

The word "lithosphere" is derived from the Greek *lithos*, meaning stone. Historically, the lithosphere was considered to be the solid crust of the earth, as distinguished from the atmosphere and the hydrosphere. The words "crust" and "lithosphere" were used interchangeably to mean the unmoving, rocky portions of the earth's surface. Advances in the understanding of the structure of the earth's interior, resulting mostly from seismology, have forced the redefinition of old terms. "Crust" presently refers to the rocky, outer "skin" of the earth, containing the continents and ocean floor. "Lithosphere" is a more comprehensive term that includes the crust within a thicker, rigid unit of the earth's outer shell. To appreciate the reason for this redefinition, it is necessary to learn about the nature of the earth's interior.

Except for the upper 3 or 4 kilometers, the earth's interior is inaccessible to humans. Therefore, indirect methods, such as studying earthquakes and explosions, are used to learn about the inside of the earth. Earthquakes and explosions, both conventional and nuclear, generate two types of energy waves: compressional (P) waves and shear (S) waves. P waves travel faster than do S waves and are generally the first waves to arrive at an observation station. The speed of a wave, however, depends on the rock through which it travels. When seismic waves encounter a boundary between two different rocks, some energy is reflected back, and some is transmitted across the boundary. If the rock properties are very different, the transmitted waves travel at a different speed and their travel path is bent, or refracted. This phenomenon can be illustrated by placing a pencil in a glass of water. Light in water travels at a speed different from that of light in air, so light is refracted, or bent, as it travels from water to air. Thus, the pencil appears to be bent. P and S waves are reflected and refracted as they travel through the earth. Waves following different paths travel at different speeds.

Since 1900, seismologists have studied P and S waves arriving at different locations from the same earthquake. They discovered three distinct layers in the earth: the crust, the mantle, and the core. The boundaries separating these layers show abrupt changes in both P- and S-wave speeds. These changes in wave speeds provide information about the earth's interior. Scientists studying the theory of traveling elastic waves, such as earthquake waves, related the speed of waves to the physical properties of the material through which they travel. It was found that S waves do not travel through liquids. From this finding, scientists concluded that the earth's core had a liquid outer region and a solid inner region. Other scientists measured the P- and S-wave speeds of many different rocks and provided clues to the kind of rocks found inside the earth.

The quantity and quality of seismological and related information have grown rapidly since the end of World War II. There has been an increase in the number of seismological observatories and in the quality of seismographs, the instruments that record the arrivals of seismic waves. The methods of explosion seismology, developed for use in the search for oil and gas, have also been applied to the lithosphere. Experimental rock studies have been undertaken at higher and higher temperatures and pressures. In addition, the development of high-speed computers has enabled scientists to handle the vast amounts of data being generated and to test more complex models of the earth's properties with the observed seismic data. The combined use of explosion seismology, earthquake studies, and the experimental and theoretical studies of rocks has provided a very detailed picture of the seismic structure of the crust and upper mantle.

The continental crust averages 30-40 kilometers thick and is divided into two main seismic layers. One layer, the upper two-thirds of the crust, has P- and S-wave speeds corresponding to those of granitic rocks. The speeds increase slightly in the bottom third of the continent, corresponding to rocks of basaltic composition. The average oceanic crust is 11 kilometers thick and is of basaltic composition. Beneath both continental and oceanic crust, the P- and S-wave speeds increase sharply. This boundary between the crust and mantle is called the Mohorovičić discontinuity, or Moho. The Moho marks a compositional change to a dense, ultramafic rock called peridotite.

At an average depth of 100 kilometers, the S-wave speed decreases abruptly. It remains low for about 100-150 kilometers. This region is called the low velocity zone (LVZ). Laboratory experiments have shown that seismic-wave speeds, particularly those of S waves, decrease in rocks containing some liquid. The LVZ in the mantle indicates a zone of partial melting, perhaps 1-10 percent melt. The presence of the melt reduces the overall strength of the rock, giving the region its name, "asthenosphere," from the Greek *asthenes*, meaning "without strength."

The partially molten asthenosphere is very mobile, allowing the more rigid lithosphere above it to move about the earth's surface. The boundary between the lithosphere and the asthenosphere does not mark a change in composition; it marks a change in the physical properties of the rocks. The lithosphere defines this region of crust and mantle from the mantle region below by its seismic-wave speeds and its physical properties.

Seismic-wave speeds and earthquake distribution provide information about the lithospheric plates and the boundaries between them. Like the earth's crust, lithospheric plates are not the same everywhere. For example, the Pacific plate contains primarily oceanic crust, the Eurasian plate is mostly continental, and the North American plate contains both continental and oceanic crust. The lithosphere is thinnest at spreading centers, or regions where two plates are moving away from each other, such as the Mid-Atlantic Ridge and the East Pacific Rise. Here, the asthenosphere is close to the surface and the melt portion pushes upward, separating the plates and creating new lithosphere. Shallow earthquakes occur as the new crust is cracked apart. In areas such as western South America or southern Alaska, two plates are coming together, with the oceanic lithosphere being thrust under the continental plate. Earthquakes occur as deep as 700 kilometers as one plate slides under the other. Along the California coast, two plates slide past each other along faults that cut through the lithosphere. Earthquakes are common, and the faults can move several meters at a time. Where two continental plates, India and Eurasia, have collided, the crust is highly faulted and 65 kilometers thick. Earthquakes in and near the Himalaya are numerous, often occurring along deep fault zones.

Although earthquakes are most common along plate boundaries, they can also occur within lithospheric plates. Some earthquakes are related to newly forming boundaries. The Red Sea is believed to be a recently formed spreading center pushing the Arabian Peninsula and Africa apart. Some earthquakes result from the movement along ancient geologic faults buried within the crust. The causes of some earthquakes, however, such as the one in 1886 in Charleston, South Carolina, remain unknown.

Structural details within plate regions cannot be determined by earthquake studies alone. P and S waves generated by explosions are reflected and refracted by layers within the lithospheric plates. Regional studies show the upper lithosphere to be highly variable. In mountainous regions, such as the Appalachians or the Rocky Mountains, the continental crust is thicker than average and shows much layering. In the midcontinent and the Gulf of Mexico regions, the crust consists of thick layers of sediments and sedimentary rocks. Oil companies, combining the data from many controlled explosions, discovered petroleum and natural gas within these layers from the changes in P- and S-wave speeds. Other regional seismic studies have found ancient geological features deep within the crust. Similarities in the seismic structure between these and other known features can uncover potential sites of much-needed natural resources. The discovery of the oil fields of northern Alaska was prompted by the area's structural similarity to the Gulf of Mexico, a known source of oil and gas.

The seismic structure of the lower lithosphere is less well known. Early studies show that it is also highly variable and that crustal structures are often related to features deep in the lithosphere. Much work, however, remains in unraveling the details of the lithosphere.

Methods of Study

Scientists use a number of seismic techniques to study the lithosphere. They use P and S waves generated by earthquakes that travel through the earth (body waves) and along the earth's surface (surface waves). Reflection and refraction seismology uses seismic waves generated by explosions to study the continental and oceanic lithosphere. Data from experimental studies of rocks are used to relate seismic speeds to specific kinds of rocks. Computers help analyze the vast amounts of seismic data and are used to develop models to aid in the understanding of the earth.

The use of P and S waves from earthquakes is the oldest method of studying earth structure. The time at which P and S body waves, reflected and refracted by the layers in the earth, arrive at different distances from the same earthquake is related to the average speed at which the waves travel. The arrival time of surface waves also depends on the layer speeds. Using seismic waves from many earthquakes, seismologists can determine the seismic structure of the lithosphere.

In regions with numerous earthquakes, seismologists record P and S waves using many portable seismographs, instruments that record seismic-wave arrivals. The scientists can then determine a more detailed regional structure. Earthquakes, however, do not occur regularly everywhere on the earth. Until an average regional structure is known, it will be difficult to determine the precise location and time of an earthquake.

Explosions as a source of seismic waves to study crustal structure have been developed and used extensively by the oil industry. With an explosive source, its location and time of detonation can be precisely controlled. Two basic techniques using artificial sources are reflection seismology and refraction seismology. Refraction seismology studies the arrivals of waves that are refracted, or bent, by the layers in the crust. The scientist determines an average velocity structure for an area by recording the time the first waves arrive at receivers located varying distances from the explosion. To determine deep structure, the distance between the explosion and the receivers must be very large. Reflection seismology allows a deeper look into the crust by studying reflections from many different layers. The seismic-wave receivers do not need to be placed as far from the source as they must in refraction studies. The reflection technique combines the results from many explosions, producing a picture of the earth's layers. This method is used extensively in the search for oil and gas. The techniques of reflection and refraction seismology have been applied to the lithosphere. Long reflection and refraction profiles have been acquired over geologically interesting but little-understood regions.

Seismic waves are vibrations traveling around and through the earth. Because of friction, these vibrations eventually stop, and seismic waves no longer travel. Earthquakes and explosions generate waves that vibrate at many frequencies. The earth slows each frequency differently. As a seismic wave travels through different rocks, the shape of its vibrations recorded on a seismograph is related to the properties of the rocks through which it travels. The analysis of seismic waveforms has shown differences between waves generated by earthquakes and by explosions.

To understand the lithosphere, it is necessary to know about rocks. Using a hydraulic press, scientists squeeze rocks in the laboratory to pressures and heat them to temperatures present deep within the earth. They then measure the rock's physical properties at these conditions. Experimentally measured P and S speeds are compared to wave speeds determined from earthquakes and explosions to infer the kind of rocks and the conditions that exist within the earth. The complexity of the lithosphere, however, does not allow simple answers.

To aid the scientists in their studies, computers are used to develop models— simplified representations—of the earth. By making changes in the model, the scientist can study changes in computed seismic properties and compare them to the observed earth properties. Changes in the model are made to resemble the earth more closely. In modeling the lithosphere, scientists incorporate data from a wide range of sources, such as earthquake studies, experimental rock studies, and geologic maps. The computer allows the earth scientist to test more complex models in an effort to provide a better understanding of the lithosphere.

Context

Understanding the seismic structure of the lithosphere helps in understanding nature. The movement of the lithospheric plates about the earth creates mountain ranges, causes earthquakes, and devours ocean basins. Because much of the earth is inaccessible, seismic waves, generated by earthquakes and explosions, are used to look deep within the earth to provide a picture of the earth's structure. For the earth scientist, increased knowledge of the seismic structure of the lithosphere helps in unraveling the processes by which geologic features are formed.

Increased knowledge of the lithosphere is important to the average person for three reasons: First, earthquakes are caused by movements between and within the lithospheric plates. Every year, lives are lost and millions of dollars in damage occur because of earthquakes and earthquake-related phenomena. Detailed knowledge of the lithosphere helps scientists understand where and how earthquakes occur. This information can lead to regional assessment of the potential for earthquakes and earthquake-related damage. Knowledge of the earthquake potential of a region can result in the improvement of local building codes and the evaluation of existing emergency preparedness plans. Earthquake-hazard assessment can also aid in prediction by determining the probability of future earthquake occurrence. Some success in long-term predictions has been seen in Japan and China. Eventually, the increased understanding of the lithosphere may lead to the short-term prediction of earthquakes.

Second, detailed knowledge of lithospheric structure will lead to the discovery of potential sites of needed natural resources, such as oil, gas, and coal; metals, such as iron, aluminum, copper, and zinc; and nonmetal resources, such as stone, gravel, clay, and salt. Scientists are beginning to unravel the relationship of tectonic features to the formation of many mineral deposits. Detailed knowledge of the structure of the lithosphere from seismic studies can uncover deeply buried features that may provide new sources for critically needed resources.

Finally, in the interest of preserving life on earth and the earth itself, better knowledge of the lithosphere can lead to a nuclear test ban treaty. Scientists require detailed information on the seismic structure of the lithosphere to locate and identify earthquakes and nuclear explosions. More structural information will also lead to better identification of the differences between these two types of seismic wave sources. An accurate and reliable means of distinguishing between earthquakes and nuclear explosions is critical for the verification of any nuclear test ban treaty.

Bibliography

Bakun, William A., et al. "Seismology." *Reviews of Geophysics* 25 (July, 1987): 1131-1214. A series of articles summarizing research in seismology in the United States from 1983 to 1986. Reviews recent findings and unresolved problems in all areas of seismology. Articles are somewhat technical but suitable for the informed reader. Extensive bibliographies.

Bolt, Bruce A. *Earthquakes*. New York: W. H. Freeman, 1988. A popular, illustrated book on the many features of earthquakes. Chapter topics include the use of earthquake waves to study the earth's interior and earthquake prediction. A bibliography and index are included. Suitable for the layperson.

Bullen, K. E., and B. A. Bolt. *An Introduction to the Theory of Seismology*. 4th ed. New York: Cambridge University Press, 1985. Introductory sections of most chapters provide historical and nonmathematical insight into the subject, suitable for the general reader. Contains a selected bibliography, references, and an index. (Designed as a text for the advanced student with a mathematics background.)

Mutter, John C. "Seismic Images of Plate Boundaries." *Scientific American* 254 (February, 1986): 66-75. An article on the application of explosion seismology to the study of plate boundaries. Summarizes the method of seismic reflection profiling. Shows results of studies across different plate boundaries. Well illustrated. Suitable for the general reader.

Pitman, Walter C. "Plate Tectonics." In *McGraw-Hill Encyclopedia of the Geological Sciences*. New York: McGraw-Hill, 1978. A brief summary of plate tectonics, discussing evidence for the theory and an explanation of causes of present-day features. Cross-referenced, illustrated, with bibliography. Suitable for the general reader.

Press, Frank, and Raymond Siever. *Earth*. 4th ed. San Francisco: W. H. Freeman, 1986. A book for the beginning reader in geology. Of interest are chapter 17, "Seismology and the Earth's Interior," and chapter 19, "Global Plate Tectonics: The Unifying Model," for an overall understanding of the importance of the lithosphere. Illustrated and supplemented with numerous marginal notes. Chapter bibliographies and glossary.

Smith, Peter J., ed. *The Earth*. New York: Macmillan, 1986. A well-illustrated, comprehensive guide to the earth sciences for the general reader. Chapter 3, "Internal Structure," describes historical development of the current view of the earth's lithosphere. Chapters 1, 2, and 5 provide related material. Includes glossary of terms.

Thomson, Ker C. "Seismology." In *McGraw-Hill Encyclopedia of the Geological Sciences*. New York: McGraw-Hill, 1978. A brief summary of the principles of seismology. Discusses methods of determining earth structure and of detecting nuclear explosions and describes related research. Cross-referenced and illustrated, with bibliography. Suitable for the interested general reader.

Pamela R. Justice

Cross-References

LITHOSPHERIC PLATES

Type of earth science: Geology
Field of study: Tectonics

Lithospheric plates are large, distinct, platelike segments of brittle rock. They are composed of upper mantle material and oceanic or continental crust. The seven major and numerous minor plates fit together to form the outer crust of the earth.

Principal terms

ASTHENOSPHERE: a layer of the mantle in which temperature and pressure have increased to the point that rocks have very little strength and flow readily

DENSITY: the mass of a given volume of material as compared to an equal volume of water

FELSIC: rocks composed of the lighter-colored feldspars, such as granite

ISOSTASY: the balance of all large portions of the earth's surface when floating on a denser material

LITHOSPHERE: the outermost portion of the globe, including the mantle above the asthenosphere

MAFIC: rocks composed of dark, heavy iron-bearing minerals such as olivine and pyroxene

MANTLE: the layer of the earth between the crust and the outer core

Summary of the Phenomenon

The lithosphere is the sphere of stone or outer crust of the earth. It is composed of seven major platelike segments and numerous smaller ones. These lithospheric plates fit together in jigsaw-puzzle fashion. The recognition of the existence of these plates and their distinct boundaries has led to the theories of plate tectonics and continental drift.

Lithospheric plates are layered. The bottom layer is the rigid upper portion of the mantle. The upper mantle is composed of dense, grayish green, iron-rich rock. Some plates have another solid layer of oceanic crust. This crustal rock is composed primarily of basalt. Some plates consist of only upper mantle and a thin covering of oceanic crust, while other plates have mantle material, oceanic crust, and continental crust. The continental crust is primarily granitic and is less dense than the basalt of the oceanic crust. Until recently, it was assumed that all plates had a continuous layer of oceanic crust and that continental crust was an additional layer, riding on the top. That no longer appears to be the case. The continental crust may be underlain by areas of oceanic crust in a discontinuous fashion, but the two crustal types are actually complexly intermingled.

The upper crustal rocks range from 12 kilometers thick over the ocean plains to more than 30 kilometers thick on the continental masses. The Mohorovičić discontinuity defines the boundary between the crust and upper mantle. This boundary is recognized because sound waves, called seismic waves, suddenly accelerate at this boundary. The lithospheric plates, including the rigid upper mantle, are 75 to 150 kilometers thick. They float on the asthenosphere, which is a deeper portion of the mantle. The rock of the asthenosphere is under such pressure and increased temperature that it has little strength and can readily flow in much the same fashion as warm candle wax. The contact between the plates and the asthenosphere is marked by a sudden decrease in the speed of seismic waves.

The ability of the lithospheric plates to float on the asthenosphere is a key to understanding them. In much the same way that ice floats on water, the plates float on the material below them. Ice is able to float because it is less dense than water. As ice forms, it crystallizes and expands to fill more space. A given volume of ice has less density than the same volume of water. The density of the different layers of the earth increases toward the solid iron and nickel core. The lower mantle floats on the outer core, the asthenosphere floats on the lower mantle, and the lithospheric plates float on the asthenosphere.

The plates fit together along margins. There are generally considered to be only three types of plate margin: ridges, trenches, and transform faults. Ridges, such as the Mid-Atlantic Ridge, are characterized by rifts or spreading centers. Trenches are margins where one plate is being forced below another and are the deepest areas of the ocean floor. Transform faults, such as the San Andreas fault in California, are areas where two plates are sliding alongside each other. The complex interactions of the lithospheric plates have led to the formation of the continents as they now exist. The plate margins do not necessarily follow the continental outlines. Continents may be composed of more than one plate. All the rocks and minerals that are on or near the surface are located on these plates. Geologic processes such as mountain building, earthquakes, and volcanism can be observed at or near the plate margins.

Both types of crustal material, oceanic and continental, form through crystallization. This process is dependent on time, temperature, and pressure. As a molten material cools, a complex series of reactions occurs. The denser minerals crystallize early in the cooling of a molten material. If there is sufficient time in the cooling process, these early-formed dense minerals will gradually react with the remaining molten materials to form less dense minerals.

At the ridge margin of a plate, molten rock rises to the surface as two plates spread apart. The cold ocean waters cool the molten material that wells up. The dense minerals with small crystals are all that form from the molten rock. The mafic material thus formed is called basalt and is welded onto the oceanic crust. Molten material does not always reach the surface rapidly, as it does in a volcanic eruption or at a sea-floor spreading center. In many cases, molten rock will well up under a resistant rock layer and rise no farther. Since it did not reach the surface, it cannot cool quickly. When this occurs, the dense mafic minerals again form first. In this case, however, they have time to react further with the molten rock. As the cooling slowly proceeds, the felsic minerals begin to crystallize. Given sufficient cooling time, a less dense rock such as granite will form. Because it is less dense, the granite takes up more volume than an equal weight of basalt and becomes the major component of continental crust.

The same molten material, depending upon the time that it has to cool, can form either the mafic basalts of the oceanic crust or the granitic continental crust material. If a lithospheric plate composed of continental crust collides with a plate composed of oceanic crust, the plate with the continental crust will ride up over the denser oceanic crust, forming a trench margin. An area where the oceanic crust is pushed below continental crust in this fashion is called a subduction zone.

When two plates of continental material collide, neither can be subducted. If they do not begin to slide alongside each other, the compressive forces will form mountains. These mountains cannot rise higher than their isostatic balance. They must either be eroded by wind and water or sink back into the asthenosphere. The eroded pieces of rock, called sediment, are transported to lower areas called basins. As the sediment becomes more deeply buried, the pressure of overlying sediments causes them to lithify or become sedimentary rock. These sedimentary rocks have considerable pore space between the individual grains of sediment or silt and therefore are not very dense. They become additional continental crust material.

If the sedimentary rocks are buried deeply enough, the pressure and increased temperature will begin a process called metamorphism. The rock begins to grow larger crystals. The metamorphic process is temperature- and pressure-dependent. With enough heat and pressure, it is possible to metamorphose the sedimentary rock back into granite. Eroded sediments also become soils that provide nutrition for plants. The plants in turn give off oxygen and create a breathable atmosphere.

The continental crust is the most observable of the two crustal types. What is known about it by far exceeds what is known about oceanic crust. Theories that adequately explained the crustal processes do not explain what has recently been learned about the ocean floors.

The composition of the lithospheric plates includes most of the known minerals and rocks. The plates together form the sphere of stone that is the earth's surface. The interactions of the plates create some of the most impressive of the geologic phenomena, from earthquakes to volcanoes.

Methods of Study

Lithospheric plates fit together to form the crust or rock surfaces of the earth. The study of the surface of the earth and its composition is an extremely broad subject. It includes many of the subdisciplines of geology and oceanography. The study of the earth's surface and extraction of economic minerals have existed since mankind's earliest times. Flint or obsidian used in toolmaking were early trade items. Mining geology and mineralogy are almost as old. The early Greeks and Romans wrote books on geology.

Humans have used minerals and the metallic minerals since prehistory. Much knowledge of the earth is essentially a by-product of what was learned during the search for minerals, mineral ores, and gems. Something as simple as the formation of a nail requires iron ore and carbon. Mining geologists assay ores looking for economic deposits, and mineralogists study minerals.

Geophysicists bounce sound waves through the earth to determine subsurface structures. With the use of seismographs, they listen to earthquakes to pinpoint their locations. They also measure the gravity and magnetic field of specific areas of the earth. Petroleum geologists search for oil and gas by drilling into the earth's surface. Their interpretation of drill cuttings and core samples provides information about ancient environments. Volcanologists study volcanoes. They employ lasers to measure any minute movements on the surface of a volcano. They also use seismographs to detect the earthquakes that may signal an onset of volcanic activity. Because of the potential devastation of volcanoes, prediction has become increasingly important. Petrologists examine rocks to understand the earth processes that formed them. Their primary tools are the scanning electron microscope and X-ray diffraction machines.

Geochemists analyze the chemical composition of rocks and minerals and the reactions that may have caused their formation and dissolution. Paleontologists study fossilized life forms, while paleoecologists study ancient environments. Planetary scientists investigate meteorites and moon rocks to increase understanding of the earth and its lithospheric plates. Much of what is known about the mantle material is a result of the study of meteorites.

Much early geologic work was done on the more readily accessible continental crust. Recently, scientists have made considerable progress in the study of the oceanic crust. Early exploration of the ocean floor was through simple depth measurements from ships. Sailors lowered a weighted line over the side of a ship and physically measured the depth to the sea floor. The echo sounders developed in the early 1900's allowed for more rapid measurements of the ocean depths. In time, continuous profiles of the sea floor were made. Instead of the featureless plain that was expected, oceanic ridges, deep trenches, and numerous submerged volcanoes appeared.

Dredging is an old but ongoing method of sampling the surface of the ocean floor. The deep-diving bathysphere paved the way for bathyscaphes and other high-technology submersibles. Much recent work has been done with television cameras. A major find was made by a geologist in the late 1970's. A sea-floor volcanic vent actually had life forms subsisting on the chemically rich waters near it. Until this time, it had been assumed that all life on the earth was dependent on photosynthesis. This initial television discovery of chemosynthetic life forms shocked the scientific community.

Drilling on the ocean floor has been accomplished by drill ships such as the *Glomar Challenger*. The cores of the deep ocean floor indicated a much younger oceanic crust than had been expected. Much that was learned about the oceanic crust simply did not fit with the scientific theories of the day. Serious rethinking had to be done, and many theories had to be radically changed.

Context

Lithospheric plates are the brittle rocks that float on the hot, plastic asthenosphere. They fit together to form the crust of the earth. Each step people take is either on the surface of a lithospheric plate or on something that is directly or indirectly made from one. Weathered surface rock provides the soil in which plants grow. The plants provide a breathable atmosphere and sustain animal life. The interaction of lithospheric plates leads to earthquakes, volcanic activity, and tidal waves. These impressive geologic displays have caught man's imagination since earliest times.

Since the lithospheric plates form the solid surface of the earth, in a real sense everything humans touch is related to them. Even something as unlikely as plastic is made from petroleum products extracted from the earth's crustal rocks. Coal, oil, and gas are burned to provide heat and electricity. Minerals extracted from lithospheric plates become the gold that makes jewelry, crowns teeth, and is part of circuit boards and computer chips. The minerals and compounds extracted from the lithospheric plates provide the iron for skyscrapers, cars, and car fuel. The coal, oil, and gas are formed by complex interactions of ancient plant life during the rock-forming processes that have occurred during the formation of upper portions of the lithospheric plates. The surface of the earth and its ongoing geologic processes also affect the weather.

The study of the composition and motion of lithospheric plates has created nearly all the body of knowledge in the field of geology. Numerous subdisciplines have arisen to study specific areas of geology. Study of the oceanic crust is relatively new, and recent discoveries are changing commonly accepted views of the earth. As views change, more discoveries seem to become possible. As more is learned about the earth's surface, views must be altered and upgraded to explain the phenomena observed.

Bibliography

Glen, William. *Continental Drift and Plate Tectonics*. Columbus, Ohio: Charles E. Merrill, 1975. A college-level introductory text, this volume covers the concepts of lithospheric plates and their formation and motion. Although technical, the material is introduced in a fashion that does not require a background in geology. Includes a very good index and an extensive supplementary-reading reference section.

Gross, M. Grant. *Oceanography*. 2d ed. Columbus, Ohio: Charles E. Merrill, 1971. Designed as an introductory-course text in oceanography for the college student. The first three chapters discuss oceanic plates and the sea floor, or oceanic crust. The historical section on sea-floor study and current methodology is valuable, as is the index and an extensive supplementary reading list.

Marvin, Ursula B. *Continental Drift*. Washington, D.C.: Smithsonian Institution Press, 1973. Taking a historical approach, Marvin provides considerable discussion of plates and plate theory, covering old theories and explaining their progression toward new ones; includes discussion of the views that disagree with current theory. Index and extensive bibliography. For college-level readers.

Miller, Russell. *Planet Earth: Continents in Collision*. Alexandria, Va.: Time-Life Books, 1983. A clear and excellently illustrated introduction to lithospheric plates and plate tectonics. Extensive historical background is provided, and the concepts are introduced in a logical fashion. Good index and extensive bibliography. For advanced high school and college readers.

Walker, Bryce. *Geology Today*. 10th ed. Del Mar, Calif.: Ziff-Davis, 1974. An excellent introductory text for the study of lithospheric plates, crustal rocks, plate movement, and geologic processes. The progression of concepts is clear and logical, and the volume is exceptionally well illustrated and indexed. The bibliography includes listings of other technical reference books.

_____. *Planet Earth: Earthquake*. Alexandria, Va.: Time-Life Books, 1982. Offers some exceptional illustrations of lithospheric plates. Chapter 5, "Dreams of Knowing When and Where," contains a good discussion of equipment and methodology used to determine plate movement. Well indexed, with a good bibliography for additional reading. For high school and introductory college students.

_____. *Planet Earth: Volcano*. Alexandria, Va.: Time-Life Books, 1982. Although much of this book is about the surface effects of volcanoes, there are several technical sections. Focus is primarily on the formation of the basaltic portions of lithospheric plates. The methodology discussed in chapter 5, "Monitoring the Earth's Heartbeat," is particularly valuable. Good index and bibliography.

Raymond U. Roberts

Cross-References

Continental Crust, 261; Continental Growth, 268; Continental Rift Zones, 275; The Lithosphere, 1380; Ocean Basins, 1785; The Ocean Ridge System, 1826; The Oceanic Crust, 1846; Plate Margins, 2063; Plate Motions, 2071; Plate Tectonics, 2079; Subduction and Orogeny, 2497.

LUNAR CRATERS

Type of earth science: Planetology
Field of study: Large solar system bodies

Most lunar craters are the erosion scars of debris left over from the origin of the solar system colliding at high velocities with the surface of the moon. Studies of the sizes and time distributions of lunar impact craters allow scientists to make estimates of the same process acting on the earth, where much of the evidence has been removed by erosion. Volcanic craters enable researchers to determine the eruption characteristics and thermal evolution of the moon.

Principal terms

BASIN: a large (greater than a 350-kilometer diameter on the moon) impact crater; some restrict the term to craters with multiple rings forming a bull's-eye pattern

CALDERA: a circular depression of volcanic origin, greater than 1 kilometer in diameter

EJECTA: the material excavated by an impact event and deposited around and within a crater; some may be ejected at a sufficiently high velocity to escape the lunar gravitational field

REGOLITH: (from the Greek, meaning "blanket stone") a thin layer of fragmented rock material at the surface of the moon

SECONDARY CRATER: a crater resulting from impact of material thrown out of a primary impact crater

SINUOUS RILLE: a riverlike channel produced by lava flowing across the lunar surface

SPECTROSCOPY: the science of determining the absorption or radiation characteristics of electromagnetic radiation at specific wavelengths

Summary of the Phenomenon

All of the large lunar craters are named; many of these names are attributable to a 1651 publication by Giambattista Riccioli in which they appear on a map drawn by P. Grimaldi. Riccioli divided the nearside of the moon into octants. This map was drawn with the aid of the "Galilean" rather than the "astronomical" telescope so was not inverted. On this map, Octant 1 extended from the ten o'clock to just past the eleven o'clock position and was succeeded clockwise by the other seven octants. The craters were named for astronomers, beginning with the most ancient in Octant 1 and concluding with Riccioli's contemporaries in Octant 8. This practice has continued to the present, with the restriction that a crater is named for a scientist no longer living.

Lunar craters are of three origins. There are those directly excavated by the impact of a meteorite, there are those called secondaries that result from the impact of material excavated to form the crater of the primary meteorite impact, and there are those of volcanic origin. Up until the return of lunar samples, the scientific community had been sharply divided into those who believed the majority of lunar craters to be of impact origin and those who believed the majority to be volcanic in origin. The evidence gained as a result of the Apollo missions has established that the vast majority of lunar craters are of impact origin, resulting from collisions of the moon with meteors, asteroids, comets, and minor planets at velocities of from 5 to 50 kilometers per second (10,000 to 100,000 miles per hour).

No one has counted the total number of lunar craters, as they range in size from the microscopic to the giant (2,500 kilometers in diameter) South Pole-Aitken basin. It has been estimated that there are about 1,850,000 craters with diameters in excess of 1 kilometer on the lunar surface and 125 with diameters greater than 100 kilometers. A 3,200-kilometer-diameter Procellarum basin has been tentatively identified which, if placed over a map of the United States, would stretch from Washington, D.C., to western Utah and from Brownsville, south Texas, up into central Canada. At the other end of the scale, microscopic impact craters are produced on the moon because of the lack of a lunar atmosphere. Similar-sized particles rapidly burn up in the earth's atmosphere.

Primary impact craters increase in morphological complexity with increasing size. Small craters are bowl-shaped, with a well-defined, generally circular rim, smooth interior walls, and have a depth-to-diameter ratio of one-fifth to one-sixth. The floor of a fresh crater is invariably at a lower elevation than the preexisting terrain. The rim of the crater is surrounded by a generally circular continuous ejecta blanket, followed outward by the discontinuous ejecta blanket. This discontinuous ejecta often takes the form of rays that radiate outward from a zone close to the center of the primary impact site. An exception is found in craters produced by oblique impacts. These craters are generally elongate and have ejecta blankets preferentially distributed downrange or exhibiting a bilateral symmetry, with "wings" on either side of the crater.

An abrupt change in the crater's shape takes place at a diameter of about 16 kilometers in the maria (dark lava expanses) and 21 kilometers in the highlands. At larger diameters, craters develop terraces on the interior walls, have a generally broad, level floor interrupted by small hills and mounds, develop a central peak, have a less uniform rim elevation, and have a depth-to-diameter ratio reduced to about one-fortieth. Flows and ponds, which are often seen both within and exterior to these craters, are impact melts resulting from liquefaction of the impactor and target rocks. At diameters in excess of 140 kilometers, the central peak becomes modified into a centralized peak ring. At diameters in excess of 350 kilometers, multiple rings of alternating elevated and depressed terrains—the giant multiring basins—are witnessed.

Secondary impact craters are generally less regular than primaries because they are formed at lower collisional velocities, an upper limit being the lunar escape velocity of 2.4 kilometers per second, at which speed objects ejected from the surface would leave the moon's gravitational field. The size of the secondaries is largely dependent on the size of the primary. The largest secondary has a diameter of between 2 and 5 percent of that of the primary. Generally, secondaries have smooth interior profiles and are shallower than primaries of the same diameter. They also differ from primaries in that their distribution is nonrandom. They frequently occur in linear or curving chains, patches, or clusters surrounding the primary. Another common feature of secondaries is the presence of a herringbone pattern produced by small ridges ploughed up by impacting objects closely spaced in both time and distance. The apex of the V shape points back toward the primary.

Many large lunar craters were once considered to be analogous to terrestrial calderas. Calderas form as a result of collapse following evacuation of a large, near-surface magma chamber. Analyses of returned lunar volcanic materials established, however, that they were derived from great depths (150-400 kilometers), with little evidence for residence at shallow levels for any extended periods. True lunar volcanic craters are primarily recognized on the basis of their distribution, which, like that of secondaries, is nonrandom. Volcanic or endogenic (of internal origin) craters are found at the summits of volcanic domes and cones, at the heads of sinuous rilles, or in association with linear fractures. The craters are generally small (less than 20 kilometers in diameter) and have outlines that range from circular to elliptical or highly irregular. Some volcanic craters are surrounded by a halo of dark surface deposits believed to consist of pyroclastic materials ejected during strombolian- or vulcanian-style eruptions.

Impact craters are the product of an instantaneous geologic event, yet the lunar surface has been subjected to the formation of these features for at least the last 4.2 billion years. Many lunar craters have thus become highly modified from their original pristine form. Since the moon lacks an atmosphere, this modification results primarily from two agents: later impacts and volcanism. An impact has two principal effects. First, it will result in the total or partial obliteration of any crater smaller than itself that was located within the area of the younger crater. Second, ejecta from the younger crater will erode the walls and infill the floors of craters surrounding itself. At the extreme, the ejecta deposits could totally infill the pre-existing surrounding craters. The net result of this process is that older craters are shallower than are newer ones of similar size. The effects of volcanism on impact craters are largely restricted to areas around and within the major maria. A commonly held misconception is that an impact event can trigger the release of magma from the lunar interior. Although the relationship between depth and diameter of the large basins is a subject of much debate, there are very few who believe that the original impact cavities extended to a depth greater than that of the lunar crustal thickness of 75 kilometers. Moreover, there is good evidence that volcanism within any single large basin extended over a time frame of several hundred million years—which is difficult to reconcile with an instantaneous impact event. The reason for the association of volcanic material with impact craters is that the crater floors are topographic lows and closer to the part of the interior from which the volcanic materials were derived.

One feature attributed to volcanic modification of impact craters is the presence of floor fractures. These features are primarily found on the level floors of craters with diameters of 30 to about 100 kilometers and consist of radial and concentric, spider-web-like arrangements of fractures. They are attributed to uplift of the crater floor by subfloor intrusions of magma. Some of these magma bodies found outlets to the surface and, with limited volcanic output, resulted in the formation of volcanic dark-halo craters aligned along the floor fractures. The crater Alphonsus is a typical example. With more extensive volcanism, the floor of the crater becomes flooded with lava until even the central peak becomes buried. At this point, there is too thick an overlying lava pile, and the magma seeks alternative routes to the surface around the periphery of the crater. Some craters have experienced post-flooding floor fracturing, which results from the sinking of the dense, thick lava pile or posteruptive intrusion, leading to renewed uplift. Flooding of the larger basins appears to have begun within the central low and later extended to the topographic lows between the mountain rings. Small impact craters were constantly being created during the period of basin filling. Many of these craters were either partially or totally covered by younger lava flows.

Methods of Study

Because impact craters are instantaneous events, they are superb geologic time markers. Any material on which an impact crater and its ejecta are superposed is older than the crater; any material overlapping the crater or its ejecta is younger. Analysis of these relationships led to the development of the lunar stratigraphic column consisting of five systems. The pre-Nectarian system, comprising all lunar surface features, formed prior to excavation of the Nectaris basin and succeeding systems defined by formation of the Imbrium basin and the Eratosthenes and Copernicus craters.

Primary impact crater densities indicate the relative ages of different units on the lunar surface: the more craters, the older the surface. Craters employed in such studies are usually larger than 4 kilometers in diameter, and the densities are obtained by the extremely tedious task of simply counting them on a photograph. Crater density divided by the average crater-production rate gives the approximate absolute age of the surface units. In the case of the moon, a calibration curve for production rate can be obtained by comparing the radiometric age of samples returned from the landing sites with the crater-count statistics of those sites. These data indicate an exponential decline in crater production from about 4 billion years ago to the present. The details of crater production prior to about 4 billion years are the subject of debate but, because most of the lunar surface postdates this period, the debate is of little relevance to age determinations.

Small craters (less than 3 kilometers in diameter) have also been used for dating purposes. These techniques are based on the fact that the morphologies of small craters are modified in a consistent manner with time. One of these, called the D_L

method, is based on the interior slope of the crater. As craters become progressively infilled, the length of the shadow cast by the rim decreases. For a given illumination angle, it is therefore possible to define the largest crater within an area that has reached a specified shadow limit. If a crater in another area is wider than the limit, the second area is older.

The predictable depth-diameter relationships of fresh impact craters allow the determination of some of the third-dimensional characteristics of lunar surface features. If a crater has been flooded by a younger lava flow, the extent of departure of that crater from the dimensions of a similarly sized fresh crater can be employed to determine the thickness of the lava (or other material). The effectiveness of this method is limited by the accuracy of the topographic data.

The material forming the lunar highlands has a different composition from that of the maria and results in pronounced spectroscopic differences. By analyzing the spectroscopic signatures of ejecta blankets of craters superposed on the lunar maria, it is possible to determine if a crater excavated solely basaltic material or if it penetrated into the crust beneath. The depth-diameter relationship of the crater can then be employed to ascertain the mare thickness.

Mineralogical and geochemical analyses of returned lunar samples have played a large role in scientists' understanding of the physical processes involved during an impact event. Indirectly, lunar craters have also provided information on the deep lunar interior, because the impacts of both natural and man-made objects have generated seismic waves recorded by the Apollo seismic network.

Context

The heavily cratered surface of the moon provides a scenario for what was also taking place at a time for which scientists have no rock record for the earth. They have learned that, the farther back in time, the number of objects that hit the moon increases exponentially until around 4 billion years ago. In addition, the study of lunar craters has influenced the conceptualization that meteorite impacts may have played a role in terrestrial mass extinctions and thereby the evolution of life. It has been suggested that because the moon contains so many craters, a large number of age determinations of the impact events could provide information concerning a hypothesized correlation between impact bombardment and cyclic extinctions. Analyses of the sizes and distribution of volcanic craters have provided data concerning the internal thermal evolution of the moon and the stress distributions within the upper lunar crust. In addition, study of the morphologies of impact craters allows scientists to determine the effects of impacts within a gravitational field one-sixth that of the earth and on a body with no atmosphere. Much of the work by Ralph Baldwin in formulating the characteristics of impact craters was based on data from small terrestrial man-made explosions. Scientists are now able to predict fairly accurately the consequences of very large explosions on land, into water, or in space as a result of lunar impact crater studies.

It has been suggested that the permanently shadowed floors of some near-polar craters may be reservoirs for trapped volatiles such as water. Such resources, if present, would play an important role in the location of a manned lunar base. Furthermore, impact craters have played the major role in forming the lunar regolith. This loosely aggregated material could be mined with limited mechanical processing. Conversely, the myriad craters on the lunar surface pose a major hazard for safe surface travel and will probably result in unavoidable detours for initial manned expeditions. Both structures and persons would have to be protected against the small impacting bodies that rain onto the lunar surface but from which humans are shielded by the earth's atmosphere.

Bibliography

Baldwin, R. A. *The Measure of the Moon*. Chicago: University of Chicago Press, 1963. The first nine chapters outline the characteristics of both lunar and terrestrial, man-made, and natural craters. Written in pre-metric-system times, it requires mathematical (though simple) conversions. Suitable for advanced high school and college students.

Basaltic Volcanism Study Project. *Basaltic Volcanism on the Terrestrial Planets*. Elmsford, N.Y.: Pergamon Press, 1981. Chapter 8 provides a detailed account of the derivation of surface ages of the various bodies of the solar system by impact crater analyses. College-level and above.

Melosh, H. J. *Impact Cratering: A Geologic Process*. New York: Oxford University Press, 1989. A good synthesis of research information related to the impact process. Mathematics separated out in text and in two appendices. Aimed at graduate student and research audiences.

Merrill, R. B., and P. H. Schultz, eds. *Multiring Basins*. Elmsford, N.Y.: Pergamon Press, 1981. The proceedings of a conference devoted to analysis of the large impact structures on the various planets and satellites. Twenty separate articles. Well-indexed. Research-level only.

Roddy, D. J., R. O. Pepin, and R. B. Merrill, eds. *Impact and Explosion Cratering*. Elmsford, N.Y.: Pergamon Press, 1977. Very thick book devoted to the impact process and its products. Represents a good summary statement of impact cratering work undertaken up until the mid-1970's. Research-level only.

Wilhelms, D. E. *The Geologic History of the Moon*. U.S. Geological Survey Professional Paper 1348. Washington, D.C.: Government Printing Office, 1987. Full of photographs of lunar craters supplemented with an outstanding text based on more than twenty years of lunar geological mapping by the author. Research-level book but understandable to the dedicated high school student. A must-have book for those interested in the moon.

James L. Whitford-Stark

Cross-References

Asteroids, 98; Astroblemes, 106; Comets, 253; Igneous Rock Bodies, 1131; Lunar

LUNAR HISTORY

Type of earth science: Planetology
Field of study: Large solar system bodies

The moon's cratered surface has slowly evolved over the past 4.6 billion years primarily because of meteoritic impact. Observations made by astronomers with ground-based telescopes and by studies carried out by the Apollo project as well as direct studies of moon rocks have revealed much about this formation process.

Principal terms

ANORTHOSITE: a low-density igneous rock, pale yellow in color and consisting mostly of plagioclase, that comprises most of the outer crust of the moon

BASALT: an igneous rock that ranges from light to dark gray in color and consists mostly of plagioclase and several other minerals found in the lunar dark areas called maria

BASINS: circular regions on the moon that are hundreds of kilometers in diameter and are caused by gigantic explosive impacts by large meteorites

BRECCIA: a rock found primarily in the lunar highlands that became "welded" or "cemented" as a result of fusing action caused by the heat of meteoritic impact

DIFFERENTIATION: a process whereby molten rock separates according to density during the early, hot primordial stages of a planet's formation; it formed a double-layered lunar crust

HIGHLANDS: densely cratered regions on the lunar surface, which when seen with the naked eye take on a pale yellow color; they are primarily anorthositic breccia

IGNEOUS ROCK: a rock of volcanic origin that has formed by molten rock cooling and solidifying

IMPACT CRATERS: craters formed by the impacts of meteorites

KREEP-NORITE: a rock formation occupying small regions of the lunar surface, caused by the release of lava from liquid pockets of deep lunar crust as a result of meteoritic impacts

MARIA: dark, mostly circular-shaped basaltic regions on the moon that fill the largest impact craters, called basins, or the low-lying regions around these basins

PROTO-SUN: the sphere of gas that contracted out of interstellar gas between four and five billion years ago to become the sun and planets

Summary of the Phenomenon

The moon's surface has evolved into its present state as a result of meteoritic impact over the eons since the solar system formed. In contrast, the earth's surface has been molded and shaped primarily as a result of geologic activity brought on by heat transfer from its molten core. One can argue that these very different surfaces, the earth's constantly changing, eroding surface and the moon's relatively tranquil, slowly changing surface, are a direct result of the mass or amount of material in the planet. Low-mass planets acquire surfaces with low geological activity, whereas more massive planets continuously undergo a considerable amount of such activity.

As seen from the earth, with a small telescope or even with the unaided eye, two distinct regions on the moon are apparent. The pale yellow regions called the highlands and the gray-blue, roughly circular regions called maria were both named by Galileo in 1609. *Maria* is Latin for "seas" (*mare* is the singular), and Galileo, assuming that the regions he saw were bodies of water, thus named them. Even with the sole aid of binoculars or small telescopes, the moon's largest craters are evident in great numbers. These craters occupy the highland areas and are distinctly rare in the maria.

Virtually without exception, the craters on the moon are impact craters, the result of meteoroids blasting into the moon's surface at speeds equal to or greater than 10 kilometers per second. The largest of these impact craters, called basins, are in some cases multiple, ringlike structures resembling a bull's-eye pattern. The large structures observed in the highlands and borders of the maria that resemble mountain ranges are the rims of these large basin craters. Many of them are identified by the circular dark mare within their crater walls. They are referred to with names such as Mare Imbrium (the Sea of Rains) and Mare Crisium (the Sea of Crises).

As a result of an impact, both the meteoroid and the underlying surface are subject to rapid, intense heating. All the energy of motion must be translated into other forms, namely heat and shock waves, since the motion is brought to an abrupt stop. In a fraction of a second, the outer regions of the meteoroid and some surface material are vaporized, and the resulting high-temperature, dense gas explodes violently. This activity results in a crater surrounded by a rim, composed of most of the material that was ejected from the resulting hole. Beyond the rim, arranged in a sun-burst or spray pattern, is the ejecta blanket.

There are thought to have been six states in the evolution of the moon: the origin of the moon, the separation of the moon's crust, the first age of igneous activity, the great bombardment period, the second age of igneous activity, and the quiescent period. The origin of the moon is the stage that is least understood. Astronomers, physicists, geologists, and mathematicians have struggled and debated over the origin of the moon for at least two centuries. A satisfactory theory has yet to be found, although scientists are reasonably certain about some aspects of origin. The earth and the moon formed about the same time, shortly after the proto-sun (the very early stage of the sun, which contracted by gravity out of interstellar material) some 4.6 billion years ago. The earth and the moon formed relatively near each other (at a distance that is small compared to the distance between planets). This knowledge is based on the chemical composition found in moon rocks and the overall pattern of chemical composition found in moving from the inner to the outer solar system.

A modern hypothesis of the lunar origin is called the large impact hypothesis. It gained favor among scientists and then became subject to intense investigation and scrutiny. The idea is that two large primordial, planet-sized bodies had a brushlike collision, which resulted in the larger of the two spinning off a large ring system and the smaller of the two breaking up within the ring system. Subsequently, the ring system fell partially onto the larger body, completing the formation of the earth and also partially condensed by accretion into the moon. This theory has many features that are consistent with the knowledge that the earth and moon formed near each other and explains the similarity of the earth's crust to the composition of the moon. It also explains why the earth's moon is so much larger in proportion to its parent planet than any other satellite in the solar system.

The second stage of evolution, the differentiation of the crust, occurred during the early stages of origin, when the moon was still molten in its outer layers. This condition occurred from the heat of formation and was prolonged by constant bombardment of meteorites striking the moon's outer layers. In this early stage of the solar system, much debris was still in the form of a complex set of rings around the sun. Chunks of the debris, composed of meteoroids, fell onto the surfaces of the moon and other planets. These meteoritic showers were especially furious and frequent in the early solar system.

Since the outer layers of the moon were molten, the lighter minerals tended to float, and the heavier ones tended to sink. This means that heavy igneous material, such as the mineral basalt, would sink, whereas lighter igneous material, such as the mineral anorthosite, would float. The moon's crust differentiated into an igneous shell with an inner zone of basalt and an outer zone of the lower-density igneous rock anorthosite. Nearly all specimens collected by Apollo can be put into three categories: mare basalt, found in the maria; KREEP-norite, with an unusually high content of potassium (K), rare earth elements (REE), and phosphorus (P); and the anorthosite group. The latter two are found in the lunar highlands.

As the moon's surface solidified, several pockets or subsurface pools of KREEP-norite remained molten because of slight differences in chemical composition within the crustal rock. Certain impurities would form crystals with lower melting temperatures and thus remain liquid. Some of the darker shades of pale yellow rock highland material, surrounding the maria, are KREEP. Coincidentally, meteorites struck above some of these liquid pockets and fractured the solid rock. The cracks and fractures formed would occasionally lead to one of these pools, and the release in pressure would cause the liquid to "creep out" onto the surface. This episode of igneous activity is the third stage of lunar evolution.

Continuously during the first 500 million years and the first four stages, meteorites of all sizes struck the moon. The largest impacts formed multirimmed supercraters, hundreds of kilometers in diameter, called basins. The meteoroids responsible may have been huge rocks 150 to 200 kilometers in diameter. The fourth stage, the great bombardment period, overlaps all the other stages. Its place-ment in the list is based on the concept that this age is still easily identified by the largest fossil craters still visible today. Earlier bombardments have had their craters obliterated by more recent impacts. Many of the largest craters observed in the highlands date back to impacts during this period. This is also true of many of the large basins, which in turn are often accompanied by the gray-blue colored maria.

Since the mass of the moon is low compared to that of the earth, the moon lost most of its internal heat of formation and the heat provided by radioactive decay in a short time, perhaps less than 800 million years after its origin. The earth, being eighty-one times more massive than the moon, has retained much of its heat, as a result of radioactive decay in its interior. Although the moon still has a molten core, it does not transfer a substantial heat flow to the surface, as it once did.

Between 3.8 and 3.1 billion years ago, then, only the lower basaltic strata of the separated crust was heated. The largest impacts, slightly after and during this stage, formed large fractures that in some cases reached down to the lower basaltic lay-ers. This allowed the heated (turned molten) basalt to flow as lava to the surface and fill in the low-lying areas in and around the basins. This accounts for the gray-blue basaltic maria. All these maria have generally circular shapes, with one exception, the Ocean of Storms. This pancake shape is what one would expect from flows into large, almost circular craters. Since basalt has a higher density than anortho-site, these pancaked lava flows have been detected by the effect their gravity has on satellites orbiting the moon. As a result of their localized pull of gravity, they have been named mascons (mass concentrations).

These events mark the second great igneous period. The flow of basalt onto the lunar surface apparently came in stages, since astrogeologists can identify younger flows atop older flows. The age of the flows can be identified by comparing the frequency of impact craters found in the flows and also the wrinkle structures in the maria that identify the border of a flow. Finally, after the first 1 billion years, the igneous activity ceased and impacts gradually became less frequent. This quiescent period lasted more than 3 billion years to the present time.

All the features on the moon's surface can be shown to be caused by impacts—directly, as in the case of a crater, or indirectly, as in the case of KREEP or a mare. There are no mountains on the moon. All the mountainlike features are partial or quite complete rims of basins or craters. The partial rims have been obliterated by more recent impacts. Another mountainlike feature often seen at the center of a well-preserved or relatively fresh (young) crater results from the focus of a shock wave reflected and focused by the rim formation during impact back toward the im-pact center. The arrival of the reflected shock wave apparently heaves the center of the crater upward.

The surface of the moon today is covered with a finely pulverized rock called regolith. The regolith varies in depth from 5 to 10 meters in young maria (3.1 billion years old) to perhaps 20 to 25 meters or more in the highlands (more than 4.2 bil-lion years old). The regolith has been formed by the constant churning and mixing from particles impacting through the ages, ranging in size from micrometeorites to meteoroids large enough to form the largest craters. Crater rims, having both a sharp (young) and a rounded, smoothed (old) appearance, are evidence of this same kind of slow erosive process caused by impacts.

Close microscopic inspection of the regolith reveals evidence of impacts and the moon's evolutionary history. The regolith consists of tiny pieces of anorthosite, anorthositic breccia, basalt, basaltic breccia, a variety of glasslike, irregularly shaped particles, and small, spherically shaped glass beads. The glass is believed to be produced by the heat and shock of impact resulting in a fused metamorphic, glasslike rock. The spherical beads result from liquid drops thrown out during the splash of ejection shortly after impact. The drops freeze or solidify before falling back to the surface and are found as small, spherical glass beads.

The dark maria, which are mostly circular in shape, are giant crater rims called basins that formed from titanic impacts, from the leftover debris in the formation of the solar system about 4 or more billion years ago. The maria themselves were the results of lava flows from the deep crust that occurred somewhat after the impacts, between 3.8 and 3.3 billion years ago. Over the past 3.3 billion years, the main changes on the lunar surface have been color changes in the maria. They have been impacted by meteorites ranging in size from dust particles to massive chunks of rock. This bombardment has had the effect of adding various shades of gray to the maria. The white anorthositic breccia is found in the highlands, and the battleship-gray basalt is found in the maria.

One might imagine highly energetic impacts that might have occurred about 4 billion or more years ago. These impacts led to the subsequent mare formation and the formation of the moon's layers as described by the six major stages of lunar evolution. The figure shows a cross section of the lunar interior, noting the various layers discussed in the six stages of lunar evolution. Apollo landing sites were chosen strategically on the basis of obtaining as much information as possible about these layers.

Methods of Study

The Apollo astronauts studied the surface geology of the moon and placed experiments on the lunar surface to study moonquakes in hopes of getting information about the lunar interior. Moon rocks brought back to the earth played a major role, if not the most important role, in the understanding of the evolution of the lunar surface. Fragmented pieces of lunar rock provide many clues to lunar history. Geologists can easily identify several distinct rock types in such a sample. Some of the gray pieces are the well-known igneous rock basalt. Some of the very white pieces are brecciated anorthosite. Breccia is a type of rock that has been fragmented and welded together with immense heat. Other pieces are glasslike substances and still others resemble glass beads. These basic rock types provide an understanding of the evolution of the moon's surface as brought about by eons of meteoritic bombardment. The Apollo studies, together with previous space and ground-based

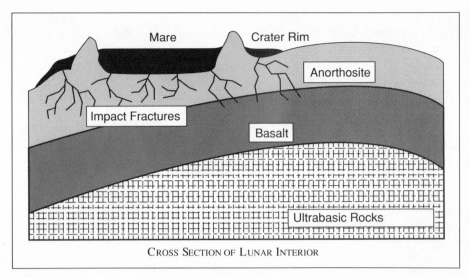

CROSS SECTION OF LUNAR INTERIOR

telescopic studies, have allowed scientists to construct an evolutionary history of the lunar surface.

All lunar samples are geologically processed. Their composition was established by igneous processes inside the moon. No primitive or primordial lunar material (material that existed on the moon's surface soon after the formation of the moon) is likely to have survived the turbulent early history of the moon. Primordial material from which the moon was formed should be about 4.6 billion years old. The earth and moon, moreover, formed in the same general region. This is indicated by the specific abundances of certain types of atoms, especially those of oxygen. Abundances are good indicators of position from the sun in the inner solar system. Lunar and crustal terrestrial rocks have very similar abundances. The overall density of the moon is similar to the density of the earth's crust. This is one of the reasons scientists in the past speculated that the moon came from the earth.

Context

Scientists' knowledge of the history of the lunar surface has helped unravel and untangle the still mysterious circumstances that led to the origin of the solar system, the planets in general, and the earth-moon system in particular. It is important to understand the history of the moon in that it provides information about the history of the earth. Because of the moon's ancient surface, questions that cannot be answered by examining the youthful terrestrial surface have been answered by lunar studies.

Furthermore, detailed studies of lunar rocks have led to a much deeper understanding of the probable chemical composition of the solar nebula and the protosun. This is important not only because it helps explain the process by which the sun and planets formed but also because it provides specific clues and observations that increase scientists' understanding of star formation in general. Astronomers now believe that planetary formation is a natural consequence of star formation because of their studies of the moon's history and its detailed composition.

Anomalous abundances found in both lunar and terrestrial rock of particular chemical elements have led directly to speculations about the origin of the solar system. Some chemicals in the rare earth group strongly indicate that a supernova explosion may have contaminated the gas and dust from which the solar nebula formed with chemical debris from deep within the exploding star. Some astronomers suggest that the shock of the supernova blast wave actually triggered the contraction of the solar nebula into the formation of the sun and planets.

Understanding the lunar surface also has the potential of future exploitation. The moon might someday be used as a space station, an astronomical observatory, or a space colony. The moon would also be an excellent source of minerals, since virtually all lunar rocks are rich in the metal titanium and would supply much more of this metal than could be mined on earth in even the richest deposits.

Bibliography

Abell, George O., David Morrison, and Sidney C. Wolff. *Exploration of the Universe*. 5th ed. Philadelphia: Saunders College Publishing, 1987. This elementary astronomy textbook is considered by many astronomers to be one of the finest available. It is written in a traditional style, and the chapter on the moon includes several good photographs, images, and diagrams.

Briggs, Geoffrey, and Frederick Taylor. *The Cambridge Photographic Atlas of the Planets*. Cambridge, England: Cambridge University Press, 1982. A series of excellent photographs and images taken both from earth-based telescopes and spacecraft. The lunar photographs taken by the Apollo astronauts and the images taken by the Lunar Orbiter spacecraft are particularly striking.

Kaufmann, William J., III. *Discovering the Universe*. New York: W. H. Freeman, 1986. This short volume is intended for introductory astronomy courses of one semester's duration at the college level. The chapter on the moon is very lucid and is filled with spectacular diagrams and photographs.

Kosofsky, L. J., and Farouk El-Baz. *The Moon as Viewed by the Lunar Orbiter*. NASA SP-200. Washington, D.C.: Government Printing Office, 1970. A fine collection of lunar images taken from the Lunar Orbiter satellite series. They consist of both overall global images and selected high resolution detailed images of particular areas on the moon.

Morrison, David, and Tobias Owen. *The Planetary System*. Reading, Mass.: Addison-Wesley, 1987. A very up-to-date textbook at the beginning college level introducing scientific knowledge of the solar system. The chapters on the moon, which concentrate on lunar history and geology, are particularly readable.

Pasachoff, Jay M. *Astronomy: From the Earth to the Universe*. 3d ed. Philadelphia: Saunders College Publishing, 1987. This is one of the finest astronomy textbooks. The presentation and format are visually impressive and very detailed. The chapter on the moon is highly recommended.

Seeds, Michael A. *Foundations of Astronomy.* 2d ed. Belmont, Calif.: Wadsworth, 1988. An extremely well-written textbook. The chapter on the moon has some highly understandable colored diagrams that specifically identify lunar history and lunar geology concepts.

Snow, Theodore P. *The Dynamic Universe: An Introduction to Astronomy.* 3d ed. St. Paul, Minn.: West Publishing, 1988. This visually spectacular volume has many good diagrams and photographs in the chapter on the moon. It is very readable and informative.

Wilhelms, Don E. *The Geologic History of the Moon.* Professional Paper 1348. Denver, Colo.: U.S. Geological Survey, Books and Open-File Reports Section, 1987. A detailed publication on the current knowledge of lunar history with a strong emphasis on what has been learned as a result of the space program.

James Charles LoPresto

Cross-References

Asteroids, 98; Igneous Rock Classification, 1138; Igneous Rocks: Anorthosites, 1152; Igneous Rocks: Basaltic, 1158; Lunar Craters, 1393; Lunar Maria, 1408; Lunar Rocks, 1414; Crystallization of Magmas, 1420; The Origin of Magmas, 1428; Tektites, 2512.

LUNAR MARIA

Type of earth science: Planetology
Field of study: Large solar system bodies

The lunar maria achieved international prominence in 1969 when the astronaut Neil Armstrong stepped onto the surface of the Sea of Tranquillity. The location had been carefully planned to allow safe access and departure and to afford constant telecommunication contact with the earth. It provided the first sample of the surface of another orbiting body in space.

Principal terms

IMPACT BASIN: a large cavity produced by a meteorite impact

IMPACT BRECCIA: angular, fragmental rock produced by meteorite impact

TRANSITION GROUP METALS: elements occupying the central columns of the periodic table; unlike the main group elements, they can have one, two, or three valence electrons

VISCOSITY: a measure of the ability to flow; a substance with low viscosity flows easily

Summary of the Phenomenon

Mare (plural, *maria*) is the Latin for "sea"; the term reflects seventeenth century ideas about the nature of the lunar surface. In a like manner, there is an Oceanus Procellarum (Ocean of Storms), some areas called Lacus (lake), others called Sinus (bay), and still others called Palus (marsh). Returned lunar samples have established not only that there is no surface water on the moon but also that the moon as a whole has so little water that there are not even hydrated minerals in the rocks. In reality, the maria are areas occupied by basaltic lava flows. These lavas occupy approximately 16 percent of the lunar surface, with 80 percent located in the equatorial area always turned toward the earth—a total of more than 6 million square kilometers. Although extensive, the mare basalts probably represent less than 1 percent of the total lunar crustal volume.

Volcanoes form some of the highest features on the earth, but the majority of the lunar lavas are situated in low regions. These lows were excavated by meteorite impacts which left craters varying in size from microscopic to 2,500 kilometers in diameter. The larger of these craters, called basins, were later filled by lavas to form the maria. Smaller craters, particularly those immediately surrounding the near-side maria, also became the sites of lava eruptions. Estimates of the thicknesses of the mare lavas range from less than 100 meters in the shallowly flooded craters to perhaps 10 kilometers in the larger basins. The depth of basalt fill appears to be related to the age of the impact-basin-forming events, the deeper fill being found in the younger basins. Nearly thirteen hundred separate eruption locations have been identified. This number does not include those buried by their own or younger erupted materials. The true number of eruption sites may be closer to thirty thousand.

Returned lunar samples have radiometric ages which fall within a range of 3 to 4 billion years. The presence of basaltic fragments in breccias produced by the large-basin-producing impacts dating from about 4 billion years and of dark materials excavated by impacts from beneath a younger impact depositional cover indicate that the age of volcanism extends further back in time than the ages of the returned samples. Furthermore, ages determined by crater-counting techniques have indicated the presence of lavas perhaps as young as 2 billion years. Thus, although now long absent, the majority of volcanic eruptions on the moon took place over a time span of about 1 billion years. Additionally, crater-counting data indicate that individual maria may have witnessed eruptions for a similar time span, the older materials being deeply buried near the center of the basins. Crater counting and superposition relationships have led to the erection of a relative time scale based on the time of formation of large impact craters and basins. The subdivisions of this time scale in order of decreasing age are pre-Nectarian, Nectarian, Early Imbrian, Late Imbrian, Eratosthenian, and Copernican. Two-thirds of the near side mare surface is of Late Imbrian age; much of the remainder is of Eratosthenian age. Early Imbrian, Nectarian, and pre-Nectarian lavas could have been buried by impact ejecta and younger lavas; Copernican-aged lavas are restricted to small areas of the western near side.

Morphological evidence for volcanism is found in the form of lava-flow fronts, sinuous rilles, mare domes, cones, and pyroclastic deposits. Measured flow fronts have heights which average about 30 meters but range from 10 to 63 meters. It is highly probable that thinner flows once existed, but they have been subject to obliteration by more than 2 billion years of meteorite impact erosion. Flow fronts outline individual eruptions more than several hundred kilometers in length. The great size of these features is attributable to the extremely low viscosities of the erupted materials and their high-volume output rate. Sinuous rilles superficially resemble terrestrial river channels and range from hundreds of meters to 3 kilometers in width and a few kilometers to 300 kilometers long. These features are believed to be lava channels or collapsed lava tubes. The Apollo 15 mission involved exploration at the edge of one of these structures, Hadley Rille. More than three hundred mare domes have been identified on the moon. They have shapes and dimensions comparable to small terrestrial shield volcanoes. Conical structures are common in the Marius Hills volcanic complex within Oceanus Procellarum but are relatively rare elsewhere. It is believed that these structures are the lunar equivalent of a terrestrial Strombolian eruption style.

Pyroclastic deposits on the moon can be subdivided into two major groups: dark halo deposits and regional dark mantle deposits. Dark halo deposits extend to ranges of about 5 kilometers from an endogenic crater. Dark mantle deposits cover areas of up to 40,000 square kilometers. The Apollo 17 mission returned samples of this pyroclastic material in the form of orange "soil." The stratigraphy and compositional variations of lunar pyroclastic materials suggest an age range comparable to the mare basalts. Three areas with abnormally high concentrations of volcanic features exist in Oceanus Procellarum and are called volcanic complexes: the Marius Hills, Rümker Hills, and Aristarchus Plateau-Harbinger Mountain regions. Other features, less definitively attributable to volcanism, include irregular plateaus, mare ring structures, and a number of craters with morphologies drastically different from those of "normal" impact craters.

Compositionally and texturally, the returned lunar mare samples are basaltic lavas and glasses. Samples from each landing site are unique in terms of their major and minor element chemistry. Additionally, different chemistries can be recognized in the basalts at each site. General distinctions have been drawn between high, intermediate, low, and very low titanium basalts and feldspathic basalts. It must be remembered that samples have been returned from only six mare sites. Fortunately, basalts are rich in the transition group metals (particularly iron and titanium), which are capable of identification by the way they alter electromagnetic radiation in the visible wavelengths. It has therefore been possible to map the distribution of compositionally different basaltic materials across the near side of the moon on the basis of their spectral characteristics. More than one dozen spectrally different units have been identified. There appear to be no simple age-composition relationships or composition-location relationships. For example, there are both old and young titanium-rich basalts and there are titanium-rich basalts in both the eastern and the western hemispheres of the moon.

There are also dome-shaped features on the lunar surface whose shapes and spectral characteristics serve to distinguish them from mare domes. These features have heights of up to slightly more than 1 kilometer and areas of up to 500 square kilometers. They are all close to the highland-mare boundary in Oceanus Procellarum. Their spectra have suggested a comparison with KREEP basalts, which are basalts rich in potassium, rare earth elements, and phosphorus. If of volcanic origin, their shapes would indicate formation by higher-viscosity materials or at lower volumetric eruption rates than mare basalts. Stratigraphic analysis indicates that they were emplaced at the lunar surface at the same time that basaltic eruptions were taking place elsewhere.

In summary, volcanic activity, perhaps dominated by KREEP-rich materials, preceded the development of the younger large impact basins. The cavities created by the large impacts became the sites of basalt deposition, and the deeper, central portions of the basins were the first to be filled. Widespread flood-type volcanism was locally accompanied by the eruption of more volatile-rich pyroclastic material. With progressive infilling, the magma had an increasingly difficult task in penetrating the thick, high-density basin fill, so volcanism shifted to the periphery of the basins, found outlets in the floors of circumbasinal craters, and overflowed into the surrounding terrains.

Methods of Study

The locations and stratigraphic relations of the lunar maria have been determined by geologic mapping using earth-based and orbital photographs as the data base.

Relative ages of different surface units have been determined by measuring the number of impact craters of a given size within a specified area or by determining the extent to which craters of a given size have been modified with respect to fresh, similarly sized craters. Both of these techniques rely on the fact that the moon is under constant bombardment by meteorite particles, so that the longer an area has been exposed at the lunar surface, the more craters it will have and the more the preimpact surface will be affected by erosion and deposition. In some cases it is possible to identify the secondary craters—craters created by material excavated by a primary impact—of a large impact. These secondary craters (and the primary crater) have to be younger than the material into which they impacted. It is by mapping these relationships that scientists have established the lunar stratigraphic column. The advantage of the return of lunar samples was that the relative ages calculated by the cratering techniques could be related to the absolute ages determined by radiometric dating. Furthermore, the exposure times (rather than crystallization or metamorphic ages) of the returned samples at the lunar surface have been established by determining their amounts of solar-derived particles. Sizes of such structures as lava-flow fronts have been determined by measuring the lengths of shadows and through the use of the lunar laser altimeter carried aboard orbiting spacecraft. These data have been compiled to make topographic maps.

Many techniques have been employed to determine the thickness of the mare basalts. One geophysical technique relies on the fact that the mare basalts have a greater density than the surrounding highlands materials. This greater density results in the maria's exerting a greater gravitational pull on a spacecraft, causing minute changes in its orbital motions. This phenomenon led to the discovery of strong pulls over the younger circular impact basins and the formulation of the name "mascons," for mass concentrations. Morphometric techniques for determining mare thicknesses rely on the fact that impact craters have regular and predictable dimensional characteristics. For example, a fresh, bowl-shaped crater has a depth equal to one-sixth its diameter. If an impact crater has penetrated a mare surface and excavated pre-mare materials from beneath, then the mare must be less thick than one-sixth of the crater diameter. Similarly, if all pre-mare craters with less than a specific diameter have been buried by lava, then, again, a minimum depth can be established. At the larger end of the scale, it is possible to take a topographic map of a relatively unflooded young basin, such as the Orientale Basin, and artificially, to raise the lava level parallel to the contours until the basin looks like the more deeply flooded basins. The height difference is then a measure of the mare infill thickness in the more deeply flooded basin.

The composition of the mare basalts has been established by standard geochemical techniques applied to returned samples. More moonwide data have been obtained from orbital geochemical experiments. Information on radon and polonium variations was gathered by the alpha-particle spectrometer; details of the uranium, potassium, and thorium concentrations and the elemental abundances of oxygen, silicon, iron, magnesium, and titanium were determined by the gamma-ray spectrometer; and aluminum, silicon, and magnesium variations were determined using the X-ray fluorescence data. Various forms of photographic and reflectance spectroscopy techniques have been employed by earth-based observers to determine transition element variations, mineral compositions, and glass contents of the mare surfaces facing the earth.

Context

The maria form the least rugged terrain on the moon, so they are conducive to the safe landing of spacecraft. These flat areas would also facilitate lunar exploration through the use of surface craft. They are most abundant on the earth-facing hemisphere, where continuous telecommunications are possible with the earth. Excavation of the maria to produce dwellings would not be very difficult. Alternatively, natural shields to solar radiation, such as lava tubes, could be turned into habitation sites. Several techniques have been proposed for the mining of mare basalts to be used as raw materials for the construction of spacecraft in earth orbit and to provide sustenance for lunar inhabitants. These factors make the maria primary candidates for the establishment of a permanent, manned lunar base.

A far-side mare site would be an ideal location for the construction of an astronomical observatory. Communications with earth-based stations would necessitate a more complex satellite system than that required by a near-side base, but at the same time, the shielding from terrestrial electromagnetic radiation provided by the bulk of the moon would enable clear views of distant galaxies.

From a scientific viewpoint, the surface materials of the maria provide a diary of solar activity and small meteorite impacts extending over the past few billion years. This information has been removed from terrestrial rocks by erosion, deposition, and the recycling of oceanic plates. Detailed study of the maria can therefore furnish information about what was taking place in the near-earth solar system from the time of emplacement of the oldest surviving terrestrial rocks, through the development of unicellular organisms, to the arrival of humans. These data cannot be obtained from the surface of Venus, because of the thick atmosphere of that planet; neither will Mars serve, because of the effects of wind erosion, ice formation, and, perhaps, past erosion by river systems. The moon is a unique natural laboratory, and the maria provide the most favorable sites for a manned laboratory.

Bibliography

Baldwin, Ralph B. *The Measure of the Moon*. Chicago: University of Chicago Press, 1963. This book served as the reference work to those directly involved with the scientific planning of the manned and unmanned lunar landings. Most valuable for the correlations it identifies between impact cratering phenomena and man-made explosions. Suitable for advanced high school and college students.

Lunar and Planetary Institute, Houston, Texas. *Basaltic Volcanism on the Terrestrial Planets*. Elmsford, N.Y.: Pergamon Press, 1981. An indispensable text for any studies of planetary geology. Entire chapters are devoted to petrology and geochemistry, remote sensing, surface morphologies, radiometric dating, and crater studies. For college-level readers.

Mendel, W. W. *Lunar Bases and Space Activities in the Twenty-first Century*. Houston: Lunar and Planetary Institute, 1985. Eighty-eight articles dealing with the scientific, industrial, and social and political value of establishing a lunar base. The articles are short and of varying degrees of complexity.

Mutch, Thomas A. *Geology of the Moon*. Rev. ed. Princeton, N.J.: Princeton University Press, 1972. A very readable textbook for advanced undergraduate and graduate students. Describes the moon from a stratigraphic viewpoint, with the newly acquired Apollo results forming the last chapter.

Schultz, Peter H. *Moon Morphology: Interpretations Based on Lunar Orbiter Photography*. Austin: University of Texas Press, 1974. A post-Apollo photographic encyclopedia of lunar surface features. Not a book to be read from cover to cover, but each of its pages can be read individually. Aimed primarily at a research-level audience.

Taylor, Stuart R. *Planetary Science: A Lunar Perspective*. Houston: Lunar and Planetary Institute, 1982. An extremely literate summary of the information derived from analyses of lunar samples and an attempt to synthesize those data with photogeologic information. The author concentrates on the more controversial interpretations of lunar geology. Extensive, sometimes annotated bibliographies at the end of each chapter. For college-level audiences.

Wilhelms, Don E. *The Geologic History of the Moon*. Professional Paper 1348. Denver, Colo.: U.S. Geological Survey, Books and Open-File Reports Section, 1987. This volume synthesizes the author's vast accumulated knowledge of mapping the lunar surface with information derived from every other field of lunar research. An essential source for budding lunar scientists and a reference source for specialists needing to put their work in perspective. A research-level book, but intelligible to the adventurous college student. Heavily illustrated.

James L. Whitford-Stark

Cross-References

Igneous Rocks: Basaltic, 1158; Lunar Craters, 1393; Lunar History, 1400; Lunar Rocks, 1414; Meteorite and Comet Impacts, 1623; Plate Tectonics, 2079; Remote Sensing and the Electromagnetic Spectrum, 2166; Future Resources, 2182; Stratigraphic Correlation, 2485; Volcanoes: Flood Basalts, 2630; Volcanoes: Shield Volcanoes, 2681; Volcanoes: Types of Eruption, 2695; X-Ray Fluorescence, 2744.

LUNAR ROCKS

Type of earth science: Planetology
Field of study: Large solar system bodies

Lunar rocks are among the materials brought to earth from the surface of the moon during the Luna and Apollo space programs of the 1960's and 1970's. They were studied and analyzed by scientists in a successful effort to enhance understanding of the physical nature of the moon and its origins. All samples have been cataloged according to a variety of criteria relating to mineralogy, crystallography, geochronology, geochemistry, magnetism, radioactivity, and other characteristics.

Principal terms

ALPHA PARTICLE: a helium nucleus emitted during the radioactive decay of uranium, thorium, or other unstable nuclei

BRECCIA: a rock consisting of sharp fragments held in a fine-grained material

CRYSTAL: a solid made up of a regular periodic arrangement of atoms; its form and physical properties express the repeat units of the structure

GABBROS: igneous rocks rich in magnesium

GLASS: a solid with no regular periodic arrangement of atoms; that is, an amorphous solid

IGNEOUS ROCK: a rock formed by the cooling of molten volcanic material

ISOTOPES: atoms of the same element with identical numbers of protons but different numbers of neutrons in their nuclei

ISOTROPIC: having properties that are the same in all directions; the opposite is anisotropic—having properties that vary with direction

MARE: a large dark area on the surface of the moon

PETROGRAPHY: the description and systematic classification of rocks

PRIMARY MINERALS: those minerals formed when magma crystallizes

REGOLITH: the surface layer of the moon

SILICATE: a substance whose structure includes silicon surrounded by four oxygen atoms in the shape of a tetrahedron

SPHERULES: fluidlike, regularly shaped glass particles

VESICULAR: blistered, or containing bubblelike cavities

Summary of the Phenomenon

When direct exploration of the surface of the moon began during the 1960's, scientists around the world looked forward with great anticipation to the study and analysis of materials brought back to earth from the lunar surface by the manned space missions of the Apollo program and the unmanned programs of the Soviet

Union such as the Luna. As new and different material arrived at the completion of each successive mission, an astonishing wealth of information about the origin and physical character of the moon began to accumulate.

Using the latest scientific techniques to analyze soil and rock gathered during the missions, researchers were able to identify the basic elements and minerals that comprise the moon's surface; using that knowledge in combination with other information gathered by remote-sensing technology and sophisticated photography techniques over several decades, they were able to extrapolate information about the origin of the moon. Perhaps most important, they were able to determine with some accuracy a chronology of events in lunar evolution. While there are still many unsolved mysteries about the moon and its history, it is remarkable how many data were gathered from the study of moon rocks: pieces of the material found on the lunar surface. Moon rocks are defined as surface materials that exceed 1 centimeter in diameter. Anything smaller is considered moon soil, although it is unlike earth soil, which usually contains large amounts of decayed organic material and moisture. On the moon, the lack of atmosphere and organic material gives the soil a composition similar to dry, clean sand. It is probably powdered rock, created when large objects impacted violently with the surface of the moon over the millennia.

Rock at the surface of the moon is rich in calcium and aluminum. Below 20 kilometers, the surface is not broken so extensively as it is near the top. The upper mantle is from 200 to 300 kilometers thick and contains high concentrations of magnesium and iron silicate, pyroxene, and olivine. There is reason to believe that the core is iron-rich and produced a global magnetic field during the early days of the moon's history. Most of the radioactive materials on the moon are located at or near the surface. The two major activities that have resulted in the character of the lunar surface are volcanism and meteor impacts. Lowland regions exhibit evidence that there has been great volcanic activity on the moon, and across the lunar landscape there is evidence that impacts have resulted in broad redistribution of rock and soil. Occasionally that activity has resulted in the breaking up of bedrock and basalt breccias that formed previous to later redistribution, recrystallization, or both.

Each of the lunar missions that returned to earth with samples of moon rock expanded the body of knowledge about the geological character of the moon's surface. Each mission landed at a different location on the lunar surface to ensure that as broad a collection of materials as possible would be acquired given the limited number of missions planned and the limited payload capacity available on returning spacecraft. For the purposes of lunar exploration, two primary regions of the moon were identified. Generally speaking, the lunar highland is that region that is light on the surface on the moon. The maria constitute that portion of the lunar surface that is dark. The highland is generally composed of the remnants of ancient volcanic cones and the ridges of giant impact craters. The maria are surface areas characterized by volcanic chamber depressions and impact crater basins. The analysis of rocks collected at various spots within each of the two regions demonstrates that each has unique physical characteristics.

Moon rock can be categorized in two ways, crystallized, or igneous, rocks and breccias. The igneous rock encountered on the lunar surface is most often volcanic in origin and appears to have been scattered over wide areas during violent eruptions. Some specimens are believed to have been thrown from 100 kilometers to 1,000 kilometers, either during eruptions or as a result of meteor impact. Certain highland samples contain evidence of the existence of plutonic rock, formed when volcanic material cools below the surface.

The Apollo 17 crew, working with the benefit of knowledge gained in previous manned and unmanned missions, further subcategorized lunar rock as follows: basalts, dark matrix breccias, glass-bonded agglutinates, vesicular green-gray breccias, blue-gray breccias, layered, foliated, light-gray breccias, and brecciated gabbroic rocks. The distribution of moon rock material is different for highland and mare regions. In the highlands, the surface consists of approximately 10 percent plutonic rock, 85 percent breccias, and 5 percent volcanic material, primarily basalts. Mare regions contain 90 percent volcanic basalts and 10 percent breccias.

It is important to note that the number of minerals identified on the moon is dwarfed by the number found on earth; this difference probably results from the moon's lack of atmosphere, particularly oxygen and moisture, which often interact with elements in the weathering process to form minerals. There are some two thousand minerals on earth, while there are only two hundred known to exist on the moon. The number of primary minerals, however, is similar on both bodies. The principal minerals discovered on the moon at the regolith level include clinopyroxene, plagioclase, olivine, ilmenite (by far the most abundant, 15-20 percent by volume), trydymite, cristobalite, and orthopyroxenes. Three new minerals have been identified, including armalcolite, pyroxferroite, and tranquillityite. It is interesting to note that armalcolite was named for the three astronauts on the Apollo mission that returned with it: Neil Armstrong, "Buzz" Aldrin, and Michael Collins. Armalcolite has since been found on earth; it is formed when crystallization occurs in the absence of moisture and oxygen.

Ancient orange glass beads, thought to have been spewed out during volcanic eruptions, have given scientists a glimpse of what constitutes the core of the moon's interior. These beads contain high levels of lead, zinc, tellurium, and sulfur and are thought to have originated as deep as 300 kilometers into the center of the moon. Lunar rock samples have been individually but not uniformly rich in such elements as aluminum, magnesium, potassium, phosphorus, titanium, iron, chromium, and zirconium. Some lunar rocks are referred to as glassy agglutinates. These rocks are believed to have been formed when volcanic action or meteoric impact caused fine rock dust to weld together, a process known as impact melting. Their appearance ranges from dark opaque to transparent. Other rocks have different origins but are covered by glassy materials thought to have formed and been distributed in the same manner. While the great majority of collected lunar rocks are igneous, there is some evidence that a metamorphosis has occurred as a result of shock settling of soil, caused by meteor impact and vibrations that occur during the course of violent volcanic activity.

Breccias appear to contain material that has been ejected by impacts or volcanic eruption. There are two types: soil breccia and ejecta blanket breccia. Soil breccia is composed of the same materials that exist as soil in a particular region. It probably results from the shock of meteor impact. Soil breccia is also characterized by weak cohesion. Ejecta blanket breccias are thought to have been formed when volcanically ejected materials fused together to form a layer of rock that later underwent various forms of thermal metamorphism. The composition of such rock varies with the depth at which it has been found or at which it is thought to have originated.

The primary source of lunar erosion appears to have been impact cratering, although solar wind and cosmic-ray effects have also altered the character and composition of surface materials. Some lunar samples show cosmic-ray bombardment over long periods of time that has resulted in the alteration of the surface of the sample. The same activity has been useful in helping scientists determine how long a particular sample fragment was in the same location and at what level it has resided within the regolith.

Scientists have also determined with some confidence the age of the moon and the time of the earliest crystallization of moon rock formations. Isotopic dating techniques indicate that the earliest crystallization occurred more than 4 billion years ago and that most volcanic activity appears to have spanned some 600 million years.

Methods of Study

Before the first direct contact with the surface of the moon occurred, much was known about the composition and origin of that surface from sophisticated technology capable of analyzing materials from afar. Those techniques included remote-sensing processes involving the visible, infrared, and microwave bands of the electromagnetic spectrum. Yet, the understanding derived from this technology was limited until actual samples of surface materials were brought to earth by the moon explorers. Scientists could then compare the data from the remote-sensing experiments with direct observations to determine what it was that they were seeing at the time. Radar, which was used in determining the physical nature of the moon's surface, was successful in establishing that it was loose, a mixture of sand and broken rock. Infrared studies confirmed that the surface was porous and exhibited low thermal conductivity. Photometric and polarimetric studies further refined the knowledge of the character of the surface by establishing that it contains high concentrations of iron-rich basalts (confirmed by the Apollo missions).

Once the first lunar samples arrived, scanning electronic microscopes were used to photograph them, an important step in categorizing individual sample fragments. Samples were also sieved to determine the relative abundance of materials in a particular location. In this way, researchers were able to determine where some materials were more abundant than others on the surface when collected using the same procedure. Some samples were cross-sectioned for better observation of stratification, if it existed. Many were tested using standard chemical analysis techniques to determine the chemical nature of the materials. X-ray fluorescence analyses were also conducted to determine the relative concentrations of specific elements or components. Isotopic and carbon dating techniques were used to determine the relative ages of specific samples and to attempt a chronology of the events that have affected the evolution of the materials under study.

Context

There is enormous scientific interest in the moon. Many scientists believe that it may hold the key to a better understanding of the physical nature of the solar system—indeed, of the universe itself. Perhaps more important, it may hold the key to a better understanding of the origin of planet Earth and of its relationship to other objects in the universe. Lunar rocks have given scientists the first window into that unknown sphere, helping them to understand the nature of planetary formation. The Luna and Apollo programs demonstrated for the first time that many accepted ideas about the moon and its composition were accurate, though many others were not. They also demonstrated that the earth and its moon have much in common. Except for the lack of a lunar atmosphere of similar composition to that of earth, they would probably have evolved in much the same way.

Another significant outcome of the study of lunar rock samples has been the unequivocal knowledge that certain elements, metals, and other valuable materials exist in abundance on the moon and may be important to future generations on earth. Perhaps more important, however, is the knowledge gained of how specific elements interact under conditions that rarely exist on earth: namely, with little oxygen and no water. The moon has now become a giant laboratory that is helping scientists to understand the nature of chemical and geological evolution and order.

Bibliography

"Apollo 11—Lunar Science Conference." Washington, D.C.: American Association for the Advancement of Science, 1970. A good look at the techniques and technology employed in the analysis and study of moon samples.

Cortright, Edgar M., ed. *Apollo Expeditions to the Moon*. NASA SP-350. Washington, D.C.: Government Printing Office, 1975. An excellent summary of the major accomplishments and milestones achieved during the Apollo years. Contains a number of anecdotes by many of those who participated in the project, including astronauts and key engineers and scientists. Well illustrated.

Firsoff, V. A. *Strange World of the Moon*. New York: Science Editors, 1962. This short book is an intriguing look at the moon from the eyes of a scientist before the Apollo program. Useful in understanding how far science has progressed since the arrival of moon rocks for analysis.

Glass, Billy P. *Introduction to Planetary Geology*. New York: Cambridge University

Press, 1982. A very good primer on the nature of the universe as it can be understood through the eyes of the geologist. Contains a good section on the moon surface samples acquired during the space era. Illustrated, indexed.

Musgrove, Robert G., comp. *Lunar Photographs from Apollos 8, 10, and 11*. NASA SP-246. Washington, D.C.: Government Printing Office, 1971. Excellent photographs of the lunar surface and its landmarks. Particularly useful in understanding the texture of the surface and the nature of its physical composition.

National Aeronautics and Space Administration. *Preliminary Science Report: Apollo 14*. NASA SP-272. Washington, D.C.: Government Printing Office, 1971.

_____. *Preliminary Science Report: Apollo 15*. NASA SP-289. Washington, D.C.: Government Printing Office, 1972.

_____. *Preliminary Science Report: Apollo 16*. NASA SP-315. Washington, D.C.: Government Printing Office, 1972. Each of these three reports is the official report on the scientific findings from the mission indicated. Excellent references.

_____. *Preliminary Science Report: Apollo 17*. NASA SP-330. Washington, D.C.: Government Printing Office, 1973. The official report of the findings relative to the surface materials brought back by the Apollo 17 mission. Contains an excellent description of those materials and their composition. The text is supported by excellent photographs of samples.

Michael S. Ameigh

Cross-References

CRYSTALLIZATION OF MAGMAS

Type of earth science: Geology
Field of study: Petrology, igneous

Magma is a naturally occurring liquid usually composed of silicate material with suspended minerals that either concentrate or reject elements, thereby either depleting or enriching the liquid in a given element. This process gives geologists a means to understand how some elements are concentrated in the minerals or liquids to form potential economic deposits.

Principal terms

BASALT: a dark igneous rock containing plagioclase feldspar, pyroxene, or olivine; it contains mineral grains too small to see with the naked eye as well as various amounts of larger minerals

CLINOPYROXENE: a calcium, iron, and magnesium silicate mineral

FELDSPAR: a silicate mineral categorized as either plagioclase feldspar, containing calcium, sodium, and aluminum, or alkali feldspar, containing potassium, sodium, and aluminum

FRACTIONAL CRYSTALLIZATION: the process by which minerals form in a magma and either float or settle from the magma, depending on whether they are lighter or heavier than the magma

GARNET: a magnesium, iron, and aluminum silicate mineral

MINERAL: a naturally occurring substance with a more or less constant composition and thus constant physical properties that reflect that composition

OLIVINE: a silicate mineral containing iron and magnesium

QUARTZ: a silicate mineral containing only silica

SILICATE MINERALS: minerals composed of silicon, oxygen, and other metal ions, such as potassium, sodium, calcium, magnesium, iron, and aluminum

VISCOSITY: a measure of how readily a fluid flows; the more viscous a fluid is, the less easily it flows

Summary of the Phenomenon

Magmas are composed of a liquid, derived from the melting of silicate rocks at great depth, as well as suspended minerals. The minerals slowly form and grow larger. They sink if they are heavier than the liquid, and they float if they are lighter than the liquid. This is somewhat analogous to what happens if water is placed in the freezer section of a refrigerator. The temperature of the water drops until ice (analogous to a mineral in the magma) begins to form. Ice is unusual in that it is a solid that is less dense than the liquid from which it forms; therefore, it floats instead of sinking. Most minerals sink from the silicate liquids from which they are forming, since they are denser than the liquids. Also, the composition of the ice is the same as that of the water. As long as both ice and water are present in the container, the temperature remains at 0 degrees Celsius.

Magmas are more complex than water, as they contain many more substances. In contrast to water crystallizing to ice at a constant temperature, magmas crystallize several kinds of minerals over a range of temperatures. Also, magmas are exceedingly hot, as they may range in temperature from 600 to 1,200 degrees Celsius. What happens to a crystallizing silicate magma composed of many substances can be compared to what would happen if table salt (sodium chloride) were added to the crystallizing water analogy. If table salt (analogous to a mineral) is added to water (analogous to the magma) by stirring, the salt will dissolve up to a point at which no more salt will dissolve. As the water is cooled in the freezer, more solid salt will form and settle to the bottom of the water, as the salt is denser than the water. Eventually, a temperature will be reached at less than 0 degrees Celsius in which salty ice (a second mineral) will begin to form from the salty water. Thus, the mixture behaves in a fashion more similar to that of minerals crystallizing from silicate liquids.

The kinds and sequences of minerals crystallizing from the magma depend on the liquid composition, the total pressure, the kinds of vapor (for example, carbon dioxide or water vapor), and the pressure of the vapor. The kinds of minerals crystallizing will in turn influence the composition of the gradually decreasing amount of magma.

Suppose a magma exists at a shallow depth of about 5 kilometers below the surface of the earth. Further suppose that this magma is similar in composition to lavas erupted in the Hawaiian Islands called basalt. A mineral called olivine (magnesium and iron silicate) is often one of the first minerals to crystallize out of these basaltic magmas. Olivine contains more magnesium and less silicon than does the basaltic magma; therefore, the lesser amount of remaining liquid becomes more depleted in magnesium and more enriched in silicon. Another mineral called plagioclase (calcium, sodium, and aluminum silicate) may also begin to crystallize with the olivine. The plagioclase is more enriched in calcium and aluminum and depleted in silicon than the magma. Thus, crystallization and separation of plagioclase will result in the depletion of calcium and aluminum and enrichment of silicon in the remaining magma. Plagioclase has a density similar to that of the magma, and it may float or sink depending on whether it is less or more dense than the surrounding magma. Many other elements are not incorporated into the olivine and plagioclase as they undergo fractional crystallization and gradually become more concentrated in the magma.

As the magma changes composition, it may begin to crystallize other minerals, and olivine may stop crystallizing. For example, quartz (all silica) may crystallize from the last bits of the magma left after most of the liquid has solidified. The magma may not increase much in silicon if minerals enriched in silicon, such as quartz, are crystallizing. In some magmas, the last small amounts of liquid left after crystallization may contain a considerable amount of water vapor and unusually large concentrations of some normally rare elements. These rare elements may sometimes form minerals not normally found in most rocks, and they may be economic to mine.

The pressure at which a magma crystallizes may also influence the kinds of minerals that form. Suppose the basaltic magma discussed above crystallized at an exceedingly high pressure, corresponding to a depth of about 60 kilometers below the surface of the earth. Instead of olivine, garnet (magnesium, iron, and aluminum silicate mineral) may be the first mineral to crystallize. Clinopyroxene (calcium, magnesium, and iron silicate mineral) may then shortly join the garnet crystallizing from the magma. No plagioclase or olivine would ever crystallize, as would have occurred at lower pressure. The crystallization and removal of garnet and clinopyroxene would result in a much different change in the composition of the remaining magma from that which would occur at lower pressure. For example, the garnet and clinopyroxene are more concentrated in silicon than the basaltic liquid, and thus the liquid would decrease in silica during fractional crystallization rather than increase, as it would at lower pressure.

The starting composition of the magma will also influence the kinds of minerals that crystallize and in turn influence how the composition of the remaining magma will crystallize. For example, a silicate-rich magma of granitic composition will crystallize different minerals at lower pressures from those of the basalt. The granitic magmas also contain much lower magnesium and iron concentrations and higher potassium concentrations than those of basaltic magmas. Correspondingly, the granitic magmas crystallize more silica-rich and potassium-rich minerals, such as quartz and the potassium-rich feldspars, than do those of basaltic magmas.

The crystallization of minerals from granitic magmas may result in much different changes in composition of the remaining granitic magmas from those of the basaltic magmas. For example, some of the last fractions from the granitic magmas may contain much water vapor and produce exceedingly large crystals of quartz, feldspar, and many rare minerals, such as beryl (a beryllium and aluminum silicate), tourmaline (a complex silicate mineral with boron, sodium, lithium, and aluminum among the many elements), or spodumene (a lithium and aluminum silicate). At other times, gases rich in water vapor may bubble out of these last bits of granitic magmas, much like the gases in a soft drink, and carry out many rare elements not normally concentrated in most rocks. These hydrothermal, or hot water, deposits may form a variety of mineral deposits with minerals such as molybdenite (a molybdenum ore) or wolframite (a tungsten ore).

The presence of water vapor in the magma may also affect the temperature of crystallization, influence the kinds of minerals that crystallize from the magma, and influence the viscosity and settling rates of minerals. The presence of water vapor drastically lowers the melting point of the silicate rocks or crystallization temperature of the silicate magmas. Indeed, some magmas would not exist in nature if water vapor were not present, as the temperature in the earth would not be high enough to keep the silicate magma liquid. Also, if water vapor suddenly boils out of a magma with suspended crystals, the magma may suddenly freeze to such a fine material that individual crystals may be too small to be seen. The resultant rock would contain the large, early-formed crystals in a fine-grained rock. Some minerals, such as biotite (a potassium, magnesium, iron, and aluminum silicate), have water as an essential part of the mineral. Thus, biotite cannot form without the presence of water vapor in the magma.

Water vapor also breaks down the long chains of silicate atoms in the magma and makes them shorter. This in turn allows the magma to flow more easily, or become less viscous. Less viscous magmas may flow more readily to the surface to form volcanic rocks, or minerals may settle faster in a less viscous magma.

Methods of Study

Unfortunately, geologists cannot directly sample magma below the earth's surface to see how it crystallizes. An understanding of how magmas crystallize is derived primarily from experiments in furnaces that approximate the high temperature and pressure that are likely to exist below the surface of the earth. This information can then be related to the solid igneous rocks gradually exposed by erosion or to lavas being extruded in volcanoes. Geologists only see these end products of crystallization and never see magma undergoing fractional crystallization.

Basalt extruded from volcanoes often contains large crystals (1 to 10 millimeters across) of feldspar, pyroxene, or olivine, suspended in a very dark-colored and fine-grained (crystals less than 0.8 millimeter across) or glassy material called the groundmass. In addition, the tops of solidified lavas often contain abundant holes representing the loss of gases from the lava flows. Water vapor is one of the main kinds of gases bubbling out of the lavas. Geologists thus assume that the large crystals of feldspar, pyroxene, and olivine crystallized at some depth below the surface and contained a large amount of dissolved water vapor.

There may also be a series of lava flows piled on top of one another that have differences in composition when they are analyzed. Geologists would like to understand how these compositional differences among lavas are formed. Could they be related to the crystallization of the large crystals settling out of the basaltic magma by fractional crystallization, thus gradually transforming the composition of the magma? Could the compositional differences among the lavas be related to different degrees of melting of the solid rocks that formed the basaltic magmas? How do the dissolved gases bubbling out of the basaltic magma change the composition of the magma?

Some geologists conduct experiments in furnaces at the high temperatures and pressures corresponding to various depths within the earth to see how natural basalts crystallize or to see which solid rocks melt to produce the basaltic magmas. The process might involve placing a natural basalt in a furnace at a known temperature and pressure until all the basalt melts, for example, at 1,200 degrees Celsius. Then the basaltic liquid could be cooled to a slightly lower temperature and suddenly cooled to a very low temperature. The kinds, amounts, and composition of the minerals and the composition of the glass (the liquid forms a glass when rapidly cooled) could then be determined.

The composition of minerals and glass may be determined using an electron microprobe. This instrument shoots a narrow beam of electrons onto a small portion of the mineral or glass. Each element gives off a characteristic energy of radiation that identifies that element. The intensity of the radiation depends on the amount of the element in the sample so that the concentration of the element may be determined. Thus, the mineral and glass compositions may be measured. The experiment may continue at a series of lower temperatures until all the magma crystallizes. The changing composition and kinds of minerals forming from the basaltic magma can thus be precisely related to the changing composition of the basaltic magma.

Similar experiments for the same basalt can then be done at different pressure or composition of vapor coexisting with the basaltic liquid to determine the effect of changing these parameters on the composition and kinds of minerals forming from the liquid. Also, natural rocks that differ in composition from that of the first basalt may be crystallized over a range of temperature, pressure, and fluid composition to determine their effect on the course of the crystallization.

If the compositional differences among a series of lavas piled on top of one another are similar to the changing composition of the glass during the experimental crystallization of a basalt, then the compositional changes in the series of lava flows could be a result of fractional crystallization. The experiments do not prove that the series of lavas formed by fractional crystallization; they merely show that this is one possible way that the lavas may have formed. The lavas, for example, might have formed by different degrees of melting of the same rock. Sometimes, geologists have to prove that all but one of the possible hypotheses for the formation of a series of rocks cannot be true. The possibility left after all other hypotheses have been rejected then becomes the most attractive hypotheses for the formation of a series of lavas.

The crystallization experiments described above were done on very complex natural rocks, and the results are often difficult to understand. Thus, geologists sometimes experiment on rock materials with fewer elements than those in the natural rocks. Once these simpler experiments are understood, other elenents can be added to these rock materials to see how they affect the experiments. Some of the first melting and crystallization experiments in furnaces were done on pure minerals, then on mixtures of two minerals, and finally on mixtures of three or more minerals. For example, a single mineral such as magnesium-rich pyroxene was discovered to melt at a constant temperature to a liquid with the same composition, just like the ice-water melting described previously. Calcium-rich plagioclase also melted at a constant but different temperature from that of the pyroxene. A surprising result occurred when the minerals were then mixed together in various ratios and melted. Any ratio of the mixture of minerals melted at a lower temperature than that of either of the separate minerals (analogous to the salt-ice mixture described previously). Also, the composition of the silicate liquid formed during the melting was usually different from that of the mineral mixture. As the degree of melting increased, the temperature increased, and the composition of the liquid became closer to that of the original solid mixture. Experiments such as this made geologists realize that even though individual minerals have exceedingly high melting points by themselves and cannot melt at reasonable temperatures within the earth, mixtures of minerals (especially in the presence of water vapor) have much lower melting points and can therefore melt and crystallize at temperatures thought to exist within the earth.

Context

Geologists believe that the crystallization of minerals from magmas is a major process that causes elements to increase or decrease in magmas, depending on whether they are rejected or concentrated in the minerals settling from the magma. This process creates rich mineral deposits that can be found in many parts of the world. For example, the Muskox Intrusion, a body of rock formed in Canada by solidification of magma below the surface of the earth, contains high nickel contents in portions of the intrusion that contain a considerable amount of the mineral olivine (concentrated nickel). The olivine and the mineral chromite settled from the magma at different rates, leaving the chromite concentrated in other layers.

Chromite-rich portions can also be found in the large intrusions of the Stillwater complex in Montana, the Great Dyke of Rhodesia, and the Bushveld complex of South Africa. The Great Dyke and the Bushveld complex have chromite layers that can be traced for scores of kilometers. They are the major sources of chromium for the world, and they are also mined for platinum and other elements with similar chemical properties. Chromium is used with steel to give it hardness and toughness and make it resistant to chemical attack.

Unlike nickel or chromium, other elements such as tungsten, tin, beryllium, the rare earth elements, molybdenum, boron, lithium, niobium, tantalum, and uranium are not concentrated in most minerals crystallizing from magmas, and these elements gradually become more concentrated in the smaller amounts of remaining liquid. Eventually, some of these elements may concentrate in the last portions of the crystallizing granitic magma and may form economic deposits of minerals enriched in these elements. For example, potentially economic deposits of beryllium may occur in the mineral beryl, niobium or tantalum may occur in the mineral columbite, and lithium may occur in the mineral spodumene. Beryllium is used as an alloy with copper to increase the hardness, strength, and fatigue resistance of copper. The mineral beryl may be many different colors, and it has been used as a gemstone. Tantalum and niobium are used for alloys in steel. Tantalum makes steel resistant to chemical corrosion, and niobium helps steel resist high temperatures. Lithium is used in grease to help it keep its lubricant properties over a range of temperatures.

Sometimes, fluids rich in water vapor may bubble out of the magmas and carry out elements—such as tin, copper, tungsten, antimony, gold, silver, and bismuth—that form hydrothermal deposits. Wolframite, a mineral rich in tungsten, may form in hydrothermal deposits formed at the highest temperatures. Tungsten is used to harden steel used at high speeds in tools, valves, and similar apparatuses. Native gold or silver is more likely to form in hydrothermal deposits at a lower temperature than wolframite. Gold and silver are used for ornamental purposes. Gold is also a monetary standard and is used in dental and scientific applications. Silver is used in photographic film and electronic equipment.

Bibliography

Best, M. G. *Igneous and Metamorphic Petrology.* San Francisco: W. H. Freeman, 1985. This college-level geology text provides a brief, general overview of processes affecting the formation of magmas. A useful, well-written introduction for the general reader.

Bowen, N. L. *The Evolution of Igneous Rocks.* Princeton, N.J.: Princeton University Press, 1928. This is a classic study describing the first experiments undertaken to understand how magmas crystallize. Much of the book is technical, but the chapters on diversity of igneous rocks and fractional crystallization are quite accessible to the nonscientist.

Craig, J. R., D. J. Vaughan, and B. J. Skinner. *Resources of the Earth.* Englewood Cliffs, N.J.: Prentice-Hall, 1988. An excellent book for the layperson who has had some high school science and is interested in ore deposits. Chapters 6 and 7 contain a discussion of metals concentrated by magmatic crystallization. For each element, there are sections on its history and uses, its geologic occurrence and ore minerals, and its production and reserves. A glossary is included.

Dietrich, R. V., and B. J. Skinner. *Rocks and Rock Minerals.* New York: John Wiley & Sons, 1979. One of many books that give information on the identification and origin of minerals and rocks for readers with a minimal science background. A reader with a high school course in chemistry can better appreciate the chemical information. There is a section at the beginning of chapter 4 on the crystallization of magmas.

Foord, E. E., and R. F. Martin. "Amazonite from the Pikes Peak Batholith." *The Mineralogical Record* 10, no. 6 (1979): 373-384. This article describes minerals formed in the late stages of crystallization of the Pikes Peak Batholith. *The Mineralogical Record* is written for the mineral collector or lay reader with an interest in minerals. It contains many beautiful photographs of minerals.

Leicht, W. C. "The History of Crystallized Gold in California." *The Mineralogical Record* 18, no. 1 (1987): 33-40. This is one of many articles in *The Mineralogical Record* on hydrothermal minerals associated with a large granite intrusion. This entire issue is on gold, and it has many spectacular photographs of naturally occurring gold.

Press, F., and R. Siever. *Earth.* San Francisco: W. H. Freeman, 1974. This is one of many introductory textbooks in geology for college students. It has a chapter on igneous rocks that includes a large section on the crystallization of magmas.

Robert L. Cullers

Cross-References

Experimental Petrology, 662; Feldspars, 698; Igneous Rocks: Basaltic, 1158; Igneous Rocks: Batholiths, 1165; Igneous Rocks: Granitic, 1180; Igneous Rocks: Ultramafic, 1207; The Origin of Magmas, 1428; Water in Magmas, 1433; Orthosilicates, 1969; Phase Changes, 2042; Phase Equilibria, 2049; Silica Minerals, 2365.

THE ORIGIN OF MAGMAS

Type of earth science: Geology
Field of study: Petrology, igneous

Magma is a naturally occurring molten rock material that originates ultimately within the earth's mantle but also within the crust and migrates in the subsurface via both intrusion and extrusion. Recognition of the origin of magmas is essential in understanding the complex relationship between volcanism and regional deformation processes, or plate tectonics.

Principal terms

ASSIMILATION: the incorporation and digestion of solid or fluid foreign material

ASTHENOSPHERE: that portion of the earth that comprises the part of the upper mantle where isostatic adjustments occur, magma may be generated, and seismic waves are strongly attenuated

CONTAMINATION: the process whereby the chemical composition of a magma is altered as a result of assimilation of inclusions or the surrounding rock being intruded

CRYSTALLIZATION: the formation and growth of a crystalline solid from a liquid or gas

DIFFERENTIATION: the process of developing more than one rock type from a common magma

EXTRUSION: the emission of magma or lava and the rock so formed onto the earth's surface

INTRUSION: the process of emplacement of magma and the rock so formed in preexisting rock

ISOTOPE: one of two or more species of the same chemical element where the element has the same number of protons but different number of neutrons and, therefore, different mass

LITHOSPHERE: that portion of the earth that comprises the crust and part of the upper mantle where deformation at geologic rates occurs

MAGMATIC EVOLUTION: the continuing change in the chemical composition of a magma during its ascent

Summary of the Phenomenon

Magma is a naturally occurring mobile rock material consisting of a liquid silicate phase, with or without a solid phase of suspended crystals, and entrained gases. Largely a molten heterogeneous material, magma originates within the earth's upper mantle or lower crust. The earth's crust in part is largely a product of magmatic processes within the mantle that began at least 3.8 billion years ago and are evidenced today in certain areas such as the sea floor and in some continental regions. Magmas encompass a considerable range in composition and almost invariably contain one or more solidus phases (feldspar, pyroxene, olivine, and so on) that are enclosed in a silicate melt whose properties, notably viscosity and temperature, are related to its composition. Extrusion is the process whereby magma cools at the surface and forms extrusive rocks. Volcanic (surficial) rocks are derived from magmas that erupted as lava from volcanic vents that have solidified. In contrast, intrusion is the process whereby magma cools at depth (deep-seated) and forms intrusive rocks. Plutonic rocks, which are derived within the crust—notably below volcanic regions where temporary reservoirs of magma exist—are good examples of intrusive rocks. It is inferred that such bodies solidify completely without ever reaching the surface.

The earth is subdivided into the crust, mantle, and core. Based on geophysical evidence, the earth consists of solid material, with the exception of the outer core. The crust extends to a depth of 30-50 kilometers under most continental regions and less than 10-12 kilometers under most oceanic regions. The mantle is below the crust and is characterized by an abrupt increase in seismic velocities. The transition, referred to as the Mohorovičić discontinuity, from the crust to the mantle represents an important change in bulk composition and mineralogy from essentially an andesite-basaltic continental crust and basaltic oceanic crust to a mantle of peridotite. The upper layers of the earth include the asthenosphere and portions of the lower lithosphere. The asthenosphere includes that portion of the upper mantle or layer of weakness that comprises the part of the upper mantle where isostatic adjustments occur, magma may be generated, and seismic waves are strongly attenuated. Overlying the asthenosphere is the lithosphere, which includes the crust and that portion of the upper mantle or layer of strength where deformation at geologic rates occurs. The thickness of the lithosphere is on the order of 100 kilometers. The boundary between the lithosphere and asthenosphere is the low-velocity zone, at depths ranging from about 100 to 200 kilometers.

The solid mantle is composed principally of the rock referred to as peridotite. Peridotite is a general term for a coarse-grained, dense plutonic rock composed chiefly of olivine with or without other mafic mineral constituents. These other constituents include pyroxenes but also amphiboles and micas with little or no feldspar. The ultimate source of all magmas is a result of partial melting of the solid preexisting rock, notably the mantle. Pressure and temperature conditions in the asthenosphere are such that a small increase in temperature or decrease in pressure can induce partial melting of peridotite within ranges of about 10-30 percent. Melting is concentrated within the uppermost 150-250 kilometers of the mantle.

Partial melting can be induced in several ways, most clearly by the increase in temperature. Melting is, however, rarely complete. Most melts probably coalesce to form discrete magma bodies that migrate away from the source area, leaving some residue behind; thus, the resulting chemical composition of the magma differs from that of the source material. Partial melting of the originally solid crust or mantle allows for the diverse variety of igneous rock types observed. Only a very small fraction of igneous rocks are representative of primary magmas. Primary variation occurs when magmas of different composition are created at the source, which accounts for the variation in igneous rocks, including differences in composition and type of materials being melted in the source region, degree of partial melting, and conditions under which melting has taken place.

Although the diversity in igneous rocks can be explained in terms of these primary variations, secondary variations (where different magmas subsequently evolved from a common parent) are also very important, as they reflect the magmatic evolution of the igneous rocks. These secondary processes include magmatic differentiation, whereby more than one rock type is developed from a common magma. The incorporation and digestion of solid or fluid foreign material during magma ascent, referred to as assimilation, can also result in the development of a different rock type if, in fact, the chemical composition of a magma is significantly altered. The altering of magma chemistry via assimilation is referred to as the process of contamination. Mixing of magma types can also change the overall chemistry such that once solidified, an intermediate rock type is developed. When a magma chemistry is altered simultaneously by solidifying or crystallizing within the cooler portions of the magma body while also melting portions of the surrounding rocks encompassing the body (the process of zone melting), the evolved rock type can also be changed. Within plutonic rocks, evidence of differentiation, sometimes of contamination, and rarely of magma mixing has been found. With volcanic rocks, however, these processes are more difficult to detect.

Magma generation is closely associated with tectonic processes. Basaltic magmas, for example, are generated by direct partial melting of mantle peridotite. This magma type is most abundant beneath active oceanic ridges, which are the sites where lithosphere plates are being formed. In fact, the oceanic crust is basically basaltic in composition and composed of volcanic rocks solidified from magma erupted on the ocean floor. These rocks are underlain by basaltic dikes, which reflect fissures or conduits for molten magma. These dikes are in turn underlain by gabbros and cumulate layers, which are evolved rocks that have formed when large amounts of crystals settled out of a cooling magma.

Andesitic magmas are generated above subduction zones, where lithospheric plates converge. Subduction zones are long, narrow belts where one lithospheric plate descends beneath another. In this case, the melting of peridotite within the mantle is complicated by the presence of wet sediments and basalts that comprise the descending oceanic or lithospheric plate. These magmas thus tend to be more silica-rich and are responsible for the formation of new continental crust, which grows by progressive accumulation of andesitic volcanic rocks above and dioritic intrusive rocks below.

Granitic magmas to a large extent are generated above subduction zones. The processes at work here include both partial melting at the base of the andesitic crust and differentiation, the process of developing more than one rock type from a common magma of andesitic or even basaltic magmas that have been modified by some mixing with crustal material.

True primary magmas are of basaltic composition, as they can only be generated by partial melting of peridotite within the mantle. In contrast, andesites and granites can be formed either by differentiation of basaltic magmas or by direct partial melting within the mantle or crust. In fact, almost all other igneous rocks evolve in this manner, reflecting the complex interrelationship of these two fundamental processes. The study of both terrestrial meteorite impact craters and lunar rocks returned by the Apollo space program has demonstrated that igneous-looking rocks can also be produced by the melting of rocks by meteorite impact.

Methods of Study

The information gained regarding the origin of magmas has almost entirely been gleaned from the study of their product igneous rocks. Through the study of the mineral composition and texture achieved in igneous rocks, the evaluation of these rocks from their site of origin to place of residency can be achieved. Extensive studies are conducted on igneous rocks in surveying the range of chemical compositional variations, notably volcanic rocks. These approximate to liquid compositions, although they do differ in the content of volatile constituents such as water and carbon dioxide, which may be lost during eruption. Plutonic rocks do not always give good indications of liquid compositions because of the role of crystal accumulation processes.

The data on igneous rocks include field relations, textural relationships, mineral composition, and geochemistry. In addition, experimental petrology suggests how igneous systems might be expected to behave. Systematic investigation of igneous rocks began in the mid-nineteenth century with the rise of the microscopic study of mineral composition and textural relationships. In the early twentieth century, an emphasis was placed on the genetic relationships of igneous rocks and trying to understand the way in which different rock types form and how an initially formed magma may become compositionally differentiated to give rise to a variety of different rock types. Currently, igneous rocks are studied to gain information regarding processes at depth and the nature of the upper mantle. Thus, igneous rocks are studied to understand the evolution of magmas, igneous processes in general, and the nature of source materials from which magmas are derived.

Rocks undergo melting and fractionation over a wide range of temperatures and pressures. Thus, natural rock types including peridotite, eclogite, and various basalts are melted experimentally. The type of melts produced depends first on the conditions of melting and, second, on the fractionation processes after melting. Deciphering the degree of partial melting is necessary, as source rocks do not melt instantaneously, nor does the solid phase go into the melt simultaneously. Melts of rocks are produced by subjecting rocks to various pressures. For example, by varying the conditions of melting, different basalt types can be produced. Peridotite, for example, has a very wide melting range but remains partially solid at temperatures several hundred degrees above the temperature at which melting begins. On the other hand, eclogite has a very limited melting range, sometimes going from almost completely crystallized to completely molten within a temperature rise of as little as 25 degrees Celsius.

Context

Knowledge concerning the processes involved in the origin of magmas and the subsequent rock types formed is essential in understanding the formation and evolution of the earth's crust. By understanding these processes on earth, scientists are able to apply this information to the study of other planets within the solar system.

Economically, many mineral deposits of igneous affiliations result from hydrothermal solutions, which directly or indirectly are derived from magma as a consequence of magmatic processes such as crystallization and differentiation. Thus, a relationship exists between magma and mineral deposits. This relationship is demonstrated by the occurrence of igneous rocks that are themselves characterized as ores, depositions of mineral deposits from volcanoes and hot springs, and mineralizations along perimeters of igneous bodies.

Bibliography

Carmichael, Ian S., et al. *Igneous Petrology*. New York: McGraw-Hill, 1974. Chapter 1, "Magma and Igneous Rocks," and chapter 7, "Sources of Magma: Geophysical-Chemical Constraints," are recommended. A well-known reference presenting in-depth discussion of both the diversity of igneous rock types and their evolution and magma evolution.

Hall, Anthony. *Igneous Petrology*. New York: John Wiley & Sons, 1987. A standard text discussing the general aspects of the occurrences, composition, and evolution of igneous rocks and magmas.

Jensen, Mead L., and Alan M. Bateman. *Economic Mineral Deposits*. 3d ed. New York: John Wiley & Sons, 1981. Chapter 4, "Petrology of Mineral Deposits: Magmas, Solutions, and Sediments," and chapter 5, "Magmatic Concentrations," are recommended. A standard and easy-to-read, well-illustrated text discussing the occurrence and formation of mineral deposits.

Smith, David G., ed. *The Cambridge Encyclopedia of Earth Sciences*. New York: Crown, 1981. Chapter 5, "Earth Materials: Minerals and Rocks," gives a brief but good discussion of the relationship between magma source and rock type. A well-illustrated and carefully indexed reference volume.

Stephen M. Testa

Cross-References

Continental Growth, 268; Earth's Mantle, 555; Hot Spots and Volcanic Island Chains, 1079; Igneous Rock Bodies, 1131; Lithospheric Plates, 1387; Crystallization of Magmas, 1420; Water in Magmas, 1433; The Ocean Ridge System, 1826; Subduction and Orogeny, 2497; Volcanism at Spreading Centers, 2607; Volcanoes: Flood Basalts, 2630.

WATER IN MAGMAS

Type of earth science: Geology
Field of study: Petrology, igneous

Water promotes melting deep in the earth's crust, where magmas are generated, and abets their intricate ascent toward the surface. When magmas survive, the available water determines the explosive nature of a volcanic eruption. Exceptional buildup of water in magma may ultimately assist the crystallization of spectacular, gem-quality minerals.

Principal terms

CONVECTION: the movement of portions of a liquid medium as a result of density differences caused by heating

DIAPIR: an unstable mass of magma ascending in the earth's crust

GRANITE: an even-textured, light-colored igneous rock made up of quartz and two feldspars, with variable amounts of micas and dark minerals

HYDROUS MINERAL: a naturally occurring chemical compound with a regular atomic structure that contains water molecules

MAGMA: partially or completely molten liquid that upon cooling crystallizes into a crystalline or glassy igneous rock

RETROGRADE BOILING: boiling caused by crystallization; it occurs at constant pressure with falling temperature

Summary of the Phenomenon

Only small amounts of water are needed to affect the evolution of magmas in the earth's crust. Although dissolved water content may be most commonly less than 2 percent by weight in magma, the amount is better appreciated from its concentration on a volume basis. That 2-percent-by-weight water, depending on the magma composition, will range from 6 to 17 percent by volume. Therefore, water is a significant component of magma.

Water effects on magma vary with geologic environments. Magma behavior resulting from water at shallow depths and in volcanoes contrasts with its behavior in deeper magmas associated with, for example, the formation of granites. Mafic magmas, those high in iron and magnesium, contain much smaller amounts of water in comparison to silicic magmas, or those high in silica and alkalies. In addition, the presence of water in the form of a liquid or vapor will profoundly alter the evolution of magma in the earth's crust. When water cannot be absorbed further by a magma, the excess becomes vapor. This water vapor becomes entrained as a gaseous "bubble" carried along in the magma as it advances in the crust. The type of magma, the form of the water that is contained in the magma, and the depth of that magma in the earth's crust thus constrain the overall role of water.

Examination of the role of water in magmas at great depths suggests melting as a dominant effect. Water facilitates melting to generate granitic magmas in the earth's lower crust up to 80 kilometers. Water permits melting to occur at much lower temperatures, for example, near 630 degrees Celsius for water content that is 2 percent by weight in magma. Otherwise, temperatures in excess of 1,000 degrees Celsius would be required and granitic magmas would be less likely to ascend into the upper crust. Enormous bodies of exposed granites at the earth's surface testify to the amount of magma once formed at depth that has ascended.

A prevalent source of water for melting is the dehydration of hydrous minerals. The most common hydrous minerals include micas and amphiboles. Muscovite, a mica that melts at a relatively low temperature, may release sufficient water to induce melting as shallow as 14 kilometers and as deep as 56 kilometers. Higher temperatures are required to release water from amphiboles. Following the liberation of water, the original minerals change their composition. A residue of unmelted rock plus new minerals, especially sillimanite and potassium feldspars, remain as evidence of this past melting event. Geologists call this type of melting anatexis.

A second source of water is thought to be from a descending slab of crust that has been previously altered near the sea floor. Hydrous minerals are created from the exchange of seawater with hot volcanic gases. If this crustal segment is carried to greater depths by the mechanism of plate tectonics, more water will then be available.

A minimum melt is generated and may either solidify or crystallize at the initial site of generation or move upward. At this point, the way that the magma is transported toward the surface will depend on the delicate balance between amount of water, form of water, composition of the magma, and temperature. Too little water will inhibit melting if temperatures are maintained, and insufficient magma will be available. Too much water will cause the premature crystallization of the magma and it will "freeze" in its tracks.

The buoyant mass of magma, called a diapir, ascends by remaining less dense than the surrounding cooler rocks. It may be viewed as a tadpole-shaped glob of molten liquid slowly pushing its way upward. The surrounding rocks are more viscous than the diapir and will tend to retard its advance unless melting can continue. Water in the magma will facilitate this rise by creating a partially molten, lubricating boundary layer. Scientists have calculated this lubricating envelope to measure only 5 to 10 centimeters thick, yet this thickness is sufficient to promote buoyancy of the diapir.

Eventually, temperatures in the rising magma cool and crystals form. The size of crystals will depend on the rate of cooling. Slower cooling promotes larger crystals, and rocks will be coarse-grained. The presence of free water vapor in the magma will significantly affect the rate of cooling. Imagine a pressure cooker deep in the earth's crust, say, at a depth of 25 kilometers. At that depth, the magma can absorb almost 12 weight percent of water before free water vapor is present. This free water vapor permits the magma to cool rather quickly, between about 650 and 630 degrees

Celsius, and crystals will be small. If the pressure cooker contains less water, say, 2 weight percent, no free water vapor is available. As a result, the magma cools more slowly over a wide temperature interval, about 1,000-630 degrees Celsius. In this situation, large crystals, often of gem quality, form.

A special process occurs during the final history of a magma when it is confined at depth or has been transported only a few kilometers from its source of melting. Residual pockets of water will accumulate from boiling when temperature falls at constant pressure—which is contradictory to normal boiling. The reason for this retrograde boiling is that those minerals crystallizing first are anhydrous, leaving behind higher water concentrations in the remaining magma. The capacity for the last batch of magma to absorb water is exceeded. At constant pressure in a closed or confined system, this excess water will boil. Exceptionally coarse-grained rocks with crystal-lined cavities form. Geologists call these water-rich pockets pegmatites. Atoms of rare elements can diffuse much more readily in a water-rich magma than in a silicate-rich magma. Significant concentrations of residual elements will form in the last water-rich magmas. Some of this residual water will not remain in cavities but instead will be driven out and assist in fracturing the enclosing rock. This water behaves as a supercritical fluid and may migrate far away from its parent magma. Eventually, rich deposits of metals may be deposited as veins.

At shallow levels in the crust—that is, less than 3 kilometers—water plays a different role in magma. Volcanic eruptions prove that some magma reaches the surface of the earth. Water-induced processes in shallow magma reservoirs beneath volcanoes largely determine the explosive behavior of future eruptions. Inside magma chambers, water permits elements to diffuse upward, and eventually the magma is zoned into chemically distinct layers. Within each zone, convection overturns older magma with newer magma. Some zones near the roof of the magma chamber may be rich in water and, if close to the surface, may pose the greatest potential for explosive eruptions. Voluminous floods of gas-rich lavas seen in the Yellowstone region in Wyoming and Idaho are thought to have originated in such a manner. This layering process induced by water-rich magmas at shallow depths can be seen in the volcanic material erupted. Periodic eruptions from these zoned magma chambers have produced sequences of different rock types.

The ability of magma to flow is controlled in part by water. Magma is known to be composed of a loose atomic arrangement of silicon and oxygen. This silicate network, or polymer, may be additionally modified by other elements. It contributes to the viscous nature of magmas. If water enters the magma, however, the network will be depolymerized and bridges of atoms are broken. The result is a more fluid magma.

Water vapor is the predominant gas in volcanoes. The eruptive behavior of magma is strongly dependent on the expansion of gas in a rising magma. Beneath a volcano, the magma reservoir may vary in its viscosity over time. Vesiculation, or the ability to form and coalesce gas bubbles, will vary according to the viscous nature of magma. The low pressure of gas that expands freely in a fluid magma limits the violence of an eruption. The magma velocity may be high, but the "frothy" nature of the gas will have dissipated before it discharges from the volcanic vent. Quite the opposite is evident in very viscous magmas that collect in volcanic plumbing systems. Water-vapor bubbles remain intact and expansion is inhibited until the uppermost neck of the volcano is reached. A sudden drop in pressure at the vent causes a violent eruption. Like that of a cannon, the discharge is rapid and a cataclysmic eruption may ensue.

Methods of Study

Estimation of the water content in magma is derived from direct measurement, experiments, thermodynamic calculations, and geologic observations. Measurements of a quenched magma collected during volcanic eruptions can yield water estimates. The amount of water trapped in the volcanic glass is often determined gravimetrically. Gravimetric analysis involves the weighing of the sample after the fluids have been driven off by heat. Additional methods are available to measure these fluid inclusions. One promising method involves crushing the sample in a vacuum or in a stream of helium. Liberated water is converted to acetylene before being pumped into a gas chromatograph. Inside the gas chromatograph, the acetylene will be adsorbed onto a column sensitive only to acetylene; a highly sensitive helium detector collects the ions generated from the collision of acetylene and helium.

Experiments measuring the amount of water present at different pressures and temperatures have been conducted in a hydrothermal pressure vessel, or "bomb." To determine the solubility of water in a magma as a function of pressure and temperature, rock powder and water in known proportions are placed in an inert metal foil capsule, which is welded shut and placed in this "bomb," which is a hollow, high-strength alloy steel vessel fitted with tubes to carry fluids under pressure from a pump. The vessel is placed in a furnace. After each experiment at a given temperature and pressure, the sample is either quickly quenched with compressed air or dropped into a bucket of water. If the sample melt does not absorb all the available water, the water vapors are frozen into the quenched glass as vesicles or bubbles. The water content can thus be determined at various pressures and temperatures for different rock types; geologists then can extrapolate water content of magma to depths in the earth's crust.

In lieu of experimental data, thermodynamic calculations are used to estimate water content in magmas. This method is applicable only to those mineral assemblages whose chemical relations are known. The calculations are based on the idea that some minerals require water to exist at a particular pressure and temperature. If the pressure and temperature change, the amount of water must also change in order that the minerals remain unchanged.

Geological observations of volcanic products ejected by an eruption offer a promising method of estimating water contents. Careful field measurements of the size, shape, and distribution of volcanic fragments plus the physical dimensions of the volcanic vent can lead to an estimate of the gas-flow rate. Because water vapor is the predominant gas involved, the amount of water involved in the eruption can be estimated. Even the sizes of ancient gas bubbles or vesicles in a rock can be measured to determine estimates of water content.

Actual water contents measured in volcanic eruptions agree with estimates obtained in experiments and from calculations. Confirmation of water amounts at deeper pressures remains tenable. If the geology at depth were well known, then possibly experimental data could be extrapolated more confidently.

Context

Traces of water tens of kilometers beneath the earth's surface can influence whether a volcano will erupt violently, if at all. Small amounts of melting eventually lead to the creation of magma chambers beneath volcanoes. Tremendous quantities of magma inch their way upward toward the surface with the aid of water. Volcanic eruptions are powerful displays of magma reaching the surface.

One of the principal reasons that eruptions in Hawaii can be viewed safely is that the water-vapor pressure has been diffused well beneath the vent at the surface. The most prolific eruptions in historical times have been from Kilauea, as miles of fluid magma have poured onto the Hawaiian landscape. This fluid lava has been pumped from a deep reservoir very poor in water. On the other hand, eruptions at Mount St. Helens awoke many geologists to the need to forecast potential hazards. Destructive volcanic eruptions are fueled by high water pressure. The amount of water required in a magma reservoir prior to explosive activity needs to be better understood. Careful measurement of water being discharged from volcanoes and found in earlier ejected rocks may reveal the answer to this mystery.

Many magmas will experience a limited ascent and will eventually freeze beneath the earth's surface. Many of these granitic rocks are exposed after millions of years of erosion. To the casual observer, these rocks appear quite similar, but to the gem collector and exploration geologist, they may indicate the presence of emeralds, rubys, and rare metals. At rare localities, cavities of once-boiling water in deep magmas are evidenced by spectacular gem-quality minerals.

Bibliography

Baker, D. R. "Depth and Water Content of Magma Chambers in the Aleutian and Mariana Island Arcs." *Geology* 15 (1987). The reader can discover a practical application of measuring water contents in magmas. The Aleutian and Mariana regions of the Pacific are home to many active volcanoes. This article describes the ascent of magma and the water content of these magma-chamber pressure cookers.

Decker, Robert, and Barbara Decker. *Volcanoes*. New York: W. H. Freeman, 1981. This introduction to the nature and power of volcanoes is rich with examples of active volcanoes worldwide. Processes involved in the generation of magma are discussed with many illustrations. Suitable for high school readers.

Fairbridge, Rhodes Whitmore, ed. *The Encyclopedia of Geochemistry and Environmental Sciences*. New York: Van Nostrand Reinhold, 1972. An excellent summary of water and gases occurring in magmas, with emphasis on discharges from volcanoes. Many additional references related to the behavior of water are given.

Hall, Anthony. *Igneous Petrology*. New York: Halsted Press, 1987. A comprehensive review of earth processes that generated a wide variety of igneous rocks. Each chapter discusses a different rock group. The role of water in magmas is emphasized in the sections on granites. Text is college-level, but the illustrations are useful to the general reader.

William C. Sidle

Cross-References

Experimental Petrology, 662; Fluid Inclusions, 726; Crystallization of Magmas, 1420; The Origin of Magmas, 1428; Pegmatites, 2025; Phase Changes, 2042; Phase Equilibria, 2049; Volcanoes: Types of Eruption, 2695.

MAGNETIC REVERSALS

Type of earth science: Geophysics
Type of study: Geomagnetism and paleomagnetism

The investigation of earth's magnetic field history, as recorded by diverse rock types, has disclosed that the magnetic field changes position relative to the surface of the earth. The information accumulated from the study of these reversals is used to explain many of the events that have occurred in the history of the earth, such as continental collisions.

Principal terms

BASALT: dark-colored, fine-grained igneous rock frequently found beneath the sediment covering the ocean floor

DETRITAL REMANENT MAGNETIZATION (DRM): sedimentary rock magnetization acquired by magnetic sediment grains aligning with the magnetic field

NORMAL POLARITY: orientation of the earth's magnetic field so that a compass needle points toward the Northern Hemisphere

POLARITY: orientation of the earth's magnetic field relative to the earth

REVERSE POLARITY: orientation of the earth's magnetic field so that a compass needle points toward the Southern Hemisphere

THERMAL REMANENT MAGNETIZATION (TRM): magnetization acquired as a magma's magnetic material becomes permanently magnetized

Summary of the Phenomenon

Research into the history of the earth's magnetic field has revealed that the field has flipped polarity many times in the past. Presently, the field is oriented so that a compass needle points toward the Northern Hemisphere of the earth. This orientation is known as normal polarity. If a compass needle were to point toward the south, that would indicate a reverse polarity. The flipping, or reversal, of the field involves the exchange of pole positions from Northern Hemisphere to Southern, either normal to reverse or reverse to normal.

To determine whether the polarity change is a real field change or simply a modification in a rock's magnetic-recording mechanism, numerous rocks were analyzed to ascertain their magnetic characteristics and to determine whether these alter over time. Only a very small percentage of the rocks studied, including an igneous rock from Japan, displayed a self-reversing tendency. This find persuaded geophysicists that self-reversing tendencies in rocks do not need to be considered in the study of the field's history. Therefore, geophysicists do not have to test every rock to determine whether it self-reverses.

Geologists must still verify that the polarity changes are real phenomena that are consistent from one region of the earth to another. They make use of the fact that when magnetic grains form in magma, they magnetically align themselves with the magnetic field present at that time. This type of rock recording of magnetic direction is known as thermal remanent magnetization (TRM), and the best recorder is rock of basaltic composition.

The Hawaiian Islands are the site of basaltic rock formed from magma that has sporadically erupted from the Hawaiian volcanoes over a period of millions of years. The island of Hawaii is a large volcano that sits several kilometers below sea level and rises several kilometers above sea level. Measured from base to summit, Hawaii is the highest mountain in the world.

A detailed polarity history of the island is difficult to develop because volcanic eruptions are intermittent, with several thousands of years between eruptions; however, an overall appreciation of the field changes can be acquired by sampling the distinct layers located in the eroded sides of the volcanoes. Back in the laboratory, an "absolute" date for the rocks can be obtained using radioactive-dating procedures. Relative dates—the sequence of occurrence for the samples—can also be established, as sample A is from a layer that lies below sample B, and so on. Relative dating helps assure that the absolute dates are correct. If sample A has an absolute date of 120,000 years and sample B a date of 140,000 years, but sample B is located physically above sample A in the volcano, then something is wrong. Accurate dating is an important aspect in the establishment of the polarity time scale.

By using a magnetometer, the polarity and the field direction of the sample can be determined. If the field points down, the polarity is normal. A field that points up indicates a reversed polarity. Once enough data have been collected (several hundred samples), the sample polarities can be plotted against the sample date. In this manner, the polarity history can be determined for the past 4 million years.

The fact that field reversals are a worldwide occurrence and instantaneous from a geological perspective permits the establishment of the field of magnetostratigraphy for correlating rock layers from various continents. In piecing together the earth's history as revealed in the rocks, it is necessary to know what is occurring around the world at approximately the same time. In order to accomplish this feat, ways have been developed to correlate rocks in one area with rocks in another area. One way is by using index fossils, which are fossils that are widespread and common but which lived for only a short time. The problem is that index fossils are limited in distribution and cannot be used for correlating between continents. Magnetostratigraphy bypasses this difficulty.

The polarity scale shows that from 4 million to 3.3 million years ago, the field was reversed. This period is called the Gilbert reverse epoch (the major periods are named for scientists who have advanced the discipline of magnetism). The field was normal until 2.5 million years ago during the Gauss normal epoch, except for a brief period of reversed polarity around 3 million years ago, known as the Mammoth reverse event. The Matuyama reverse epoch continued until 700,000 years ago. This epoch contained two normal events: the Olduvai, around 2 million years ago; and the Jaramillo, about 1 million years ago. The Brunhes is the present-day normal epoch. Other normal or reverse events may have been present in these epochs.

Geophysicists are compelled to find other methods that verify the validity of the polarity scale and to extend and add more detail to the existing scale. One technique utilizes the sediment layer covering most of the ocean basin. This sediment can record magnetic field direction by the mechanism of detrital remanent magnetization (DRM). Long sediment cores are obtained from various areas in the ocean, and the magnetic polarity of areas along the length of the individual cores is measured. Again, a pattern of polarity changes is evident. Radioactivity cannot efficiently date the layers of the core. Fortunately, the sediment is laid down very slowly, and this rate is measurable. The rate is on the order of millimeters per one thousand years; thus, a layer 10 millimeters from the surface was deposited approximately 15,000 years ago. Polarity is plotted against calculated age, and analysis shows that the sediment-based data correspond well with the land-based scale.

In the 1950's, magnetometers were towed behind ships that sailed over the oceanic ridge to the south of Iceland. The data were plotted on a map of the research area, and something strange became evident: The recorded magnetic field varied over the area. The map revealed a striped pattern of weaker and stronger field intensities that was aligned parallel to the ridge, now known as magnetic sea-floor stripes. Fred Vine and Drummond Matthews, working together, and Lawrence Morley, working alone, realized that polarity changes caused the stripes.

In the mid-1960's, a revolution in the earth sciences was occurring with the development of the theory of plate tectonics. Scientists theorized that the earth's surface rock was split into plates of thin but considerable area. These plates had boundaries that interacted in several possible ways: They could move together, or converge; they could move apart, or diverge; or they could slide past each other in an area known as a transform fault. At the diverging boundary, the motion should produce a breach between the plates, but none was found. Investigation disclosed that the volcanically active oceanic ridge was the diverging boundary and that basaltic magma quickly filled any gap. New plate material is formed at this diverging boundary, and the cooling magma records the magnetic field present at the time of cooling by thermal remanent magnetization (TRM). The cooled magma moves away parallel to the ridge as the plates diverge. The magnetic field of basaltic rock that recorded the earth's magnetic field during a period of the reversed polarity cancels some of the earth's present-day field. This cancellation produces an area of lower-intensity field parallel to the ridge. The rock recording normal polarity adds to the earth's field, resulting in a strong intensity stripe.

The last polarity change 700,000 years ago was represented by rock that was located many kilometers from the center of the ridge. By dividing that distance by 700,000 years, the rate at which the plate is forming can be calculated. That value is approximately 2-5 centimeters per year depending on which portion of the ridge is being measured. This rate is comparable to how fast human fingernails grow. As a result of this movement, North America, which is west of the ridge, is now about 25 meters farther west of Europe, which is east of the ridge, than when Christopher Columbus sailed in 1492.

Other research has extended the polarity scale back hundreds of millions of years. This extension permits the identification of long-term trends depicting the manner in which the field has changed polarity. The field has remained very stable, with few polarity changes, several times in the past. In the Pennsylvanian period of the late Paleozoic era, for example, the field was predominantly in the reversed position; the field was normal for a long time in the Cretaceous period of the Late Mesozoic era. At other times, including the present Cenozoic era, the field has flipped many times.

Methods of Study

The procedure used to study magnetic reversals depends on the area of investigation. Land-based investigations are straightforward: The researcher chooses a likely site and conducts preliminary research to ascertain whether others have studied the area and whether the site will yield samples appropriate for study. If an area displays promise, the required rock samples are obtained. The rock should not be severely weathered, as that may alter the magnetic or radioactive components of the rock, which could lead to incorrect results. The sample is collected using a gasoline-powered drill with a tube-shaped, diamond-tipped drill bit. The resulting sample is a cylinder of rock still attached at its base to the original rock. A brass tube, the size of the drill bit, is slipped over the cylinder. Brass is used because it is nonmagnetic and will not alter the sample's magnetic characteristics. Attached to the tube is a small platform on which is placed a Brunton compass, used to measure the orientation of the sample. The compass is very important, as sample orientation, the sampling site latitude and longitude, and the magnetic field direction of the sample are needed to calculate the sample's pole position. An orientation mark is made on the sample with a brass rod, and the sample is broken from the original rock. An identification number is assigned, which is carefully recorded along with all other pertinent information.

In the laboratory, the samples are prepared for the measurement of the rock's magnetic field direction by cutting them into lengths of 2.5 centimeters; thus, several small samples are obtained from each core, which can be used for dating purposes and for verifying the sample's polarity. Scientists do not rely on one measurement but make multiple assessments of a characteristic to ensure sample integrity. Because they are basalt samples, the rocks' magnetic directions are measured by a spinner magnetometer. A spinner works similarly to an electrical generator in that the sample is spun at high speed near coils of wire. The magnetic sample induces an electric current in the coils that is proportional to the strength of the sample's magnetic field. The rock's magnetic field direction is determined from these signals.

Usually, a computer performs the calculation of the final pole position using sample orientation, site latitude and longitude, and rock field direction. This pole position is plotted on a graph known as a stereonet, which is a two-dimensional representation of the earth's surface. Normal polarity poles plot in the Northern Hemisphere of the stereonet and those of reversed polarity in the Southern.

The basalt is also analyzed to determine its age. The amount of a suitable radioactive element (the parent isotope) and the amount of the element into which the radioactive element decays (the daughter isotope) are measured. The sample's age is calculated from these measurements.

The sediment polarity scale is more difficult to obtain, because the cores come from the ocean bottom—3 kilometers below sea level, in some places—using a coring device that is dropped from a ship. Back in the laboratory, samples are taken along the length of the core. Their position on the core is measured, as their distance from the top of the core determines the age of the sample. The original core is not oriented as it is taken from the sea floor, because the scientist is not interested in the sample's pole position. The scientist is interested in the sample's polarity, and an unoriented core will yield that information.

The sediment has a weak magnetic field, so a superconducting magnetometer is used for the measurements. When some materials are cooled close to absolute zero, near the boiling point of liquid helium, they have no resistance to electrical current. Superconducting magnetometers that can detect small magnetic fields, such as those of sediment, employ these materials. Again, the polarity of the sediment sample is determined from the magnetometer readings.

The detection of the sea-floor stripes is a simple but tedious endeavor that requires the towing of a magnetometer "fish" several hundred meters behind a ship along parallel tracks across the area of interest. The magnetometer is towed to prevent the detection of ship-related magnetic fields. The readings—signal strength and ship's position—are plotted on a map and the stripe patterns are observed.

Context

The fact that the earth's magnetic field has reversed many times in the past is important because it verifies the theory of plate tectonics. Before the plates rupture, the rock layers along the potential rift area dome upward; to relieve the pressure, the dome splits in a three-armed rift. Two of the arms expand in length and join arms from other domed areas. These joined arms form the boundary between the two plates; the third arm fails to enlarge but forms a wedge-shaped basin that fills with sediment. Over time, organic material in the sediment is converted to petroleum. These sources of petroleum were unknown until the development of the theory of plate tectonics. Understanding plate tectonics also increases the understanding of earthquakes and their origin, which could lead to their prediction and even to their control.

Bibliography

Cox, Allan, ed. *Plate Tectonics and Geomagnetic Reversals*. San Francisco: W. H.

Freeman, 1973. Cox was a leader in establishing the magnetic polarity scale for the past 4 million years. In this book, he provides fascinating introductions to chapters that are composed of seminal papers concerning magnetic reversals and their contribution to the development of the theory of plate tectonics. The papers are advanced for the average reader, but have many graphs, diagrams, and figures that merit attention. The introductions are good, as they reveal the human side of scientists in their quest for knowledge.

Garland, G. D. *Introduction to Geophysics*. 2d ed. London: W. B. Saunders, 1979. Used as text for introductory geophysics, this book contains in sections 21.4 through 21.6 very readable material on magnetic reversals, magnetic anomalies, and the magnetic character of the oceans and continents. The many figures and graphs are of interest to the general reader.

Glen, William. *The Road to Jaramillo: Critical Years of the Revolution in Earth Science*. Stanford, Calif.: Stanford University Press, 1982. A history of the plate tectonics revolution of the mid-1950s to the mid-1960's. Chapter 6 is devoted to the evolution of the magnetic polarity scale. Chapter 7 deals with magnetic sea-floor stripes and their interpretation. Other chapters are also important, such as chapter 5, with its discussion of the participants in the earth science revolution.

Jacobs, J. A., R. D. Russell, and J. T. Wilson. *Physics and Geology*. 2d ed. New York: McGraw-Hill, 1974. The previous edition, *Geology and Physics*, was written when the theory of plate tectonics was emerging as the major theory of terrestrial phenomena such as earthquakes. The text was leaning toward the acceptance of the theory but did not show a deep confidence in it. This text was used as an introductory geophysics text but is now outdated. Provides a source of insight into the problems that plagued the development of the theory. Formidable for the average student, as there is considerable mathematics in some chapters, though chapter 8, "Geomagnetism," contains a minimum of equations and many figures and graphs. One problem is the method of reference citation—the author's name and the reference year are placed within the text, which makes for tiresome reading because there are many citations.

Kennett, J. P. *Marine Geology*. Englewood Cliffs, N.J.: Prentice-Hall, 1982. Pages 71-78 are devoted to magnetostratigraphy and magnetic reversals. The text is a veritable all-you-need-to-know book about marine geology: plate tectonics, oceanic structure, sediments, margins, and history. Various dating methods are also described. Very readable, with no mathematics and some figures.

_____, ed. *Magnetic Stratigraphy of Sediments*. Benchmark Papers in Geology, vol. 54. Stroudsburg, Pa.: Dowden, Hutchinson, and Ross, 1980. A memorial edition to Norman Watkins, who was intimately involved with the research aimed at the development of plate tectonic theory via the study of magnetization of sediments. A collection of seminal papers concerned with the magnetic stratigraphy of sediments, which relies on the fact of magnetic reversals. As a collection, the reading is uneven, as some papers are very involved, while others are less technical. The editor provides short essays at the beginning of each chapter. Graphs, tables, figures, and diagrams abound.

Lapedes, Daniel N., ed. *McGraw-Hill Encyclopedia of Geological Sciences*. New York: McGraw-Hill, 1978. Pages 704-708, under the heading "Rock Magnetism," provide a concise description of many aspects associated with rock magnetism: how rock magnetization occurs, the present field, magnetic reversals, secular variation, and apparent polar wandering, among others. Very readable, with no mathematics and a fair number of graphs, tables, and figures.

Motz, Lloyd, ed. *Rediscovery of the Earth*. New York: Van Nostrand Reinhold, 1979. As a collection of articles for the nonscientist by renowned scientists in their respective fields, the text makes very interesting reading and is augmented with many colorful illustrations. The chapter "The Earth's Magnetic Field and Its Variations" was written by Takesi Nagata, who has written hundreds of articles on diverse aspects of geophysics besides the earth's magnetic field.

Stephen J. Shulik

Cross-References

The Origin of Earth's Magnetic Field, 532; Secular Variation of Earth's Magnetic Field, 540; Earth's Magnetic Field at Present, 548; The Geologic Time Scale, 874; Geothermal Phenomena and Heat Transport, 906; Igneous Rocks: Basaltic, 1158; Magnetic Stratigraphy, 1446; The Ocean Ridge System, 1826; The Oceanic Crust, 1846; Plate Tectonics, 2079; Radioactive Decay, 2136; Radioactive Minerals, 2143; Rock Magnetism, 2217; Stratigraphic Correlation, 2485; Volcanism at Spreading Centers, 2607.

MAGNETIC STRATIGRAPHY

Type of earth science: Geophysics
Field of study: Geomagnetism and paleomagnetism

The earth's magnetic field has fluctuated between a polarity like that of today's field ("normal") and one completely opposite ("reversed") thousands of times in the last 600 million years. The magnetic minerals in erupting lavas and in settling sediments align with the prevailing field at the time the rock forms and thus record the earth's polarity history. The pattern of polarity changes in a thick sequence of rock and can be matched from area to area, providing scientists with a very powerful tool of correlation.

Principal terms

CORRELATION: matching the sequence of events (distinctive layers, fossils, magnetic polarity intervals) between two stratigraphic sections

CURIE POINT: the temperature at which a magnetic mineral locks in its magnetization

MAGNETIC DOMAIN: a region within a mineral with a single direction of magnetization; mineral grains smaller than about 100 microns contain only one domain, while larger grains can contain several domains

MAGNETIC POLARITY TIME SCALE: the geologic history of the changes in the earth's magnetic polarity

MAGNETIC REMANENCE: the ability of the magnetic minerals in a rock to "lock in" the magnetic field of the earth prevailing at the time of their formation

PALEOMAGNETISM: the study of the ancient magnetic field of the earth, as recorded by magnetic minerals in rocks

RADIOMETRIC DATING: the estimation of the numerical age of a rock by measuring the decay of radioactive minerals, such as uranium, rubidium, or potassium

STRATIGRAPHY: the study and interpretation of geologic history from layered rock sequences (usually sedimentary)

Summary of the Phenomenon

A compass shows that the earth's magnetic field lines point toward the North Pole, but 800,000 years ago, a compass needle would have pointed to the South Pole. The earth's magnetic field has apparently changed polarity thousands of times in the geologic past, and an excellent record of its history extends back over the last 150 million years. This history is recorded in the magnetic minerals of rocks that were deposited or erupted in the geologic past.

Several minerals common in the earth's crust are known to be magnetic, but the most important are the iron oxides magnetite and hematite. Magnetite contains three atoms of iron and four of oxygen; hematite contains two atoms of iron and three of oxygen. When a magma cools, the magnetic domains (areas within a crystal that have the same magnetic direction) within crystals align with the field at that time and lock in that direction as the rest of the rock crystallizes. This process is known as thermal remanent magnetization (TRM). Since TRM is formed by cooling, it is found only in igneous and metamorphic rocks. The only igneous rocks that are commonly layered and capable of stratigraphic study are lava flows. Stacked sequences of lava flows were the source of the first discovery that the earth's magnetic field had reversed. The temperature at which this magnetization is locked in is known as the Curie point. For magnetite, the Curie point is about 578 degrees Celsius, but for hematite, it can be as high as 650 degrees Celsius. The actual Curie point varies with the variation in iron and titanium content in the mineral.

When rocks with magnetic minerals are eroded, the magnetic grains become sedimentary particles that are transported by wind and water. As these particles settle, they too align with the prevailing field. As the rest of the sediment is hardened into rock, the sedimentary rock records the direction of the field at the time it was formed. This is known as detrital (or depositional) remanent magnetization (DRM). Since most stratigraphic sequences are sedimentary, most magnetic stratigraphy is concerned with the DRM of sediments.

After a rock is formed, it is possible for water seeping through it to oxidize the iron and precipitate new minerals (particularly hematite and iron hydroxides, such as goethite). Since these new minerals are formed by chemical activity, the magnetic field they lock in is known as chemical remanent magnetization (CRM). These minerals lock in a magnetic field that records the time of chemical alteration rather than the time of the formation of the rock. This magnetization is usually a secondary, "overprinted" one that obscures the original magnetization, which is the most interesting to the paleomagnetist.

Thick sequences of lava flows or layers of sediments that span long periods of time record the changes in the earth's magnetic field through that time interval. By sampling many levels through such a sequence, the paleomagnetist can determine the magnetic sequence, or magnetic stratigraphy, of that local section. Under the right conditions, the magnetic pattern of a section is distinctive. It can be matched to the pattern in a number of other sections of approximately the same age, and these sections can be correlated by the polarity changes. If the pattern is long and distinctive enough and its numerical age can be estimated (usually by radiometric dating), then it is possible to match the pattern to the worldwide magnetic polarity time scale and to estimate an even more precise age.

The worldwide magnetic polarity time scale was first developed in the 1960's, when a group of scientists found that all lava flows with potassium-argon dates less than about 700,000 years were normally magnetized (like the present earth's field), and those older than 700,000 years were usually reversely magnetized (opposite the present earth's field). They began to seek out more and more lava flows around the world, sampling them for both their magnetism and their potassium-argon age. In about five years of sampling, they found a consistent pattern: All rocks of the same age had the same magnetic polarity, no matter where they were located. This immediately suggested that their magnetic properties were caused by worldwide magnetic field reversals rather than by local peculiarities of the rocks themselves.

Continuous sequences of lava flows that could be dated, however, were not available for time periods older than about 13 million years. What was needed was a terrestrial process that continuously recorded the earth's magnetic field behavior and could be dated. Such a process was discovered in the early 1960's at the same time that magnetic polarity reversals were documented. The crust of the ocean floor is constantly pulling apart, and the gap is filled by magma from the mantle below. When the magma cools it locks in the magnetic polarity prevailing at the time. Continual sea-floor spreading pulls apart this newly cooled crustal material and carries it away from the mid-ocean ridge, causing new magma to fill in the rift, to cool, and to lock in a new polarity. This process of cooling, magnetization, and spreading acts as a "tape recorder" that produces a magnetic record of the present field at the center of the ridge and progressively older fields away from the ridge crest. In a few places in the ocean basin, this ocean-floor "tape recording" goes back about 150 million years.

The steady spreading of oceanic plates provides the only continuous record of the changes in the earth's magnetic field between 13 million and about 150 million years ago. In 1968, the first attempt was made to construct a magnetic polarity time scale. Using the known rates of spreading of several mid-ocean ridges, scientists extrapolated several oceanic spreading records back to about 100 million years and placed tentative dates on all the polarity events that were recorded. Since 1968, many attempts have been made to date this polarity time scale more precisely. Ironically, most of the new dates have shown that the original 1968 extrapolation was remarkably good, and new versions of the time scale differ very little from the first version. This proves the assumption that sea-floor spreading is a relatively steady, constant process.

In the last decade, magnetic stratigraphy has proven to be one of the most powerful tools of correlation and dating available. It has many features that other methods of correlation do not. Unlike correlation by distinctive rock units or by the changes in fossils through time, magnetic polarity changes happen on a worldwide basis and can be recorded in any type of rock (lavas or marine or nonmarine sediments) formed at that time. No rock type is formed worldwide, and fossils are restricted by the environments in which they lived. Thus, rocks formed in both the oceans and land can be directly correlated by magnetic stratigraphy, even though the rock sequences are different and they do not share the same fossils.

Another unique feature of magnetic stratigraphy is that polarity changes take place within about 4,000-5,000 years, which is considered instantaneous in a geological sense for any event that occurred more than about a million years ago. Thus, a polarity zone boundary represents a worldwide, geologically instantaneous "time plane" that can be used as a very precise marker wherever it is found. By contrast, the changes in fossil assemblages in a stratigraphic section can seldom resolve events down to a few thousand years, and radiometric dates typically have analytical errors that are anywhere from hundreds of thousands to millions of years.

The major limitation of magnetic stratigraphy is that most magnetic patterns are not unique. When paleomagnetists sample a rock, they get only normal or reversed polarity, not a numerical age. To date a sequence, some other form of dating must be used to place the magnetic pattern on the magnetic polarity time scale. For example, a sequence of "normal-reversed-normal" is not unique by itself; it has occurred many times in the geologic past. If, however, a distinctive set of fossils or a radiometric date can constrain that pattern to a certain period in earth history, then there may be only one part of the magnetic polarity time scale that matches that pattern at that particular point in time. This match gives a more precise age estimate than does the fossil or radiometric date alone.

Methods of Study

Paleomagnetists study ancient magnetic fields by sampling rocks of the proper age and rock type. If it is a lava or other very hard rock, they use a portable drill that collects a short core about 2 centimeters in diameter. Lavas tend to be strongly magnetized compared to other rock types. If the rock to be sampled is a softer sedimentary rock that might break up while drilling, then simple chisels and scrapers are used to extract a hand sample. Sediments tend to have magnetizations that are weaker than those of lavas by a factor of one hundred to one thousand. In addition, only fine-grained sediments (siltstones, claystones, fine sandstones, and limestones) record a remanence; coarse sandstones have more than one magnetic domain within each magnetic grain, which cancel one another out. In both cases, the direction of the present earth's magnetic field is marked on the sample, so it can be compared with the direction recorded in the rock.

The samples are then measured in a device called a magnetometer, which determines the direction and intensity of the field recorded by the sample (its natural remanent magnetization, or NRM). Some magnetometers are portable, but they are only suitable for measuring strongly magnetized lavas. Most labs now use a superconducting cryogenic magnetometer. Its sensing area is kept at 4 degrees Celsius above absolute zero (-269 degrees Celsius) so that it is superconducting, or has almost no resistance to electrical current. When a sample is lowered into the sensing area, even weak magnetic fields in the sample cause changes in electrical current, which are then converted into a magnetic signal.

Typically, the field direction found in the sample (NRM) is a composite of several different magnetic fields. For example, if the rock were deposited during a period of reversed polarity, it may still have a young magnetic overprint acquired during the normal polarity that is seen today. The interaction of these two directions may give an NRM that is neither normal nor reversed, but some intermediate direction. To get rid of unwanted overprinting, the samples must be treated with high temperatures (thermal demagnetization) or high external magnetic fields (alternating field demagnetization), which destroys the less stable (and presumably young overprinted) component of the magnetization. After each treatment at progressively higher temperatures or progressively higher applied fields, the sample is measured again. Interpreting the change of direction and strength of the magnetic component during this stepwise demagnetization enables the paleomagnetist to decide which magnetic mineral is the carrier of the magnetic remanence and also which temperature or field is best for magnetically "cleaning" samples.

After magnetic cleaning, each sample produces a direction that presumably represents the field direction at the time the rock was formed. This remanence is known as the primary, or characteristic, remanence. Because several samples are taken of each lava flow or of each sedimentary bed, the directions of all of the samples from a given site are averaged to omit random "noise." The more tightly all the directions from a site cluster, the more reliable they are likely to be. There are statistical methods that measure this clustering and allow the paleomagnetist to determine the quality of the data. Data that cluster poorly or give nonsensical results can be rejected.

Context

Magnetic stratigraphy has become one of the most powerful tools of dating geologic events. It is critical to understanding geologic history and provides a much greater understanding of certain aspects of the geological past than was previously possible. For example, there has been great controversy over how fast evolution takes place or when mass extinctions occurred. By more precisely dating the sequences in which these events are recorded, scientists can determine rates of evolution much more precisely or determine a much more accurate date for the timing of a mass extinction, which may, in turn, allow the determination of the causes of these events and resolve many long-standing controversies. Magnetic stratigraphy has been used to date the long history of evolution of fossil mammals and dinosaurs in the terrestrial environment and the details of the evolution of the world ocean in marine sections. In many marine sections, the use of magnetic stratigraphy has allowed precise dating of climatic changes, particularly the glacial-interglacial fluctuation of the last ice age. This precise dating, in turn, has allowed scientists to determine that the glacial-interglacial cycles were controlled by changes in the earth's orbital motions, and they thus deciphered the cause of the ice ages. A better understanding of how some of these events (climate change, ice ages, mass extinctions) occurred in the past will help scientists to decide if such events are likely to happen again in the near future.

Bibliography

Boggs, Sam, Jr. *Principles of Sedimentology and Stratigraphy.* Columbus, Ohio: Charles E. Merrill, 1986. A college-level textbook on stratigraphy and sedimentology, which devotes a chapter (chapter 15) to magnetic stratigraphy. This chapter, although brief and not concerned with the practical aspects of magnetic stratigraphy, does give one of the few up-to-date accounts available in any stratigraphy textbook.

Cox, Allan, ed. *Plate Tectonics and Geomagnetic Reversals*. San Francisco: W. H. Freeman, 1973. A collection of the classic papers that led to the plate tectonics revolution, edited by a man who was responsible for the paleomagnetic data that propelled it. It includes many of the pioneering papers that first described the reversals of the earth's magnetic field as well as the discovery of the magnetic polarity time scale and sea-floor spreading. One of its best features is the editorial introductions, which place the papers in historical context.

Cox, Allan, and R. B. Hart. *Plate Tectonics: How It Works*. Palo Alto, Calif.: Blackwell Scientific, 1986. A college-level textbook that explains many facets of plate tectonics, with examples and problem sets. Several chapters give an excellent discussion of paleomagnetism.

Glen, William. *The Road to Jaramollo: Critical Years of the Revolution in Earth Sciences*. Stanford, Calif.: Stanford University Press, 1982. A history of the plate tectonics revolution, recounting the important individuals and their discoveries that led to the discovery of continental drift and sea-floor spreading. The development of the magnetic polarity time scale was a key part of this, and the rivalry between various labs in discovering and dating the magnetic reversals is described in detail.

Kenneth, J. P., ed. *Magnetic Stratigraphy of Sediments*. Stroudsburg, Pa.: Dowden, Hutchinson, and Ross, 1980. An anthology of classic papers on magnetic stratigraphy. Most of the papers deal with magnetic stratigraphy of marine sediments and their application to paleo-oceanographic problems, but some also cover terrestrial magnetic stratigraphy. The editor wrote introductions that place all the papers in historical context.

Lindsay, E. H., et al. "Mammalian Chronology and the Magnetic Polarity Time Scale." In *Cenozoic Mammals of North America*, edited by M. O. Woodburn. Berkeley: University of California Press, 1987. This chapter contains one of the best reviews of the practical aspects of magnetic stratigraphy as applied to terrestrial sections. Although it is written on the professional level, it assumes little or no background in rock magnetism.

McElhinny, M. W. *Palaeomagnetism and Plate Tectonics*. New York: Cambridge University Press, 1973. One of the most popular college textbooks on paleomagnetism. Although some of the text is outdated, it contains an excellent discussion of the field as it was at that time.

Prothero, D. R. *Interpreting the Stratigraphic Record*. New York: W. H. Freeman, 1989. A college-level textbook on stratigraphy, containing a chapter on magnetic stratigraphy. The discussion on magnetic stratigraphy is considerably clearer, more thorough, and more up-to-date than that by Boggs.

_____. "Mammals and Magnetostratigraphy." *Journal of Geological Edu-*

cation 36 (1988): 227. A nontechnical article detailing the practical aspects of terrestrial magnetostratigraphy. It also reviews the progress on the terrestrial, fossil-mammal-bearing record up to the time of the article.

Tarling, D. H. *Palaeomagnetism: Principles and Applications in Geology, Geophysics, and Archaeology.* London: Chapman and Hall, 1983. One of the best books available on paleomagnetism. It discusses magnetic stratigraphy on a much more general level than does McElhinny. A good first resource in reading about the subject.

Donald R. Prothero

Cross-References

Earth's Magnetic Field at Present, 548; The Geologic Time Scale, 874; Magnetic Reversals, 1439; Rock Magnetism, 2217; Stratigraphic Correlation, 2485.

MAMMALS

Type of earth science: Paleontology and earth history

Mammals are four-legged backboned animals distinguished by a number of unique characteristics, including hair, constant warm body temperature, mammary glands, and specialized teeth that are replaced only once. Mammals first descended from a group of animals known as synapsids, or mammal-like reptiles, about 200 million years ago but remained small (mouse-sized) and unspecialized until the dinosaurs died off about 65 million years ago. They then underwent a huge evolutionary radiation, that is, spread into different environments and diverged in structure.

Principal terms

CENOZOIC ERA: the period of geologic time from about 65 million years ago to the present

GENUS (plural, GENERA): a group of closely related species; for example, *Homo* is the genus of humans, and it includes the species *Homo sapiens* (modern humans) and *Homo erectus* (Peking Man, Java Man)

MAMMARY GLANDS: the glands that female mammals use to nurse their young

MARSUPIALS: mammals that give birth to a premature embryo that then finishes its development in a pouch

MONOTREMES: primitive mammals, such as the platypus and spiny anteater, that lay eggs and have other archaic features

ORDER: a group of closely related genera; in mammals, orders are the well-recognized major groups, such as the rodents, bats, whales, and carnivores

PLACENTALS: mammals that carry the embryo in the mother until it is born in a well-developed state; it is nourished in the womb by a membrane (the placenta)

SYNAPSIDS: the mammal-like reptiles that lived from about 300 to 200 million years ago and evolved into mammals

Summary of the Phenomenon

Mammals are a group of vertebrates (animals with backbones) that have been the dominant animals on land and sea since the dinosaurs died out about 65 million years ago. Indeed, the present period of geologic time, the Cenozoic era, is often called the Age of Mammals. About 4,170 species of mammals are alive currently, but at least five times that many are now extinct. About 1,010 genera of mammals are living but, according to a 1945 tabulation, an additional 2,000 genera were extinct, and that number has greatly increased since 1945. Mammals have been very successful in occupying a great variety of terrestrial and aquatic ecological niches. They include terrestrial meat-eaters and plant-eaters, tree dwellers, burrowing forms, and even aquatic forms. The largest terrestrial mammals today are elephants, but the extinct hornless rhinoceros *Paraceratherium* was much larger, reaching 6 meters at the shoulder and weighing about 20,000 kilograms. The largest mammals, however, are whales; they can weigh up to 150,000 kilograms in the case of the blue whale, which is larger than even the largest dinosaurs.

Living mammals are easily distinguished from all other vertebrates by a number of unique evolutionary specializations. Unlike other vertebrates, mammals have hair, are equipped with mammary glands to nurse their young, and bear live young (except for the most primitive egg-laying mammals, the platypus and spiny anteater). Mammals maintain a constant, relatively high body temperature. They have a four-chambered heart and a very efficient digestive and respiratory system, which includes a diaphragm in the chest cavity to aid in breathing. Mammals develop rapidly as juveniles and then stop growing when they reach adult size, unlike other animals, which grow continuously through life.

Fossil mammals, however, are known only from their fossilizable parts, which are mostly their teeth and bones. Their fossil record can be traced back to their ancestors, the synapsids, or mammal-like reptiles, which are known as far back as 300 million years ago. Fossil mammals are usually distinguished from their ancestors by a number of skeletal features. These features include specialized teeth that are replaced only once (comparable to our "baby teeth" and adult teeth), a jaw joint between the dentary and squamosal bones, and a middle ear that is composed of three bones (the hammer, anvil, and stirrup).

As the large synapsids were being replaced by the dinosaurs about 210 million years ago, mammals evolved as tiny, mouse-sized animals that fed on insects. Mammals remained thus for almost 150 million years, living in the nooks and crannies of the world of the dinosaurs, who dominated the planet. A number of different "experimental" groups of insectivorous (insect-eating) mammals lived during this time, but all went extinct. About 100 million years ago, the three major groups of living mammals evolved. These include the monotremes, the marsupials, and the placentals.

The monotremes are the egg-laying mammals, the platypus and the spiny anteater of Australia and New Guinea. The more advanced mammals bear live young. One group, the pouched mammals, or marsupials, give birth to a premature, partially developed embryo. The embryo then climbs to the mother's pouch and fastens to a nipple, where it finishes its development. The most familiar marsupials are the kangaroo, koala, Tasmanian devil, and opossum, although there have been many other types of marsupials in the past, and many are still alive today in Australia and South America. Where marsupials lived in isolation with no competition from placental mammals, they have evolved into many different body forms, which converge on the body forms of their ecological equivalents in the placentals. In Australia presently, there are marsupial equivalents of cats, wolves, mice, flying squirrels, rabbits, moles, tapirs, and monkeys. Among extinct marsupials of South America were the equivalents of lions and of saber-toothed cats. As similar as these animals look to their placental equivalents in their external body form, they are not related to true cats, wolves, or the rest, as they are all pouched mammals.

Unlike marsupials, placentals must carry the embryo in the womb through its full development. To allow this, the embryo is nourished by an extra membrane surrounding it in the womb. This membrane, the placenta, is shed when the baby is born and is part of the "afterbirth." This mode of reproduction makes the placental baby less vulnerable than a marsupial baby, but it means that the mother is more vulnerable, as she must carry a larger embryo a longer time. A female marsupial can also reproduce faster, as she can carry one baby in a pouch and be pregnant with another.

After the extinction of the dinosaurs about 65 million years ago, the planet was ready for a new group of large animals to evolve and take over the vacant ecological niches. Placental mammals underwent a tremendous diversification until they occupied many ecological niches, and some reached the size of sheep. Most, however, were no larger than a cat. The placentals split into the edentates (anteaters, sloths, armadillos, and their relatives) and the rest of the mammalian orders (groups of genera). Like marsupials, edentates had their greatest success in isolation in South America, although presently the armadillo is successfully spreading northward. The most successful placentals in the Northern Hemisphere in the early Cenozoic were the archaic ancestors of the insectivores (moles, shrews, hedgehogs, and their extinct relatives), primates (lemurs, monkeys, apes, humans, and their extinct relatives), the carnivores (meat-eating mammals), and a great number of extinct, archaic orders that have no living descendants.

About 54 million years ago, in the Eocene epoch, some of the modern orders of mammals began to appear. They were still small and unspecialized and would not be easy to recognize today. Some of these groups included the rodents (mice, rats, squirrels, guinea pigs); the even-toed hoofed mammals, or artiodactyls (pigs, camels, deer, cattle, antelopes, giraffes, and their relatives); and the odd-toed hoofed mammals, or perissodactyls (horses, rhinos, tapirs, and their extinct relatives). These groups lived along with many archaic groups that are now extinct, so the Eocene world had a strange mixture of modern and archaic mammals. During the Eocene, the first bats began to fly and the first whales to swim.

About 38 million years ago, the world's climate got much cooler and more extreme. The tropical rain forests that had dominated the world in the Eocene were replaced by more mixed vegetation, including open grasslands. As a consequence, most of the archaic groups of mammals died out, and they were replaced by a great diversification of mammals from living groups. The archaic forms were mostly leaf-eaters that could not survive the loss of the tropical forest or tree-dwelling forms, such as the ancient primates. At this time, the first true dogs, cats, elephants, rhinos, tapirs, camels, pocket gophers, rabbits, and shrews appeared. Although still very archaic representatives of their respective orders, the mammalian communities began to take on a more modern look. From this point on, environments (like the East African savanna today) were dominated by perissodactyls, artiodactyls, carnivores, rodents, rabbits, and insectivores.

Since the end of the Eocene, the world's climate continued to get cooler and more extreme. More and more forests were replaced by open grasslands, and the mammals evolved in response to the changing environment. Most of the larger plant eaters (perissodactyls and artiodactyls) had to develop ever-growing molars to chew tougher grasses and long legs to escape their predators by running. This development can be seen not only in the evolution of the horse, but also in the rhinos, camels, and the many artiodactyls that chew their cud (including antelopes, deer, sheep, and cattle). Carnivores became more specialized into ambush hunters (cats), pack hunters (dogs), bone-crushing scavengers (hyenas), and a specialized type, the sabertooths, which evolved four different times independently. Rodents became the most common mammals of all, and they dominate the burrowing, ground-foraging, and tree-dwelling ecological niches.

During the last 5 million years, the earth's climate has become increasingly severe as the ice ages developed. Many mammals became extinct, while others became adept at migrating away from ice sheets or developed thick coats of hair (such as the woolly mammoth and woolly rhino) in order to live in glaciated regions. The most severe extinction of large mammals happened only 10,000 years ago, when the ice sheets retreated and the present interglacial period began. Whether this extinction was attributable to the change in climate or to the severe overhunting by prehistoric humans is still disputed. Since that time, many mammals have been wiped out by overhunting, by the destruction of habitat, or by competition from mammalian "weeds" (such as rats, rabbits, and goats) that accompany human habitation. The extinction of mammals has reached its worst levels during the last two centuries, as human populations have exploded to more than 5 billion. Only a pitiful remnant of the once-rich assemblage of mammals that dominated the earth for 65 million years is left presently, and much of it is endangered in the wild.

Methods of Study

Because only the hard parts of the mammals commonly become fossils, mammalian paleontologists specialize in studying bones and teeth. Ideally, the paleontologist would study complete skeletons, but these are rarely found, as scavenging and stream erosion break up and scatter them. Most paleontologists thus make do with teeth, jaws, and skulls. Teeth, in particular, are valuable, as they are the hardest and most durable tissue in the body and thus are the most resistant to breakdown by erosion and stream abrasion. In addition, teeth are highly diagnostic of species and are influenced by the diet of the animal. Therefore, the paleontologist can not only identify a mammal by its teeth but also learn much about its ecology.

A paleontologist starts searching in sedimentary beds of the appropriate age and environment (river-channel sandstones and floodplain mudstones), particularly those that have produced fossil mammals in the past. The best results occur in areas with desert climates and badlands exposures, as there are few plants to cover the rocks and the erosion is fast enough that new fossils are exposed each year. The most successful method is to prospect, or to walk head-down with the eyes "fastened" to the ground, for as many hours and days as it takes until bones or teeth are seen. When fossils are found, they may not be worth collecting if they are too fragmentary or are unidentifiable. If the fossil is worthwhile, the paleontologist collects not only the fossil itself but also exact data about where it occurred and at what stratigraphic level (so that it can be used for dating). The most common mistake made by amateurs is to collect a fossil without carefully noting this information.

Occasionally, mammal fossils are large enough or fragile enough that special methods are necessary. In this case, the paleontologist digs around the exposed fossil and clears the rock around it until it is almost free, resting on a thin pedestal of rock. Then it is encased in a "jacket" of burlap and plaster of paris, much like the plaster cast used to set broken limbs. When the plaster cast is dry and hard, the fossil is removed from the pedestal, and more plaster and burlap seal it in the cast. When it reaches the lab, technicians can open the cast and carefully clean away the excess rock, treating the fossil with hardener and preservative as they expose it.

Fossils of small mammals (particularly rodents, rabbits, primates, and insectivores) are too tiny to see while prospecting. These fossils are more often collected by finding a rich, bone-producing level from which bags of fossil-rich material are then filled. This material is later placed in a wooden box with a window-screen bottom and allowed to soak in a stream. The water washes out all the silt and clay, leaving a concentrate of pebbles and fossils. This concentrate can then be dried and spread out on a table to be sorted through by hand.

Context

Mammal fossils are scientists' only record of more than 200 million years of evolution. Mammals have the most complete fossil record of any vertebrate group, so they are excellent organisms to demonstrate the processes of evolution, ecological convergence (such as that between certain marsupials and placentals), and the development of modern species (such as the modern horse from its Eocene ancestor). Because humans are mammals, the study of their evolution and how they originated from other mammals interests most people.

Additionally, fossil mammals are practically the only fossils that are common in terrestrial sediments. Because mammals evolve very rapidly, each bed in a terrestrial sedimentary sequence can have slightly different mammals. Thus, mammal fossils are the most useful for dating terrestrial deposits of the last 65 million years. Also, as mammals are relatively mobile, they have been used to reconstruct ancient geography. When certain mammals from one continent first appear in the rocks on another continent, scientists are aided in reconstructing when the continents were connected by land bridges and when they were isolated. The ecology of many fossil mammals can be reconstructed from their anatomy by comparing them with living mammals. In this case, the fossil mammals from a particular deposit can be used to infer the ancient environment in which those sediments were deposited.

Bibliography

Carroll, Robert L. *Vertebrate Paleontology and Evolution*. New York: W. H. Free-man, 1988. A complete, well-illustrated textbook on fossil vertebrates. Includes several chapters on fossil mammals. Although written at the college level, some parts can be understood by the general reader.

Colbert, Edwin H. *The Evolution of the Vertebrates*. New York: John Wiley & Sons, 1980. The best general book on vertebrate evolution for the nonspecialist.

Halstead, L. B. *The Evolution of the Mammals*. London: Peter Lowe, 1978. A colorfully illustrated book for the general reader that has great visual appeal, although much of the information is inaccurate or out-of-date.

Kurtén, Björn. *The Age of Mammals*. New York: Columbia University Press, 1972. A general book written on the level of the advanced general reader. Unfortunately, it does not have many illustrations, and it has become very dated.

MacDonald, David W., ed. *The Encyclopedia of Mammals*. New York: Facts on File, 1984. An excellent, colorful review of the living mammals, with some very good sections on extinct mammals as well.

Savage, R. J., and M. R. Long. *Mammal Evolution: An Illustrated Guide*. New York: Facts on File, 1986. A beautifully illustrated account of mammal evolution for the general reader. It groups the mammals by their ecology, however, rather than by their normal classification, and contains some inaccuracies.

Woodburne, Michael O., ed. *Cenozoic Mammals of North America: Geochronology and Biostratigraphy*. Berkeley: University of California Press, 1987. A valuable review of the dating and correlation of strata by fossil mammals. Intended for the advanced college student and the paleontologist.

Donald R. Prothero

Cross-References

MANGANESE NODULES

Type of earth science: Economic geology

Manganese nodules are growths of metal-yielding elements that accumulate in the oceans. Associated with active rift areas, the nodules are formed by precipitation from seawater and by interactions with biological organisms. Their economic potential for development as strategic metal reserves has increased the importance of the nodules to humans.

Principal terms

ACCRETION: the growth of materials by the addition of new material from a surrounding fluid

NODULE: a spherically shaped, concentrically layered hard mass found on the sea bottom, composed of metallic ions accumulated on seed material

OXIDIZING CONDITIONS: environmental situations in which elements react quickly to the availability of oxygen or other electron-rich atoms

PRECIPITATION: the settling out of ions, elements, or chemical compounds dissolved in a solution as a result of changes in the environment, such as temperature, pressure, or chemical concentrations

SCANNING ELECTRON MICROSCOPY: a technique for resolving extremely small details and for watching crystals grow; electrons are passed over an active surface, then are focused by magnets to give a visual image

VERNADITE and TODOROKITE: typical rare minerals tying up copper, nickel, and cobalt in nodules, derived from continental ore deposits

WHITE and BLACK SMOKERS: vents near active undersea spreading centers, from which large amounts of hot fluids and dissolved substances escape from deeper layers inside the earth

Summary of the Phenomenon

One of the numerous discoveries of the expedition of HMS *Challenger* of 1873-1876 was that of unusual and plentiful sorts of rocks referred to as manganese nodules, retrieved from the ocean by bottom dredging. These nodules, as analyzed first by Sir John Murray, were found to be surprisingly high in manganese localized on red clay, with additional traces of limestone and accretions of diverse heavy metals such as iron, titanium, and chromium. Upon examination, the manganese nodules, measuring 1 to 15 centimeters in diameter, were found to be essentially a conglomeration of heavy metals and other chemical compounds formed around a basic particle acting as a catalyst, or seed nucleus, for crystallization. This centerpiece, represented quite often by a shark's tooth, a piece of bone, or other small, round objects, acts as a condensation center, allowing a surface out onto which the dissolved elements and molecules in solution can precipitate from the surrounding ocean waters. Larger nodules are the result of the gradual growth of such layers on the seed nucleus over long periods of time.

The phenomenon of manganese nodules, however, was not new to geology. Stony concretions of manganese and iron had been used in Sweden for a long time, more than ten thousand tons being mined from Swedish lakes in the year 1860 alone. Professional chemical and mineralogical studies there indicated that the nodules regrew within a cycle of thirty to fifty years, totally replacing the dredged materials. Swedish scientists found that, in the normal oxidizing conditions found in freshwater lakes, with very low rates of sedimentation from surrounding materials, if center seeds such as spores, bark, or clay particles were present, iron and manganese would precipitate as the water met the relevant conditions of temperature and pressure. Growth was continuous and often accelerated by currents sweeping the lake floor, keeping the nodules available at the surface for the further deposit of ions. Such growth ceased when sediments were able to accumulate rapidly on the lake floor.

In the seas, manganese is found in numerous places and in several forms. In red clays found on the ocean bottom, the element occurs in higher concentration than it does normally in igneous rocks. In other sediments, it occurs principally as manganese dioxide in fine grains, in coatings, and as matrices for other rocks in the process of formation. Although some nodules are large in size, the bulk of manganese is distributed in red clays, igneous rocks, and limestone. The dark colors of the red clays of the Indian and Pacific oceans, for example, have been attributed to the manganese content.

The nodules themselves, with an average content of 29 percent manganese dioxide and 21.5 percent iron oxide, grow by accretion. Slices through the rock show laminations of different shades and textures, indicating differing precipitation rates and chemical compositions of the surrounding waters over time. Found worldwide, manganese nodules, particularly those with the highest metallic concentration, occur in bands running from the north equatorial Pacific to southeast Hawaii to Baja California. Scientists estimate that in the Pacific area alone, one and a half trillion tons of nodules are present, with a rate of formation of some ten million tons per year. A comparable amount are found in the Indian Ocean, with those of high nickel-copper counts discovered adjacent to the equator. Atlantic nodules have much lower strategic metal concentrations. Such distribution and abundance of elements—in addition to manganese—suggest that the water and overlying sediments may control the ultimate composition of the nodules. In the Pacific, diatomaceous and radiolaran siliceous oozes underlie the rocks. In more northern areas, which demonstrate less biological productivity in the surface waters, the nodules have higher iron and lower nickel-copper concentrations where the formed concretions are resting over pelagic red clays. Indeed, analysis indicates that chemical differences exist between the top water-contacted layer of the nodule and the bottom sediment-immersed layer. The bottom layers test higher in manganese, nickel, and copper; the top layers, in iron and cobalt. Fluctuations in concentration through sectionalized nodules can be accounted for by the episodic rolling over the sea floor.

Manganese nodules contain small, poorly crystalline minerals, the types of which depend on their location in the ocean. The material vernadite, with trivalent cobalt, is found in nodules from seamounts and shallow seas; todorokite, with divalent nickel and copper, is found in rocks from siliceous oozes. Divalent manganese-bearing todorokites come from continental ore deposits.

The addition of ions causes the nodules to grow, apparently at a very slow rate. Radium, via the mechanism of absorption by manganese peroxide, is included in the nodules; in the concentric layers it falls off rapidly with increasing depth below the nodule surface, indicating duration of formation for each layer. Other isotopes used for determining growth rates include thorium 230, beryllium 10, and potassium 40. Isotopic measurements indicate a growth rate of a few millimeters per million years. The mystery of this growth process, when the burying red clay sediments accumulate at a thousandfold faster rate, was solved by time-lapse sea-floor photography and sedimentological studies. Both methods showed that the periodic rolling of the nodules, keeping them at the sediment-seawater interface, was accomplished by the high populations of organisms burrowing in the underlying sediments.

Several hypotheses have been proposed for the formation of manganese nodules, the earliest dating back to the time of Murray (1891). These hypotheses include slow precipitation from seawater, deposition from submarine volcanic disturbances, and diagenesis (remobilization) from sediments. Chemical analysis has shown that, compared to normal volcanic rock concentration of manganese, a five- to tenfold concentration of manganese would be required to give the amount found in Pacific red clays. Manganese is leached out of solid materials when it is in a reduced state in acid solutions; the opposite, an alkaline solution in oxidizing conditions, tends to precipitate manganese out as insoluble manganese dioxide. Nodules form, without redissolving into the water, in areas of seamounts and in oceanic deposits where there are even slight amounts of limestone with high alkalinity. Small nodules form this way, as slow precipitates.

In the 1960's, the investigation of the mid-oceanic ridge and of enclosed ocean basins yielded data about the formation of metals. Hot brines above metal-bearing muds were found, particularly near the East Pacific Rise. Water running through those ridge-axis hot springs and flank hydrothermal areas becomes supersaturated with manganese and other metals it dissolves by virtue of a temperature of 400+ degrees Celsius. Deposits of materials dropping out of solution cluster in basins near active spreading centers, known now as black (lacking manganese) or white smokers. Basic metal ions derive from those fluids emitted at the sea floor. White smokers cause the material to be deposited within the rock as cold water percolates downward. Manganese precipitates out when the water cools below white-smoker temperatures; floating in the water column, it then reprecipitates on the sea floor. In general, as the cold seawater travels down into the basaltic crust, it heats, dissolves more metals, and rises to the surface. The leached-out metals are then contributed to the nodule concentrations of iron, cobalt, copper, nickel, and manganese as sulfides and oxide ions.

Methods of Study

Numerous investigative techniques have been used to understand both the chemical makeup and the formation process of manganese nodules. Rock samples have been collected by bottom dredging, either by use of simple dredging sacks or by use of submersibles with grappling arms for retrieving specimens.

Once the samples are in the laboratory, a diverse range of analytical techniques are used to determine the chemistry of the nodules. Microchemical analysis starts on sectioned specimens. The chemical composition can be determined using diverse techniques, such as atomic absorption spectroscopy, in which a small sample is burned and the emitted light is analyzed to give concentrations, or ultraviolet spectrophotometry, using light of ultraviolet frequencies that passes through a solution of the nodule in fluid. Chemical analysis for metallic ions can be achieved by affixing concentrations on the order of parts per million or, in some cases, parts per billion. Such chemical work has revealed differences between nodules as well as within nodules themselves, providing information on the spacing of the nodules and on their movement in regard to the water-sediment interface. Such analyses provide fluctuating concentration values for manganese, iron, nickel, copper, cobalt, and other metals, as well as information on the matrix of the red clays and other components, thus furnishing clues to the origin of the rocks.

The minerals found in the nodules, such as todorokite or feroxyhyte, are best studied by use of the geologic polarizing microscope for identification. This instrument, using polarizing lenses that can be aligned at diverse angles to each other, can be used to identify crystals by their color changes and indices of refraction when viewed in polarized (single-plane) light. Each type of mineral responds differently to the light; the various changes as the light's plane of polarization is turned indicate a particular mineral type.

The growth and fine detail of minerals in the nodules can be investigated more precisely by using the scanning electron microscope. In this technique, high-speed electrons are bounced off the surface to be viewed, the returning particles focused by the action of magnetic fields to give a detailed picture, at ultrafine resolution, of the crystal's growing surface. Such observations point to a biological source for the metals in the nodules and to remobilization of the nodules by the underlying organisms in the sediments.

Geophysical, chemical, and physical studies are done to investigate the formation process. Radioactive decay counters measure rates of nuclear breakdown in radioisotopes to find the rate of growth of the nodules. Time-lapse photography, both in the laboratory and on the sea floor, shows how organisms move the nodules, causing them to roll periodically and thus not be buried by accumulating sediments.

Such studies of the rates of siliceous ooze or of oceanic red clay sediment deposition give vital information on the sediment-seawater interface and how it changes over time. Chemical and geological laboratory experiments, using conventional chemical tools, show how metals are adsorbed onto the surface of clays or are organically complexed in biological matter settling to the sea floor. In simple chemical experiments using reducing environments, manganese and iron oxides oxidize organic debris to give soluble, positively charged ions such as divalent manganese, iron, nickel, and copper in the pore water of the sediment, making them available for accumulation in the nodules. Further oxidation studies show how manganese and iron are produced to insoluble hydrated forms that accumulate on the nodules themselves. Detailed chemical studies of minerals found in the white smokers on the sea bottom, particularly those minerals left behind in the cracks, and studies of the microscopic "bubbles" associated with the original fluid left trapped in the crystals give a detailed look at the possible source for ores to be found inside the nodules.

Modern oceanographic science has been able to detail accurate maps indicating where the nodule abundance and associated metal concentrations are highest and where the mining of such minerals would be most economical. It has been suggested that mining of the nodules in deep water could be achieved by giant deep-sea vacuum cleaners, a technique entirely feasible from an engineering standpoint. During the summer of 1970, several companies tested such processes, which allow nodules to be recovered at costs low enough to make a profit. Deposits on land, however, have higher manganese and iron concentrations, complicating the retrieval picture. Three basic systems have been designed for the future: an airlift, a hydraulic lift without air, and a mechanical lift called the continuous-line bucket system. Theoretically, these extended hoses, fitted with spread nozzles, would pass over the sea bottom, using simple suction to remove the supersurface nodules.

Context

Manganese nodules have been shown to have economic importance. Formed by accretion around spherical objects, the nodules, besides containing 20 percent manganese and 15 percent iron or more, have significant enrichments in nickel, copper, cobalt, zinc, molybdenum, and other elements considered important for strategic reasons. Through various chemical and physical techniques, the basic mechanisms of formation seem to be understood, including the dissolving and redeposition of terrestrially derived manganese and the emission as a hot-water-dissolved substance from white smokers found in the undersea volcanic rift areas.

Manganese nodules show enormous economic potential. Besides the maganese oxide phases accumulating on the surface of the nodules, there are numerous other ions that are bound up in the rock and mineral phases as essential constituents in the crystal structures forming within the nodules.

By understanding the distribution and chemical concentration of manganese nodules, geochemists achieve a more detailed picture of the makeup of the earth, particularly below the surface, and of the process of mineral enrichment. This knowledge provides vital clues in the search for elements and compounds considered essential for the survival of technological civilization. That information also sheds light on such diverse topics as the origin of the earth, the formation of the continents, and the planetary evolution over time.

Bibliography

Anderson, Roger. *Marine Geology: An Adventure into the Unknown.* New York: John Wiley & Sons, 1986. An introduction to the features of marine geological sciences, this work emphasizes modern knowledge built on plate tectonics. Excellently written, the book provides a detailed account of the black and white smokers of the sea bottom, including a discussion of the strange organisms found there. Contains numerous charts and pictures and an extensive bibliography. For general audiences.

Burns, G., ed. *Marine Minerals.* Washington, D.C.: Mineralogical Society of America, 1979. A vastly detailed account of the variety of rocks and minerals found on the sea floor, this work furnishes an in-depth analysis of chemical elemental distribution. Numerous graphs and tables facilitate data handling. Not for beginners, but a wide range of topics and information provide guidelines for further research.

Glasby, G. P., ed. *Marine Manganese Deposits.* New York: Elsevier, 1977. A collection of papers on the types and quantities of manganese deposits found under various conditions. Manganese nodules—their origin, relationship to continents and organisms, growth rates, and chemical compositions—are discussed. Provides extensive tables and charts as well as references. Detailed reading, but a good starting point for further research on numerous topics.

Ingmanson, Dale, and William J. Wallace. *Oceanography: An Introduction.* 3d ed. Belmont, Calif.: Wadsworth, 1979. A general source of information on the oceans, with several chapters specifically about the geology of the sea floor. The formation of features, such as nodules, is related to current theories of sea-floor spreading and the evolution of the oceans. Excellent photographs and diagrams. Well written for the layperson.

Seibold, E., and W. Berger. *The Sea Floor: An Introduction to Marine Biology.* New York: Springer-Verlag, 1982. An excellent introduction to marine geology, detailing the types of materials, geologic features, and complex evolution of the ocean bottom. The interaction of organisms, weather, sediments, and humans is explained lucidly. Well written, with numerous charts and pictures. Additional references are listed.

Smith, Peter J., ed. *The Earth.* New York: Macmillan, 1986. A delightful book, filled with pictures and explanatory diagrams, this work describes the structure of the earth and its evolution. Manganese nodules are discussed both as a typical deposit and as a possible resource for human development. Additional references and a glossary are provided.

Trask, Parker Davies, ed. *Recent Marine Sediments.* Mineola, N.Y.: Dover, 1965. This work records a symposium on the origins and features of sea sediments. Extremely detailed, the section on special sediment features describes the formation of nodules and other deposits found in the world's oceans. An excellent section on methods of study, including mineral analysis, X-ray methods, and bottom-sampling apparatus, is provided. Extensive references. Reading may be difficult for the layperson.

Arthur L. Alt

Cross-References

Elemental Distribution in the Earth, 391; Hydrothermal Mineralization, 1108; Igneous and Contact Metamorphic Mineral Deposits, 1124; Industrial Metals, 1216; Iron Deposits, 1254; Ocean-Floor Drilling Programs, 1804; The Oceanic Crust, 1846; Platinum Group Metals, 2086; Earth Resources, 2175; Future Resources, 2182; Strategic Resources, 2188; Sedimentary Mineral Deposits, 2296.

MARINE TERRACES

Type of earth science: Geology
Field of study: Geomorphology

Marine terraces are ancient (fossil) coastlines that result from several different modes of origin. They are a common coastal feature worldwide and are presently at elevations well above or well below present-day sea level. Global cycles of sea-level change and tectonic uplift and subsidence of coasts are responsible for creating multiple sets of parallel marine terraces. Global sea-level history and tectonic history of coastal areas can be determined by the study of the age and elevation of marine terraces.

Principal terms

BARRIER ISLAND: a long, low sand island parallel to the coast and separated from the mainland by a salt marsh and lagoon; a common coastal feature on depositional coasts worldwide

BIOABRASION: physical and chemical erosion or removal of rock as a result of the activities of marine organisms

GUYOT: an oceanic volcano, presently submerged far below sea level, with a top that has been beveled flat by wave erosion; the tops of some guyots are capped by coral reefs at or near their summits

INNER EDGE POINT: the landward edge of a wave-cut terrace at the base of the sea cliff; the elevation of this point is the position of highest sea level during formation of the terrace

ISOSTATIC READJUSTMENT: rapid tectonic uplift or subsidence of continental areas in response to the addition or removal of the weight of overlying deposits of glacial ice or seawater

LITHOSPHERE: the outer shell of the earth, where the rocks are less dense but more brittle and coherent than those in the underlying layer (asthenosphere)

NOTCH or NIP: an erosional feature found at the base of a sea cliff, the result of undercutting by wave erosion, biobrasion from marine organisms, and dissolution of rock by groundwater seepage

PLEISTOCENE EPOCH: the time of earth history, from about 2 million to 10,000 years ago, during which the earth experienced cycles of warming and cooling, resulting in cycles of glaciation and sea level change

STRANDLINE: the position or elevation of the portion of the shoreline between high and low tide (at sea level); usually synonymous with "beach" and "shoreline"

SUBSIDENCE: the sinking of a block of the earth's lithosphere because of a force pushing it down; coastal areas undergoing rapid subsidence tend to be submerged below sea level

TECTONIC: pertaining to large-scale movements of the earth's lithosphere

UPLIFT: the rising of a block of the earth's lithosphere because of a force pushing it up; coastal areas undergoing uplift tend to emerge above sea level

WAVE-CUT BENCH: a gently seaward-sloping platform cut into the bedrock of a coast by wave erosion and landsliding; wave-cut benches are proof of sea-level variations and tectonic uplift and subsidence of coastal areas

Summary of the Phenomenon

The coastline of continents and islands represents a fundamental boundary between the earth's solid landmass and the constructional and destructional energy of the sea. The landforms in coastal areas are the result of continuous dynamic interaction between these competing geological agents. Marine processes of erosion and sedimentation construct a shoreline profile on the edge of the landmass that defines the strandline, a narrow zone of wave- and tide-washed coast. The coastal strandline usually exhibits a gently sloping platform with its top at an elevation between high and low tides; it is often bounded by adjacent steeper slopes and is a reliable indicator of sea level. Familiar strandline features are beaches, coral reefs, and wave-cut platforms, strandline platforms cut into the bedrock by wave erosion.

If erosion and sedimentation were the only active geological conditions, most coasts would have a single type of strandline landform whose position remained constant through time. The volume of seawater in the world's oceans, however, fluctuates directly with changes in the volume of ice in continental glaciers, causing sea level to rise and fall in response. As the average temperature of the earth's atmosphere rises or falls, glacial ice on the continents melts (sea-level rise) or accumulates (sea-level fall) in response to the temperature change. The temperature of the surface ocean reacts in a similar manner: Warming causes expansion of the seawater (sea-level rise); cooling results in contraction (sea-level fall). It has been estimated from oxygen isotope evidence in deep-sea cores that worldwide sea level has been 430-530 feet lower than today several times during the last 2-3 million years of earth history. There is also abundant physical evidence for large-scale sea-level excursions. On the Atlantic coast of the United States, elephant teeth 25,000 years old have been dredged up by fishermen from more than forty locations on the continental shelf, some as far as 75 miles offshore. Three-thousand-year-old oak tree stumps rooted in life position and many cultural artifacts used by coastal American Indians have also been found below sea level in this region.

The landmasses are also surprisingly dynamic, rising or falling in elevation in response to a variety of tectonic factors. On some coasts, isostatic readjustment results in uplift and subsidence. The weight of increasing thicknesses of overlying glacial ice or seawater will cause the earth's lithosphere to be depressed downward; when the weight is removed, the landmass will rebound upward. Volcanic activity will cause expansion (uplift) when the earth's lithosphere is heated; contraction (subsidence) occurs as the lithosphere cools. An extreme example of this effect is the guyot, an inactive volcanic seamount that has subsided far below sea level as the hot lithosphere on which it formed cooled and contracted. Guyots have been beveled flat by wave erosion and rimmed with banks of dead coral reef during the period when their tops were in shallow water. Coastal landmasses also undergo uplift and subsidence in response to the forces of plate tectonic movement. Although usually a slow, incremental process, a sudden, rapid coastal uplift occurred in Prince William Sound, Alaska, during the 1964 "Good Friday Earthquake," which resulted in elevation of a wave-cut platform one-quarter mile wide.

During the Pleistocene epoch (about 2 million to 10,000 years ago), strandline features formed on coasts worldwide that were strongly influenced by these complex and rapidly changing geologic conditions. Most coasts are not tectonically stable (located at one elevation) for a very long period of geologic time, and processes of landscape erosion and decay often act much more slowly than the rates of sea-level and land-level change. Abandoned strandline features, or "fossil coasts," are common to many areas of the world. First recognized in nineteenth century Europe, parallel sets of these distinctive landforms are present on cliffs and coastal hills at elevations high above present-day sea level and on the ocean floor far below present-day sea level. Many contain marine fossils (discovered by Leonardo da Vinci about A.D. 1500), demonstrating their marine origin, and create a steplike topographic profile of the terrain, leading up the seaward-facing hills. These features are referred to as marine terraces and are found on many coasts worldwide both above and below sea level.

Because their formation requires time, strandline landforms usually form when coastal uplift/subsidence and sea-level change are in balance and the position of the strandline is relatively stable for a period of thousands of years, a situation referred to as a sea-level stillstand. In many areas, sea level tends to vary in cycles separated by stillstand events, during which marine terraces can develop. Occasionally, the processes of terrace formation will destroy or obscure an older terrace, so most coasts exhibit only one or two terraces. An unbroken flight of marine terraces climbing inland indicates a coast that is being continuously uplifted. One of the most striking and well-developed sequences of marine terraces in the world is on the seaward slopes of the Palos Verdes Peninsula of southern California. Here, thirteen distinct terrace levels, from 50 to 1,480 feet in elevation, form a complete record of coastal uplift and sea-level change spanning several hundred thousand years.

Submarine terraces have been reported from many parts of the world at depths several hundred feet below present-day sea level. Submerged terraces are usually better preserved than are elevated marine terraces because, being underwater, they are less affected by processes of erosion and landscape degradation. Because they are obscured from view and more difficult to study than are terraces on land, less is known about them. The most distinctive submerged wave-cut platforms are present at depths of −130 to −200 feet off the southwest coast of Great Britain, at −560 to −660 feet off northern Australia, and a sequence of at least five terraces at depths of −500 to −700 feet off the southern California coast and its nearshore islands from Santa Barbara to San Diego. Study of marine terraces at these anomalous elevations worldwide has been used to document sea-level variations and the tectonic uplift and subsidence of coastal landmasses through time and to estimate the magnitude of these changes.

There are several types of marine terraces, differing in their mode of formation. Processes of coastal erosion form marine terraces on coasts where the shoreline is backed by a steep, irregular cliff, where the supply of sediment is too limited to build beaches, and where nearshore waters are so shallow that waves break directly on the sea cliff. The base of the cliff is continuously pounded by the full force of the waves, resulting in very large impact pressures. Beach cobbles and abrasive sand-laden water are hurled at the base of the cliff. The force with which these stones attack the cliff is difficult to exaggerate; there are reports of beach cobbles thrown 150 feet above sea level and of others raining down on the roof of a lighthouse-keeper's cottage.

Wave-cut platforms result from the rapid horizontal cutting away of rock at the base of a sea cliff. Wave erosion quarries a notch into the base of the sea cliff, which undercuts and oversteepens the cliff until landsliding causes the cliff to collapse; this loose rubble is rapidly carried away by the waves and is a source of new rocks to continue wave attack. In some places, notch formation is aided by the bioabrasion activities of marine organisms that live attached to and feed on rocky shores and that secrete chemicals to help dissolve the rock or abrade it away with rasping feeding appendages. Dissolution of the rock is sometimes aided by groundwater seeping out of the base of the sea cliff. The net effect of this process is the landward retreat of the sea cliff and formation of a platform that slopes gently seaward (0-3 degrees). The boundary between the "step" of a wave-cut terrace and the steeper "riser" of the sea cliff that terminates its landward edge is called the inner edge point. The elevation of this point is the position of highest sea level during formation of the feature, and it is used to calculate the height of ancient sea levels in marine terraces.

The platform is continually abraded by the waves transporting sand down the coast, and its width is determined by the amount of landward sea-cliff erosion. The rate of sea-cliff retreat can be surprisingly rapid. Average rates on the California coast exceed 6 inches per year for hard rock cliffs and up to 3 feet per year in cliffs composed of soft, unconsolidated sediment. The coast of East Anglia, Great Britain, experiences up to 13 feet of sea-cliff retreat annually. Continuous records are available for the Huntcliff coast of Yorkshire, Great Britain, at a former Roman signal station where the cliff has retreated 100 feet in eight hundred years.

Overlying many elevated wave-cut platforms is a mantle of unconsolidated sediment, referred to as coverhead. This material, deposited by a combination of terrestrial and marine sedimentary processes, buries the abraded platform surface and may be as much as 100 feet thick. Typical coverhead deposits include a basal layer of well-sorted beach sand, rounded beach cobbles, and marine fossils—the shoreline sediments left on the platform as sea level retreated. These basal strand-line sediments are often covered by a heterogeneous deposit composed of poorly sorted rock debris, soil, and stream gravel deposited by sediment washing or landsliding down from the sea-cliff slopes above and by coastal streams building their alluvial fans toward the coast.

Marine terraces are also formed by sediment deposition, which usually occurs on relatively flat coasts with a wide continental shelf where the energy of approaching waves is dissipated by friction with the shallow sea bottom. In areas such as the Atlantic and Gulf coasts of North America and the Netherlands, rivers transport large quantities of mud and sand into coastal waters. Waves and wind currents pile sand into a long, narrow strandline feature known as a barrier island, a common landform found fringing low-lying coasts worldwide. Once formed during a still-stand of several thousand years, a barrier island will migrate landward as sea level rises. Waves and tidal currents cause barrier sand to wash over the top of the island or around its ends, moving it grain-by-grain landward with the rising sea. When sea level begins to fall, the barrier does not migrate seaward but is left behind inland of the new strandline, where it remains as a record of the former high stand of sea level; this feature is usually referred to as a beach ridge. Subsequent to sea level falling and the strandline moving seaward, river and marsh sediment is often deposited on the seaward side of the abandoned barrier. When sea level again rises to its former position, a new barrier island migrates with it; this island is, in turn, abandoned on the coast at the highest position of sea level. If the new barrier migrates far enough inland to reach the older remnant barrier, it will be welded onto it, forming a wide composite barrier island composed of two or more barrier islands.

Throughout the Pleistocene, sediment deposition has widened the Atlantic and Gulf coastal plains, and repeated cycles of sea-level rise and fall have formed concentric arcs of abandoned barrier islands stretching inland more than 30 miles from the present-day coast. These beach ridge barrier islands are a type of marine terrace, each recording an ancient high stand of sea level. One of the most promi-nent is Trail Ridge in southern Georgia, a sand ridge more than 36 miles long that encloses a low swampy area on its landward side known as the Okefenokee Swamp. Submarine beach ridges are less common than their inland counterparts but have been reported from western Brittany at depths of up to −660 feet.

In tropical areas where the coastal waters are warm all year and clear of sus-pended mud, corals will flourish and often form massive reefs. Reefs that grow during a long stillstand will become large and well developed, with a gently sloping top that corresponds to sea level. These coastal depositional features are also found stranded above the shoreline when sea level falls or the landmass rises, resulting in reef terraces. This type of marine terrace is most common on island coasts but is also present on the coasts of the Mediterranean and Red seas and on the Yucatan Peninsula of Mexico.

Methods of Study

The location, elevation, and shape of marine terraces are determined by standard field-mapping and land-surveying techniques and by study of aerial photographs and satellite imagery. The time of formation, or age, of marine terraces is routinely determined by analyzing fossils found in terrace sediments with any of several reliable methods. Some terraces, particularly older ones, cannot be accurately dated because they do not contain well-preserved fossils. Carbon 14 is the most commonly used radioactive isotope for dating organic remains. The carbon 14 technique is highly accurate if done on pristine fossil material, and it has been used to date relatively young terraces containing corals, mollusks, and fossilized plant matter found within coverhead or reef deposits. This technique is expensive, and when samples have been chemically altered since they were formed, the technique can be unreliable. A less precise but useful and less expensive method has been developed using the amino acids present in the protein "glue" (called conchiolin) found within the calcium carbonate shell structure of marine mollusks. The amino acid dating technique takes advantage of the alteration of amino acid molecules within the conchiolin as they age. Because the rate of alteration varies with climate and other local factors, a standard dating curve must be constructed for each region in which the method will be used. This curve is usually calibrated using carbon 14 dates, and all other samples are compared to it to ascertain their age. Both of these methods are limited by the short half-life of the carbon 14 isotope (5,730 years) and can be used only on terraces less than about 60,000 years old. Older terraces are dated using other radioactive isotopic techniques. The uranium decay series is particularly effective and is widely employed on both coral and mollusk fossils. Using the thorium-ranium and protactinium-uranium ratios, marine terraces as old as 640,000 years have been documented.

Knowledge of marine terrace ages has proved useful in land-use planning applications, such as evaluating whether particular earthquake faults or coastal landslides have been recently active, but their greatest contribution has been in the study of sea-level change during the Pleistocene. Once the terraces from a single stretch of coast are dated, a simple graph is constructed using the present-day elevation of the inner edge point (for wave-cut terraces) or its upper surface (for reef and beach ridge terraces). The points on the graph show the location of the strandline relative to the coastal land surface during sea-level stillstands at various times during the last several hundred thousand years; the curve that connects these points is an estimate of the relative sea-level variations for that location.

Context

Because marine terraces at successively higher elevations are increasingly older, a simple conclusion is that ancient high stands of sea level stood at elevations much higher than sea level today and that sea-level oscillations have become less and less pronounced with time. When the marine terrace sea-level curves from many areas worldwide are compared with one another, however, there is virtually no correlation between the various curves. This finding shows that the world's coastal landmasses are rising and subsiding independent of one another and of global sea-level oscillations. Studies of late Pleistocene sea-level history using independent evidence indicate that the highest sea-level stillstands within the last 400,000 years were only about 5-10 feet higher than present sea level. This demonstrates that coastal areas with late Pleistocene marine terraces are being tectonically uplifted at rates exceeding the rate of sea-level rise.

There have been many attempts to separate the confusing and often complicated effects of coastal uplift from the Pleistocene oscillations of sea level by analysis of marine terrace sea-level curves. The best results have come from studies on coasts that have experienced steady tectonic uplift during the Pleistocene. In this situation, once a terrace forms at a high stand of sea level, it is raised up above the destructional forces of the sea as the uplifted coast steadily emerges. The island of Barbados in the eastern Caribbean and the Huon Peninsula in New Guinea both have spectacular flights of well-preserved marine terraces. The marine terrace sea-level curves derived from these coasts show cycles of sea-level rise and fall superimposed on a fairly simple uplift history. As expected, the terraces were arranged in a pattern of increasing elevation with increasing age. Using reliable independent evidence of Pleistocene glacial-ice and ocean-volume changes derived from oxygen isotopes in deep-sea cores, average rates of constant tectonic uplift were first assumed and later were calculated for both areas. When the amount of tectonic uplift was subtracted for each terrace, the resulting oscillations of the marine terrace sea-level curves showed a cyclic pattern that corresponds remarkably well with global climatic fluctuations during the last 400,000 years. They also show that sea level has not been significantly higher than its present-day elevation for the last 150,000 years. The timing of these sea-level cycles corresponds very well with variations in the earth's orbital movements about the sun, a suspected cause of Pleistocene glacial cycles (ice ages) and sea-level change. Because much is known about the history of Pleistocene sea-level variations from marine terrace data and other types of studies, dates of marine terraces are also used to determine the tectonic uplift or subsidence history of coastal areas. In tectonically active areas, such as the coast and offshore islands of southern California, coastal uplift rates several feet per century have been documented by the combined relationships of the elevation and age of marine terraces.

Bibliography

Davis, J. L. *Geographical Variation in Coastal Development*. London: Longman Group, 1977. A general text comparing geomorphic features in coastal regions worldwide.

Hearty, P. J., and P. Aharon. "Amino Acid Chronostratigraphy of Late Quaternary Coral Reefs: Huon Peninsula, New Guinea, and the Great Barrier Reef, Australia." *Geology* 16 (July, 1988): 579-583. A technical article describing the application of the amino acid dating technique to the classic coral reef terraces of the

Huon Peninsula and a comparison of the results with uranium-series ages. *Geology* is a monthly publication of the Geological Society of America.

Moore, W. S. "Late Pleistocene Sea-Level History." In *Uranium Series Disequilibrium: Applications to Environmental Problems*, edited by M. Ivanovich and R. S. Hannah. Oxford, England: Clarendon Press, 1982. Half of this chapter in an advanced textbook is a description of state-of-the-art terrace dating techniques written in a technical style. Included is a summary of all known dates for fossil-bearing marine terraces all over the world that is slightly easier to read.

Oaks, R. Q., Jr., and N. K. Coch. "Pleistocene Sea-Levels: Southeastern Virginia." *Science* 140 (May 13, 1963): 979. A technical article containing an excellent description of uplifted beach ridges on the Atlantic coastal plain of the United States. Also describes ages and dating techniques and their use in determining sea-level history.

Pethic, J. *An Introduction to Coastal Geomorphology*. Baltimore: Edward Arnold, 1984. Written primarily for the Western European region, this advanced text contains several good sections on the formation of marine terraces, their use in sea-level and tectonic uplift studies, and the correlation of terrace data with other studies.

Sharp, R. P. *Coastal Southern California*. Dubuque, Iowa: Kendall/Hunt, 1978. Written by a legendary southern California field geologist and teacher, this guide is easily understood and used by the nongeologist. Contains the route and descriptions for several day trips of geological investigation that any active and curious individual would find worthwhile.

Sheldon, J. S. *Geology Illustrated*. San Francisco: W. H. Freeman, 1966. Well illustrated with dramatic black-and-white photographs (both ground level and aerial), this book uses an encyclopedia-like format to describe a wide variety of geological processes and landforms. Sheldon is known all over the world for his excellent aerial photography and his clear, concise treatment of geological information in his educational films and materials.

Shepard, F. P. *Geological Oceanography*. New York: Crane, Russak, 1977. A classic and very readable text, with descriptions and explanations of a variety of coastal features by one of the greatest oceanographers in the history of the science.

James L. Sadd

Cross-References

Climate, 217; Coastal Processes and Beaches, 240; Geochronology: Radiocarbon Dating, 840; The Geomorphology of Wet Climate Areas, 890; Continental Glaciers, 967; Ice Ages, 1115; Ocean Waves, 1839; Paleoclimatology, 1993; Reefs, 2158; Sea Level, 2267; Seamounts, 2274; Stable Isotopes: Oxygen 18/Oxygen 16, Deuterium/Hydrogen, and Carbon 13/Carbon 12 Ratios in Rocks, 2456; Transgression and Regression, 2534.

MARS' ATMOSPHERE

Type of earth science: Planetology
Field of study: Large solar system bodies

Atmospheric studies contribute to understanding the histories of the planets. Because many similarities exist among the atmospheres, the study of one planet may contribute to the understanding of another. The atmosphere of Mars, with its simple structure, can be used to model certain aspects of Earth's atmosphere and is therefore a valuable aid in comprehending the past, present, and future of that atmosphere.

Principal terms

ESCAPE VELOCITY: the speed an object must have in order to escape the gravitational field of a planet, moon, or star

MASS SPECTROMETER: an instrument specifically designed to find compounds and identify them according to their masses

TROPOSPHERE: the lowest level of an atmosphere; it contains the highest density of material in the atmosphere and displays turbulent winds and chemical mixing

Summary of the Phenomenon

One goal of modern scientists is to unravel the history of the Earth, the solar system, and the universe. Because all data must be recorded in the present, conditions and processes of the past must be inferred from current conditions and processes. Scientists construct a model of an atmosphere's history from those inferences and use that model to project the future for the atmosphere. The model is revised as better data are gathered.

Astronomers generally assume that the terrestrial planets (Mercury, Venus, Earth, and Mars) have had two atmospheres. The primitive atmospheres would have existed soon after the formation of the planets and would have had distinctly different compositions from those that exist today. These atmospheres contained hydrogen, helium, and other lightweight compounds with speeds near or above the escape velocities of terrestrial planets. Consequently, the primitive atmospheres would be lost over a reasonably short time.

Secondary atmospheres developed as nitrogen, carbon dioxide, water, and argon were released from the planetary interiors as molten rock outgassed and volcanoes erupted. Volcanoes on Earth emit mostly carbon dioxide and water. Because scientists assume that the planets formed from the same cloud of material, they also assume that the gases coming from the interiors of different planets would be similar. Therefore, the secondary atmospheres of Venus, Earth, and Mars should contain the same compounds, but the specific quantities of those compounds should vary as conditions on the planets vary. Venus should have mostly water vapor because it is nearer the sun and has a higher surface temperature than does Earth. Mars should have mostly solid water because its distance from the sun makes it a colder planet than Earth.

Until the space program sent explorers to Mars, there was no accurate method for determining the pressure, composition, and temperature profile of its atmosphere. Mars would be expected to have a thin atmosphere, with its low escape velocity of 5.0 kilometers per second. Most estimates made during the first half of the twentieth century were between 1.2 and 1.8 pounds per square inch. (Atmospheric pressure at sea level on Earth is 14.6 pounds per square inch.) This pressure is high enough for liquid water to exist on the surface of Mars as long as the temperature is not above 310 Kelvins. Most scientists did not believe that Mars could retain much water, but if the pressure estimates were accurate, the existence of water on Mars could not be eliminated from models of the planet and its atmosphere. The composition of the Martian atmosphere was difficult to determine from Earth because the Earth's own atmosphere obscured much of the information that comes from the planet. Because the atmospheres of the terrestrial planets were expected to be similar, astronomers looked for nitrogen, oxygen, water, and carbon dioxide. Nitrogen is very difficult to observe, so no one was surprised when it was not detected. Astronomers, however, expected to find a significant amount of nitrogen when a spacecraft arrived at the planet. Earth-bound telescopes also failed to detect oxygen or water but found carbon dioxide. Astronomers used this information and their assumptions to predict that the Martian atmosphere was largely nitrogen with some carbon dioxide present.

During the late 1960's, a series of United States Mariner spacecraft flew past Mars and found that the atmospheric pressure was less than 0.09 pound per square inch. Roughly 95 percent of the atmosphere was carbon dioxide, with 1-3 percent nitrogen. Many astronomers concluded that Mars was dead and moonlike. More recent analysis of the Martian atmosphere has shown its composition to be 95.3 percent carbon dioxide, 2.7 percent nitrogen, 0.13 percent oxygen, 0.03 percent water, and 1.6 percent argon, with trace amounts of krypton and xenon.

Average temperatures at the surface of Mars are about 215 Kelvins. The warmest spot on the planet may reach 300 Kelvins near noon, but the temperature dropped to less than 192 Kelvins at the Viking 2 landing site. The polar regions are much colder. Liquid water will not exist under these conditions. During the summer days, however, the surface temperature is high enough for liquid water to exist briefly. Because the vapor pressure of water in the atmosphere is very low, this liquid water evaporates quickly. As winter begins, the water molecules freeze to cold dust particles in the atmosphere. Carbon dioxide molecules also attach themselves during the cold nights, and when the particles have enough mass, they fall to the surface. The temperatures during the day are high enough to vaporize the carbon dioxide but not the water. Pictures of the soil around the Viking 2 lander show a frost of these water-ice-coated dust grains. Clouds or ground fog of water ice crystals form about half an hour after dawn in areas heated by the sun. Beyond latitudes of 65 degrees, winter conditions cause carbon dioxide to freeze and a polar hood of carbon dioxide clouds and haze hangs over the polar regions. The coldest regions on Mars are the poles during winter. Polar caps made of carbon dioxide ice change size as the seasons change, but a permanent cap of water ice remains at each pole, where the temperatures never get warm enough to allow water to melt or vaporize. The permanent cap at the south pole is smaller than the one at the north pole because Mars is much nearer the sun during the south pole's summer than during summer in the northern hemisphere. The total atmospheric pressure changes by 26 percent seasonally because of the vaporization/condensation cycle of carbon dioxide at the poles. Much of the carbon dioxide vaporized at one pole moves toward the other pole and precipitates there.

High-pressure systems form during the summer months in a hemisphere, and low pressure develops during the winter. The pressure difference will be the greatest when it is summer in the southern hemisphere and winter in the northern hemisphere. Large-scale wind currents flow toward the north pole during northern winter and toward the south pole during southern winter. Dust particles picked up by these winds cause large-scale dust storms. These storms cause little erosion because the thin Martian atmosphere can carry only small dust particles. Viking 1 measured wind gusts up to 26 meters per second as a dust storm arrived. The most vigorous storms may involve wind velocities greater than 50 meters per second.

Some data imply that the Martian atmosphere was denser at one time than is presently observed. Channels (not canals) found by the Mariner spacecraft have the same appearance as channels formed on Earth by flowing water. Many craters show more erosion than is possible with the current atmosphere. Indirect evidence indicates that significant quantities of nitrogen, water, and carbon dioxide have been outgassed from the Martian interior. Many astronomers thus believe that the Martian atmosphere was once denser and warmer than now and that it became moist periodically as polar caps melted. Rivers may have flowed during these periods. As time passed, the pressure gradually decreased as water vapor and carbon dioxide were lost from the atmosphere. Those losses reduced the capacity of the atmosphere to retain heat. A change in the tilt of Mars' rotational axis and a change in Mars' orbital path also reduced the temperature. As temperatures dropped, the water from the atmosphere was permanently trapped in the polar caps. Eventually, much carbon dioxide was also deposited in the polar caps, and the current cycle of vaporization and condensation was established.

Methods of Study

Astronomers face the challenge of collecting data on objects that are millions of miles away. Earth-based telescopes collect light that is analyzed for relevant information. This technique, however, often does not provide the precision needed for study of planets. The advent of the space program gave astronomers new opportunities to gather data as sophisticated spacecraft traveled to the remote parts of the solar system. Mariner 4 took the first close-up spacecraft photos of Mars on July 15,

1965. Additional Mariner spacecraft studied Mars from space, and each of the two Viking missions sent a lander to the surface while leaving an orbiting craft to gather data and to serve as an information link between the lander and Earth.

Although the Mariner spacecraft had determined that carbon dioxide was the main component of the Martian atmosphere, concentrations of other compounds present in small amounts were still unknown. As the Viking landers descended through the atmosphere, they looked for nitrogen, argon, and other elements whose molecular weight was less than 50. A mass spectrometer, an instrument specifically designed to find compounds and identify them according to their masses, analyzed the atmosphere at altitudes above 100 kilometers. Nitrogen was discovered with an abundance of 3 percent. Argon, an inert gas, was found with an abundance of 1.6 percent. Another instrument, the retarding potential analyzer, showed that many hydrogen and oxygen ions were escaping from the atmosphere. Because these two elements combine to form water, their loss can be expressed in terms of water loss. Roughly 240,000 liters of water were lost each day.

The gas chromatograph mass spectrometer was to be used in analyzing gases emitted from experiments with the soil samples; however, it was also used to find krypton and xenon, which could not be detected by the upper atmosphere mass spectrometer because their concentrations were too low. The concentrations of these gases were enriched by a procedure in which Martian air was pumped into the sample chamber where carbon dioxide and carbon monoxide were removed. By repeating this process several times, krypton and xenon concentrations were increased to measurable levels.

The meteorology boom contained sensors to measure temperature, wind direction, and wind velocity. These sensors are thin bimetallic wires. As they change temperature, they induce an electric current. The size of this current determines the temperature. Wind cools the wires; by measuring the current passed through the wires to warm them to their original temperature, the velocity of the wind can be determined. Wind direction is measured by monitoring which of the sensors is cooling faster. Atmospheric pressure was measured by a sensor containing a thin metal diaphragm. The amount of movement of the diaphragm was used to determine the pressure.

Context

Planetary exploration has as its broad goals the search for life and for clues concerning the origin of the solar system. Atmospheric conditions that include the presence of water and nitrogen must exist in order for the basic materials for life to exist. The dense, hostile atmosphere of Venus destroyed any hope of finding life there. The Martian atmosphere resembles Venus' atmosphere more than Earth's; in fact, Venus and Mars each have about 95 percent carbon dioxide and 3 percent nitrogen, but the pressure on Venus is more than nine thousand times the pressure on Mars. Although there is evidence that water once flowed on the Martian surface and that the atmosphere was once thicker than it is now, there is no conclusive evidence that there has been enough water in the atmosphere to cause rain. The conditions for the development of life do not seem to have existed in the Martian atmosphere.

Further exploration of the planet will be conducted by unmanned spacecraft. Astronomers would also like to send humans to explore and perhaps colonize Mars. What benefits would come from exploration? Because the Martian atmosphere has a simple structure and because there are no bodies of water to affect the air flow, the atmospheric movement follows predictable patterns. Study of this simple system can lead to a better understanding of the more complex atmospheres of Earth and perhaps Venus. On Earth, this understanding could lead to better prediction of weather patterns, increased agricultural production, and decreased danger from natural disasters. Because carbon dioxide plays an important role in the greenhouse effect, study of the Martian atmosphere could reveal important information on how to deal with the increasing concentration of carbon dioxide in Earth's atmosphere.

Astronomers also believe that a better understanding of Earth's atmosphere will help them to draw conclusions about the possible existence of other planets like Earth in other solar systems. If life can form from inorganic matter, a careful study of the atmospheres on Earth and Mars could set limits on the range of conditions suitable for life to exist. The study may even conclude that life cannot spontaneously erupt from nonliving matter. Such a conclusion would require a total revamping of modern scientific thought.

Bibliography

Briggs, G. A., and F. W. Taylor. *The Cambridge Photographic Atlas of the Planets*. New York: Cambridge University Press, 1982. A collection of the best photographs taken by space probes from the United States and the Soviet Union. In addition to the captions accompanying the photos, a discussion of the important features of each planet and its satellites is provided. General audience.

Chapman, Clark R. *Planets of Rock and Ice: From Mercury to the Moons of Saturn*. Rev. ed. New York: Charles Scribner's Sons, 1982. A description and comparison of the planets in light of the data collected from the space probes. A small number of photographs. General audience.

Ciaccio, E. J. "Atmospheres." *Astronomy* 12 (May, 1984): 6. Excellent review of the atmospheric data of the planets and moons. Includes color photos and diagrams of atmospheric characteristics. *Astronomy* magazine is for amateur astronomers, with many articles such as this one written for a general audience.

Hartmann, W. K. *Moons and Planets*. 2d ed. Belmont, Calif.: Wadsworth, 1983. Excellent coverage of all the bodies of the solar system. Many photos and diagrams; intended as a textbook. College-level audience with some background in physics and math.

Moore, Patrick. *Guide to Mars*. New York: W. W. Norton, 1977. An interesting discussion of Mars that includes historical development of information about the planet. Describes the pre-Mariner data through the Viking missions. Some black-

and-white photos; several maps. General audience.

Morrison, David, and Tobias Owen. *The Planetary System*. Reading, Mass.: Addison-Wesley, 1988. A discussion of data from each of the planets. Contains a large number of photographs and line drawings. Although intended as an astronomy textbook, it provides good reading for anyone with an interest in the solar system. Some sections require a good science background.

Trejo, Paul E. *Introductory Astronomy: The Solar System*. Dubuque, Iowa: Kendall/Hunt, 1986. This book is intended as an introductory astronomy text. Trejo discusses general astronomical principles before zeroing in on the solar system. Contains a limited number of photographs and line drawings; planetary data are summarized well. General audience, with some background in science helpful in spots.

Washburn, Mark. *Mars at Last!* New York: G. P. Putnam's Sons, 1977. A description of the exploration of Mars. Includes much anecdotal material about people involved with various modern missions as well as early studies of the planet. Washburn captures the excitement of the scientists awaiting the landing of Viking 1. General audience.

Dennis R. Flentge

Cross-References

The Atmosphere's Evolution, 114; The Atmosphere's Global Circulation, 121; The Atmosphere's Structure and Composition, 128; Climate, 217; The Greenhouse Effect, 1004; Mars' Craters, 1480; Mars' Polar Caps, 1487; Mars' Valleys, 1494; Mars' Volcanoes, 1500; Mars' Water, 1508; Remote Sensing and the Electromagnetic Spectrum, 2166; Elemental Distribution in the Solar System, 2434; The Origin of the Solar System, 2442; Venus' Atmosphere, 2587; Wind, 2730.

MARS' CRATERS

Type of earth science: Planetology
Field of study: Large solar system bodies

Examination of Mars' craters reveals the history of its atmosphere and cyclic planetary meteorology, as well as details about Mars' weathering processes and much about its current weather cycles.

Principal terms

BASIN: a large, typically flat-bottomed crater formed by the impact of a very large body

CRATER MORPHOLOGY: the structure or form of craters and the related processes that developed them

DEGRADATION: the process of crater erosion from all processes, including wind and other meteorological mechanisms

EJECTA: the material ejected from the crater of a meteoric impact

EOLIAN EROSION: a mechanism of erosion or crater degradation caused by wind

PEDESTAL CRATER: a crater that has assumed the shape of a pedestal as a result of the wind's unique shaping processes

RAMPART CRATER: a type of crater found most often on Mars and produced by some subsurface shaping mechanism that causes a unique, rampart-type wall formation

SUPERIMPOSITION: craters that are formed within other craters, such as those formed when a meteor falls inside or on the walls of an existing crater

Summary of the Phenomenon

Earth-based telescopic observations of Mars cannot reveal its distinct surface features. The distance is too great and the combined effects of Earth's and Mars' atmospheres reveal only indistinct and blurred splotches of color. The first distinct images of the planet's surface came from the United States' space probe Mariner 4 on July 14, 1965. The probe sent back to Earth nineteen photographs of the Martian surface, quite unrefined by the standards of the 1990's but exceptionally revealing nevertheless. In the twenty-two minutes that it took to transmit the photographs, centuries of speculation about Mars was laid to rest. The most surprising and pronounced of the Mariner 4 revelations was the extensive cratering of the Martian surface, a finding few planetologists expected.

There are two classes of craters on any planet or other terrestrial body: impact craters, caused by meteors or comets impacting the surface, and volcanic craters. On the known bodies of the solar system, including Mars, the impact craters outnumber volcanic craters by many thousands of times.

Earlier views of the planet Mercury and the detailed knowledge of Earth's moon depicted both bodies as heavily cratered. Most of this cratering occurred in the earliest 500 million years, when the planets formed by accretion out of the primordial material that formed the bodies of the solar system and the sun. During this period, the planets were heavily bombarded from space by meteors and planetesimals caught in the gravitational pull of the newly forming planets.

Earth, on the other hand, is not heavily cratered, although it was subjected to the same rate of incoming meteors; Earth's thick atmosphere burns up and destroys any incoming body of less than 1,000 kilograms in mass. Earth's widespread weather also quickly erases any meteoric crater. Any trace of a meteor falling into the ocean is either totally erased or largely mediated by the water. On airless, inactive bodies, however, there are few mechanisms to erase cratering, even though some occurred billions of years ago.

From Earth-based telescopic observations, it was widely expected before 1965 that there was enough weathering on Mars to have erased most of its primordial cratering. Mariner 4 clearly showed that this was not the case. The most immediate implication was that Mars was far less active meteorologically and geologically than was initially thought. Later, both extreme views were mediated by data from later space probes and more detailed studies, which showed that Mars has an active weathering process, though not as vigorous as that of Earth.

It has been shown that Mars is a unique planet, different in important ways from Earth, the Moon, or Mercury. The study of its craters has been remarkably useful— acting as geological clocks, the craters provide information dating vast planetary regions, periods of meteorological activity, and volcanoes. The craters have even suggested typical allegories to possible water reserves beneath the planet's surface. Its primordial craters, still intact in certain regions and erased in others, give a remarkably intact, long-term surface history of Mars.

The space probes that followed Mariner 4 were Mariners 6 and 7 (1969), Mariner 9 (1971-1972), and Vikings 1 and 2 (1976-1977). These spacecraft provided greatly improved images of Mars and returned data over long periods of time, including detailed meteorological observations from both orbit and the surface. From this information, a detailed assessment of Martian cratering and morphology was accomplished. Some of the most elemental assessments of crater morphology include crater size, composition of ejecta, composition and behavior of impacted terrain, modification processes of the crater, and its effect on surrounding craters and terrain. These findings may lead to a determination of the crater's age, that of surrounding crater fields, and even the age of the impacted terrain. As a planetary whole, assessments are made of crater sizes, numbers, distribution, and ages within selected planetary areas.

The largest craters, typically caused by very large impacting bodies (such as asteroids), are called basins. The largest such basin on Mars is called Hellas Planitia; with a diameter of 1,600 kilometers and a depth of 3 kilometers, it is the deepest point on the planet's surface. (As large as it is, it is still not the largest known in the solar system. The lunar basin called Oceanus Procellarum—the Ocean of Storms—has a diameter of some 2,500 kilometers.) Other such large features are Isidis (1,400 kilometers) and Argyre (900 kilometers).

The most common type of crater found on Mars is called a rampart crater, first described by planetary geologist J. F. McCauley in 1973. Rampart cratering seems almost unique to Mars. This interesting morphology consists of a central crater wall with an ejecta pattern that resembles a resolidified flow pattern radiating outward from the crater wall as a low ridge and radial striae. This flow pattern hints that the impact actually liquefied the subsurface materials, causing them to flow away from the impact point, then resolidify as a rampart or gently sloping wall. The causes of this fluidized ejecta are thought to have been entrapment of atmospheric gases in the ejecta or, more significantly, water in the ejecta material, such as permafrost, which acts as a lubricant, allowing the materials to flow away from the impact point. The latter concept is a favorite one of those who hope to discover immense amounts of water locked up in the subsurface deposits as permafrost. Since rampart cratering is prevalent on much of Mars, such planetary-wide deposits of permafrost would be a very positive sign for eventual human colonization of the planet.

One of the most unusual craters found on Mars is the pedestal crater. The pedestal crater was formed by weathering action which cut away at the base of the crater until it had given the crater the appearance of being a pedestal. The unique meteorology and geology required to produce such craters are found on Mars between 40 and 60 degrees north latitude.

In examining craters on Mars, planetologists are able to define the crater's age, and hence that of the surrounding terrain, through a process of observing certain of its characteristics. The process of a crater wearing down is called degradation. Examining the original impact that formed the crater is a starting point; a new crater with little or no degradation is one with sharp edges and fresh ejecta outlying its central diameter. As the crater degrades through natural processes (erodes), the rim loses its sharpness and the walls slump and lose definition. Ultimately, the walls may form gullies and eventually become completely degraded to surface level. In the final stage, the crater is hardly noticeable over the terrain, and some planetary scientists even call such a crater a ghost.

On Earth, the most profound degradation process is weathering, which can erase even large craters quickly, in geologic terms. On Mars, such processes are substantially slower. Since liquid water does not flow on the Martian surface, weathering processes are confined to wind erosion, or eolian processes. It is estimated that eolian erosion is responsible for filling in craters on Mars at the rate of 0.0001 centimeter per year. From these crater studies, there is considerable evidence that such erosion has slowed in the planet's recent geologic past. The last period of relatively heavier erosion occurred roughly 600 million years ago, according to some crater studies.

The interior morphology of Martian craters is highly variable. It is typically dependent on the mass of the incoming meteor and the composition of the impact site. In smaller craters, the bottom usually assumes a more spherical shape. In larger craters, the central region of the crater flattens out until, in craters greater than 25 kilometers in diameter, a central peak is formed. Such flatness is often caused by the impacting body liquefying the impacted crust or by magma welling up from the planet's interior to fill in the impact crater.

By examining craters formed within other craters in a process called superimposition, planetary geologists are able to determine the age of whole regions of Mars' surface. With an overall planetary comparison, which includes mass crater counts, it has been discovered that there are areas that have changed little since Mars was formed, while other regions, notably volcanic regions, have changed in the recent geologic past.

In some of the most fascinating crater studies accomplished to date, scientists have attempted to determine the age of what appears to be massive river channels on Mars. Although conditions on Mars at present will not allow liquid water to exist on the planet's surface, it appears that water once flowed in an extensive series of channels. Planetary geologists have examined craters that overlie the enigmatic channels. They range in age from 3.5 billion years to as young as fewer than 200 million years, strongly suggesting that the channels have been formed on a cyclic basis throughout the geologic history of Mars.

On Mars can be observed the largest volcanic craters in the known solar system, volcanoes from ten to one hundred times larger than the largest volcano on earth, Mauna Loa in Hawaii. Four very large volcanic craters exist in close proximity in the Tharsis region. The largest volcano is Olympus Mons, a 200-million-year-old volcano with a crater 80 kilometers across. (These Martian volcanoes, called shield volcanoes after their earthly counterparts, have craters nested inside one another.) Three other Tharsis volcanoes are roughly alike in size, all much larger than Mauna Loa. The crater on Arsia Mons is 140 kilometers in diameter (compared to Mauna Loa's 2.8 kilometers), the largest Pavonis Mons crater is 45 kilometers in diameter and 5 kilometers deep (compared to Mauna Loa's 0.2 kilometer of depth), and the largest of the Ascraeus Mons craters is roughly the same diameter as the largest Pavonis Mons crater. The volcanic plains spreading away from the Martian volcanoes are dated according to crater distribution. The youngest is Pavonis Mons, credited with 80 million years.

Methods of Study

The means for collecting aggregate crater data is orbital photography from interplanetary spacecraft. Almost all such data collected to date have come from the United States' probes: Mariners and Vikings. The techniques for analysis are dependent on the aim of the study. For example, a statistical counting method borrowed from other applications, called a frequency distribution, is used to determine the number of craters located over a given area. This information may lead to determination of the age of the area under study given a uniform crater deposition rate.

Other statistical counting methods include cumulative distribution, logarithmic incremental distributions, and incremental frequency distributions, all of which are specific methods of presenting collected crater population data. Some appear as graphs, others as numerical tables, and some data presentations are simple maps showing locations of craters over a given area. In the largest distribution sampling exhibit, the entire planet of Mars is presented with its crater distributions marked.

All of these are unique representations designed to give the researcher information in a specific way so that the concept under study, such as the age of an area, can be efficiently viewed. Inferences are made from this statistical presentation about such broad concepts as crater production and erosion.

The most desirable study technique is ideally one enhanced by physically visiting the site and taking in situ measurements. Yet in the absence of these data, orbital crater studies have provided ample sources of information for developing credible theories about Mars' many puzzles.

The techniques used for determining aging are rather obvious ones. Planetologists have arrived at a rate of cratering for Mars that is equivalent to three hundred meteors, of one kilogram or larger, striking each square kilometer every million years. From this baseline of impacts, current photographs can be compared to establish which areas are very old and which are newer geological formations. The logical extension of such knowledge is the ability to date such formations as plains, volcanic flows, and stream beds, as well as to establish a baseline for regional eolian erosion.

Context

The study of Martian craters allows planetary scientists to determine from orbital photographs many varied characteristics of Mars. From information relating present conditions on Mars all the way back to its earliest geological history, crater studies have allowed much of the planet's chronology to be traced. Orbital studies of Mars' craters may lead to answers about the planet's most significant geological history, such as whether water ever existed on Mars in liquid form, what formed the vast river channels and canyons, and what happened to the water. Such questions form the pivotal inquiry into what man will have to do to survive on Mars should this neighbor planet be colonized.

Crater studies address questions of importance relative to Earth's own history and future. Planetologists seek to understand why Mars is so different from Earth and what indeed happened to its once apparently abundant water. Such questions of planetary history relate to what may one day happen on Earth. If the scientific community is able eventually to draw enough parallels from the study of other planets, it may be able to apply rigid mathematical projections to Earth's own future based on present conditions and trends.

The uniqueness of Mars lies directly in the story told by its craters. Because Mars supplies in some areas a complete history of its surface extending almost to the time of its formation and in a remarkable continuum to other regions as recent as a few tens of millions of years, Mars offers a single time compendium of the solar system itself. A complete study of Mars should yield secrets that date the solar system's entire history in an account from the first epochs to the most recent.

Bibliography

American Geophysical Union. *Scientific Results of the Viking Project*. Washington, D.C.: Author, 1978. This is a compendium of articles about the Viking project as published in the *Journal of Geophysical Research*. It consists of detailed, technical articles from the journal about the assessments of data from the Viking landers on the surface of and in orbit around Mars. It is a technical journal but is suitable for college-level readers.

Barbato, James P., and Elizabeth A. Ayer. *Atmospheres*. Elmsford, N.Y.: Pergamon Press, 1981. This book is a well-thought-out, highly developed analysis of the atmospheres of twelve planets and moons of the solar system. The list includes Earth, Mercury, Venus, Mars, Jupiter, Io, Ganymede, Saturn, Titan, Uranus, Neptune, and Pluto. The treatment of Mars' atmosphere includes a discussion of winds and other erosional factors. It is suitable for a general readership but would appeal to a more technical audience as well.

Beatty, J. Kelly, et al., eds. *The New Solar System*. Cambridge, Mass.: Sky Publishing, 1982. This beautifully illustrated and well-crafted book was intended to bring the most recent planetary discoveries to light in a single source. It reports Martian cratering in detail. It is written for the general reader and is extensively illustrated.

Ezell, Edward, and Linda Ezell. *On Mars: Explorations of the Red Planet, 1958-1978*. NASA SP-4212. Washington, D.C.: Government Printing Office, 1984. This book is an official NASA history of the Viking program from the original ideas in 1958 to the culmination of the project some twenty years later. It is a detailed assessment of the political and technical history but also discusses details of the instruments that photographed Mars from orbit and the surface instruments that measured the winds. It is written for all readers and is generally nontechnical.

Hartmann, William K., and Ron Miller. *Out of the Cradle*. New York: Workman Publishing, 1984. This combination picture book and narrative of future human exploration discusses Mars as a logical next step for human exploration and settlement after the moon. It speculates on the struggle of future colonists on Mars. The book is written for the general reader and is illustrated with the artist's conception of future Mars bases and explorers.

Joëls, Kerry Mark. *The Mars One Crew Manual*. New York: Ballantine Books, 1985. This facsimile of what a future Mars explorer's crew manual may look like is an excellent reference for what the future colonist may find on arrival at Mars. It also includes a discussion of the environment of Mars, the ground conditions, and the craters. It is written for all backgrounds and is illustrated.

Miles, Frank, and Nicholas Booth. *Race to Mars—The Harper & Row Mars Flight Atlas*. New York: Harper & Row, 1988. This is also a futuristic Mars crew manual which relates the more or less exact process of a flight to Mars and what the expedition members will encounter while there. This book is exquisitely photographed and illustrated with a very detailed discussion of Mars' cratering. It is written for all readers.

Mutch, Thomas A., et al. *The Geology of Mars*. Princeton, N.J.: Princeton University Press, 1976. This technical book is written in textbook style and is accessible to those with a college-level science background. It is a complete analysis of the recovered Viking data in a geological narrative, with illustrations, photographs, and tables.

Dennis Chamberland

Cross-References

The Geologic Time Scale, 874; Lunar Craters, 1393; Lunar Maria, 1408; Mars' Atmosphere, 1474; Mars' Volcanoes, 1500; Mars' Water, 1508; Meteorite and Comet Impacts, 1623; Meteors and Meteor Showers, 1666; The Origin of the Solar System, 2442; Volcanoes: Calderas, 2614; Volcanoes: The Hawaiian Islands, 2638; Volcanoes: Shield Volcanoes, 2681.

MARS' POLAR CAPS

Type of earth science: Planetology
Field of study: Large solar system bodies

In 1666, Giovanni Cassini observed Mars' surface and described two polar caps, the planet's most visible features. These caps have been studied extensively since, both telescopically and by means of the Viking and Mariner space probes.

Principal terms

LOWELL BANDS: dark areas on the periphery of the Martian polar caps in summer

MILLIBAR: one thousand dynes per square centimeter; a dyne is a small unit of force that will cause a body of 1 gram to accelerate at 1 centimeter per second per second

PERIHELION: in a planet's orbit, its nearest point to the sun

SUBLIMATION: the transformation of a solid directly into a gas or a gas directly into a solid, passing through no liquid stage

WATER ICE THEORY: the theory that the polar caps of Mars are composed of water in solid form

Summary of the Phenomenon

When Giovanni Cassini observed the polar caps of Mars in 1666, little was known about the planet's surface features. A decade before Cassini, the Dutch astronomer Christiaan Huygens suggested the presence of polar caps on Mars, but it was not until 1672 that he actually saw the planet's south polar cap, Mars' most apparent feature when one views it through a telescope. No one before Cassini had seen the polar caps in detail, because no instrument had existed to allow sufficient magnification.

Early astronomers, who, after the invention of the telescope, were able to observe some of the surface features of Mars, reached conclusions based on analogies with Earth, the only planet whose atmosphere and chemical composition they knew in detail. It is not surprising, then, that the Martian polar caps were presumed to be like the polar caps found on Earth: composed of ice, snow, hoarfrost, or a combination of these forms of water. This theory presupposes that Mars has water, a requisite for life, and therefore the individual components of water, hydrogen and oxygen. This notion gave rise to the popular theory that Mars could support life in some form, a theory that was subsequently brought into considerable question and that remained controversial even after the Viking and Mariner missions to Mars.

In 1719, the Italian astronomer Giacomo Maraldi discovered that the polar caps are not centered at Mars' precise geographical poles. Maraldi also divined from his observations that the south polar region of Mars has a much greater mass than its northern counterpart. Subsequent research and observation has substantiated Maraldi's theories, revealing that the planet's north polar cap lies about 64 kilometers from its geographical north pole and that the south polar cap lies some 400 kilometers from the geographical south pole. This phenomenon occurs because of the planet's elongated orbit, which makes its relationship to the sun very different from Earth's.

The present atmosphere of Mars is known to be such that there can be no accumulated areas of liquid water, such as lakes, ponds, rivers, or oceans. Considerable evidence suggests, however, that the "canals" of Mars were cut by flowing liquid, presumably water in liquid form. Most evidence demolishes the theory that these channels were forged by lava flowing from the planet's volcanoes. Current theory indicates, rather, that in one stage of the planet's evolution, water in liquid form was plentiful.

When everything astronomers knew about Mars came from their observations through telescopes, they could gather substantial information about the polar caps; they were at odds, however, in their interpretations of these data. They could not always be sure what they were seeing. They also had little means of knowing with any certainty the depth of the polar caps. Some scientists thought that they were hundreds of feet deep; others thought the caps were merely thin coverings of hoarfrost. Common sense supported the latter idea. The argument was that if a thin layer of hoarfrost covered the poles, it would, under warmer conditions, condense and form clouds. On the other hand, if the polar caps were composed of fairly deep layers of solid water, where would the melting residue run during the warmer season? The atmosphere of Mars was then thought to be almost totally dry, yet observations through telescopes clearly showed that in the summer, the polar caps seemed to melt partially. Certainly they diminished in size, and the areas surrounding them assumed a dark coloration, suggesting that water was mixing with minerals and dust at the periphery of the thawing area and causing what looked like a moist condition.

The south polar cap covers an area of more than 10 million square kilometers in winter and at times extends almost halfway to the Martian equator. Even a minimal thawing would produce water in great quantity, especially if the water ice ran to great depths; yet, no water from the polar cap appeared through the telescope to have penetrated other areas of the planet, which seemed dusty and dry.

Faced with this anomaly, scientists could do little to verify their theories until a different sort of evidence, the kind provided by the Mariner and Viking missions, became available in quantity between 1965 and 1977, when activity in the space program was at its peak. Viking 2 measured some of the temperatures of the north polar cap with a high degree of certainty and discovered that the temperatures in its dark surrounding areas had a range of between -38 and -33 degrees Celsius and that the white, presumably frozen, areas had a range between -63 and -68 degrees Celsius. These temperatures exceed the -79 degrees at which carbon dioxide sublimates into a solid.

The atmosphere of Mars, thought until the Mariner 4 flyby in 1965 to be about 85 millibars, was proved to be a thin 10 millibars; Earth's atmosphere at sea level is

1,000 millibars, or 1 bar. The Martian atmosphere is comparable to Earth's atmosphere at about 24,000 meters, where the pull of gravity is all but lost. Such an atmosphere does not permit freestanding water, indicating that if the Martian atmosphere had always been the way it is now, the planet could never have had water and the polar caps would necessarily be composed of some other substance.

Thinking of this sort gave rise to the theory that the polar caps were composed of solid (frozen) carbon dioxide, or dry ice. Percival Lowell advanced such a theory as early as 1895; other eminent astronomers considered it more likely than the water theory as late as 1971, when Mariner 9 was uncovering data that would soon vitiate, although not completely eliminate, the carbon dioxide theory. Mariner 4, when it made its flyby of Mars in 1965, had returned data suggesting that the Martian atmosphere was composed largely of carbon dioxide under weak pressure. This information caused some astronomers to cast their lots with Lowell's theory that carbon dioxide in its frozen state covered the polar caps but that when the temperature rose, it became, through sublimation, gaseous and returned to the atmosphere as mist or fog. This explanation helped to account for the haze often observed over the polar regions.

Data that Mariner 9 transmitted substantiated the theory that the present Martian atmosphere accommodates no accumulations of liquid water. The same mission, however, collected various rock samples in which liquid water was found to be locked. It also presented incontrovertible evidence that the polar caps are composed largely of ice and are minimally 0.8 kilometer deep, indicating clearly that the Martian climate has changed through the eons and that it was once such that liquid water, now locked in the polar caps in solid form, was abundant.

The earliest space missions carried out research only on the north polar cap, but they managed to dispel a substantial number of misconceptions about Mars, among them the mistaken idea that the planet is totally dry. The data sent back suggest that in the northern latitudes above 60°, the atmosphere is quite moist; the atmosphere over the north polar cap has twenty times the water vapor that the atmosphere over the equatorial regions contains. During the Martian summer, surface ice exposed to the sun evaporates in the morning, causing a mist that seems to condense, resulting later in the day in precipitation. Although these data were gathered exclusively over the north polar cap, there was little reason to think that the south polar cap differed significantly. At perihelion, the planet's closest approach to the sun, the north polar cap does not face the sun directly but is tilted away from it. This tilt prevents it from getting the full impact of the sun's rays, which would, presumably, melt a polar cap composed of frozen water.

The space probes of Mars indicate that over the long term, water is quite plentiful on the planet. The climate of Mars must be viewed over eons; the planet is now much drier than it once was, and scientists think that it will evolve through this period to one in which conditions resemble what they were when the Martian atmosphere allowed the accumulation of water in bodies similar to the ones on Earth.

It is now widely accepted that portions of both of the major early theories about the polar caps were true. Although the evidence is strong that deep layers of water ice cover the polar regions and although it is known that the deep crater Korolev in the north polar cap is filled with water ice, many astronomers think that during certain seasons, there are thin coatings of carbon dioxide that sublimate into the gaseous state and cause the clouds or mists that have been observed over the polar caps.

Methods of Study

In the three and a half centuries that the polar caps of Mars have been observed, descriptions of the caps have moved from the highly speculative to the soundly scientific. In this period, astronomers have moved from primitive optical telescopes to incredibly complex telescopes of enormous size and capable of detecting invisible radiation, strategically placed to focus on the sky and on the planets. Mars has been the most intriguing planet for most astronomers to explore, because it is sometimes a relatively close 56 million kilometers from Earth. It is also the planet that most resembles Earth in its surface features, although its atmosphere currently precludes advanced life.

The Viking and Mariner missions solidified human knowledge of Mars. Telescopic evidence suggested to many that, because of reflections detected from the polar caps, the caps must be composed of water ice. When the earlier Mariner missions presented evidence favoring the carbon dioxide theory, astronomers were forced to rethink their earlier stands. Later expeditions, however, offered convincing evidence in favor of the water ice theory. When Viking 1 landed, it not only photographed the surface extensively and transmitted the pictures to Earth but also deployed an arm that dug into the Martian surface and analyzed the composition of the materials it uncovered. Finding water locked in Martian rocks established clearly the former existence of water on the planet.

Mariner 9 was placed into orbit around Mars in 1971, and it sent back more than seven thousand pictures. It photographed the south polar cap continuously from November, 1971, until March, 1972, capturing the waning of the polar cap as summer advanced. These pictures provided extremely varied information and reiterated the water ice theory.

Context

Human curiosity about Mars has been great. The question whether there is now or could ever be life on Mars has long been a matter of conjecture. If there is, was, or will be life on Mars, that life would likely be confined to organisms much smaller and less complex than anything resembling human beings. To sustain animal or vegetable life, it is presumed, some minimal atmosphere must exist and water must be present. Research into the polar caps of Mars provides evidence that water is plentiful in the planet's frozen polar caps, but the same research suggests that the planet is much drier than Earth, that its atmosphere is so rarefied that it cannot support complex organisms, and that its temperatures, although much less forbidding than those on Jupiter or Venus, are not conducive to life.

In the second quarter of the twentieth century, Eugene M. Antoniadi, a Greek-born astronomer who spent his professional life in France, explained the dark areas on the periphery of the polar caps in summer, designated the "Lowell bands" for astronomer Percival Lowell. Antoniadi thought that the fringes of the ice fields were reduced in brightness by grasses and bushes that grew in the periphery, presupposing by such a contention the existence of life on Mars and of an atmosphere that would support life. This theory has been disproved, but it reflected the widespread notion that life exists on Mars—although not in the form of the "little green men" that some works of science fiction describe.

Space-probe exploration of the polar caps of Mars has revealed that water in some form exists on Mars and suggested that water in liquid form was once more plentiful there than it is currently. The channels of Mars are now generally thought to have been forged through the eons by flowing water, and the presence of the polar ice caps supports this theory. These explorations have also presented evidence that the atmosphere of Mars has changed drastically from what it once was. Climatic change may one day produce a Mars quite different from the present planet. Astronomers who make such projections, however, caution that they are talking about millions, perhaps hundreds of millions, of years. Mars is unlikely to change in easily perceptible ways within the lifespan of a single human now living.

Bibliography

Carroll, Michael W. "The Changing Face of Mars." *Astronomy* 15 (March, 1987): 6-22. Carroll presents convincing data to support the contention that there is water on Mars. He considers not only the polar caps but also evidence found in the channels and in rock samples.

Chapman, Clark R. *The Inner Planets: New Light on the Rocky Worlds of Mercury, Venus, Earth, the Moon, Mars, and the Asteroids*. New York: Charles Scribner's Sons, 1977. Chapman writes at a level that makes his information, which is thoroughly researched, accessible to the nonspecialist. His discussion of the atmospheric conditions of planets is intriguing for the sharp contrasts it presents. The material is presented with meticulous fairness and objectivity. Generous illustrations and photographs. Excellent index.

Glasstone, Samuel. *The Book of Mars*. Washington, D.C.: National Aeronautics and Space Administration, 1968. Contains a useful history of Mars up to the Mariner missions. Mars exploration to 1967 is covered accurately and with excellent illustrations. Includes such topics as the avoidance of contamination of Mars and the possibility of life on Mars. Much of the book's speculative material was disproved by future exploration, particularly the Viking 1 mission in 1976. The book, well indexed and illustrated, is accessible to laypersons.

Hartmann, William K., and Odell Raper. *The New Mars: The Discoveries of Mariner 9*. Washington, D.C.: National Aeronautics and Space Administration, 1974.

Although its information was rendered somewhat outdated by the Viking missions, this book is valuable for its detailed information about the material uncovered by Mariner 9. Includes numerous photographs; they will be useful for students of the polar caps, because Mariner 9 photographed the south polar cap steadily for four months. Some background in astronomy would be helpful.

Knight, David C. *The First Book of Mars: An Introduction to the Red Planet*. Rev. ed. New York: Franklin Watts, 1973. Aimed at the nonspecialist and particularly at the young reader, this well-illustrated, well-indexed book is never condescending. Knight does not avoid complex matters but presents them clearly. Some of the information has been superseded by the Viking missions' findings.

Leighton, R. B. "The Photographs from Mariner IV." *Scientific American* 214, no. 4 (1966): 54. These photographs of the north polar cap encouraged the incorrect perception that the polar caps consisted of solid carbon dioxide that sublimated into a gas at higher temperatures.

Lowell, Percival H. *Mars and Its Canals*. New York: Macmillan, 1906. Lowell speculates that the polar caps are composed of carbon dioxide, a theory that regained its vogue after Mariner 4's pictures suggested an absence of water in substantial quantities in the polar caps. The book has historical interest for sophisticated readers.

Michaux, C. M. *Handbook of the Physical Properties of the Planet Mars*. Washington, D.C.: National Aeronautics and Space Administration, 1967. Although Michaux was working with flawed data, as was proved by space ventures in the decade after his book appeared, the material on the polar caps is striking and well presented. Valuable for readers with some background in astronomy.

Moore, Patrick. *Guide to Mars*. New York: W. W. Norton, 1977. A reliable book on Mars and Mars exploration, this compact volume provides an excellent chapter that focuses on the Martian ice caps, plains, and deserts. The material on the Mariner and Viking missions and their results is indispensable to any serious student of the polar caps or of Mars in general. Necessary historical information is skillfully woven into the text.

Richardson, Robert S. *Exploring Mars*. New York: McGraw-Hill, 1954. It is interesting to compare this dated book with later ones that indicate clearly the enormous progress that has been made in understanding Mars. The material on the polar caps is limited but valuable. The index is extensive and accurate.

Spangenberg, Ray, and Diane Moser. "The Secret Ice of Mars." *Space World* W-2-266 (February, 1986): 14-15. This article, using computer analysis of Viking data, discusses the water ice residues found on the planet, notably in the polar caps, and strengthens the theory that Mars once had abundant water.

R. Baird Shuman

Cross-References

Aerial Photography, 17; The Atmosphere's Structure and Composition, 128; Cli-

MARS' VALLEYS

Type of earth science: Planetology
Field of study: Large solar system bodies

Like Earth, Mars has valleys exhibiting complex geological histories, including flowing water, hill-slope processes, and structural control. Unlike Earth, yet similar to the Moon, Martian valleys may be as old as 4 billion years.

Principal terms

GEOMORPHOLOGY: the study of landforms on planetary surfaces and the processes responsible for their origin

GEOTHERMAL: pertaining to the heat of the interior of a planet

GREENHOUSE EFFECT: the condition that develops in a planetary atmosphere whereby radiatively active gases, such as carbon dioxide, hold heat that enters the atmosphere by solar radiation; the warming effect is similar to that inside a glass enclosure such as a greenhouse

GROUNDWATER: the water that occurs in the subsurface of a planet; it particularly applies to the subsurface zone that is saturated with such water

IMPACT CRATER: a generally circular depression formed on the surface of a planet by the impact of a high-velocity projectile such as a meteor, asteroid, or comet

MODEL: a simulation of a phenomenon that is difficult to observe or specify by direct means; models abstract from phenomena under study those qualities that the investigator perceives to be essential for understanding

PERMEABILITY: the property or capacity of porous geological materials to transmit fluids; it indicates the relative ease of fluid flow through a medium for some energy gradient through that medium

SAPPING: a natural process of erosion at the bases of hill slopes or cliffs whereby support is removed by undercutting, thereby allowing overlying layers to collapse; spring sapping is the facilitation of this process by concentrated groundwater flow, generally at the heads of valleys

Summary of the Phenomenon

Valleys are low-lying, elongate troughs on planetary surfaces that are surrounded by elevated ground. On Earth, valleys often contain a stream with an outlet. Valleys on the Moon, however, are completely dry, and are thought to have been created mostly by subsurface forces. Some lunar valleys may also form by chains of craters left by impacting meteors. About two hundred years ago, the origin of valleys on Earth was very controversial. In 1788, the Scottish naturalist James Hutton disputed the prevailing opinion that valleys formed by cataclysmic flooding, specifically the Noachian flood of biblical accounts. Hutton hypothesized that valleys formed gradually through the erosive action of the rivers and streams that lay on their floors. The fluvial origin of most valleys was subsequently demonstrated by detailed geomorphological work over the next century.

In 1972, spacecraft images revealed the presence of channels and valleys on Mars that appeared very similar to those on Earth. On the Moon, which lacks significant water and other volatile chemical components, valleys are very different. Some, called sinuous rills, have formed by the erosive action of lava. Others are structural depressions formed as blocks of land dropped between fractures. Such valleys also occur on Mars and Earth, but are much less common than the fluvial forms.

On Mars, a very interesting inversion of scale occurs for channels and valleys. Channels are those troughs in which fluid flow completely surrounded the depression that confined it. Martian channels are up to 200 kilometers wide and 2,000 kilometers long. The channels are much larger than networks of small valleys in the ancient, heavily cratered uplands of the planet. The valleys are typically a few kilometers wide and several hundred kilometers long. Both Martian channels and Martian valleys are extremely ancient by terrestrial standards but are comparable in age to many features on the Moon. The valleys formed early in the planet's history—by analogy to the Moon, more than 3.5 billion years ago—when rates of impact cratering were much higher than they are at present. The channels are somewhat younger, extending in age from about 3 to 0.5 billion years ago.

Martian channels were formed by immense flows of fluid that emanated from zones of collapsed topography known as chaotic terrain. This fluid seems to have burst onto the surface as immense floods of water plus considerable sediment. In the extreme cold of the Martian environment, the water would have partly frozen to form ice jams driven by the turbulent water. Local blockades of ice may have induced secondary floods, and the ice itself could have flowed in a manner somewhat similar to terrestrial glaciers. The processes of cataclysmic water outburst were probably repeated over long periods of time. These floods were probably generated from ground ice in the subsurface, perhaps heated by volcanic activity.

One of the enigmas about flowing water on Mars is the present surface environment of the planet. The atmospheric pressure is only about 0.7 percent of the terrestrial atmospheric pressure. The temperatures measured at the Viking landing sites on the planet ranged from -30 degrees Celsius by day to -80 degrees Celsius at night. Under these conditions, any standing body of water would rapidly vaporize and freeze. Rapid outbursts of water that formed the large channels, however, could have been maintained because of the relatively short duration of the flow events.

The existence of small valley networks of the heavily cratered terrains of Mars poses a problem for scientists. The valleys have short tributaries that end in abrupt valley heads, similar to the box canyons of the western United States. This valley form is believed to be caused by spring sapping. Sapping is the process whereby groundwater undercuts hill slopes; the groundwater apparently emerged as springs at the heads of the valleys, providing a subsurface source for flow.

One way to have maintained the groundwater flow that sustained Martian valley growth would have been for precipitation (rain or snow) to have fallen in the headwater areas. Water infiltrating the ground would then have recharged the groundwater flow system. This mechanism, however, requires a very different climate for Mars from the one observed today; the atmosphere has to be warm and dense enough to hold considerable water. Atmospheric scientists have constructed theoretical models of such an ancient, hypothetical atmosphere for Mars. They conclude that increased amounts of carbon dioxide may have been present early in the planet's history. The carbon dioxide could have contributed to a greenhouse effect, whereby the planetary surface is warmed by trapping incoming solar radiation as heat. An alternative mechanism for maintaining groundwater flow to the valley networks would be for geothermal systems to drive the flow by convective, or circulating, heat. Subsurface volcanic rocks would supply the heat, circulating the groundwater in a manner similar to that in areas of hot springs, such as Yellowstone. Water flowing in the valleys would cool, seep into the ground, and recharge a recirculating system driven by volcanic heat. This mechanism would not require a dense, warm atmosphere early in the planet's history.

Both the channels and valleys of Mars are modified by many other processes besides water flow. Because these features have hill slopes, a variety of gravity-induced slope adjustment forms are present; called mass movements, these slope adjustments include landslides, flows of debris, and slow creep of slope materials. All these processes may have been facilitated by water and ice mixed with the rock materials. Movement of debris onto the channel and valley floors, in some cases, completely conceals evidence of fluvial action that originally cut into the landscape.

Wind action is also facilitated by the confinement of valleys. The wind erodes fine sediment, producing a lineated topography that parallels prevailing directions. The eroded materials may locally accumulate as sets of sand dunes, or they may be more broadly distributed as sheets of deposited sand or dust.

Valleys also served as troughs along which erupted lavas descended from volcanic source areas. Indeed, Martian volcanoes serve as excellent sites in which to observe the evolutionary sequence of valley development on Mars. The volcanoes vary in age and in the character of their surfaces, thereby providing a kind of natural experiment on the formation of valleys. Studies of fluvial valley development on volcanoes indicate that incision by flowing water occurs only when the very permeable lava flows of the volcanoes are altered to have less permeable surfaces. Lowered surface permeability arises from volcanic ash that mantles local areas. Channels forming on this ash incise into the volcano. As valleys form by enlargement of these zones, the incision is able to tap groundwater in the permeable lava flows. This groundwater further sustains valley growth in a headward direction by sapping. Eventually, the volcano is dissected by a mature network of valleys adjusted to the water flow system that is sustaining their growth.

Many mysteries still surround the valleys on Mars. While most valley networks are very old, older indeed than most rocks on Earth, some are quite young. Very well developed valleys occur on the relatively young Martian volcano Alba Patera. The valleys are restricted to a local area of volcanic ash. It may be that water was introduced by local precipitation, perhaps related to outburst flooding in the large channels.

Also puzzling is the fact that the large channels on Mars contain landforms that are very different landforms from those generally seen on Earth. The best Earth analogy to the outflow channels is a region called the Channeled Scabland in Washington State. This area of flood-eroded basalt was generated by immense glacial lake outbursts during the ice ages. The Channeled Scabland has more similarities to the Martian channels than does any other region on Earth. Mars has additional surprises, including an abundance of linear grooves and a lack of depositional forms.

Methods of Study

The channels and valleys of Mars were discovered by remote-sensing observations generated from spacecraft. Despite Percival Lowell's accounts of Martian "canals" nearly one hundred years ago, telescopic views of the planet were inadequate to interpret the presence of channels and valleys. It was not until 1972, when the Mariner 9 spacecraft returned the first high-resolution pictures of them, that the importance of the valleys was realized.

Ages of the valleys are interpreted by the numbers of superimposed impact craters. Then, by analogy to known cratering rates and histories on the Moon, ages can be assigned to the Martian landforms. The genesis of the valleys must also be determined by analogy. The interpreter of the pictures of the valleys must have a broad familiarity with natural landscapes, which is used to infer causes for the combinations of features seen in the channels and valleys. Often the details of planetary landforms are somewhat different from what is generally known from terrestrial experience. On Mars, such lack of correspondence arises from the lower gravitational acceleration, the low surface pressure, and the low temperature.

The details of Martian landforms are analyzed on maps that show relationships and patterns. Geological maps elucidate the time sequence of development, and geomorphological maps show genetic relationships among the planetary features. Quantitative measurements can be made of the landform shapes, which can be compared to measurements on similar-appearing terrestrial features.

Model building is the activity whereby an explanation of the valley is provided in a form that extracts significant elements from the natural complexity of the phenomenon. The model may be expressed in abstract mathematical terms, it can involve laboratory hardware, or it can simulate the sequence of landform development through various kinds of analogy. In all cases, however, the model is used to express in simple, predictable terms the complexity of the real-world system under investigation. Models are only as good as their correspondence to the natural system, so successful model building requires an intimate knowledge of the system under investigation. This knowledge must be continually checked against new inferences about that system gained through ongoing investigation.

Context

The valleys of Mars reflect immense environmental changes that occurred on the planet. The surface conditions presently are too cold and the atmosphere too thin for water to exist in its liquid state. Yet, in the past, during selected epochs of its planetary history, Mars was able to sustain an active hydrological cycle that produced river valleys similar to those on Earth. Because the small valleys occur throughout the heavily cratered terrains of the planet, the scale of environmental change must have been global.

Earth has also been affected by global environmental change. Numerous times over the past several million years, the planet has experienced decreased global temperatures with associated glaciation. During glacial advances, hydrological conditions were profoundly changed. Most recently, the global change of interest on Earth has become the warming associated with artificially increased levels of carbon dioxide and other trace gases in the atmosphere. Thus, like Mars, Earth oscillates between periods of increased warmth and cold. By comparing the theories that explain such cycles, scientists hope to understand exactly how the environmental change occurs and thus to develop a means of predicting future change that will affect humanity on its home planet.

In a broad sense, the development of humankind has been linked to discoveries associated with exploration and with the migration of peoples to new lands; the space program is the most modern manifestation of such trends. When the channels and valleys of Mars were discovered, they stimulated an immense scientific effort to explain the conditions on Mars that made flowing water possible in the past. Scientists generally agree that most of the water on Mars is now locked up in its subsurface, frozen as ground ice in layers of thick permafrost. There is speculation that, if Mars could be made warm, perhaps by inducing plant growth or by releasing trapped carbon dioxide, it is not inconceivable that Martian rivers could be made to flow again—they might even sustain a population of emigrants from Earth.

Bibliography

Baker, Victor R. *The Channels of Mars*. Austin: University of Texas Press, 1982. This 198-page book provides a complete review of scientific ideas about channels and valleys on Mars. Abundantly illustrated with pictures of Martian landforms, diagrams illustrating processes, and interpretive maps. Considerable discussion of possible terrestrial analogues to features on Mars. Also provides general review material on the history of Mars studies, the general geology of Mars, and implications for global environmental change on the planet.

_____. "Planetary Geomorphology." *Journal of Geological Education* 32 (June, 1983): 236. This 11-page review paper describes the techniques and approaches to studying landforms on the terrestrial planets. Lists sources of information on planetary surfaces, including the libraries of planetary data supported by the National Aeronautics and Space Administration.

_____, ed. *Catastrophic Flooding: The Origin of the Channeled Scabland*. Stroudsburg, Pa.: Dowden, Hutchinson and Ross, 1981. This book reprints many scientific papers dealing with the cataclysmic flood origin of the Channeled Scabland region of Washington State. Its 360 pages also contain information on the scientific analogy between the Channeled Scabland and the channels on Mars.

Carr, Michael H. *The Surface of Mars*. New Haven, Conn.: Yale University Press, 1981. A well-illustrated summary of Mars geology, this book extensively features pictures from the Viking orbiter spacecraft. There is a major chapter on channels and valleys, but all the important landforms of Mars are discussed in some detail. This 232-page book is the best starting point for an in-depth review of modern ideas about the geology of Mars.

Greeley, Ronald. *Planetary Landscapes*. Winchester, Mass.: Allen & Unwin, 1985. This book provides a review of the geomorphology of planetary surfaces throughout the solar system. Compares the processes among multiple planetary bodies with an emphasis on properties of individual planets and moons. Channels and valleys on Mars are seen in the broader context of surfaces on the various planets.

Murray, Bruce G., Michael C. Malin, and Donald Greeley. *Earthlike Planets: Surfaces of Mercury, Venus, Earth, Moon, Mars*. New York: W. H. Freeman, 1981. This 387-page book emphasizes a comparative planetology approach to the study of the planetary surfaces. All the major planetary processes are covered. Martian channels are treated as enigmatic features that defy easy explanation. Their occurrence is considered in the broader context of general planetary geology.

Mutch, Thomas A., et al. *The Geology of Mars*. Princeton, N.J.: Princeton University Press, 1976. This 400-page book was produced at the beginning of the Viking mission to Mars as a summary of knowledge up to that time. Reflects the discovery of Martian channels by the Mariner 9 mission in 1972. Although many of the ideas in the book have been superseded by analysis of the Viking results, its reading provides a good background in the evolution of scientific thinking about Mars. Many of the problems identified remain unresolved.

Victor R. Baker

Cross-References

Mars' Atmosphere, 1474; Mars' Volcanoes, 1500; Mars' Water, 1508; River Valleys, 2210.

MARS' VOLCANOES

Type of earth science: Planetology
Field of study: Large solar system bodies

The discovery of mammoth volcanoes on Mars as a result of images returned by the National Aeronautics and Space Administration's Mariner and Viking unmanned spacecraft has led to an intensified study of Martian volcanic characteristics and activities. It is believed that this study will help scientists to determine the relationship between Earth and Mars and to develop a unified theory about the origin and evolution of the solar system.

Principal terms
CALDERA: the sunken crater at the summit of a volcano caused by the internal collapse of magma
CRUST: the outermost shell of a planet, next to the mantle
EJECTA: material thrown out of a volcano during eruption; molten rocks
LAVA: molten magma from the interior of a volcano thrown out through breaks in the sides or top
MAGMA: molten rock material formed deep in a planet's interior; when thrown out of a volcano, it becomes known as lava
SCARP: a vertical or near-vertical cliff, often extending for many kilometers
TECTONICS: the study of the processes that formed the structural features of the earth's crust; it usually addresses the creation and movement of immense crustal plates
THARSIS DOME: an immense bulge in the Martian crust in the Tharsis region of the planet; it is raised 11 kilometers above the Martian surface

Summary of the Phenomenon

Volcanoes on Mars are generally larger then those on Earth. In fact, one should approach the planet with the understanding that all of its major features are gigantic, including its craters, plains, valleys, volcanoes, and polar caps. That is one of Mars' overall characteristics, and the enormous size of the Martian volcanoes is typical.

Observed Martian volcanoes seem to group themselves into two distinct regions (see figure): in the Tharsis region, atop the Tharsis Dome, and in the region known as Elysium, a large topographic region of crustal upheaval. Volcanoes in other areas tend to be smaller and older than those in these two regions, although the dispersion of Martian volcanoes is not broad. Sixteen principal volcanoes have been identified in these two prime areas, both of which are mostly in the planet's northern hemi-

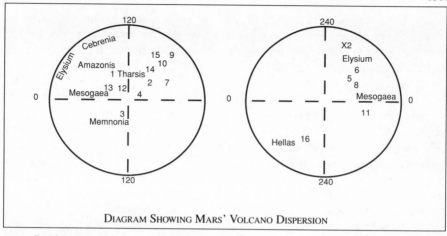

DIAGRAM SHOWING MARS' VOLCANO DISPERSION

SOURCE: Data from *National Geographic* 173 (February, 1973), map.

sphere. According to researchers, there are very few or no volcanoes in the other regions of Mars, although the reason for this absence is not completely understood. Scientists speculate that the Martian crust is much thicker, overall, than Earth's crust and that it is much more difficult for magma to punch a hole through its surface. Also, the rigid Martian crust does not allow for tectonic plate movement such as that which occurs on Earth.

Volcanoes on Mars are created in the same manner as terrestrial volcanoes, either by eruption through a central tunnel or by eruption through side vents in the volcano's walls. There is ample evidence that both processes have been at work on Mars in its long geologic past. In the first process, material from the planet's interior pushes up, overflows, and then cools rapidly, creating an upside-down cone with a hole in the top that eventually seals, plugging the eruption tunnel. In the second instance, magma oozes through breaks in the volcano's flanks, called vents. The major characteristics of Martian volcanoes, however, are very different from those of terrestrial volcanoes.

Researchers studying Mars have determined that there is no tectonic movement, or shifting of gigantic "plates" of crustal expanse, on Mars as there is on Earth. As a result, material from Mars' interior continues to erupt through the exact same tunnel over and over again, constantly building the volcano higher and wider. On Earth, on the other hand, a volcano is likely to be moved from its original spot, drifting away by the long-term motion of tectonic plates. This movement seals the magma tunnel deep inside the volcano, preventing further eruption.

The second process, the eruption of magma through side vents in the volcano's flanks comes about by the interior materials bursting through the weakest points in the sides of the volcano. This kind of process occurs on Mars as on Earth, but the result is usually quite different. On Mars, lava flowing down the sides of the volcano spills beyond the volcano's base perimeter, creating vast lava plains that completely surround the volcano. Once again, because the volcano stays in one place, repeated eruptions through the side vents cause the lava plain to continue to grow broader and broader. On Earth, the buildup is considerably slower, if it occurs at all, because the volcano is moved away from its original eruption site by tectonic movement.

The volcanoes on Mars dwarf those on Earth. The largest of the Martian volcanoes are part of a grouping of about eight near the equator in the Tharsis Bulge, or Dome. One of the four biggest is (1) Olympus Mons (the numbers refer to the volcano dispersion diagram), a shield volcano judged to be about 27 kilometers high and 600 kilometers in diameter. The other three lie in a nearly straight line to the east of Olympus Mons. Beginning with the northernmost, their names are (2) Ascraeus Mons, (4) Pavonis Mons, and (3) Arsia Mons. Although they are not as spectacular as Olympus Mons, their sizes are still quite impressive.

The Martian calderas, large craters at volcanoes' summits caused by settling of the magma in their interiors, are similarly immense. The caldera of Olympus Mons, for example, is a highly complex collection of features measuring about 3 kilometers deep and 25 kilometers across, with its walls set at a slope of about 32 degrees. The complex is the result of repeated caldera collapse after extrusions of magma settle and stop. The calderas of Martian volcanoes are unique, at least in the inner planets, in having many circular fractures surrounding the main caldera. In addition, the entire Olympus Mons structure is surrounded by a scarp, or cliff, which at some points is 6 kilometers high. In numerous places, there is ample evidence that lava has flowed over the sides of the scarp. These scarp lava overflows are often referred to as "flow drapes" and are quite common to Martian volcanoes; they extend the main volcano structure into the surrounding lava plain, often for many hundreds of kilometers. The flow drapes at Olympus Mons extend the volcano structure at least 1,000 kilometers outward over the rigid surrounding planetary crust. Flow drapes indicate that the scarp was formed before the time of the eruption of the magma which created the lava flows, and they help geologists to determine the age of the volcano and the extent of the extrusion of magma.

Terracing is a feature that is highly pronounced on the slopes of Martian volcanoes, created by the front lines of immense lava flows churning down a volcano's sides. Multiple terracing is often seen; it results from repeated eruptions, which create well-defined blankets of lava. Olympus Mons exhibits many such terracing features. It is difficult to imagine the enormous volume and extent of the rolling lava required to produce the many examples of terracing on this volcano.

Arsia Mons rises some 16 kilometers above the Tharsis Dome with a caldera measuring 140 kilometers in diameter. The caldera is surrounded by concentric rings of hummocky topography, some of which are graben (long, linear depressions usually found between two parallel faults). The lava flow reaches at least 1,500 kilometers into the surrounding plain, often covering earlier features of the region. The images from the Mariner 9 mission, especially, disclose many lava-flow fronts and ridges where the rolling lava came to a stop. Repeated eruptions on Mars have thrown out truly copious amounts of lava, which, in turn, have formed far-reaching, relatively smooth plains adjacent to the volcano cones. These plains may extend hundreds of kilometers or, as in the case of Alba Patera (number 14 on the volcano dispersion diagram), more than 1,700 kilometers out from the central cone. Although relatively flat, these plains most often show many lava-flow patterns, such as ridges and hummocks at the leading edges of flows.

The flow of lava down the flanks of a volcano can take many different forms, and all these forms are present on Mars. The thickness of the lava, steepness of the slope, and presence or absence of barrier features all cause the downward spread of lava to take different forms and speeds, creating a variety of patterns. Fine-edged flows, flat-topped flows, and flow ridges can be seen in various volcano complexes. The ages of lava flows can be determined by the presence or absence of craters and other features on the volcanoes' flanks; numerous craters, for example, would indicate that the flows are relatively older and that the craters were formed after the lava flow, whereas lava that creeps into or flows over preexisting craters indicates that the flow came after the crater was created. Some ancient Martian volcanoes, such as Tyrrhena Patera (number 11), exhibit features that have been degraded by time, sometimes so much so that it is impossible to determine the location of the primary volcano. Other features of some volcanoes suggest the downward flow of ash rather than of lava.

The properties of Martian volcanoes are important for scientists to study because they tell of the planet's present and past geology, providing clues to the planet's age, formation, and activity. Considerable study of the volcanoes has disclosed that there is no tectonic plate activity associated with Mars and that the crust is far more rigid than Earth's; that while there is a scarcity of volcanoes on Mars in comparison with the large number on Earth, they do help to establish theories about Mars' age and evolution; and that volcanic ejecta can reveal something of the activities deep within Mars' crust and of the composition of material in the planet's mantle.

In sum, volcanoes on Mars are somewhat different from volcanoes on Earth. Martian volcanoes are significantly larger. The volcano cone is created differently, and the absence of tectonic movement allows a Martian volcano to stand over the same site for millions of years. Earth volcanoes in the process of eruption spew out lava in large amounts, yet Martian volcanoes eject lava in still larger amounts. When lava flows down the sides of a terrestrial volcano, it is affected by the landscape—streams, trees, and boulders which may deflect the flow pattern this way or that. On Mars, however, the flanks of volcanoes have no such barriers; instead, they have impact craters and the patterned buildup of previous lava flows. Finally, terrestrial volcanoes do not change size appreciably; those on Mars, however, keep growing bigger.

Methods of Study

Planetologists have enlisted a wide range of analytical techniques to study Martian volcanoes. The most obvious and by far the most productive have been the images of the Martian surface gained through six highly successful unmanned missions conducted between 1965 and 1976 by the United States' National Aeronautics and Space Administration (NASA): Mariners 4, 6, 7, and 9 and Vikings 1 and 2. These flyby, orbiting, and surface-landing missions produced a huge amount of photographic material with which geologists have begun to piece together a profile of Mars' evolution based on the study of volcanoes. The study of volcanoes is especially enlightening because it allows a view of material that originated from deep inside the planet.

By comparing Mars' topographic features with similar features on Earth, scientists can gain an enormous amount of information in a short time. By applying geometry to shadows and large-scale topography, they can determine the sizes and trace the short- and long-term development of evolutionary features. This information is critical in the case of volcanoes; lava-flow patterns, especially, are revealing about the structural evolution of volcanic sites and the surrounding terrain. Photographic evidence can be enlarged to a surprising degree, and very often, extremely detailed images can be studied simultaneously by scientists all over the world. The paper prints are the result of a new and extremely promising technique known as remote-sensing technology—the acquisition of data at a distance by mechanical or electronic means. In this technique, television cameras aboard the mission spacecraft gather the image and convert it into digital data, which are separated into shades of gray and then transmitted across space to receiving antennae on Earth. In special receiving stations, the digital data are put together again and stored in computers. The data are permanent, can be recalled from the computers at any time, and can be manipulated by computer operators. Shadow areas can be lightened or darkened, color can be added and shaded, and mathematical computations can be applied to various features, all revealing the true nature of the topography.

The Viking landers, which descended to the surface of Mars, contained a multitude of scientific instruments that recorded data about wind direction and velocity, surface and atmospheric temperatures, the sizes of windblown material, the composition of Mars' soil, and even the viscosity of the soil. An arm was extended from each spacecraft (there were two landers, each settling at a different location on Mars); at the end of the arm was a specially designed scoop that dug a trench in the planet's surface. By analyzing the characteristics of the trench, scientists could deduce such information as the ability of the soil to cling together, whether or not other surface material slid into the trench, and the strength it took to dig the trench. Also, a series of three instruments aboard the landers received the collected soil, analyzed it chemically, and determined its composition. These data were collected in numerical format and radioed back to Earth, allowing scientists to create a profile of the Martian environment. The profile was then applied to other regions on the planet, such as those where volcanoes existed. The picture of Mars that developed from these instrumented explorations is one of a cold, lifeless wasteland without the kind of environment that would allow humans to survive even for a short time.

Context

If scientists could decipher how Mars evolved into the planet it is today, they could compare it to Earth and to the other planets and, perhaps, reach a greater understanding of Earth's past and future. One of the keys to unraveling Mars' mysteries is volcanic activity; it is a critical measure of what is or is not happening both on the planet's surface and deep inside its interior. Martian volcanoes are instrumental in the creation of other topographic features, such as extensive lava plains and scarps. Most volcanoes are located in a relatively confined area on Mars, and scientists want to know why volcanoes are not formed in other locations as well. Close study of Martian volcanoes could give scientists some clues about the interior properties of the planet and allow them to gain new insights into Mars' internal dynamics.

Commercially, Mars may harbor wealth in the form of natural resources. The Martian surface is characterized by planetwide iron deposits and iron oxide, from which Mars derives its pinkish-orange coloration. Other critical minerals and resources may exist there as well. It is important, therefore, to understand reasons for the present dispersion patterns of volcanoes in order to determine how volcanic actions affect mineral deposits and perhaps to predict future volcanic eruptions in mineral-rich areas.

For many thousands of years, humankind has been preoccupied with the possibility of extraterrestrial life. During the past two hundred years, Mars has been considered a place where intelligent beings might be living. Surveys of the solar system have shown that none of the other planets can sustain human life; yet, evidence of some kind of lower-order life may eventually be found. Beyond this reason for exploration, the study of other planets, especially Earth's "sister" planets, Venus and Mars, will shed light on the origin and real nature of the universe.

Mars and, indeed, all planets must be viewed as a system of interacting forces, so that they can be compared from a systematic viewpoint. Scientists, therefore, ask the following questions: What are the driving elements in the forces which sculpt, change, and characterize each planet, especially volcanic action? Is there a common thread among volcanic activities on all the planets and their satellites? How do these elements and forces behave on Earth? The study of Mars, then, has enabled scientists to arrive at a new method known as earth system science.

Bibliography

Arvidson, Raymond E., et al. "The Surface of Mars." *Scientific American* 238 (March, 1978): 76-89. For schools and students without access to NASA publications, this magazine article is excellent, although written in a more popular style. It features superb photographs and careful text.

Corliss, William R. *Viking Missions to Mars.* NASA SP-334. Washington, D.C.: Government Printing Office, 1974. The author of this compact reference work has managed to tell nearly the entire Viking-to-Mars story with good illustrations and crisp language. The reader is led through the entire scenario, and meaningful photographs of the Martian surface are provided. Chapter 2, "Viking's Target: Mars," shows the planet in detail, using photos from previous Mariner missions, and allows the reader to begin thinking in terms of comparisons with Earth features. The booklet is ideal for high-school students and lay readers. Includes a good bibliography.

French, Bevan M., Stephen P. Maran, and Eric G. Chipman. *A Meeting with the Universe: Science Discoveries from the Space Program.* NASA EP-177. Washington, D.C.: Government Printing Office, 1981. This lavishly illustrated volume puts Mars and its enigmatic volcanoes in the context of the many discoveries of NASA's "golden age of planetary exploration" of the 1960's and 1970's. Full-color charts and diagrams, terse text, a table of contents and an index, and an all-inclusive viewpoint awake the reader to the excitement of scientific discovery. Offers insight into the overall structure of the cosmos. Suitable for high-school students and adult lay readers.

Hartmann, William K., and Odell Raper. *The New Mars: The Discoveries of Mariner 9.* NASA SP-337. Washington, D.C.: Government Printing Office, 1974. A companion volume to *Viking Orbiter Views of Mars* and an overview of the startling Mariner 9 mission, this book is an excellent research work covering basic geology and planetology, comparing Martian and terrestrial features. It contains background data about Mars and its study, an explanation of the Mariner 9 mission sequence, and interpretations of the best of the mission's visual and scientific results. Graphs, charts, drawings, and photographs. Suitable for general audiences.

National Aeronautics and Space Administration. *Viking 1, Early Results.* NASA SP-408. Springfield, Va.: National Technical Information Service, 1976. The first scientific results of the Viking 1 Lander are chronicled in this booklet that represents a "first look" at the instrument and photographic evidence collected by a highly successful mission. Contains many mission photographs from both the Lander and the Orbiter. Charts, diagrams, maps, and graphs all contribute to a valuable reference work. For the advanced high school or college student.

National Aeronautics and Space Administration, Viking Lander Imaging Team. *The Martian Landscape.* NASA SP-425. Washington, D.C.: Government Printing Office, 1978. A definitive reference work about a major planetary exploration mission. The book contains superb photographs, some stereoscopic (a pair of glasses is provided), and is written for the layperson. The team of writers describes all the main events of the missions of both Landers. For comparisons with volcanic regions, and a good explanation of Martian topography in general, this book is unsurpassed. Includes charts, diagrams, and tables of mission data.

Spitzer, Cary R., ed. *Viking Orbiter Views of Mars.* NASA SP-441. Washington, D.C.: Government Printing Office, 1980. The purpose of this book, written by the scientists who designed and supervised the missions, is to provide a glimpse of the dramatic Martian landscape as viewed by the Viking Orbiter spacecraft. It achieves its goal, in clear pictures that are breathtaking in their scope. An ample amount of text written to explain each photograph is a welcome aid to serious readers. The reader with a good grasp of high-school earth science will find this book a delight. For the scholar, the book is a starting point for getting acquainted with Mars. Includes cardboard glasses to be used for numerous stereoscopic views throughout the book.

Thomas W. Becker

Cross-References

Iron Deposits, 1254; Mars' Atmosphere, 1474; Mars' Craters, 1480; Mars' Polar Caps, 1487; Mars' Valleys, 1494; Mars' Water, 1508; Remote Sensing and the Electromagnetic Spectrum, 2166; Future Resources, 2182; The Origin of the Solar System, 2442; Volcanoes: Calderas, 2614; Volcanoes: Eruption Forecasting, 2622; Volcanoes: Shield Volcanoes, 2681; Volcanoes: Stratovolcanoes, 2688; Volcanoes: Types of Eruption, 2695.

MARS' WATER

Type of earth science: Planetology
Field of study: Large solar system bodies

Knowledge of how much water there once was on Mars and how much remains would shed light on the history of Mars and the solar system, the possible development of life in Mars' past, and ways of providing resources for future Mars colonists.

Principal terms

EJECTA: the material ejected from the crater made by a meteoric impact
MASS WASTING: the downslope movement of material; it may be caused by the water-softening of soil
PERMAFROST: permanently frozen soil which is laced with water ice
POLYGONAL GROUND: the distinctive geological formation caused by the repetitive freezing and thawing of permafrost
REGOLITH: the layer of soil and rock fragments just above the solid planetary crust
SATURATION: the condition of the atmosphere when water is at the point of precipitation
SPRING SAPPING: a process in which water flows out of subsurface springs to surface level, forming a stream bed as it flows downslope
THERMAL EROSION: the erosion of water ice from a solid state to vapor
THERMOKARST: geological formations, resembling surface depressions, caused by the melting of subsurface ice or permafrost
WATER OF HYDRATION: molecular water that is bound in the crystalline structure of surface rocks

Summary of the Phenomenon

There is water on Mars. How much water and exactly where it is has become the center of many questions about the planet. In 1971, the U.S. space probe Mariner 9 returned photographs of Mars which clearly showed that the surface of the planet had been extensively scarred sometime in its distant past, probably by liquid water flowing over it. Subsequent detailed investigations by the U.S. Viking probes in 1976 confirmed this evidence and added voluminous data to support the idea that liquid water had at one time existed on or close to the planet's surface.

Yet, under present conditions, it is impossible for water to exist in the liquid form on the planet's surface. The highest temperature recorded at the Viking landing sites on the warmest summer days was −29 degrees Celsius, and the average temperature is much colder elsewhere on the planet. It fell to −123 degrees at the site of the Viking 2 lander during the Martian winter. Even if it were warm enough for liquid water to exist, it would quickly vaporize in the low atmospheric pressure of Mars.

The atmospheric pressure at the Viking lander sites (the locations where the U.S. probes made a soft landing on the planet's surface) was less than one one-hundredth of the earth's atmospheric pressure at sea level. This pressure compares to that found at an altitude of about 35 kilometers above the earth, nearly four times the altitude of Mount Everest.

The water directly measured by the orbiting Viking probes was in the form of water vapor in the atmosphere. There was also evidence that water exists in the solid form—as ice in subsurface permafrost, in the Martian polar caps, in the surface rocks and soil, in clouds and fog, and as frost.

The amount of water vapor discovered in the Martian atmosphere was quite low compared to earth standards. At the Viking lander sites, the atmosphere was 0.03 percent water vapor. This amount compares to the percentage of water vapor at an altitude of 9 or 10 kilometers on earth. Mars is so dry that if all the water vapor in the atmosphere of the planet could be condensed into a solid block of water ice, it would measure only about 1.3 cubic kilometers. (That is but a tiny fraction of the water vapor in the earth's atmosphere.) The Viking probes measured the part of the Martian atmosphere with the greatest amount of atmospheric water vapor, which was the area nearest the planet's north pole.

Even though the Martian air is dry by earth standards, because of the low atmospheric pressure, it is near a saturated state; daily temperature variations cause the water vapor to condense in the form of ice fogs, clouds, and frost. The fog is quite tenuous; typical Martian fogs are about half a kilometer in depth, and if they were completely condensed into water, they would form a layer only a single micron thick. Frosts of water vapor, sometimes mixed with frozen carbon dioxide to form an ice called clathrate, form on the planet's surface seasonally.

The Martian poles are repositories of water ice and frozen carbon dioxide. The depth of water ice at the north and south poles varies. The north polar cap is estimated to be one meter to one kilometer deep. The south cap is less affected by the Martian summers, and its estimated thickness is 0.23 to 0.50 meter. It is primarily solid carbon dioxide. The amount of water ice in the caps is unknown. Polar water ice directly exposed to the Martian environment can undergo a deterioration by sunlight from solid directly to vapor by a process called thermal erosion.

Estimates show that Mars' original water, outgassed from the planet's interior by volcanism (as on the earth), may have been sufficient to cover the planet with a layer some 46 meters deep. Most of it, however, was lost over the course of the planet's history in a process called molecular dissociation. High-energy ultraviolet sunlight split the water molecules into hydrogen and oxygen atoms, which were eventually lost to space. The equivalent of nearly 270,000 liters of liquid water is lost this way each Martian day. Orbital photographs show, however, that the surface is extensively scarred by what appear to be channels whose only earthly analogue is caused by running water. Since liquid water requires an atmospheric pressure and temperature much greater that those which now exist on Mars, it is thought that the planet's conditions must once have been sufficiently different to allow water to flow.

As the orbital Viking probes circled Mars, they mapped the seasonal variations of water vapor over the planet. It was discovered that as the spring and summer temperatures rose, water vapor levels increased also. Most scientists agree that the source of this water vapor was ground deposits of water. The water is encapsulated either in frozen aquifers or within the soil itself. Such frozen ground is called permafrost. The permafrost is located in the regolith of Mars; the depth of this upper layer of ice-laden soil is variable. The permafrost in the polar regions may be up to 8 kilometers deep; in the equatorial regions, it may extend to 3 kilometers.

The existence of large areas, perhaps planetwide areas, of permafrost is supported by orbital images which show four distinct geological formations: meteoric impacts display a kind of fluid ejecta, flowing away from the main crater, not seen on the moon or the planet Mercury. It indicates that the energy of the meteoric impact melted the permafrost. Another formation is called polygonal ground. These distinct polygonal shapes observed from a high altitude are caused by the repeated freezing and thawing of permafrost on or near the surface. Mass wasting (on earth, often called landslides or mudslides) consists of distinctive downslope movements of soil, possibly caused by water softening. Finally, a geological phenomenon called thermokarst was observed on Mars. It is caused by the underground melting of permafrost or underground ice formations, which leads to sinkholes or collapsed surface features.

In addition to permafrost, water is locked molecularly into the crystalline structure of the Martian soil and rocks. The Viking landers discovered that 0.1 to 1 percent of the surface materials consist of water of hydration. This tightly bound water can be released only by heating of the materials.

Many of the stream formations may have been caused by spring sapping during a planetary warming cycle. Spring sapping offers evidence of hidden, frozen deposits of ice that may thaw during warm cycles.

Methods of Study

Most of the information regarding water on Mars came from five U.S. spacecraft: the Mariner 9 orbiter, two Viking orbiters, and two Viking landing craft. Two broad categories of information were gathered: direct and indirect.

The direct evidence for Martian water came from orbiting instruments which measured atmospheric water vapor over seasonal periods and actually photographed the Martian polar caps, fogs, and cloud formations. The landing craft directly measured water vapor on the surface of Mars. They photographed seasonal frost deposits and clouds while measuring water of hydration by heating rock and soil samples. The instrument on the orbiter that measured the water vapor was called the Mars atmospheric water detector. It examined reflected solar radiation from the Martian surface at a spectral band of 1.4 microns.

The Viking lander instrument that analyzed the Martian soil for water was called the gas chromatograph mass spectrometer. Soil samples were taken from the surface of the planet by a robotic arm which directed the sample to a heating chamber. The soil was heated to 500 degrees Celsius, and the materials driven off by the heat were analyzed. It was discovered, after a series of samples had been analyzed, that between several tenths of a percent and several percent of the surface material was water. Some of the water was believed to be loosely absorbed on the surface, but it was likely that a significant fraction was accounted for by water of hydration.

Indirectly, scientists inferred much about the Martian water repositories through comparing orbital photographs with high-altitude photographs of the earth. Nearly all investigators were convinced that the only known mechanism that could form the clearly defined river and stream beds was running water. This observation, coupled with simplified dating techniques of counting craters in stream beds to determine approximate ages, enabled speculation about cyclic Martian warming trends. These periodic warming trends could conceivably cause subsurface ice deposits to melt, and subsequent atmospheric pressure increases could allow the water to flow over the Martian landscape, cutting the stream formations in the soil.

Examination of ejecta patterns all over the planet led to speculation that permafrost was a planetwide manifestation. Comparison of earthly geologic formations of polygonal ground, mass wasting, and thermokarst with their Martian counterparts provided evidence for the widespread nature and even depth of the Martian permafrost layer. Photographs of cloud and fog formation over the planet during subsequent orbits enabled the calculation of temperatures, saturation levels, and even the content of cloud and fog banks. After the lander data had verified the orbital photography, a highly accurate picture of Martian water deposits was formulated.

Context

The question of what happened to Mars' water is of critical importance to the next generation of space explorers. It is also important to understanding how earthly water reserves are balanced on a planetwide scale. That nearly an entire planet's water resources, consisting of many trillions of liters, should simply vanish is critical not only to Mars' history but also to Earth's future. Although the mechanisms of planetary water loss are understood, it is important to study Mars to learn exactly how and where the planet absorbed its remaining water resources, using techniques which could be used to locate Earth's diminishing freshwater resources by space observations. Scientists may also learn how permafrost water deposits are linked to the contamination of water by soil salts and other impurities and how long-term climatic cycles lead to planetwide weather changes. If the earth tilted only a few degrees, extreme global changes could be introduced which could have ramifications for the planet's long-term weather patterns.

Perhaps the most direct knowledge to be gained, however, is whether future colonists will be able to use what water there may be on Mars. This water will be vital for the establishment of a Mars colony and will ultimately determine its size and usefulness. The water that is obtained from atmospheric distillation, the permafrost, the water of hydration, mining aquifers, or the polar caps will be used for a multitude of purposes, including drinking, agriculture, cooling equipment, washing and cleaning, and the breaking down of molecular water into atomic hydrogen, for fuel, and oxygen, for breathing. Water on Mars may become one of the most significant aspects of "the desert planet."

Bibliography

American Geophysical Union. *Scientific Results of the Viking Project.* Washington, D.C.: Author, 1978. A compendium of articles about the Viking project published in the *Journal of Geophysical Research.* It consists of technical assessments of data returned by the Viking landers and orbiters. Includes several discussions of water on Mars and in the Martian atmosphere. Detailed, but suitable for college-level readers.

Barbato, James P., and Elizabeth A. Ayer. *Atmospheres: A View of the Gaseous Envelopes Surrounding Members of Our Solar System.* Elmsford, N.Y.: Pergamon Press, 1981. This book is a well-thought-out, highly developed analysis of the atmospheres of twelve planets and moons of the solar system. The list includes Earth, Mercury, Venus, Mars, Jupiter, Io, Ganymede, Saturn, Titan, Uranus, Neptune, and Pluto. The discussion of Mars' atmosphere includes a description of the planet's atmospheric water reserves. It is suitable for a general readership but would appeal to a more technical audience as well.

Beatty, J. Kelly, Brian O'Leary, and Andrew Chaikin. *The New Solar System.* Cambridge, England: Cambridge University Press, 1981. This beautifully illustrated and well-crafted book was intended to bring planetary discoveries to light in a single source. It covers the Martian water question in detail and extends it to a discussion of such ideas as life on Mars and the possibility of long-term Martian seasons. Written for the general reader.

Ezell, Edward Clinton, and Linda Newman Ezell. *On Mars: Exploration of the Red Planet, 1958-1978.* Washington, D.C.: Government Printing Office, 1984. This book is an official history of the Viking program, from its conception in 1958 to the culmination of the project some twenty years later. It is a detailed assessment of the program's political and technical history, but it also discusses details of the instruments that scanned for water, the Martian environment, and subsequent findings on the planet. It is written for all readers and is generally nontechnical.

Hartmann, William K., and Ron Miller. *Out of the Cradle: Exploring the Frontiers Beyond Earth.* New York: Workman, 1984. This combination picture book and narrative discusses Mars as a logical next step for human exploration and settlement after the moon. It depicts the struggle of future colonists on Mars and includes a discussion of where these colonists might get water for survival. The book is written for the general reader and is illustrated with artists' conceptions of future Mars bases and explorers.

Joëls, Kerry Mark. *The Mars One Crew Manual.* New York: Ballantine Books, 1985. This "facsimile" of what a future Mars explorer's crew manual might look like includes a discussion of the Martian environment, ground conditions, and water.

It is written for readers of all backgrounds and is illustrated.

Miles, Frank, and Nicholas Booth. *Race to Mars: The Harper & Row Mars Flight Atlas.* New York: Harper & Row, 1988. Another rendition of a future Mars crew manual, this book describes a flight to Mars and what the expedition members might encounter there. It includes a detailed discussion of Mars' water and its importance to future explorers. Illustrated.

Dennis Chamberland

Cross-References

Aquifers, 71; The Atmosphere's Structure and Composition, 128; Climate, 217; Clouds, 224; Floods, 719; The Greenhouse Effect, 1004; The Hydrologic Cycle, 1102; Mars' Atmosphere, 1474; Mars' Craters, 1480; Mars' Polar Caps, 1487; Mars' Volcanoes, 1500; Phobos and Deimos, 2058; Precipitation, 2108.

MASS EXTINCTIONS

Type of earth science: Paleontology and earth history

Mass extinctions demonstrate that the evolution and extinction of life are not smooth but rather interrupted by mass dyings as a result of as yet poorly understood causes. Mass extinctions seem to be an integral part of the overall pattern of life processes on the earth.

Principal terms

ECOLOGY: the study of the relations between organisms and their environments

ENVIRONMENT: the conditions affecting the existence, growth, and overall status of an organism

ERA: one of the major divisions of geologic time, including one or more periods

GEOLOGIC RECORD: the history of the earth and its life as recorded in successive layers of sediment and the fossil specimens they contain

NICHE: in an ecological environment, a position particularly suited for its inhabitant

PERIOD: the fundamental unit of the geologic time scale

PLATE TECTONICS: the theory and study of the formation and movement of the sections that make up the outer portion of the earth, which move independently over the interior

STRATIGRAPHIC TIME SCALE: the history of the evolution of life on earth broken down into time periods based on changes in fossil life in the sequence of rock layers; the time periods were named for the localities in which they were studied or from their characteristics

Summary of the Phenomenon

The extinction of animal species appears to be as much a part of the pattern of life on earth as is the evolution of new species. Indeed, the two processes go hand in hand, as new species fill the environments vacated by dying ones. Extinction is so common that more than 99 percent of the species that have ever lived are now extinct. At periods throughout the earth's history, extinctions of numerous and widely varied species have occurred within a relatively narrow range of time. Climatic changes, worldwide catastrophic events, and changing sea levels lead the list of possible causes of these mass extinctions. A species cannot be considered separately from the environment in which it lives. A change in the environment may occur faster than the organism can adapt and evolve along with it. This species may become extinct, while another species will develop to fill the environmental niche left behind. Thus, it appears that the ability of a species to survive may depend upon its ability to adapt quickly to changing conditions.

The pattern holds true for both plant and animal life. Mass extinctions of plant and of animal life, however, do not seem to coincide. In the plant world, there have been three revolutions in principal plant forms. Each evolved quickly, and once a major group of plants was established, it continued for millions of years. Animal life is marked by frequent extinctions; mass extinctions of animal life appear successively throughout the geologic record. In fact, it is these very extinctions that have, in many cases, provided the reference points that separate one geologic period from another. Catastrophic extinctions and revolutionary changes in animal life have occurred at least six and perhaps as many as nine distinct junctures in the history of the earth. Hundreds of minor extinctions have occurred as well.

The earliest known mass extinction occurred some 650 million years ago toward the end of the Precambrian eon. Animal and plant life was primitive at this time, and it is possible that chemical changes in the atmosphere were occurring as the oxygen-producing plants developed. At the time of the mass extinction, more than 70 percent of the forms of algae disappeared. The end of the Cambrian period, about 500 million years ago, is generally seen as the first of the major extinctions of life. More than half of the existing species of animal life vanished at this time. At the end of the Devonian period, 360 million years ago, many types of fish became extinct, along with 30 percent of the animal life on the planet. The largest mass extinction in the earth's history happened some 248 million years ago at the end of the Permian period. This extinction also marked the end of the Paleozoic era. Half of all the families of animal life were exterminated. This included 75 percent of all the amphibian families and 80 percent of the reptiles. Marine life, however, was hit hardest. Many families of shellfish, microscopic plankton, and other forms of marine life became extinct. It took 15-20 million years for animal life to recover to anywhere near the previous variety. Another mass extinction took place at the end of the Triassic period some 213 million years ago. Up until this time, primitive amphibians and reptiles had dominated the land. By the end of the period, they had dropped out and were replaced by the early dinosaurs. It could appear that competition with the dinosaurs led to the demise of these creatures, but other extinctions took place at this time, particularly in the oceans, which point to a more general cause.

The most studied and best-known mass extinction occurred at the end of the Cretaceous period some 65 million years ago. It is known mostly for the disappearance of the dinosaurs, but it also marks the extinction of many other forms of life, including many ocean reptiles, shelled creatures called ammonites, and forms of microscopic plankton. In all, a quarter of all the known families of animals were eliminated. In this extinction, as is true with previous extinctions, there was a gradual decline in diversity among animal life for tens of millions of years before the final extinction at the end of the period.

The latter part of the Tertiary period, 10,000 years ago, saw the extinction of the giant land mammals. From the woolly mammoth and the mastodon to the sabertooth cats, all perished. There is some evidence that implicates humankind in the extinction of these giant mammals. With organized hunting and the use of fire, it is conceivable that early humans played a role in the decimation of animal populations. Remnants at ancient kill sites show that thousands of animals were killed at a single hunt. Even in historical times, it has been seen that with the arrival of primitive people to a new area, extinctions of indigenous life forms follow.

Although it has not been proven that humankind is reponsible for the extinctions of the giant mammals toward the end of the Tertiary period, there is little doubt as to its role in the most recent mass extinction of life. The twentieth century has witnessed a widespread extinction of life forms resulting from the explosive spread of the human species. While human demand for space increases, available habitats for other animals diminish. Remote areas that were once the havens of wildlife are now being penetrated by hunters, farmers, lumbermen, fishermen, and developers. Those areas devoid of humans are visited by the products of civilization—acid rain, air and water pollution, and destruction of the ozone layer. Thus, humankind is directly or indirectly responsible for the extinctions of more than 450 species of animals, and many more are endangered.

Current extinctions aside, why should a large percentage of life on earth die out suddenly? The question can be misleading. For example, "suddenly" is a relative term when applied to geologic events. Changes happen over thousands of millions of years. An abrupt change in layers of sediment may indicate a change that took place over a period of a few days or a few million years. It is difficult to determine from the geologic evidence how sudden "suddenly" was.

Although it was long known that mass extinctions occurred from time to time throughout the earth's history, the causes were thought to be unknowable for lack of definitive evidence until high levels of the element iridium were found at the boundary marking the end of the Cretaceous period. With the possibility of testable evidence, the study of mass extinctions was opened again in earnest, and new relationships among available data began to be formed. As mass extinctions were documented exhaustively, what appeared to be a cyclic pattern emerged. According to one study, exterminations of life occurred about every 26,000 years. The periodicity remains in question, and theories range from an orbiting death star to the fact that random extinction events create an intrinsic periodicity.

Something in the earth's environment definitely changes at the time of a mass extinction. Many theories begin, then, by determining the changing conditions at the time of the extinction. Although valid, a weakness in this method is that the earth's environment is constantly in a state of flux. In whatever time period one examines, changes are bound to be found. It is therefore merely speculation whether any particular change or set of changes was sufficient to cause a mass dying. In addition, it seems that mass extinctions cannot be studied from the perspective of a single species or even a single extinction event. Only by studying them as a whole can scientists determine patterns that may explain them. In general, mass extinctions kill species on the land and in the oceans at the same time. They strike hardest at large animals on the land. Freshwater animals are generally left unscathed, as well as large cold-blooded land animals (assuming that theories indicating that the dinosaurs were warm-blooded are correct). Plants are not affected as severely as animals. Any theory of mass extinction must therefore address these issues.

Two theories have emerged which seem to handle the criteria. Neither theory is new, but each has received renewed interest with the emerging evidence. One popular theory invokes a global catastrophe with a celestial origin. Impacts by meteorites or comets are proposed to be responsible for at least the mass extinction which killed the dinosaurs, if not others. The theory accounts for the extinctions as well as for survivors, and evidence of a rare mineral found in meteorites was discovered in rock layers from the Cretaceous period, leading to fresh interest in the theory. The deciding factor in the acceptability of the theory is the suddenness of the extinctions, which on a geologic time scale would have occurred virtually instantaneously.

The other theory has to do with the changing sea levels of the earth, a theory from the 1920's in which interest revived in the light of the theory of plate tectonics. As the sea level drops, warm, shallow seas recede. The habitat of some marine animals is eliminated, while chemical changes in the deeper ocean water cause other extinctions. On land, bridges appear between areas that were once separated by water, and the migration of animals follows. Competition for available habitats is generated among species that were previously separated, also leading to extinctions. The drifting together and breaking apart of continents would dramatically affect habitats. It has been shown that in general, the arrangement of continents affects the variability of climate, the variety of species on land, and the nature of habitats along the continental shelves in the ocean. Changes in these factors over long periods of time would lead to extinctions of animal species.

There is no single or simple answer to the cause of mass extinctions. The pivotal question seems to be whether they occurred instantaneously, requiring a single catastrophic event, or over an extended period. In a period of several million years, many changes will occur in the environment, some of them catastrophic. Volcanoes erupt, meteorites strike, climates change, and continents drift. There is no doubt that catastrophes occur, but how they affect life on earth is as yet poorly understood.

All things considered, it is most likely that mass extinctions occur as a result of a combination of many factors, including catastrophic ones, happening over long periods of time. Perhaps a cyclic pattern exists, or perhaps species survival is a matter of playing the odds on a changing planet. Yet, if the earth is considered to be a living organism, it is no wonder that as the planet ages and evolves, the life it supports also changes.

Methods of Study

The major clues to unravel the pattern of life on earth come from the study of the geologic record. The sequential layering of rocks, their deformation and erosion, allow scientists to construct a history of the processes the rocks have undergone. By analyzing the chemical composition of layers of rock and sediment and studying the nature of the fossil remains in them, scientists can begin to understand what forms of life existed during which time periods and when (and sometimes how) they became extinct. It was discovered that the layers could be dated by the decay of radioactive elements and that, in this way, the ages and periods of geologic time could be dated accurately.

Of all the fossils in the geologic record, fossils of tiny marine animals give the clearest picture of mass extinctions. Produced prolifically in the world's oceans, they settled among the sediment on the ocean floor and fossilized in layers. These layers tell the story of how the creatures developed, diversified, flourished, and finally when they ceased to exist. Found in diverse areas of the world, from desert to mountainous regions, the fossils also tell the story of the movement of continents. Certain of them form such a complete record that their forms and types can be used to date sediments all over the world. While fossil remains of land animals can also be dated and related to specific time periods, these larger fossils are much scarcer and therefore do not present as complete a picture.

By studying traces of magnetism preserved in rock along with fossil deposits, geologists can chart the drifting of the continents in the distant past. The emergence of the theory of plate tectonics has provided scientists with a framework for understanding why the earth's environment and all its features are in a constant state of change. This changing environment is a key clue to periodic mass extinctions.

Besides the rise and fall of fossil species, other characteristics of the geologic layers can be measured. The relative abundances of certain elements indicate the processes that may have been occurring at the time the deposits were laid down. An example is the iridium found at the site of the extinction of the dinosaurs. Iridium is uncommon on the earth but is found in certain types of meteorites, which has led many scientists to believe that the extinction of the dinosaurs was caused by the impact of a comet or meteorite. Particles of soot were also found in the layers from that time period, suggesting that a large part of the earth may have been burned. Shocked quartz, indicating violent activity, also supported the theory.

The story of life found in the geologic record leaves scientists with myriad clues but few answers. It is as if they had millions of minute pieces to an enormous puzzle; collecting the pieces does not solve the puzzle. The various clues must be interpreted, seen in the light of their historical significance, and put together in fresh ways. As patterns emerge in the study of mass extinctions, the clues are beginning to fall into place, and an understanding of the dynamics of life on earth is emerging.

Context

In the evolution of life, mass extinctions are pivotal events. Whether suddenly or over millions of years, the entire course of life changes gears and, where one pattern had been flourishing, another takes its place. In this context, the human presence on the earth can be seen as nothing short of a remarkable accident. If any of the great exterminations of the past had simply not happened, the inhabitants of the earth today might be quite different. The intelligence and unique consciousness of self that are human trademarks might never have developed or might have evolved in a different form.

As no other animal species ever has, humans study and document the history of life. Nevertheless, they are, inescapably, participants as well. As scientists begin to understand the patterns that exist in evolution, humankind is faced with serious implications for the species. With the knowledge of the nature of its interaction with the environment, humanity is the only species with the ability to foresee its own possible extinction. What is more, humans may be the only species with the ability to bring about or to avoid its own extinction.

There is little that could be done to prevent the type of sudden, catastrophic event that is one possible cause of mass extinctions. An impact by a comet or asteroid could occur at any time, with little warning. In studying how such an impact would bring about extinctions, however, scientists have been able to draw parallels to the possible effects of a nuclear war. By injecting massive amounts of dust into the atmosphere, combined with light-absorbing soot from resulting worldwide fires, the human race might create for itself a "nuclear winter" which it would fail to survive.

If mass extinctions were caused by slow, gradual changes in the environment, the implications for humankind might be even more insidious. Humans have been actively altering their environment since the beginning of civilization but do not know enough about the subtle ecological balance to understand how they might be permanently affecting it. Considering the effects of overpopulation, deforestation, and the many ways humans pollute their own habitat, they may already have tipped the balance toward eventual extinction. With some evidence of the damage to the environment, however, processes may yet be set in motion to reverse it.

Bibliography

Bakker, Robert T. *The Dinosaur Heresies.* New York: William Morrow, 1986. An expert on current theories concerning the dinosaurs explains them in an easy-to-read and interesting way. Dinosaurs are studied in terms of their place in geologic history, and their extinction is explained as part of a larger pattern. The pattern is compared to other mass extinctions in the history of the earth.

Calder, Nigel. *The Restless Earth.* New York: Viking Press, 1972. An illustrated and easily understood reference on the theory of plate tectonics as seen in the context of geology as a whole. Discusses the effects of continental drift on habitats on land and in the oceans. Also overviews the history of the earth from a geological and paleontological perspective.

Chorlton, Windsor. *Ice Ages.* Planet Earth Series. Alexandria, Va.: Time-Life Books, 1983. A beautifully illustrated and fascinating account of the nature and activity of glaciation in the history of the earth. Discusses the effects of glaciation on plant and animal life, including the development of humankind. Addresses the theories of cosmic causes for the ice ages and for mass extinctions.

Colbert, Edwin H. *Dinosaurs: An Illustrated History.* Maplewood, N.J.: Hammond, 1986. Portrays the natural history of the dinosaurs, their beginnings, evolutionary development, how they influenced the environment in which they lived, and their extinction. Well illustrated.

Man, John. *The Natural History of the Dinosaur.* New York: Gallery Books, 1978. A well-written and informative volume directed toward the general reader. Provides an overview of the discovery of dinosaur fossils and discusses theories of dinosaur extinction.

Miller, Russell. *Continents in Collision.* Alexandria, Va.: Time-Life Books, 1983. A nicely illustrated volume written for the general reader with an interest in earth science. Describes the dynamic processes of the earth, how they have been discovered, and their implications on the present and future earth.

Press, Frank, and Raymond Siever. *Earth.* 4th ed. San Francisco: W. H. Freeman, 1986. A very complete text on the history of the earth designed to be used as a beginning geology text at the college level. Presents a broad range of topics. Major topic areas are the earth's formation, the fossil record, surface processes, and internal processes.

Wilford, John Noble. *The Riddle of the Dinosaur.* New York: Alfred A. Knopf, 1985. A well-written, sparsely illustrated account of the life and death of the dinosaurs. More in-depth than most books about dinosaurs, the book deals with each area of the study of the dinosaurs, discusses the various and sometimes controversial ideas concerning them, and comes to a synthesis without espousing a particular conclusion.

Divonna Ogier

Cross-References

Biostratigraphy, 173; The Evolution of Life, 655; The Fossil Record, 760; Geochronology: Radiocarbon Dating, 840; The Geologic Time Scale, 874; Gondwanaland and Pangaea, 982; Ice Ages, 1115; Meteorite and Comet Impacts, 1623; Paleobiogeography, 1984; Paleoclimatology, 1993; Plate Tectonics, 2079.

MASS SPECTROMETRY

Type of earth science: Geochemistry
Field of study: Analytical techniques

Mass spectrometry is the technique used for determining particle abundances by their mass and charge characteristics in an evacuated electromagnetic field. Its principal uses in the earth sciences are in determining the isotope ratios of light, stable substances and in measuring the isotopic abundances of radioactive and radiogenic substances.

Principal terms

ABSOLUTE DATE or AGE: the numerical timing of a geologic event, as contrasted with relative, or stratigraphic, timing

GEOCHRONOLOGY: the study of the absolute ages of geologic samples and events

HALF-LIFE: the time required for a radioactive isotope to decay by one-half of its original weight

IONS: atoms or molecules that have too few or too many electrons for neutrality and are therefore electrically charged

ISOCHRON: a line connecting points representing samples of equal age on a radioactive isotope (parent) versus radiogenic isotope (daughter) diagram

ISOTOPE: a species of an element having the same number of protons but a different number of neutrons and therefore a different atomic weight

NUCLIDE: any observable association of protons and neutrons

RADIOACTIVE DECAY: a natural process whereby an unstable, or radioactive, isotope transforms into a stable, or radiogenic, isotope

Summary of the Methodology

The golden decade of physics, from 1896 to 1906, saw the critical discoveries and experiments that resulted in the quantitative analysis of charged particles by mass. One hundred years ago, experiments with cathode rays led to their identification as streams of electrons by Eugen Goldstein, Wilhelm Wien, and Joseph John Thomson. Using the earliest application of mass analysis, Thomson identified the two isotopes of neon, neon 20 and neon 22. This work was followed in 1918 and 1919 by A. J. Dempster and F. W. Aston, who designed mass spectrographs which were used in succeeding years to determine most of the naturally occurring isotopes of the periodic table.

In 1896, Antoine-Henri Becquerel presented his discovery of the phenomenon of radioactivity to the scientific community in Paris. This finding was followed rapidly by the seminal work of Marie Curie in radioactivity, a term she coined. Her discovery of the intensely radioactive elements radium and plutonium led Ernest

Rutherford to delimit three kinds of radioactivity—alpha, beta, and gamma—and, in 1900, led Frederick Soddy to formulate a theory of radioactive decay. Soddy later proposed the probability of isotopes, the existence of which was demonstrated on early mass spectrographs and mass spectrometers.

Rutherford and Soddy's theory of the time dependence of radioactive decay, followed by breakthroughs in instrumentation for the measurement of these unstable species and their radiogenic "daughter" nuclides, caught the attention of early geochronologists and had a revolutionary effect on the study of geology. In 1904, Rutherford proposed that geologic time might be measured by the breakdown of uranium in uranium-bearing minerals, and a few years later, Bertram Boltwood announced the "absolute" ages of three samples of uranium minerals. The ages, which approximated half a billion years, indicated that at least some earth materials were much older than had been thought, an idea developed by Arthur Holmes in his classic *The Age of the Earth* (1913). Holmes's early time scale for the earth and his enthusiasm for the developing study of radioactive decay were not met with instant acceptance by most contemporary geologists, but eventually, absolute ages would become the prime quantitative components in the field of geology. After the early study of the isotopes of uranium came the discovery of other unstable isotopes and the formulation of the radioactive decay schemes that have become the workhorses of geochronology. The theory of the radioactive decay of the parent, or unstable, nuclide (or the growth of the daughter, or stable, nuclide) developed in the early 1900's has not changed; it is still the basis for geochronologists' measurement of time. This field is one of the arenas for the use of mass spectrometry.

The other use of mass spectrometry in the earth sciences results from isotopes' potential to fractionate, or change their relative abundance proportions, during geological processes, for physicochemical reasons other than radioactive decay and radiogenic buildup. Fractionation not resulting from radioactive decay (stable isotope fractionation) comes about because the thermodynamic properties of molecules depend on the mass of the atoms from which they are made. The total energy of a molecule can be described in terms of the electronic interactions of its atoms and the other energetic components of these atoms, such as their rotation, vibration, and translation. Molecules which contain in their molecular configurations different isotopes will have differing energies, because of the different energy components (usually vibrational and rotational) that are mass-dependent. The total energy of molecules also decreases with decreasing temperature; at zero Kelvin, or absolute zero, this energy has a finite value known as its zero-point energy. The vibrational component of energy, the most important factor in fractionation, is inversely proportional to the square root of its mass. A molecule with the heavier of two isotopes will have a lower vibrational energy and thus a lower zero-point energy than a similar but lighter isotope molecule. Other factors being equal, the chemical bonds of a molecule with lighter isotopic composition will be more easily broken than those of the heavier isotope analogue, and the heavier molecule thus will be less reactive chemically.

Geologic processes that result in stable isotopic fractionation are the redistribution of isotopes as a function of isotopic exchange; nonthermodynamic (kinetic) processes that depend on the amounts of the species present during a reaction; and a range of strictly physical processes, including diffusion, evaporation, condensation, adsorption, desorption, crystallization, and melting. Physical conditions such as these undoubtedly were much more intense during preaccretion events, such as star formation, than during more typical "geologic" processes, such as sedimentation or volcanism; consequently, fractionation effects are observable in primitive materials, such as some components of relatively unprocessed meteorites. These materials show extremely interesting stable isotope fractionation effects even among the heaviest elements.

As commonly used, the term "mass spectrometer" refers to an instrument in which beams of ionized isotopes are separated electrically. (The earlier, more qualitative mass spectrograph focused ion beams onto a photographic plate.) Mass spectrometers have three common elements: a source component, wherein elemental species are ionized so that they can be accelerated electrically; an analyzer section, where isotopic species are separated by their mass-charge ratio; and a collector assembly, where the ion beams are quantitatively measured.

The most common instrument in geologic use is the magnetic-sector machine, in which a uniform magnetic field is bound in a region, or sector, commonly by a stainless steel tube that can be evacuated to very low pressures to prevent sample contamination. The source region may consist of a solid source; a purified and spiked sample of a heavy element is introduced in the solid state onto a filament of purified metal such as tantalum or rhenium, and the filament is heated electrically until a sufficient percentage of the element is ionized for efficient measurement. Alternatively, the source may be a gas; in this case, the desired, commonly light, elements in a gaseous state are introduced into an evacuated region and bombarded with electrons to produce a sufficient percentage of ionized species for acceleration into the analyzer section of the instrument. The ionized species are accelerated electrically through a series of slits, onto which variable electric potentials can be applied for the purpose of acceleration and focusing, so that a well-defined, focused beam of the element or its gaseous compound is beamed into the analyzer tube.

The analyzer sector, commonly constructed so that the lowest pressure possible can be maintained and the least number of contaminant species will be struck by the focused beam, is bent at angles of 90 or 120 degrees and passed through an electromagnetic field capable of efficient separation of the ion beams by their mass-to-charge ratios. (Where the charges are uniform, as is usual in earth science research, the separation is, as desired, only by mass.)

The collector assembly commonly consists of a Faraday cup; the separated isotope beams enter, hit the metal cup, and impart unit charges to the cup as the atoms are neutralized. The resulting direct current is exceedingly low and, in many instruments, must be converted to an alternating current so that the intensity of the signal can be increased for measurement with a strip-chart recorder or, more commonly, for digital readout. Accelerating voltage in the source assembly is adjusted with the magnetic field in the analyzer sector (commonly monitored and controlled with a very precise gaussmeter) so that a beam of a unique charge-to-mass ratio (or of a unique mass, for ions of the same charge) passes through a final slit into the collector. Ions entering the collector are neutralized by electrons that flow from ground to the metal collector cup, across a resistor whose voltage difference is amplified and measured with a digital or analogue voltmeter. These data are exhibited as a strip-chart readout or, more commonly, as digital output that is computer-collected and reduced for analysis. The collection of large numbers of highly precise isotopic ratios in computer-reduced digital form has made possible the modern use of mass spectrometry in the earth sciences and the determination of isotopic parameters that would not otherwise have been obtainable.

Other types of mass spectrometry have been used in earth science work, such as time-of-flight mass spectrometry, but their uses have been limited. Still other methods undoubtedly will become of increasing importance to the earth sciences; some of these have opened studies that would not have been possible with more traditional equipment. Accelerator mass spectrometry employs the use of a particle accelerator or cyclotron as the mass analyzer; it is useful primarily to make high-abundance measurements for cosmogenic nuclides such as carbon 14. Ion probe mass spectrometry involves the combination of a microbeam probe (using ions, rather than the lighter electrons, as "bullets" for ionization) and a magnetic-sector mass spectrometer. This highly sophisticated technique has made possible the accurate isotopic analysis of very small regions of minerals in thin section. Resonance ionization mass spectrometry holds much promise in earth science studies because of its potentially high ionization efficiency and, therefore, sensitivity. Other possible mass spectrometric practices may include high-accuracy isotope dilution analysis utilizing a plasma ion source, and ion cyclotron resonance (Fourier transform) mass spectrometry. The supermachine of the future may combine some or even all of these potential advances.

Applications of the Method

Although some modern methods of determining absolute time do not involve isotopes, most do, and the standard method for their quantitative measurement is by mass spectrometry. Because the various radioactive nuclides useful in geochronology are also varied in their chemical characteristics, several instruments and techniques are involved. The principal mechanics of spectrometry, however, are mainly the same. The standard method involves placing the purified samples of the materials in question as solids on purified metal filaments and inserting the loaded filaments into a solid-source mass spectrometer. Evacuated to very low pressures, the spectrometer source regions are made so that the metal filaments can be heated to the point that the rubidium or strontium ionizes. The charged, ionized sample is accelerated through a series of collimating slits into the high-vacuum analyzing tube, where it encounters a controlled electromagnetic field. The beams of ions are separated by charge-mass ratios into beams of separated isotopes; as the charge of the elements is the same for each atom, however, the ions in this case are separated on the basis of mass only. Specific isotopic beams, controlled by the magnetic field, are channeled through more collimating slits to the collector part of the spectrometer. Commonly, a Faraday cup is used to analyze the number of atoms of each isotope by conversion of each atomic impact into a unit of charge, which is amplified, often with a vibrating reed electrometer. A digital readout is then produced. The actual output is isotope ratio measurements, which are converted by a mathematical program to the required parameters for determining time.

Scientists determine the age graphically, with the use of an isochron diagram, in which isotope ratios collected in the spectrometer are used as coordinates. A line known as an isochron connects points representing samples of equal ages. An isochron has an age value indicated by its slope on the figure; a horizontal isochron has a zero-age value, while positive slopes of successively greater degree have increasingly greater ages. A single mineral or rock is represented by only one point in the diagram; therefore, for an isochron to be drawn, an estimate of the sample's initial isotopic composition would be necessary. Ages calculated this way are termed "model ages."

Stable isotope fractionation, or the enrichment of one isotope relative to another in a chemical or physical process, also has earth science applications. The two processes of this sort are equilibrium fractionation, which is useful in determining geologic paleotemperatures, and kinetic (nonequilibrium) fractionation, which is useful in establishing biologically mediated geochemical processes, such as the bacterial utilization of sulfur. Isotopic fractionation in these processes is measured by the fractionation factor α, defined as A/B, where A is the ratio of the heavy to the light isotope in molecule A, and B is that ratio for molecule B. Although α may be calculated theoretically, in geologic use it is derived mainly from empirical data. This factor, which is largely dependent on the vibrational energies of the molecules involved, is a function of temperature; thus, it is a measure of ambient geologic processes.

Many earth science applications of stable isotope fractionation are in use, but perhaps the best-known example is the use of oxygen isotope ratios to establish paleotemperatures of ancient seawater. Surface seawater, in at least partial equilibrium with the atmosphere, contains oxygen with a characteristic isotopic composition. This composition is provided by the ratio of the most abundant species: oxygen 18 and oxygen 16. Marine plants and animals, such as foraminifera, that build their hard parts out of components dissolved in seawater, such as calcium, carbon, and oxygen (as in calcium carbonate), utilize oxygen that is isotopically characteristic of the seawater. Although this process also depends on other, incompletely understood, factors, it is primarily a function of water temperature. Therefore, the ratio of oxygen 18 to oxygen 16 in the foraminifera is a measure of the water temperature. Because the calcium carbonate does not readily reequilibrate with ambient water after it is precipitated, it retains its characteristic isotopic composition after sedimentary burial for many millions of years. Isotopic data collected from foraminifera recovered from deep-sea cores are therefore used to record water temperatures (and consequently, climate) of the geologic past. More than any other paleothermometry device, this application has been extremely useful in providing a record of global temperature changes, especially of the past glacial periods, for use in constructing and testing quantified models of the causes of climate change.

For this application, the sample is introduced into the source region of the mass spectrometer as a gas, commonly carbon dioxide. Ionization of the gas may be accomplished by bombardment of the molecules with electrons. The positively charged ions created are accelerated through collimating slits into the analyzer section of the spectrometer. In this type of gaseous analysis, use is made of the double-focusing mass spectrometer, in which the isotopic composition of the sample is determined relative to that of the standard in iterative, alternating measurements.

Context

The revolution in the earth sciences, largely a result of the plate tectonics paradigm which was introduced in the early 1960's, was preceded by an even more important revolution, one that received little fanfare. In the 1940's and 1950's, earth science began to be significantly influenced by quantitative investigations which may be considered to have provided the quantitative foundation for the plate tectonic revolution. Of these studies, none was more significant than the use of mass spectrometry for determining absolute ages of minerals and rocks and, later, for paleothermometry. Absolute-age determinations gave a firm basis for paleontology and established not only the earth's antiquity but also a quantitative sequencing for its rocks and sediments—the geologic time scale.

Mass spectrometers still consist of the basic source, analyzer, and collector sections, but many advances have been made, so it is now possible to obtain extremely precise ratio measurements of tiny pieces of material in a relatively short time. Ion probe mass spectrometers allow these measurements on *in situ* samples in thin sections that, concomitantly, can be studied petrologically. Accelerator mass spectrometry makes possible the precise measurement of cosmogenic nuclides such as radiocarbon on tiny samples. The developing field of resonance ionization mass spectrometry will further instrument efficiency and sensitivity. Supermachines of the future may be able to combine the principal attributes of all these modern spectrometers. The continued crucial position of mass spectrometry in the earth sciences seems assured.

Bibliography

Duckworth, H. E. *Mass Spectrometry*. Cambridge, England: Cambridge University Press, 1958. An older, very technical but informative treatise on the basic principles of mass spectrometry. Suitable for college-level readers.

Faure, Gunter. *Principles of Isotope Geology*. 2d ed. New York: John Wiley & Sons, 1986. An excellent, though technical, introduction to the use of radioactive and stable isotopes in geology, including an introductory treatment of mass spectrometric principles and techniques. The work is well illustrated and indexed. Suitable for college-level readers.

Levin, Harold L. *The Earth Through Time*. 3d ed. Philadelphia: Saunders College Publishing, 1988. Chapter 5, "Time and Geology," reviews the geologic time scale and then turns to techniques for determining absolute age. It offers a history of early attempts at geochronology, an overview of radiometric dating, and a discussion of the principal dating methods. There is a simple description and diagram of a mass spectrometer. Easy to read and suitable for high school students.

Smith, David G., ed. *The Cambridge Encyclopedia of Earth Sciences*. Cambridge, England: Cambridge University Press, 1981. Chapter 8 in this clearly written text contains a section on mass spectrometry and its uses. Other analytical techniques are also discussed. Includes a table of trace element abundances in common rocks and minerals. For general audiences.

E. Julius Dasch

Cross-References

MERCURY

Type of earth science: Planetology
Field of study: Large solar system bodies

Mercury, the closest planet to the sun, highly resembles Earth's moon. Much that is known about this planet was obtained from experiments on board and photographic images returned by the unmanned Mariner 10 spacecraft, which completed three flybys of Mercury.

Principal terms

CALORIS BASIN: the largest known structure on Mercury; it is similar to the Moon's Imbrium Basin

EJECTA: the arrangement of surface and subsurface material thrown out during the formation of an impact crater

IMPACT CRATER: a depression, usually circular, in a planetary surface caused by the high-speed impact of rocky debris or comet nuclei

INTERCRATER PLAIN: terrain consisting of gently rolling plains littered with small secondary craters; the crater density is higher than in a smooth plain

SCARPS and RIDGES: linear surface features which suggest evidence of planetary tectonic processes

SMOOTH PLAIN: a formation that is relatively flat, with a sparsely cratered surface

Summary of the Phenomenon

Mercury is the closest planet to the sun. It completes one revolution about the sun in only 87.97 days. Mercury's orbit has a mean distance of only 0.387 astronomical unit (1 AU is the mean earth-sun distance), an eccentricity of 0.206, and an inclination of 7 degrees with respect to the ecliptic plane. Mercury rotates about an axis with no obliquity and has a period of 58.65 days. The ratio of Mercury's rotational period to its revolution period is almost precisely two to three. Mercury's mass is 3.30×10^{23} kilograms, and its mean radius is 2,439 kilometers; therefore, Mercury's mean density is 5,420 kilograms per cubic meter. Mercury's most prevalent features are its craters. Degradation of original craters has resulted from secondary impact and ballistic infilling, seismic activity resulting from impacts, lava flows, and isostatic readjustment.

Mercury's surface appears remarkably similar to that of Earth's moon; both are heavily pocked with impact craters. (Mercury's radius is about 50 percent larger than the Moon's.) Closer examination, however, reveals many important differences between the surfaces of Mercury and the Moon. The Moon has many more color variations on its surface than does Mercury. Mercury's albedo, or reflectivity, is 0.12, a brightness similar to that of the lunar highlands on the Moon's front face.

Although there are 20 percent albedo contrasts across Mercury's surface, it lacks the dark maria and filled craters so prevalent on the Moon. On both worlds, younger craters are often higher in albedo and surrounded by prominent ejecta blankets and bright rays. On Mercury, most craters are less than 200 kilometers across. Many of the larger craters are double-ringed with flat floors that are usually shallower than their lunar counterparts. Central peaks are found in intermediate-sized craters, but larger circular features tend not to have central peaks. Other lunar features are absent or rare on Mercury. There appears to be no evidence of volcanic domes, cinder cones, or lava-flow fronts on Mercury. Rilles on the planet are usually straight rather than sinuous, are quite deep, and are as wide as 6 kilometers.

Mercury is surrounded by an extremely tenuous atmosphere of helium, argon, and neon. High daytime surface temperatures coupled with a low escape velocity lead to degassing, as the average thermal kinetic energy is sufficient to effect atmospheric escape in a relatively short period of geologic time. The average planetary surface temperature is 452 Kelvins, but the maximum daytime temperature is about 700 Kelvins (at closest approach to the sun) and the minimum nightside temperature is 90 Kelvins. Mercury exhibits the greatest equatorial temperature variation—more than 600 Kelvins—of any planet.

Mercury has a magnetic field only 1.6 percent as strong as Earth's. The origin of the magnetic field is uncertain. A metallic core composed primarily of iron would be consistent with both the observed density and the magnetic field; however, Mercury's slow rotational speed could be too slow to generate currents in the core even if it is molten. Mercury's small magnetic field interacts with the solar wind. Mariner 10 recorded a moderately strong "bow shock" that traps energetic solar wind particles.

Although Mercury's surface resembles the Moon's, its mean density is closer to that of Earth. It is believed that, in proportion to its size, Mercury contains, in its core, double the amount of iron found in any other world in the solar system. High iron content would be consistent with the formation of Mercury by solar nebula condensation close to the sun. (Heavy elements would be more attracted to the early protosun than would lighter elements.) The existence of a magnetic field suggests that the iron has undergone differentiation and formed a hot, convecting core. The formation of the iron core would have generated heat in addition to the original radiogenic heat, causing expansion and melting of the entire mantle. This process would have had to occur before the era of intense cratering, because Mercury lacks surface expansion features and numerous preserved lava-flow formations. According to one model of Mercury's interior, the planet's asthenosphere cooled quickly and thickened, possibly disappearing altogether. Mercury's lithosphere could extend down to the iron core, hundreds of kilometers below the surface. There is evidence to support such a model. After core formation, the planet would have cooled and contracted, resulting in a decrease in radius perhaps as large as one or two kilometers. Compression of the surface would then cause thrust faults (the result of one rock unit slipping over another). Observed thrust faults on Mercury indicate a 2-kilometer contraction.

Mercury's surface physiography can be classified into four major terrain types: heavily cratered terrain, smooth plains, intercrater plains, and hilly and lineated terrain. The intercrater plains are believed to be the oldest material on the surface, predating the era of intense impact cratering. Smooth plains represent the youngest material.

Smooth plains, located principally in the northern hemisphere near the large feature called the Caloris Basin, are flat, lightly cratered surfaces akin to lunar maria. Craters in the smooth plains are typically sharp-rimmed and only 10 kilometers across, at most. Some smooth plains fill the floors of large craters. Often, the plains have sinuous ridges, an aspect shared by lunar maria. Regardless of their location on the surface, Mercury's smooth plains have equal impact-crater frequency, which indicates that the smooth plain features were all formed at about the same time. Smooth plain features are believed to be volcanic in origin. There are too many smooth plains for them to have resulted from a single catastrophic impact or to be ejecta from the large Caloris Basin. Similarities between lunar maria and smooth plains suggest a common origin. Lunar maria are volcanic in nature, so smooth plains on Mercury are believed to be volcanic, also.

Intercrater plains, believed to be the oldest material on Mercury, compose the largest physiographic feature on the planet. These plains have a greater crater density than smooth plains. The craters that pockmark the rolling plains are typically less than 10 kilometers in diameter and generally represent secondary rather than primary impacts. Intercrater plains were formed by a variety of different events occurring over long periods. These plains are probably primordial crust that has been subjected to impact cratering, but their origin is by no means clear. The variety of intercrater plains suggests several alternative origins.

Heavily cratered terrain is reminiscent of the lunar highlands, areas of many overlapping craters. Crater diameters vary between 30 and 200 kilometers. Ejecta deposits cannot be clearly identified with individual craters because of high degrees of overlap and disruption. This variety of terrain was formed as the era of intense bombardment was ending.

Hilly and lineated terrain is found directly opposite the Caloris Basin on Mercury and may have been formed by the Caloris impact. This terrain, often referred to as "weird terrain," covers about 250,000 square kilometers and is made of hummocky hills 5 to 10 kilometers wide at the base and 0.1 to 1.8 kilometers high. Seismic energy from the Caloris impact broke this region into hills and depressions.

The Caloris Basin is the largest single surface feature revealed by the Mariner 10 photographs. More than 1,300 kilometers across, Caloris resembles the Moon's Imbrium Basin and may represent an important event in Mercury's history, just as Imbrium does for the Moon. The basin is rimmed by mountains 30 to 50 kilometers wide and several kilometers high. Inside the basin are smooth plains scarred by small craters, ridges, and grooves indicative of lava flows modified by tectonic activity.

Methods of Study

Mercury reveals few of its secrets to visual observation from Earth. Because it is so close to the sun, it is often hidden by solar glare and can be seen only briefly, telescopically, at twilight. Astronomers once incorrectly assumed that Mercury did not rotate as it revolved around the sun. Few surface features were known before the Mariner 10 encounters; indeed, for all intents and purposes, all that is known about Mercury was obtained through scientific investigations performed by the Mariner 10 spacecraft. The probe was equipped with seven primary experiments; they involved high-resolution television imaging, infrared radiometry, radio wave propagation, extreme ultraviolet spectroscopy, magnetometry, plasma detection, and charged particle flux measurements.

Mercury's atmosphere was studied, using the ultraviolet experiment, during a solar occultation. The instrument measured the drop in intensity of ultraviolet radiation from the sun as Mercury's disk and tenuous atmosphere obscured it. Those data provided a profile of the atmospheric concentration above the planet's surface. Other atmospheric data were gathered by monitoring radio waves emitted by Mariner 10 as it passed behind Mercury and then reemerged. The infrared radiometer, fixed to the spacecraft body on the sunlit side, had apertures which shielded the detectors from direct solar radiation. This experiment determined Venusian cloud temperatures as well as measuring surface temperatures on Mercury. Heat-loss data obtained as Mariner 10 crossed the planet's terminator (the line separating daylight from darkness) helped scientists to infer information about the planet's surface material composition. Surface brightness temperature was measured in a pair of spectral ranges, 34 to 55 micrometers and 7.5 to 14 micrometers, which represented temperatures of 80 to 340 Kelvins and 200 to 700 Kelvins.

Mariner 10 measured Mercury's magnetic field with a magnetometer package consisting of two three-axis sensors placed at different spots on a 6-meter-long boom. The use of two sensors provided the capability to isolate the spacecraft's own magnetic field from the weak field of the planet. Magnetic field measurements in interplanetary space were also made.

High-resolution images of a planetary surface can provide a wealth of information concerning the planet's past, its geologic activity, and its surface composition. Mariner 10's television imaging system included two vidicon cameras attached to telescopes. The assembly was mounted on a scan platform which permitted the horizontal and vertical movements necessary for precise pointing. Cassegrain telescope systems were used in the imaging system. Powerful enough to resolve ordinary print at a distance of more than 400 meters, this system provided narrow-angle, high-resolution images. The television system also included an auxiliary optical system to obtain wide-angle, lower-resolution photography. This system was mounted on each of the television cameras. Experimenters were able to switch from narrow-angle to wide-angle imaging by moving the position of a mirror on the system's filter wheel. The vidicon cameras had 9.8-by-12.3-millimeter apertures and could make exposures of between 3 milliseconds and 12 seconds. Analogue signals from the vidicon camera readout were digitized for transmission to Earth receiving stations. An individual television image consisted of 700 vidicon scan lines, with each scan line consisting of 832 pixels.

The principal objectives of Mariner 10's television imaging program included the collection of data useful in studying Mercury's planetary physiography, the precise determination of Mercury's radius and rotation rate, the evaluation of Mercury's photometric properties, and the categorization of the morphology of surface features. Television scans were made of the space surrounding Mercury in an attempt to locate unknown satellites, but none was found. This system was also used for studies of Venus and Comet Kohoutek.

Context

Although the existence of a wandering star later named "Mercury" (the Romanized name of the Greek god Hermes, patron of trade, travel, and thieves) was known since antiquity, the vast majority of man's knowledge of the planet closest to the sun has been obtained in the second half of the twentieth century from ground-based observations and three Mariner 10 spacecraft encounters in 1974 and 1975. Timocharis is considered to have registered the first recorded observation of Mercury, in 265 B.C. Very little more was learned about the planet until after the invention of the telescope. Observation of the phases of Mercury was first reported in 1639 A.D. by the Italian astronomer Zupus. Telescope technology improved, and evidence of surface features was found in the early 1800's, when the astronomers Karl Ludwig Harding and Johann Schröter measured albedo variations. It was not until the early 1960's that Mercury's rotation rate was precisely measured by radar observations. The unmanned Mariner 10 spacecraft obtained the first close-ups of the planet. Photographs obtained during this flyby mission began the geologic analysis of Mercury.

Mariner 10, the final spacecraft in the Mariner series, was launched on November 3, 1973, at 12:45 A.M. eastern time atop an Atlas-Centaur launch vehicle from launch complex 36B at Cape Canaveral. This spacecraft became the first to use gravity assists by large solar system bodies to direct its trajectory to multiple photographic targets. It was recognized that the alignment of Earth, Venus, and Mercury was such that a single spacecraft could be launched between 1970 and 1973 from Earth toward Venus and then reach Mercury. Giuseppe Colombo of the Institute of Applied Mechanics in Padua, Italy, noted during an early 1970 U.S. Jet Propulsion Laboratory conference on the approved Mariner 10 mission that a 1973 launch opportunity existed in which the spacecraft could enter an orbit with a period nearly twice that of Mercury. That meant that a second Mercurian encounter was possible. Mariner 10 was indeed placed on a trajectory that permitted multiple encounters with Mercury, and this success demonstrated the feasibility of gravity-assist trajectories. The technique would prove invaluable to the Voyager probes, which were sent to the outer solar system.

Shortly after Mariner 10's escape from Earth orbit, its planetary science experiments were activated to verify their operating condition. Mosaic photographs returned to Earth indicated that the spacecraft was in good condition to image a moonlike world with high-quality camera systems. Mariner 10 came within 5,794 kilometers of Venus on February 5, 1974. During eight days of photography, the spacecraft returned 4,165 images of Venus and a wealth of data about the Venusian atmosphere. After another forty-five days of interplanetary cruising, the spacecraft reached the mission's principal target: the planet Mercury. Mariner 10 began taking photographs on March 23, 1974, reaching its closest approach, 5,790 kilometers, on March 29. The spacecraft then passed behind Mercury, to the nightside. More than two thousand photographs were obtained on this first encounter. Mariner 10's trajectory returned the spacecraft to Mercury on September 21, 1974; this time, it came as close as 50,000 kilometers. The probe completed a third encounter in March, 1975, before running out of fuel and entering a solar orbit.

Bibliography

Beatty, J. Kelly, Brian O'Leary, and Andrew Chaikin. *The New Solar System*. Cambridge, England: Cambridge University Press, 1981. A beautifully illustrated overview of all the major objects in the solar system, this volume is a collection of chapters written by various experts in the field of planetology. Extensive bibliography.

Chapman, Clark R. *The Inner Planets: New Light on the Rocky Worlds of Mercury, Venus, Earth, the Moon, and the Asteroids*. New York: Charles Scribner's Sons, 1977. An excellent overview of the terrestrial planets, incorporating astronomical and spacecraft data. Planetology is presented in a manner accessible to the layperson.

Cross, Charles A., and Patrick Moore. *The Atlas of Mercury*. New York: Crown, 1977. This reference book summarizes pre-Mariner 10 knowledge of the solar system and Mercury. It details the Mariner 10 design and data-taking procedures. Includes extensive maps of Mercury's surface and a thorough glossary. For general audiences.

Davies, Merton E., Stephen E. Dwornik, Donald E. Gault, and Robert G. Strom. *Atlas of Mercury*. NASA SP-423. Washington, D.C.: National Aeronautics and Space Administration, Scientific and Technical Information Office, 1978. Provides an excellent description of Mariner 10 and its mission. Includes a full atlas of spacecraft photography of Mercury. An essential reference for the planetary science enthusiast or researcher, accessible to general audiences.

Dunne, James A., and Eric Burgess. *The Voyage of Mariner 10: Mission to Venus and Mercury*. NASA SP-424. Washington, D.C.: National Aeronautics and Space Administration, Scientific and Technical Information Office, 1978. This book offers an elegant description of the first spacecraft mission directed to the planet Mercury. Prepared by the Jet Propulsion Laboratory, the text is complete with information on spacecraft operations and data returns. Photographs of Mercury abound. For general audiences.

Greeley, Ronald. *Planetary Landscapes*. Boston: Allen & Unwin, 1985. This text includes chapters on all the planets except Neptune and Pluto. There is extensive use of spacecraft data throughout. It provides explanations of solar system geology and planetary morphological processes, and space- and ground-based photographs are abundant. An excellent reference for the serious researcher.

Short, Nicholas M. *Planetary Geology*. Englewood Cliffs, N.J.: Prentice-Hall, 1975. Suitable for use as a text in high school earth sciences curricula, this book describes a vast number of geological processes seen throughout the solar system. It is heavily weighted toward lunar, Venusian, and Martian studies. Includes a particularly good description of cratering processes.

Whipple, Fred L. *Earth, Moon, and Planets*. Cambridge, Mass.: Harvard University Press, 1971. This text is somewhat dated, particularly with regard to Mercury and the outer planets, but it offers an excellent overview of planetary geology. Particularly useful appendices. Suitable for the layperson.

David G. Fisher

Cross-References

Earth's Differentiation, 525; Geothermal Phenomena and Heat Transport, 906; Heat Sources and Heat Flow, 1065; Lunar Craters, 1393; Lunar Maria, 1408; Elemental Distribution in the Solar System, 2434; The Origin of the Solar System, 2442; Venus' Atmosphere, 2587; Venus' Surface, 2593.

THE MESOZOIC ERA

Type of earth science: Geology
Field of study: Stratigraphy

The Mesozoic era is a major episode in earth history during which a primitive flora and fauna and physical environment changed progressively toward more familiar conditions. Also, continents and ocean basins nearly achieved their present configuration. It is characterized by dinosaurs and other large reptiles.

Principal terms
EPICONTINENTAL SEA: a sea covering part of a continental block; such seas generally are less than 200 meters deep and are the depositional site of most exposed sedimentary rocks
GONDWANALAND: an ancient, large continent in the Southern Hemisphere that included Africa, South America, India, Australia, and Antarctica
LAURASIA: an ancient, large continent in the Northern Hemisphere that included North America and Eurasia
PANGAEA: the supercontinent containing all continental crust that existed at the beginning of the Mesozoic
PERIOD: a unit of geological time comprising part of an era and subdivided, in decreasing order, into epochs, ages, and chrons
RIFTING: a process of faulting and basaltic intrusion occurring where crustal plates separate during continental drift; may cause mountains
SUBDUCTION: a process by which one crustal plate rides over another, which descends and melts, generating molten rock that then intrudes the deformed plate above; it causes mountains
SYSTEM: the rocks deposited during a period, which is defined by age of the rocks making up its system
TETHYS: a seaway embayed into Pangaea between the southeast corner of Asia, the western end of the Mediterranean, and the southeast end of Pangaea

Summary of the Phenomenon

The Mesozoic era and system are respectively a major subdivision of geologic time and the rocks of that age. The Mesozoic began about 225 million years before the present and ended about 65 million years before the present. It was preceded by the Paleozoic era and followed by the Cenozoic era and is divided into three periods: Triassic (about 225-180 million years before the present), Jurassic (about 180-144 million years before the present), and Cretaceous (about 144-65 million years before the present).

All the continents were gathered in a single large landmass, the supercontinent

Pangaea, at the beginning of the Triassic period. South America, Africa, Antarctica, Australia, New Zealand, Arabia, and Peninsular India previously formed the super-continent Gondwanaland during the Carboniferous (about 350-285 million years before the present), while North America, Greenland, Eurasia (less Peninsular India), and Borneo formed Laurasia. Laurasia and Gondwanaland merged during the Permian (about 285-225 million years before the present) by welding northwest Africa and South America to the south and east margin of North America. At this time, the Atlantic Ocean and Gulf of Mexico did not exist, but a large wedge-shaped seaway, Tethys, separated the former Laurasia and Gondwanaland blocks between the Mediterranean and opening to the east. The equator transected Mexico, the Sahara Desert, and northern India, continuing eastward to divide the Tethys seaway. The South Pole was slightly offshore of the western base of the Palmer Peninsula, and the North Pole was in eastern Siberia.

During the Late Triassic, Pangaea began to break up as North America moved away from Europe and northwest Africa. The resultant narrow North Atlantic Ocean and Caribbean-Gulf of Mexico widened in the Jurassic and Cretaceous, reaching something near the present size and shape by the end of the period. Starting in the Jurassic, North America pulled away from South America, leaving a Caribbean-Gulf of Mexico seaway connecting the Atlantic and Pacific. The South Atlantic opened later in the Cretaceous, resulting in a relatively narrow strait be-tween Africa and South America by the end of the Mesozoic. The Late Triassic also was the time during which India, Australia, and Antarctica began moving away from Africa as a single block. India separated from the Australian-Antarctica block as movement continued and, in the Late Jurassic, Madagascar split from Africa. Later, Cenozoic, movement divided Antarctica and Australia and fused Peninsular India to Asia, eventually resulting in the present configuration of lands surrounding the Indian Ocean.

By the end of the Cretaceous, the equator passed just north of South America, crossed Africa at the southern margin of the Sahara, clipped the southwest corner of Arabia, traversed India along a north-south line through western India, and crossed Sumatra and Java. The North Pole was in the Arctic Ocean off western Siberia, and the South Pole lay within Antarctica.

Movement of the continents and opening of ocean basins caused compressional deformation of the earth's crust accompanied by massive igneous intrusion. The Andes and the mountains of western North America resulted from North and South America moving westward over oceanic crust in the Pacific Basin. Thrust faulting, folding, and batholithic (igneous) intrusion began in the Late Jurassic from Califor-nia and Nevada northward to British Columbia and Alaska. This process continued during the Cretaceous, spreading to South America, the Palmer Peninsula, and northwest Antarctica. Similar deformation associated with subduction also took place along the northern margin of the Tethys seaway from the Mediterranean through the Balkans, Caucasus, and into Indonesia. Rifting along the east coast of North America from Nova Scotia to Florida caused fault-block mountains and major basaltic flows as the Atlantic Ocean began opening in the Triassic and early Jurassic. Similar rifting with mountain making and basaltic flows occurred in South Africa, India, and Australia as the eastern part of Gondwanaland fragmented during the Late Triassic through the Cretaceous.

Triassic sedimentary deposits are characterized by terrestrial red beds laid down on the supercontinent, Pangaea, under arid climatic conditions. These conditions occur between paleolatitudes (lines of latitude shown on the present pattern of land and sea where those lines existed in the past) from 10 to 30 degrees north and south. Thus, red beds were deposited north of the equator, from the north coast of Africa through Spain and Germany to the Ural Mountains and northwestward into Britain and Scandinavia. Similar rocks in East Greenland and southwestern North America are part of the same belt, as well as red beds in the rift valley system between Nova Scotia and Florida. Red beds and evaporites (salt and associated minerals precipitated from evaporating water) also accumulated in a parallel southern belt in Brazil, South Africa, Madagascar, eastern India, Australia, and Antarctica. Triassic marine rocks are sparse because Pangaea stood well above sea level during most of the Triassic, but fairly complete sequences do occur between the Alps and southern China along the northern margin of the Tethys seaway. Similarly, marine Triassic sediments occur in the Alps and western Cordillera of North America, which then were on the continental side of a subduction zone. Epicontinental seas encroached on both the Americas and Eurasia from these bordering areas, leaving marine rocks interbedded with the great red bed accumulations on their western and southern margins.

Growth and expansion of spreading centers as Pangaea began breaking up probably caused the advance of epicontinental seas in the Jurassic through Middle Cretaceous. Resultant marine sedimentary rocks are widespread in North America from the Rocky Mountains westward and in western Europe. In addition, growth of mountain ranges along continental margins, as a result of either subduction or collision, led to extensive alluvial (river or stream) deposition. Also, relatively deep sea deposition continued in subduction zones bordering the Pacific and the northern shore of Tethys. Epicontinental seas also encroached on the western Americas prior to the Late Jurassic and were responsible for extensive deposits in western Europe. As the North Atlantic opened, Late Jurassic deposits first filled the Nova Scotia to Florida rift zone and then overlapped the continent in the Middle Jurassic and into the Cretaceous. Also, a great evaporite basin in the Gulf of Mexico area accumulated Jurassic salt deposits. Rising mountains from California to western Canada shed extensive alluvial deposits eastward as far as central Kansas during the latest Jurassic. Widespread alluvial deposits associated with basalt flows in India, Australia, Antarctica, Madagascar, and New Zealand. Terrestrial, coal-bearing rocks also border the northern and western shores of marginal seas from Iran to Siberia.

Processes responsible for Jurassic depositional events accelerated in the Cretaceous, with maximum expansion of epicontinental seas in the middle of the period. Drying and filling of most of these seas followed as a result of expanded mountain making toward the end of the Cretaceous. Thus, deep-water, continental margin deposition continued around the Pacific perimeter and on the southern margin of Eurasia until these basins were engulfed by growing mountain chains. Epicontinental seas expanded over Europe west of the Urals, western and northern Africa, central Australia, western and northern South America, and on the Atlantic coast of North America. In addition, a new seaway opened between the Arctic Ocean and the Gulf of Mexico, separating the rising mountains of the western Cordillera from the eroded stumps of the Appalachians. Widespread chalk deposits characterize these seas in areas remote from actively rising mountains, including the notable chalk cliffs of Dover and Normandy. The rising western North and South American mountains, however, shed abundant detritus to their east in the form of alluvial plains, deltas, and muddy marine deposits, which very nearly filled the North American midcontinent seaway by the end of the Mesozoic. Most, but not all, of the other Cretaceous epicontinental seas either dried up or were greatly constricted at the end of the period or early in the Tertiary.

Early Mesozoic plants resembled those of the preceding Paleozoic. Primitive Carboniferous coal swamp plants persisted in restricted moist environments in the Northern Hemisphere but died out at the end of the Triassic. Cycadeoids, gingkos, conifers, and ferns dominated Triassic through Early Cretaceous floras, with the cycads, primitive conifers—including the auracariaceans of the Petrified Forest— and gingkos first expanding in the Triassic. This plant life was joined by more modern conifers and early relatives of cypress in the warmer, moister Jurassic and Early Cretaceous. Abruptly, in the middle of the Cretaceous, modern broad-leaved trees appeared and quickly dominated the forests. Thus, Late Cretaceous forests closely resembled those of the present.

Large amphibians, along with an expanding contingent of reptiles, constituted the terrestrial vertebrate fauna at the beginning of the Triassic period. Phytosaurs (large crocodile-like reptiles) were the dominant reptiles, but the first dinosaurs appeared in the Late Triassic, along with the first ichthyosaurs (porpoiselike reptiles), nothosaurs (ancestors of plesiosaurs), and the first turtle. The first frogs also were Triassic. Mammal-like reptiles (reptiles with skeletons similar to mammals), living mostly in the Southern Hemisphere, declined during the Triassic but probably gave rise to the first mammals late in the period. One small animal, *Protoavis*, is variously thought to have been a peculiar dinosaur or the first bird.

Rapid dinosaur diversification in the Jurassic led to bipedal (two-footed) and quadrupedal (four-footed) forms as well as both herbivores and carnivores. *Brachiosaurus*, a quadrupedal herbivore, was probably the largest land animal of all time. Other, bizarre, nondinosaurian, reptiles also appeared in the Jurassic. Ichthyosaurs and the first plesiosaurs (large animals with long necks and tails and four paddles for limbs) became abundant in the seas, and the first batlike pterosaurs invaded the skies. The only mammals were small, inconspicuous, and generalized. *Archaeopteryx*, largely because feather fossils are preserved, generally is considered to be the first bird.

Dinosaurs continued to dominate terrestrial Cretaceous faunas but began a slow decline culminating in extinction at the end of the period. Large sauropods (quadrupedal, herbivorous saurischians, saurischians being "reptile-hipped" dinosaurs) declined throughout and disappeared before the end of the period. Theropods (bipedal saurischians with short forelimbs), including *Tyrannosaurus*, the largest known terrestrial carnivore, also declined, but a few persisted to the end of the period. Ornithischians ("bird-hipped" dinosaurs) include a number of quadrupedal herbivores. One of these, *Triceratops*, with its distinctive three horns and fringed neck, persisted to the very end of the Cretaceous. Other, bipedal, ornithischians include the duckbilled dinosaurs. Pterosaurs also declined to extinction at the end of the period, but one of them, *Quetzalcoatlus*, was a giant, having a wingspan of 10 meters. Ichthyosaurs declined, but plesiosaurs were abundant, along with giant lizardlike mosasaurs in the marine fauna. All, however, became extinct at or before the end of the Cretaceous. The Cretaceous also saw the rise of turtles, snakes, lizards, and crocodilians—all currently prominent reptiles. Mammals of the time included both marsupials (mammals retaining the newborn in a pouch on the mother's abdomen) and placentals (mammals in which the young are not nurtured in a pouch). All of them were small, resembling modern shrews and insectivores, but include the ancestors of all modern mammals. Cretaceous birds are rare, but a diversity of toothed birds are known, including the flightless, marine, diving bird *Hesperornis*. More modern birds appear in the very latest Cretaceous.

Chondrostian fish (ray-finned, but with largely cartilaginous skeletons) diversified greatly in the Early Triassic as sharks declined and more primitive fish characteristic of the Paleozoic persisted in low numbers and variety. Cartilaginous fish, including sharks, continued to be dominant in the Jurassic, but holostean fish gave rise to the first teleosts (bony fish) in the Late Jurassic. This group continued to expand and diversify in the Cretaceous and persists to the present.

Primitive insects occur sporadically in Triassic through Middle Cretaceous fossil faunas, but were reduced to a minor role by an explosive appearance of very modern-appearing insects accompanying the appearance of broad-leaved forest trees in the Middle Cretaceous.

Marine invertebrates suffered extensive extinction in the Permo-Triassic transition. The Paleozoic corals, trilobites, and graptolites completely disappeared, and other groups, such as brachiopods, bryozoans, and crinoids, were decimated. By Late Triassic, however, new organisms had occupied the environments inhabited by the extinguished animals. Modern corals, not at all closely related to Paleozoic corals, already were constructing reefs. The old bryozoans were replaced by new bryozoan types, and the reduction in brachiopods was matched by expansion among the pelecypods (clams, oysters, and scallops). Ammonites, descended from a single group of shelled cephalopods surviving into the Early Triassic, quickly evolved into many species, so much so that the Mesozoic is known as the age of ammonites as well as the age of dinosaurs. Other characteristic organisms appeared during the Jurassic and Cretaceous, including rudistid clams (giant pelecypods that built reefs), a wide variety of echinoids (sea urchins and sand dollars), globigerinids and other planktonic foraminifera (single-celled animals secreting shells), and coccoliths (single-celled, planktonic algae secreting minute carbonate plates), along with crabs, shrimp, and lobsters. Globigerinids and coccoliths became sufficiently abundant in the early part of the Late Cretaceous to cause worldwide deposition of chalk and chalky limestone.

At the end of the Mesozoic, many organisms had become extinct, including dinosaurs and ammonites. These extinctions, though not as extensive as those at the end of the Paleozoic, are the reason for recognizing separate Mesozoic and Cenozoic eras. Not all the characteristic Mesozoic animals that failed to survive into the Cenozoic, however, became extinct at the very end of the period. In addition, very little change occurred in the flora, as the major change took place in the middle of the Cretaceous.

Close examination of the rocks at the Mesozoic-Cenozoic boundary as defined by occurrences of planktonic foraminifera, coccoliths, ammonites, and dinosaurs has uncovered the widespread occurrence of a thin layer containing anomalous concentrations of iridium and, more questionably, sooty material and minerals of the sort associated with meteoritic impacts. This evidence has been used to advance a theory that the end-of-Cretaceous extinctions were caused by meteoritic impact, perhaps through drastic cooling caused by vast quantities of dust and smoke thrown into the atmosphere. Physical evidence of an actual impact has not convinced all researchers, however, and many paleontologists do not feel that the gradual disappearance of the Mesozoic fauna can readily be explained by an instantaneous event, even though it might be synchronous with the final extinctions.

Mesozoic rocks are rich in mineral fuels. Coal is sparse in the Triassic, reflecting the aridity of the time. Much coal, however, occurs in the Jurassic of Asia, deposited on alluvial plains north of the Tethyan orogenic belt, and even more extensive deposits in the Cretaceous of North America and northern South America are in a similar position relating to the growing western American mountains. Jurassic and Cretaceous oil and gas are very important, especially around the Gulf of Mexico and in the Persian Gulf region. Triassic ore deposits are rare because of little mountain building and igneous intrusion, but Jurassic and Cretaceous metallic ores are very extensive. The gold of the California Mother Lode is in Jurassic rocks, and many of the precious and base metal reserves of the Rocky Mountains and the Andes are Cretaceous. Similarly, the mountains formed elsewhere on the Pacific Rim and on the northern margin of the Tethys are rich in metallic ores. Finally, the diamond pipes of southern Africa are Cretaceous.

Methods of Study

Mesozoic history has been unraveled through application of general geological principles of petrography (study of the origin of rocks), stratigraphy (study of the relationships between rock bodies), structural geology (study of deformation of the earth's crust), and paleontology (study of fossils).

Individual masses of rock of similar character (formations, intrusions, or metamorphic terrains) are defined, and their distribution is mapped on and below the earth's surface. Each rock body then is interpreted as the record of an event in earth history, such as the accumulation of a beach, intrusion of molten rock material, or alteration of a part of the earth's crust by extreme deformation or deep burial. Interpretation is accomplished through application of the principle of uniformitarianism, which states that the nature of past geologic events must be inferred from knowledge of present-day chemical, physical, and biological processes. For example, rocks displaying the same materials and sedimentary structures seen on a modern mud flat are assumed to have originated as deposits on a mud flat.

Analysis of geometric relationships between formations and other rock bodies, their stratigraphy, allows scientists to place the events that they represent in chronological succession and to outline the geographic extent of past environments. Thus, the succession of formations at a given point records a succession of events occurring at that point according to the principle of superposition. Superposition states that a rock unit covering or disrupting another rock unit is the younger of the two, and that events responsible for faulting (breaking) or folding layers of rock are more recent than the events responsible for the affected rock units. For example, delta muds succeeded by beach sands, which are overlain in turn by marine muds containing fossils, indicate expansion of the sea onto the land. Furthermore, the position of the beach deposits over an area records the advance of the strandline, or shoreline, over time.

Structural geologists plot the faults, folds, and igneous intrusions that tell when and where mountains formed during the Mesozoic as well as throughout geologic time. Mesozoic time is defined as the time during which Mesozoic organisms were in existence. Thus, appearance of ammonites above occurrences of Paleozoic fossils indicates the beginning of the Mesozoic record in a succession of rocks. The abrupt disappearance of ammonites or dinosaurs similarly signals the end of the Mesozoic. Meticulous description of fossils and careful noting of their range of occurrence within rock sequences make possible determination of the beginning and end of the Mesozoic. Furthermore, the three Mesozoic periods and systems (rocks representing a period) and their subdivisions down to the most minute increments of time, chrons, which are represented by zones of rock, are all defined by fossil occurrences. In addition to ammonite zones, zones based on globigerinids and, in the Cretaceous, on coccoliths, provide the most refined time scale. The average length of a Cretaceous chron defined by an ammonite zone is only 900,000 years—much less than a reasonable percentage of expected error in a radiogenic age determination. These fossil-defined chrons, though the most discriminant available units of time, do not provide dates in years before the present for geologic events. They reveal only the succession of events, not their duration in years.

Spontaneous decay of unstable isotopes of certain elements provides a means of determining the rock's age in years. In using radiogenic isotopes, it is assumed that the element in question was originally present in the mineral under analysis in a fixed proportion and that the ratio of radiogenic isotopes to nonradiogenic isotopes was the same as in presently known minerals. It is also assumed that decay proceeded at a constant rate as known presently. Furthermore, it is assumed that no radiogenic material or decay products have been added or subtracted from the rock in question subsequent to its original formation. If all of this is true, then the amount of decay product in comparison to the amount of undecayed radiogenic isotope provides a means of calculating the time in years required to produce the present state of affairs. Dates derived in this way may then be used to determine the age in years of the rocks containing the fossils used in zoning the Mesozoic. Also, in spite of the margin of error inherent in the radiogenic technique, the average length of chrons included within a major time unit, such as a period, can be determined with reasonable accuracy. In actual practice, however, widely differing dates for the initiation of time periods are frequently advanced, mostly because of additions or losses of radiogenic and/or decay product in specific samples or because of difficulty in relating radiogenic dates, which are mostly derived from unfossiliferous igneous rocks, to fossil-determined temporal subdivisions. Nevertheless, substantial progress has been made, and most dates for the periods and their major subdivisions are now reasonably well known. Further cooperation among geologic mappers, paleontologists, and radiogenic dating specialists will, undoubtedly, bring continued improvement.

Context

The Mesozoic era is a major subdivision of geologic time, beginning about 225 million years before the present and ending about 65 million years before the present. It follows the Paleozoic and is succeeded by the Cenozoic era. The Mesozoic is defined as the time during which the rocks and fossils of the Triassic, Jurassic, and Cretaceous periods were deposited.

During the Mesozoic, the world's flora and fauna evolved from the archaic plants and animals of the Paleozoic to creatures of very nearly modern aspect. Primitive Paleozoic plants characteristic of the Coal Measures (Late Paleozoic coal-bearing rocks) first were replaced by cycads and early conifers during the Triassic to Middle Cretaceous. At that time, modern forest trees suddenly appeared and have persisted to the present. The formerly dominant large amphibians were reduced to a subordinate role with the appearance of a spectacular assemblage of dinosaurs and other large reptiles constituting the Late Triassic through Cretaceous "dinosaur" fauna. These reptiles then all became extinct, clearing the way for the rise of modern mammals in the Cenozoic. The first small and obscure mammals evolved from a group of mammal-like reptiles in the Triassic but were never an important component of the fauna during the Mesozoic. The oldest generally recognized bird is Jurassic, but Mesozoic birds remained rare and were very unlike modern birds, having teeth for the most part. The modern insect fauna began to appear in the Middle Cretaceous, apparently adapted to the new forest plants that also evolved at that time. In the oceans, relatively modern corals, clams, oysters, scallops, crabs, lobsters, and other marine invertebrates evolved in the Mesozoic. Ammonites, however, appear at the beginning of the Mesozoic, and their disappearance marks the end of the period.

World geography also underwent change, from a situation in which all the world's continents were fused into a single supercontinent, called Pangaea, to a nearly modern map of the oceans and continents. In the process, North and South America separated from each other and from Pangaea, thus initiating the Atlantic Ocean and, as a strait connecting Atlantic and Pacific, the Gulf-Caribbean basin. In addition, Antarctica, Australia, Peninsular India, Madagascar, and the other lands around the Indian Ocean separated from one another and from Africa. By the end of the Mesozoic, most of these landmasses had moved to approximately their present positions, with the exception of Peninsular India, which had yet to join the Asian continent.

Subduction (the overriding of one plate of the earth's crust by another) of oceanic crust beneath continents caused major mountain making on the periphery of the Pacific Ocean and on the southern margin of Europe and Asia. The western American cordillera and the Andes formed between the Middle Jurassic and the Early Cenozoic in this manner. Also, extensive mountains rose on the south side of the Eurasian continent, beginning in the Late Mesozoic but culminating, for the most part, in the Cenozoic. A different kind of mountain caused by rifts, fault blocks, and extensive lava piles, formed where the continents split apart. Features of this sort border the east coast of North America and southern Africa and also occur in southeastern Australia, on Peninsular India, and in Antarctica.

Many of the world's metallic mineral deposits are associated with mountain ranges formed by subduction during the Jurassic and Cretaceous. Major accumulations of coal and petroleum also occur in Jurassic and Cretaceous rocks.

Bibliography

Arkell, W. J. *Jurassic Geology of the World*. Edinburgh: Oliver and Boyd, 1956. A summary description of the Jurassic rocks of the world, their location and age, as determined in detail by fossil content. A professional work with an extensive bibliography.

Kummel, Bernhard. *History of the Earth: An Introduction to Historical Geology*. 2d ed. San Francisco: W. H. Freeman, 1978. A brief account of all of the rocks of the earth's crust, including the Mesozoic, and their history. Also, a history of life. This beginning, college-level text antedates plate tectonic theory but is still the best comprehensive description of all the world's Mesozoic rocks and fossils in a single volume.

Levin, Harold L. *The Earth Through Time*. 3d ed. Philadelphia: Saunders College Publishing, 1988. A history of the earth, emphasizing North America. Especially good account of the fossil record. A beginning college text.

Seyfert, Carl K., and Leslie A. Sirkin. *Earth History and Plate Tectonics*. 2d ed. New York: Harper & Row, 1979. A history of the earth, including the Mesozoic, emphasizing plate tectonics (evolution of continents and ocean basins). Also covers other aspects of the earth's history. A college text of moderate technical level.

Stanley, Steven M. *Earth and Life Through Time*. 2d ed. New York: W. H. Freeman, 1989. All aspects of the earth's history, including the Mesozoic, are covered in this book. Especially comprehensive for the history of life; good coverage of Europe. A beginning college text, easy to read but not superficial.

Ralph L. Langenheim, Jr.

Cross-References

Biostratigraphy, 173; The Cenozoic Era, 202; Continental Growth, 268; The Cretaceous-Tertiary Boundary, 303; Dinosaurs, 370; The Evolution of Life, 655; The Geologic Time Scale, 874; Gondwanaland and Pangaea, 982; Island Arcs, 1261; Mass Extinctions, 1514; Micropaleontology: Microfossils, 1674; Ocean Basins, 1785; The Oceanic Crust, 1846; Paleobiogeography, 1984; Paleoclimatology, 1993; The Paleozoic Era, 2018; Stratigraphic Correlation, 2485; Subduction and Orogeny, 2497.

METAMICTIZATION

Type of earth science: Geology
Field of study: Mineralogy and crystallography

Metamictization breaks down the original crystal structure of certain rare minerals to a glassy state by radioactive decay of uranium and thorium. It is accompanied by marked changes in properties and often water content. Many minerals start to lose their radioactive components upon metamictization. Those that do not may be candidates for synthetic rocks grown from high-level nuclear wastes in order to isolate them until they are safe.

Principal terms

ALPHA PARTICLE: a helium nucleus emitted during the radioactive decay of uranium, thorium, or other unstable nuclei

CRYSTAL: a solid made up of a regular periodic arrangement of atoms; its form and physical properties express the repeat units of the structure

GLASS: a solid with no regular periodic arrangement of atoms; that is, an amorphous solid

GRANITE: a light-colored igneous rock made up mainly of three minerals, two feldspars, and quartz, with variable amounts of darker minerals

ISOTOPES: atoms of the same element with identical numbers of protons but different numbers of neutrons in their nuclei

ISOTROPIC: having properties that are the same in all directions—the opposite of anisotropic, having properties that vary with direction

PEGMATITE: a very coarse-grained granitic rock, often enriched in rare minerals

SILICATE: a substance whose structure includes silicon surrounded by four oxygen atoms in the shape of a tetrahedron

SPONTANEOUS FISSION: uninduced splitting of unstable atomic nuclei into two smaller nuclei, an energetic form of radioactive decay

X RAY: a photon with much higher energy than light and a much shorter wavelength; its wavelength is about the same as the spacing between atoms in crystal structures

Summary of the Phenomenon

Metamict minerals are an anomaly. They have the form of crystals, but in all other ways they resemble glasses. They fracture like glass, are optically isotropic like glass, and to all appearances are noncrystalline. Yet minerals cannot grow without an ordered crystalline arrangement of their constituent atoms—even metamict ones. The term "metamict" is from the Greek roots *meta* + *miktos*, meaning "after + mixed." It aptly describes minerals that must originally have grown as crystals and subsequently have been rendered glassy by some process that has destroyed their original crystallinity. Scientists and gem collectors have known of metamict minerals for hundreds of years, but only relatively recently, with the discovery of radioactivity and all its effects, has the cause of metamictization become clear. The discovery that all metamict minerals are at least slightly radioactive and that metamict grains have more uranium or thorium than do their nonmetamict equivalents led to the realization that radiation damage resulting from the decay of uranium and thorium causes metamictization. Although controversial at first, the concept of radiation damage is now so easy for scientists to accept that the puzzle is not why some minerals become metamict, but why others with relatively large concentrations of uranium and thorium never do.

The varieties and chemical compositions of minerals that undergo metamictization are quite diverse. Yet all metamict minerals share several common properties: they are all radioactive, with measurable contents of uranium, thorium, or both; they are glassy, brittle, and fracture like glass; they are usually optically isotropic for both visible and infrared light; they are amorphous to X-ray diffraction; and they often have nonmetamict equivalents with the same form and essentially the same composition. Finally, compared to their nonmetamict equivalents, they have lower indices of refraction, are more darkly colored, are softer, are less dense, are more soluble in acids, and contain more water. In those minerals that exhibit a range of metamictization from crystalline to metamict, partially metamict samples have intermediate properties. For example, X-ray diffraction patterns of zircon show that radiation damage causes it to swell markedly in proportion to accumulated radiation damage up to the point of total metamictization. Beyond that point, the structure is so disordered that it can no longer diffract X rays, even though a continued decrease in density indicates further expansion. Changes in other properties parallel the decrease in density. Partially metamict zircons that are heated at temperatures well below the melting point recrystallize readily to grains that are aligned with their original form, while those that are completely metamict recrystallize just as readily, but not to the original alignment. Several other metamict minerals recrystallize in the same way, but many produce mixtures of different minerals on heating because either they are outside their fields of stability or their compositions have changed subsequent to metamictization.

Metamict minerals belong to only a few broad groups of chemical compounds. In each group, some have uranium or thorium as the dominant metal ion present, but most have only small amounts substituting in the crystal structure for other ions, such as zirconium, yttrium, and the lanthanide rare earth elements (REE), which just happen to have similar sizes and charges. This is known as isomorphous substitution and is common in most mineral groups.

The largest group of metamict minerals are yttrium-, REE-, uranium-, and thorium-bearing complex multiple oxides of niobium, tantalum, and titanium. All the metal-oxygen bonds in these minerals have about equal strength and about equal susceptibility to radiation damage. As it happens, most of these minerals have little resistance to metamictization and are commonly found in the metamict state.

Samarskite, brannerite, and columbite are examples of complex multiple oxide minerals. Samarskite is always totally metamict and compositionally altered with added water. It usually recrystallizes to a mixture of different minerals on heating, making its original structure and chemical formula hard to determine. Brannerite can range from partially to totally metamict. It has been found to be the primary site for uranium in some 1,400-million-year-old granites from the southwestern United States. In those rocks, it was recrystallized as recently as 80 million years ago, but even in that geologically short period of time, it has become metamict again. Columbite is never more than partially metamict. Apparently, the presence of iron in its formula helps prevent metamictization from progressing as far as it does in other niobates. These minerals are generally found in coarse-grained pegmatites associated with granites. They may also be found as accessory minerals within the granites themselves, but even when they account for most of the rock's uranium or thorium, they are so rare that it takes special concentrating techniques simply to find a few grains.

Silicates are the largest group of minerals in the earth's crust, but they account for only the second largest number of metamict minerals. They are characterized by having very strongly bonded silicon-oxygen groups in their crystal structures. Each silicon ion is surrounded by four oxygen ions in a tetrahedral (three-sided pyramid) shape. The chemical bonding between silicon and oxygen in the tetrahedral group is considerably stronger than the bonding between oxygen and any other metal ions in the structure and is more resistant to radiation damage. The only silicates susceptible to metamictization are those in which the tetrahedral groups are not linked to form strong chains, sheets, or networks that make the structure resistant to radiation damage. The most commonly occurring metamict mineral is zircon, a zirconium silicate with isolated tetrahedral groups. Only a small amount of uranium can substitute for zirconium in the structure, up to about 1.5 percent, but it is usually less than 0.5 percent. Up to about 0.1 percent of thorium can also be present. These small amounts are sufficient to cause zircon to occur in a wide range of degrees of metamictization. Zircon is only one member of a group of silicates that grow with essentially the same crystal structure and subsequently become metamict. Thorite (thorium silicate) and coffinite (uranium silicate) also belong to that group. They each require about the same amount of radiation damage as does zircon to become metamict, but because their concentrations of radioactive elements are much higher, metamictization occurs much more quickly.

Phosphates are the smallest group of metamict minerals, and they are usually found only partially metamict. One of particular interest is xenotime (yttrium phosphate), which has the same crystal structure as zircon. It commonly occurs in the same rocks as zircon, with equal or even greater contents of uranium and thorium, but is usually much less radiation damaged. Similarly, monazite (a rare earth phosphate) has the same structure as huttonite, a mineral with the same composition as thorite, and takes up about the same amount of uranium and considerably more thorium than does zircon but is seldom more than slightly damaged. Apparently, the substitution of phosphorus for silicon in these structures makes the phosphates less susceptible to metamictization than are the equivalent silicates.

Although all metamict minerals are radioactive, not all radioactive minerals are metamict. Besides the phosphates, there are several other radioactive minerals that are never found in the completely metamict state. Among them are the oxides of uranium (uraninite), thorium (thorianite), and cerium (cerianite); fluorocarbonates such as bastnaesite and parisite; and some fluorides. These minerals must be less susceptible to the accumulation of radiation damage than are the metamict minerals. It may be that they undergo self-repair as fast as they are damaged. One thing that most have in common is that they do not retain the products of radioactive decay within their structures.

In order to understand metamictization fully, one must also understand how the radioactive decay of uranium and thorium damages crystal structures. In nature, uranium and thorium are both made up of a number of isotopes. Their most common isotopes are uranium 238, uranium 235, and thorium 232. Each of these isotopes decays, through a series of emissions of alpha particles, into an isotope of lead—lead 206, lead 207, and lead 208, respectively. The alpha particle is emitted from the decaying nucleus with great energy, and the emitting nucleus recoils simultaneously in the opposite direction. The energy transmitted to the mineral structure by the alpha particle and the recoiling nucleus is the major cause of radiation damage. The alpha particle has a very short range in the mineral structure (only about 20 wavelengths of light) and imparts most of its energy to it by ionizing the atoms it passes. Near the end of its path, when it has slowed down enough, it can collide with hundreds of atoms. The much larger recoil nucleus has a path that is about a thousand times shorter, but it collides with ten times as many atoms. Thus, the greatest amount of radiation damage is caused by the recoil nucleus rather than the alpha particle itself. Both particles introduce an intense amount of heat in a very small region of the structure, disrupting it but also increasing the rate at which the damage is spontaneously repaired. The accumulation of radiation damage depends on a balance between the damage and self-repair processes. In simple terms, radioactive minerals that remain crystalline have high rates of self-repair, while those that become metamict do not.

Another contribution to radiation damage in uranium-bearing minerals is the spontaneous fission of uranium 238, in which its nucleus splits into two separate nuclei of lighter elements. That process is much more energetic than is alpha emission, but it happens at a much lower rate. It probably produces only about one-tenth to one-fifteenth the damage that alpha emission and alpha recoil cause. The radiation damage done by the decay of uranium and thorium is not always confined to the metamict mineral itself. The decay process also involves the emission of gamma rays that penetrate the surrounding rock, often causing the development of dark halos in the host minerals. Metamict grains are also often surrounded by a thin, rust-colored, iron-rich rim at their contact with other minerals. These rims are enriched in uranium and lead that have leaked out of the damaged grain as well as the iron from the surrounding rock. These phenomena draw dark outlines around radioactive grains and make them easy to spot in most granites and pegmatites.

Methods of Study

Scientists have used a diverse range of analytical techniques to study the metamictization phenomenon, including X-ray diffraction and other X-ray methods, electron diffraction, high-resolution electron microscopy, and infrared spectroscopy. X-ray diffraction results from the reinforcement of X-ray reflections by repeated planes of atoms in a crystal. The diffraction pattern is characteristic of each crystal structure and depends on the spacing of the planes. The strength of diffraction peaks depends on the atomic density in the diffracting planes and on the regularity of the crystal structure. If the structure is damaged, both the intensity and the sharpness of the diffraction peaks decrease. Glasses produce no X-ray diffraction pattern, because there is no long-range order or regularity in their structures and thus no planes of atoms on which X rays can diffract. They are said to be "X-ray amorphous."

X-ray diffraction studies of metamict minerals have shown them to resemble glasses in being devoid of a regular crystal structure. In partially metamict samples, the spacing between planes increases and the regularity of the structure decreases with progressive radiation damage. For example, in some 570-million-year-old zircons, 0.25 percent uranium is enough to make them X-ray amorphous—completely metamict. Much older zircons from other localities with higher uranium contents, however, yield X-ray patterns that reveal them to be only slightly damaged. In those areas, a relatively recent geologic event caused the zircons to be completely recrystallized with partial loss of lead, produced by radioactive decay of uranium and thorium, but little or no loss of uranium or thorium themselves.

Once a mineral is X-ray amorphous, X-ray diffraction is not as effective as is X-ray absorption spectroscopy for studying its structure. The way that a material absorbs X rays depends on the spacing of the atoms in it. X-ray absorption spectroscopy has shown that the spacing between adjacent ions is little changed in metamict minerals, but the regularity at greater distances has been lost. It has also shown that among complex multiple oxides, their crystal structures are highly regular and easily distinguished, but their metamict structures are nearly indistinguishable. Thus, the oxides all approach the same glassy state on metamictization.

Electron diffraction from single grains of metamict minerals yields results very similar to those of X-ray diffraction techniques. For example, it has been shown that partially metamict zircons are made up of misaligned crystalline domains that are destroyed with progressive metamictization.

High-resolution electron microscopy allows the scientist to examine a mineral's structure directly. While actual atoms cannot be seen, the regularity of the array of atoms making up the structure can. Applied to zircons, this technique has shown that fission particles from the spontaneous fission of uranium 238 leave long tracks of disruption behind them as they pass through the crystal structure. In partially metamict zircons, highly disordered damaged patches (called domains) are interspersed with undamaged domains. As metamictization proceeds, the damaged domains begin to overlap and eventually wipe out all remaining crystalline domains.

Infrared spectroscopy is a powerful tool for studying the bonds between atoms in minerals. The absorption of infrared light by a crystal structure depends on the strength and regularity of bonds within the structure. Infrared study has shown that the silicon-oxygen bonds of the tetrahedral groups in zircon remain intact to a large extent even in metamict samples, while the regularity of virtually every zirconium-oxygen bond has been disturbed. Thus, silicon remains surrounded by four oxygen atoms even in the most metamict zircons when the regularity of the formerly crystalline structure has been destroyed. Infrared spectroscopy is also often used to study the occurrence of water in minerals. Because most metamict minerals are enriched in water to some extent, its role in producing or stabilizing the metamict state is a question of some interest. Infrared studies of zircons in a wide range of metamict states show that while there is no water in their structures, small amounts of hydroxyl are common. The existence of "dry" zircons in all states from crystalline to metamict, however, shows that neither water nor hydroxyl is necessary to the metamictization process. The tendency for metamict zircons to have more hydroxyl than do less damaged samples suggests that hydroxyl enters zircons only after metamictization has opened up their structures sufficiently for it to diffuse in.

Context

Metamict minerals are important to people for two principal reasons. First, some gemstones, such as zircon, occur in the metamict state, and several others, such as topaz, can be enhanced in appearance by irradiation. Metamict gemstones are often considerably more valuable than the crystalline varieties, because the anisotropic optical properties of the crystalline gems make them look "fuzzy" inside and less beautiful than the isotropic metamict stones. Radiation damage also often imparts color to the gemstone, increasing its value. (Artificial means of imparting color to gemstones by irradiation have been developed, but the gem often fades back to its original color with time. Consequently, it is best to know the entire history of a colored gem, or have it examined by a knowledgeable and trustworthy expert, before investing large amounts of money in it.)

Second, and ultimately more important, the understanding of metamictization may someday be invaluable to the safe disposal of high-level nuclear wastes. Ways must be found to keep high-level wastes from leaking into the environment and poisoning groundwater for a period of at least ten thousand years—after which they will have lost most of their radioactivity. The only way that scientists can determine what could conceivably lock up hazardous, highly radioactive atoms for that length of time is to examine results of long-term experiments on potentially leak-proof containers—solid materials that could be grown from the radioactive wastes that would be impervious to alteration, breakdown, or damage. The "experiments" of that duration are those that have already occurred in nature: radioactive minerals that have been damaged internally for millennia. Geochemists have found that some minerals retain their radioactive elements over millions of years despite metamictization, while others do not. Synthetic analogues of the ones that do may be grown from a mixture of the radioactive elements and added compounds to produce man-made rocks that are resistant to leaching and that have the potential to trap the hazardous substances for the required time.

Bibliography

Deer, W. A., R. A. Howie, and J. Zussman. *Rock-Forming Minerals.* Vol. 1A, *Orthosilicates.* 2d ed. New York: Longman, 1982.

——————. *Rock-Forming Minerals.* Vol. 1B, *Disilicates and Ring Silicates.* 2d ed. New York: Longman, 1986.

——————. *Rock-Forming Minerals.* Vol. 5, *Non-Silicates.* New York: Longman, 1962. These are part of a five-volume set that describes the most important rock-forming minerals. Metamict minerals are covered in the three volumes listed: oxides and phosphates in volume 5, silicates in the expanded volumes 1A and 1B. The discussion of metamictization in the volumes for zircon and allanite is especially lucid and complete. As a whole, the work is well written, very well illustrated, and well indexed—an indispensable reference for geologists. Suitable for college-level students.

Fleischer, M. *Glossary of Mineral Species.* 5th ed. Tucson, Ariz.: The Mineralogical Record, 1987. This glossary is an alphabetical listing of all currently accepted mineral names and formulas, along with the now-accepted assignments of discredited names. Includes separate lists of important mineral groups as well as the chemical word-formulas for several minerals. Does not include a list of minerals by chemical contents. Not indexed or illustrated and has a minimum of text. Suitable for anyone needing the formula of a particular mineral, but less suitable for identifying a mineral from its composition.

Hurlbut, C. S., Jr., and G. S. Switzer. *Gemology.* New York: John Wiley & Sons, 1979. A well-illustrated and complete introduction to gemstones, describing the methods of study of gems. A good introduction to mineralogy for the nonscientist, this volume includes a section with descriptions of minerals and other materials prized as gems. Suitable for high-school-level readers.

Mitchell, R. S. "Metamict Minerals: A Review, Part 1. Chemical and Physical Characteristics, Occurrence." *The Mineralogical Record* 4 (July/August, 1973): 177.

——————. "Metamict Minerals: A Review, Part 2. Origin of Metamictization, Methods of Analysis, Miscellaneous Topics." *The Mineralogical Record* 4 (September/October, 1973): 214. This pair of articles on metamict minerals covers the process of metamictization in great depth without becoming overly technical.

The Mineralogical Record is written for lay mineral and gem collectors as well as for earth scientists. Its editorial aim is to cover the famous mineral and gem localities of the world with state-of-the-art photography. Several issues have become collector's items. Suitable for anyone interested in gems or minerals.

Smith, David G., ed. *The Cambridge Encyclopedia of Earth Sciences*. New York: Crown Publishers, 1981. Chapter 5, "Earth Materials: Minerals and Rocks," gives a good description of the areas of mineralogy essential to an understanding of metamictization, although there is no discussion of metamict minerals. The text is suitable for college-level readers not intimidated by somewhat technical language. A well-illustrated and carefully indexed reference volume.

James A. Woodhead

Cross-References

Earth's Oldest Rocks, 561; Electron Microscopy, 601; Gem Minerals, 802; Geochronology: Fission Track Dating, 826; Groundwater Pollution, 1028; Infrared Spectra, 1232; Ionic Substitution in Minerals, 1245; Physical Properties of Minerals, 1681; The Structure of Minerals, 1693; Nuclear Waste Disposal, 1758; Radioactive Decay, 2136; Radioactive Minerals, 2143; Stable Isotopes: Water-Rock Interactions, 2462; X-Ray Powder Diffraction, 2751.

METAMORPHIC ROCK CLASSIFICATION

Type of earth science: Geology
Field of study: Petrology, metamorphic

Metamorphic rocks bear witness to the instability of the earth's surface. They reveal the long history of interaction among the plates that comprise the surface and of deep-seated motions within the plates. Among the metamorphic rocks are found many ores and stones of value to human civilization.

Principal terms

CONTACT METAMORPHISM: metamorphism characterized by high temperature but relatively low pressure, usually affecting rock in the vicinity of igneous intrusions

FOLIATION: a texture or structure in which mineral grains are arranged in parallel planes

METAMORPHIC FACIES: an assemblage of minerals characteristic of a given range of pressure and temperature; the members of the assemblage depend on the composition of the protolith

METAMORPHIC GRADE: the degree of metamorphic intensity as indicated by characteristic minerals in a rock or zone

METAMORPHISM: changes in the structure, texture, and mineral content of solid rock as it adjusts to altered conditions of pressure, temperature, and chemical environment

PELITIC ROCK: a rock whose protolith contained abundant clay or similar minerals

PRESSURE-TEMPERATURE REGIME: a sequence of metamorphic facies distinguished by the ratio of pressure to temperature, generally characteristic of a given geologic environment

PROTOLITH: the original igneous or sedimentary rock later affected by metamorphism

REGIONAL METAMORPHISM: metamorphism characterized by strong compression along one direction, usually affecting rocks over an extensive region or belt

TEXTURE: the size, shape, and relationship of grains in a rock

Summary of the Phenomenon

A significant part of the earth's surface is made up of rocks quite different from sedimentary or igneous rocks. Many of them have distinctive textures and structures, such as the wavy, colored bands of gneiss or the layered mica flakes of schist. They often contain certain minerals not found or not common in igneous or sedimentary rocks, such as garnet and staurolite. Studies of their overall chemical composition and their relations to other rocks in the field show that they were once igneous or sedimentary rocks, but, being subjected to high pressure and temperature, they have been distorted and altered or recrystallized through a process called metamorphism. Metamorphism involves both mechanical distortion and recrystallization of minerals present in the original rock, the protolith. It can cause changes in the size, orientation, and distribution of grains already present, or it can cause the growth of new and distinctive minerals built mostly from materials provided by the destruction of minerals that have become unstable under the changed conditions. The chemical components in the rock are simply reorganized into minerals that are more stable under higher pressure and temperature.

Metamorphic rocks can be classified in a purely descriptive fashion according to their textures and dominant minerals. Because the growing understanding of metamorphic processes can be applied to interpret the origin and history of the rocks, they are also classified according to features related to these processes. The most common classification schemes, in addition to the purely descriptive, categorize the rocks by general metamorphic processes, or metamorphic environments; by the original rocks, or protoliths; by metamorphic intensities, or grades; by the general pressure and temperature conditions, called facies; and by the ratios of pressure to temperature, called pressure-temperature regimes.

The oldest classification is purely descriptive, based on the rock texture (especially foliation) and mineral content. Foliation is an arrangement of mineral grains in parallel planes. The most common foliated rocks are slate, schist, and gneiss. In slate, microscopic flakes of mica or chlorite are aligned so that the rock breaks into thin slabs following the easy cleavage of the flakes. Schist contains abundant, easily visible flakes of mica, chlorite, or talc arranged in parallel; it breaks easily along the flakes and has a highly reflective surface. Gneiss contains little mica, but its minerals (commonly quartz, feldspar, and amphibole) are separated into different-colored, parallel bands, which are often contorted or wavy. The foliated rocks can be described further by naming any significant minerals present, such as "garnet schist." Nonfoliated metamorphic rocks lack parallel structure and are usually named after their dominant minerals. Common types are quartzite (mostly quartz), marble (mostly calcite), amphibolite (with dominant amphibole), serpentinite (mostly serpentine), and hornfels (a mixture of quartz, feldspar, garnet, mica, and other minerals). Quartzite breaks through its quartz grains, whose fracture surfaces give the break a glassy sheen. Marble breaks mostly along the cleavage of its calcite crystals, so that each flat cleavage surface has its own glint. Hornfels often exhibits a smooth fracture with a luster reminiscent of a horn.

The second classification of metamorphic rocks is based on the general processes that formed them or the corresponding environments in which they are found. The recognized categories are usually named regional, contact, cataclastic, burial, and hydrothermal metamorphism.

Regional metamorphism is characterized by compression along one direction that is stronger than the pressure resulting from burial. The compression causes foliation, typified by the foliated rocks slate, schist, and gneiss. These rocks are found in extensive regions, often in long, relatively narrow belts parallel to folded mountain ranges. According to the theory of plate tectonics, folded mountain ranges like the Appalachians and the Alps began as thick beds of sediments deposited in deep troughs offshore from continents. The sediments were later caught up between colliding continents, strongly compressed, and finally buckled up into long, parallel folds. The more deeply the original sediment is buried, the more intense is the metamorphism. Clay in the sediment recrystallizes to mica, oriented with the flat cleavage facing the direction of compression. Thus, pelitic or clay-bearing sediments become slates and schists with foliation parallel to the folds of the mountains. At higher temperatures, the mica recrystallizes into feldspar, and the feldspar and quartz migrate into light-colored bands between bands of darker minerals so that the rock becomes gneiss. At yet higher temperatures, some of the minerals melt (a process called anatexis), and the rock, called a migmatite, becomes more like the igneous rock granite.

Contact metamorphic rocks are commonly found near igneous intrusions. Heat from the intrusive magma causes the surrounding rock, called country rock, to recrystallize. Though the rock is under pressure because of burial, there is usually no tendency toward foliation because the pressure is equal from all directions. Some water may be driven into the rock through fine cracks or, conversely, water may be driven from the rock by the heat. Especially mobile atoms such as potassium can migrate into the rock and combine with its minerals to form new crystals (a process called metasomatism). Usually, however, the chemical content is not greatly altered, and recrystallization chiefly involves atoms from smaller crystals or the cement migrating into larger, crystals or forming new minerals. In quartz sandstone, for example, the quartz crystals grow to fill all the pore space in a tight, polygonal network called crystalloblastic texture, and the rock becomes quartzite. Similarly, the tiny crystals in limestone or dolomite grow into space-filling calcite crystals, forming marble or, if other minerals are present, the mixed rock called skarn. Pelitic rocks recrystallize to hornfels, containing a variety of minerals, such as quartz, feldspar, garnet, and mica.

Cataclastic (or dynamic) metamorphism occurs along fault zones, where both the rock and individual grains are intensely sheared and smeared out by stress. In deep parts of the fault, the sheared grains recrystallize to a fine-grained, finely foliated rock called mylonite.

Burial metamorphism occurs in very deep sedimentary basins, where the pressure and temperature, along with high water content, are sufficient to form fine grains of zeolite minerals among the sedimentary grains. The process is intermediate between diagenesis, which makes a sediment into a solid rock, and regional metamorphism, in which the texture of the rock is modified.

Hydrothermal metamorphism (which many prefer to call alteration) is caused by hot water infiltrating the rock through cracks and pores. It is most common near volcanic and intrusive activity. The water itself, or substances dissolved in the water, may be incorporated into the crystals of certain minerals. One important product is serpentine, formed by the addition of water to olivine and pyroxene, which is significant in sub-sea-floor metamorphism.

A third classification is based on the original rocks, or protoliths. This classification is possible because relatively little material is added to or lost from the rock during metamorphism, except for water and carbon dioxide, so the assemblage of minerals present depends on the overall chemical composition of the original rock. The most abundant protoliths are pelitic rocks (from clay-rich sediments, usually with other sedimentary minerals), basaltic igneous rocks, and limestone or other carbonate rocks. Each kind of protolith recrystallizes into a different characteristic assemblage of minerals. The categories can be named, for example, metapelites, metabasalts, and metacarbonates.

Metamorphic intensity, or grade, is the basis for a fourth classification scheme. As the pressure and temperature increase, certain minerals become unstable, and their chemical components reorganize into new minerals more stable in the surrounding conditions. The presence of certain minerals, called index minerals, therefore indicates the intensity of pressure and temperature. The grades most commonly used are named for index minerals in pelitic rocks; in the late nineteenth century, they were described by George Barrow in zones of metamorphic rocks in central Scotland. These Barrovian grades, in order of increasing intensity, are marked by the first appearances of chlorite, biotite, garnet, staurolite, kyanite, and sillimanite.

A fifth classification scheme categorizes the rocks according to the intensity of pressure and temperature, or facies, without reference to protoliths. The concept of facies was developed by Penti Eskola, working in Finland about 1915, who enlarged on the work of Barrow in Scotland and V. M. Goldschmidt in Norway. Eskola realized that each protolith has a characteristic mineral assemblage within a given facies, or range of pressure and temperature. The facies are named for one of the assemblages within a specified range of conditions; for example, the greenschist facies, named for low-grade metamorphosed basalt, refers to equivalent low-grade assemblages from other protoliths as well. Other examples are the amphibolite facies, the range of pressures and temperatures that would give the staurolite and kyanite grades in pelitic rocks; and the granulite facies, which corresponds to extreme conditions bordering on anatexis.

Finally, the facies themselves, or the metamorphic assemblages in them, can be classified according to ratios of pressure to temperature, called pressure-temperature regimes. The greenschist, amphibolite, and granulite facies include mineral assemblages of increasing metamorphic intensity whose pressure and temperature rise together approximately as they would with increasing depth under most areas of the earth's surface. This sequence is sometimes referred to as the Barrovian pressure-temperature regime because Barrow's metamorphic grades in pelitic rocks fall in these facies. In another regime, called the Abukuma series after an area in Japan, the temperature is much cooler for any given pressure. The blueschist facies, characterized by blue and green sodium-rich amphiboles and pyroxenes, is typical of this series. The converse situation, a regime in which temperature rises much faster than pressure, corresponds to contact metamorphism, and is called the hornfels facies.

Methods of Study

Initial studies of metamorphic rocks are almost always done in the field. The tectonic or structural nature of the region suggests the processes to which the rock has been subjected. For example, an area of folded mountains can be expected to exhibit regional metamorphism; a volcanic area, some contact metamorphism; and a fault zone, some cataclastic metamorphism. Some features are obvious at the scale of an outcrop, such as banding and foliation, or the halo of recrystallized country rock abutting an igneous intrusion. Some textural features, such as foliation, large crystals such as the garnet in garnet schist, or the luster of a fracture surface as in quartzite or marble, are easily seen in a hand specimen. Similarly, a preliminary estimate of mineral content can be made from a hand specimen.

Many features, however, are best seen in thin section under a petrographic microscope. Usually all but the finest grains can be identified. From the relative abundance of the various minerals and their known chemical compositions the overall chemical composition of the rock can be calculated. The protolith can then be identified by comparing the calculated composition to the known compositional ranges of igneous and sedimentary rocks.

Textures seen under the microscope reveal much about the history of the rock. Foliation, for example, usually indicates regional metamorphism. A space-filling, polygonal texture can show contact or hydrothermal recrystallization, and a crumbled, smeared-out cataclastic texture indicates faulting.

Certain minerals such as staurolite or kyanite indicate the grade of metamorphism. Metamorphism is a slow process, however, especially at low temperatures, and conditions sometimes change too rapidly for the mineral assemblage to come to equilibrium. It is not uncommon to find crystals only partially converted into new minerals or to find lower-grade minerals coexisting with those of higher grade. At low grade, some structures of the original rock, such as bedding, may be preserved. Even the outlines of earlier crystals may be seen, filled in with one or more new minerals. High-grade metamorphism usually destroys earlier structures.

All metamorphic rocks available for study are at surface conditions, so the pressures and temperatures that caused them to recrystallize have been relieved. If conditions were relieved slowly enough, and especially if water was available, the rock may have undergone retrograde metamorphism, reverting to a lower grade and thus adjusting to the less intense pressure and temperature. Retrograde metamorphism is usually not very complete, and some evidence of the most intense conditions almost always remains. For example, the distinct outline of a staurolite crystal might be filled with crystals of quartz, biotite mica, and iron oxides.

More recent methods of investigation sometimes applied to metamorphic rocks are X-ray diffraction and electron microprobe analysis. The pattern of X rays scattered from crystals depends on the exact arrangement and spacing of atoms in the crystal structure, which is useful for identifying minerals. X-ray diffraction can be used to identify crystals that are too small or too poorly formed to be identified with a microscope. The microprobe can analyze the chemical composition of crystals even of microscopic size. Determination of exact composition or of variation in composition within growth zones of a single crystal can be especially useful for identifying variations in conditions during crystal formation.

Context

Most people encounter metamorphic rocks while traveling through mountains and other scenic regions. Recognizing these rocks is easier if one has a general idea of where the various types occur and how they appear in outcrops.

Regional metamorphic rocks are best exposed in two kinds of localities: the continental shields and the eroded cores of mountain ranges. Ancient basement rocks of the continental platform, composed of regionally metamorphosed and igneous rocks, are exposed in shields without a cover of sedimentary rock. The Canadian Shield, extending from northern Minnesota through Ontario and Quebec to New England, is the major shield of North America. Similar shields are exposed in western Australia and on every other continent. The old, eroded mountains of Scotland and Wales contain abundant outcrops in which some of the pioneering studies of metamorphic rocks were conducted. The Appalachians have even larger exposures, extending from Georgia into New England. Somewhat smaller outcrops occur in many parts of the Rocky Mountains and the Coast Ranges. The foliated rocks schist, slate, and gneiss make up the bulk of these exposures. Rock cleavage parallel to the foliation is an important clue to recognizing outcrops of these rocks; slopes parallel to foliation tend to be fairly smooth and straight, while slopes eroded across the foliation are ragged and steplike. Bare slopes of schist can reflect light strongly from the many parallel flakes of mica. Slate is usually dull and dark-colored but characteristically splits into ragged slabs. The colorful, contorted bands of gneiss are easily recognized.

Contact metamorphic rocks are much less widespread and are generally confined to areas of active or extinct volcanism. The Cascades and the Sierra Nevada show many examples, but some of the best exposures are found near ancient intrusives in the Appalachians and in New England. Contact metamorphic rocks are more of a challenge to recognize because they generally lack foliation. The best clue is physical contact with a body of igneous rock. They often form a shell or halo around an igneous body, most intensely recrystallized at the contact and extending outward a few centimeters to a few kilometers (depending mostly on the size of the igneous body), until they eventually merge into the surrounding unaltered country rock. The halo is generally similar to the country rock but, because it is recrystallized, it is usually harder, more compact, and more resistant to erosion. Broken surfaces can be distinctive. Depending on the nature of the country rock, one might look for the glassy sheen of fractured quartzite, the glinting cleavage planes of marble, or the smooth, hornlike fracture of hornfels.

Hydrothermally altered rocks from sub-sea-floor metamorphism, when finally exposed on land, are found among regional metamorphic rocks and appear much like them except for the greenish-gray colors of chlorite, serpentine, and talc. Terrestrial hydrothermal alteration is most easily recognized in areas of recent volcanic activity. Good examples are exposed in the southwestern United States, such as the so-called porphyry copper deposits. Many such areas contain valuable deposits, and so may have been mined or prospected. The outcrops are often much fractured and veined near the intrusion. Where alteration is most intense, the rock may appear bleached; farther from the intrusion, it may have a greenish hue because of low-grade alteration. Quartz and sulfide minerals such as pyrite are common in the veins, but weathering often leaves a rusty-looking, resistant cap called an iron hat or gossan over the deposit.

Rocks formed by cataclastic and burial metamorphism require specialized equipment for their recognition. Zones many miles wide containing mylonite, the product of cataclastic metamorphism, are exposed along the Moine fault in northwestern Scotland (where mylonite was first studied) and along the Brevard fault, extending along the Appalachians from Georgia into North Carolina. Examples of burial metamorphic rocks are found under the Salton Sea area of California and the Rotorua area of New Zealand.

Bibliography

Bates, Robert L. *Geology of the Industrial Rocks and Minerals*. Mineola, N.Y.: Dover, 1969. Somewhat technical but readable and practical descriptions of the geological occurrence and production of metamorphic rocks and minerals (among others), listing their principal uses. Representative rather than comprehensive. Topical bibliography and good index.

Compton, Robert Ross. *Manual of Field Geology*. New York: John Wiley & Sons, 1962. A standard undergraduate text with a chapter devoted to the interpretation of metamorphic rocks and structures in the field. Some knowledge of mineralogy is assumed. The illustrations are helpful.

Ehlers, Ernest G., and Harvey Blatt. *Petrology: Igneous, Sedimentary, and Metamorphic*. New York: W. H. Freeman, 1982. Undergraduate text in elementary petrology for readers with some familiarity with minerals and chemistry. Thorough, readable discussion of most aspects of metamorphic rocks. Abundant illustrations and diagrams, good bibliography, and thorough indices.

Pough, Frederick H. *A Field Guide to Rocks and Minerals*. 4th ed. Boston: Houghton Mifflin, 1976. The best of the most widely available field guides, authoritative but easy to read. Color plates of representative mineral specimens, and sufficient data to be useful for distinguishing minerals. Very brief description of rocks, including metamorphic rocks. Elementary crystallography and chemistry are presented in the introduction.

Strahler, Arthur N. *Physical Geology*. New York: Harper & Row, 1981. The chapter on metamorphic rocks is a good intermediate-level approach to classification and metamorphic processes. Related chapters on geological environments may interest the reader. Excellent bibliography for the beginning student, with thorough glossary and index.

Tarbuck, Edward J., and Frederick K. Lutgens. *The Earth*. 2d ed. Westerville, Ohio: Charles E. Merrill, 1987. One of the better earth science texts for beginning college or advanced high school readers. Good elementary treatment of metamorphic rocks and, in other chapters, of related environments. Color pictures throughout are excellent. Bibliography, glossary, and a short index.

James A. Burbank, Jr.

Cross-References

Foliation and Lineation, 747; Hydrothermal Mineralization, 1108; Igneous and Contact Metamorphic Mineral Deposits, 1124; Metamorphic Rocks: Blueschists, 1561; Metamorphic Rocks: Pelitic Schists, 1570; Metamorphic Textures, 1578; Metamorphism: Anatexis, 1586; Contact Metamorphism, 1594; Metamorphism: Metasomatism, 1599; Regional Metamorphism, 1606; Sub-Sea-Floor Metamorphism, 1614; Petrographic Microscopes, 2034; Plate Tectonics, 2079.

METAMORPHIC ROCKS: BLUESCHISTS

Type of earth science: Geology
Field of study: Petrology, metamorphic

Blueschists are a class of metamorphic rocks that recrystallize at depths of 10-30 kilometers or more where ocean-floor-capped lithosphere rapidly subducts into the interior of the earth. Blueschists are important because they contain minerals indicating that metamorphism occurred under conditions of unusually high confining pressures and low temperatures. Their presence in mountain belts is the primary criterion for recognizing ancient subduction zones.

Principal terms

ACCRETIONARY PRISM: the accumulation over time of variably deformed and metamorphosed sediments and ocean islands near a trench at a subduction zone

GEOTHERM: a curve on a temperature-depth graph that describes how temperature changes in the subsurface

LITHOSPHERE: the outer rigid shell of the earth that forms the tectonic plates, whose movement causes earthquakes, volcanoes, and mountain building

METAMORPHISM: the alteration of the mineralogy and texture of rocks because of changes in pressure and temperature conditions or chemically active fluids

PROGRADE and RETROGRADE METAMORPHISM: metamorphic changes that occur primarily because of increasing and then decreasing temperature conditions

RECRYSTALLIZATION: the formation of new crystalline grains in a rock

SUBDUCTION: the process of sinking of a tectonic plate into the interior of the earth; deep-ocean trenches and volcanic arcs form at subduction zones

TECTONISM: the formation of mountains because of the deformation of the crust of the earth on a large scale

TRENCH: a long and narrow deep trough on the sea floor that forms where the ocean floor is pulled downward because of plate subduction

VOLCANIC ARC: a linear or arcuate belt of volcanoes that forms at a subduction zone because of rock melting near the top of the descending plate

Summary of the Phenomenon

Blueschists are a distinctive class of metamorphic rock containing one or more of the minerals lawsonite, aragonite, sodic amphibole (glaucophane), and sodic pyroxene (omphacite and jadeite plus quartz). These minerals indicate that recrystallization occurred in the temperature range of 150-450 degrees Celsius and pressures of 3-10 kilobars or more. Blueschists of basaltic composition typically contain abundant glaucophane, a mineral that can give a rock a striking blue color. Other minerals commonly found in blueschists include quartz, mica, chlorite, garnet, pumpellyite, epidote, stilpnomelene, sphene, and rutile. The abundance of these and rarer minerals depends, as it does in all metamorphic rocks, upon rock composition, the exact pressures and temperatures of recrystallization, and the nature of chemically active fluids that have affected the rocks.

Blueschists in one place or another display a remarkably wide variety of structural features. In the field, many are complexly deformed, with intricate folding and refolding of compositional layering at scales of millimeters to tens of meters. Commonly, folded rocks also display a thickening and thinning of the layering, forming an interesting structure known as boudinage. Many blueschists are faulted, some so intensely that they are fragmented rocks known as breccias. When flaky minerals such as mica are lined up at the microscopic scale, a rock has a scaly foliation known as a schistosity. A parallel alignment of rod-shaped amphiboles gives the rock a lineation. Blueschists typically have schistosities, and many also have lineations. The development of these features depends upon the magnitude of penetrative rock flowage by microscopic crystal deformation concurrent with metamorphic recrystallization (a geologic process known as dynamic metamorphism). Although most blueschists were so highly deformed during metamorphic recrystallization that all original features in the rocks were destroyed, some retain relict features from the rock's premetamorphic history, such as ripple marks, delicate fossils, or volcanic flow layering. Blueschists bearing these features were recrystallized but not highly deformed. Hence, the diversity of minerals and deformational features of the class of rocks known as blueschists is great. Many are truly blueschists, but some are neither blue in color where glaucophane is lacking nor schistose in texture when deformation was minor.

Laboratory experiments show that metamorphic recrystallization near 200 degrees Celsius causes anorthite (calcium-rich plagioclase) in combination with water to recrystallize as lawsonite at approximately 3 kilobars, calcite to transform to aragonite at 5 kilobars, and albite (sodium-rich plagioclase) to recrystallize as jadeite plus quartz near 7 kilobars. At higher temperatures, these changes occur at higher pressures. Experiments combined with other measures of metamorphic temperature conditions indicate that most blueschists were metamorphosed at temperatures of 150-450 degrees Celsius and minimum confining pressures of 3-10 kilobars, respectively. Metamorphic pressures of 3-10 kilobars correspond to burial depths for recrystallization of 10-30 kilometers. Thirty kilometers is near the base of typical continental crust. Ultra-high-pressure blueschists containing relics of the mineral coesite, a dense mineral having the same composition as quartz forming at extremely high confining pressures, have been found in small areas of the Alps, Norway, and China. Laboratory experiments indicate that confining pressures of 25-30 kilobars are required to transform quartz to coesite. Although coesite-bearing blueschists are rare, their occurrence is very important because they indicate that some blueschists recrystallized at depths of 75-90 kilometers, depths in the earth which are very near the base of the lithosphere.

The mineralogy of blueschists indicates that the metamorphic conditions for their formation within the earth would be equivalent to geothermal gradients of 10-15 degrees Celsius per kilometer depth or less. Such ratios of temperature to depth do not exist in the interior of normal lithospheric plates, because geothermal gradients are typically 25-35 degrees Celsius per kilometer depth. The plate tectonic setting for the generation of blueschists is thus very unusual.

Regional terranes of blueschist extending for hundreds of kilometers in length and tens of kilometers in width are found in California, Alaska, Japan, the Alps, and New Caledonia. Smaller bodies of blueschist that are probably remnants of once-extensive terranes are found at numerous other sites around the world. Blueschists are found as fault-bounded terranes juxtaposed against deposits of unmetamorphosed sediments, igneous batholiths, or sequences of basalt, gabbro, and peridotite thought to be fragments of ocean crust (ophiolites) or other metamorphic terranes. The common feature of all occurrences is that they are regions that were probably the sites of ancient lithospheric plate convergence, a tectonic process commonly known as subduction. Subduction carries surficial rocks into the depths of the earth, where the increase in pressure and temperature causes metamorphism. Plate convergence involves localized shearing action between the descending plate and the overriding plate. As a result, blueschists and associated rocks typically undergo a complex deformational history, sometimes forming chaotic mixtures known as mélanges where deformation was particularly intense. It is of special interest that nearly all extensive blueschist terranes are of Mesozoic age or younger (less than about 250 million years).

Sites of plate subduction in the modern world are marked by ocean trenches, great earthquakes, and arcs of andesitic volcanoes. The region between the trench and volcanic arc is known as the arc-trench gap. Typically a forearc basin is on the arc side of the gap and an accretionary prism is on the trench side. The forearc basin sits atop the overriding plate and becomes filled largely with basaltic to andesitic volcanic debris generated in the nearby arc. Forearc basin deposits are essentially undeformed and unmetamorphosed. In striking contrast, the accretionary prism is directly above the descending plate and consists largely of variously deformed and metamorphosed sediments that were bulldozed off the descending plate during plate convergence. Most typically, blueschists are found in the arcward parts of an accretionary prism, locally faulted directly against forearc basin deposits.

The unusual conditions of very low temperatures for a given depth of burial can develop within subduction shear zones because plate convergence at speeds of tens of kilometers per million years (centimeters per year) transports cold lithosphere downward faster than the earth's interior heat is conducted upward through it. As a result, after a few tens of millions of years of subduction, the front of the overriding plate cools, and the local geothermal gradients become greatly depressed (less than 10 degrees Celsius per kilometer depth). After fast plate convergence has occurred for a few tens of millions of years, temperatures less than 200 degrees Celsius at depths of 30 kilometers or more can be attained. The subduction zone metamorphism that creates blueschists is also known as high-pressure/low-temperature metamorphism.

Because blueschists are found within accretionary prisms, it is important to understand how prisms grow and deform. Subduction accretion occurs by both offscraping and underplating. Offscraping is the process of trenchward growth or widening of the prism by addition at its toe of incoming sediments and seamounts (which are ocean islands such as Hawaii). It occurs by bulldozer-like action that causes the incoming pile of oceanic and trench-axis sediments to be folded and thrust-faulted. Offscraped rocks are weakly metamorphosed with the development of zeolite-group minerals and, at somewhat greater depths, the minerals prehnite and pumpellyite. Underplating is the process of addition of material to the bottom of a prism and, at greater depths, the bottom of the overlying crystalline plate. Underplating thickens and uplifts the overriding block and occurs concurrent with the shearing motions driven by the movement of the descending plate. Blueschists form in the region of underplating.

The presence of blueschists at the surface of the earth directly indicates that some subduction zones were "two-way streets," along which surficial rocks were not only subducted down to but also uplifted back from depths of 30 kilometers or more. The relationship of the uplift and exposure of blueschists to the growth of an accretionary prism is rather obscure, however, because active trench slopes are submerged beneath deep water and sites of slow sediment deposition. Most of the down-and-up motion is by some combination of fault slippage and pervasive rock flowage. Surficial erosion is a minor contributor to the uplift process.

Underplating appears to be the basic process that drives both the thickening of accretionary prism and the uplift of included masses of blueschist. Underplating by itself, however, does not bring blueschists nearer the surface. The presence of a steep trench slope (5-10 degrees) causes a prism to thin by gravity-driven downslope spreading, much like a glacier thins as it flows down a mountain. Prism thinning seems to occur by a combination of normal faulting and rock flowage. Over a period of tens of millions of years, underplating-driven thickening at the base of the prism and gravity-driven thinning near the surface of the prism would slowly uplift a large terrane of blueschist near the edge of the overriding plate. The actual exposure of blueschist bedrock over a substantial area typically occurs only after subduction ceases and the top of the prism has become exposed to erosion.

The type of high-pressure/low-temperature metamorphism varies with depth. At the shallower depths of offscraping, temperatures and pressures are low, and only zeolites, prehnite, and pumpellyite develop. Surficial rocks subducted to depths of 10-30 kilometers and temperatures of 150-350 degrees Celsius are continuously metamorphosed into blueschists. At depths of 30-40 kilometers and more, and at higher temperatures, the blueschists turn into the class of rock known as eclogite. Eclogites of basaltic composition are composed largely of dense garnet and sodic pyroxene (omphacite).

The sequence of change from the zeolite to prehnite-pumpellyite to blueschist and finally to eclogite mineral assemblages is known as prograde metamorphism. Rocks in accretionary prisms commonly show all gradations of the progressive sequence. Overall, prograde metamorphism causes a general decrease in rock water content, destruction of the original minerals by recrystallization, increase in rock density, and increase in size of recrystallized crystals. At depths where the basalts and gabbros in the ocean crust (or ophiolite) at the top of the descending plate change from blueschist into eclogite, there is a large increase in the bulk density of the descending plate. This transformation decreases the buoyancy of the descending plate to such an extent that it may be the primary driving force of plate subduction and mantle convection.

One important aspect for understanding subduction zone metamorphism is that thermal modeling calculations using computers indicate that the pressure-to-temperature ratios during prograde metamorphism will change rapidly during the early stages of subduction. That is a result of the fact that the overriding plate contains heat that is lost when it flows down into the cold descending plate. The low-temperature geothermal conditions that characterize subduction zone metamorphism will stabilize after a few tens of millions of years of fast plate convergence. Thus, the temperature conditions at any particular depth will change over time, and most higher temperature (350-450 degrees Celsius) blueschists must have recrystallized along the base of the overriding plate during the early stages of subduction. Another significant conclusion is that because the mechanical response of rocks to deformation is also a strong function of temperature, the pattern of faulting and rock flowage will also change with time. That is important for understanding the origin of subduction-zone earthquakes.

When the descending plate reaches depths of 100-125 kilometers, magmas are generated near its upper surface. They rise to the surface to form a volcanic arc of basaltic to andesitic composition. The presence of ultra-high-pressure blueschists directly confirms that some sediments are actually dragged down to (and returned from) very near the typical depths of arc magma origin. Recent isotopic studies of the element beryllium in volcanic arc magmas show that some subducted sedimentary material is actually melted and incorporated into arc magmas. The intrusion of hot arc magmas near the surface and the eruption of volcanoes causes heating of the wall rocks, creating contact metamorphic rocks and regional metamorphic rocks known as greenschists and amphibolites. This near-surface prograde metamorphism is of a low-pressure/high-temperature type. As a result, many ancient subduction zones are delineated on a regional scale by parallel belts of high-pressure/low-temperature and low-pressure/high-temperature metamorphic belts, a distinctive association known as paired metamorphic belts.

Plate convergence stops either when the relative motions between the descending and overriding plates become such that the margin becomes a transform plate margin or when a buoyant continent or island arc is conveyor-belted into a trench and "plugs up" the subduction zone. Transform plate motion occurs largely by horizontal movement along steep faults, a type of movement known as strike-slip faulting. The change from subduction to transform motion began along the California coastline about 30 million years ago with the generation of the San Andreas fault system. The San Andreas strike-slip fault is causing the offset and dismemberment of the accretionary prism known as the Franciscan subduction complex. Blueschists in the California Coast Ranges are now juxtaposed against unmetamorphosed forearc basin sediments and even igneous intrusions of the associated volcanic arc of which the Sierra Nevada is a remnant. In the process, some fault blocks rise and blueschists are eroded while others subside and blueschists become buried, reheated, and remetamorphosed as more normal geothermal conditions are reattained (a process known as retrograde metamorphism). The collision of the continent of India with Asia, starting about 50 million years ago, has plugged a subduction zone on a southern edge of Asia and created the Himalaya. Such mountainous uplift leads to extremely rapid erosion of the accretionary prism caught between the continental blocks. Postsubduction destruction of blueschists by either erosion or retrograde metamorphism is the probable explanation for why most extensive terranes of blueschist are of Mesozoic age or younger.

Methods of Study

Geologists study blueschists in the field, in the confines of the laboratory, and with computer modeling. Fieldwork involves going to the sites where blueschists are exposed in rock outcrops. Geological maps are made to show the field relations between blueschists and associated rocks. The first stage of geological mapping is recording on a topographic map the distribution of the major types of rocks, the orientation of bedding, and the locations and orientations of major faults and folds. Representative rock samples are collected for later laboratory study. The second stage of mapping is typically of much smaller areas. These detailed maps delineate additional variations in the types of rocks, the orientation of minor faults and folds, and associated schistosities and lineations. This stage of analysis usually provides the basis for determining the detailed movement patterns of the blueschists during subduction-zone deformation.

Laboratory studies of blueschists include the analysis of thin sections of the rock samples collected in the field, the geochemical studies of rock and mineral compositions, and experiments to determine the stability limits of minerals under different conditions of pressure, temperature, and fluid composition. Thin sections of the rocks are examined under polarized light with a petrographic microscope. Different minerals display different colors and other optical properties that enable their identification. Thin-section analysis also enables the recognition of microscopic folds and faults, the detailed nature of schistosities and lineations, the nature of deformed crystals, and the types of inclusions of older crystals in younger ones such as garnet. Liquid inclusions of metamorphic fluids trapped in crystals can also be examined and analyzed. These observations provide clues as to the nature of both prograde and retrograde metamorphism.

Minerals, particularly finely crystalline ones, are also identified by X-ray diffraction. The analysis of the scattering pattern of a beam of X rays focused upon the sample enables the researcher to identify minerals and, for minerals such as feldspar, pyroxene, or chlorite, to estimate their elemental composition. The elemental composition of powdered rock samples is commonly determined using X-ray fluorescence. A focused X-ray beam causes atoms in a powder to emit other X rays whose type and intensity depend upon the types and amounts of atoms in the powder. The elemental composition of individual mineral grains is determined by analysis with the electron microprobe. A beam of high-energy electrons is focused on a 100-square-micron portion of a crystal in a highly polished thin section. As for X-ray fluorescence, the type and intensity of emitted X rays depend upon the types and amounts of atoms in a small spot in the crystal. Measurement of the composition of many spots in a traverse across a crystal enables determination of the variation in mineral composition from its core to rim, a variation known as compositional zoning. Zoning is a sensitive measure of the pressure and temperature history of the growing minerals and, hence, both their prograde and retrograde metamorphic history.

Mass spectrometers are used to determine the isotopic ratios of the component minerals of blueschists for the calculation of the age of metamorphism. Isotopic ratios of neodymium 143 to neodymium 144 and strontium 87 to strontium 86 are indicators of the geologic setting in which igneous rocks were erupted. Measurements of the ratios of oxygen 18 to oxygen 16 in coexisting minerals are indicators of the temperature of metamorphic recrystallization. The age of metamorphism for blueschists is determined from the analysis of radioactive isotopes and their daughter decay products in certain crystals. Examples are potassium 40, which decays into argon 40; rubidium 87, which decays into strontium 87; and uranium 238, which decays into lead 206. The measurement of the ratio of parent to daughter elements in either the whole rock or component minerals can be used to calculate the metamorphic age or ages of the rocks.

Experiments are conducted under controlled conditions in the laboratory to determine the stability limits and compositional relations for minerals at different pressures, temperatures, and fluid compositions. The goal is to simulate physical conditions deep in the earth. Experiments show that minerals such as aragonite, lawsonite, and jadeite plus quartz are stable only at high ratios of pressure to temperature conditions. Experimental studies are also performed to determine how the ratios of oxygen isotopes in quartz and other minerals vary with different temperatures and oxygen pressure conditions. The ratio of iron and magnesium in garnet and pyroxene also varies in a systematic manner with different pressure and temperature conditions. Laboratory calibration of elemental and isotopic compositions of minerals under controlled laboratory conditions is the basis for estimating the pressures and temperatures of metamorphism.

Computer simulations of the temperature conditions within subduction zones give an understanding of how temperatures change with time. Computer models that employ the principles of continuum mechanics are used to simulate the long-term tectonic deformation of an accretionary prism and the uplift of blueschist terranes. Geochemical computer models employ the principles of thermodynamics and are used to calculate what types of minerals should develop during prograde and retrograde subduction-zone metamorphism.

Context

The study of blueschists is important because they are direct indicators of the geologic processes that occur deep within subduction zones that become mountain belts. Their creation indicates that abnormally cold geothermal conditions develop arcward of the ocean trenches where rapid plate convergence occurs for tens of millions of years. Their preservation indicates that tectonic movements by faulting, folding, and rock flowage can be such that they become uplifted to near the surface while geothermal conditions remain very cold. Understanding the deformational history of blueschists is important because many of the world's largest and most destructive earthquakes occur at subduction zones at the very depths where blueschists are forming today. An understanding of how they deform and recrystallize during their downward and upward paths in ancient subduction zones will eventually provide new understanding of how destructive subduction-zone earthquakes are nucleated and, hence, better earthquake prediction.

Subduction zones are the sites where ocean-floor-capped lithosphere plunges back into the earth to be recycled. Blueschists are direct indicators that some of the sediment on top of the descending plate is also dragged to near the base of the lithosphere. Their presence in paired metamorphic belts is the primary way that geologists recognize ancient subduction zones. Blueschists are a key part of the geologic story of how continents grow by the addition of accretionary prisms along their edges.

Bibliography

Cox, Allan, ed. *Plate Tectonics and Geomagnetic Reversals*. San Francisco: W. H. Freeman, 1973. This book is a collection of papers discussing the basic principles of the theory of plate tectonics and how it was developed. Chapters are introduced by short articles that discuss the importance of the following group of papers. The text is suitable for college-level students.

Davis, George H. *Structural Geology of Rocks and Regions*. New York: John Wiley & Sons, 1984. A structural geology textbook that discusses how folds, faults, and rock flowage occurs. Chapter 6 covers the theory of plate tectonics and contains a short section on blueschists and their occurrence. The text is suitable for college-level students.

Ernst, W. G. *Earth Materials*. Englewood Cliffs, N.J.: Prentice-Hall, 1969. An elementary earth science book that discusses rocks and minerals. Sections on regional metamorphism, chemistry of metamorphic rocks, physical conditions of metamorphism, and metamorphism and the rock cycle include discussions specifically referring to blueschists. The text is suitable for high school students.

Ernst, W. G., ed. *Subduction Zone Metamorphism*. Stroudsburg, Pa.: Dowden, Hutchinson and Ross, 1975. A collection of technical papers that cover the topic of subduction-zone metamorphism around the world. Most of the papers focus on blueschists. The editor has written a series of summaries that introduce groups of related papers and explain their relative importance. The text is for advanced college-level students.

Evans, Bernard W., and Edwin H. Brown, eds. *Blueschists and Eclogites*. Boulder, Colo.: Geological Society of America, 1986. This book reports the nature of blueschists and eclogites at many sites around the world. Contains numerous pictures and diagrams of structures and mineral textures found in blueschists. The text is suitable for advanced college-level students.

Hallam, A. *A Revolution in the Earth Sciences*. New York: Oxford University Press, 1973. An elementary earth science book that discusses continental drift and the theory of plate tectonics. Blueschists are discussed in the chapter on the origin of mountain belts. The text is suitable for high-school-level readers.

Miyashiro, Akiho. *Metamorphism and Metamorphic Belts*. New York: John Wiley & Sons, 1973. An advanced textbook on metamorphic petrology that contains much discussion of blueschists, their occurrence, and their plate tectonic setting. The text is for advanced college-level students who want to understand the principles that control the formation of minerals in metamorphic rocks.

Press, Frank, and Raymond Siever. *Earth*. 4th ed. San Francisco: W. H. Freeman, 1986. An extremely well-written, well-illustrated introductory textbook on earth sciences. The chapter on plutonism and metamorphism contains a discussion of blueschists. An extensive glossary of geological terms is included. The text is aimed at students at the advanced high school and freshman college levels.

Windley, B. F. *The Evolving Continents*. 2d ed. New York: John Wiley & Sons, 1984. This book focuses on the origin and evolution of the continents. Several sections on blueschists are listed in a comprehensive index. The text is for college-level students.

Mark Cloos

Cross-References

Continental Growth, 268; Displaced Terranes, 377; Earthquake Distribution, 421; Experimental Petrology, 662; Foliation and Lineation, 747; Geothermometry and Geobarometry, 922; Island Arcs, 1261; Metamorphic Textures, 1578; Contact Metamorphism, 1594; Regional Metamorphism, 1606; Mountain Belts, 1725; Plate Margins, 2063; Plate Tectonics, 2079; Stable Isotopes: Fractionation Processes, 2449; Subduction and Orogeny, 2497.

METAMORPHIC ROCKS: PELITIC SCHISTS

Type of earth science: Geology
Field of study: Petrology, metamorphic

Pelitic schists are formed from fine-grained sedimentary rocks. They are an important metamorphic rock type because they undergo distinct textural and mineralogical changes that are used by geologists to gauge the temperatures and pressures under which the rocks are progressively modified.

Principal terms

EQUILIBRIUM: a situation in which a mineral is stable at a given set of temperature-pressure conditions

INDEX MINERAL: an individual mineral that has formed under a limited or very distinct range of temperature and pressure conditions

ISOGRAD: a line on a geologic map that marks the first appearance of a single mineral or mineral assemblage in metamorphic rocks

METAMORPHIC ZONE: areas of rock affected by the same limited range of temperature and pressure conditions, commonly identified by the presence of a key individual mineral or group of minerals

MICA: a platy silicate mineral (one silicon atom surrounded by four oxygen atoms) that readily splits in one plane

MINERAL: a naturally occurring chemical compound that has an orderly internal arrangement of atoms and a definite chemical formula

PROGRESSIVE METAMORPHISM: mineralogical and textural changes that take place as temperature and pressures increase

SEDIMENTARY ROCK: a rock formed from the physical breakdown of preexisting rock material or from the precipitation—chemically or biologically—of minerals

SHALE/MUDSTONE: sedimentary rock composed of fine-grained products derived from the physical breakdown of preexisting rock; shales break along distinct planes and mudstones do not

TEXTURE: the size, shape, and arrangement of crystals or particles in a rock

Summary of the Phenomenon

Metamorphism literally means "the change in form" that a rock undergoes. More precisely, metamorphism is a process by which igneous and sedimentary rocks are mineralogically, texturally, and, occasionally, chemically modified by the effects of one or more of the following agents or variables: increased temperature, pressure, or chemically active fluids. Pelitic schists have long been recognized as one of the best rock types to gauge and preserve the wide range of mineralogical and textural changes that take place as metamorphic conditions progressively increase. It is perhaps easiest to understand the conditions under which metamorphism occurs by excluding those conditions that are not generally considered metamorphic. At or near the earth's surface, sedimentary rocks form from the physical or chemical breakdown of preexisting rocks at relatively low pressures and temperatures (less than 200 degrees Celsius). Igneous rocks form from molten material at high temperatures (650-1,100 degrees Celsius) and at low pressures for volcanic rocks to high pressures for those formed at great depth. The conditions that exist between these two are those that are considered metamorphic.

Although all the agents of metamorphism work together to produce the distinctive textures and minerals of regionally metamorphosed rocks, each has its own special or distinctive role. Temperature is considered the most important factor in metamorphism. It is the primary reason for recrystallization and new mineral growth. Two types of pressure affect metamorphic rocks. The pressure caused by the overlying material and uniformly affecting the rock on all sides is referred to as the confining pressure. An additional pressure, referred to as directed pressure, is normally caused by strong horizontal forces. While confining pressure has little apparent influence on metamorphic textures, directed pressures are considered the principal reason that several types of metamorphosed rocks develop distinctive textures. Chemically active fluids are important because they act both as a transporting medium for chemial constituents and as a facilitator of chemical reactions during metamorphism. As metamorphic conditions increase, fluids play an important role in aiding metamorphic reactions, even though they are concurrently driven out of the rocks. Most metamorphic rocks preserve mineral assemblages that represent the highest conditions achieved. As metamorphic conditions start to fall, reactions are very slow to occur because adequate fluids are normally not available. If the metamorphism involves significant additions and losses of constituents other than water, carbon dioxide, and other fluids, this process is referred to as metasomatism. For example, if the magnesium content of a rock markedly increases during metamorphism, this is referred to as magnesium metasomatism.

Geologists recognize several types of metamorphism, but one, regional metamorphism, is predominant. Regional metamorphism takes place at depth within the vast areas where new mountains are forming. The products of regional metamorphism are exposed in a variety of places. One of the best is on shields—broad, relatively flat regions within continents. There, the thin veneer of sedimentary rocks has been stripped away, exposing wide areas of deeply eroded ancient mountain belts and their regionally metamorphosed rocks, complexly contorted and intermingled with igneous rocks. The cores of older eroded mountain belts, such as the Appalachians and the Rockies, also commonly expose smaller areas of very old regionally metamorphosed rocks. Pelitic schists mainly occur in regionally metamorphosed rocks. They may also occur in contact metamorphic deposits, which are small, baked zones that formed immediately adjacent to igneous bodies that invaded pelitic rocks as hot molten material. In contrast to the thousands of square kilometers typically occupied by regionally metamorphosed rocks, individual contact metamorphic deposits are rarely more than several kilometers wide.

Fine-grained sedimentary rocks (shales and mudstones) that formed from the physical breakdown of other rock types were once commonly referred to as pelites. Although the terms "pelite" and "pelitic" are largely absent in modern treatments of sedimentary rocks, they are widely used in the literature on metamorphism. Pelitic rocks undergo very marked textural and mineralogical changes that geologists use to gauge the conditions of formation in a particular area. "Schist," as used in the term "pelitic schist," has several definitions. The name may be applied broadly to any rock that is foliated or contains minerals that have a distinct preferred planar orientation. "Schist" also has a much narrower definition, referring only to foliated, coarse-grained rocks in which most mineral grains are visible to the unaided eye. This foliation, or preferred orientation, is imparted upon the rock because of deformation and recrystallization in response to a pronounced directed pressure at elevated temperatures.

The development of foliation is the most diagnostic feature of rocks that have undergone regional metamorphism. Directed pressure produces a variety of foliations that change as a function of the conditions of formation. An unmetamorphosed pelitic rock is typically a very fine-grained, soft rock that may or may not be finely layered (containing closely spaced planes). At low temperatures and pressures (low grades of metamorphism), pelitic rocks remain fine-grained, but microscopic micaceous minerals form or recrystallize and align themselves perpendicular to the directed pressure. That produces a dense, hard rock called a slate, which readily splits parallel to the preferred orientation. Any layering may be partially or totally obliterated. The accompanying texture is called a flow or slaty cleavage. At slightly higher conditions, micaceous minerals become better developed but remain fine-grained. The foliated rock produced takes on a pronounced sheen and is referred to as a phyllite. As conditions continue to increase, grain size increases until it is visible. This change produces a texture referred to as a schistosity, and the rock is called a schist. At very high conditions, the micas that were diagnostic of lower conditions start to become unstable. The rock, referred to as a gneiss, remains foliated but does not readily split as the slates, phyllites, and schists do. The foliation, or gneissosity, takes the form of an alternating light and dark banding. At higher conditions, gneissic rocks gradually grade into the realm where igneous rocks form.

The first study to show that a single rock type can undergo progressive change on a regional scale was that of British geologist George Barrow toward the end of the nineteenth century in the Highlands of Scotland, southwest of Aberdeen. His work indicated that pelitic schists and gneisses contained three discrete mineralogic zones, each represented by one of three key minerals: staurolite, kyanite, and sillimanite. Barrow suggested that increasing temperature was the controlling agent for the zonation observed. Later work by Barrow and other geologists confirmed this hypothesis and broadened the mapping over the entire Highlands, revealing additional mineral zones that formed at lower metamorphic conditions. From lowest to highest temperatures, several mineralogical zones were recognized. In the chlorite zone, there are slates, phyllites, and mica schists generally containing quartz, chlorite, and muscovite. In the biotite zone, mica schists are marked by the appearance of biotite in association with chlorite, muscovite, quartz, and albite. Biotite occurs in each of the higher zones. A line marking the boundary of the chlorite and biotite zones is referred to as the biotite isograd. (An isograd is a line that marks the first appearance of the key index mineral that is distinctive of the metamorphic zone.) In the almandine (garnet) zone, mica schists are characterized by the presence of almandine associated with quartz, muscovite, biotite, and sodium-rich plagioclase. The garnet first appears along the almandine isograd and occurs through all the higher zones. In the staurolite zone, mica schists typically contain quartz, muscovite, biotite, almandine, staurolite, and plagioclase. In the kyanite zone, mica schists and gneisses contain quartz, muscovite, biotite, almandine, kyanite, and plagioclase. Staurolite is no longer stable in this zone. In the sillimanite zone, mica schists and gneisses are characterized by quartz, muscovite, biotite, almandine, sillimanite, and plagioclase. Sillimanite forms at the expense of kyanite.

These zones—also called Barrovian zones—are recognized throughout the world. The accompanying figure hypothetically illustrates the approximate ranges of the common mineral zones in pelitic rocks. Path 1 indicates the typical temperature and pressure conditions along which a Barrovian mineral sequence forms. Path 2 shows a sequence of mineralogical zones more diagnostic of contact metamorphic deposits or a very low-pressure regionally metamorphosed sequence. It should be noted that

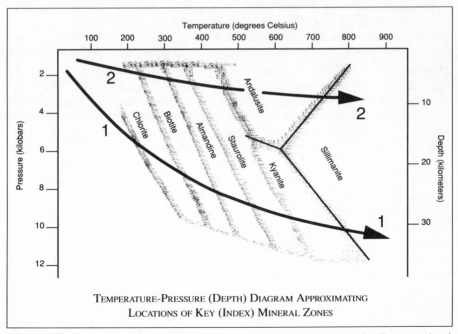

TEMPERATURE-PRESSURE (DEPTH) DIAGRAM APPROXIMATING
LOCATIONS OF KEY (INDEX) MINERAL ZONES

NOTE: Path 1 illustrates a typical Barrovian sequence; path 2 is typical of a very low-pressure regionally metamorphosed sequence.

the minerals andalusite, kyanite, and sillimanite have identical compositions; each, therefore, has its own conditions of equilibrium as shown in the figure. The key distinction between the two sequences shown in the figure is that the Barrovian type includes kyanite and sillimanite zones at higher temperatures, whereas in the lower pressure type (path 2), kyanite is absent and the andalusite and mineral zones are present.

Methods of Study

The study of pelitic schists can be conducted from a number of perspectives. The foundation of all studies, however, is the kind of fieldwork that George Barrow conducted in Scotland, which includes careful mapping, sample collection, rock description, and structural measurement.

Once the data and samples are returned to the laboratory, other methods of investigation may be employed. Rocks are commonly studied under the binocular microscope or powdered and/or made into thin sections to be analyzed in polarized light transmitted through the sample beneath the petrographic microscope. The preparation of the standard thin section involves several steps: cutting a small block of the sample so that it is 2.7 millimeters by 4.5 millimeters on one side; polishing one side and glueing it to a glass slide; and cutting and grinding the glued sample to a uniform thickness of 0.03 millimeter. Observations and descriptions of these thin sections are essential to the study of pelitic rocks because they commonly provide information about the interrelationships among the minerals present and clues to the metamorphic history of the sample.

Whole-rock chemical analyses of pelitic rocks are also important. Standard analytical procedures, atomic absorption, and X-ray fluorescence spectroscopy are all methods used to determine the amounts of the elements within these rocks. Chemical analyses of individual minerals also provide important information about pelitic rocks. Although mineral analyses have traditionally been conducted by the same analytical techniques as whole-rock analyses, problems obtaining material pure enough for analysis have plagued scientists. Since the 1960's, almost all published mineral analyses have been produced on the electron microprobe, which greatly improves the accuracy of the analyses. These whole-rock analyses and individual mineral analyses are commonly plotted together in several ways on triangular graph paper in order to illustrate the kinds of mineral associations that can exist at different metamorphic conditions.

In experimental petrology, metamorphic minerals are grown under a variety of controlled equilibrium conditions to provide geologists with a better understanding of the actual conditions for their formation. Although such studies have greatly enhanced knowledge of naturally occurring metamorphic reactions, the field is not without controversy. The behavior of the reactions kyanite to sillimanite, andalusite to sillimanite, and kyanite to sillimanite as temperatures increase provides a fitting story of the great complexity of this endeavor (see figure). Since the late 1940's, at least a dozen different studies have been conducted on these minerals that occur in pelitic schists. The various studies are not in agreement, so many geologists remain deeply divided about the exact conditions under which these three minerals are stable.

Physical chemistry and thermodynamics provide geologists with tools to predict how minerals in idealized, simplified chemical reactions theoretically behave. Such comparisons are extremely important in making judgments about more complex natural environments.

Context

The only important pelitic rock type that is useful as such is very low-grade slate that is quarried for flagstone, roofing material, countertops, blackboards, billiard tables, and switchboard panels. Yet, pelitic rocks do contain a number of minerals that are extracted for their usefulness.

Staurolite, almandine-garnet, corundum, and kyanite are all minerals from pelitic rocks that have some use as gemstones. In addition, staurolite crystals grow together and may form a cross, which are sold as amulets called fairy stones, although most objects sold as "fairy stones" are not genuine staurolite. (The name "staurolite" is derived from the Greek word meaning "cross" because of the mineral's diagnostic cruciform twin.) The gem forms of corundum occur as two important varieties: the ruby and the sapphire. The ruby is characteristically red; sapphires, which are traditionally considered blue, occur in a wide variety of colors. Corundum also has limited use as an abrasive, particularly for the production of optical lenses. Garnet, from pelitic schists, also has some use as an abrasive for sandblasting and spark plug cleaning. In addition, sillimanite and kyanite are used as refractory (high-temperature) materials in porcelain and spark plugs.

Graphite is another mineral that may occur in or is associated with pelitic schists. Deposits near Turin, Italy, occur in micaceous phyllites, schists, and gneisses. Graphite has a variety of uses, including the production of refractory crucibles for the making of bronze, brass, and steel. It is used with petroleum products as a lubricant and blended with fine clay in the "leads" of pencils. It is also used in steel, batteries, generator brushes, and electrodes, and for electrotype.

Another relatively uncommon mineral, pyrophyllite, is found in very low-grade pelitic rocks and has properties and uses similar to those of talc. Pyrophyllite is used in paints, paper, ceramics, and insecticides, and as an absorbent powder. A special variety of pyrophyllite, called agalmatolite, is prized by the Chinese for the carving of small objects.

Bibliography

Bates, Robert L. *Geology of the Industrial Rocks and Minerals*. Mineola, N.Y.: Dover, 1969. A reference book that deals with rocks and minerals that are extracted because of their economic importance. Slate, graphite, pyrophyllite, kyanite, and corundum, all products of metamorphosed pelitic rocks, are considered in terms of their properties and uses, production, and occurrences. Includes an index and an excellent bibliography.

Dietrich, Richard V., and B. J. Skinner. *Rocks and Rock Minerals*. New York: John Wiley & Sons, 1979. A college-level book that focuses on the description and identification of rocks and minerals through simple methods intended for use in the field. Chapter 6 provides a good overview of metamorphism, emphasizing the important role that pelitic rocks play in the study of regional metamorphism.

Ehlers, Ernest, and H. Blatt. *Petrology: Igneous, Sedimentary, and Metamorphic*. San Francisco: W. H. Freeman, 1982. An upper-level college text that deals with the descriptions, origins, and distribution of igneous, sedimentary, and metamorphic rocks. Pelitic rocks figure prominently in the treatment of the occurrences, graphic representations, the processes of metamorphism, and the mineral changes during metamorphism. Includes a index and bibliographies for each chapter.

Ernst, W. G. *Earth Materials*. Englewood, N.J.: Prentice-Hall, 1969. A compact but excellent introduction to the study of rocks and minerals. Chapter 7, which treats metamorphism, emphasizes the importance of textural and mineralogical changes that pelitic rocks undergo during regional metamorphism. Chapter 2 also briefly addresses the mineral reactions among the index minerals kyanite, sillimanite, and andalusite.

Gillen, Cornelius. *Metamorphic Geology*. Winchester, Mass.: Allen & Unwin, 1982. A readable, well-illustrated introduction to metamorphism that focuses on textures and field relationships. Provides a good discussion of pelitic rocks and Barrovian zones. Also emphasizes the strong tie between metamorphic processes and mountain-building events. Includes a glossary and a short bibliography.

Mason, R. *Petrology of the Metamorphic Rocks*. Winchester, Mass.: Allen & Unwin, 1978. A college-level text intended for the second-year geology student that deals with metamorphic rocks from the perspective of descriptions in the field and beneath the petrographic microscope. Discussion of pelitic rocks covers both regional and contact metamorphism. A glossary, bibliography, and index are included.

Miyashiro, Akiho. *Metamorphism and Metamorphic Belts*. New York: John Wiley & Sons, 1973. An excellent college-level text that treats several types of metamorphism but focuses on regional metamorphism. Early in the text, emphasis is on the mineralogical reactions that occur in pelitic rocks (and other rock types) that best illustrate the concepts of progressive metamorphism. Includes an index and a fine bibliography.

Tennisen, A. C. *Nature of Earth Materials*. 2d ed. Englewood Cliffs, N.J.: Prentice-Hall, 1983. A text written for the nonscientist that covers the nature of atoms and minerals and igneous, sedimentary, and metamorphic rocks. Also includes a section on the uses of these materials. Well illustrated. Bibliography and subject index are included.

Winkler, H. G. F. *Petrogenesis of Metamorphic Rocks*. 5th ed. New York: Springer-Verlag, 1979. An upper-level college text that addresses the chemical and mineralogical aspects of metamorphism. Emphasizes the principle that mineral reactions in common rock types can be used to determine metamorphic conditions. Separate chapters deal with pelitic and other important rock types. Includes index and short bibliographies after each chapter.

Ronald D. Tyler

Cross-References

Foliation and Lineation, 747; Metamorphic Rock Classification, 1553; Metamorphic Textures, 1578; Contact Metamorphism, 1594; Metamorphism: Metasomatism, 1599; Regional Metamorphism, 1606; Mountain Belts, 1725.

METAMORPHIC TEXTURES

Type of earth science: Geology
Field of study: Petrology, metamorphic

Metamorphic textures are important criteria in the description, classification, and understanding of the conditions under which metamorphic rocks form. Textures vary widely and develop as a result of the interaction between deformation, recrystallization, new mineral growth, and time.

Principal terms

COHERENT TEXTURE: an arrangement that allows the minerals or particles in a rock to stick together

CRUST: the outermost layer of the earth, composed of rocks with comparatively low densities

FOLIATION: a planar feature in metamorphic rocks

MICA: a silicate mineral (one silicon atom surrounded by four oxygen atoms) that splits readily in only one direction

SHIELD: a large region of stable, ancient rocks within a continent

STRAIN: deformation resulting from stress

STRESS: force per unit of area

TECTONICS: the study of the processes and products of large-scale movement and deformation within the earth

TEXTURE: the size, shape, and arrangement of minerals or particles in a rock

Summary of the Phenomenon

In the classification and description of sedimentary, igneous, or metamorphic rocks, texture is a very important factor. Texture has a relatively straightforward definition—it is the size, shape, and arrangement of particles or minerals in a rock. How texture is related to the rock fabric and rock structure may be confusing. Rock structure is sometimes used to refer only to features produced by movement that occurs after the rock is formed. Rock fabric sometimes refers to both the structure and the texture of crystalline (most igneous and metamorphic) rocks. There is so much disagreement that the three terms are used interchangeably. Yet, although there is no agreement on the categories of metamorphism, some are more generally accepted than others. Regional, contact, and cataclastic are the three principal types. Shock, burial, sub-sea-floor, and hydrothermal metamorphism tend to be more controversial and are not considered significant.

Metamorphic textures develop in response to several factors, the most influential being elevated temperatures and pressures and chemically active fluids. In each type of metamorphism, the relative influence of each of these three factors varies greatly.

Generally, the effect of temperature on metamorphism is easy to understand. Converting dough to bread by baking provides a common analogy. The roles of pressure and fluids, however, are more difficult to explain. Two types of pressure, confining and directed, play a role in metamorphism. Confining pressure is the force exerted on a rock at depth by the overlying material. Directed pressure is a larger force exerted by some external factor, usually tectonic in origin. Of these two types, directed pressure produces more apparent textural changes in metamorphic rocks. The primary role of chemically active fluids is to facilitate the metamorphic reactions and textural changes that occur.

Of all the types of metamorphism, the most pervasive is regional metamorphism. Regional metamorphism occurs in the roots of mountain belts as they are forming. Thousands of square kilometers can be involved. Temperature and directed pressure are the critical agents in producing the new mineral assemblages and textures distinctive of this type of metamorphism. The most diagnostic feature in regionally metamorphosed rocks is a planar fabric, which forms as platy and elongate minerals develop a preferred orientation. This planar fabric, or foliation, generally forms only in the presence of (and in an orientation that is perpendicular to) the directed pressure. Directed pressure may also impart a linear element on some rocks. This lineation may develop because elongate minerals or groups of minerals are recrystallized, deformed into a preferred direction, or both. Lineations may also develop where two planar fabrics intersect. Of all the different rock types, shales and other fine-grained rocks are the most sensitive to increasing conditions of metamorphism and show marked textural changes as metamorphic conditions increase. Not all regionally metamorphosed rocks develop foliations or lineations; many rock types show very little textural change from the lowest to highest conditions of metamorphism.

As metamorphism begins, shale is converted to slate, which diagnostically splits along smooth surfaces called cleavage. Cleavage takes two forms: flow cleavage and fracture cleavage. Flow cleavage is a pervasive or penetrative fabric; directed pressure influences every portion of the rock, with most of the micaceous minerals undergoing recrystallization. A variety of penetrative fabrics characterize regionally metamorphosed rocks formed at different metamorphic conditions. In fracture cleavage, the distinct planar fractures are separated by discrete, relatively undeformed segments of rock.

At the lowest grades of regional metamorphism, as the penetrative fabric develops in slate, very fine-grained micaceous minerals start to grow in a preferred orientation, thus producing planes of weaknesses along which the slate readily splits. At slightly higher metamorphic conditions, the micaceous minerals continue to form. The rock typically takes on a pronounced sheen, although the individual mineral grains remain mostly too small to see with the unaided eye. This texture is referred to as a phyllitic texture, and the rock is called a phyllite. As metamorphic conditions continue to increase at ever greater depths, the micaceous minerals eventually grow large enough to be seen with the naked eye, and the preferred orientation of these platy minerals becomes obvious. This texture is referred to as a schistosity, and the rock is called a schist. As the conditions of metamorphism approach very high levels, the micaceous minerals start to break down to form other minerals that are not platy, and the rock begins to lose its property to split along foliation surfaces. A new type of foliation develops, however, because light and dark minerals tend to separate into alternating bands. This banded texture is characteristic of rocks called gneisses, and the texture is referred to as a gneissosity. At even higher conditions, rocks begin to melt in a process called anatexis. Anatexis occurs at conditions that are considered to be at the interface between metamorphism and igneous processes.

Although not as pervasive as regional metamorphism, contact metamorphism is of interest because many of its deposits are economically important. Contact metamorphism occurs in areas of relatively shallow depths where a hot, molten igneous body comes in contact with the cooler rock that it has invaded. The metamorphism takes place outside the margins of the igneous mass, with temperature as the key agent of metamorphism and recrystallization as the dominant process modifying the original rock. The area metamorphosed around the intrusion is called the aureole. The size of this aureole is a function of the size, composition, and temperature of the igneous body, as well as the composition of the host rock and depth of the intrusion. The intensity of the metamorphism is greatest at the contact between the two rock bodies and decreases away from the source of heat. Aureoles may be as thin as a meter or as wide as 2-3 kilometers.

A number of rock types and textures are characteristic of contact metamorphism. Most rocks produced by contact metamorphism are fine-grained because the processes by which they were formed are relatively short-lived. Typically, the aureole is made of a hard, massive, and fine-grained rock called a hornfels. Characteristically, the hornfels is more fine-grained than is the rock that was metamorphosed. The uniform grain size gives the rock a granular appearance, particularly when magnified; this texture is termed granoblastic or hornfelsic. Since hornfels undergo no deformation, textures in the original rock may be preserved, even when recrystallization is complete.

When shales are metamorphosed, very large crystals of minerals such as andalusite and cordierite may develop in an otherwise fine-grained granoblastic rock. These large crystals constitute a porphyroblastic texture and are themselves called porphyroblasts. When schists or slates are subjected to contact metamorphism, remnant porphyroblasts or ovoid masses of mica may produce a spotted appearance, and the rock is named a spotted slate or schist. If the aureole contains silicon-rich carbonate rocks (impure limestones), much coarser textures are likely to form at or near the contact of the igneous body. These coarser-grained rocks are termed tactites or skarns.

The third type of metamorphism is cataclastic or dynamic metamorphism, which occurs in fault or deep-shear zones. Directed pressure is the key agent, with temperature and confining pressure playing variable roles. The textures in cataclastic rocks are divided into four groups: incoherent, nonfoliated, mylonitic, and foliated-recrystallized. Incoherent texture develops at very shallow depths and low confining pressures. Based on the degree of cataclasis (from least to most), fault breccia and fault gouge are the rock types formed. Nonfoliated (or mortar) texture forms coherent rocks typified by the presence of porphyroclastic minerals (large crystals that have survived cataclasis) surrounded by finely ground material. Rocks with this texture lack obvious foliations. Also included in this group are cataclastic rocks with glassy textures. Unusually intense grinding produces enough frictional heating to melt portions of the rock partially. Mylonitic texture occurs in coherent rocks that show a distinct foliation (flow structure). The foliation typically forms because alternating layers show differing intensities of grinding. Textural subdivisions and rock names are based on the degree of grinding, such as protomylonite (least amount of grinding), orthomylonite, and ultramylonite (most amount of grinding). The final group is the foliated-recrystallized textures. Cataclastic rocks that illustrate considerable recrystallization are also typically foliated. The degree of grinding determines the rock name. Mylonite gneiss shows the least cataclasis, while the blastomylonite is more crushed.

Shock metamorphism is the rarest type of metamorphism. It is characteristically associated with meteorite craters and astroblemes. Astroblemes are circular topographic features that are inferred to represent the impact sites of ancient meteorites or comets. Some geologists consider shock metamorphism as a type of dynamic metamorphism because in both, directed pressure plays the essential role, whereas temperature may vary from low to extremely high.

A number of textural features are associated with shock metamorphism. Brecciation (breaking into angular fragments), fracturing, and warping of crystals are common. On a microscopic scale, the presence of two or more sets of deformation lamellae in quartz crystals is considered conclusive evidence of a meteorite impact. (Deformation lamellae are closely spaced microscopic parallel layers that are partially or totally changed to glass or are sets of closely spaced dislocations within mineral grains.) Shock metamorphism is also detected when minerals are partially or completely turned to glass (presumably with and without melting) and when shatter cones are present. Shatter cones are cone-shaped rock bodies or fractures typified by striations that radiate from the apex.

Methods of Study

Although much of the work of describing metamorphic textures comes from the field of metamorphic petrology, the means of studying how these textures, fabrics, or structures are generated is more within the area of structural geology called structural analysis. Structural analysis, in turn, relies heavily on the fields of metallurgy, mechanics, and rheology to describe and interpret the process by which rocks are deformed. Structural analysis considers metamorphic textures and larger features, such as faults and folds, from three different perspectives: descriptive analysis, kinematic analysis, and dynamic analysis. Synthesis of the information obtained from these three analyses typically leads to comprehensive models or hypotheses that explain problems concerning metamorphic textures.

Descriptive analysis is the foundation of all studies of metamorphic textures because it involves both fieldwork and laboratory analysis. In descriptive analysis, geologists consider the physical and geometric aspects of deformed rocks, which include the recognition, description, and measurement of the orientations of textural elements. Typically, descriptive analysis involves geologic mapping, in which geologists measure the orientations of metamorphic structures with an instrument that is a combination compass-clinometer. (A clinometer is an instrument or scale used to measure the angle of an inclined line or surface in the vertical plane.) These structural measurements are plotted in a variety of ways to determine if the data show any statistical significance. Characteristically, these field studies may also include analysis of aerial photographs (taken vertically from aircraft to minimize distortion) or satellite imagery to determine if textures or structures that are evident on the microscopic scale, or those of a rock outcrop, are related to much larger patterns.

In the laboratory, descriptive analysis of metamorphic textures can involve several techniques. One of the most important involves the petrographic microscope, in which magnified images of textures result from the transmission of polarized light through thin sections of properly oriented rock specimens. The thin section is a paper-thin slice of rock (usually 0.03 millimeter thick) that is produced by gluing a small cut and polished block of the rock specimen to a glass slide. This block, commonly a little less than 2.7 millimeters by 4.5 millimeters, is then cut and ground to the proper thickness.

Kinematic analysis is the study of the displacements or deformational movements that produce features such as metamorphic textures. Several types of movement are recognized, including distortion and dilation. The study of distortion (change of shape) and dilation (change of volume) in a rock is called strain analysis. Strain analysis involves the quantitative evaluation of how original sizes and shapes of geological features are changed. Although strain commonly expresses itself as movement along preexisting surfaces, distortion also creates new surfaces such as cleavages and foliations in metamorphic rocks.

Dynamic analysis attempts to express observed strains in terms of probable patterns of stress. Stress is the force per unit of area acting upon a body, typically measured in kilograms per square meter. Although dynamic analysis is the most hypothetical phase of structural studies, the theoretical and experimental aspects of dynamic analysis provide important contributions to the study of the kinds of structural changes that metamorphic rocks undergo. One important area of study in dynamic analysis involves experimental deformation of rocks under various levels of temperature, confining pressure, and time. Such experiments are typically conducted on short cylindrical specimens on a triaxial testing machine, which attempts to simulate natural conditions with the variables controlled. By jacketing specimens in impermeable coverings, pressures can be created hydraulically to exceed

10 kilobars, which are comparable to those near the base of the crust. Dynamic analysis also involves scale-model experiments, using clays and other soft substances to attempt to replicate naturally occurring structural features.

Context

Although a number of metamorphic minerals and rocks are used by society, in most cases, the metamorphic textures of these materials play no role in their utility. One notable exception is slate. Because metamorphic processes impart a strong cleavage to this very fine-grained rock, it readily splits apart along these thin, smooth surfaces. The combination of grain size, cleavage, and strength makes slate useful in a number of products, including roofing shingles, flagstones, electrical panels, mantels, blackboards, grave vaults, and billiard tables. Most other metamorphic rocks, however, have foliations or other textural features that make the rocks structurally weak, and limit their usefulness.

In other cases, however, metamorphic rocks are useful because they lack pronounced foliations or do not readily break along planes of weakness. Many widely used marbles, particularly those quarried in Italy, Georgia, and Vermont, are products of regional metamorphism. They are prized in part because they are generally massive (lacking texturally induced planes of weakness) and can be cut into very large blocks. Several quartzites and gneisses also tend to be massive enough to be used as dimension stone or as aggregate because of high internal strength and relative chemical inertness.

Aside from direct usage, metamorphic textures are also of considerable concern in construction and mining in areas where strongly foliated rocks exist. One particular example illustrates the types of problems that metamorphic textures can create if not recognized and adequately treated. In 1928, four hundred people were killed in a flood in an area near Los Angeles, California. The flood occurred when the St. Francis Dam collapsed only one year after it had been built. The builders had failed to recognize that the eastern side of the dam was constructed on regionally metamorphosed rocks that had foliations paralleling the steep valley sides. Numerous rockslide scars should have alarmed the builders, but all were overlooked. The textural factors were never proven to have caused the collapse of the dam, because the builders had made other errors; however, the foliated rocks certainly must have contributed to the disaster.

For the same reasons, problems can develop in mountainous or hilly regions when construction occurs where weak, intensely foliated metamorphic rocks exist. When road or railway cuts are excavated through foliations inclined toward these cuts, rock slides are possible. In some cases, the roads can be relocated, or, if not, slide-prone slopes may be modified or removed. In other places, slide-prone exposures or mine walls and ceilings can be pinned and anchored.

Construction of buildings in metamorphic areas also requires careful evaluation. Where weak foliations parallel slopes, it must be determined whether the additional weight of structures and water for lawns and from runoff are likely to induce rock slides or other forms of slope instability. If so, land-use plans and zoning restrictions need to be adopted to indicate that these areas are potentially hazardous.

Bibliography

Best, Myron G. *Igneous and Metamorphic Petrology*. San Francisco: W. H. Freeman, 1982. A readable advanced college-level text that generally should not be beyond the general reader who wants to learn more about metamorphic textures. This illustrated treatment of metamorphism includes the topics of mineralogy, chemistry, and the structure of metamorphic rocks. Both field relationships and global-scale tectonic associations are discussed.

Davis, George H. *Structural Geology of Rocks and Regions*. New York: John Wiley & Sons, 1984. An uppper-level geology text that provides an excellent treatment of the deformational features in metamorphic rocks. Includes chapters on descriptive, kinematic, and dynamic analyses. Provides a well-illustrated treatment of cleavage, foliation, and lineation. Good bibliography and author and subject index.

Dietrich, Richard V., and B. J. Skinner. *Rocks and Rock Minerals*. New York: John Wiley & Sons, 1979. This short, readable college-level text provides a relatively brief but excellent treatment of regional, contact, and cataclastic metamorphic rocks, with good coverage of metamorphic textures. Very well illustrated. Includes a subject index and a modest bibliography.

Ernst, W. G. *Earth Materials*. Englewood Cliffs, N.J.: Prentice-Hall, 1969. Chapter 7 in this very fine, compact, introductory-level book provides a succinct treatment of the topic of metamorphism. Metamorphic structures, cataclastic rocks, contact metamorphism, and regional metamorphism are all briefly discussed. Includes a subject index and a short bibliography.

Hyndman, Donald W. *Petrology of Igneous and Metamorphic Rocks*. 2d ed. New York: McGraw-Hill, 1985. A college-level text intended for the undergraduate geology student. Not overly technical. Hyndman clearly covers the traditional themes (categories, processes, and conditions) necessary to understand metamorphic rocks. Text provides information on the locations and descriptions of metamorphic rock associations. Includes an index and an exhaustive bibliography.

Spry, A. *Metamorphic Textures*. Oxford, England: Pergamon Press, 1969. Advanced college-level text that treats metamorphism in terms of textural changes and largely disregards chemical interactions. Although parts of the blook may be beyond the introductory reader, several chapters deal with very basic principles. Provides excellent illustrations and photographs. Includes an extensive bibliography and author and subject indexes.

Suppe, John. *Principles of Structural Geology*. Englewood Cliffs, N.J.: Prentice-Hall, 1985. A well-illustrated college text intended for the geology major. Chapters 10 and 11 provide clear discussions of "Fabrics" and "Impact Structures," respectively, that are very readable and that do not generally require

extensive background to understand. Includes a bibliography and subject index.
Williams, Howel, F. J. Turner, and C. M. Gilbert. *Petrology: An Introduction to the Study of Rocks in Thin Sections*. 2d ed. San Francisco: W. H. Freeman, 1982. Although the bulk of this upper-level college text deals with the description of textures and mineral associations in igneous, sedimentary, and metamorphic rocks beneath the petrographic microscope, the authors provide excellent, understandable descriptions of the major types of metamorphism and associated textures.

Ronald D. Tyler

Cross-References
Astroblemes, 106; Experimental Rock Deformation, 669; Folds, 739; Foliation and Lineation, 747; Metamorphic Rock Classification, 1553; Metamorphic Rocks: Pelitic Schists, 1570; Contact Metamorphism, 1594; Regional Metamorphism, 1606; Mountain Belts, 1725; Stress and Strain, 2490.

METAMORPHISM: ANATEXIS

Type of earth science: Geology
Field of study: Petrology, metamorphic

As a crustal process, anatexis records the thermal culmination of prograde regional metamorphism and produces most of the granitic plutons and migmatites in mobile belts less than 600 million years old. Anatectic melting probably accounts for the major tracts of granulite facies rocks in Precambrian shield areas.

Principal terms

LIQUIDUS TEMPERATURE: the temperature at which the last crystal of a rock disappears into the melt phase

MAGMA: molten rock material that crystallizes (solidifies) to form igneous rocks

METAMORPHIC CULMINATION: the point in time when the thermal maximum is reached during a prograde metamorphic event

MINIMUM MELT: the composition of the initial melt, formed at the solidus temperature, during progressive heating of a rock

MOBILE BELT: a linear belt of igneous and deformed metamorphic rocks produced by plate collision at a continental margin

PROGRADE METAMORPHISM: recrystallization of regional-scale solid rock masses induced by rising temperature

REFRACTORY MINERAL: a mineral with a sufficiently high melting temperature that is unaffected by anatexis and remains in the solid residue

REGIONAL METAMORPHIC FACIES: the particular pressure-temperature conditions under which metamorphism occurred

RETROGRADE METAMORPHISM: the reversal of prograde mineral reactions caused by the reintroduction of water and/or carbon dioxide during the period of declining temperature following metamorphic culmination

SOLIDUS TEMPERATURE: the temperature at which melting begins

Summary of the Phenomenon

Anatexis refers to any process that leads to gradual melting of preexisting crustal or mantle rocks. In general, solid rocks near but below their solidus temperatures can be induced to melt in response to a temperature increase or a pressure decrease (decompression) or by a change in chemical composition (especially the addition of water)—or combinations of these processes. Since all common rocks are granular aggregates of several mineral species, each with its own melting behavior, melting of the total rock is a heterogeneous process. Therefore, a rock subject to slow progressive heating will melt in a stepwise fashion over a temperature interval determined by the melting points of the least and most stable minerals in the rock. The temperature at which melting begins is the solidus temperature; the temperature at which the last crystal disappears into the melt phase is the liquidus temperature. For most rocks, this melting interval extends over a range of about 200-250 degrees Celsius. Between the solidus and liquidus temperatures, a rock system consists of a melt, which is enriched in the more soluble and lowest-melting-point components, and a coexisting solid residue of the more refractory minerals. This condition of partial melting or partial fusion has become synonymous with anatexis and is responsible for the generation of magma in both the mantle and the crust.

Experiments have clearly shown that anatexis plays a major role in the production of basaltic magma from peridotite parent rock in the earth's upper mantle. Most discussions of anatexis, however, concern processes operating in the crust in which partial melting is viewed as the culmination of regional metamorphism. In this context, the term "ultrametamorphism" is also used synonymously with "anatexis." As a crustal phenomenon, anatexis occurs under confining pressures that generally are less than 10 kilobars (roughly the pressure at a depth of 35 kilometers). This limit could extend as high as 15 kilobars if exceptional crustal thickening is produced by the governing plate-collision event. Experiments indicate that melting will begin in a wide variety of common metamorphic rocks under moderate pressures (4-7 kilobars) when the temperature reaches the vicinity of 700 degrees Celsius. These temperature-pressure conditions are attained only near the upper limit of the amphibolite facies of regional metamorphism. Upper amphibolite facies rocks, in general, mark the highest grades of metamorphism attained in Phanerozoic mobile belts (those less than 600 million years old). Thus, no crustal rock may be subjected to anatexis without first undergoing progressive metamorphism through greenschist facies and amphibolite facies conditions.

A large amount of experimental data show that the initial composition of an anatectic melt is that of granite. Granite is the "minimum melt" in any parent rock that contains both quartz and feldspar. In the region where melting occurs, the product will be a mixture of granitic melt and solid residual material. The melt-to-solid ratio depends upon the degree of melting (1 percent, 5 percent, 20 percent, and so on), which is a function of temperature, confining pressure, bulk composition of the parent rock, and the availability of free water. Among these controlling variables, water content is paramount because even small quantities of water (relative to rock saturation) significantly depress the solidus of a rock and therefore facilitate anatexis. Given enough free water, almost any rock will melt during high-grade metamorphism; under dry conditions, anatexis is virtually impossible in the crust.

The solid-melt mixture resulting from a significant degree of partial melting forms a low-density "mush" with a strong tendency to rise from the melt site, en masse, and form granitoid plutons or even volcanic rocks if it can successfully reach the surface before complete crystallization. The dynamics of rising magma bodies

Earth Science

and their crystallization history in transit are major subjects of study in igneous petrology. The metamorphic petrologist, however, is concerned with the conditions that lead up to melting and the geological traits of the melt site itself.

In deeply eroded mobile belts of Phanerozoic age, conditions of peak metamorphic intensity are best recorded by pelitic schists of the upper amphibolite facies. These "pelites" are the metamorphic equivalents of common clay-rich shales and mudstones transformed into garnet-mica schists containing the distinctive zone mineral sillimanite. If this sillimanite zone is traversed in the direction of increasing metamorphic intensity, one normally encounters pods, veins, lenses, and small, discontinuous layers of granitic rock with increasing frequency. These rocks of "mixed" igneous-metamorphic appearance are migmatites, the origin of which has been debated for nearly a century. Migmatites are classified on the basis of the relationship between the leucosome (light-colored, granite-looking material) and the melanosome (dark mica-rich/amphibole-rich material with metamorphic texture). There is broad agreement on the anatectic origin of migmatites and associated S-type granites (granites with a sedimentary parentage) in the sillimanite zone of regional metamorphic belts. For these migmatites, the leucosome is interpreted as the crystallization product of an anatectic melt, and the melanosome is interpreted as the refractory components of parent rock depleted in low-melting-point constituents (essentially quartz and alkali feldspar). The salient feature of migmatites as a rock class is the bewildering range of structural relationships existing between the leucosome and melanosome components. These very complexities are interpreted by some geologists as further evidence of origin by anatexis. They argue that a correlation exists between the degree of partial melting of the parent rock and the degree of complexity and intimacy manifested by the leucosome and melanosome. A common pattern is that of stromatic migmatites, in which the leucosome forms thin, discontinuous layers more or less parallel to the schistosity of the enclosing rock. Veinitic migmatites exhibit a melanosome densely traversed by a network of tiny leucosome veinlets. Nebulitic migmatites, common in some localities, are characterized by poorly defined "patches" of leucosome that pass by gradations, over a transition distance of a few centimeters, into vaguely defined melanosome patches. It is important to bear in mind that migmatites are exceptionally diverse in their features and mode of occurrence. The majority occur in vast Precambrian terranes where evidence for a simple origin by anatexis is lacking or equivocal. Such migmatites may be products of a number of subsolidus mechanisms; among these are metasomatism, metamorphic segregation coupled with polyphase folding, and injection by unrelated granitic magmas followed by intense deformation.

In contrast to Phanerozoic mobile belts, ancient Precambrian shield terranes are dominated by metamorphic rocks of basic composition that record temperature/pressure conditions of the granulite facies. Most of these terranes are bounded either by major faults or profound unconformities and do not exhibit rocks transitional to the lower-grade amphibolite facies. Minor lenses and zones of amphibolite facies rocks do occur within granulite terranes, but these are almost invariably the result of postmetamorphic rehydration of the granulites. Typical Archean (older than 2.5 billion years) and Proterozoic (older than 600 million years) granulites exhibit compositional layering deformed by large-scale recumbent folds. Migmatites, in the form of granitic lenses, are commonly present within layered granulite sequences, but there are no transitions from high-grade migmatized rocks to unmigmatized rocks of lower grade, as in Phanerozoic mobile belts. In fact, there is rarely an indication of the downgrade or upgrade directions. Pelitic and carbonate rocks are conspicuously rare or absent in granulite terranes.

The field relations and traits of Precambrian granulites have long puzzled geologists. Their study is seriously hindered by the lack of stratigraphic markers (destroyed by deformation) and the rarity of areas recording the transition to amphibolite facies conditions. Darjeeling, India, and Broken Hill, Australia, are two localities where this important transition has been recognized and studied. Granulite facies rocks are recognized by a definitive mineral assemblage which, for basic rocks, consists of clinopyroxene, orthopyroxene, and plagioclase. This assemblage may be accompanied by a variety of minor phases, including quartz, garnet, cordierite, sillimanite, kyanite, alkali feldspar, calcite, and olivine. Hornblende and biotite are absent or, at most, rare. This mineralogy reveals the outstanding characteristic of all granulite facies rocks: They are virtually anhydrous. They are, in fact, the driest rocks on earth.

Laboratory melting experiments indicate that the refractory residue produced by a significant degree (perhaps 20-30 percent) of partial melting would possess properties similar to those of basic granulite facies rocks. These include anhydrous character, low radioactivity, relatively high density, and refractory mineralogy. The key link between anatexis and granulites is the behavior of water during melting. Prograde reactions under upper amphibolite-granulite facies conditions will certainly liberate small amounts of water by the successive destruction of muscovite, biotite, and hornblende (all hydrous phases). Once liberated, this water depresses the solidus temperature of the enclosed rock and permits melting. As temperature increases at any given pressure in the range 4-10+ kilobars, water is released in a stepwise fashion by the dehydration reactions, inducing further melting. This situation has the appearance of a runaway "crustal meltdown," and it would be, except for one important factor. Water, in the presence of an undersaturated silicate melt, is very efficiently absorbed by that melt, which effectively removes it from the presence of the restite. This stabilizes or even raises the solidus temperature of the rock enclosing the melt. At these pressures, granitic melts can absorb nearly 10 percent water (by weight); as a result, the rate of melting rapidly diminishes to zero. If the water-bearing granitic melt is capable of upward movement, it leaves behind a highly desiccated, refractory residue such as granulite facies rocks. The rarity of pelitic and carbonate lithologies in granulite terranes appears to be the result of metamorphism, dehydration reactions, anatexis, and the mobilization of granitic magma. Increasing evidence suggests that Precambrian granulite terranes represent the "root zones" of major batholith systems that have since been removed by erosion. Seismic data from the root zones of present-day batholiths such as the Sierra Nevada tend to support this hypothesis.

Methods of Study

Significant volumes of granitic migmatites and plutons are normally encountered in zones of highest metamorphic grade in Phanerozoic mobile belts. Vast amounts of experimental data indicate that, given the availability of water, prograde metamorphism to upper amphibolite facies conditions should culminate with anatexis. In many well-studied localities, granites and migmatites are restricted to upper amphibolite facies host rocks (including the northeastern United States, southern Greenland, Scotland, and the Black Forest of Germany). In the past, the mere spatial association of these rocks was accepted as evidence of crustal fusion during prograde metamorphism (that is, ultrametamorphism), but that is no longer the case. Modern studies have returned to the field in the classic localities to find evidence for availability of sufficient water to form the exposed granites.

The question of water availability arises because the trifling amount of pore water retained in amphibolite facies rocks is insufficient to produce melting under the prevailing pressure and temperature conditions. It follows, therefore, that dehydration reactions involving muscovite must supply the needed water. The difficulty with this reasoning is that once a granitic melt appears, it can absorb up to about 10 percent water (by weight) from the surrounding rocks. To sustain the melting process, an ever-increasing burden is placed on concurrent dehydration reactions. Many geologists question whether this "water budget" will permit large volumes of granitic magma to form.

The formation of sillimanite, a distinctive needlelike mineral, is a key factor in modern field studies. In most areas, sillimanite appears initially by the simple reaction: kyanite $\rightarrow$ sillimanite. Traversing up-grade from the rocks which are recording that reaction, researchers frequently discover that the rocks have undergone a second sillimanite-producing reaction that involves the breakdown of muscovite: muscovite + quartz $\rightarrow$ sillimanite + potassium feldspar + water. By careful study, the geologist draws lines on a geological map, delineating the appearance of sillimanite by both of these reactions. These lines are known as the first sillimanite isograd and the second sillimanite isograd, respectively. The second reaction is the key water-producing reaction that must precede melting if it occurs. It is demonstrated by mapping the first appearance of the pair sillimanite + potassium feldspar. Migmatites frequently appear very close to this isograd and are usually interpreted as evidence for the reaction: muscovite + quartz + water $\rightarrow$ sillimanite + melt. This third reaction constitutes anatexis, or ultrametamorphism, and could be expected to occur at depths of about 15 kilometers and temperatures in the vicinity of 700 degrees Celsius if water is available. This reaction must cease if the melt absorbs all the available water. Such is the paradoxical relationship between anatexis and regional metamorphism. The melt formed by the third reaction would be close in composition to the granite minimum but, because it would likely contain a refractory assemblage of biotite, hornblende, garnet, and plagioclase crystals, its bulk composition (melt + solid residue) could be closer to granodiorite. If the second and third reactions can produce sufficient melt volume, the melt may segregate, collect, and rise a small distance to form a granitic pluton. If it does not segregate and collect efficiently, migmatites are the likely result. Melts that remain immobile until they are water-saturated have a very limited capacity for upward movement (decompression induces crystallization). The potential for rising is also limited by the fact that as the second and third reactions are taking place, the entire rock mass is being intensely deformed by regional compression.

Beyond demonstrating a water-producing reaction such as the second reaction, the case for ultrametamorphism also requires proof that the appearance of granitic plutons is synchronous with, or slightly later than, metamorphic culmination and that the resulting granitic rocks have S-type traits (traits that indicate sedimentary parentage). Syntectonic plutons are recognized by their poor development or lack of thermal aureoles, semiconcordant contacts with enclosing rocks, and shared late-stage deformational features with their metamorphic parent rocks. The S-type characteristics will be reflected in the rock chemistry, in the mineralogy (especially the presence of garnet, cordierite, and muscovite), and by abundant unmelted inclusions of metamorphic rock.

Context

All rocks are subject to partial melting, or anatexis. In fact, the earth's crust developed largely in response to partial melting of the upper mantle. Once a stable crust developed, its maximum temperature and thickness were limited by anatectic melting of the crustal rocks. The plate tectonics theory provides a satisfying basis for understanding large-scale mass transfer between the crust and mantle and the critical role played by anatexis. In all spreading-plate systems, anatectic magmas are generated at both leading and trailing plate margins. At present, new oceanic crust is forming at a rate of 3×10^{16} grams per year along oceanic-ridge axes. This new crust is basaltic in composition and derived by partial melting of underlying mantle peridotite. Additions to the continental crust occur on an even larger scale along continental margins in plate-collision settings. The most obvious manifestation of crustal growth in collisional settings is intensive, andesite-dominated volcanism, such as that currently taking place in the Andes of South America. Less obvious but more important contributions to crustal growth occur beneath the thick volcanic cover of youthful mobile belts such as the Andes. At depth, deformed sequences of metasedimentary rocks are intruded by gigantic granitic batholiths of anatectic origin.

As a crustal process, anatexis is logically viewed as the ultimate stage of progressive metamorphism and is often termed ultrametamorphism. In mobile belts, partial melting of metasedimentary rocks occurs at intermediate depths (amphibolite facies conditions) to form S-type granitic batholiths such as those that dominate the mountainous terrains of Western Europe and the Far East. These batholiths represent recycled crustal material rather than mantle-derived additions to the crust. They are, nevertheless, major components of many mobile belts and hosts to important metallic ores (tin and tungsten especially). In contrast, I-type granitic batholiths are produced by anatexis of metaigneous rocks at substantially greater depths (granulite facies conditions). The production of I-type granitoids is poorly understood but most likely involves melt contributions from the lowermost crust, the subducted slab associated with plate collisions, and the "mantle wedge" separating these two regimes. Most authorities agree that I-type plutonism involves significant volumes of mantle-derived melt and is, therefore, a major factor in crustal growth.

The production and destruction of oceanic crust appears to be balanced on a global basis (that is, subduction cancels ocean-ridge volcanism), but it is clear that the ratio of continental to oceanic crust has not remained constant throughout geological time. The past 2.5 billion years have witnessed major, episodic, lateral growth and thickening of continental crust around each of the world's ancient Precambrian shields. This record of growth clearly requires sustained production of I-type granitic magmas by anatexis.

Bibliography

Best, Myron G. *Igneous and Metamorphic Petrology*. New York: W. H. Freeman, 1982. A popular university text for undergraduate majors in geology. A well-illustrated and fairly detailed treatment of the origin, distribution, and characteristics of igneous and metamorphic rocks. Chapter 4 treats granite plutons and batholiths, and chapter 12 treats a broad spectrum of metamorphic topics; pages 421-427 are recommended for an overview of regional metamorphism in mobile belts.

Fyfe, W. S. "The Generation of Batholiths." *Tectonophysics* 17 (March, 1973): 273-283. An influential article by one of the major figures in petrological research. An overview of anatectic thinking that can be understood by college-level readers familiar with igneous and metamorphic processes. The periodical *Tectonophysics* will be found in major university libraries.

Presnall, D. C. "Fractional Crystallization and Partial Fusion." In *The Evolution of the Igneous Rocks: Fiftieth Anniversary Perspectives*, edited by H. S. Yoder, Jr. Princeton, N.J.: Princeton University Press, 1979. A technical article dealing with theoretical aspects of rock melting and crystallization of silicate melts. Not for readers without a strong background in geology or chemistry.

Press, Frank, and Raymond Siever. *Earth*. 4th ed. New York: W. H. Freeman, 1986. Chapter 15, "Plutonism," and chapter 17, "Metamorphism," provide readers with no background in geology an introduction to igneous and metamorphic processes. The concept of partial melting is introduced in chapter 15; migmatites are mentioned in chapter 17.

White, A. J. R., and B. W. Chappel. "Ultrametamorphism and Granitoid Genesis." *Tectonophysics*, November 15, 1977: 7-22. An excellent article providing an overview of S-type and I-type granite genesis by the authors who first recognized these distinctions (now regarded as fundamental). Not overly technical, but requires some background in geology. This particular issue is entirely devoted to anatexis (ultrametamorphism), so those interested in the topic should scan its contents. This periodical is found in major university libraries.

Wiley, P. J. "Petrogenesis and the Physics of the Earth." In *The Evolution of the Igneous Rocks: Fiftieth Anniversary Perspectives*, edited by H. S. Yoder, Jr. Princeton, N.J.: Princeton University Press, 1979. Reviews fifty years of progress in experimental petrology. Production of basaltic magma (page 506) and granitic magma (page 511) by partial melting are concisely summarized from the experimental viewpoint. Technical—requires prior knowledge of melting phenomena.

Winkler, Helmut G. F. *Petrogenesis of Metamorphic Rocks*. 3d ed. New York: Springer-Verlag, 1974. A traditional text for undergraduate majors in geology. Chapter 18 deals with anatexis, migmatites, and granite magmas in some detail. This reference should be consulted after Press and Siever and before the more technical works.

Yardley, Bruce. *An Introduction to Metamorphic Petrology*. New York: Halsted Press, 1989. An excellent undergraduate text, with a good index and very extensive, current references. Chapter 3 deals with metamorphism of pelitic rocks, including anatexis and migmatization. The author is a prominent leader in migmatite research.

Gary R. Lowell

Cross-References

Continental Crust, 261; Continental Growth, 268; Igneous Rocks: Batholiths, 1165; Igneous Rocks: Granitic, 1180; The Origin of Magmas, 1428; Metamorphic Rock Classification, 1553; Metamorphic Rocks: Pelitic Schists, 1570; Regional Metamorphism, 1606; Plate Tectonics, 2079; Subduction and Orogeny, 2497.

CONTACT METAMORPHISM

Type of earth science: Geology
Field of study: Petrology, metamorphic

Contact metamorphism is caused by the temperature rise in rocks adjacent to magmatic intrusions of local extent that penetrate relatively shallow, cold regions of the earth's crust. Many economically important metallic mineral deposits occur in contact metamorphic zones.

Principal terms

AUREOLE: a ring-shaped zone of metamorphic rock surrounding a magmatic intrusion

CONTACT METAMORPHIC FACIES: zones of contact metamorphic effects, each of which is characterized by a small number of indicator minerals

CONTACT METAMORPHISM: the change in mineralogy and/or composition of rock as a result of high temperatures around magmatic intrusion of limited extent

HORNFELS: the hard, splintery rocks formed by contact metamorphism of sediments and other rocks

LITHOLOGY: the general physical type of rocks or rock formations

Summary of the Phenomenon

Contact metamorphic rocks are moderately widespread; they occur at or near the earth's surface, where magmas of all kinds intrude low-temperature rocks. Minerals in contact metamorphic rocks are similar to those in regional metamorphic rocks of comparable metamorphic grade. Contact metamorphic effects are divided into facies (zones), each of which is characterized by a small number of concentric indicator mineral rings surrounding an intrusive rock. Nonsymmetrical zones imply special conditions, such as less (or more) chemically or thermally reactive rocks or a nonvertical intrusive body.

Development of contact metamorphic facies reflects both the history of pressure and temperature changes and the bulk-rock chemistry. Thus, by stating that a rock belongs to a particular facies, scientists convey much about the rock's history. This information is vital to exploration for metallic and industrial minerals that commonly occur in contact metamorphic aureoles and for general understanding of regional geology.

Contact metamorphic mineral facies have counterparts with regional metamorphic zones. In addition to the bulk chemical composition of a rock, temperature and pressure are two variable factors. These two factors can be independent. Thus, for example, one can find low-pressure, high-temperature facies or, alternatively, high-pressure, low-temperature facies. With contact metamorphism, these facies occur very close to the intrusive rock. With regional metamorphism, however, the effect is widespread and may not be related to an intrusive rock.

Contact metamorphic rocks are recognized by their location adjacent to igneous bodies and by evidence indicating a genetic temporal relationship. Contact metamorphic rocks are commonly massive. Granitic rocks are the most common intrusive material. The most frequent depth of the solidification of a granitic magma is 3 kilometers, corresponding to a load pressure of 800-2,100 bars. There are intrusions that solidify at a greater or shallower depth; a depth of 1 kilometer corresponds to a load pressure of 250 bars. Consequently, the load pressures effective during contact metamorphism range from 200 to 2,000 bars in most cases. In contrast, load pressures prevailing during regional metamorphism are generally greater.

When a magma intrudes into colder regions, the adjacent rocks are heated. If the heat content of the intruded magma is high and the volume of the magma is not too small, there will be a temperature rise in the bordering rock that lasts long enough to cause mineral reactions to occur. The rocks adjacent to small intrusions of dikes and sills are not metamorphosed (only baked), whereas larger plutonic rocks give rise to a distinct contact aureole of metamorphic rocks. Several zones of increasing temperature are recognized in contact aureoles.

The contact metamorphic zones surround the intrusion in generally concentric rings that approximate the shape of the intrusion. Those zones which correspond to the highest-temperature minerals are closest to the intrusion; the zone corresponding to the lowest temperature is located farthest from the intrusion. The lowest-temperature contact metamorphic zone gradually grades into unmetamorphosed country rock.

Contact metamorphic rocks are characteristically massive because of lack of deformation; most are fine-grained except for a special variant called a skarn. Skarns may contain metallic mineralization in sufficient concentration that they can be worked for a profit. Such mineral concentrations are called ores.

Contact metamorphic rocks lack schistosity. The very fine-grained, splintery varieties are called hornfels. The large metamorphic gradient, decreasing from the hot intrusive contact to the unaltered country rock, gives rise to zones of metamorphic rocks differing markedly in mineral constituents. The intensity and mineral assemblage in contact metamorphic zones are dependent on several factors: the chemical composition of the intrusive rock; its temperature and volatile content; the composition and permeability of the host units; the structural or spatial relationship of the reactive units to intense contact effects and solutions conduits, or traps; and the pressure or depth of burial.

Argillaceous limestone is usually receptive to contact metamorphism, as its diverse rock chemistry is amenable to mineral development over a broad set of physical and chemical conditions. A typical contact metamorphic mineral assemblage formed from rocks originally of this composition is a plagioclase-garnet-epidote rock. This kind of rock frequently hosts important ore deposits. Shale usually converts to hornfels that is characterized by the minerals cordierite, biotite, and chlorite and that is essentially nonreactive and nonpermeable. Member lithology usually does not host ore deposits. Porous limestone is often exceptionally susceptible to solution and to replacement by ore. Rocks formed from this material contain magnetite, garnet, and pyroxene.

Clean, massive limestone has only thin, contact metamorphic zones developed in it. Clean limestones merely recrystallize, forming coarse-grained marble in the highest-temperature contact metamorphic zones adjacent to an intrusion. Dolomite is usually poorly mineralized and nonreactive. Siliceous dolomite, however, may act as a good host, with assemblages characterized by tremolite, diopside, serpentine, and talc. Mafic rocks, such as andesites, diabases, and diorites, can be reactive hosts capable of producing some types of ore deposits. Secondary biotite is the key alteration mineral in mafic rocks. It is associated with ore minerals and is present in lieu of sericite as the alteration product. The biotite zone may be very broad.

Contact metamorphic facies are identified by the mineral assemblages that are developed in the metamorphosed rocks. Albite and chlorite are the contact metamorphic minerals restricted to the albite-epidote hornfels facies. Calcite, epidote, and talc also occur in this facies. Andalusite may occur in the highest-temperature part of the albite-epidote hornfels.

Anthophyllite-cummingtonite is restricted to the hornblende hornfels facies. Muscovite is present in this facies as well as in the albite-epidote hornfels facies and sometimes in the lowermost pyroxene hornfels facies. Grossular-andradite garnet and idocrase, sometimes with vesuvianite, biotite, and almadine garnet, are present here as well as in the pyroxene hornfels facies. Sillimanite may occur in the highest-temperature part of the facies at higher pressure; staurolite may occur in high-pressure, iron-rich rocks. Calcite is present, but not with tremolite-actinolite or epidote or plagioclase. Under certain chemical compositions of the original rocks, other minerals that may be present include anthophyllite, cummingtonite, phylogopite, biotite, diaspore, and scapolite.

Orthoclase with andalusite or sillimanite is restricted to the pyroxene hornfels facies. Sillimanite is present here and also in the upper hornblende hornfels facies. Hyperstine and glass present in the pyroxene hornfels may also be present in the sanidinite facies. Muscovite is present only in the lowest-temperature part of the facies. For silica-deficient rocks in the pyroxene hornfels facies, dolomite, magnesite, and talc may occur only in the lowest-temperature part of the facies or at high carbon dioxide pressures.

Diagnostic minerals of the sanidinite facies are sanidine, mullite, tridymyte, and pigeonite. In silica-deficient rocks at this facies, wollastonite, grossularite, and plagioclase are present. Other minerals that may occur under special conditions are perovskite, spinel, diopside, and pseudobrookite.

Methods of Study

Contact metamorphic zones are studied by standard geologic techniques, including the preparation of geologic maps through field study. Aerial photographs and satellite images are frequently used to identify contact metamorphic zones through detecting rock alteration in the contact metamorphic zone. Satellite sensors measure, analyze, and interpret electromagnetic energy reflected from the earth's surface for subsequent computer analysis. Geophysical techniques (gravity and electrical methods) are used to locate mineralized zones containing relatively heavy metallic ore minerals. The gravity contrast of these zones can be measured with surface instruments and then mapped. Some of these same minerals, particularly the ore minerals, transmit electric current in an anomalous manner. These anomalies plotted on base maps may be an additional clue to the presence of ore deposits in contact metamorphic zones.

Subsequent laboratory work involves the determination of mineral relationships by studying thin slices of rock through which light passes under a microscope (petrography). Frequently, the chemistry of entire rock samples is determined to help scientists understand the presence or absence of minerals as a guide to mineral exploration and to the composition of the original rock. Because of significant advances in laboratory instruments, detailed mineral chemistry analyses are routinely performed that determine chemical makeup of microvolumes of minerals. These determinations permit the earth scientist to understand the conditions under which the contact metamorphic zones formed and to interpret the history of the contact metamorphic zone.

This information provides critical insight into the potential for metallic ore deposits within the contact metamorphic zone. Such deposits are explored by means of surveys that detect and record variations in geochemistry, gravity, and plant types and abundances. Anomalously high element concentrations in rocks, soils, and plant tissues may indicate mineral deposits that are not exposed. Many ore deposits have an anomalous gravity signature because of heavy associated silicate minerals and metallic minerals. Maps of localized variations may lead to subsurface exploration, which is conducted by drilling techniques. Continuous cylindrical samples, to a depth of as much as several thousand feet, are taken, and the study of such subsurface samples leads to the evaluation of possible minable concentrations of certain metals and other elements used by modern civilizations.

Context

Contact metamorphic zones frequently contain metallic mineral deposits without which modern civilization could not exist. Many significant mineral deposits worldwide occur in these zones. The metals extracted from deposits of this type include tin, tungsten, copper, molybdenum, uranium, gold, silver, and, in some cases, refractory industrial metals. Specialized surveys assess the potential of metallic ore deposits before expensive subsurface sampling by drilling.

Recognition and understanding of the contact metamorphic environment can lead to a significantly improved understanding of regional geology and the regional geologic history. In some areas, contact metamorphic zones are associated with igneous intrusives of only one geologic age. Specialized laboratory studies provide supporting data to determine the geologic history and potential for economic mineralization.

Bibliography

Hyndman, D. E. *Petrology of Igneous and Metamorphic Rocks*. New York: McGraw-Hill, 1972. Suitable for introductory-level college education in the earth sciences. Key concepts are summarized at the ends of chapters. Appropriate for advanced students with teacher guidance.

Pough, F. H. *A Field Guide to Rocks and Minerals*. 4th ed. Boston: Houghton Mifflin, 1976. Provides an excellent overview of the environments in which minerals are formed and found, and simple laboratory tests that can be conducted in the field or laboratory. Offers the user a basic grasp of the subject of mineralogy. Profusely illustrated.

Sorrella, C. A. *Minerals of the World*. Racine, Wis.: Western Publishing, 1973. This well-illustrated softcover book presents an excellent overview of rocks and minerals. It provides information about the minerals expected in a variety of environments, including contact metamorphic zones.

Winkler, H. G. F. *Petrogenesis of Metamorphic Rocks*. 4th ed. New York: Springer-Verlag, 1976. An introductory text at the college level. Portions may be of interest to advanced students.

Jeffrey C. Reid

Cross-References

Aerial Photography, 17; Experimental Petrology, 662; Metamorphic Rock Classification, 1553; Metamorphic Textures, 1578; Regional Metamorphism, 1606; Earth's Resources, 2175.

METAMORPHISM: METASOMATISM

Type of earth science: Geology
Field of study: Petrology, metamorphic

Metasomatism is produced by circulation of aqueous solutions through rock undergoing metamorphic recrystallization. The solutions cause chemical losses and additions by dissolving and precipitating minerals along their flow paths. Metasomatic processes have produced the world's major ore bodies of tin, tungsten, copper, and molybdenum, as well as smaller deposits of many other metals.

Principal terms

AQUEOUS SOLUTION, HYDROTHERMAL FLUID, and INTERGRANULAR FLUID: synonymous terms for fluid mixtures that are hot and have a high solvent capacity, which permits them to dissolve and transport chemical constituents; they become saturated upon cooling and may precipitate metasomatic minerals

CONTACT METASOMATISM: metasomatism in proximity to a large body of intrusive igneous rock, or pluton; the intensity of metasomatism increases as igneous contact is approached

DENSITY: the ratio of rock mass to total rock volume; usually measured in grams per cubic centimeter

METEORIC WATER: surface water that infiltrates porous and fractured crystal rocks; the same as groundwater

PERMEABILITY: the capacity to transmit fluid through pore spaces or along fractures; high-fracture permeability is generally requisite for metasomatism, as porosity is greatly reduced by metamorphic recrystallization

POROSITY: the ratio of pore volume to total rock volume; usually reported as a percentage

PROGRADE METAMORPHISM: recrystallization of solid rock masses induced by rising temperature; differs from metasomatism in that bulk rock composition is unchanged except for expelled fluids

RECRYSTALLIZATION: a solid-state chemical reaction that eliminates unstable minerals in a rock and forms new stable minerals; the major process contributing to rock metamorphism

REGIONAL METASOMATISM: large-scale metasomatism related to regional metamorphism; the intensity of regional metasomatism is usually mild and difficult to discern from original variations in rock composition

Summary of the Phenomenon

Metasomatism is an inclusive term for processes that cause a change in the overall chemical composition of a rock during metamorphism. Such processes may be described as positive or negative depending upon whether a net gain or a loss is produced in the affected rock body. Where chemical changes are slight, the minerals in the original rock remain unchanged or register only very subtle changes. On the other hand, intense metasomatism may result in total destruction of the original mineral assemblage and its replacement by new, and different, minerals. In these extreme cases, metasomatism is usually difficult to detect, particularly if large rock volumes are affected. Metasomatic effects are most obvious when the original rock texture and mineral assemblage is partially destroyed. In such cases, the resulting rock will exhibit an unusually large variety of minerals as well as microscopic evidence of incomplete chemical reactions. In normal metamorphic reactions, chemical migration occurs on the scale of a single mineral grain (a few millimeters at most) during recrystallization. In contrast, metasomatism involves chemical transport on the scale of a few centimeters or more. In areas where metasomatism has been intense, it can often be demonstrated that the scale of chemical transport ranged from about 100 meters to as much as several kilometers. It is the movement of chemical components through rocks on this larger scale which distinguishes metasomatism from metamorphism. Dehydration (water-releasing reaction) and decarbonation (carbon dioxide-releasing reaction) are the commonest types of chemical reactions during metamorphism at the higher grades. These reactions certainly produce significant changes in rock composition and involve large-distance chemical transport, but because they typify normal prograde metamorphism, they do not constitute metasomatism. If, on the other hand, water and/or carbon dioxide were reintroduced into a rock which had previously experienced prograde metamorphism, this would constitute a fairly common type of metasomatism.

The reshuffling of the chemical components into new mineral assemblages during metamorphism, particularly when gaseous phases are lost, necessitates major changes in rock volume (usually volume reductions) and a corresponding change in rock porosity and density. Metasomatic replacement of a metamorphic rock will induce additional changes in volume (either reductions or increases), porosity, and density. Although metasomatism is defined as a process of chemical change, physical changes in rock properties also occur, and these are an essential aspect of metasomatism. For convenience, introductory textbooks treat metamorphic and metasomatic reactions as "constant volume" processes. This assumption may hold true in specific instances, but it has no general validity, particularly when volatile constituents are involved in the reactions. It has been demonstrated on theoretical grounds that chemical transport on the scale of a few centimeters or more requires the presence of an intergranular pore fluid that can effectively dissolve existing minerals and deposit others while the rock as a whole remains solid. The relative mobility of this fluid phase leads to two theoretical types of metasomatism: diffusion metasomatism and infiltration metasomatism. In diffusion metasomatism, the chemical components move through a stationary aqueous pore fluid permeating the rock by the process of diffusion. The effects are limited to a distance of a few centimeters from the surface of contact between rocks of sharply contrasting composition. This process cannot produce large-scale metasomatic effects. Infiltration metasomatism involves a mobile aqueous fluid that circulates through pores and fractures of the enclosing rock and carries in it dissolved chemical components. This fluid actively dissolves some existing minerals and deposits new ones along its flow path. The scale of infiltration metasomatism is thus determined by the circulation pattern of the fluid, and rock compositions over distances of several kilometers can be easily altered. For convenience, the term "metasomatism" will be used in place of "infiltration metasomatism" and the effects of diffusion metasomatism will be ignored.

The degree of chemical change that accompanies recrystallization is closely related to the fluid/rock ratio prevailing during the process. Since regional metamorphism is a deep-seated process, a low fluid/rock ratio generally prevails, and the process is "rock-dominated" in the sense that minerals dominate the composition of the fluid circulating through the rocks. A significant degree of metasomatism under such conditions is unlikely unless the fluid is very corrosive. Small quantities of fluorine or chlorine can produce corrosive aqueous fluids, but these elements are rarely important in regional metamorphism. Contact metamorphism, however, occurs close to the earth's surface, where large volumes of groundwater circulate in response to gravity. Groundwater will mix with any water given off by a high-level crystallizing pluton; it follows that contact metamorphism takes place under conditions of high fluid/rock ratio. Such a process will be "fluid-dominated" in the sense that the circulating fluid will exert control over the compositions of the minerals formed by recrystallization. These conditions are highly favorable for metasomatism.

Intense, pervasive metasomatism will develop under the following conditions: when energy is available to provide temperature and pressure gradients to sustain fluid movement; when a generally high fluid/rock ratio prevails; when the aqueous fluid has the solvent capacity to dissolve minerals in its flow path; and when the enclosed rocks possess, or develop, sufficient permeability to permit fluid circulation. These conditions must be sustained for a sufficient time period, or recur with sufficient frequency, to produce metasomatism.

Such conditions are commonly attained in rocks adjacent to large bodies of intrusive igneous rock, or plutons, particularly those which expel large quantities of water. As an example of contact metasomatism, consider the effects produced in the fractured roof zone of a peraluminous, or S-type granite pluton. Hot water vapor, concentrated below the roof by crystallization, is often enriched in corrosive fluorine accompanied by boron, lithium, arsenic, silicon, tungsten, and tin. This reactive fluid migrates up fractures, enlarging pathways by dissolving minerals and seeping into the adjacent rock. The result is a network of quartz-muscovite-topaz-fluorite replacement veins that may contain exploitable quantities of tin, tungsten, and base metal ore. Fluorine-dominated metasomatism is known as greisenization. Greisen effects may extend 5 to 10 meters into the wall rocks from vein margins.

Within this zone, the original rock textures, minerals, and chemical composition will be profoundly modified by metasomatism. In many cases, the entire roof of the granite pluton is destroyed and replaced by greisen minerals. Some of the world's major tin and tungsten deposits—such as those in Nigeria, Portugal, southwest England, Brazil, Malaysia, and Thailand—were formed by just such a process. On a larger scale, spectacular sodium and potassium metasomatism develops adjacent to intrusions of ijolite and carbonatite plutons. This intense alkali metasomatism is called fenitization and is developed on a regional scale in the vicinity of Lake Victoria in East Africa. In this region, ijolite-carbonatite complexes are plentiful, and aureoles, or ring-shaped zones, of fenite extend outward 1 to 3 kilometers from the individual plutons. The width of the fenite zone around a source pluton is largely determined by the fracture intensity in the surrounding rocks; where they are highly fractured, large-scale, and even regional, fenitization is present. Massive, unfractured rocks resist fenitization, and the resulting aureoles are narrow. Metasomatism around ijolite intrusions is dominated by the outflow of sodium dissolved in an aqueous fluid expelled by the magma and an apparent back-flow migration of silicon to the source intrusion. A typical result would be an inner zone, 20 to 30 meters wide, of coarse-grained "syenite fenite" composed of aegirine, sodium feldspar, and sometimes nepheline. Beyond the outer limit of this zone, there would be a major aureole of shattered host rock veined by aegirine, sodium amphibole, albite, and orthoclase, which might extend well beyond 1 kilometer from the parent intrusion. Fenitization around carbonatite intrusions is dominated by potassium metasomatism, which converts the country rocks into orthoclasite (a coarse-grained metasomatic rock composed almost exclusively of potassium feldspar). The resulting fenite aureole is typically less than 300 meters wide and is roughly proportional to the diameter of the parent carbonatite. The chemical composition of the country rocks appears to exert little influence on the progression of fenitization. The rocks adjacent to ijolite intrusions are driven toward a bulk chemical composition approaching that of ijolite, while those adjacent to carbonatite intrusions are driven toward orthoclasite regardless of their initial composition.

Methods of Study

Intensely metasomatized rocks usually exhibit mineral zoning, which is more or less symmetrical around the passageways that controlled fluid migration. These passages may be networks of vein-filled fissures, major fault zones, shattered roof zones of igneous plutons, or the fractured country rocks adjacent to such plutons. Emphasis is placed on fracture permeability as a control of fluid migration, as most metamorphosed rocks have negligible porosity. The metasomatic mineral zones are often dominated by single, coarse-grained mineral species, which is obviously "exotic" with respect to the original mineral assemblage. Inner zones often cut sharply across outer zones, and the resulting pattern reflects a systematic increase in metasomatic intensity as the controlling structure is approached. By means of foot traverses across the metasomatized terrain, geologists carefully map the mineral zoning pattern and its controlling fractures. Such maps provide insight into the fracture history of the area, show the distribution and volume of the metasomatic products, and indicate the relative susceptibility of the various rock types present to the metasomatic process. If ore bodies are present, geologic maps provide essential information for exploring the subsurface extent of the ores through drilling. They also provide a basis for systematically sampling the metasomatic zones as well as the country rock beyond the limit of metasomatism; the unaltered country rock is called the protolith.

The sample collection provides material for study in the laboratory after field studies are complete. A paper-thin slice is cut from the center of each rock sample and is mounted on a glass slide for microscopic examination. From such examinations, the scientist can identify both fine- and coarse-grained minerals and can determine the order of metasomatic replacement of protolith minerals.

The objectives in a study of metasomatism are to determine the chemical changes that have taken place in the altered rocks and to reconstruct the history of fluid-rock interaction. To this end, it is essential to determine the chemical compositions of the various protoliths affected by metasomatism so that additions and losses in the metasomatized rocks may be calculated. The ideal protolith is a rock unit that is both chemically uniform over distances comparable to the scale of zoning and highly susceptible to metasomatism. Considerable attention must, therefore, be devoted to the study and sampling of protoliths during the field stage of a project. Ideally, the samples should be collected just beyond the outer limit of metasomatism in order to avoid metasomatic contamination and to minimize the effect of a lack of protolith uniformity. Unfortunately, it is only possible to approximate the position of this outer limit in the field, because the decreasing metasomatic effects merge imperceptibly with the properties of the unaltered protolith. Sampling problems are further compounded in study areas where rock exposures are poor or where exposed rocks are deeply weathered. Rock weathering promotes chemical changes indistinguishable from metasomatism, so weathered samples cannot be accepted for chemical study. The sample requirements for metasomatic research are more stringent than for any other type of geological study, and meeting them always taxes the ingenuity of a geologist.

The samples, having been cut in half for the microscope slides, are then prepared for chemical analysis and for density measurement. One half is stored "as is" in a reference collection for future use. The other half is cleaned of all traces of surface weathering and plant material. The samples are then oven-dried, and bulk densities are obtained by weighing and coating them with molten paraffin (to seal pore spaces), followed by immersion in water to determine their displacement volumes. Next, the samples are crushed and ground to fine powder. The average mineral grain density is determined by weighing a small amount of rock powder and measuring its displacement volume in water. The porosity of each sample is determined, and the powdered samples (20-30 grams each) are then sent to a laboratory specializing in quantitative chemical analysis. Because it is desirable to study as many as sixty-five different chemical elements, the laboratory will use several modern instrumental techniques as well as the traditional "wet method" to determine their concentrations.

Modern studies use the mass balance approach which relates the physical, volumetric, and chemical properties between the altered rocks and their protoliths. As an example, consider a particular element in a given volume of protolith. The mass of this element is the product of volume × bulk density × element concentration. If the element is totally insoluble in the circulating fluid, then its mass must remain constant during metasomatism of the enclosing rock. It follows that for this immobile element, the product of volume × bulk density × element concentration in the altered rock must equal that of the parent protolith. This provides an objective test for determining which elements were mobile and which were immobile during the metasomatic event. From this point, it is a simple matter to calculate gains and losses of each element for the altered rocks.

Context

Metasomatic deposits of a wide range of metals and industrial minerals are commonly found at or near the contact between igneous plutons and preexisting sedimentary rocks. Ore deposits concentrated by contact metasomatic processes have, in the past, been described under many names; now they are collectively known as skarn deposits. Skarn deposits are major sources of tungsten, tin, copper, and molybdenum. Important quantities of iron, zinc, cobalt, gold, silver, lead, bismuth, beryllium, and boron are also mined from skarn deposits. Additionally, such deposits are a source of the industrial minerals fluorite, graphite, magnetite, asbestos, and talc. For the most part, skarn deposits are found in relatively young mobile belts that are not yet deeply eroded. The most productive skarns are generally those in which granitic magma has invaded sedimentary sequences dominated by layers of carbonate rocks.

The physical and chemical principles of metasomatism have been deduced by research geologists over many decades from thousands of individual field and laboratory studies. Most of these studies, like those of the East African fenites, were unrelated to economic mineral deposits. The knowledge derived from the studies, however, is put to practical use by economic geologists who explore remote areas in search of new skarn deposits or who exploit known skarn ores at producing mines. These economic geologists test, on a daily working basis, the theoretical hypotheses and generalizations formulated by research geologists concerned with metasomatism.

Bibliography

Burnham, C. W. "Contact Metamorphism of Magnesian Limestones at Crestmore, California." *Geological Society of America Bulletin* 70 (1959): 879-920. A classic account of metasomatism at one of the best-known mineral-collecting localities in the world, having more than one hundred species of rare minerals. This periodical can be found in university libraries. Written for professional geologists but can be understood by those with some knowledge of geology.

Einaudi, M. T., L. D. Meinert, and R. J. Newberry. "Skarn Deposits." In *Economic Geology: Seventy-fifth Anniversary Volume*. El Paso, Tex.: Economic Geology Publishing, 1981. A comprehensive review of skarn deposits and skarn theory written for professional geologists. The text is technical, but the extensive bibliography is useful to those interested in learning more about specific types of skarn and skarn localities.

Fyfe, W. S., N. J. Price, and A. B. Thompson. *Fluids in the Earth's Crust*. New York: Elsevier, 1978. The best overview of the theoretical side of fluid-rock interaction. The authors argue that subduction and sea-floor spreading may be viewed as large-scale metasomatic processes, the end product of which is the earth's crust. Written for advanced students of geology or chemistry. Extensive bibliography.

LeBas, Michael John. *Carbonatite-Nephelinite Volcanism: An African Case History*. New York: John Wiley & Sons, 1977. A detailed account of the geology in the Lake Victoria region of East Africa, containing excellent descriptions of volcanoes and calderas formed by recent alkalic and carbonatitic magmas. Fenites are discussed throughout in great detail. Can be understood by those with a modest background in geology, provided that they first familiarize themselves with the nomenclature of alkalic rocks.

Mason, Roger. *Petrology of the Metamorphic Rocks*. Winchester, Mass.: Allen & Unwin, 1978. A very good college-level text dealing with major aspects of metamorphism. Chapter 5 is devoted to contact metamorphism and metasomatism. Excellent glossary and index.

Press, Frank, and Raymond Siever. *Earth*. 4th ed. New York: W. H. Freeman, 1986. Chapter 17 introduces the high school and college reader without a geology background to the subject of metamorphism and metasomatism. Metasomatism is treated in very general terms. Good index and illustrations.

Taylor, Roger G. *Geology of Tin Deposits*. New York: Elsevier, 1979. An overview of tin deposits. Chapter 6 deals authoritatively with metasomatism and its application to exploration for tin. Requires some background in geology and chemistry.

Gary R. Lowell

Cross-References

REGIONAL METAMORPHISM

Type of earth science: Geology
Field of study: Petrology, metamorphic

Regional metamorphism, which takes place in the roots of actively forming mountain belts, is a process by which increased temperatures and pressures cause a rock to undergo recrystallization, new mineral growth, and deformation. These changes diagnostically cause minerals to develop a preferred orientation, or foliation, in the rock.

Principal terms

EQUILIBRIUM: a situation in which a mineral is stable at a given set of temperature-pressure conditions
IGNEOUS ROCK: a rock formed from the cooling of molten material
MICA: a platy silicate mineral (one silicon atom surrounded by four oxygen atoms) that readily splits in one plane
MINERAL: a naturally occurring chemical compound that has an orderly internal arrangement of atoms and a definite formula
SEDIMENTARY ROCK: a rock formed from the physical breakdown of preexisting rock material or from the precipitation, chemically or biologically, of minerals
SHALE: a sedimentary rock composed of fine-grained products derived from the physical breakdown of preexisting rock material
STRAIN: change in volume or size in response to stress
STRESS: force per unit of area
TEXTURE: the size, shape, and arrangement of crystals or particles in a rock
ZEOLITES: members of a mineral group with very complex compositions: aluminosilicates with variable amounts of calcium, sodium, and water

Summary of the Phenomenon

Metamorphism is a process whereby igneous or sedimentary rocks undergo change in response to some combination of increased temperature, pressure, and chemically active fluids. Several types of metamorphism are recognized, but regional metamorphism is the most widespread. Regionally metamorphosed rocks in association with igneous rocks make up about 85 percent of the continents. In order to describe regionally metamorphosed rocks and to understand the processes by which they form, one must understand two properties of these rocks: texture and composition. Texture refers to the size, shape, and arrangement of crystals or particles in a rock. Composition refers to the minerals present in a rock.

The effect of temperature and pressure on texture and composition is aided by fluids. Fluids transport chemical constituents and facilitate chemical reactions that take place in the rocks. As metamorphic conditions increase, metamorphic reactions readily occur if fluids are present; however, fluids are gradually driven off as recrystallization reduces open spaces. Once fluids are eliminated and temperatures and pressures decrease, the reactions generally occur very slowly. Therefore, in most metamorphic rocks, the minerals preserved are those that represent the highest temperatures and pressures attained, assuming equilibrium when adequate fluids were still available.

Regionally metamorphosed rocks characteristically develop distinctive textures, largely because of the role of two types of pressure in concert with elevated temperatures: confining pressure, or the force caused by the weight of the material overlying a rock, and a stronger directed pressure, or a horizontal force created by mountain-building processes.

As metamorphism commences, rocks become deformed, and original features are strongly distorted or obliterated. Original minerals either recrystallize or react to form new minerals and develop a pronounced preferred orientation, or foliation, in response to the directed pressure. Preferentially aligned platy minerals (such as the micas), formed during the early stages of metamorphism, enhance the development of foliation. Foliation assumes different forms depending on the degree of metamorphism.

Although the minerals in most rock types characteristically develop preferred orientations, shales and other fine-grained rock types display more distinct changes of texture. Shales undergo textural changes as they pass from conditions of low-grade metamorphism (low temperatures and pressures) at shallow depths to high grades (higher temperatures and pressures) deeper in the earth. At low grades of regional metamorphism, microscopic platy minerals grow and align themselves perpendicular to the orientation of the directed pressure. This realignment allows this fine-grained rock, called a slate, to split or cleave easily along this preferred direction. Under somewhat higher metamorphic grades deeper in the earth, the platy minerals continue to develop parallel arrangements in response to the directed pressures, but the resultant mineral grains, typically the micas, are now large enough to be identified with the unaided eye. This texture, a schistosity, forms in a rock called a schist. At higher grades, the platy minerals react to form new minerals, and a gneissic texture develops. This texture is distinguished by alternating layers of light and dark minerals that give the rock, called a gneiss, a banded appearance.

Just as textural changes in metamorphic rocks are generally predictable as grade increases, minerals also appear or disappear in a systematic sequence and become even better gauges of the conditions of metamorphism. A progression of key minerals in shales, called index minerals, form as the grade of metamorphism increases. These index minerals, therefore, occur in rocks metamorphosed at a given range of temperature-pressure conditions. When mapped in the field, areas containing index minerals are called metamorphic zones. As the metamorphic grades increase, the typical sequence of the index minerals is chlorite, biotite, garnet, staurolite, kyanite, and sillimanite.

Since metamorphic zonation, based on index minerals, relies on the presence of shales, if shales are not abundant, zonation can be limited. Fortunately, another type of metamorphic zonation is recognized that is not based on single minerals in one rock type but on sequences of mineral assemblages in groups of associated rocks within ranges of temperature-pressure conditions. These ranges of temperatures and pressures in which diagnostic mineral assemblages in different rock types may exist are called metamorphic facies. The zeolite facies represents the lowest conditions of regional metamorphism. At the lowest extremes of this facies, conditions considered sedimentary merge with those that are metamorphic. This facies is named for the zeolite group of minerals that form within this facies. As metamorphic conditions increase, the assemblages of minerals distinctive of the zeolite facies break down, and new assemblages form that are distinctive of either the blueschist or the greenschist facies. As the names of these facies imply, the textures formed under these conditions are commonly schistose, and a number of the minerals impart either blue or green tints to the rocks in their respective facies. In a given area of regional metamorphism, it is typical to find rocks that represent a sequence of metamorphic facies that follow either of two pathways. One path has temperature increasing relatively more rapidly than pressure, so the combination of facies that it crosses is referred to as a low pressure/high temperature sequence. Assemblages that represent an alternate pathway, in which temperature increases more slowly relative to pressure, are termed a high pressure/low temperature sequence.

By understanding how mountains are formed, scientists can learn how regionally metamorphosed rocks are generated. Regional metamorphism occurs in the roots of actively forming mountain belts. Linear zones thousands of kilometers long and hundreds of kilometers wide can be involved. It will take millions of years before the products of regional metamorphism are exposed in the Andes or Cascades. On all the continents, however, broad areas of exposed rocks, called shields, now reveal the products of numerous ancient mountain-building events.

In the 1960's, the concept of plate tectonics revolutionized geology and scientists' understanding of the processes in regional metamorphism. For decades, geologists have known that the earth is divided into several concentric layers. The outermost zone, the crust, consists of relatively low-density rocks and averages 35 kilometers thick on the continents and 10 kilometers thick under the oceans. Beneath the crust is the mantle (nearly 3,000 kilometers thick), and then the core.

With the advent of plate tectonics, another important subdivision was recognized. The upper 60-100 kilometers, which includes the crust and a portion of the upper mantle, behaves in a relatively rigid fashion and is composed of about twenty pieces that move independently of one another. This rigid zone is called the lithosphere, and the pieces are called lithospheric plates. Because each plate is moving relative to its neighbors, three types of boundaries with other plates exist: those in collision, those pulling apart, and those sliding by one another. The rigid lithosphere appar-

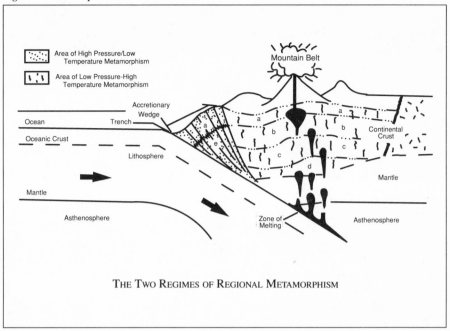

THE TWO REGIMES OF REGIONAL METAMORPHISM

NOTE: Inferred locations of metamorphic facies: *a*, zeolite; *b*, greenschist; *c*, amphibolite; *d*, granulite; *e*, blueschist.

ently floats on a soft plastic layer, called the asthenosphere, that extends from 60-100 kilometers to at least 250 kilometers into the mantle.

Regional metamorphism is restricted to margins in collision, called convergent boundaries. The collision of two lithospheric plates produces several profound effects (see figure). One plate subducts, or sinks, under the other but manages to crumple the edge of the continent into a mountain belt. An oceanic trench forms at the point of contact. As one plate plunges downward, melting occurs where temperatures sufficiently rise. The molten material rises through the lithosphere to produce volcanoes at the surface and masses of igneous rock at depth. It is in this realm—extending from the zone of collision to well beyond the igneous bodies— that regional metamorphism occurs. Within this area, two distinct sequences of regional metamorphism develop. The figure illustrates that the high pressure/low temperature sequence forms in the region nearest the trench. As sediments and volcanic rocks are carried rapidly (in geological terms) downward into the subduction zone, they attain relatively high pressures but remain relatively cold because they have not had the time to heat up. The minerals that form in these high-pressure conditions are those of the zeolite and blueschist facies. If the downward movement continued uninterrupted, the rocks would eventually heat up. Before that can happen, however, thin, cold slabs with high-pressure mineral assemblages within them are chaotically pushed or thrust back toward the surface. Why this thrusting occurs is not entirely clear, but it is not uncommon to find a region 100 kilometers wide, adjacent to a trench, composed entirely of highly deformed high pressure/low temperature facies rocks. This region is called an accretionary wedge because of its inferred shape in a vertical slice through the earth. It is this material that allows the continents to grow larger through time.

Methods of Study

The study of regionally metamorphosed rocks is conducted from several different perspectives. At the core of these studies are the field observations. Descriptions of rock units and structures provide information on how these rocks have formed. Much of this fieldwork is synthesized into a geological map.

In the laboratory, samples from the field are studied by a variety of physical and chemical methods. Studies with the petrographic microscopic yield information on mineral compositions and textural relationships that provide clues for classifying and determining modes of origin for these rocks. X-ray powder diffraction techniques are commonly used to identify metamorphic minerals not readily identified by visual inspection. Since metamorphic rocks are markedly changed texturally and mineralogically from their original state, chemical analysis provides data that can be compared to probable premetamorphic rock types. Standard classical chemical methods of analysis may be used, but a number of more sophisticated, faster, and simpler spectrographic methods are popular. Atomic absorption and X-ray fluorescence spectroscopy are two of the more widely applied techniques to determine elemental abundances, although emission spectrographic and neutron activation analyses are also used. Another important tool is the electron microprobe. Most published mineral analyses are generated by electron microprobe analyses. Mass spectroscopic analyses also provide information on the distribution of isotopes in metamorphic rocks and minerals. These data are useful in determining age and conditions of formation.

Rock deformation experiments provide information about the mechanical properties of metamorphic rocks. Rock samples subjected to stress and strain tests yield data on properties such as plasticity, strength, and viscosity. These data are particularly important in understanding how directed pressures influence textures. Another phase of the study of metamorphic rocks is experimental petrology. Here, metamorphic minerals are synthesized under controlled-equilibrium conditions. From these studies, geologists gain knowledge about the actual ranges of stability of these minerals in naturally occurring environments. The study of the crystal chemistry and thermodynamics provides information regarding actual conditions of formation and potential reactions. The roles of variables—such as entropy, volume change, and heats of reaction—provides clues to the behavior of mineral assemblages at varying temperature and pressure conditions. Theoretical petrology, the treatment of data on metamorphic rocks by mathematical models or the principles of theoretical physics, also provides important information in the study of regional metamorphism.

In addition to analyzing the samples collected, scientists analyze field data in the laboratory. Statistical analysis of orientations of foliations and other structural features is greatly facilitated by the computer. Laboratory analyses are recast to generate a variety of graphical treatments to check for chemical trends or metamorphic facies relationships.

Context

The products of regional metamorphism touch people's lives in many ways. Marbles, gneisses, and slates are used as building and cut ornamental stones, and some quartzites, marbles, and gneisses are used as aggregate. The minerals graphite, talc, vermiculite, and asbestos are four of the more commonly used mineral products of regional metamorphism, whereas wollastonite, garnet, kyanite, emery, and pyrophyllite are mineral products of limited use. Graphite is most commonly used in the metallurgical industry, with lesser amounts used as lubricants, in paints, in batteries, as pencil "leads," and in electrodes. Talc is also a product with diverse uses. The ceramics industry is the largest consumer, followed by paint and paper manufacturers. Vermiculite is a common product in thermal and acoustic insulation. Asbestos, despite concerns about its health risks, remains a very important fire-retardant material.

Regionally metamorphosed rocks provide certain advantages in construction but also present unique engineering problems. A scan of the skyline of the Island of Manhattan in New York City reveals that the largest skyscrapers are restricted to several areas of the island, surrounded by expanses of much shorter buildings. The reason that buildings such as the Empire State Building occupy only certain areas is that they sit directly on structurally strong regionally metamorphosed rocks that occur at or near the surface. In other areas of the island, these rocks are too deeply buried, and the overlying sediments are too weak, to support the larger structures. In other cases, inclined foliations paralleling slopes in hilly or mountainous regions represent potential planes of slippage that can give way and produce massive rock slides, particularly when road, mine, or dam construction modifies the landscape. In areas where foliations are not adequately taken into account, the cost can be millions of dollars in repairs and/or great loss of life. Special techniques and restrictive measures need to be applied when construction occurs in areas where foliations present potential problems.

Many scenic places reveal regionally metamorphosed rocks, so understanding the features in these rocks and how they formed can enhance appreciation of these landscapes. Whether amid the rocks at the bottom of the Grand Canyon or in the center of New York City's Central Park, one stands on the deeply eroded roots of mountain ranges that once (more than a billion years ago) rose to heights equivalent to the Himalaya today.

Bibliography

Bates, Robert L. *Geology of the Industrial Rocks and Minerals*. Mineola, N.Y.: Dover, 1969. Readable text that concentrates on the occurrences and uses of rocks and minerals. Key chapters 4, 9, and 11 deal with metamorphic rocks, metamorphic minerals, and minor industrial minerals, respectively. All provide excellent summaries of how the products of regional metamorphism are utilized. Includes an index and good bibliography.

Dietrich, R. V., and B. J. Skinner. *Rocks and Rock Minerals*. New York: John Wiley & Sons, 1979. A college-level book that describes rocks and minerals in very clear, concise terms, emphasizing simple identification techniques. Gives an excellent but succinct overview of metamorphic rocks and their conditions of formation, notable occurrences, and uses.

Ernst, W. G. *Earth Materials*. Englewood Cliffs, N.J.: Prentice-Hall, 1969. A short, highly regarded introductory-level book that uses crystal structures, the concepts of chemical equilibria, physical chemistry, and thermodynamic principles to explain the formation of minerals in the three major rock types. This textbook is concerned with the stability of metamorphic mineral assemblages and textures in terms of temperature-pressure conditions.

Gillen, Cornelius. *Metamorphic Geology: An Introduction to Tectonic and Metamorphic Processes*. London: Allen & Unwin, 1982. This short, well-illustrated book provides an introduction to metamorphism and indicates the strong relationships among mountain building, plate tectonics, and metamorphic processes. Regional examples are largely European, but this is one of the few introductory-level texts that is fully devoted to metamorphism. Includes glossary and short bibliography.

Mason, R. *Petrology of the Metamorphic Rocks*. London: Allen & Unwin, 1978. In addition to short sections on experimental and theoretical petrology, isotope and electron-microprobe analyses, the focus of this second-year college-level text is the description of metamorphic rocks in the field and under the microscope. This illustrated book of modest length is written from the perspective of a European geologist.

Miyashiro, A. *Metamorphism and Metamorphic Belts*. New York: John Wiley & Sons, 1973. Readable college-level text that deals with the basic concepts, characteristics, and problems of metamorphic geology. Focuses on the use of shales and specific igneous rocks to help explain metamorphism. Summarizes classic metamorphic belts throughout the world.

Tennisen, A. C. *Nature of Earth Materials*. 2d ed. Englewood Cliffs, N.J.: Prentice-Hall, 1983. A text written for the nonscientist that covers the nature of atoms and minerals as well as igneous, sedimentary, and metamorphic rocks. Also includes a section on the uses of these materials. Well illustrated, with a bibliography and subject index.

Ronald D. Tyler

Cross-References

SUB-SEA-FLOOR METAMORPHISM

Type of earth science: Geology
Field of study: Petrology, metamorphic

Sub-sea-floor metamorphism of oceanic ridge basalts by magma-driven, convecting seawater induces significant changes in the chemical composition of both rock and circulating fluid. These changes are a major factor in the exchange of elements between the lithosphere and the hydrosphere and play a critical role in the origin of exhalative ore deposits.

Principal terms

BLACK SMOKERS: active hydrothermal vents along sea-floor ridges, which discharge acidic solutions of high temperature (350 degrees Celsius or more), volume, and velocity, charged with tiny black particles of metallic sulfide minerals

CONVECTION: fluid circulation produced by gravity acting on density differences arising from unequal temperatures within a fluid; the principal means of heat transfer where fluids of low thermal conductivity are concerned

METASOMATISM: chemical changes in rock composition that accompany metamorphism; significant metasomatism almost invariably involves the presence of an aqueous fluid

OPHIOLITE COMPLEX: an assemblage of metamorphosed basaltic and ultramafic igneous rocks intimately associated with unmetamorphosed marine sediment; the rocks originate and are metamorphosed at marine ridges and are subsequently emplaced in mobile belts by plate-collision tectonics

PILLOW BASALT: a submarine basaltic lava flow in which small cylindrical tongues of lava break through the chilled surface, break up into pods, and accumulate downslope in a formation resembling a pile of sandbags

REGIONAL METAMORPHIC FACIES: the particular pressure and temperature conditions prevailing during metamorphism as recorded by the appearance of a new mineral assemblage; those facies relevant to ocean-ridge processes are (from lowest to highest intensity) zeolite facies, prehnite-pumpellyite facies, greenschist facies, and amphibolite facies

THERMAL GRADIENT/GEOTHERMAL GRADIENT: the rate of temperature increase with depth below the earth's surface

WATER-TO-ROCK RATIO: the mass of free water in a given volume of rock divided by rock mass of the same volume; processes occurring at water-to-rock ratios less than 50 are considered to be "rock-dominated," while those greater than 50 are "fluid-dominated"

Summary of the Phenomenon

The sea-floor spreading process generates an estimated 3×10^{16} grams of new basaltic crust per year along the world's ocean ridge system. Magma rising from the mantle produces this juvenile ocean-floor crust, which consists of upper layers of permeable lavas and lower layers of dike networks cutting gabbroic intrusive bodies. The thermal gradients and permeabilities of rocks in the vicinity of ocean ridges are both high, resulting in an environment favorable for convective cooling of the rock sequence by circulating seawater. Intensive studies of heat-flow patterns across ocean ridge systems in the early 1970's confirmed that large-scale seawater circulation through hot basaltic crust is actually occurring. During the same period, advances in structural and chemical studies of ophiolite complexes on land led geologists to conclude that these peculiar rock sequences are fragments of oceanic crust and upper mantle that were tectonically emplaced by plate collisions. A principal line of evidence used to support this conclusion is the fact that ophiolitic basaltic rocks had been metamorphosed and intensely veined prior to emplacement. The ophiolitic metabasalts were, in fact, identical in all respects to samples obtained in dredge hauls along the axial valleys of ocean ridges. As a result, a new form of rock metamorphism, regional in extent but totally restricted to the marine ridge environment, was recognized. The first scientific paper describing this phenomenon in a comprehensive and unified fashion appeared in 1973; in this landmark paper, the newly recognized metamorphic process was referred to as sub-sea-floor metamorphism. Subsequent researchers in this field have introduced alternative terms to refer to the subject, such as "submarine hydrothermal alteration" and "ocean-ridge metasomatism." For historical reasons, the original terminology is the most convenient, but, for brevity, "sub-sea-floor metamorphism" will be reduced to the acronym SFM.

If large volumes of normal seawater circulate convectively through hot basalt in close proximity to rising basaltic magma, it follows that chemical reactions between rock and seawater should alter the initial compositions of both. It also follows that the rock will be cooled by continued influx of unheated water and that the water circulating through the rocks will be heated by contact with the rock along its flow path. It is important to recognize that SFM is a process involving both heat and mass transfer. Geochemists were quick to realize that large-scale, continuous alteration of ridge basalts by convecting seawater could have profound effects on the exchange of chemical elements between the earth's lithosphere and hydrosphere. This hypothesis was tested by direct sampling of discharge fluids from submarine hot springs (350-400 degrees Celsius) in the Galápagos Rift and the East Pacific Rise (21 degrees north latitude) by manned submersibles in 1977 and 1979. It was found that, compared with normal seawater, these hot springs vent a fluid that is distinctly acidic; strongly depleted in magnesium (Mg) and sulfate (SO_4); enriched in silica (SiO_2), calcium (Ca), and hydrogen sulfide (H_2S); and enriched in a wide range of metallic elements. These compositional differences are the result of rock-seawater interaction and prove that SFM involves large-scale metasomatism. This is in marked contrast to regional metamorphism in continental mobile belts, which is a quasi-isochemical process.

Samples recovered by dredging the steep escarpments of submarine ridge valleys represent the common regional metamorphic facies (zeolite, prehnite-pumpellyite, greenschist, and amphibolite), but the vast majority record the conditions of the greenschist facies. Most samples are metabasalts with mineralogy indicative of a temperature range of 100-450 degrees Celsius and very low pressures (400-500 bars) relative to continental metamorphism. The original mineralogy of ridge basalts, which consists of tiny crystals of calcic plagioclase, clinopyroxene, and olivine set in a glassy matrix, is converted by SFM to complex mixtures of actinolite, tremolite, hornblende, albite, chlorite, epidote, talc, clay, quartz, sphene, and pyrite that, however, tend to preserve the original igneous texture of the rock. Such assemblages are well known in basaltic rocks of continental mobile belts and ophiolite complexes, and they record greenschist facies conditions. For the majority of samples, greenschist facies metamorphism has produced an alteration assemblage which consists of albite-actinolite-chlorite-epidote and is accompanied by a small amount of quartz and pyrite. The major mineralogical transformations recorded in these rocks appear to be plagioclase to albite to chlorite or to albite plus epidote; plagioclase plus clinopyroxene to chlorite plus epidote; olivine to chlorite plus pyrite; clinopyroxene to actinolite; and matrix glass to chlorite plus actinolite.

The intense hydrothermal veining observed in some dredge samples and especially in ophiolite complexes appears to record former high fracture-permeability, which is prerequisite to extensive basalt-seawater interaction. The major vein minerals are chlorite, actinolite, epidote, quartz, pyrite, and, less commonly, sulfides of iron, copper, and zinc. On the basis of mineralogy, greenschist facies alteration is described as chlorite-rich (chlorite greater than 15 percent of rock, epidote less than 15 percent) or epidote-rich (epidote greater than 15 percent, chlorite less than 15 percent). Chlorite-rich alteration is dominant in the dredge-haul samples recovered so far, and this preponderance is taken to mean that the chlorite-forming reactions occur at lower temperatures and closer to the seawater-basalt interface, where seawater influx of the basaltic crust begins. In other words, the transition from chlorite-rich to epidote-rich alteration records prograde metamorphism that, in the case of ridge basalts, correlates with increasing depth and temperature.

The mechanics of ridge-basalt emplacement ensure that all such rocks have an opportunity to react with seawater and undergo metasomatism. Although the chemical composition of average mid-ocean-ridge basalt (MORB) is very well known, it is unlikely that it reflects exactly the pristine composition of the initial magma. The metasomatic nature of SFM has mainly been determined on the basis of dredge samples of pillow basalt. Individual pillows typically exhibit intensely altered rims and cores of relatively fresh basalt. On this basis, it is known that chlorite-rich alteration shows greater departures from parent-rock composition than does the higher-grade epidote-rich alteration. Chlorite-rich samples exhibit significant gains of magnesium and corresponding losses of calcium, but their state of oxidation is, for the most part, unaffected by the alteration process. Epidote-rich samples generally undergo minor losses of magnesium and gains of calcium but become somewhat oxidized by the alteration reactions.

Laboratory experimentation with basalt-seawater reactions in the temperature range of 150-350 degrees Celsius indicates that magnesium is removed from seawater and held in magnesium-rich secondary phases (especially chlorite) at the water-rock interface. The extent of this reaction depends on both temperature and water-to-rock mass ratio. At water-to-rock ratios less than 50 (in other words, rock-dominated conditions), magnesium removal from seawater is complete, the reaction rate being proportional to temperature. The form of this reaction is suggested by

$$3Mg^{++} + 4SiO_2 + 4H_2O = Mg_3Si_4O_{10}(OH)_2 + 6H^+$$
$$\text{(talc)}$$

where talc is used as a simple chemical analogue for the more complex formulas of the chlorites that actually form. Note that H^+ (positively charged hydrogen) appears on the product side of this reaction; this outcome means that the seawater solution will be acidic as long as magnesium remains in solution to drive the reaction. For rock-dominated conditions, however, magnesium is soon depleted and the acidic conditions associated with the reaction are short-lived. However brief, the acidic stage is important because it permits the circulating seawater to leach metallic elements from the enclosing basalt. At water-to-rock ratios in excess of 50 (that is, fluid-dominated conditions), magnesium cannot be completely removed from solution, so that the acidic, metal-leaching conditions of the reaction are maintained indefinitely. Electrical neutrality of the solution is balanced by the loss of calcium, sodium, and potassium from basalt because these elements are not utilized in the formation of chlorite. In contrast, iron and aluminum are retained in the rock because they participate in the formation of chlorite. The rate and magnitude of the reaction both increase with temperature and, because thermal gradients near ridges are very high, it would be expected that magnesium-metasomatism would be restricted to relatively shallow crustal depths. This limitation exists because fluids downwelling from the crust-seawater interface would become quickly heated.

For temperatures in excess of 350 degrees Celsius, experiments predict that magnesium-metasomatism will be replaced by sodium-metasomatism of a slightly more complex nature. In this case, seawater sodium (Na) replaces calcium in plagioclase crystals of basalt, which in turn permits the liberated calcium to form epidote and maintain acidic conditions independent of the fluid-to-rock ratio. This reaction takes the form:

$$Na^+ + 2CaAl_2Si_2O_8 + 2SiO_2 + H_2O = NaAlSi_3O_8 + Ca_2Al_3Si_3O_{12}(OH) + H^+$$
$$\text{(calcium-plagioclase)} \qquad \text{(albite)} \qquad \text{(clinozoisite)}$$

where clinozoisite is a simple analogue for epidote. This reaction shows that the more albite forms, the more calcium is recycled from plagioclase to epidote, and the more acidic the aqueous solution becomes. This reaction depends upon the availability of silica, which must be supplied to the solution by the rock. Because basalts with glassy matrices are more susceptible to silica leaching than comparable rocks with crystalline matrices, it is expected that sodium-metasomatism (albitization or spilitization) is most pronounced in basalts that were formerly glassy.

The complex fluids currently venting from submarine ridge hot springs are viewed as the end product of a sequence of chemical reactions that begin with seawater infiltration of hot, fractured basalt some distance from the ridge axis. Convective circulation, supported by magmatic heat, drives the downwelling fluids to depths of perhaps 1 or 2 kilometers, during which time they are heated to temperatures in excess of 350 degrees Celsius and react extensively with the surrounding rocks. The fluids ultimately are returned to the sea floor by upwelling through narrow, focused zones along ridge axes and discharged into the sea as highly evolved hot-spring solutions. Many chemical and physical details of this complex process are yet to be explained, but it seems clear that a calcium-fixing reaction, such as the second reaction described, must play a major role in producing the high-temperature, acidic, metal-charged solutions that vent from ridge-crest hot springs.

Methods of Study

Prior to the late 1970's, scientific data were largely gathered along ocean ridges from specially designed research ships operating on the surface. The methods utilized included bathymetry, heat-flow and magnetic measurements, dredge sampling, and core drilling of bottom sediments and ridge basalts. It is impossible to overemphasize the success of these techniques, which provided the confirming evidence for sea-floor spreading and the foundation for modern plate tectonic theory. A new era began, however, in 1977, when the manned submersible *Alvin* was utilized to make direct observations of submarine hydrothermal activity along the Galápagos Rift. That was soon followed by the immensely successful 1979 RISE expedition, which used *Alvin* to photograph and sample the amazing "black smokers" on the East Pacific Rise. Manned submersibles, supported by conventional research vessels, offer many advantages. Chief among them are that small-scale geological phenomena may be directly observed and revisited to study temporal effects; a wide range of geophysical data may be measured directly on the sea floor; samples of sediment, fluid, and rock may be collected and re-collected directly from precisely known sample sites; the physical characteristics of each data-measurement site can be observed and described; and interactions between biological and geological systems can be observed.

Direct sea-floor observations, coupled with detailed laboratory experimentation on basalt-seawater reactions, are extremely valuable as a means of investigating processes operating at the rock-seawater interface along ocean ridges where crustal growth occurs. Additional data derive from studies of hot brines in deep boreholes of active geothermal areas such as Salton Sea (California), Iceland, and New

Zealand. Useful as these approaches are, their value from a metamorphic perspective is limited because they cannot tell how metamorphic conditions vary with depth beneath the rock-seawater interface; neither do they predict the effects of prolonged (for example, over millions of years) rock-seawater interaction. Full characterization of SFM as a petrologic process requires traditional geological study of rocks on land that record the entire range of SFM effects. Fortunately, such rocks, known as ophiolite complexes, are relatively common in major orogenic belts such as the Alps, Appalachian-Caledonian system, and numerous circum-Pacific mountain ranges.

Ophiolites are now considered to be fault-bounded slices of ancient metamorphosed sea floor and upper mantle rock that have been thrust onto continental margins as a result of plate collisions. The ideal ophiolite sequence is equivalent to the ideal succession of rock types formed along active ocean ridges between the upwelling asthenosphere and the sea floor. This ideal sequence is 2-10 kilometers thick and includes three distinct components: a lowermost zone of ultramafic mantle rocks, which represent the refractory residue produced by partial melting of the upper mantle and extraction of basaltic magma; an overlying zone of crustal ultramafic cumulates formed by crystal settling on the floors of former magma chambers; and roof-zone basalts, tapped from the underlying magma chambers, which grade from sheeted-dike complexes upward into submarine lava flows, pillow basalts, and admixed marine sediments.

Many ophiolite localities have been closely studied. Usually they are linear rock bodies, elongate parallel to the continental margin at the time of their emplacement. The ideal "ridge-stratigraphy" is never complete because of the intense structural dismemberment that attends their emplacement. The thickest and most complete ophiolite sequences are probably the Vourinos ophiolite of Greece and the Troodos complex of Cyprus. These well-studied bodies are both about 1,700 meters thick, but most ophiolites are thinner and correspondingly less complete. Nearly all ophiolites are intensely deformed and have undergone one or more overprinting metamorphic events subsequent to SFM. In spite of such difficulties, ophiolite studies continue to contribute to the growing body of knowledge of SFM. As an example, consider the ophiolites in the eastern Ligurian Apennine mountain range near Genoa, Italy. Here, the sequential appearance of chlorite, pumpellyite, epidote, and hornblende in a pillow lava assemblage 225 meters thick records a prograde metamorphic episode that field evidence indicates occurred prior to tectonic emplacement. These pillow lavas are now upside-down as a result of recumbent folding during emplacement, but, when restored to their original stratigraphic position, it is clear that the metamorphic mineral assemblage formed in response to a steep thermal gradient that increased downward. The metamorphic temperature interval deduced for the Ligurian pillow lava sequence is 180-400 degrees Celsius; the maximum temperature of 400 degrees Celsius occurred at a depth of only 300 meters below the rock-seawater interface, which equates with an amazing geothermal gradient of 1,300 degrees Celsius per kilometer. Elsewhere, these same rocks yield a slightly lower thermal gradient of 900 degrees Celsius per kilometer. Such gradients are five to eight times those measured at active oceanic rifts (about 170 degrees Celsius per kilometer) and suggest that the Ligurian SFM took place in close proximity to a magma chamber. A thermal gradient of about 150 degrees Celsius per kilometer has been determined for the Troodos ophiolite on Cyprus. These data indicate that SFM occurs in response to a wide range of thermal gradients, a result that is entirely consistent with the sporadic nature of volcanic activity along the axes of active submarine ridges.

Context

"Sub-sea-floor metamorphism" refers to the chemical and mineralogical changes produced in ridge basalts and underlying ultramafic rocks by reaction with heated seawater. Although still in its infancy as a field of study, this branch of metamorphic petrology is contributing to the understanding of chemical mass balance between the earth's hydrosphere and lithosphere. More important, from the economic point of view, studies of sub-sea-floor metamorphism have greatly advanced knowledge of the important "volcanic-exhalative" class of ore deposits.

Volcanic-exhalative ore bodies are major stratabound metallic deposits that precipitate directly onto the sea floor from metal-laden solutions discharged by submarine hot springs. The resulting ores are mineralogically variable but are generally sulfide-rich and, for this reason, are often called massive sulfide deposits even though many contain substantial quantities of metallic oxides, carbonates, and sulfates. Of the several types of exhalative ore deposits now recognized, the Cyprus-type is most closely identified with igneous and metamorphic processes operating along submarine ridges. On the island of Cyprus, massive sulfide copper-zinc ores are hosted by ancient, metamorphosed, sea-floor rocks called ophiolites and blanketed by a thin layer of iron-manganese-rich marine chert. The Cyprus ores are lensoidal to podlike bodies, 200-300 meters across and up to 250 meters thick. The largest of these massive sulfide lenses contain 15-20 million tons of ore that typically assays about 4 percent copper, 0.5 percent zinc, 8 parts per million each of silver and gold, 48 percent sulfur, 43 percent iron, and 5 percent silica. The minerals comprising the ore are mainly pyrite and chalcopyrite accompanied by minor sphalerite and marcasite.

Cyprus-type massive sulfides are of worldwide occurrence, and hundreds of these deposits are now known. As a class, they constitute a major mineral resource produced as a by-product of sub-sea-floor metamorphism. They are considered, by most geologists, to form directly on the sea floor from the discharge of black smokers such as those discovered by manned submersibles along the East Pacific Rise. The smokers are 2- to 10-meter-high chimneys that pump dense, black plumes of hot (350 degrees Celsius), acidic (pH = 4), metal-laden brine onto the sea floor. The turbulent black plumes, for which this special class of hot spring is named, are composed of fine particles of pyrite, pyrrhotite, and sphalerite. Calculations indicate that, at their present high flow rates, ten black smokers such as those operating on the East Pacific Rise could produce the largest known Cyprus-type massive sulfide body in only two thousand years.

Bibliography

Best, M. G. *Igneous and Metamorphic Petrology.* New York: W. H. Freeman, 1982. A popular university text for undergraduate majors in geology. Well-illustrated and fairly detailed treatment of the origin, distribution, and characteristics of igneous and metamorphic rocks. Sub-sea-floor metamorphism is covered on pages 427-432, but the treatment is somewhat dated in this rapidly developing field.

Fyfe, W. S., N. J. Price, and A. B. Thompson. *Fluids in the Earth's Crust.* New York: Elsevier, 1978. The best overview available of the theoretical side of fluid-rock interaction. The authors argue that subduction and sea-floor spreading may be viewed as large-scale metasomatic processes, the end product of which is the crust. Written for advanced students of earth sciences. Extensive bibliography.

Guilbert, J. M., and C. F. Park, Jr. *The Geology of Ore Deposits.* New York: W. H. Freeman, 1986. A splendid edition of a traditional text for undergraduate majors in geology. Chapter 13 treats ore deposits formed by submarine volcanism in comprehensive fashion. Cyprus-type ore bodies are specifically described on pages 598-603. Excellent index and illustrations.

Haymon, R. M. "Growth History of Hydrothermal Black Smoker Chimneys." *Nature* 301 (1983): 695-698. A brief technical article describing the chemistry and mineralogy of the black smokers discovered by the 1979 RISE expedition. This prestigious British science magazine can be found in most university libraries.

Humphris, S. E., and G. Thompson. "Hydrothermal Alteration of Oceanic Basalts by Seawater." *Geochimica et Cosmothimica Acta* 42 (January, 1978): 107-125. This paper is a major contribution to the growing field of sub-sea-floor metamorphism, although it requires some background in geochemistry. The authors examine the long-term implications of chemical exchange between seawater and the lithosphere.

Mottl, M. J. "Metabasalts, Axial Hot Springs, and the Structure of Hydrothermal Systems at Mid-Ocean Ridges." *Geological Society of America Bulletin* 94 (1983): 161-180. An excellent article that summarizes the status of sub-sea-floor metamorphism. Although technical, much can be gained from this article by college-level readers who have some background in this subject area. This periodical will be found in any university library.

Seyfried, W. E., Jr. "Experimental and Theoretical Constraints on Hydrothermal Alteration Processes at Mid-Ocean Ridges." *Annual Review of Earth and Planetary Sciences* 15 (1987): 317-335. This review paper is on the status of sub-sea-floor metamorphism. Emphasis is on experimental aspects of basalt-seawater interaction. Technical, with some background in geochemistry needed. This journal is an annual periodical, published in hardcover book form, and should be found in most major libraries.

Spiess, F. N., and RISE Project Group. "East Pacific Rise: Hot Springs and Geophysical Experiments." *Science* 207 (March 28, 1980): 1421-1432. This article is the report on the 1979 RISE expedition that discovered the now-famous black smokers and explored the rift system in the vicinity of 21 degrees north latitude by manned submersibles. Recommended for general readers.

Spooner, E. T. C., and W. S. Fyfe. "Sub-Sea-Floor Metamorphism, Heat, and Mass Transfer." *Contributions to Mineralogy and Petrology* 42, no. 4 (1973): 287-304. This paper is the classical work in the ophiolite terrane of the Ligurian Apennines that established a unified model for sub-sea-floor metamorphism. Essential reading at a modest technical level.

Yardley, B. W. D. *An Introduction to Metamorphic Petrology.* New York: John Wiley & Sons, 1989. An excellent undergraduate text with a good index and extensive current references. For college-level readers, a good place to begin studies of any type of metamorphism.

Gary R. Lowell

Cross-References

Heat Sources and Heat Flow, 1065; Hydrothermal Mineralization, 1108; The Lithosphere, 1380; Water in Magmas, 1433; Metamorphism: Metasomatism, 1599; Regional Metamorphism, 1606; The Ocean Ridge System, 1826; The Oceanic Crust, 1846; Ophiolites, 1954; Volcanism at Spreading Centers, 2607; Volcanoes: Flood Basalts, 2630.

METEORITE AND COMET IMPACTS

Type of earth science: Planetology
Field of study: Small solar system bodies

The hypervelocity impact of a meteorite or comet on a planetary surface destroys the impacting body and produces a crater that is many times larger than the impacting body. Impact has been responsible for shaping many planetary surfaces and may have caused climatic and biotic changes on the earth.

Principal terms

ASTEROID: a small, rocky body in orbit around the sun; a minor planet

COMET: a small body in orbit around the sun that has a fuzzy appearance and often develops a long tail as a result of release of gas and dust as the solid core is heated by sunlight

COMPLEX CRATER: an impact crater of large diameter and low depth-to-diameter ratio caused by the presence of a central uplift or ring structure

HYPERVELOCITY IMPACT: impact involving an object that is traveling faster than the speed of sound in the impacted material and producing compressive shock waves

METEORITE: a rock of extraterrestrial origin that has fallen on the earth's surface; most meteorites are believed to be fragments of asteroids

SHOCK WAVE: a compressional wave formed when a body undergoes a hypervelocity impact; it produces abrupt changes in pressure, temperature, density, and velocity in the target material as it passes through

SIMPLE CRATER: a small impact crater with a simple bowl shape

TARGET MATERIAL: material, generally rock, that is hit by a projectile or impacting body

Summary of the Phenomenon

Most objects swept up by the earth as it orbits the sun are vaporized, or at least appreciably slowed down by the earth's atmosphere; however, large objects such as asteroids or comets, with masses greater than about 100 metric tons, can hit the earth's surface still traveling at close to their velocity in space (generally between 10 and 40 kilometers per second). Such objects can explode on impact and produce a depression in the earth's surface called an impact crater. Although impact craters are relatively rare on the earth's surface, studies of other planetary bodies, such as Mercury and Mars, as well as the Moon, indicate that impact cratering is a major geological process in the solar system. The relatively low number of impact craters on the earth is a result of the earth being a geologically active planet; as a consequence, impact craters are generally quickly destroyed by other processes, such as gradation, tectonism, or volcanism.

Impact craters have been widely recognized as impact features only in the latter part of the twentieth century. They can be confused with other features, such as volcanic craters; many older impact craters have been so deeply eroded that only a circular area of deformation remains. The first crater to be identified as having an impact origin is Meteor (or Barringer) Crater in Arizona. This crater was first suggested to be an impact crater in 1891 by G. K. Gilbert, a well-known American geologist, and Marcus Baker. Gilbert also proposed that the lunar craters were formed by meteoroid impact. He later changed his mind about Meteor Crater and suggested that it was formed by volcanism. D. M. Barringer, however, supported the view that the crater had been formed by the impact of a large nickel-iron meteorite, fragments of which were found scattered around the crater. Barringer attempted to develop the crater as a commercial enterprise for the recovery of nickel-iron. He was not successful in using the crater as a source of iron, but the crater is now widely accepted as an impact crater largely as a result of his publications in the early 1900's. By 1928, only two impact craters had been recognized, and both were associated with meteorite fragments.

In the 1960's, shock metamorphic effects were recognized, and their identification became an important criterion for identifying impact craters. Shock metamorphism refers to the changes that take place in rock material as a result of high temperature and pressure generated during a high-velocity impact event. The recognition of shock metamorphism as a criterion for identifying impact structures has led to the discovery of more than one hundred impact structures since 1960.

The size and morphology of an impact crater depend initially on the size and velocity of the impacting body and on the nature of the surface or target material. The forward motion of small meteoroids is stopped by the earth's atmosphere, and the object falls to the earth, where it can be collected as a meteorite. Such objects do little damage on impact. Larger objects can retain a portion of their forward velocity and can penetrate into the ground, particularly if the meteorite lands in soft material such as soil or sediment. The resulting feature is called a penetration funnel. A number of craters of this type are found in Campo del Cielo, Argentina, associated with fragments of a nickel-iron meteorite.

Large impact craters or explosion craters are produced during hypervelocity, or hypersonic, impact events. During such an event, the impacting body explodes and a crater is produced that is many times the diameter of the impacting body. Hypervelocity impacts occur when the impacting body hits the surface, traveling at a velocity that exceeds the velocity of sound in the target material—that is, greater than several kilometers per second for most rock material. Upon impact, the kinetic energy of the impacting body is transferred to the earth's surface in the form of intense shock waves. The kinetic energy of a moving body is equal to one-half its mass times its velocity squared. Thus, a nickel-iron meteorite with a diameter of 20 meters, weighing about 32,000 metric tons, traveling at a velocity of 20 kilometers per second, would impart about 6.4×10^{15} joules of energy into the target rock. This amount of energy is equivalent to approximately one and a half million tons of dynamite and would be about seventy-five times more powerful than the atom bomb that was dropped on Hiroshima.

Three stages are recognized in the formation of an impact crater: compression, excavation, and postcratering modification. The compression stage is initiated when the projectile (the meteorite or comet) makes contact with the ground. Two compressional shock waves are produced: One travels back through the impacting body, destroying it, and one moves through the ground. At the initial point of contact, pressures exceeding a megabar can be produced, which results in deformational stresses that are orders of magnitude greater than the strength of rock material. High temperatures are generated by the shock wave and increase with increasing shock pressure. At shock pressures greater than about 250 kilobars, most rock types will be crushed; above about 500 kilobars, rock material will begin to melt. At pressures exceeding 1,000 kilobars, rock will be vaporized. The high pressure and temperature produced during the passage of the shock wave distinguish impact from other geological processes.

The compressional shock wave moves out radially into the ground, and the pressure and temperature drop off exponentially from the initial point of contact. Thus, near the initial point of contact, the pressure and associated temperature are high enough to vaporize rock material completely. Surrounding that, a larger volume of rock is melted; surrounding that, a much larger volume of rock is crushed by the passage of the shock wave. For impact events that form craters larger than about 1 or 2 kilometers in diameter, the shock pressures and temperatures are great enough to melt and/or vaporize the impacting body completely.

The excavation stage begins with the development of rarefaction waves that follow the compressional shock wave. During passage of the rarefaction waves, the rock material is decompressed and set into motion. Rock material moves upward and outward, leading to ejection of rock and the development of a transient cavity. Rock material near the point of impact is ejected first. This material is subjected to the highest pressure and temperature and is therefore in the form of vapor and melt. It also has the highest velocity and thus is thrown farthest from the crater. As the cavity grows, the ejected material (ejecta) is derived from progressively greater distances from the initial point of contact and is thus subjected to progressively lower pressure and temperature and has progressively lower ejection velocity. Thus, the rock excavated from the greatest depth experiences the lowest pressure and temperature and lands nearest the crater.

The postcratering modification stage involves changes that occur after the crater is formed. These changes include slumping of the crater walls, isostatic adjustments, and erosion and infill of the crater. This stage can continue over a long period of time and eventually leads to obliteration of the crater. Old impact scars left after the crater has been removed by erosion have been called astroblemes (star wounds).

The ejecta forms an ejecta blanket and secondary craters surrounding the primary impact crater. A continuous blanket of ejecta extends out from the crater a distance of one to two crater diameters. The ejecta blanket is thickest next to the crater and thins outward. Rocks from shallow depths in the crater are deposited first, followed by rocks from progressively deeper depths, resulting in a reversed stratigraphy in the ejecta blanket. Beyond the ejecta blanket, the ejecta is discontinuous and large blocks of rock form low-velocity craters, called secondary craters, which often occur in clusters or loops.

The surface around the impact crater is elevated above the surrounding surface to form a rim. The raised rim is a result of a variety of processes. The rock adjacent to the crater is crushed by the shock wave and thus takes up more volume, which causes the land surface next to the crater to be elevated. In addition, the ejecta blanket is thickest next to the crater. Furthermore, in some impact craters, the surface rock originally inside the crater was lifted up and thrown back over itself to form an overturned flap. This also adds to the elevation of the land surface immediately adjacent to the crater.

Some of the melt stays inside the crater, and some of the ejecta falls back inside the crater. The melt flows to the floor of the crater and is covered with an ejecta layer that insulates it and prevents it from cooling rapidly. As a result, the melt layer crystallizes and forms a layer of melt rock that has texture similar to that of an igneous rock. The melt rock can be distinguished from normal igneous rocks by the presence of inclusions showing evidence of shock metamorphism, by their unusual compositions corresponding to a mixture of the target rocks, and, in some cases, by contamination from the impacting meteorite. The ejecta that falls back into the crater forms a layer of fragmental rock called a fallback breccia.

In map view, most impact craters are circular; in cross section, the profile of a crater varies with size. Smaller craters have simple bowl shapes with a depth-to-diameter ratio of about 1:5. Larger craters are more complex and have lower depth-to-diameter ratios because of the presence of a central uplift or interior rings. On earth, the transition from simple to complex craters takes place at a crater diameter of about 2-4 kilometers. The central uplift may be the result of postshock rebound of the crater floor, gravitational collapse of crater rim material, or both.

More than one hundred impact craters have been identified on the earth. Known terrestrial impact craters range in diameter from less than 1 kilometer to about 140 kilometers and in age from less than 100,000 to nearly 2 billion years. Twelve impact craters still have meteorite fragments associated with them, and in every case the meteorite is an iron or stony iron. All the craters with associated meteorite fragments are small (less than 2 kilometers in diameter) and young (less than 1 million years old). Meteoritic contamination of the melt rocks in some of the larger impact structures indicates that at least some of them were probably formed by stony meteorites.

The rate of crater formation has decreased with time. Immediately after the planets were formed, the cratering rate was exceedingly high, but the rate decreased exponentially with time until about 3 billion years ago. Since then, the rate has been fairly uniform. It is estimated that for the last 100 million years, a crater larger than

10 kilometers was formed on the average of about every 100,000 years, while a crater larger than 100 kilometers was formed about every 50 million years. Most of the craters were probably formed by meteorites rather than by comets, but many of the larger craters may have been formed by comets.

Methods of Study

Knowledge of impact craters and the cratering process comes from the study of known impact craters, experiments with man-made explosions, laboratory experiments with high-velocity projectiles, and theoretical studies. Many of the known impact craters have been studied and mapped extensively in order to develop criteria for recognizing impact structures. Meteor Crater in Arizona is the best-known and most studied impact crater. Many shock metamorphic features were first recognized there and then later used as criteria for identifying other impact structures that no longer have meteorite fragments associated with them.

High-speed motion pictures of explosions, using chemical explosives and nuclear devices, have been studied in order to understand the cratering process. Crater formation can also be observed on a smaller scale by observing the impact of missiles and on an even smaller scale by impacting projectiles in the laboratory. Such studies can be used to relate impact-cratering effects to known conditions of impact velocities, projectile properties, and target conditions. These studies indicate that under average conditions, the diameter of the impact crater is about ten to twenty times the diameter of the impacting body. Such information cannot be obtained from the study of impact craters, as the velocity and mass of the projectiles are not known.

The formation of large impact craters (greater than 1 kilometer in diameter) requires more energy than the largest nuclear bomb explosion. Thus, these large events cannot be studied directly, but computer programs have been developed in an attempt to model what might happen during a highly energetic impact. Some scientists have suggested that during a large impact event, involving kilometer-sized impacting bodies, a fireball is formed that can carry material up through the atmosphere and eject it into space at velocities close to or exceeding the earth's escape velocity.

Studies of lunar impact craters have been used to calibrate crater formation rates over time. The lunar highlands were formed about 4.5 billion years ago, while the different mare (lunar sea) surfaces were formed between 3 and 4 billion years ago. Since their formation, these surfaces have not been modified by degradation processes or tectonism. By determining the number of impact craters per unit area on these various surfaces, which have been radiometrically dated, scientists have been able to determine the rate of formation of impact craters through time.

Context

If scientists' current theories concerning the origin of the planets is correct, then the planets were formed by the accretion of asteroid-sized bodies called planetesimals. The early history of the planets and their satellites was dominated by meteoroid bombardment. The surfaces of the Moon, Mercury, parts of Mars, and many of the satellites of the outer planets attest an early history of intense bombardment. The number of craters per unit area has been used to determine the relative ages of different regions on a planetary surface. The large circular basins on the Moon and on planetary bodies are believed to be the results of asteroid impacts. Some scientists have even argued that the earth's moon was formed as a result of a Mars-sized body colliding with the earth. Most of the atmospheres and hydrospheres of the terrestrial planets (Earth, Venus, Mars) may have been contributed during the late stage of accretion by cometary impacts. Some scientists have speculated that the first organic molecules that led to the development of life on the earth were brought in by impacting meteorites or comets.

Impact has played a major role in the earth's history. During the first half-billion years of the earth's history, impact cratering was the dominant process in shaping the face of the globe. Impact may have also played an important role in the geologic history of the earth over the last few billion years. It has been suggested that large impacts might have triggered mantle plumes that led to extensive volcanism and may have caused the breakup of continents and initiated continental drift. Furthermore, impacts are probably responsible for the formation of a group of unusual glass objects called tektites.

It has even been suggested that large impacts might be the cause of climatic changes, mass extinctions, and geomagnetic reversals. Large impacts might cause extinctions in a variety of ways. Nitrogen oxide can be produced by shock heating of the atmosphere by an impacting body, which would lead to the development of acid rains. The impact of comets could introduce large quantities of gases or chemicals, such as ammonium, that could poison the environment. Large impacts can throw huge quantities of dust into the atmosphere that would block out sunlight, preventing photosynthesis and possibly even triggering an ice age. The impact of a 10-kilometer-diameter asteroid at the end of the Mesozoic era, about 65 million years ago, is thought to have been responsible for a mass extinction. It has been proposed that periodic increases in comet impacts have been responsible for mass extinctions that occur approximately every 26 million years. Evidence suggests that at least three large impact events might be associated with reversals of the earth's magnetic field.

Astronomers have shown that a large number of asteroids in earth-crossing orbits could in the future collide with the earth. These objects range in diameter from less than 1 kilometer to about 10 kilometers. The impact of a 10-kilometer body would produce a crater more than 100 kilometers in diameter and would destroy everything within a few hundred kilometers of the crater. It has even been suggested that a large impact event might be mistaken for a nuclear bomb attack and that such an event could trigger a war.

Some large impact structures have economic value. The 140-kilometer-diameter Sudbury impact structure in Ontario, Canada, is the primary source of most nickel and is also a source of copper and other metals. Several billion dollars worth of metals have been recovered from this structure since it was discovered in 1883. At least one buried impact crater has provided a trap for petroleum. The Boltysh structure in the Ukraine is a buried 25-kilometer-diameter impact structure that contains about 3 billion tons of oil shale. Several oil-producing structures in North America are also suspected as being of impact origin.

Bibliography

Classen, J. "Catalogue of 230 Certain, Probable, Possible, and Doubtful Impact Structures." *Meteoritics* 12 (1977): 61. As indicated by the title, this article is essentially a list of certain and possible impact craters. The author gives data on crater location, size, age, and evidence for an impact origin, where present. He also gives an extensive reference list.

French, Bevan M., and Nicholas M. Short, eds. *Shock Metamorphism of Natural Materials.* Baltimore: Mono Book, 1968. A collection of papers dealing with cratering mechanics and shock metamorphism. The papers vary in degree of difficulty.

Horz, Friedrich, ed. "Meteorite Impact and Volcanism." *Journal of Geophysical Research* 76 (August 10, 1971). A collection of papers dealing with impact structures and shock metamorphism. Most of the papers are fairly technical.

Roddy, D. J., R. O. Pepin, and R. B. Merrill, eds. *Impact and Explosion Cratering.* Elmsford, N.Y.: Pergamon Press, 1977. A collection of papers on cratering mechanics and impact craters on various planetary bodies. The papers vary in degree of difficulty, but some should be suitable for advanced high school students.

Shoemaker, E. M. "Impact Mechanics at Meteor Crater, Arizona." In *The Solar System.* Vol. 4, *The Moon, Meteorites and Comets,* edited by B. M. Middlehurst and G. P. Kuiper. Chicago: University of Chicago Press, 1963. A classic paper on Meteor Crater and its origin. Suitable for high school readers.

Silver, Leon T., and Peter H. Schultz, eds. *Geological Implications of Impacts of Large Asteroids and Comets on the Earth.* Special Paper 190. Denver, Colo.: U.S. Geological Survey, 1982. A collection of papers on impact cratering and the effects of large impacts on the climate and life with emphasis on the events that occurred about sixty-five million years ago, at the end of the Mesozoic era (the age of the dinosaurs). These papers vary in degree of difficulty, but some are suitable for advanced high school students and undergraduates.

Billy P. Glass

Cross-References

Asteroids, 98; Astroblemes, 106; Comets, 253; Lunar Craters, 1393; Mars' Craters, 1480; Mass Extinctions, 1514; Paleoclimatology, 1993; Tektites, 2512.

METEORITES: ACHONDRITES

Type of earth science: Planetology
Field of study: Small solar system bodies

Achondrites are stony meteorites containing abundant silicate minerals that have formed as a result of igneous processes on small planetoids or asteroids. They closely resemble basaltic rocks found upon the earth and moon. Meteorites in general could serve as a new source of raw materials and may have had an effect upon the evolution of living creatures upon the earth.

Principal terms

ACHONDRITE: a stony meteorite that contains mostly silicate minerals and a small amount of metal formed from the cooling of molten rock

BASALT: a type of igneous rock that contains an almost equal abundance of small plagioclase feldspar and pyroxene minerals

BRECCIA: a rock composed of a random mixture of angular fragments of other rocks and minerals

CRYSTALLIZATION: the process by which minerals are formed at various temperatures and pressures, resulting in an orderly arrangement of their atoms

CUMULUS CRYSTALS: dense minerals within liquid magma that accumulate by gravity upon the floor of the magma chamber

METAMORPHISM: a process by which heat and pressure is applied to a rock without causing it to melt

SOLAR NEBULA: the disk-shaped cloud of hot dust and gas from which the solar sytem formed

Summary of the Phenomenon

Meteorites found on the earth are solid materials left over from the formation of the solar system. Achondrites are an important variety of meteorite, as they closely resemble certain common terrestrial, or earth, rocks. Meteoroids are defined as any extraterrestrial samples of matter that exist in orbit around the sun. A meteoroid becomes a meteor when it begins to vaporize at an altitude of about 100 kilometers above the earth, as a result of friction with the air molecules of the earth's atmosphere. A meteor is usually observed as a bright but brief streak of light in the night sky and is commonly known as a shooting star. A meteor becomes a meteorite when it survives the fiery passage through earth's atmosphere, later to be discovered and recovered as a solid mass. Every year the earth receives about 363 metric tons of meteorite dust.

Meteorites can be divided into three groups based upon the abundance of metals and silicate minerals they contain. These groups are the irons, stony irons, and stones. The irons exist as mixtures, or alloys, of two metallic, iron-nickel minerals known as kemacite and taenite. The stony irons are transitional between the irons and the stones, and they consist of abundant silicate minerals mixed with metallic minerals in roughly equal amounts. Stone meteorites are composed of silicate and oxide minerals with minor amounts of metal. They can be further subdivided into two different groups known as the chondrites and achondrites. Achondrites are not as abundant as chondrites. They are dissimilar both in chemical composition and in texture from chondrites, as they lack oxide mineral droplets called chondrules. Achondrites were generally formed by the solidification of pods of molten rock called magma chambers and have therefore crystallized as igneous rocks. These rocks most likely originated on or within a small planet-sized body or large asteroid. In appearance, some achondrites have large crystals that result from slow cooling as intrusive rocks below the surface. Another type, having small crystals, was formed by rapid cooling on or close to the surface of the parent body. Both types are similar to igneous rocks on the earth. As such, some resemble lava flows, as they are riddled with many holes caused by gases that escaped under low pressure.

Most achondrites contain a small amount of metal (less than 10 percent) in the form of iron and nickel alloys and are rich in one or more silicate minerals such as olivine (a magnesium-iron silicate), pyroxene (an iron-magnesium-calcium silicate), and plagioclase feldspar (a calcium-sodium-aluminum silicate) in varying proportions. Other minerals, such as spinel or chromite (iron-magnesium-aluminum-chromium oxides), are also found. Some achondrites show evidence of collision with other meteors in space, resulting in a rock called a breccia. Breccias and other rocks show the effects of shock metamorphism: The pressure of impact causes the rocks to break apart and the minerals to shatter or deform, while the heat generated causes mineral and rock fragments either to melt slightly or to fuse together, depending upon its intensity.

In general, achondrites resemble a rock called basalt, which is a very common dark-colored igneous rock found upon the earth and moon. With a few exceptions, achondrites are older and have an abundance of rare isotopes that are very different from the rocks found upon either the moon or the earth.

As a group, achondrites can be subdivided into seven types based upon their texture and chemical composition. First and most abundant are the eucrites. They are similar in appearance to fine-grained terrestrial basalts, and they contain roughly equal amounts of certain calcium-rich silicates such as plagioclase feldspar and pyroxene minerals. In a hand specimen, a few eucrites exhibit a texture called cumulate, which shows the accumulation of coarse-grained crystals within a magma chamber. Still others contain many holes formed by escaping gases that closely resemble terrestrial basaltic lava flows, which is known as vesicular texture. The majority of eucrites have been fragmented into cohesive masses that contain mixed pieces from other meteorite types such as a diogenite or an iron meteorite. Therefore, eucrites probably existed as shallow intrusive and extrusive igneous rocks that also show the effects of shock metamorphism. The small variation of major chemical elements within all eucrites suggests their formation upon the same parent body.

The age of creation for eucrites has been determined using radioactive rubidium-strontium isotope techniques at 4.5-4.6 billion years old, indicating crystallization very early in the history of the solar system.

A diogenite is an achondrite that has a chemical composition similar to an igneous earth rock called a pyroxenite, which has an abundance of the mineral pyroxene. Texturally, diogenites have coarse-grained crystals that indicate slow, deep cooling below the surface. Based upon laboratory melting experiments using actual achondrite samples, these crystals probably formed by cooling and crystallization from the same magma that previously produced a eucrite or by the more extensive melting of some eucrite source. Chemically, diogenites consist of metamorphosed accumulations of a particular magnesium-rich but calcium-poor pyroxene mineral known as a bronzite along with minor amounts (less than 10 percent) of plagioclase feldspar crystals and some metallic iron. The crystals from this rock type have become chemically homogeneous as a result of the thermal heating of metamorphism. Like some eucrites, diogenites have been found shattered or mixed with pieces of other meteorites (eucrites), resulting in a solid rock of broken and angular crystals; this mixing indicates that both rock types formed on the same parent body.

Howardites are a variety of achondrite that represent mixtures of many different meteorite types. They consist of crushed pieces from eucrites and diogenites, and they also contain about 2-3 percent by weight of pieces from chondritic meteorites. Texturally, howardites closely resemble the lunar soil. Under high magnification, a howardite's exterior surface is covered with small micrometeorite craters that contain impact-generated glasses, evidence of their formation and existence on the surface of the parent body.

SNCs (pronounced "snicks") are a small, unusual, and highly controversial group of related achondrites that include the shergottites, nakhlites, and chassignites. The name "shergottite" comes from the town of Shergotty in the state of Bihar in India, where this strange meteorite fell in 1865. Since that time, a few others like it have been found. As a group, the shergottites are similar to slow-cooled, coarse-grained igneous rocks rich in pyroxene and plagioclase minerals, known as diabase on the earth. The feldspar mineral found within the shergottites, however, is replaced by a non-earth mineral called maskelynite, which is a type of feldspar mineral whose orderly atomic structure has become disorganized from a shock impact. Other minerals to be found are pyroxenes (calcium-rich augite and calcium-poor pigeonite), calcium- and sodium-rich plagioclase feldspars, oxidized iron in the form of magnetite, minor olivine, and a rare water-bearing amphibole mineral named kaersutite. Texturally, the shergottites are cumulates with elongated pyroxene crystals that have a preferred orientation, which is probably the result of flowage of newly formed crystals within the magma while still in a hot liquid state. Their geologic history records crystallization in a relatively earth-like oxygen-rich environment, a period of intense shock metamorphism and high-intensity heating probably caused by impact, as indicated by numerous quickly cooled glass fragments. The radiometric age determinations on some of its minerals reveal an age of 1.3 billion years, and an analysis of trapped gas bubbles within some minerals detects the presence of noble gases such as xenon, krypton, and argon. The source of the shergottite magma has a very similar chemical composition to that of earth's mantle, which suggests that this achondrite type had a complex, multistage formational history upon some body in space, different from that from which the eucrites and diogenites formed.

The nakhlites are similar to terrestrial coarse-grained igneous rocks known as gabbros. Mineralogically, these meteorites are rich in augite, contain minor olivine and plagioclase feldspar, and have a few strange sulfide minerals and some metallic iron. Compared to the shergottites, all these minerals lack shock features, show no evidence of thermal metamorphism, and have a very young radiometric age of 1.4 billion years. Although their overall chemistry is different from that of the shergottites, nakhlites are believed to have been derived from either the same or a similar parent body.

Chassignites are meteorites named for the first specimen that was found in Chassigny, France, in 1815. Several other specimens have since been found in other localities around the world. The few existing samples studied show that they are composed of abundant olivine crystals with minor amounts of pyroxene, plagioclase feldspars, and kaersutite that also show alteration by shock metamorphism. In a hand specimen, chassignites closely resemble terrestrial olivine-rich rocks called dunites. In 1974, a single strange meteorite called Brachina was found in Australia; it may be related to the chassignites because of similarities in mineralogy. Brachina has a fine-grained texture, contains 80 percent olivine and 10 percent plagioclase feldspar, lacks hydrous minerals, is unshocked, and is 4.5 billion years old. Despite intensive study, the origin of the chassignites is unknown.

Collectively, the SNCs contain cumulus crystals and a large percentage of volatile gases and elements, which indicates formation upon a planetlike or planet-sized body with a stronger gravitational field than that of the moon. As a group, they have an average age of 1.3 billion years old, as determined by radioactive dating techniques. The abundance and variety of rare gases trapped within small bubbles in these meteorites is very similar to those gases found within the Martian atmosphere; scientists have therefore suggested that the SNCs originated on the planet Mars. They have proposed that a large meteor impact upon the Martian surface early in its geologic history, that hit at the correct angle and speed, could cause material to be thrown up into the atmosphere at a velocity of greater than 5 kilometers per second and to be sent out into space; these Martian rocks were eventually attracted by the earth's gravitational field.

Ureilites, another variety of achondrite, were named for the town of Novo Urei in the Soviet Union, where in 1886 the first specimen was found. They consist of fairly large and abundant crystals of magnesium-rich olivine, minor clinopyroxene, and rare plagioclase feldspar set within smaller crystals composed of graphite, iron-rich metal, halite, sylvite, and troilite. In some specimens, the olivine shows a preferred orientation from crystal settling while molten; thus, ureilites exhibit variable textures. Most specimens have undergone intense high-pressure shock metamorphism that resulted in the formation of small diamonds from the graphite. Ureilites are the only achondrites that contain these tiny crystals, whose source of carbon is unknown.

Aubrites, also known as the enstatite achondrites, are composed predominantly of a magnesium-rich pyroxene mineral called protoenstatite and of rare plagioclase feldspar crystals. Texturally, aubrites have large crystals, indicating slow cooling, but their origin and place of formation remain unexplained.

Methods of Study

The body or bodies from which achondrites formed remains undiscovered. Extensive mineral and chemical studies suggest that most achondrites may be derived from a single, small, water-free planetoid or asteroid. Based upon meteorite melting experiments in the laboratory, the partial melting of a parent body with an overall chondrite composition could produce a eucrite. Other experiments, using partially melted olivine and feldspar-rich igneous rocks, produced magmas that under the proper conditions could form both diogenites and eucrites. Melting can easily take place in the low-pressure environment of space, provided that enough heat is generated by the decay of short-lived radioactive isotopes, such as aluminum 26, that were once abundant in these rocks.

Applying processes similar to those that formed the earth, a parent body may be modeled that could become extensively melted and partially separated into a thin, crude upper crust of eucrite material atop a crustal diogenite layer; a mantle of relatively thick, mixed SNC material; and a small, metallic iron-nickel core. Planetary geologists have estimated that the parent body for the achondrites may measure up to 100 kilometers in size (asteroid-sized), where pressures on the interior core region would not be more than 2 to 3 kilobars. The mixing of eucrites and diogenites to form howardites probably occurred via meteorite impact, excavation, and lithification on or close to the surface of the parent body. Because the abundance of rocks rich in olivine is very low in scientists' present collection of achondrites, the parent body for these rocks must still be intact somewhere. Scientists hypothesize that the identity of this parent body may be either the asteroid known as 4 Vesta, which is 539 kilometers in diameter, or the asteroid referred to as 1915 Quetzalcoatl. Both choices are based upon an analysis of the light reflected off these asteroids, which is similar to that reflected from samples of eucrites and diogenites. The issue will be resolved once an automated satellite is flown to one of the nearby earth-orbiting asteroids and a sample is returned for further study.

Meteorites arrive daily on the earth in sizes ranging from specks of dust to huge masses weighing several thousand kilograms. The vast majority fall into the ocean, never to be recovered, or into remote, uninhabited areas to be discovered much later. Some are found in farmers' fields or in woodland areas near large cities. Most meteorites are "finds"; that is, they were not observed in the sky prior to landing. Others, called "falls," are seen streaking across the sky like bright fireballs and can be tracked to their impact sites. Regardless, most achondrites are passed by unnoticed, because they closely resemble ordinary earth rocks. Usually, the iron meteorites make up most of the finds, as they have a strange appearance and a high density that immediately attracts attention to them.

The best locale in which to find meteorites is Antarctica. In this remote and relatively uninhabited ice-covered continent, meteorites stand out starkly as black rocks against a white background of snow and ice. Because of the extreme cold and lack of liquid water in this region, nearly all varieties of meteorites are found perfectly preserved. Once a meteorite is located by scientists, its exact location is recorded and marked on a map, using longitude and latitude. Next, the specimen is photographed from several different angles and given a field catalog number for future reference. Meteorites are usually named for the closest town or post office in the vicinity where they are found; however, in the case of Antarctica, the name of the nearest mountain range, valley, or glacial moraine is used.

In the laboratory, the specimen is weighed and measured, its density determined and its physical appearance described. Thin sections are made from small chips of the meteorite for viewing under a petrographic microscope. The passage of light and its behavior through the individual minerals of the rock as observed in the microscope assist in the determination of the mineral's identity. The overall texture of the rock and the distribution and abundance of each mineral present in the meteorite are described in order to place it into a classification system. The bulk chemical composition of the meteorite and a detailed analysis of its individual minerals can be made using an electron microprobe. Under an electron beam, the atoms within the mineral give off energy in the form of X rays; the intensity and wavelength of these X rays are dependent upon the type of elements present within the sample and thus act as mineralogical fingerprints. The meteorite is then fully analyzed in order to determine its overall chemistry and elemental distribution and thus determine the processes that created it in space.

Thus, meteorites have provided evidence for three different solar system processes: reactions that occurred in the solar nebula prior to the formation of the planets, information on processes occurring in planetlike bodies, and collisional (impact) events that occurred between interplanetary objects, involving shock mechanisms, fragmentation of rocks, and the fusion of its fragments. Continued study of the achondrites, along with other meteorite types, may someday unlock the secrets of how the planets formed 4.7 billion years ago.

Context

Meteors represent the building blocks of planets, and they exist as a new frontier for the mining of valuable metallic and nonmetallic ores. They can be used instead of scarce earth resources that require environmentally harmful extraction and processing techniques. Useful elements that can be extracted from the stony or achondrite meteorites include iron, nickel, cobalt, and diamonds. Specific minerals could be mined from meteors and processed in the space environment, using giant smelters that could be powered by the sun at little or no cost. The lack of gravity would allow the production of homogeneous materials that would be impossible to prepare within earth's gravitational field. Similarly, the low temperature of space is conducive to the rapid casting and cooling of molten materials into specific forms. In a pure space environment, the potential for creating new compounds and materials using meteorites as the raw materials is boundless. Unfortunately, the ideal area in which to search for and collect the most abundant meteors is located far from the earth. Most meteors that encounter the earth's atmosphere are probably wandering fragments that came from a group of rocky debris known as the Apollo asteroids, which exist in the area between the orbits of Mars and Jupiter. Thus the use of meteors for mining purposes must await future technology to overcome this vast distance.

Meteorites called carbonaceous chondrites are relatively rare and primitive, but they have been found to contain certain complex organic molecules called amino acids. These acids are necessary in order to form deoxyribonucleic acid (DNA)—thus they are the building blocks of life and heredity. If this material can form and exist in the harsh environment of space, then the precursors to life may have initially formed beyond the earth and later arrived here by way of a meteorite impact. If this hypothesis is correct, then life may exist upon some of the other planets within the solar system.

Achondritic meteorites may have affected the evolution of life on the earth at various times during its geologic history. Based upon the fossil record 65-70 million years ago during the Cretaceous period of the Mesozoic era, the dinosaurs and many other life forms suddenly became extinct upon this planet. Evidence suggests that their extinction may have been related to the impact of a large stony meteorite upon the earth. The force of this impact could have thrown up a large cloud of dust, smoke, and ash that probably lasted between six months and one year. A cloud of this type would have effectively prevented the solar radiation from reaching the earth, thus quickly cooling the planet. This would have had dire consequences for reptilian animals, who could not regulate their internal body temperatures. Moreover, it would have rapidly destroyed the bulk of the plant population by preventing photosynthesis from occurring. The effect of plant destruction would have been felt along the entire length of the food chain, ultimately resulting in the mass extinction of many organisms. The extinction event is evidenced with a thin layer of clay that occurs at a point in geologic time between the Cretaceous and Tertiary periods; below this layer, microscopic life forms are very abundant, while above it they have decreased drastically in number. Within the clay is a precious metal called iridium. Iridium is rare in earth rocks but abundant in achondritic and iron meteorites. Although several other possible explanations for the iridium abundance in the clay layer have been proposed, most geologists agree that a meteor impact was the source of this rare metal. Preliminary studies of several other mass extinction events prior to that of the Cretaceous period suggest that this kind of event may not be unusual in the earth's geological history.

Bibliography

Burke, John G. *Cosmic Debris: Meteorites in History.* Berkeley: University of California Press, 1986. This book examines the role of meteorites in science history, from their origin as "thunderstones," their folklore and myths, and their curators and collectors to their role in current research. Many footnotes, a few photographs, and a detailed bibliography. Nontechnical and written for the general reader.

Dodd, Robert T. *Thunderstones and Shooting Stars: The Meaning of Meteorites* Cambridge, Mass.: Harvard University Press, 1986. A thorough, clearly written review of the latest information on all types of meteorites. Chapter 9 discusses achondrites and their parent bodies and how they relate to the origin of the planets.

Glass, Billy P. *Introduction to Planetary Geology.* New York: Cambridge University Press, 1982. An introductory college textbook that describes research prior to 1982. Chapter 4 is a general overview of the origin and ages of meteorites and extraterrestrial dust. Written for the reader with some science background.

Hutchison, Robert. *The Search for Our Beginning: An Enquiry, Based on Meteorite Research, Into the Origin of Our Planet and Life.* New York: Oxford University Press, 1983. A clear and easy-to-read nontechnical book that describes the various types of meteorites and the information they provide about the solar system. Illustrated with many photographs of meteorites. Highly recommended.

McSween, Harry Y., Jr. *Meteorites and Their Parent Planets.* Cambridge, England: Cambridge University Press, 1987. A thorough description of all types of meteorites, their chemistry, origin, history, and scientific importance. Many terms are clearly defined within the text, which is well written and nontechnical.

Moore, C. B. *Meteorites.* Boston: Houghton Mifflin, 1971. This small paperback is recommended for the general reader with no scientific background. Well written and illustrated with many line drawings and black-and-white photographs.

Steven C. Okulewicz

Cross-References

METEORITES: CARBONACEOUS CHONDRITES

Type of earth science: Planetology
Field of study: Small solar system bodies

The carbonaceous chondrite meteorites are the most primitive remnants of the primeval nebula from which the sun, earth, and all other bodies of the solar system originated. The hydrocarbon molecules present in these meteorites indicate the types of carbon-bearing molecules that most likely were present on the primitive earth and may have been the building blocks of life.

Principal terms

AMINO ACIDS: relatively simple compounds of carbon and oxygen that are the building blocks of proteins

FISSION TRACKS: regions of damage to a crystal along the path taken by a moving ion, usually a fragment resulting from fission decay or a cosmic ray

HYDROCARBONS: molecules containing hydrogen, carbon, and oxygen

ISOTOPES: atoms of the same chemical element that have different numbers of neutrons and thus a different atomic weight

OLIVINE: a silicate mineral of magnesium and iron that is common in chondritic meteorites

SOLAR NEBULA: the cloud of gas and dust that collapsed to form the solar system

Summary of the Phenomenon

The carbonaceous chondrites are a class of meteorites that are both chemically and physically primitive. They are chemically primitive in that, except for the elements hydrogen, oxygen, carbon, and the noble gases, the proportions of the elements in these meteorites are very similar to those observed in the sun. They are physically primitive in that the carbonaceous chondrites escaped the thermal alteration, exposure to heat that causes changes in chemical composition and mineralogy, that affected almost all the meteorites in the other classes. Because of the primitive nature of the carbonaceous chondrites, they are thought to be the best samples currently available of the condensing nebula out of which the sun, earth, and other solar system objects formed. Thus, the carbonaceous chondrite composition is generally taken as the starting point for models of the formation and subsequent evolution of the earth.

The carbonaceous chondrites are relatively scarce, constituting only 7 percent of all the meteorites recovered after they have been observed falling. They are composed of millimeter-sized chondrules, individual particles whose mineralogy and texture indicate their crystallization from molten material, set in a matrix of finer-grained material. The carbonaceous chondrites are easily distinguished from all other meteorites by their dull black color, friability, generally low density, and almost total lack of nickel-iron grains, but not all carbonaceous chondrites are alike. Differences in composition, mineralogy, and texture allow the carbonaceous chondrites to be separated into four distinct types.

The most primitive type of carbonaceous chondrite, called the "CI" type, is extremely rare, being represented by only five meteorites. Of these, only Orgueil, a fall of about 127 kilograms, is large enough for widespread study. The others, Ivuna (0.7 kilogram), Alais (with little remaining of a 6-kilogram fall), Tonk (7.7 grams), and Revelstoke (only 1 gram), are all very small.

The CI carbonaceous chondrites are different from all other chondrites, both carbonaceous and ordinary, in that they lack chondrules and consist almost entirely of low-temperature minerals, particularly clays. The other three carbonaceous chondrite types consist of a matrix, similar in chemical composition to bulk CI material, mixed with chondrules and aggregates of high-temperature phases, minerals that form at high temperatures from a condensing gas and that exhibit a depletion in volatile elements from what is observed in CI matrix. As the abundance of high-temperature material increases from about 1 percent in the CI meteorites to almost two-thirds of the meteorite, the similarity of the bulk composition to that of the sun decreases. All four types of carbonaceous chondrites can be considered as mixtures of a matrix of primitive composition with a high-temperature component, chondrules and aggregates, depleted in the more volatile elements.

At one time, it was thought that the high-temperature material might be derived from the matrix by heating, which would eliminate the volatile material. Recent studies, however, show significant differences between the chemical and isotopic compositions of the high-temperature and low-temperature components of the carbonaceous chondrites, which make it impossible to derive one from the other by any simple process.

Much of the recent research on carbonaceous chondrite meteorites has focused on understanding the process by which these objects formed from the solar nebula, the gas and possibly dust that collapsed to form the sun, earth, and other solar system objects. As the most primitive relics of the formation process currently available for laboratory analysis, the carbonaceous chondrites have been used to determine the chemical composition of the solar nebula, to establish the sequence and duration of events in the formation process, and to establish the temperatures characteristic of the process.

This scientific investigation benefited from two major meteorite falls in 1969. In February, 1969, the Allende carbonaceous chondrite fell in northern Mexico, and about 2,000 kilograms of material were recovered for analysis. Later in 1969, an even more primitive carbonaceous chondrite, Murchison, fell in Australia. In addition, the return of lunar samples in 1969 spurred the development of research laboratories for the study of extraterrestrial materials. With the end of the Apollo lunar landing program, many of these laboratories shifted their emphasis to meteorite research and began to use highly sophisticated instruments perfected for the lunar sample analysis for the study of meteorites.

Analysis of the meteorites has provided significant estimates of the age of the solar system and thus of the earth as well. Radioactive indicators in the meteorites suggest that the rocky bodies of the solar system formed 4.55 billion years ago. Similar indicators provide evidence that the formation process, from gaseous nebula to solid rocks, took only a few hundred million years and perhaps even less.

Organic matter (chemical compounds of carbon, nitrogen, and oxygen) has been detected by spectroscopic methods in comets, on some asteroid surfaces, and on some planetary satellites. Study of the properties of this organic matter would provide indications of the organic material likely to have been present on the earth at the time life developed on this planet. The meteorites, particularly the carbon-rich chondrites, have been subjected to intensive examinations to determine whether they contain samples of this organic matter.

The search for organic matter in the carbonaceous chondrites was hampered for decades by the organic contamination of these meteorites from the time of their recovery until their analysis. By the time of the fall of Murchison in 1969, meteorite researchers were aware of the contamination problem and efforts were made to preserve samples for organic analysis. In addition, several laboratories had recently developed procedures and instrumentation to search for organic material in returned lunar samples. Methods to distinguish terrestrial contaminations from extraterrestrial organic material were developed for the lunar sample analysis program. The first analyses of the Murchison meteorite provided evidence for the presence of amino acids, which are the building blocks of proteins. Subsequent analysis of carbon in the organic matter indicated that the isotopic composition, the ratio of carbon 13 to carbon 12, was inconsistent with terrestrial contamination. It has now been demonstrated that several carbonaceous chondrites contain a varied suite of organic compounds. These same organic compounds have been duplicated in laboratory experiments by purely chemical processes and consequently are not evidence for life in space, but they are taken to indicate the types and variety of organic material likely to have been present on the earth to serve as building blocks for life.

Methods of Study

Scientists have employed a variety of techniques and instruments to uncover the secrets contained in the carbonaceous chondrite meteorites. The chemical compositions, mineralogies, isotopic ratios for individual elements, present radioactivity, and molecular abundances have all been determined. Because of the small amount of carbonaceous chondrite material available for scientific study, especially of the rare CI type, many of the techniques employed to examine these meteorites have benefited greatly from the sophisticated instrumentation developed in support of the lunar sample analysis program.

The observation that the carbonaceous chondrites are primitive, that is, relatively unaffected by thermal processes, was established by detailed chemical analyses of individual mineral grains. The effect of prolonged heating is to cause the compositions of minerals of the same type to equilibrate, meaning that all grains of the same mineral from a single meteorite would have approximately the same composition if the meteorite were heated above the equilibration temperature. Such an effect is seen in most ordinary chondrites.

The compositions of small mineral grains are usually determined using an electron microprobe, an instrument that bombards the sample with an intense beam of electrons and detects the X rays emitted by the sample. When struck by an electron, each element emits X rays of specific energies. Thus, the number of X rays emitted at the energy characteristic of the element iron gives the iron abundance in the sample. When the mineral grains in the carbonaceous chondrite meteorites are examined by this technique, nearby grains of olivine, the most easily altered of the major minerals in the matrix, exhibit a relatively wide range of compositions. In the Allende meteorite, for example, magnesium-rich olivine chondrules are found in direct contact with iron-rich matrix olivine. Such contacts eliminate the possibility that significant thermal events have occurred since the time at which the Allende meteorite was formed.

Observation of radioactive effects can also indicate the thermal history of these meteorites. The elements uranium and plutonium decay by nuclear fission, a process by which the nucleus splits into two fragments, each about one-half the mass of the original nucleus. These fragments fly apart with high energy, traveling a few thousandths of a centimeter before coming to rest. The host material can be damaged along the path of each fragment. This damage, called a fission track, is more easily attacked by reactive chemicals than is the surrounding mineral. After this chemical etching, the fission tracks can be observed through a microscope. This damage, however, can be healed by heating. Thus, if fission tracks are revealed by chemical attack, the mineral has not been heated above the healing, or annealing, temperature subsequent to the fission event. The presence of tracks from uranium and plutonium fission in minerals from the carbonaceous chondrites indicates that they have not been heated above a few hundred degrees Celsius since their formation.

Similar radioactive processes can be used as clocks, providing a way to determine the ages of these meteorites. One such clock depends on the radioactive decay of rubidium 87, one of two long-lived or stable isotopes of the element rubidium, into strontium 87, one of the four stable isotopes of strontium. About one-half of any initial sample of rubidium 87 decays to strontium 87 in 49 billion years. In any given sample, if the abundance of rubidium 87 as well as the amount of strontium 87 produced by radioactive decay could be measured, the elapsed time, or age, required for that amount of decay would be determined. In practice, application of this radioactive clock is complicated by a number of factors, including the migration of the strontium 87 from its decay site because of heating and the fact that not all the strontium 87 in the sample is from rubidium 87 decay. When appropriate corrections are made for these effects, however, the rubidium-strontium clock, as well as similar clocks using different pairs of radioactive elements, give a consistent picture that the carbonaceous chondrites formed 4.55 billion years ago. Results for the oldest rocks on the moon give essentially the same age. The extensive thermal activity in the early history of the earth has apparently destroyed most or all evidence of the earliest rocks to form on this planet, but the observation that both the meteorites and the oldest lunar rocks have a common age suggests that the entire solar system, including the earth, formed at that time.

Radioactive elements also provide clues to the duration of solar system formation. Decay of aluminum 26, which is reduced to one-half of its starting abundance in only 720,000 years, produces magnesium 26. Magnesium has three stable isotopes, which are usually found in fixed ratios to one another, but the ratio of magnesium 26 to the other two isotopes of magnesium will increase when aluminum 26 decays. In some of the high-temperature aggregates from the Allende meteorite, significant enrichments in magnesium 26 were found by mass spectrometry. Detailed examination of the minerals containing these enrichments showed that the size of the magnesium 26 enrichment increased in proportion to the aluminum concentration in that mineral. This suggested that radioactive aluminum 26 was incorporated into the mineral and subsequently decayed to magnesium 26. For this to be true, however, the high-temperature aggregates would have to have formed within a few million years of the isolation of the solar nebula, or most of the aluminum 26 would already have decayed. Thus, the high-temperature aggregates in Allende and some other carbonaceous chondrites provide evidence that mineral grains condensed very early in the solar system formation process.

Context

The carbonaceous chondrite meteorites appear to have experienced only minor alteration since their formation from the collapsing gaseous cloud that became our solar system. These meteorites preserve a record of that early era of solar system history. The chemical composition of the least altered of these meteorites is almost identical to the composition of the sun, except for a few gaseous elements. Thus, the carbonaceous chondrite composition is taken to indicate the bulk composition of the earth, which cannot be measured directly since the earth's core, where the metal is thought to be concentrated, is inaccessible.

Radioactive clocks in the carbonaceous chondrites indicate that they formed 4.55 billion years ago. The consistency of this age with the age of the oldest rocks brought back by Apollo missions from the moon is taken to indicate that the entire solar system, including the earth, formed at that time. Isotopic relics of other radioactive elements, now extinct, demonstrate that some minerals in the carbonaceous chondrites formed within a few million years of the isolation of the solar nebula from addition of new galactic radioactive isotopes.

The carbonaceous chondrites also contain organic molecules, including amino acids, which are the building blocks of proteins. Although there is no evidence of biological activity on the parent body of the carbonaceous chondrites, these or similar organic molecules are likely to have been available on earth to serve as building blocks for the development of life.

Bibliography

Dodd, Robert T. *Meteorites: A Petrologic-Chemical Synthesis.* London: Cambridge University Press, 1981. This is a well-illustrated summary of the mineralogical and chemical analyses of all types of meteorites. Chapter 2 focuses on the chondritic meteorites and their relation to one another. Chapter 3 describes the properties of the carbonaceous chondrites, their relationship to the solar nebula, and the possibility that they contain presolar grains. This text is suitable for college-level readers who have at least a minimal background in earth science.

_____. *Thunderstones and Shooting Stars: The Meaning of Meteorites.* Cambridge, Mass.: Harvard University Press, 1986. This reference book explains why there is a scientific interest in meteorites and summarizes what is known about them. It includes chapters on the chondritic meteorites and on the parent bodies of these meteorites. While written as a college-level text, this book provides detailed explanations of the phenomena and techniques of analysis without requiring the reader to have an earth science background.

Hutchison, Robert. *The Search for Our Beginning: An Enquiry, Based on Meteorite Research, Into the Origin of Our Planet and Life.* Oxford, England: Oxford University Press, 1983. This book summarizes the present state of scientific knowledge about the earth, the moon, and the inner planets and describes how the knowledge gained from the study of meteorites has shaped the theories for the origin and evolution of the inner solar system. This illustrated work is intended for general readers.

Kerridge, John F., and Mildred S. Matthews, eds. *Meteorites and the Early Solar System.* Tucson: University of Arizona Press, 1988. This work is a collection of articles by sixty-nine contributing authors describing the current state of meteorite research as it relates to early solar system processes. Although all types of meteorites are described, this book focuses on the chondritic meteorites and what they tell scientists about the early solar system. The book is well illustrated; it is written as a text or reference for graduate students studying meteoritics but provides a detailed review and comprehensive bibliography of the major topics in meteorite research accessible to general-level readers.

Mason, Brian. *Meteorites.* New York: John Wiley & Sons, 1962. This book emphasizes the chemical and mineralogical measurements made on the meteorites and describes the relationship between meteorites and other objects in the solar system. It provides a state-by-state listing of all the meteorites collected in the United States, including the exact location, year of recovery, weight, and type.

Nagy, B. *Carbonaceous Meteorites.* New York: Elsevier, 1975. This book describes the carbonaceous chondrite meteorites with particular emphasis on the carbon-rich phases, and discusses the long effort to identify organic compounds in meteorites. Intended as a college text, this book is suitable for readers with a high school science background.

Wasson, John T. *Meteorites: Classification and Properties.* New York: Springer-Verlag, 1974. This book is intended as a college-level introduction to meteorite research and classification by type. The emphasis is on interpretation of the chemical and mineralogical data. This book is well illustrated and includes a tabulation of all meteorites known by the early 1970's, with the type of each meteorite indicated. Appendix C lists each carbonaceous chondrite known at the time of publication.

_____. *Meteorites: Their Record of Early Solar-System History.* New York: W. H. Freeman, 1985. This college-level text is less technical than Wasson's 1974 book. This well-illustrated volume describes the formation processes for the different meteorite types and attempts to link the different meteorite groups with their appropriate parent bodies. Chapter 7 provides an extensive discussion of the chondritic meteorites, including the carbonaceous chondrites.

George J. Flynn

Cross-References

Asteroids, 98; Elemental Distribution in the Earth, 391; Earth's Age, 490; The Evolution of Earth's Composition, 496; Electron Microprobes, 596; Geochronology: Fission Track Dating, 826; Geochronology: Rb-Sr Dating, 848; Meteorites: Chondrites, 1645; Radioactive Decay, 2136; Elemental Distribution in the Solar System, 2434; The Origin of the Solar System, 2442; Stable Isotopes: Oxygen 18/Oxygen 16, Deuterium/Hydrogen, and Carbon 13/Carbon 12 Ratios in Rocks, 2456.

METEORITES: CHONDRITES

Type of earth science: Planetology
Field of study: Small solar system bodies

Chondrites belong to a class of meteorites known as the stony meteorites. This classification is based on the approximate ratio of greater than 80 percent silicate (rock-forming) minerals to less than 20 percent metallic minerals. Chondrites are the most common type of meteorite.

Principal terms

BARRED-OLIVINE CHONDRULES: generally small spherules (1 to 5 millimeters) consisting of the mineral olivine, forming parallel bars with interstitial glass

CARBONACEOUS CHONDRITES: stony meteorites that are slightly metamorphosed agglomerates containing chondrules, unmelted aggregates, and volatile-rich matrix materials

ENSTATITE CHONDRITES: a rare group of recrystallized agglomerates whose textural features and mineralogy represent conditions of thermal metamorphism under reducing conditions

GLASS: a solid consisting of a disordered pattern of atoms, which represents a rapid cooling from a molten state; in meteorites, it is found in chondrules and within the matrix as fragments

INCLUSIONS: objects of similar size, with rounded or irregular shapes, that have textures and mineralogies suggestive of unmelted aggregates of solid particles, indicative of a primitive origin

MATRIX: the fine-grained material that surrounds both chondrules and inclusions; it consists of hydrous silicate minerals, troilite, magnetite, and other lower-temperature phases

ORDINARY CHONDRITES: a classification of chondrule-bearing stony meteorites based on the distribution of iron among its various oxidation states

PORPHYRITIC CHONDRULES: generally small spherules (1 to 5 millimeters) with crystals of the minerals olivine and pyroxene set into a glass matrix

RADIATING PYROXENE CHONDRULES: generally small spherules (1 to 5 millimeters) composed of excentroradial pyroxene crystals, often resembling a fanlike growth pattern

Summary of the Phenomenon

Stony meteorites are the most abundant of the three groups of meteorites and come closest to resembling terrestrial rocks in their appearance and chemical composition. The major portion of these meteorites consists of the silicate minerals olivine, pyroxene, and plagioclase feldspars. Metallic nickel-iron grains occur in varying amounts and are accompanied by an iron-sulfide mineral called troilite, which is very rare on earth.

Aside from being the most abundant meteorite type, stony meteorites have the greatest variety in composition, color, and structure. One particular structural feature called chondrules divides the group into two main subgroups: the chondrites, those with chondrules, and achondrites, those without. Many scientists believe that these small, rounded, nearly spherical chondrules may represent the oldest material in the solar system. In terms of age, stony meteorites represent both the oldest and the youngest material of extraterrestrial origin. In the Allende meteorite, small, white grains were found to be 4.61 billion years old. One of the meteorites believed to be a rock blasted off the surface of Mars has an age of between 700 million and 1 billion years. In yet another type of stony meteorite, from the group known as the carbonaceous chondrites, organic compounds such as amino and fatty acids are found. Some scientists believe that meteorites such as these are responsible for the origin of life on earth. These carbonaceous chondrites may have had their origin in comets, although scientists are not yet certain that this is the case.

The study of stony meteorites is very important. In their basic characteristics, these meteorites represent materials that formed in a region of the solar system far removed from earth. They can reveal much about the conditions that existed when the solar system was formed. The chondrites in particular reveal a set of unique conditions that may have lasted only a short period of time and therefore may be the key to understanding how the terrestrial planets came to exist.

The chondrite classification of stony meteorites represents approximately 86 percent of all meteorite falls. The word "chondrite" is derived from the Greek word *chondros*, meaning grain. This is most appropriate, since chondrites are partially composed of well-rounded grains called chondrules that contain generally high-temperature silicate minerals. These chondrules range in size from less than a millimeter to just under a centimeter. As seen in the meteorite's structure, they can be either whole or partial and are embedded within a matrix of fine-grained opaque minerals and glass. The minerals olivine and pyroxene are the main constituents, along with the interstitial glass. These mineral phases with their varying textures, along with the interstitial glass, are indicative of rapid cooling from a high-temperature liquid. The most common types of chondrules are the barred-olivine, the excentroradial "feathery" pyroxene, and the porphyritic olivine and pyroxene varieties.

Mineralogically, the chondrites are principally composed of 45 percent olivine, 25 percent pyroxene, 10 percent plagioclase, 5 percent troilite, and 2 to 20 percent nickel-iron alloy minerals (kamacite and taenite). Chondrites that tend to be poorer in olivine have a correspondingly higher metal content, and the reverse is also true. This fact makes possible a preliminary classification scheme based on the ratio of reduced iron to oxidized iron. From this ratio, division is made into three basic groups: the H (high iron content), the L (low iron content), and the LL (low iron-low metal). Based on the fact that these three groups account for more than half of the known meteorites, they are collectively called the ordinary meteorites. Two other groups are also recognized, but they represent relatively rarer meteorites. The first is the enstatite chondrites (E), so named for the predominance of the mineral enstatite. The last group is the carbonaceous chondrites (C), which derive their name from the varying amounts of carbon found in their bulk chemistry, far exceeding the normal trace amounts that are found in the ordinary chondrites.

The principal differences in the mineralogy of the chondrite types can be attributed to different oxidation states and are thus reflective of specific conditions of formation. The H, L, and LL chondrites are indicative of a relatively high oxidation state and can be easily separated into their respective groups on that basis. In hand specimen (the actual meteorite), a generalized classification is possible based on the amount of metal observed on a cut surface. Petrographic considerations also play a part in distinguishing specific groups, as in the case of LL type, which tends to be more brecciated (composed of rock fragments) than the other two types.

E type chondrites, on the other hand, are quite indicative of more reducing conditions. Iron is commonly found in the metallic state, comprising about 15 to 25 percent of the meteorite's composition. The principal silicate is the iron-free mineral estatite, accompanied by less common sulfide phases. As compared to the ordinary chondrites, the enstatite chondrites are quite rare and offer an interesting insight into the process of meteorite formation.

The last group of chondrites is especially interesting, since these chondrites exhibit a wide variation in their respective chemistries and conditions of formation. The carbonaceous chondrites are classified on the basis of their oxidation states and the abundance of certain volatile substances, notably carbon, sulfur, and water. Subdivision of these chondrites is made according to comparisons with certain specimens that reflect a specific chemistry and petrographic condition. The CB carbonaceous chondrites exhibit a high oxidation state, with an abundance of volatile substances; the CO types are slightly less oxidized but contain metal and sulfides; the CV type closely resemble the CO type in mineral composition and oxidation state but contain large quantities of chondrules and whitish aggregates with a high calcium-aluminum content. Collectively, these three subgroups of chondrites exhibit different conditions of formation that range from a high-temperature, low-pressure environment to one that is of lower temperature and volatile-rich. One particular type, CI chondrites, may represent the most primitive material in the solar system. Another type, CII chondrites, contain numerous organic compounds that may have served as the basis for the development of life. As a group, the carbonaceous chondrites have provided a wealth of information on many different aspects of planetary formation and the development of biological processes as they may have occurred in the early solar system.

Achondrites, the other variety of stony meteorites without chondrules, are not as common as the chondrites. In their structure, they appear as highly differentiated bodies with only trace amounts of metallic iron present. It has been suggested that achondrites had their origin in the melting of a parent meteoritic material that later recrystallized. In comparison with the common chondritic variety, the textures of achondrites are coarser, indicating a slower rate of cooling and offering support to the theory of recrystallization. Both the texture and mineralogy of the achondrites closely resemble those of common basaltic and ultramafic rocks found in the earth's crust.

The petrographic nature of chrondrites shows varying degrees of all three rock types common to the earth (igneous, sedimentary, and metamorphic), yet chondrites are distinct from any earth rock. Their basic mineralogy reveals that the chondrites were originally formed under high-temperature conditions but were later broken up and reassembled through a variation of the sedimentary process. Once incorporated into a new mass, the chondrites were subject to variations in temperatures and pressures, thus becoming metamorphosed material. It is evident that most meteorites have had a rather complex evolutionary history and can therefore provide interesting evidence for the interpretation of early solar system history.

The study of chondritic meteorites raises important questions based on variations in their chemical compositions and textural features. How did they condense from the solar nebula, and what type of parent body produced all these variations? To provide answers, a hypothetical parent body between 200 and 300 kilometers in size is proposed. This body would have been chondritic in nature and subjected to partial melting, presumably because of the short-lived radioisotope aluminum 26. Later, localized melting resulting from impact from smaller bodies and partial differentiation of magma could have produced the parent material for achondrites. Continual bombardment and subsequent melting would account for the brecciation that is common to most chondrites. This model is highly speculative but does offer a reasonable explanation for the relationship between different stony meteorite types. In addition, some of the chondrites retain some of their preparent body characteristics and offer evidence of the conditions that existed before the accretion of these asteroid-sized bodies. The chondritic meteorites play an important part in the understanding of planetary formation.

Methods of Study

The study of chondritic meteorites is conducted through the use of many different analytical techniques. The first is the determination of bulk chemical content. This can be achieved through basic wet chemical techniques or by the use of electronic instrumentation. Some of the methods most often used are neutron activation analysis and X-ray fluorescence. These methods generally produce excellent data that can be used to classify the chondrite into its basic chemical group. Where individual minerals are large enough for analysis, X-ray diffraction can be employed for a positive identification of the particular mineral phase; however, the mineral phases in the chondrite are usually too small for conventional analysis and require a more specialized approach. To achieve this, a special instrument called an electron microprobe is employed. This instrument utilizes a microscope to locate tiny mineral grains, and then X-ray bombardment will give their chemical compositions. Next, a computer will take these raw data and fit them into a proper mineral formula. This method makes it possible to determine very exact mineral phases at the microscopic level. With that information in hand, the scientist can reconstruct the meteorite's origin.

Once the meteorite's mineralogy is known, it becomes possible to employ radio-isotope dating techniques to learn the age at which the minerals crystallized. This can be achieved by use of K-Ar, Rb-Sr, and U-Th-Pb decay rates. It is from such data that meteorites have been established as the oldest known solid materials in the solar system.

To determine what has physically happened to the chondrite over the eons requires optical analysis with a petrographic microscope or an electron microscope. The petrographic microscope offers a magnified view of the physical nature of the meteorite and the minerals it contains, which in turn provides a look at features that relate to the original condition of the meteorite and the significant changes that occurred at later dates. In this technique, a thin slice (0.03 millimeter) of the meteorite is cut and adhered to a glass plate, thus permitting light to pass through. In this way, chondrules and lithic fragments can be easily seen and interpreted. Three aspects of petrology of the chondrite will be examined. First, the nature and appearance of any chondrules will be noted. Then, evidence for metamorphism and the characteristics of thermal and mechanical alteration resulting from shock will be sought. Based on this analysis, further classification will place the meteorites into specific types that represent their chemical properties, their mineral content, and the physical appearance of the chondrules and fragments present.

Experimental petrology—laboratory experiments designed to reproduce the mineralogies and textures found in chondrules—has provided valuable data to develop theories to explain chondrule formation and the accretion process of the chondrites themselves. Mathematical models and computer simulations add another dimension, helping to explain chondrite origin. By utilizing all these different techniques, the scientist can feel reasonably certain about the proposed conditions that led to meteorite formation and their relationship to planetary formation.

Context

In general, the study of meteorites has provided scientists with their first contact with extraterrestrial materials. In many instances, chondritic meteorites are very similar to certain types of earth rocks in both their chemistry and their mineralogy. By studying these meteorites, science is gaining a better perspective on the resource materials that may be available for future space explorers and colonists. Because most chondrites had their origin as fragments of small asteroids, scientists now have a very good idea of what they are made, and they do indeed represent potential resources for future mining operations. Perhaps in the near future, asteroid mining may serve as a primary source of raw materials for industry.

Aside from the fact that studies on chondritic meteorites are providing scientists with necessary information for future mineral mining, they also provide insights into the origin of the earth and perhaps even of life itself. The chondrules, which are a characteristic feature of most chondrites, have proven to be the oldest solid material in the solar system. Some of these chondrules actually contain chemical isotopes that had their origins in an entirely different solar system. Others may have compounds that formed during a supernova event that predates the solar system's formation. Detailed examination of these chondrules and their matrix material is revealing new data that describes the process of formation that eventually led to the construction of the planets. Other chondrites, like the carbonaceous chondrites, are providing evidence of organic chemistry that developed in space. From the study of these meteorites, biologists are learning about the origin of the compounds that eventually led to the beginning of life on the earth. The study of chondritic meteorites has thus provided humankind with a new perspective about its origins and about the age of the earth in relation to that of the universe. The evidence suggests that the earth is not fundamentally very different from some of the other planets.

Bibliography

Dodd, Robert T. *Meteorites: A Petrologic-chemical Synthesis*. Cambridge, England: Cambridge University Press, 1981. This book covers the range of meteorite-related topics with a detailed approach suitable for the more advanced student. It is well written and has good illustrations to support the text. Best suited for the college to graduate level.

_____. *Thunderstones and Shooting Stars: The Meaning of Meteorites*. Cambridge, Mass.: Harvard University Press, 1986. A very good introduction to the science of meteoritics at a very basic level. It is a good review of the chemical types and methods of study used to classify meteorites. In addition, there is some discussion about the importance of meteorites as a planet-shaping process and about the effect they may have on life forms throughout the ages. It is best suited for a reading level of high school to college.

Hutchison, Robert. *The Search for Our Beginning: An Enquiry, Based on Meteorite Research, Into the Origin of Our Planet and Life*. Oxford, England: Oxford University Press, 1983. A well-written introduction to meteorites and their relationship to planetary formation. The book is technical but understandable for the average reader. It is well illustrated. Suitable for high school and college-level readers.

King, Elbert A., ed. *Chondrules and Their Origins*. Houston: Lunar and Planetary Institute, 1983. A detailed series of chondrule-related articles edited by King. The articles are well written and cover a fairly wide range of topics dealing with chondrules. Good illustrations and an excellent bibliography complement the text. Good technical reference. Most suitable for undergraduate to graduate levels.

McSween, Harry Y., Jr. *Meteorites and Their Parent Planets*. Cambridge, England: Cambridge University Press, 1987. This book presents a good introduction to the science of meteoritics. It examines the nature of meteorites and their relationship to parent bodies. Good illustrations and a glossary highlight the book. Suitable for high school through college-level readers.

Mason, Brian. *Meteorites*. New York: John Wiley & Sons, 1962. This is perhaps the best of the early books on meteorites and their importance to science. Although the book is dated in the light of modern technology, it still remains as an excellent primer for the study of meteorites. It is well written and presented and is best suited for high school and college readers.

Sears, D. W. *The Nature and Origin of Meteorites*. Bristol, England: Adam Hilger, 1978. A very readable introduction to the study of meteorites, especially in historical aspects and the review of the basic concepts. The book does go quite deep into specialized areas, but it will help the casual reader gain a better perspective on the subject matter. Best suited for the college level.

Wasson, John T. *Meteorites: Their Record of Early Solar System History*. New York: W. H. Freeman, 1985. This is a well-written and well-illustrated introduction to the science of meteoritics. The author covers most of the significant topics in a clear and understandable way and offers a wealth of information for both the casual reader and the serious student. Suitable for high school and college levels.

Paul P. Sipiera

Cross-References

Earth's Oldest Rocks, 561; Earth's Origin, 569; Electron Microprobes, 596; Electron Microscopy, 601; Experimental Petrology, 662; Geochronology: K-Ar and Ar-Ar Dating, 833; Geochronology: Rb-Sr Dating, 848; Geochronology: U-Th-Pb Dating, 862; Meteorites: Achondrites, 1630; Meteorites: Carbonaceous Chondrites, 1638; Meteors and Meteor Showers, 1666; Neutron Activation Analysis, 1734; Elemental Distribution in the Solar System, 2434; The Origin of the Solar System, 2442; X-Ray Fluorescence, 2744.

METEORITES: NICKEL-IRONS

Type of earth science: Planetology
Field of study: Small solar system bodies

Nickel-iron meteorites are one of three types of meteorites. The nickel-iron classification is based on the approximate ratio of greater than 80 percent metal to less than 20 percent silicate (rock-forming) minerals. The nickel-iron meteorites are further classified by the amount of nickel in their bulk chemical composition.

Principal terms

ATAXITES: iron meteorites that contain a very high nickel content; the term is designed to indicate a lack of structure, but micro-Widmanstätten lines can be found

HEXAHEDRITES: iron meteorites that contain less than 6 percent nickel content; they usually consist of large single crystals of kamacite and may show Neumann bands when polished

KAMACITE: a form of ferritic iron containing up to 7.5 percent nickel in solid solution

NEUMANN BANDS: a textural pattern that is common to iron meteorites with less than 6 percent nickel content; they reflect deformational twinning paralled to trapezohedral planes in kamacite

OCTAHEDRITES: iron meteorites that usually contain between 6 and 16 percent nickel; the Widmanstätten structure is characteristic on etched and polished surfaces

PLESSITE: a mineralogical term used to describe a nickel-iron alloy that is neither kamacite nor taenite but is rather a mixture of both phases; it is derived from taenite during primary cooling

TAENITE: a nickel-iron alloy mineral with more than 25 percent nickel in solid solution; in octahedrite meteorites, taenite forms three-dimensional sheets that appear band-shaped in cut sections

TROILITE: an iron sulfide mineral that is common to most meteorites but is very rare on the earth

WIDMANSTÄTTEN PATTERN: a textural pattern, common to most iron meteorites containing 6-16 percent nickel, that occurs when kamacite is oriented parallel to the octahedral planes in taenite

Summary of the Phenomenon

Meteorites are materials of extraterrestrial origin that have intersected the orbit of the earth, survived passage through the atmosphere, and reached the earth's surface in various stages of preservation. Mineralogically, meteorites are composed primarily of various nickel-iron alloys, silicates, sulfides, and other minor phases. They are broadly classified into three major groups: irons, stony irons, and stones. Specific classification and further subdivision describe the individual specimen's composition and structure. In general, this basic division into three groups is based on the ratio of metallic minerals to silicate minerals. The irons consist of generally greater than 80 percent metal, the stony irons have a 50 percent metal to 50 percent stony mineral ratio, and the stones generally have greater than 80 percent stony mineral content.

Based on the actual numbers of individual specimens collected, the stony meteorites are by far the most common. That is confirmed by the number of meteorites actually observed to fall to the earth and the large number of meteorites that have been collected in Antarctica. Iron meteorites were once thought to be much more common than they actually are, based on the fact that most meteorite finds (not observed falling) were irons. This conclusion was partially correct—not because of the high in-fall rate of irons, but rather because they are very noticeable on the ground and simply stand out more than the stony variety. The Antarctic studies have now shown that irons account for less than 3 percent of the total number of recovered meteorites. Stony irons are even rarer, accounting for less than 1 percent of the total.

Iron meteorites are rare examples of nickel-iron alloy minerals that occur in the metallic state. There is no natural terrestrial equivalent for these minerals, and in fact the only native iron found on the earth is in small amounts on Disko Island, Greenland, and in Josephine, Oregon. The most common form in which iron is found is in the oxide state, as either hematite, magnetite, or limonite. In contrast, the conditions under which the meteoritic iron formed were oxygen-poor. This fact combined with that of the weight percent of the nickel alloyed with the iron indicates an extraterrestrial origin.

Iron meteorites, or siderites as they were once called, are characterized by the presence of two nickel-iron alloy phases consisting of kamacite ($Fe_{93}Ni_7$) and taenite ($Fe_{65}Ni_{35}$) combined with minor amounts of troilite (FeS) and other rare mineral phases. Based on the percentage of nickel to metallic iron present, irons are subdivided into three groups: hexahedrites, octahedrites, and ataxites. Hexahedrites represent a bulk chemical composition of 4-6 percent nickel, occurring principally as the mineral kamacite. This first group of iron meteorite consists essentially of large single crystals of kamacite. Octahedrites, which are the most common, indicate increasing amounts of nickel, appearing in the mineral form of taenite. The presence of both kamacite and taenite in octahedrites is evident upon etching with nitric acid, thus revealing a pattern of interlocking crystals with a geometric form called the Widmanstätten structure, named for its discoverer, Alois Josep Widmanstätten (1754-1849). The third group, the ataxites, has a nickel content in excess of 18 percent. Taenite and an intergrowth mixture of kamacite and taenite called plessite are the principal phases present.

The two nickel-iron alloy minerals kamacite (up to 7.5 weight percent nickel) and taenite (between 20 and 50 weight percent nickel) are the two most abundant minerals in iron meteorites. More than forty other minerals have also been identified but are present in only minor amounts. Among these minerals, diamond is the most significant. The others have no terrestrial equivalent and have been reported only from meteorite studies. The mineralogy of iron meteorites is unique also in textural appearance as a result of the relationship of the coexisting kamacite and taenite during the meteorite's cooling process. A weavelike pattern known as the Widmanstätten structure is created, resulting from the different nickel content in each mineral. The percentage of nickel is noted by the bandwidth of the Widmanstätten pattern. Nickel content is therefore an important factor in determining the extraterrestrial nature of iron meteorites. The Widmanstätten pattern does not occur in any known terrestrial rock; it is believed to be the result of slow cooling while the iron resided inside of a small asteroid-sized body. The pattern itself results from the appearance of plates of kamacite occurring in octahedral orientation as the spaces in between become filled with taenite. On a cut, polished, and etched (with nitric acid) surface, a weave, or cross-hatched pattern, appears, the individual plates varying in width according to their nickel content. This phenomenon is the result of the cooling of the molten nickel-iron alloy over a period of millions of years.

The three groups of iron meteorites are directly related to falling temperatures and the resultant rearrangement of atoms. The formation of iron meteorites begins as temperatures fall below 1,400 degrees Celsius; depending on the original amount of nickel, the three individual types are produced as certain temperatures are reached. Generally, as temperature drops, the amount of kamacite will increase as the amount of parent taenite decreases. At temperatures above 850 degrees Celsius, only taenite exists. As temperatures drop further, diffusion of nickel occurs, and the crystal structure of the taenite readjusts to accommodate the formation of kamacite. That is possible because both minerals have crystal structures with cubic symmetry, but size variations between nickel and iron will give each mineral a different crystal form. Kamacite forms a "body-centered" crystal lattice; each atom is found at the center of a cube and is surrounded by eight neighboring atoms. In contrast, taenite has an atom centered on each face of a cube, and each atom is surrounded by twelve neighboring atoms. The packing arrangement of the atoms in taenite tends to be the more efficient of the two, thus alloying it to fill the spaces between the kamacite plates.

The study of cooling rates as determined by the individual compositions of numerous iron meteorites reveals that most show a wide range. This finding implies that they originated at several different depths rather than at a single core, as once thought. If that were true, the parent body would have been relatively small (probably between 100 and 300 kilometers in diameter) and would have had a mass insufficient to melt its interior totally. Partial melting could have taken place as a result of radioactive heating from isotopes such as aluminum 26, which could create pockets of molten nickel-iron randomly scattered throughout the parent body. Later impact with similar-sized bodies could have freed them to assume independent orbits as relatively pure lumps of metal. The shock deformation lamellae noted in the hexahedrites (Neumann lines) may be evidence of such an event.

Methods of Study

Field recognition of a meteorite is not an easy task, unless one is very familiar with its distinctive characteristics. Usually the most important or obvious feature of a meteorite will be its unusual heaviness as compared to rocks of similar size. Irons are generally three times heavier than comparable earth rocks. The surface of a meteorite is fairly smooth and featureless but will often exhibit flowlines, furrows, shallow depressions, and deep cavities. One very characteristic surface feature is shallow depressions known as thumbprints, because they resemble the imprints of thumbs pressed into soft clay. Newly fallen meteorites can also exhibit a fusion crust, which shows the effects of atmospheric frictional heating upon its surface. In appearance, this crust resembles black ash, but it will weather to a rusty brown and even disappear with time. The fusion crust on iron meteorites is not particularly distinctive and does weather rapidly. One definitive property of an iron meteorite is its strong attraction to a magnet.

In most cases, confirmation of a meteorite must be made in the laboratory. A relatively simple chemical test for the presence of nickel can be made by dissolving a small amount of the specimen in hydrochloric acid. A level teaspoon of tartaric acid is added; after it has dissolved, 20 milligrams of 1 percent solution dimethyl-glyoxime in ethanol are also added. The solution is made basic by adding a 1:1 ammonium hydroxide. If the solution contains nickel, a scarlet precipitate will result. A quantitative analysis is conducted then to determine the actual weight percent of nickel. Because nickel content in meteorites falls within a very specific range, this determination will confirm the sample's identity.

Over the years, several different criteria have been used to classify iron meteorites. Some of the more obvious have been chemical, structural, and mineralogical; others include cosmic-ray exposure ages and cooling rates. The most widely used system, which goes back to the late 1800's, is based on the bandwidth of the octahedral array of kamacite as seen on a cut, polished, and etched surface. The width of these bands of kamacite is dependent on both nickel content and cooling rates. Bulk nickel content generally increases as the bandwidth of kamacite decreases, thus providing a correlation that can be used to separate individual specimens into common groups. Chemical studies for trace elements have extended this classification scheme by including analyses for gallium and germanium. A good correlation has been found between bandwidth size and gallium content, thus permitting a greater separation of iron meteorites into smaller subgroups.

Studies which classify the irons into specific types also provide clues to the meteorite's origin and the nature of its parent body. An estimation of the cooling rate for the coexisting kamacite and taenite can provide evidence of conditions at the time of the meteorite's origin. Consensus opinion places the calculated cooling rate for iron meteorites at approximately 500 degrees Celsius. This rate has been determined from crystallization experimentation in the laboratory and from direct observation of the mineral phases found in meteorites. It coincides with the bandwidth sizes of the kamacite phase and thus provides a correlation between bulk chemical data and cooling rates.

The determination of the cosmic-ray exposure age of a meteorite can provide data to theorize when the object broke out of its parent body. This technique may also lead to the matching of individual meteorite specimens to a common event. In addition, the compositions and abundances of minor and trace minerals, along with the extent of shock damage to their structures, could give a clear picture of the events which led to and occurred during the parent body's breakup. Studies such as these will inform scientists not only about the origin of the meteorite but also about the formation of the earth.

Context

Iron meteorites have played a part in the formative history of the earth and have since given evidence of what the interior of the planet may be like. Scientists speculate that the earth's interior is composed of a nickel-iron similar to that found in meteorites. These curiosities from space have had an effect on human history as well. Some of the earliest historical records from ancient Egypt speak of iron falling from the sky, and it was undoubtedly meteoritic iron that was first fashioned into tools and weapons. Studies have shown that iron tools manufactured on South Pacific Islands, where no local source of iron could be found, were actually forged from meteoritic iron. Some ancient cultures also worshiped "heavenly" iron and placed it in the burial tombs of their leaders; it was thought to be a gift from the gods and served as a symbol of wealth and power. In Europe, as the Bronze Age ended, iron actually became more valuable than gold. Perhaps in the not-too-distant future, space colonists will be mining iron asteroids to provide for their industrial resources, and iron will once again be a mainstay of industry.

Today, meteoritic iron is helping to unlock the secrets of planetary formation, and the scars of giant impacts with iron meteorites dot the earth's surface from Arizona to Australia. Perhaps the most recent testimony to the effects of a giant meteorite impact can be seen at Meteor Crater near Winslow, Arizona. Here, more than 20,000 years ago, an iron meteorite weighing more than 100,000 tons collided with the earth. The resulting crater, which measures more than 1 kilometer across and nearly 200 meters deep, was created by an object about 30 meters across but traveling at a velocity of 15 kilometers per second. The energy released at impact was tremendous, and the vast majority of the meteorite was destroyed in the process. Other meteorites have since hit the earth, but not with such a destructive force. The largest known meteorite, an iron weighing 60 tons, is still embedded in the ground where it fell in South Africa. Impacts will undoubtedly occur with varying effects in the future.

Bibliography

Buchwald, Vagn F. *Handbook of Iron Meteorites: Their History, Distribution, Composition, and Structure*. Berkeley: University of California Press, 1975. This three-volume work offers both an excellent introduction to the science of meteoritics and a general reference to specific iron meteorites. For the average reader, it provides all the basics to begin an understanding of meteorites in terms of their origin and chemical nature. For the scientist, it provides the best possible reference source for individual specimens. Most suited for college and graduate levels.

Dodd, Robert T. *Meteorites: A Petrologic-Chemical Synthesis*. Cambridge, England: Cambridge University Press, 1981. This book covers the range of meteorite-related topics with a detailed approach suitable for the more advanced student. It is well written and has good illustrations to support the text.

_____. *Thunderstones and Shooting Stars: The Meaning of Meteorites*. Cambridge, Mass.: Harvard University Press, 1986. A very good introduction to the science of meteoritics at a very basic level. It is a good review of the chemical types and methods of study used to classify meteorites. In addition, reference is made to the importance of meteorites as a planet-shaping process and to the effect they may have on life forms throughout the ages. Suitable for high school and college students.

Hutchison, Robert. *The Search for Our Beginning: An Enquiry, Based on Meteorite Research, Into the Origin of Our Planet and Life*. Oxford, England: Oxford University Press, 1983. A well-written, well-illustrated introduction to meteorites and their relationship to planetary formation. Although the book is technical, it is understandable for the average reader. Best suited for high school and college-level readers.

McSween, Harry Y., Jr. *Meteorites and Their Parent Planets*. Cambridge, England: Cambridge University Press, 1987. This book presents a good introduction to the science of meteoritics. The approach taken examines the nature of meteorites and their relationship to parent bodies. Good illustrations and a glossary highlight the book. Best suited for high school and college-level readers.

Mason, Brian. *Meteorites*. New York: John Wiley & Sons, 1962. This is perhaps the best of the early books on meteorites and their importance to science. Although the book is dated in the light of modern technology, it still remains as an excellent primer for the study of meteorites. It is well written and presented and is very usable for the average reader.

Sears, D. W. *The Nature and Origin of Meteorites*. Bristol, England: Adam Hilger, 1978. A very readable introduction to the study of meteorites, especially in its historical treatment and its review of the basic concepts. The book does go quite deeply into specialized areas, but it will help the casual reader gain a better perspective on the subject matter. Best suited for the college level.

Wasson, John T. *Meteorites: Their Record of Early Solar System History*. New York: W. H. Freeman, 1985. This book is a well-written and illustrated introduction to the science of meteoritics. The author covers most of the significant topics in a clear and understandable way and offers a wealth of information for both the casual reader and the serious student. Suitable for high school through college levels.

Paul P. Sipiera

Cross-References

METEORITES: STONY IRONS

Type of earth science: Planetology
Field of study: Small solar system bodies

There are two major types of stony iron meteorite: the pallasites and the meso-siderites. The study of pallasites provides evidence for constraints on planetary differentiation processes. The mesosiderites record a history of repeated impacts of projectiles on the basaltic surfaces of their parent body.

Principal terms

BASALT: a fine-grained, dark igneous rock composed chiefly of pyroxenes and feldspars, typically found at or near the surface of differentiated planets

BRECCIA: a rock composed of fragments from previous generations of rocks which have been cemented together

CHONDRITIC: having a chemical composition very similar to the carbonaceous chondrite meteorites

CUMULATE: an igneous rock composed chiefly of crystals which accumulated by sinking or floating from a magma

DIFFERENTIATION: the process by which a primitive planet, when heated, separates into a high-density metallic core and one or more silicate outside layers

OLIVINE: a silicate mineral of magnesium and iron which is the first major silicate to form in a cooling liquid of chondritic composition

PYROXENE: a silicate mineral of magnesium, iron, and sometimes calcium which contains more silicon than is present in olivine

Summary of the Phenomenon

Meteorites are divided into three broad categories: stone meteorites, iron meteorites, and a group called the stony irons that has both stone and iron components. These stony iron meteorites are quite rare, constituting only about 1 percent of the meteorite falls (those meteorites recovered soon after their fall to earth was observed). The stony irons are more important than their low abundance suggests, however, since they provide a link between the stones and the irons and serve as probes of certain planetary processes. There are four distinct types of stony iron meteorite: pallasites, mesosiderites, siderophyres, and lodranites. The pallasites and mesosiderites are the common stony irons; the siderophyres and lodranites are quite rare, represented by only one or two specimens each.

Pallasite meteorites are composed of millimeter- to centimeter-sized angular or rounded fragments of magnesium-rich olivine set in a continuous matrix of nickel-iron. In these meteorites, the olivine content ranges from 37 to 85 percent by volume, with the nickel-iron metal accounting for almost all of the remaining material. The minerals troilite, schreibersite, and chromite are sometimes found in small amounts.

The detailed process by which the pallasites formed is still a subject of scientific debate, but they appear to sample a boundary region where nickel-rich iron was in contact with silicate crystals, an environment analogous to the earth's core-mantle boundary. One mechanism for the formation of pallasites could have been the heating and consequent differentiation of a chondritic parent body. The high-density iron-nickel-sulfur liquid settled to the center, forming a molten core and leaving a silicate-rich mantle. As the mantle cooled, olivine, which is generally the first silicate mineral to crystallize out of cooling silicate liquids of a wide range of compositions, formed and settled to the core-mantle boundary.

The mechanism by which molten metal from the core surrounded the olivine crystals to produce the pallasite structure is not yet understood. It has been proposed that the mantle shrank as it cooled, squeezing molten metal out of the core and into the olivine-rich layer. Alternatively, the core may have contracted during cooling, causing the olivine layer to collapse into the void, giving rise to the mixing. Further cooling would have resulted in the solid pallasite material, which was excavated from the parent body by major impacts. Therefore, the pallasites are believed to provide samples of the core-mantle boundary region on earth.

Comparison of the chemistry of the pallasites with that of the earth provides some constraints on the earth's formation and differentiation process. The earth is generally assumed to have formed with the same chondritic composition as the pallasite parent body. After differentiation, the concentration of nickel in the earth's upper mantle remained at about 0.2 percent. The silicates in the pallasites are much more depleted in nickel, having a concentration of only 0.002 percent. One possible explanation for the additional nickel in the earth's outer layers is that after differentiation, additional chondritic material was added to the surface, presumably by meteoritic or cometary impact.

Constraints on the size of the pallasite parent body come from a study of how fast these objects cooled after differentiation. If two objects start at the same temperature and are allowed to cool, the smaller object will cool more rapidly, since it has a larger ratio of surface area to volume than does the larger object. The cooling rates determined for the pallasites, and the iron meteorites related to them, are consistent with formation in an object much smaller than the earth's moon, perhaps no larger than 10 kilometers in diameter. The differentiation process therefore occurred on objects of a wide variety of sizes, from the size of the earth to that of small asteroids.

The texture, composition, and cooling rate of the typical pallasites are consistent with their metal's being related to a group of iron meteorites called the IIIAB irons. If so, then samples of the pure core material of the pallasite parent body are also available.

The differentiation process believed to have occurred in the early history of the earth and of the pallasite parent body has been simulated in the laboratory by heating chondritic meteorites. As the temperature increases, the meteorites melt in stages. The first liquid to appear is composed mainly of iron, nickel, sulfur, and trace elements that have an affinity for these major elements. Because this liquid is twice as dense as the remaining silicates, it sinks to the bottom. Further melting yields liquids of basaltic composition and a solid residue of mostly olivine. The basaltic liquid, which is less dense than the solids, floats to the top. When cooled, the resulting structure has metal at the bottom, an olivine layer in the middle, and a basaltic material on top. For the earth, this process would give rise to a dense metal core surrounded by an olivine-rich mantle and covered with a basaltic crust. The absence of samples from the earth's deep interior, however, prevents direct verification of this structure.

Examination of the pallasite meteorites strongly suggests that the pallasite parent body formed with a chondritic composition, was heated, differentiated into a metallic core and silicate mantle, and subsequently cooled and solidified. Thus, the pallasites confirm that planetary differentiation, as proposed for the earth, took place on the pallasite parent body in the manner proposed for the earth.

The mesosiderite meteorites are quite different from the pallasites. They are composed of angular chunks of basaltic rocks and rounded masses of metal. The metal phases constitute 17 to 80 percent of the mesosiderites by weight. The major silicate minerals are plagioclase, calcium-bearing pyroxene, and olivine. The mesosiderites are polymict breccias; that is, they are composed of fragments of unrelated rocks. They contain pyroxene-rich fragments, like the diogenite meteorites, and fine-grained fragments of eucrite meteoritic material. The eucrites and diogenites are magmatic rocks similar, respectively, to terrestrial basalts and cumulates.

The mesosiderites appear to have formed from repeated impacts on an asteroidal surface which brought together at least three distinct types of material: diogenitic and eucritic rocks, from the surface of the asteroid, and a nonindigenous metallic component, possibly from the impacting objects. If the metal fragments in the mesosiderites are projectile material from the core of a previously fragmented asteroid, these fragments must have struck the surface of the diogenite-eucrite parent body at a very low velocity. Impacts at velocities higher than about 1 kilometer per second lead to very low concentrations of the projectile material in the resulting breccias. This low-impact velocity would suggest that the parent body exerted a very small gravitational attraction on the falling metal, indicating that the diogenite-eucrite was a relatively small asteroid, not a planet-sized object.

The mesosiderites are similar to lunar surface breccias, which are also formed by multiple impacts into basaltic rock. They allow the processes of basaltic volcanism and impact brecciation to be examined in a different solar system region and an earlier time than the lunar process.

There are other meteorites which contain mixtures of metal and silicate phases, but they are otherwise dissimilar to the pallasites and mesosiderites. The siderophyre type, represented only by the single meteorite known as Steinback, is composed of the silicate bronzite and metal. The lodranites are composed of olivine, low-calcium pyroxene, and metal. These two rare types of stony iron meteorite have not been as well studied as the pallasites and mesosiderites.

Methods of Study

The pallasite meteorites have been well studied by a variety of techniques, because, along with the iron meteorites, they provide a window on the processes and conditions in the deep interior of their parent bodies and clues to similar processes thought to have occurred on earth. Much of the evidence concerning these processes comes from detailed analyses of the chemical abundances of major and trace elements in individual minerals from each meteorite. Detailed modeling of the differentiation process suggests that certain metal-seeking trace elements will concentrate in the metallic core while other trace elements concentrate in the silicate mantle.

Early studies of the metal phases in iron and stony iron meteorites were done by examining their textures, because the abundances of the trace elements were difficult to determine. More recently, however, the abundances of these trace elements, present at the level of no more than a few atoms in every million atoms of bulk material, have been measured by neutron activation, X-ray fluorescence, and electron microprobe analysis.

Detailed measurements of the abundance of trace elements, emphasizing the elements gallium, germanium, and iridium, in the more than five hundred iron meteorites in earth collections, show twelve to sixteen distinct compositional clusters, indicating that the irons sample a minimum of twelve different parent bodies. Almost all the pallasites have metal compositions and textures suggesting that they are related to a single group of iron meteorites, the IIIAB irons. This relationship suggests that the metal in most of the pallasites samples the core of the same parent body as the IIIAB irons.

Chemical analysis of the olivine grains in the more than thirty-five known pallasites indicates that the olivine has a very narrow range of compositions. Within each meteorite, the olivine crystals are homogeneous; that is, they show no significant compositional variation from grain to grain. This narrow range of olivine compositions suggests that the grains formed from a silicate liquid of uniform composition. Most of the pallasites, then, appear to sample the core-mantle boundary of a single parent body.

A few pallasites differ from the majority in that they contain olivine, which is more rich in iron than the common pallasites. Three of these pallasites are also enriched in nickel and the trace elements germanium and iridium and depleted in gallium relative to the common pallasites. The trace element abundances suggest that these three pallasites sample a parent body different from the common pallasites; however, the metal in these three cannot be identified with any iron meteorite group.

The cooling rates of pallasite meteorites, from which the size of the parent bodies can be inferred, are determined by examination of the metal. Meteoritic metal consists of two distinct nickel-iron alloys: kamacite, an alloy that can be no more than 7 percent nickel, and taenite, which frequently has more than 20 percent nickel. The metallic liquid core generally has a higher nickel content than can be accommodated in the kamacite structure alone. As the metal cools, the amount of kamacite increases, and nickel atoms diffuse from the newly formed kamacite into the nearby taenite. Since nickel diffuses more rapidly in kamacite than in taenite, however, the nickel will build up at the kamacite-taenite boundaries. There will therefore be more nickel at the edges of the taenite than near the center. This distribution of nickel in the taenite varies with the cooling rate.

Electron microprobe analysis of the taenite grains gives the abundance of nickel as a function of distance from the edge, which allows the cooling rate to be estimated. The nickel distribution in the metal of the normal pallasites is consistent with a very rapid cooling rate, implying an extremely small parent body (less than 10 kilometers in diameter). The same technique suggests that the cooling rate of the IIIAB iron meteorites, with which the pallasites are apparently associated, was somewhat slower, implying a parent body of 200 to 300 kilometers in diameter. The reason for this difference is not yet understood.

The mesosiderites, although they are also mixtures of stone and metal, are quite different from the pallasites. The silicate portion of the mesosiderites is rich in the minerals plagioclase and calcium-rich pyroxene. These minerals melt at relatively low temperatures and are generally found on the surface of the earth and the moon. Unlike the olivine found in the pallasites, the basaltic minerals found in the mesosiderites were probably never in direct contact with the metal in the core of the parent body.

Detailed examination of the mineralogy of the mesosiderites shows that they consist of a mixture of three distinct components, each represented by a distinct type of meteorite. The silicates are fragments of both eucrite and diogenite meteorites; the metal phases resemble the iron meteorites. The eucrites are basaltlike meteorites composed mainly of calcium-poor pyroxene and plagioclase thought to have crystallized on or near the surface of their parent body. The diogenites are composed mainly of bronzite, or iron-magnesium pyroxene, which resembles the pyroxene cumulates found in the Stillwater complex and in other layered terrestrial intrusions. This combination of eucrite and diogenite fragments in the stony iron mesosiderites, and in the stone howardite meteorites, is taken as evidence that the eucrites and diogenites formed on the same parent body. The metal in the mesosiderites occurs mainly in the form of nuggets, sometimes up to 9 centimeters in diameter, or fragments. They are quite distinct from the metal veins that are continuous throughout the pallasites. Trace element analysis of the metal in the mesosiderites suggests a similarity with the IIE iron meteorites; however, the link is much weaker than that of the common pallasites with the IIIAB irons.

Context

The process of differentiation, or the melting of a primitive parent body and the concentration of iron-nickel-sulfur in the core and the lighter silicate minerals in the mantle, is believed to have taken place on earth. The study of the pallasite meteorites, which are composed of a mixture of iron-nickel core material and olivine mantle material, confirms that this process of differentiation did occur early in solar system history, at least on the pallasite parent body. Though the chemical compositions of most pallasites are consistent with a single parent body, the few pallasites of unusual composition suggest that the pallasite meteorites sample core-mantle boundaries of several parent bodies. That indicates that the differentiation process was relatively common. The good match between the postulated chemical compositions of the core and mantle and the compositions actually seen in the metal and olivine phases of the pallasites confirms the model of chemical segregation developed for the differentiation of the earth. It is believed, however, that the common pallasites sample the core-mantle boundary of a much smaller body than the earth.

The mesosiderites, although they also consist of a mixture of metal and silicates, are quite different from the pallasites. The silicates in the mesosiderites apparently sample basaltic material similar to that found in the lunar surface, in the earth's crust, and as implied by chemical measurements taken by spacecraft, on the surfaces of Mars and Venus. The iron fragments may be projectiles which struck the rocky surface of the mesosiderite parent body and were incorporated into the rock produced by the impact. The mesosiderites demonstrate that basaltic rocks similar to those on earth occur on the surfaces of some asteroids and that the impact processes that dominate the lunar landscape also occurred in the early history of solar system.

Bibliography

Dodd, Robert T. *Meteorites: A Petrologic-Chemical Synthesis*. London: Cambridge University Press, 1981. This is a well-illustrated summary of the mineralogical and chemical composition of all types of meteorites. Chapter 7 focuses on the iron and pallasite meteorites and their relation to each other. Chapter 8 discusses the eucrites and related pallasites. Suitable for college-level readers with some background in earth science.

_____. *Thunderstones and Shooting Stars: The Meaning of Meteorites*. Cambridge, Mass.: Harvard University Press, 1986. This reference book explains why there is a scientific interest in meteorites and summarizes what is known about them. It includes chapters on why planets melt and on the iron and pallasite meteorites. Although written as a college-level text, it provides detailed explanations of the phenomena and techniques of analysis that will be understood by the reader without an earth science background.

Hutchison, Robert. *The Search for Our Beginning: An Enquiry, Based on Meteorite Research, Into the Origin of Our Planet and Life*. Oxford, England: Oxford University Press, 1983. This book summarizes the state of scientific knowledge about the earth, the moon, and the inner planets and describes how the knowledge gained from the study of meteorites has shaped theories of the origin and evolution of the inner solar system. Intended for general audiences. Illustrated.

Kerridge, John F., and Mildred S. Matthews, eds. *Meteorites and the Early Solar System*. Tucson: University of Arizona Press, 1988. A collection of articles by sixty-nine contributing authors describing the state of meteorite research as it relates to early solar system processes. Section 3.2 focuses on igneous activity and the process of differentiation on the parent bodies of the iron and stony iron meteorites. The book is written as a text or reference for graduate students studying meteoritics, but it provides a detailed review and comprehensive bibliography of the major topics in meteorite research. Well illustrated.

Wasson, John T. *Meteorites: Classification and Properties*. New York: Springer-Verlag, 1974. Intended as a college-level introduction to meteorite research and classification by type, this source emphasizes the interpretation of chemical and mineralogical data. It is well illustrated and includes a tabulation of all meteorites known by the early 1970's, with the type of each meteorite indicated. Appendix C lists the pallasites and the mesosiderites.

George J. Flynn

Cross-References

Asteroids, 98; The Evolution of Earth's Composition, 496; Earth's Core, 504; Earth's Core-Mantle Boundary, 511; Earth's Differentiation, 525; Earth's Mantle, 555; Electron Microprobes, 596; Igneous Rock Bodies, 1131; Igneous Rocks: Basaltic, 1158; Meteorites: Achondrites, 1630; Meteorites: Nickel-Irons, 1652; Meteors and Meteor Showers, 1666; Neutron Activation Analysis, 1734; X-Ray Fluorescence, 2744.

METEORS AND METEOR SHOWERS

Type of earth science: Planetology
Field of study: Small solar system bodies

Meteors are the streaks of light produced by small solar system bodies (meteoroids) entering the earth's atmosphere. Fragments from asteroids produce sporadic meteors, while debris left in the orbit of a comet causes meteor showers. Both provide information about the origins of the solar system, especially if they reach the ground and are recovered as meteorites.

Principal terms

ASTEROID: one of the numerous small solar system bodies, mostly in orbits between Mars and Jupiter but including Apollo asteroids, with orbits that cross the earth's orbit

COMET: a solar system body, usually in an elongated and randomly oriented orbit, composed of rocky and icy materials that form a glowing head and extended tail when it nears the sun

FIREBALL: a very large and bright meteor (brighter than Venus) that often explodes with fragments falling to the ground as meteorites; sometimes called a bolide

METEOR: a bright streak of light in the sky, sometimes called a shooting star, produced by a meteoroid entering the earth's atmosphere at high speed and heating to incandescence

METEOR SHOWER: a large number of meteors resulting from the passage of the earth through a meteoroid stream or swarm believed to be the debris left in the orbit of a comet

METEORITE: a metallic or stony meteoroid (or combination) that survives its passage through the atmosphere as a fireball meteor and falls to the surface of the earth

METEOROID: a small solar system body, probably a fragment from a comet or asteroid, which causes a meteor when it enters the earth's atmosphere

RADIANT: the point in the sky from which a meteor shower seems to emanate, whose associated constellation provides the name for a given shower

Summary of the Phenomenon

The scientific study of meteors and their relation to meteorites did not start until the beginning of the nineteenth century. Many meteorite falls were observed and recovered earlier, but most witnesses were ridiculed, and "sky stones" were treated with suspicion. In the Bible, Joshua 10:11 records a battle in which the enemy was defeated by "stones from heaven," which may have been meteorites; Acts 20:35

refers to the image of Diana of Ephesus standing on a stone that fell from heaven. Anaxagoras, Plutarch, and several Chinese recorders from as early as 644 B.C. described stones falling from the sky. A stone preserved in a corner of the Kaaba in Mecca fell in the seventh century. The oldest authenticated meteorite in Europe—a 120-kilogram stone that fell in Switzerland in 1492—is still preserved in a museum. In spite of this evidence, much doubt remained among scientists in Europe. When a stone fell near Luce in France in 1768, it was studied by the French chemist Antoine Lavoisier and two other French scientists, who concluded that it was an ordinary stone struck by lightning.

In 1794, the Czech acoustic scientist Ernst Chladni published an account of numerous reported meteorite falls, giving strong evidence that some of them must be of extraterrestrial origin. He stated that the flight of such an object through the atmosphere caused the bright, luminous phenomenon known as a fireball. Chladni found few supporters for this idea, as most held to Aristotle's view that comets and flashes of light across the sky were atmospheric phenomena (the word "meteor" comes from the Greek word for things related to the atmosphere, as in meteorology). Chladni's cosmic theory of meteors was finally confirmed in 1798 by two students at the University of Göttingen, H. W. Brandes and J. F. Benzenberg, who had read his book. They made simultaneous observations of "shooting stars" from two different locations separated by several kilometers and used a simple triangulation method to show that the light flashes originated at least 80 kilometers above the ground from objects moving several kilometers per second from a source beyond the atmosphere. Most doubts about meteorite falls were removed after the French physicist Jean-Baptiste Biot reported an unusual fall of two or three thousand stones at L'Aigle in 1803, which eyewitnesses said was preceded by a rapidly moving fireball and explosion.

On a clear, dark night, a visual observer may be able to see about six meteors per hour. More are visible after midnight than before, increasing to a maximum just before dawn. In the 1860's, the Italian astronomer Giovanni Schiaparelli, famous for his discovery of Martian "canals," explained the increase in meteors at certain times as resulting from the earth's orbital and rotational motion. Before midnight, the observer is on the trailing side of the earth's motion and can see only those meteors that overtake the earth. After midnight, an observer is on the leading side of the earth's motion and will intercept meteors in front of it; thus, meteors will appear brighter because they are entering the earth's atmosphere at a higher velocity. Because the earth's orbital velocity is about 30 kilometers per second, and the escape velocity from the sun at the earth's orbital distance is about 43 kilometers per second, solar system objects should range in speed from 13 to 73 kilometers per second. Because no meteors have been observed with a faster speed, it is believed that they come from within the solar system rather than from interstellar space.

Most meteors become visible about 100 kilometers about the earth's surface and are completely consumed when they reach about 70 kilometers, although a few larger ones reach about 50 kilometers. Most meteors range in size from a few microns up to several millimeters. Survey estimates indicate that about 25 million meteors are bright enough to be seen over the entire earth in any twenty-four-hour period. Telescopic surveys suggest that several billion meteoroids enter the earth's atmosphere every twenty-four hours, with an average total mass of about 100,000 kilograms. Most of this is consumed in the atmosphere as meteoroids are heated by friction to incandescence, but about 1,000 kilograms per day are deposited on the earth as meteorites.

More than half of all meteors are called sporadic because they appear at any time and from any direction in the sky. The remaining meteors are associated with meteor showers that appear to radiate from a common point in the sky, called the radiant. They actually move along parallel paths but appear to diverge from the radiant—much like the divergence of railroad tracks when viewed in perspective. Meteor showers recur on an annual basis with about a tenfold increase over the usual sporadic rate. They are named for the constellation in which the radiant appears to be located. Annual showers occur when the earth crosses a meteoroid stream that fills the orbit of a comet, while periodic showers occur less frequently when the earth crosses a meteoroid swarm in the wake of a comet. The most spectacular periodic meteor showers are the Leonids, whose radiant is located in the constellation Leo. Historical records as far back as A.D. 902 mention the Leonids. A spectacular display on October 14, 934, is described in Chinese, European, and Arabic chronicles. The Japanese recorded a six-hour display in 967, and Chinese records continued to describe them every thirty-three years for several centuries.

The modern study of meteor showers began with the famous naturalist Baron Alexander von Humboldt. He observed the Leonids by chance during a trip to South America in 1799 in a two-hour display of hundreds of thousands of meteors. Humboldt was the first to suggest that these meteors might originate from a common point in the sky. The greatest Leonid display in the nineteenth century was observed in the United States and Canada on November 12, 1833. About one thousand meteors per minute were counted, and the appearance of the radiant was confirmed. The following year, two Americans, D. Olmstead and A. C. Twining, suggested that the annual Leonids were caused by the earth passing through a cloud of meteoroids each November. A few years later, the German astronomer Heinrich Wilhelm Olbers proposed that the more intense periodic meteor showers of 1799 and 1833 were caused by a denser swarm of the Leonid meteoroid stream. In 1864, H. A. Newton of Yale College reached the same conclusion independently and showed a period of recurrence of just over thirty-three years from historical records, beginning with the shower of 902. Their prediction of a spectacular display in 1866 was confirmed. Later, the English astronomer John Couch Adams, who theorized the existence of the planet Neptune, succeeded in computing the Leonid stream orbit.

In the 1860's, other meteoroid streams were identified and traced through history.

Records back to the tenth century in England recorded meteor showers associated with the festival of St. Lawrence (August 10), known as "the tears of St. Lawrence" but now identified as the August Perseids from their radiant in Perseus. In 1861, the American astronomer Daniel Kirkwood, who later discovered gaps in the asteroid belt, suggested that meteor showers result from debris left in the wake of a comet through which the earth occasionally passes. In 1866, Schiaparelli announced that the August Perseids appear to occupy the same orbit as Comet Swift-Tuttle (1862 III). Soon after, the French astronomer Urbain Leverrier and C. A. F. Peters identified the November Leonids with Comet Tempel-Tuttle (1866 I), which had a recurrence period of thirty-three years. Both the May Aquarids and the October Orionids have been associated with Halley's comet. The greatest naked-eye meteor observer was W. F. Denning, who published a catalog in 1899 of several thousand radiants, mostly of minor meteor showers of less than 10 meteors per hour, based on more than twenty years of observation.

Like comets, meteor streams may be perturbed by planets into new orbits. Those with high inclinations to the ecliptic (plane of the earth's orbit) or in retrograde orbits (opposite to the earth's motion) are least affected, such as the Leonids, Perseids, and Lyrids. After the Leonid display of 1866, the main body of the stream passed close to Jupiter and Saturn. Its associated comet could no longer be found, and only a few meteors were observed in 1899 and 1933. The comet was found again in 1965, and then, on the morning of November 17, 1966, the Leonids returned, with meteors as bright as Venus. Viewed from the western United States, they reached a maximum rate of more than two thousand per minute before dawn, producing the greatest meteor display in recorded history.

Only the bright fireball meteors, sometimes brighter than the full moon, are produced by meteoroids large enough to survive passage through the earth's atmosphere and fall to the ground as meteorites. Almost all of these are sporadic meteors; even among the fireballs, less than 1 percent yield meteorites. Dozens of meteorites fall to the surface of the earth each day, but very few are recovered. About 95 percent of "falls" (seen falling and then recovered) are classified as "stones" (about 75 percent silicates and 25 percent iron), but 65 percent of "finds" (associated meteor not observed) are "irons" (90 percent iron and 8 percent nickel), because irons are easier than stones to identify on the ground as meteorites.

Dozens of craters apparently formed by large meteorites have been identified around the world. The first such identification was made about 1900 by Daniel Barringer at Canyon Diablo in Arizona. This crater is 1.3 kilometers across and 180 meters deep, with a rim rising 45 meters above the surrounding plain. About 25,000 kilograms of iron meteorite fragments have been found in and around the crater. It is estimated that the crater was formed by an explosive impact about 50,000 years ago from a 60-million-kilogram meteorite. In 1908, a brilliant fireball meteor exploded in the Tunguska region of Siberia, leveling trees over a distance of 30 kilometers and killing some 1,500 reindeer. No large crater or meteorite has been found, but its effects were estimated to be equivalent to the explosion of a billion-kilogram meteroid. In 1972, a fireball meteor with an estimated mass of a million kilograms (10-meter size) was photographed in daylight some 60 kilometers above the Grand Teton Mountains before leaving the atmosphere over Canada.

Methods of Study

Information about meteors can be obtained with the unaided eye, but much greater scope and precision results from the use of photographic, radar (radio echo), and space-probe techniques. Modern photographic meteor observations were begun by Fred Whipple in 1936 at the Harvard College Observatory using short-focal-length, wide-angle cameras. These were later replaced by ultra-fast Super-Schmidt cameras that could detect meteors as small as a milligram. To measure the height, direction, and velocity of a meteor, simultaneous photographs of the meteor trail are taken from two stations separated by about 50 kilometers. Each photograph shows the positions of the meteor trail against the background of stars from each station so that its trajectory can be calculated by triangulation. The velocity of the meteor is measured by using a rotating shutter to interrupt the meteor trail up to sixty times per second. The velocity vector and the known position of the earth in its orbit make it possible to compute meteor orbits.

The density of a meteoroid can be estimated from its deceleration in the atmosphere, showing that most meteoroids are of lower density than are meteorites. Statistical studies have shown that meteoroids with the greatest meteor heights have average relative densities of 0.6, while another group appearing about 10 kilometers lower have relative densities averaging 2.1. The few meteoroids that penetrate deep into the atmosphere have average relative densities of 3.7. Several hundred fireball meteors have been photographed, their masses ranging from 100 grams to 1,000 kilograms, including one meteorite fall near Lost City, Oklahoma. Experiments with artificial meteors and theories of meteor burning led to estimated initial meteoroid masses from observed optical effects. Meteors comparable in light to the brightest stars have initial masses of a few grams and diameters of about 1 centimeter, producing more than a megawatt of power. Meteor showers are produced by the most fragile (lowest-density) meteoroids, and different showers produce meteoroids of different character. In general, short-period comets exposed more often to the sun produce higher-density particles than do long-period comets because of greater evaporation.

During World War II, it was accidentally discovered that meteors could be detected by radar. The radar method of studying meteors is especially valuable because it can detect meteors in daylight and is sensitive to meteoroids as small as a microgram. This method depends on the fact that meteors separate electrons from atoms, producing ionized gases that can reflect radio waves. Meteor heights can be measured from the time delay of the return signal, and velocities can be determined from the frequency shift (Doppler effect). Observations from three stations are needed to calculate a meteoroid orbit. Several important meteor showers that occur only in daylight hours were discovered by radar, including the Beta Taurids, probably associated with Comet Encke. Radar also shows that radiants can be complex structures that appear to overlap and shift positions within a few hours.

Micrometeoroids with masses of a few micrograms or less have been collected by high-altitude aircraft and rockets. Micrometeoroids are fluffy particles containing carbonaceous material different from normal meteorites but consistent with comet theories. They can be studied with microphone detectors in space probes by measuring the intensity of their collisions. The weak structure of these particles indicates that they are gently separated from their parent material, suggesting dust emitted from evaporating ice in a comet rather than violent ejection from high-temperature or colliding meteoroids. Particles of less than a milligram contribute the largest fraction of the total mass swept up by the earth each day. Rocketborne mass spectrometers have recorded metallic ions (charged atoms) of apparent meteoric origin, and meteor spectroscopy has provided chemical analysis of all the major meteor streams. These data indicate significant differences betwen cometary meteor material and the composition of meteorites.

Radioactive-dating techniques indicate that most meteorites have existed as solid bodies for about 4.5-4.7 billion years, close to the estimates for the ages of the earth, sun, and moon. This suggests that all the matter of the solar system condensed at approximately the same time. Cosmic-ray dating from the amount of unusual isotopes produced in a meteorite by cosmic rays colliding with atoms in its crystalline structure usually indicates only a few million years since its formation, presumably by some fragmentation process from a larger asteroid. Fine bands are also observed in such meteorites, similar to those that occur in metal crystals subjected to sharp collisional shock. This finding has led to the idea that meteorites probably come from asteroids that were shattered in collisions.

Context

Meteors and meteor showers not only are interesting as visual phenomena but also provide one of the most important sources of information about asteroid and comet composition and deterioration, as well as clues to the origin of the solar system. Fortunately, most meteors are caused by very small particles (less than 1 gram) and are completely vaporized high in the atmosphere. Meteors enter the earth's atmosphere with solar-system speeds and random inclinations to the ecliptic (plane of the earth's orbit); thus, it appears that most meteors are associated with comets or with asteroids that have small inclinations.

The cometary origin of most meteors is supported by the phenomena of meteor showers, which can be traced to particle swarms in various orbits with random inclinations around the sun. Many of these showers can be associated with comets or former comets and appear to be caused by particles released when cometary ices were evaporated by solar radiation. These particles either concentrate in a swarm of meteoroids behind the comet nucleus or eventually become distributed in a stream around the entire orbit of the comet. Annual meteor showers occur when the earth crosses a meteoroid stream, while more intense periodic showers occur when the earth passes through a meteoroid swarm. The densities and compositions of these meteoroids are also consistent with a cometary origin.

The few meteoroids large enough to survive their passage through the atmosphere and yield meteorites are associated with the rare fireball meteors. Their trajectories tend to have low inclinations to the ecliptic, similar to asteroids. The crystalline structure of the metal in meteorites indicates that most were formed at high temperatures and slowly cooled over several million years. Thus, it appears that they did not come from icy comets; rather, they probably originated with asteroids. Calculations show that the rocky outer shell of an asteroid would insulate its hot metallic core, causing it to cool at the very slow rate suggested by the crystalline structure of iron meteorites. Furthermore, the cooling rate in a planet is too slow to fit this observed crystal pattern.

Meteoroids in asteroidal orbits enter the atmosphere with an average velocity of about 20 kilometers per second. Most are slowed rapidly by the atmosphere. If they survive as a meteorite, they simply fall to the ground at free-fall speeds and cool rapidly, since most of the hot surface material is swept off. Meteoroids larger than about 1 million kilograms (10-meter-sized) strike the ground with most of their initial velocities, producing impact craters. A 50-meter object (100 million kilograms) can produce a 1-kilometer crater, causing widespread devastation by its shock waves and by throwing dust into the upper atmosphere with marked effects on climate and life on earth. Some evidence from large craters and geological layers of meteorite debris suggests the possibility that kilometer-sized objects strike the earth about every twenty-six million years, coinciding with major extinctions of life forms. One attempt to explain these data theorizes that the sun has a dim companion star in a twenty-six-million-year eccentric orbit. At its closest approach to the sun, its gravity would disturb many comets in the outer solar system, causing some of them to strike the earth.

Bibliography

Baugher, Joseph F. *The Space-Age Solar System*. New York: John Wiley & Sons, 1988. This college-level textbook is a readable introduction to the solar system, with an emphasis on exploration and results from interplanetary spacecraft. In addition to a good ten-page chapter on meteors and meteorites, there are also chapters on comets, asteroids, and earth collisions. A ten-page bibliography lists about five hundred references on planetary studies.

Brown, Peter L. *Comets, Meteorites, and Men*. New York: Taplinger, 1973. This book is an excellent and very readable historical study of comets, meteors, and meteorites. Six chapters on meteor showers and meteorites cover the history of these phenomena from earliest times. Appendices include a table of meteorite impact sites and the major annual meteor showers.

Burke, John G. *Cosmic Debris*. Berkeley: University of California Press, 1986. This book is a scholarly and well-documented history of meteorite and meteor discoveries and theories. Much of the book is suitable for the general reader, with interesting illustrations, but some parts are more detailed and technical. A 50-page bibliography contains about a thousand historical references.

Delsemme, A. H., ed. *Comets, Asteroids, Meteorites*. Toledo, Ohio: The University of Toledo, 1977. This book is the result of an International Colloquium on the interrelations, evolution, and origins of comets, asteroids, and meteorites. Of the seventy-five articles, twenty-two are on meteors, meteoroids, and meteorites. Although the level is quite technical, this book provides a detailed firsthand account of research results for interested students.

Glasstone, Samuel. *Sourcebook on the Space Sciences*. Princeton, N.J.: Van Nostrand Reinhold, 1965. This well-organized book on the space sciences has a good chapter on the solar system, including thirty-two pages on meteors, meteorites, and micrometeoroids. Provides a good overview for the general reader with scientific interests. Well illustrated.

Hartmann, William K. *Moons and Planets*. Belmont, Calif.: Wadsworth, 1983. This college-level textbook on planetary astronomy has a thirty-page chapter on meteorites, a chapter on comets that includes discussion of meteor showers, and a forty-page chapter on meteorite craters. It has excellent charts, diagrams, and reproductions of original paintings of space scenes by the author. An extensive bibliography includes more than 150 references on meteorites and cratering.

Joseph L. Spradley

Cross-References

Asteroids, 98; Astroblemes, 106; Comets, 253; Meteorite and Comet Impacts, 1623; Meteorites: Achondrites, 1630; Meteorites: Carbonaceous Chondrites, 1638; Meteorites: Chondrites, 1645; Meteorites: Nickel-Irons, 1652; Meteorites: Stony Irons, 1659; The Origin of the Solar System, 2442.

MICROPALEONTOLOGY: MICROFOSSILS

Type of earth science: Paleontology and earth history

Micropaleontology is the study of plant and animal fossils that are too small to be seen without magnification. These microscopic objects provide valuable information about the evolution of life on earth and about changes that have occurred on the earth's surface through time. They also have great value as index fossils and as indicators of ancient environments, data useful in the search for oil and natural gas.

Principal terms

FORAMINIFERA: single-celled, amoebalike animals

FOSSIL: remains of a once-living organism that have been naturally preserved in the earth's crust

INDEX FOSSILS: indicators of geologic age; they have short geologic (time) ranges and broad geographic distribution

ISOTOPES: atoms of an element that differ in weight because different numbers of neutrons are present in their atomic nuclei

MORPHOLOGIC EVOLUTION: changes in the body or skeleton shape of organisms through time

PARTHENOGENIC: organisms in which unfertilized females produce viable, fertile offspring without copulation with males of the species

Summary of the Phenomenon

When people think of fossils, they envision items such as the bones and teeth of dinosaurs, the petrified bones of Neanderthal man, or the shells of oysters. Micropaleontologists study the preserved remains of organisms too small to be seen with the unaided eye. It is convenient to divide micropaleontology into two subfields: animal micropaleontology and plant micropaleontology. Animal micropaleontology encompasses the study of a wide variety of fossils. In most cases, the material studied is actually the shell constructed by the once-living animal. Shells are commonly composed of calcium carbonate (the common mineral calcite), calcium phosphate (the mineral apatite, a constituent of human teeth and bones), and opaline silica (quartz with water molecules in its crystal structure). Other microscopic animals build shells from mixes of sand grains, shell fragments, and volcanic ash, all glued together with organic or mineral cement. Thus, shells are referred to as calcareous, phosphatic, siliceous, or agglutinated.

Microfossils vary in size as well as in shell composition. As a rule, few are smaller than 0.05 millimeter in diameter; most are in the range of 0.75-2.0 millimeters, and a very few are as large as 5 centimeters. Among the larger microfossils are those called nummulites, which are major constituents of the limestone used in the Egyptian pyramids. In about 450 B.C., Herodotus described them, erroneously, as mummified lentils (the food of pyramid construction crews).

Systematic study of microfossils did not begin until the early years of the nineteenth century. Alcide Dessalines d'Orbigny (1802-1857) published a paper describing some microfossils that he thought to be microscopic cephalopods related to the chambered nautilus. Subsequently, it was realized that d'Orbigny's microfossils were types of protozoans (single-celled animals) called foraminifera. Another pioneer was Christian Gottfried (1795-1876), who was the first to treat micropaleontology as a field of study. As is the case for larger fossils, microfossils can be used to determine the age of sedimentary rocks; European micropaleontologists used them for this purpose as early as 1874 and, by 1930, micropaleontology was aiding in petroleum exploration worldwide.

Many types of animals can produce microscopic shells or other hard parts which may be preserved in sedimentary rocks. Among these are protozoans, gastropods (snails), worms, crustaceans (crabs, lobsters), sponges, echinoderms (starfish, sea urchins), and fish. Protozoans contribute significantly to the microfossil record. Two are particularly useful as indicators of geologic age and of ancient environments: the foraminifera and the radiolarians. Most living foraminifera are found in the ocean, where their distribution is controlled by water temperature, salinity, depth, turbulence, light intensity, bottom conditions, availability of food, predators, parasites, and other biologic factors. Foraminifera, or forams, usually have calcareous or agglutinated shells. The largest number of species are bottom dwellers (benthic), but one group, the globigerinas, evolved to live as passive floaters (or plankton) in the surface waters of the oceans. Benthic forams have a long geologic history extending back 500-600 million years. For the last 300 million years, their shells have been significant rock formers. The rock which forms the White Cliffs of Dover is composed largely of the shells of foraminifera. Planktonic forams evolved more recently, first appearing in rocks about 175 million years old. Since planktonic species live in surface waters, ocean currents may carry them thousands of miles. This wide geographic distribution coupled with their rapid morphologic evolution makes planktonic foraminifera especially valuable as index fossils.

Radiolarians are also planktonic protozoans, but they differ from foraminifera in their soft-body-part anatomy and in their shell construction. Radiolarian shells are composed of opaline silica, are usually in the 0.05-0.5 millimeter size range, and display a bewildering array of shapes. Most are variations on three shapes: spheres, cones, or discs. Some radiolaria secrete their shells as spongy masses; others build shells of perforated sheets of silica, and still others construct lattice-work shells of great delicacy and beauty. Radiolaria are found in rocks almost 600 million years old, giving them the longest geologic range of planktonic microfossils. Mesozoic and Cenozoic radiolarians are better known than are Paleozoic ones.

Microscopic crustaceans called ostracods (or ostracodes) have a 500-million-year-long fossil record and are abundant in many sedimentary rocks. Unlike the familiar macroscopic crustaceans, ostracods encase their minute, shrimplike bodies in a pair of tiny, calcareous, bean-shaped shells 1-5 millimeters long. Outer surfaces of these shells may be smooth or they may bear spines, wartlike bumps, grooves, ridges, flanges, and pores. Hinge structures and muscle scars, found on the inner surfaces of the shells, are also useful features in distinguishing different ostracods. Although some species are planktonic, most ostracods are benthic. Living ostracods can be found from the deepest ocean floor to the shoreline and landward into lakes and streams. A few species have adapted to live on land in moist ground litter. Playa lakes in desert regions often are inhabited by ostracods. Species living in these harsh environments are often parthenogenic: Unfertilized females lay fertile eggs, which lie dormant in the muddy bottom of a dried-up lake; the next time the lake fills, the eggs hatch into a new generation of females, and the cycle continues. Dormant periods of a decade or more have been reported.

Two different kinds of toothlike structures are frequently found in assemblages of microfossils. Annelid worm jaws, called scolecodonts, are composed of a resistant organic material (chitin) and have been found in rocks up to 600 million years old. The second type are called conodonts ("cone-tooth"). Their origin is uncertain. These fossils are 0.2 to 6.0 millimeters in greatest dimension, are composed of calcium phosphate, and occur as isolated specimens or in clustered assemblages. The composition suggests that they were produced by an animal, and their distribution in sedimentary rocks suggests that these "conodont animals" (ordinal name Conodontophoridia) were marine and planktonic. They first appeared in Cambrian time, flourished through the rest of the Paleozoic, and became extinct during the Triassic period. Many micropaleontologists believe that fossils of the "conodont animal" have been found. These are roughly the size and shape of a small cigar and have paired finlike structures on the sides and an "eely" tail. In each, a cluster of conodonts is found. Perhaps the conodonts were part of a gizzardlike organ or perhaps they were claspers used in reproduction; they do not seem to have been teeth. Perhaps these clusters are the remains of the "conodont animal" in the digestive tract of another animal.

Methods of Study

While microfossils can be recovered from many types of marine sedimentary rocks, they are most abundant in fine-grained rocks such as shale. Samples of the rocks can be obtained from surface outcrops or from subsurface boreholes in the form of cores or cuttings. In collecting samples for study, care must be taken to eliminate any contamination, and accurate records of sampling localities must be maintained.

In the laboratory, a variety of techniques are used to extract the microfossils from the host rock and to clean them. Composition of the fossils, composition of the host rock, and the kind of study to be done dictate the separation methods used. Some foraminifera, for example, can be studied profitably only in thin section. To prepare them, fossiliferous samples are glued to microscope slides and are ground and polished until the rock is paper thin and the internal features of the shell can be seen. Acids are used to dissolve sedimentary rocks effectively, in order to release insoluble siliceous or phosphatic microfossils. Acetic acid will dissolve limestone without damaging conodonts, and radiolarians can be freed best by dissolving the host rock in hydrochloric acid.

Calcareous shelled ostracods and foraminifera are usually extracted from shales in the following manner. A clean, dry, crushed (to pea size) sample is soaked for thirty to sixty minutes in kerosene. The kerosene is poured off, filtered, and saved for reuse. The sample container is filled with water, and a wetting agent is added. This mixture is boiled for twenty to thirty minutes, and then it is poured through a 200-mesh screen. Fine clay particles pass through, leaving the microfossil residue on the screen. Usually it is necessary to repeat the boiling and screening process several times to yield a good, clean residue. After drying, the residue is ready for "picking." A one-grain-thick layer of residue is spread on a picking tray, which is then placed on the stage of a binocular microscope. Magnification of thirty to forty times is required. A picking brush is also needed. The micropaleontologist slides the picking tray back and forth so that all the residue is scanned. Once a microfossil is found, the picking brush and a steady hand come into play: The brush is moistened and guided to the fossil, which sticks to the brush while being transferred to a microscope slide for future study. Routinely, several hundred specimens will be picked from each sample; each specimen will be identified and tallied in the sample census. Specimens can be repicked for further study using the greater magnification of the scanning electron microscope (SEM). Thin coatings of a conductive metal are vacuum-plated on the specimens, which are then ready for SEM analysis. In a vacuum chamber, a beam of electrons is focused on the specimen; reflected electrons are collected and are converted electronically into an image of the specimen. Magnification of fifty thousand times or more is possible, and the electronic image has a three-dimensional appearance.

Probably the single most important application of microfossils is in biostratigraphy, or the use of fossils to determine the age of rocks. Fundamental to biostratigraphy has been the establishment of reference sections. These are sequences of rock that have been precisely dated and whose fossils have been described in considerable detail. Fossils from a rock sequence of unknown age are compared with fossil sequences from reference sections and the best match is obtained. Because of their rapid evolution and their broad geographic distribution, fossils of planktonic organisms are particularly well suited for this work. For example, radiolarian assemblages from Japan, West Texas, and the Ural Mountains of Eurasia can be compared directly with one another.

Using a picked collection of foraminifera, a number of other studies can be carried out. If the assemblage contains both planktonic and benthonic species, the planktonics-benthonics ratio gives a measure of water depth at the time of deposition. Another depth indicator is the ratio of calcareous-shelled benthonics to agglutinate-shelled benthonics. The diversity of the assemblage may also provide useful information. In a tropical assemblage, many species are usually present, but only a few individuals of each species occur (high diversity); in a high latitude assemblage, only a few species are present, but each is represented by a large number of individuals (low diversity). Diversity measures must be used carefully, as similar effects can be seen in relation to water depth—low diversity in very shallow or very deep water and higher diversity at intermediate depths.

Calcareous-shelled forams can also be analyzed to give a direct measure of temperature of the water in which they lived. Oxygen atoms in two forms (isotopes) occur in seawater. The ratio of oxygen 18 to oxygen 16 is a function of water temperature. When forams extract calcium carbonate from seawater and build their shells with it, the oxygen isotopes are incorporated as well. In the laboratory, the shells are converted to carbon dioxide, and the ratio of oxygen 18 to oxygen 16 is determined. The measured ratio is then plugged into a mathematical formula to calculate water temperature. A second temperature measuring-technique can be used with planktonic forams. As the animals grow, they add chambers to their shells in a spiraling pattern. In warm water, the spiral is clockwise (right-handed), and in cold water it is counterclockwise (left-handed). The coiling ratio for planktonic forams in a sample thus gives an indication of water temperature. Although this technique is less precise than isotopic measurements, it is faster and less expensive.

Studies of evolution can also be conducted using microfossils. Because planktonic animals seem to evolve faster than do benthonic ones, plankton are often preferred in these studies. Ideally, one needs closely spaced samples from a core in an area where insignificant environmental change occurred while deposition of the planktonic shells was continuous. Some lineages of Cenozoic radiolarians have been traced for several million years, during which time small morphologic changes accrued so that the descendant species are quite different from their ancestors in morphology. In some of these studies, hybridization between different but related species seems to have been recorded by the fossils.

Context

Before the advent of modern dustless chalk, every schoolchild was a microfossil collector. Old-fashioned schoolroom chalk was made from sedimentary rock (called chalk) composed mostly of calcareous microfossils. Today, people have less contact with microfossils. The gasoline that powers automobiles was refined from crude oil. When the well that produced the crude was being drilled, rock chips ("cuttings") were checked periodically for microfossils to tell the drillers the age of the rock they were drilling. Some of the soft body parts of the microscopic organisms contributed hydrocarbon molecules to the crude oil itself while their shells were being fossilized.

The Portland cement so essential in construction of road, bridges, dams, and buildings of all sorts is made from limestone. Most limestone is composed of calcareous microfossils, and microscopic shell fragments from larger animals. Inert fillers and mild abrasives in a host of common household products (foot powder, face powder, toothpaste, cleanser) are derived from chalk and other microfossil-laden sedimentary rocks.

In sediments deposited on the sea floor during the Pleistocene, microfossils document changes in the earth's climate and in the temperature of the sea as the glaciers repeatedly advanced and retreated. By understanding the temperature history of the oceans, scientists hope to understand better long-term climatic changes and to be able to predict the climatic future.

Determination of the age of sedimentary rocks beneath the deep ocean floor has proved to be a crucial line of evidence which supports the concept of sea-floor spreading, or continental drift. Microfossils are used, almost exclusively, in such determinations because they have proved to be reliable and accurate age indicators.

Bibliography

Anderson, O. R. *Radiolaria.* New York: Springer-Verlag, 1983. This volume considers the biology of living radiolarians and includes discussion of morphology, ultrastructure, physiology, ecology, and evolution. A glossary and appendix are included, as is an index. College level.

Brasier, M. D. *Microfossils.* Winchester, Mass.: Allen & Unwin, 1980. This concise volume treats fifteen groups of microfossils, emphasizing their features as seen in a microscope. Illustrated with high-quality line drawings. An appendix summarizes sampling and preparation techniques. The bibliographic entries are chiefly twentieth century articles and books. Both a general index and a systematic index are included. College level.

Fairbridge, Rhodes Whitmore, and David Jablonski, eds. *The Encyclopedia of Paleontology.* Vol. 7 in *The Encyclopedia of Earth Science.* Stroudsburg, Pa.: Dowden, Hutchinson and Ross, 1979. Microfossil groups are considered in detail in this volume. An alphabetical arrangement of fossil groups is utilized. Illustrations include line drawings, photomicrographs, and electron micrographs. A good reference list for each fossil group is included. High school or college level.

Hag, Bilal, and Anne Boersma, eds. *Introduction to Marine Micropaleontology.* New York: Elsevier, 1978. Articles by specialists on fourteen groups of microfossils. Illustrations are outstanding; indexing is thorough. A helpful glossary of terms is included. Each chapter includes lists of general references and of cited references. College level.

Kummel, Bernhard, and David Raup, eds. *Handbook of Paleontological Techniques.* San Francisco: W. H. Freeman, 1965. An indispensable volume for any paleontologist. Includes general procedures for collecting and studying most major groups of fossils. Specific techniques for collecting, preparing, and studying microfossils are included. Preparation of specimens for photography or other means of illustration is discussed. Extensive bibliographies and indexes are valuable. College to professional level.

Pokorný, Vladimír. *Principles of Zoological Micropaleontology.* Translated by K. A. Allen. 2 vols. Elmsford, N.Y.: Pergamon Press, 1963-1965. Translated from the German, this 650-page book presents an excellent overview of animal micropaleontology. Includes discussions of micropaleontological methods and of the major groups of animal microfossils. Profusely illustrated with high-quality photomicrographs and line drawings. References are grouped by chapters and include good coverage of literature published outside of North America. Fossil and subject indexes are given. College level.

William C. Cornell

Cross-References

Biostratigraphy, 173; The Cenozoic Era, 202; Deep-Sea Sedimentation, 325; Electron Microscopy, 601; The Fossil Record, 760; Fossilization and Taphonomy, 768; The Geologic Time Scale, 874; Mass Extinctions, 1514; The Mesozoic Era, 1535; Oceans: Carbonate Compensation Depths, 1855; Paleobiogeography, 1984; The Paleozoic Era, 2018; Stratigraphic Correlation, 2485.

MAGILL'S
SURVEY
OF
SCIENCE

ALPHABETICAL LIST

CATEGORY LIST

CATEGORY LIST